COMMUNISM IN CZECHOSLOVAKIA

1948–1960

Communism
in Czechoslovakia

1948-1960

BY EDWARD TABORSKY

Princeton, New Jersey
Princeton University Press
1961

Edward Taborsky was Secretary to the Foreign
Minister of Czechoslovakia in 1938. After the
Nazi invasion, he joined the government-in-
exile in England. As Personal Aide, he accompanied President Beneš to the 1943 conference
with Franklin D. Roosevelt and the 1943 and
1945 conferences with Stalin and Molotov.
From 1945 to 1948 he was Czechoslovak Envoy
to Sweden. Dr. Taborsky is now a Professor of
Government at the University of Texas.

Printed in the United States of America
by The Maple Press Company, York, Pa.

To the Memory of my Father

PREFACE

TWELVE YEARS have passed since the Communists seized power in Czechoslovakia in February 1948. In these first twelve years of its rule the communist regime of Czechoslovakia has weathered such fateful events as the death of Joseph Stalin, the man to whom the Czechoslovak Communists owed their allegiance; the dangerous era of the post-Stalin "thaw"; and the Hungarian and Polish political upheavals of 1956. According to the new Constitution of 1960, socialism has won in Czechoslovakia, the exploitation of man by man has been abolished, and the working people are "gathering forces for the transition to communism."

Thus the initial stage of the march toward the ultimate communist millenium in Czechoslovakia has been completed, and it is the purpose of the present study to review and evaluate its political results. How successful have the leaders of Czechoslovak communism been in remolding the body politic of what had once been called a bastion of democracy in Central Europe? What changes have they made in the constitutional, political, and socio-political structure of Czechoslovakia and in the Czechoslovak way of life? To what extent have they implemented their promises of better social justice, more equality, and a genuine "people's democracy"—promises which constitute the most appealing part of the Marxian dogma? How have they fared thus far in their ambitious goal of outproducing capitalism and attaining the highest living standards in the world? What have they done toward the realization of their professed aim of abolishing the exploitation of man by man? What have been the results of their colossal attempt to pattern after the image of the Marxist-Leninist *Weltanschauung* the mind and soul of a nation so thoroughly imbued with the ideas and concepts of Western democracy?

A dozen years is, of course, too short a period in which to answer with finality these and other questions concerning the success or failure of the communist experiment in Czechoslovakia. But it does permit at least an interim evaluation, particularly in view of the fact that

Czechoslovak Communists were able to do much spade work in the years 1945–1948 when they and their fellow-travelers held most of the key positions in Fierlinger's and Gottwald's cabinets.

In a way, Czechoslovakia probably constitutes a more rewarding object of study than any other of Moscow's satellites. Before her engulfment into the Soviet orbit she was the most industrialized and the least agrarian, the most urbanized and the least rural of them all. Even prior to the Second World War a number of Czechoslovak enterprises had been publicly owned and operated by central, provincial, and local authorities. The cooperative movement had a long tradition behind it. The public in general showed no marked antipathy toward government intervention in business. Reliance upon state support and subsidy was habitual even among private entrepreneurs. Until after Munich, the Communist Party of Czechoslovakia always enjoyed complete freedom to foster the communist cause—a freedom which was usually not accorded to communist parties elsewhere in prewar East-Central Europe. Since its foundation in 1921, the Communist Party has been one of the four largest political parties in the country. By 1945 practically all Czechoslovak workers and a great many intellectuals considered socialism a panacea for most economic problems. Pro-Russianism—in the sense of looking toward Russia as the main protector against any new German aggression—was fairly widespread in all walks of life. Religious belief, if deep enough, customarily imparts a high degree of immunity against communist influence, but in Czechoslovakia it was lax and rather superficial except in rural areas.

Taken together, all these factors tend to suggest that, of all Moscow's satellites, Czechoslovakia would seem to offer the most favorable conditions for the successful establishment and functioning of a Marxian system. In other words, if Marxian socialism could ever assert itself in practice as being superior to Western democracy, Czechoslovakia ought to be the right country in which to prove it. Indeed, as I know from my personal experience, this is precisely why a number of leading Czechoslovak Communists cherished the thought that Czechoslovakia was destined to become a model communist state. Indeed, Soviet leaders in recent years have considered Czechoslovakia a model people's democracy designed to serve as communism's show window.

On the other hand, except for the above-mentioned touch of superficial pro-Russianism, Czechs and Slovaks have always been definitely Western-minded and Western-oriented. Their philosophical, political, and cultural traditions are firmly rooted in Western civilization; and their leaders in every field of human endeavor have always looked toward the West rather than toward the East for inspiration and example.

Thus Czechoslovakia's present case illustrates the tragic clash between the enticing promises of a Marxian utopia and the harsh reality of Soviet-guided totalitarianism—a clash which is likely to cause its whole edifice ultimately to crumble. Also, because of her past reputation as the best working democracy of Eastern Europe, Czechoslovakia's fate reveals more vividly than that of any other Soviet satellite what happens when a Western-oriented democratic community succumbs to Marxist-Leninist totalitarianism.

This study is divided into four parts. *Part One* deals with the Communist Party of Czechoslovakia (KSČ) and its satellite "non-communist" parties. After briefly reviewing the highlights of the KSČ's history prior to 1948, it traces the changes which the Party has undergone since its seizure of power and explains and analyzes the Party's organizational and operational pattern, the nature and fiber of its leadership, and the chief problems with which it is confronted. *Part Two* is concerned with the formal government. It explores the unique nature of the Ninth-of-May Constitution, which served as a fundamental law throughout the first stage of the "socialist construction" from 1948 to 1960. It reviews the main changes enacted by the new Soviet-type Constitution of 1960 and examines the elaborate machinery of the communist "transmission belts." *Part Three* is devoted to an analysis of economic developments, which it seeks to evaluate in terms of production results, people's well-being, and human cost. *Part Four* portrays the communist effort to convert the Czechs and Slovaks to the Marxist-Leninist creed, an effort upon which hinges the ultimate success or failure of the communist experiment in Czechoslovakia as it does elsewhere behind the Iron Curtain. The last chapter is a summary of the main conclusions of the study and a brief estimate of future developments.

Throughout the volume emphasis is placed upon major trends of development and operational patterns. Attention is also paid to concepts advanced by theorists of Czechoslovak communism. However, since in their writings and pronouncements Czechoslovak Communists merely repeat Soviet-made and Soviet-interpreted precepts, I have deemed it unnecessary to clutter the book with too many such ideological derivatives which can contribute little toward a proper understanding of what has been happening in Czechoslovakia. Above all,

Communists everywhere must be judged by what they actually do rather than by what they proclaim they do.

The period under consideration begins with the communist seizure of power in February 1948 and extends to the end of 1960, thus encompassing the first twelve years of the communist rule in Czechoslovakia. However, explanatory references to developments prior to 1948 are made whenever necessary.

The sources used are mainly of two types: first, documents, books, periodicals, and other materials published by, or under the auspices of, the communist regime of Czechoslovakia; second, information obtained from non-communist and anti-communist sources, including interviews with Czechoslovak escapees, as well as reports from underground groups within Czechoslovakia. Naturally enough, these two types of evidence often disagree. The student of Czechoslovak affairs is therefore confronted with the arduous task of sifting truth from thick layers of propaganda. Because of this difficulty and the well-known secretiveness of the present Czechoslovak regime it has occasionally been impossible to find a dependable answer to some of the questions raised in this study. Whenever a query did arise, however, which is of such nature or importance that it should not be left wholly unanswered, at least a conjecture has been advanced on the basis of whatever partial documentation was available.

In concluding this preface, I wish to thank my colleagues from the Departments of Government, History, and Economics of the University of Texas for their valuable linguistic and stylistic suggestions. I would also like to express my gratitude to the Free Europe Committee for allowing me to use materials from the Committee's files and from its highly informative publications and digests, such as *Zpráva o Československu, Československý přehled, Československý zpravodaj,* and *East Europe* (formerly *News from Behind the Iron Curtain*). I am particularly grateful to Dr. Pavel Korbel of the Free Europe Committee for reading the manuscript and giving me the benefit of his most helpful comments. Finally, I am greatly indebted to the Research Institute of the University of Texas and to the John Simon Guggenheim Foundation for the fellowship which enabled me to complete this study.

Edward Taborsky

The University of Texas
Austin, Texas
February, 1961

CONTENTS

CONTENTS

PART ONE

THE COMMUNIST PARTY AND ITS NATIONAL FRONT PARTNERS

CHAPTER I

THE COMMUNIST PARTY AS A WEAPON OF REVOLUTION

"The dictatorship of the proletariat is in essence the 'dictatorship' of its vanguard, the 'dictatorship' of its Party as the force which guides the proletariat."[1] In strict accord with this fundamental maxim of communist totalitarianism, enunciated by Joseph Stalin himself, the Czechoslovak Communists promptly assumed exclusive control and political leadership the moment they vanquished their democratic opponents in the *coup d'état* of February 1948. Although purged remnants of all but one of the pre-coup non-communist parties have been allowed to vegetate, their precarious existence does not in any way detract from the full-fledged single-party dictatorship set up by Klement Gottwald and his aides. Since, therefore, the Communist Party is *the* government of the country, with formal government agencies serving only as obedient executors of Party decisions, it is appropriate to begin this study with an analysis of the KSČ, the Communist Party of Czechoslovakia.

How well or how badly is the KSČ equipped to rule? How does it actually operate as the instrument of proletarian dictatorship? Is it truly the vanguard of the working class? What is the caliber of the Party command and what is its relationship to the rank and file? How strong are the Party's ideology and moral fiber? How has it weathered the shock to which it has been exposed in the post-Stalin era? What are the major strains and problems plaguing it, and what are its main sources of strength and weakness? These are some of the questions which will be considered in the first chapters. But before this task is begun, a brief review will be made of the origins of the Party and the highlights of its developments prior to February 1948.

Origins and Apprenticeship: 1921-1938[2]

"The foundation of the KSČ [in 1921] put at the head of the working class a Party which adhered proudly to Marxism-Leninism,

[1] Joseph Stalin, *Problems of Leninism,* Moscow, 1940, p. 135.
[2] For the history of the Communist Party of Czechoslovakia prior to February 1948, see *Přehled dějin komunistické strany Československa* (An Outline of the

to the legacy of the Great October Socialist Revolution, to the banner of internationalism, and to friendship with the Soviet Union . . . . A great help and support for the solution of all the controversial and complex questions which appeared in the Czechoslovak revolutionary workers' movement was given by the Communist International, the Communist Party of the Soviet Union, and by V. I. Lenin in person at the Third Congress of the Communist International in the summer of 1921."[3]

These statements, taken from the official outline of the history of the KSČ, a Czechoslovak counterpart of the Soviet *Short Course,* reflect accurately the main characteristic of the Communist Party of Czechoslovakia, namely, its dependence on, and subservience to, the Kremlin. From its birth in 1921 through all its vicissitudes the KSČ has adhered unflinchingly to Moscow-made precepts, shifting the line whenever signals were changed by the Kremlin. Fully exploiting the broad political freedoms characteristic of T. G. Masaryk's democracy, the Communists laced the country with a network of Party cells and other units and set up their own labor unions, cooperatives, gymnastic groups, and other organizations. Unhampered by any censorship, they developed a massive Party press which became the Comintern's mouthpiece in Czechoslovakia and poured out day after day an incessant stream of vicious attacks on democratic leaders and representative institutions of the newly born Republic. In pursuance of the Leninist-Stalinist strategy of world revolution, political strikes were instigated whenever the cause of Marxism-Leninism could thereby be served. "Against your fascist police terror," said Gottwald speaking in the Czechoslovak Parliament on December 2, 1929, "we shall put up a proletarian de-

---

History of the Communist Party of Czechoslovakia), a publication of the Institute of the History of the KSČ, Praha, 1957; Jan Křen, *Československo v období dočasné a relativní stabilisace kapitalismu 1924–1929* (Czechoslovakia in the Period of Temporary and Relative Stabilization of Capitalism 1924–1929), Praha, 1957; Václav Kopecký, *30 let KSČ* (Thirty Years of the Communist Party of Czechoslovakia), Praha, 1951; Pavel Reimann, *Geschichte der Kommunistischen Partei der Tschechoslowakei,* Hamburg-Berlin, 1929. Documents pertaining to the period may be found mainly in two collections published by the Institute of the History of the KSČ: *V bojích se zocelila KSČ* (The KSČ Strengthened in the Struggle), Praha, 1956, and *Za svobodu českého a slovenského národa* (For the Freedom of the Czech and Slovak Nations), Praha, 1956. However, by their own admission, the editors of the documents left out "one-sided materials which might not be correctly understood without fuller commentaries."

[3] *Přehled dějin komunistické strany Československa,* pp. 86-87. Hereafter cited as *Přehled dějin KSČ.*

fense."[4] Every ounce of propaganda value was extracted from the few occasions in which bloodshed resulted from communist-incited clashes between workers and police.[5] Shielded by their parliamentary immunities, the communist deputies did all they could to obstruct and paralyze the work of the National Assembly, resorting upon occasion even to physical violence against their adversaries, while simultaneously using the Parliament as a convenient platform and a sounding board for communist propaganda.[6]

With the Soviet about-face in the middle thirties the KSČ steered obediently into the New Course. The inflammatory revolutionary slogans of yester-years were toned down and the "treacherous reformist leaders," who had formerly figured so prominently in the communist gallery of rogues, were invited to form a united front. "We offer the socialist parties a common struggle against hunger, fascism, and war," wrote the Central Committee of the KSČ to the executive committees of the Czechoslovak and Sudeten German Social Democratic and the Czechoslovak Socialist Parties in March 1933.[7] "The Republic can be protected only by a popular front," claimed Gottwald in December 1936.[8]

Although the Communist Party never became a member of a government coalition, it did depart from its previous obstructionist tactics and lent support to the government's efforts to strengthen the country in the face of the growing Nazi threat. For the first time in the young Republic's history the communist deputies cast their votes in 1935 for the democratic presidential candidate, Eduard Beneš, thus abandoning their hitherto consistent practice of putting up their own candidate, even though he never had any chance of winning over Czechoslovakia's George Washington, T. G. Masaryk. When the international crisis over Czechoslovakia reached its climax

[4] *Rudé právo,* April 3 and 6, 1925, June 4, 1931; *V bojích se zocelila KSČ,* pp. 290ff.

[5] *Rudé právo,* April 6, 1925; *V bojích se zocelila KSČ,* pp. 127, 130; *Rudé právo,* June 4, 1931.

[6] In particular, they used to introduce interpellations raising such demands as strict punishment of policemen interfering with the "worker's rights," requesting that pasture lands be given to small peasants, hours of work be reduced, evening and Sunday classes in apprentice schools abolished, and tariffs lowered. See *V. bojích se zocelila KSČ,* pp. 9, 18, 26, 79, 91, 109, and *Přehled dějin KSČ,* p. 134.

[7] *Rudé právo,* March 16, 1933; *V bojích se zocelila KSČ,* pp. 321ff.

[8] A speech made in the Chamber of Deputies on December 1, 1936. *V bojích se zocelila KSČ,* pp. 453ff. See also *Rudé právo,* March 31, 1935, urging a joint May Day Parade; a resolution of the Central Committee of the KSČ of December 13, 1936, for a unification of labor unions, *Rudé právo,* December 16, 1936; *Rudé právo,* July 27, 1937; *Přehled dějin KSČ,* pp. 140-141, 150, 155.

in the summer and fall of 1938, Czechoslovak Communists were among those who stood for war against Hitler rather than surrender to the Anglo-French ultimatum. Though their intransigent attitude had been prompted much more by Moscow's directives and by the Party's ulterior revolutionary designs than by concern for Czechoslovakia's national independence, Gottwald and his associates managed subsequently to draw valuable political dividends from their Munich stance.[9]

All through these years, despite the shifting lines of strategy which revealed its subservience to the Kremlin, the KSČ always ranked among the country's four strongest parties. Its greatest triumph was achieved in 1925, in the first parliamentary election after its secession from the Social Democrats, when it polled 943,000 votes and gained 41 of the 300 seats in the Chamber of Deputies. It thus trailed only 5 seats behind the leading Agrarian Party and outdistanced by 12 seats its main competitor for the workers' votes, the Social Democrats.[10] Four years later its demagoguery and fruitless negativism reduced the Party's following by almost 200,000 votes and cut its representation to 30 deputies, leaving it 9 seats behind its social democratic rivals and a full 16 seats behind the leading Agrarians. The economic depression of the thirties and the Party's switch from rigid obstructionism to greater cooperativeness during the popular-front era of world communism brought it a modest rise in popular vote to 849,000 out of the 8,231,412 votes cast in the last pre-Munich parliamentary election of 1935, i.e., 10.3 percent. The size of its parliamentary delegation, however, remained unchanged because of the over-all increase in the electorate which had occurred since 1929.[11]

Although in terms of political representation the KSČ of the interwar years ranked among the strongest communist parties outside the Soviet Union, one must not lose sight of the fact that even at the peak of its success its voting strength amounted to only 13 percent of the electorate, while actual Party membership fluctuated

[9] *Za svobodu českého a slovenského národa,* pp. 58ff., 99, 114. Hereafter cited as *Za svobodu.* See also *Přehled dějin KSČ,* pp. 169, 173; Dana Adams Schmidt, *Anatomy of a Satellite,* Boston, 1952, p. 249; Hubert Ripka, *Le Coup de Prague,* Paris, 1949, p. 4.

[10] A table of electoral results may be found in Eduard Táborský, *Czechoslovak Democracy at Work,* London, 1945, p. 85.

[11] Figures from *Statistická ročenka republiky Československé* (Statistical Yearbook of the Czechoslovak Republic), Praha, 1937, p. 279. (Hereafter cited as *Ročenka.*)

between a high of 150,000 (in 1928) and a low of 28,000 (in 1930). Furthermore, only a fraction of those who gave their votes to the Party were true Marxist-Leninists. Most of its members supported the Party because they honestly believed that the Party leadership stood for their best economic interests, for higher wages and better conditions of work, for security of employment, and for social elevation of the working man. Of all the tenets of Marxism-Leninism the only one for which they cared was industrial socialization, which they wistfully saw as a panacea for social ills. A great many workers were driven into the Party's fold by little else than the rigid social barrier which traditionally existed between manual laborers and white-collar personnel—a gulf responsible for much of the social estrangement and interclass antagonism that played into the hands of social radicals in many parts of prewar Europe.

Thus the KSČ was first and foremost a Party of those who, to paraphrase Lenin's famous dictum, were not only unwilling to "devote to the revolution . . . the whole of their lives," but were hesitant even to sacrifice for it "their spare evenings." The Party had its quota of professional revolutionaries, and its leadership was composed largely of sycophantic followers of Moscow. But not once throughout the whole existence of the pre-Munich Republic could this leadership induce the rank and file to do anything that could properly be called an attempt at revolution. Except for some brick-throwing in the course of several strikes and street demonstrations which the communist agitators had managed to misuse, Gottwald's proletarian defense consisted mainly of vitriolic verbalism, occasionally buttressed by fist-fights and inkstand-flinging in a few parliamentary sessions.

All through the first twelve years of its existence the Party was plagued by continuous factional strife and personal rivalries.[12] The Party's right wing, which was comparatively moderate, leaned toward limited cooperation with the socialist parties and wished to adapt the Party's strategy to specific conditions in Czechoslovakia. The Party's left wing relentlessly pursued an all-out revolutionary struggle and stood for rigid adherence to the Comintern's directives. Helped by a direct intervention of a Comintern emissary, D. Manuilsky, the leftists secured a majority on the Central Committee elected by the Second Party Congress in 1924. At that time a moderate

[12] A one-sided account of these strifes is given in the official *Přehled dějin KSČ*, passim; see also *V bojích se zocelila KSČ*, pp. 140ff.

group led by Bubník, a communist member of Parliament, split away from the Party and ran an abortive independent ticket in the 1925 parliamentary elections. Having failed to gain any seats, the Bubník-ites joined the Social Democrats. Another and more serious clash on Party strategy developed in the years 1925-1928. The reformist group led by Bolen and Jílek advocated a less aggressive course based on the assumption that the stabilization of capitalism would be of a longer duration, that the time was not ripe for attempts at a forcible overthrow of capitalism, and that the masses were not yet ready for decisive action. Their views were hotly opposed by a leftist group which subsequently came under the leadership of Klement Gottwald. The whole issue was taken before the Sixth World Congress of the Comintern, which threw its support behind the leftists. A special commission of the Comintern under the chairmanship of I. Gusiev, a Soviet Communist, condemned the Bolen-Jílek group for having "isolated the Party from the masses," and the Comintern's Executive Committee addressed an open letter to all members of the KSČ along these lines. It was mainly owing to this resolute Soviet intervention that the left-wingers won and that Gottwald, who had meanwhile been elected to the Comintern's Executive Committee, became the Party's Secretary General in 1929. A large-scale purge of so-called renegades and liquidators was carried out by the Party's Central Committee in June 1929. It resulted in the expulsion of many prominent Party members who were opposed to the Party's negativist rigidity and its uncritical subservience to the Comintern.

Hardly had the "right-wing liquidators" been separated from the body of the faithful when the Party leadership was confronted with a new challenge, this time from an opposite direction. A group led by Evžen Fried, and motivated by "faulty left-wing opinions regarding the conduct of the economic struggle and some intra-Party matters," accused Party leaders in the latter part of 1929 of allowing the Party line to be distorted by opportunistic tendencies.[13] While most of these left-wingers bowed to the criticism to which they were subsequently subjected by the Central Committee of the KSČ and the Executive Committee of the Comintern, the opposite was true of J. Guttman's right-wing group which rose against the Party leaders in 1933. Having been accused of misconstruing the Party's popular-front policy as "a compromise between revolutionary and reformist

[13] *Přehled dějin KSČ*, pp. 122-123.

attitudes" and thus having "capitulated in a petty-bourgeois fashion to social democracy," Guttman was expelled from the Party.[14]

Thus the history of the KSČ throughout the years of the pre-Munich Republic was characterized by an incessant struggle against heretics and by Moscow's interventions in support of those who were ready to follow unquestioningly Moscow's leadership.

The Party's political quandary was further accentuated by several other factors. The well-developed social welfare system of prewar Czechoslovakia weakened the impact of Gottwald's revolutionary tirades even at the peak of the depression. Nor could the Party's stubborn opposition to T. G. Masaryk contribute to its popularity. The short-sighted communist stratagem of opposing the candidacy of a man of such tremendous prestige as Masaryk placed the KSČ in the same camp as the Sudeten German Nationalists, who pursued similar tactics. Furthermore, the bitter hostility between the Communists and the Social Democrats, who had never forgotten nor forgiven the high-handed tactics of their communist comrades, all but killed whatever chance there might have been for a popular front on the French pattern in the late thirties. Hence the Czechoslovak Social Democrats definitely preferred collaboration with the "bourgeois" parties on their right to any partnership with their hammer-and-sickle comrades on the left, who were thus pushed into complete isolation. Nor were the Communists much more successful in their persistent endeavors to break up party coalitions and engineer governmental crises. The high degree of discipline characteristic even of non-socialist parties in pre-Munich Czechoslovakia and the pragmatic approach to politics on the part of most of the leaders of the non-communist parties made such coalitions quite resistant to Gottwald's disruptive efforts. The communist strategy of infiltration fared no better. Though the Party had complete freedom of organization, propaganda, and other political activities, its members were effectively barred from positions in state administration, police, and the officer corps of the Armed Forces.

On the other hand, the freedom with which the Party could develop conferred upon it some important advantages. While their comrades in the rest of Central-Eastern Europe, where communist parties were outlawed, had to spend most of their energies in efforts to evade the police, Czechoslovak Communists were able to operate

[14] *ibid.*, p. 142.

literally under the protection of the government. Unlike their less fortunate sister parties, they had unlimited use of the tremendous propaganda facilities of a free press. Most of the KSČ leaders were simultaneously members of the Czechoslovak legislature and were thus actually paid salaries for their subversive work. Without abandoning illegal work in the underground, the KSČ could freely train its cadres, set up its auxiliaries and front organizations, lure youth into its gymnastic clubs, and resort openly to many other deceptive activities denied communist parties elsewhere. Morever, and most important, its leaders became nationally known. As their names were continually mentioned in the press and radio news bulletins over a long number of years, the public became quite familiar with such leading figures of the communist movement as Gottwald, Zápotocký, and Slánský. This proved to be a significant asset for the communist cause when the Party made its bid for power after World War II. While communist leaders in the other East European countries were obscure figures, virtually unknown beyond the narrow circle of their fellow-conspirators, Gottwald and his colleagues were aided to no small extent by this publicity of the past and by the buildup given them by the Czechoslovak broadcasts from Moscow during the War.

Years of Exile and Underground: 1939-1945

The KSČ was outlawed in the political readjustment which was forced upon Czechoslovakia after Munich. However, its deputies continued to sit in the post-Munich rump parliament. Thus, as late as December 14, 1938, Zápotocký could use the floor of the Chamber of Deputies to deliver a pro-Soviet speech in a debate on Czechoslovakia's foreign policy.[15] After Hitler had liquidated the rest of Czechoslovakia in March 1939, the Party leaders went into hiding. Many were apprehended by the Gestapo and sent to Nazi concentration camps, among then Antonín Zápotocký, but others managed to escape abroad. Some of the latter made their way to France and England, but the cream of the Party leadership—Gottwald, Slánský, Šverma, and Kopecký—fled to Moscow, where they set up Party headquarters.

After the conclusion of the Nazi-Soviet Non-Aggression Pact of August 1939, however, their presence in the Soviet capital became

---

[15] *Těsnopisecké zprávy o schůzích poslanecké sněmovny* (Stenographic Reports of the Sessions of the Chamber of Deputies), 157th Session, December 14, 1938; *Za svobodu*, pp. 8ff.

rather embarrassing to the Soviet regime. Anxious to please Hitler and to allay the slightest suspicions of the *Führer,* Stalin had little use in the years of 1939 and 1940 for Gottwald and his colleagues. As a matter of fact, the KSČ leaders were treated almost as if they were undesirable aliens. Things improved for them after the Nazi invasion of Russia, but even then Stalin continued to hold the Czechoslovak communist leaders at more than arm's length. Since his primary interest in Czechoslovakia at that time was to deceive Beneš, Stalin was eager to demonstrate to the Czechoslovak President in a convincing fashion that he had no thought of interfering with Czechoslovak internal affairs. Nothing could help Stalin's designs better than pointedly keeping Gottwald and his associates out of any negotiations and treating them as if they were plain citizens of a foreign country given temporary asylum in the Soviet Union. During Dr. Beneš's first official visit to the Soviet capital in December, 1943, not once did Stalin or Molotov mention Gottwald, Slánský, or any other Czechoslovak Communist. Whenever some of the Gottwald group were invited to attend ceremonies, banquets, or receptions in Beneš's honor, they were relegated to the sidelines while attention was focused on Beneš and his retinue. Only toward the end of 1944 were Gottwald and his associates finally brought forward and groomed as prospective rulers of Czechoslovakia.[16] In January 1945 the process of grooming was already so advanced that, in correspondence with Beneš on the fate of Ruthenia, Stalin specifically mentioned that he had discussed the matter with "Comrade Gottwald."[17]

Besides complicating their sojourn in Moscow in the early years of their exile, Soviet policy reversals between 1939 and 1945 presented the KSČ's leadership with trying ideological problems. The worst by far was the dilemma posed by the Nazi-Soviet honeymoon of 1939-1941. How could the sudden Soviet friendliness toward Hitlerite Germany be reconciled with yesterday's anti-Naziism? Under the expert guidance of the Kremlin, the KSČ solved the unpleasant situation in true Leninist fashion by characterizing the war between Germany and the West as a clash between two imperialist camps

[16] This evaluation of the way in which the Czechoslovak Communists were treated in Moscow between 1939 and 1944 is based partly on reports from President Beneš's liaison officers in Moscow and partly on my personal observations there in 1943.

[17] For an English translation of the letter see Eduard Táborský, "Beneš and Stalin—Moscow, 1943 and 1945," *Journal of Central European Affairs,* 13, 2 (1953), p. 173.

and by denouncing Beneš as a lackey of Anglo-American imperialism. They blamed him for "sowing hatred among the Czech population toward German workers dressed in military uniforms," "driving Czech people into the English imperialistic army," "collaborating with the bankrupt Polish noblemen for the purpose of creating an anti-German and anti-Soviet Czechoslovak-Polish state," and for other activities contrary to the true interests of Czechoslovak workers.[18] Bowing to such directives, Gottwald's underlings in Czechoslovakia and in the West withdrew from collaboration with Beneš's liberation movement, which had shown great promise prior to the Hitler-Stalin pact. Nevertheless, so radical an ideological somersault did not leave the Party unscathed. While Gottwald's rigidly disciplined henchmen obeyed, many had private doubts about Stalin's wisdom and some even voiced their misgivings. The most prominent of these doubters was Vlado Clementis, one of the leading Slovak Communists who escaped to the West, later to become Czechoslovakia's Foreign Minister after Jan Masaryk's death in 1948. When the purge caught up with him in 1950, his communist accusers included in their indictment against him the charge that "he had accepted the platform of international imperialism against the Soviet Union and Stalin in 1939."[19]

When Hitler launched his invasion of Russia in June 1941 and the "imperialistic war" became "the great patriotic people's war against fascist aggressors," the Czechoslovak Communists made another about-face. "Is it not ridiculous in the extreme," wrote Lenin, "to refuse to temporize and compromise with possible (even though transient, unstable, vacillating, and conditional) allies?"[20] Pursuing their Grand Master's precept, Czechoslovak Communists promised loyal support to Beneš's government, ceased to talk about "Beneš's anti-German chauvinism" and "German workers dressed in military uniforms," traded their own "proletarian internationalism" for militant anti-German patriotism, and turned into ardent promoters of collaboration between the Soviet Union and the Anglo-Saxon Powers. In the wake of the German invasion, the Party's Central Committee

---

[18] A resolution of the KSČ's central leadership, dated December 15, 1940. See Eduard Beneš, *Paměti* (Memoirs), Praha, 1947, p. 214; also, *Za svobodu,* pp. 73ff., 92ff., 125ff.

[19] The accusation was made by the Chairman of the Slovak Communist Party, V. Široký. See *Rudé právo,* May 5, 1950.

[20] "Left-wing Communism, an Infantile Disorder," *Selected Works,* London, 1946, x, p. 111.

issued a passionate proclamation against "barbarian, bloody German fascism" and its "bestial hordes," and stated that the governments of "the most advanced nations, especially of America and England, recognized in Hitlerite fascism the most dangerous enemy of all nations and races, an enemy against whom the forces of the whole world must be united."[21] "It is not any longer a struggle of two armies, but a struggle of all the people, all the nations of the world against the band of Nazi murderers," preached an illegal edition of *Rudé právo*, published after the Nazi invasion of the Soviet Union.[22] Another issue, circulated in November 1941, reported jubilantly how in "a great historical step," the non-communist Czechoslovak Central Committee of National Resistance and the Central Committee of the Communist Party established "in brotherly cooperation a joint leading organ to our struggle for freedom."[23]

Communist good behavior was, however, only of short duration. Based solely on Leninist-Stalinist revolutionary strategy, it lasted only as long as it served communist ends. By early 1945 the situation had changed. The Red Army and the ubiquitous NKVD agents, operating on Czechoslovak soil, were supporting native Communists and obstructing political efforts of non-communists in every way. Democratic behavior on which Beneš's collaboration with the Gottwald group was predicated no longer suited the latter's designs. Nor was Stalin any longer interested in Beneš. Having fulfilled his Moscow-assigned role of showing how correctly the Soviets would treat those non-communists who harbored no enmity toward the Soviet State, the Czechoslovak President had outlived his usefulness by the end of 1944.

The changed communist attitude was amply revealed in the crucial negotiations (in Moscow in March 1945) about the formation of the new Czechoslovak Cabinet. Since I attended some of the sessions I can personally attest to what sort of negotiations they were.[24] Gottwald and his associates completely dominated the proceedings, pressing home the tremendous psychological and political advantages accruing to them from the Red Army's control over Czechoslovakia and the overt Soviet support of their cause. When the delegates of the other parties arrived in Moscow, the KSČ leaders presented them with a neatly mimeographed thirty-two-page copy of

[21] Eduard Beneš, *op.cit.*, pp. 218-220.
[22] *Za svobodu*, p. 166.
[23] *ibid.*, pp. 181-182.
[24] See also Josef Korbel, *The Communist Subversion of Czechoslovakia*, Princeton, 1959, pp. 109ff.

their complete "program of the government of the National Front of Czechs and Slovaks." This document, although filled with communist sophistry, was forced upon the democratic negotiators with only minor changes.[25] The KSČ leadership confronted the non-communist parties with a ready-made list of the new Cabinet with various posts tentatively distributed among the various groups. They chose their *marionette,* the fellow-traveling Social Democrat Zdeněk Fierlinger, for the Premiership and asserted with straight face how unselfish it was for them not to claim that top function for a Communist. They made it a *sine qua non* of their participation in the Cabinet that they obtain the key position of power, the Ministry of the Interior, which controlled the police and the whole apparatus of internal administration. They secured control over the other all-important Ministry, that of Defense, by placing at its head another of their collaborators, General Svoboda whom the Communists had raised from an unknown Lieutenant-Colonel to an almost legendary hero. Two of the staunchest Party die-hards became Ministers of Information and Education respectively, giving the Party full authority over the media of communication and thought control. Another staunch Communist was made Minister of Agriculture to strengthen the Party among the peasants by distributing vast tracts of land confiscated from the Sudeten Germans. A Communist was planted as Deputy Minister in the Ministry of Foreign Affairs so that the Party might watch closely the popular non-communist Foreign Minister, Jan Masaryk. Finally, to clinch its control, the Party secured two deputy premierships, one each for the heads of the Czech and the Slovak Communist Party, on the pretext that those were two separate parties. Thus, although the Communists held only eight out of the twenty-five Cabinet seats, they obtained, with the sole exception of the Ministry of Justice, all the key positions for the forthcoming battle for the body and soul of the Czechoslovak people.

How did they attain such spectacular success? The answer lies not only in the situation prevailing at that time in Czechoslovakia but also in the relations between Soviet Russia and the Western Powers. The Red Army was deep in Czechoslovakia. With its backing, the Communists were terrorizing their democratic opponents, setting up dreaded communist-dominated people's courts and people's

---

[25] *Program prvé domácí vlády republiky* (The Program of the First Government of the Czech and Slovak Government on Native Soil), Košice, 1945. A publication of the Ministry of Information.

committees, seizing factories, and establishing their private army, the workers' militia. The same process was evident throughout the rest of Eastern Europe. In Rumania, Vyshinsky forced King Michael to change the Rumanian Cabinet according to the Kremlin's specifications. The Polish and Yugoslav governments-in-exile, whom the Soviets did not like, were not allowed to return to their homelands. It thus became obvious that the Soviets would not tolerate in Eastern Europe any government which would not submit to communist domination. Having already seized Ruthenia, in spite of his solemn assurance in 1943 that that province would be returned to Czechoslovakia, Stalin might have at any time created a similar crisis over Slovakia. The Slovak Communists, who had meanwhile compelled the Slovak Social Democrats to fuse with them, had in fact begun a campaign for converting Slovakia into a Soviet Slovak Republic. They stopped only after receiving orders to the contrary from Kremlin agents parachuted into Slovakia, for Stalin had more ambitious plans which he did not want to jeopardize by an untimely annexation of Slovakia. Mere diplomatic protests against Soviet excesses and reminders of promises given at Teheran and at Yalta could not change the situation, and the behavior of the United States and Great Britain in 1945 clearly indicated that they did not intend to do more than that.

Under such circumstances, the hapless Beneš and the disheartened leaders of the democratic parties were at the mercy of Stalin who had by then thrown his full support behind the Czechoslovak Communists and given them an almost limitless power of political blackmail. The KSČ's leaders knew that Beneš had to comply with their requirements or risk a complete communization of Czechoslovakia while he remained deadlocked in Moscow in interminable negotiations.

"BREAKING THE BOURGEOISIE'S NECK": 1945-1948

When V. E. day came in May 1945, the Czechoslovak Communists were so powerful that they could have converted Czechoslovakia into a communist state immediately rather than wait until February 1948. Why did they wait? The reason was simple: Stalin was playing for larger stakes. Communists were gaining in France and Italy, and the Kremlin cherished a high hope that, by conquering the labor unions and gaining cooperation of the hesitant Western socialist parties, they might win "in a parliamentary fashion." The situation in China and other parts of the turbulent Far East at that time called for deft maneuvering of a similar kind rather than a determined *coup de force*. Since much could still be gained by continued repetition of the wartime tune of allied cooperation, Stalin wished to refrain as much as possible from alarming the Free World. A complete communization of Czechoslovakia, which would have led to the immediate resignation of President Beneš, might have created enough of a shock in the West to upset Stalin's subtle plans. After all, Beneš's Czechoslovakia was considered by many people in the Free World as a test case of Soviet intentions.

Submitting to Soviet guidance, the Czechoslovak communist leaders concentrated upon converting the country to communism by parliamentary means. The Party's primary purpose was to win 51 percent of the vote and thus to gain a majority in the Constituent Assembly. That would have enabled it to obtain power "legally," to institute the communist system by peaceful transition through legitimate constitutional channels, and thus to validate the Party's claim that it represented the will of the people. The whole colossal Party machine with all its auxiliaries concentrated upon the accomplishment of this paramount task. Ruthless advantage was taken of the Party's control over the air waves and of its supervision of the allocation of newsprint. The public was flooded with communist propaganda designed to convince them that the KSČ was only a benevolent group of social reformers and that no one but a few industrial and financial magnates had any need to fear it. While admitting that they stood for the socialization of big industrial enterprises, the Communists loudly professed their support of free enterprise in medium- and small-scale production. They maintained that they were actually the very best friends of private entrepreneurs, since their sole desire was to free their enterprises from the unfair and stifling competition of mammoth monopolistic corporations. They posed as staunch believers in private ownership of land by those who tilled it. They rejected in self-righteous anger insinuations that they cherished any thought of collectivizing agriculture, proudly pointing to the fact that it was a communist Minister of Agriculture who was distributing land among the peasants. For the intellectuals they depicted in rosy colors the future of creative freedom and material well-being which they had in store for scientists, writers, and others. To prove their solicitude for religion they insisted that priests and clergymen be

16

included in the category of hard-working laborers who were entitled to an extra meat ration!

To serve their purpose, the leaders of Czechoslovak communism turned upside down the Leninist conception of the Communist Party as a vanguard of the proletariat. Not only did they throw the doors wide open to those seeking admission, welcoming wholeheartedly any one and asking no questions, but they applied pressure to those who hesitated to cross the line. Peasants needing tools or fertilizer quickly found out that they would get them more easily if they joined the Party. Those eager to obtain more land soon learned that the Party membership card was the magic formula which alone seemed to be able to clear the interminable red tape. Employees of ministries and offices headed by communist chiefs and their fellow-travelers saw promotion evading them until they chose to sign the membership application blanks which were periodically placed on their desks by zealous Party agitators. This experience was shared by all those who aspired to softer or better jobs in the nationalized factories, all of which were under firm communist control. Even the allocation of an apartment by the local people's committee often called for the possession of that miracle-producing open sesame, the KSČ membership card. It is, therefore, small wonder that membership figures jumped by leaps and bounds. By the time of the Eighth Party Congress in 1946, the first Congress held since the War, the Party had 1,159,164 members as compared to the estimated 80,000 before the War.[26]

The ruthless exploitation of the advantages gained in 1945, combined with the belief on the part of a substantial number of manual workers that the Party would take good care of their material interests, brought the KSČ a major victory in the parliamentary elections of May 1946. The Party polled 38 percent of the popular vote and gained 114 out of 300 seats in the Constituent Assembly. As the leader of the biggest party, Klement Gottwald assumed the Premiership of the new twenty-six-member Cabinet, of whom nine were Communists.[27] Impressive though this communist show of strength was, it actually amounted to a Pyrrhic victory. Instead of being overawed by the big vote cast for the Party, the non-communists sighed with relief at seeing the Communists a full 12 percent behind their

[26] Gottwald's report to the Ninth Congress, *Lidové noviny*, May 27, 1949.
[27] See a table of election results in William Diamond, *Czechoslovakia between East and West*, London, 1947, p. 239; also, Hubert Ripka, *op.cit.*, p. 39.

goal of gaining an absolute majority. Their feelings were shared by a substantial number of the outwardly red "radishes" whose belief in communism was only skin-deep and who had joined the KSČ out of sheer necessity. Sensing that this was the peak of communist strength and confident that the Party would never be able to gain the coveted 51 percent, the non-communist majority began to react more forcefully against communist excesses. In the first months after the elections over 100,000 new members enrolled in the Czech Socialist Party, the most outspokenly anti-communist among the Czechoslovak parties. Similar increases were registered by the Catholic Czech Populist Party.[28] The Ministry of Justice, headed by a staunch and popular anti-communist, Prokop Drtina, began to prosecute ever more vigorously the numerous abuses of authority perpetrated by the communist-controlled police. Civic courage, the main requisite of democracy, was, after years of decline, on the rise again.

All this ran contrary to communist designs and made Party leaders realize that they could not hope to win a majority in a regular election. But they had yet another stratagem in reserve. Although the Party alone gained only 38 percent of the popular vote, the Social Democrats (Czechs and Slovaks) polled almost 13 percent. Together, the two parties adhering at least formally to Marxist socialism, obtained 153 out of 300 seats in the Constituent Assembly. If the Social Democrats could be made to cooperate and vote with the Communists, a peaceful transition to socialism was still within the realm of possibility. Hence, no stone was left unturned in the pursuit of this all-important objective. Having scored their major initial success in 1945 by planting Fierlinger and a number of other fellow-travelers in the highest offices of the Social Democratic Party, the Communists followed up these Trojan-horse tactics with a persistent campaign of wooing, cajoling, and browbeating the social democratic rank and file in factories. Distinguishing between the "honest left-wing Social Democrats" and the "treacherous right-wing elements," the communist plenipotentiaries in the factories bestowed advantages and soft jobs upon the former while they made life as difficult as they could for the latter. However, these high-pressure tactics backfired. Although some of the opportunistic and weaker elements among the functionaries allowed themselves to be bribed or coerced into submissiveness, the hard core of social democratic followers began to turn more and more anti-communist after their initial uncertainty

[28] Hubert Ripka, *op.cit.*, p. 41.

and hesitation of 1945. The communist failure to subjugate the Social Democrats culminated in November 1947, when the Social Democratic Party Congress ousted Fierlinger from the Party's Presidency by a sweeping majority of 283 to 182 and the anti-communist forces assumed control of the Central Committee.

The crushing defeat of Fierlinger and his pro-communist wing was the proverbial straw that broke the camel's back. With the leadership of the Social Democratic Party no longer in the hands of pro-communists, communist hopes to take over the government in a parliamentary manner were shattered. Only by counting the social democratic votes as their own could they ever hope to gain that 51 percent majority needed for a peaceful transition to socialism. To make things worse, all reports arriving at KSČ headquarters in the late fall and winter of 1947 indicated that the Party would lose rather than gain strength in the elections which were to be held in April or May 1948, when the two-year term of the Constituent Assembly expired. A Gallup-type poll taken in January 1948 by the Institute for Public Opinion Research under the communist-headed Ministry of Information predicted that the KSČ would obtain only some 28 percent of the popular vote as against the 38 percent it had in 1946.[29] Since the polls had been administered by the Communists themselves and a similar poll taken prior to the 1946 elections was only one-half of 1 percent off, this was gloomy news indeed.

All these ominous developments, so detrimental to the Party's chances in the forthcoming elections, were taking place at a time when Stalin had already come to the conclusion that nothing more could be gained from the West by a pretense of continued friendliness. In July 1947 the Soviet Union declared an all-out war against the Marshall Plan. Two months later the Cominform was established to launch a crusade against American "imperialism," and communist parties the world over, especially in Europe, were ordered to adopt a much more militant attitude than they had in the early postwar years. For the KSČ this spelled a much more abrupt change in tactics than it did for its sister parties in Eastern Europe. Gottwald and his collaborators had pushed the concept of "peaceful coexistence" with the "bourgeois" elements considerably further than the communist parties elsewhere in Central-Eastern Europe. On July 4, 1947, eager as they were to secure American dollars, they went so far as to vote in favor of Czechoslovak participation in the Marshall Plan

[29] Dana Adams Schmidt, *op.cit.*, p. 106.

Conference in Paris. But Moscow's condemnation of the Plan forced them to execute, almost overnight, a tactical 180-degree about-face.

Gottwald was particularly hard pressed to prove himself worthy of Stalin's trust by zealously following the new line. His heretical *faux pas* in voting for the Marshall Plan without first consulting Moscow made him extremely vulnerable. One can well imagine what reception Stalin accorded Gottwald when he summoned him to the Kremlin two days after Czechoslovakia's acceptance of the Marshall Plan invitation and ordered him to get the acceptance revoked. "I have never seen Stalin so furious," Gottwald told Masaryk and Drtina, the two non-communist Cabinet members who accompanied him to Moscow, upon his return from the interview with the Generalissimo. "He reproached me bitterly for having accepted the invitation to participate in the Paris Conference. He does not understand how we could have done it. He says that we acted as if we were ready to turn our back on the Soviet Union."[30]

Even prior to its error in accepting the Marshall Plan invitation, the KSČ leadership was criticized by other East European Communists for pushing the tactical concept of cooperation with non-communist parties too far. Tito and his aides in particular did not bother to conceal their contempt for what they considered a lack of revolutionary zeal and determination on the part of Gottwald. "What's the matter with you," one of the prominent Yugoslav Communists once barked at me, mistaking me for a Party member. "Why do you keep collaborating with those bourgeois parasites? Why don't you twist their necks as we have done?" Nor was the leadership's cautious maneuvering to the taste of some of the more radical elements within Gottwald's own Party. Speaking to the Party's Central Committee in November 1948, Gottwald defended the "correctness of the general line of the Party since 1945," but admitted that there was "impatience and even doubts" in the Party's own ranks about Party policy and that some comrades felt that the bourgeoisie should have been disposed of as early as May 1945.[31]

The Moscow-decreed switch toward increased militancy, the social democratic "betrayal of the cause of the socialist revolution," fear of serious losses in the 1948 elections, critical rumblings of the Party extremists and, last but not least, Gottwald's eagerness to make amends for his Marshall Plan blunder, and his frantic effort to regain

[30] Hubert Ripka, *op.cit.*, pp. 58-59.
[31] *Lidové noviny,* November 19, 1948.

Stalin's confidence were the major reasons behind the sudden increase in KSČ aggressiveness in 1947. Since it proved impossible to gain full control of the country through peaceful means, the inexorable logic of Marxism-Leninism called for the use of as much violence as necessary to attain the desired goal. That is exactly what happened in those crucial six days, February 20 through February 25, 1948, which pushed Czechoslovakia behind the communist Iron Curtain. In a speech delivered under the protective shield of the pre-Munich Bill of Rights in the Czechoslovak Parliament on December 21, 1929, Gottwald had this to say to his bourgeois colleagues: "You are saying that we are under Moscow's command and that we go there to learn. Yes, our highest revolutionary staff is Moscow and we do go to Moscow to learn. And do you know what? We go to Moscow to learn from the Russian Bolsheviks how to break your necks, you patriots."[32] In February 1948 Gottwald fulfilled his promise.

[32] Václav Kopecký, *op.cit.,* p. 100.

CHAPTER II

THE COMMUNIST PARTY AS
AN INSTRUMENT OF POWER
COMPOSITION AND MEMBERSHIP

HAVING YIELDED to Gottwald's ultimatum Beneš, broken and dying, left Hradčany Castle, the ancient seat of the Kings of Bohemia and, since 1918 quarters of the Presidents of Czechoslovakia—never to return. Although Beneš remained nominally the Head of State until he resigned in June 1948, the February coup rendered him powerless and the actual exercise of authority devolved on Gottwald and his communist associates. The Party's life-long ambition to overthrow capitalism and establish a dictatorship of the proletariat in Czechoslovakia was brought to fruition. The KSČ was transformed from a weapon of revolution into an instrument of power.

The circumstances by which Gottwald was carried to the pinnacle of power were vastly different from those confronting Lenin in 1917. The KSČ's leadership enjoyed in 1948 several important advantages which the Bolsheviks had not had thirty years before. Unlike their Soviet comrades of 1917, the Czechoslovak Communists had gained government experience through three years of active participation in all phases of administration prior to their seizure of power. From pre-communist days, they had at their disposal an ample supply of well-trained civil servants, most of whom, for reasons of opportunism or necessity, were ready to serve the new masters. Having managed to partially adapt the governmental apparatus to their needs in 1945-1948, Czechoslovak Communists could disregard Lenin's contention that "the working class cannot simply seize the available ready machinery of the State and set it going for its own ends."[1] On the contrary, they could utilize it forthwith for the pursuit of their goals with little or no change. They did not even have to disband the Constituent Assembly but used it, after having purged the non-communist leaders, to pass the communist-drafted Constitution. Since an experiment in Marxian socialist had been in operation for over thirty years in the

[1] Quoted after V. I. Lenin, *Sochinenia*, 3rd ed., Moscow, 1935, xxl, p. 394.

22

Soviet Union, the Czechoslovak Communists could learn from the successes and mistakes of their Soviet comrades rather than grope their way through costly trial and error or turn, as Lenin had, to the misleading experience of the Paris Commune. Unlike that of Russia in 1917, the bulk of Czechoslovak industrial production was already nationalized and largely communist controlled prior to the communist victory. Hence, solid foundations of socialism were already laid before the dictatorship of the proletariat was established. The harmful improvisation and colossal economic losses which resulted from wholesale socialization under wartime communism in Russia could therefore be avoided in Czechoslovakia. Being highly industrialized, the country had a large and well-organized working class which was quite class-conscious, viewed the private capitalist as its natural economic and political opponent, and believed, in general, in the virtues of socialization. The presence of this massive proletariat, which both Marx and Lenin visualized as the standard-bearer of the communist revolution, made Czechoslovakia a far better proving ground for an experiment in Marxism than Czarist Russia had been with her backward peasantry. There were no Kornilovs, Wrangels, or Denikins, nor any threat of outside intervention to worry the victorious Gottwald. Nor was the KSČ at the moment of its triumph plagued by any major internal dissensions and rifts like the Kamenev-Zinoviev opposition which complicated matters for Lenin after the October Revolution.

These favorable conditions, however, were offset by a few but weighty handicaps which faced the Party upon its assumption of the government. There was the embarrassing legacy of rosy promises made in the heat of competition with other parties—promises which were bound to backfire once their recipients realized that they would not or could not be implemented. There was the intense hatred engendered by the arbitrary communist behavior in the postliberation era and the painful memories of the bad conduct of the Red Army. The Party itself was overburdened with opportunists. The worst handicap which Gottwald brought with him into the conquered citadel of power, however, was his utter dependence on the Kremlin. Without Stalin's support Gottwald and his associates would never have succeeded in hoisting the red flag on Hradčany Castle. As the legendary Dr. Faustus sold his soul to Mephistopheles for the enjoyment of earthly glories, so did Gottwald pay with his own and his Party's freedom of action for Stalin's aid. It was chiefly through this dependence on the Soviet masters that the KSČ forfeited whatever chance it may have had to gradually convert its minority support into a majority. Whenever Czech and Soviet interests collided, the latter had to be met at the expense of the former. This servility toward the Kremlin brought the Party leadership further into disrepute among non-communists and made them more and more contemptible in the eyes of numerous disenchanted Party members as well.

In the wake of its victory in 1948, Klement Gottwald's Party was thus enmeshed in much the same vicious circle that had enveloped the Party of Lenin in 1918, when its leader decided to dissolve the Constituent Assembly. The Bolsheviks were then a minority and proceeded henceforth with a single-party dictatorship based on a minority. Unable to obtain the willing support of the majority, the minority had to rely primarily on force. Excessive use of coercion, however, is bound to generate hatred which makes the ruling minority seek safety in even more repression. This in turn breeds more hatred against the oppressors.

How well is the Party equipped to meet the challenging problems which confront it as the instrument of power? What changes have been made in its composition and organization? How is the Party's new role reflected in its operational patterns and principles? What developments have taken place in the Party's high command? These are some of the questions which will be considered in this and the following four chapters.

ELITISM IN THEORY AND PRACTICE

The establishment of the dictatorship of the proletariat should have put an end to the indiscriminate, wholesale recruiting of new Party members practiced in pre-February days. On the contrary, the elitist principle demanded that the sympathizers and the opportunists who were allowed to swell the Party ranks while it was striving for a 51 percent quota in 1945-1948 be promptly weeded out. In flagrant contradiction of one of the basic tenets of Leninism, however, the drive for a mass Party continued unabated after the seizure of power. "The Central Committee of the KSČ opens the gates of the Party to all honest working people who have had the opportunity to appreciate the Party's importance and its truly national mission in critical days. Leaning on the growing confidence of the people, we make it our task to increase the KSČ to two million members."[2] Responding

[2] Klement Gottwald, *Kupředu, zpátky ni krok* (Forward, Not One Step Back), Praha, 1948.

to this direct invitation by the highest Party organ, which also set aside the week between March 7 and 15 as "Gottwald's week of membership enrollment," hundreds of thousands of new converts jumped hurriedly on the Party band wagon. Another influx of new members resulted from the incorporation of the expurgated leftovers of the Social Democratic Party in the early sumer of 1948. Thus the membership soared to more than a staggering two and one-half million by November 1948, making the KSČ the largest Communist Party (at that time) outside the Soviet Union.[3]

Why Party leaders permitted the membership to rise to such unwieldy proportions, elevating one out of every three adults to the lofty status of the "vanguard of the proletariat," was never explained. Not even when the Party's Secretary General, Rudolf Slánský, subsequently admitted that it was a serious mistake was the reason given.[4] Probably their intoxication with the February victory had made Party leaders forget for a moment that the Party had moved to a new stage of development, and they let themselves be pushed by the law of continuity and by force of habit. Also, since Dr. Beneš still formally remained Head of State, they may have thought that a spectacular rise in Party membership would further solidify their victory and help them obtain the desired results in the forthcoming elections more easily. Be it as it may, such *reductio ad absurdum* of the Stalinist concept of the Party as "the General Staff of the Proletariat" could be only of short duration.

In August 1948, a new policy was begun when the Presidium of the Party's Central Committee ordered the first post-February screening of the entire membership. This resulted in the separation from the party of 107,133 members and the demotion of an additional 522,683 to the lesser status of candidates, a new category meanwhile established after the Soviet pattern.[5] Another general screening was launched in 1950, on a much larger scale. In order to achieve better results the whole procedure was thoroughly overhauled. The files of every Party member and candidate had to be reexamined. The dark spots in their past, (i.e., those years for which there was not enough material on file), were to be subjected to a particularly careful scrutiny. Each member and candidate had to appear for thorough ques-

---

[3] Slánský's report to the Party's Central Committee, *Rudé právo*, November 20, 1948.

[4] Speaking to the Ninth Party Congress in May 1949, *Lidové noviny*, May 27, 1949.

[5] *Lidové noviny*, May 27, 1949; also, *Zpráva o Československu*, i, 1 (1950), p. 2.

tioning before a special screening commission which was to recommend whether an individual was to retain his Party membership, be demoted to candidacy, stricken from the rolls, or expelled.

After this initial purge, the unholy twins, *provĕrka* and *čistka*—the screening and the ensuing expulsion of those who failed to pass—became a regular feature of Party work. This tended to serve both as the chief method of membership control and as a whip designed to make members more alive to their duties. Like the Soviet *chistka*, after which they had been patterned, they also degenerated into a weapon for the settlement of personal accounts and the liquidation of one's opponents. Supplemented by annual "controls of membership cards," which were used mainly for the elimination of those who failed to pay their dues and also as another way of ridding the Party of undesirable elements, the purges gradually reduced the Party membership to more manageable proportions.[6] Table I will make this more apparent.

TABLE I
Membership Changes, 1948-1960

	Members	Candidates	Both
November 1948			over 2,500,000[a]
May 1949	1,788,381	522,685	2,311,066[b]
August 1950			1,899,423[c]
February 1951	1,518,144	159,299	1,677,443[c]
June 1954	1,385,610	103,624	1,489,234[b]
January 1958			1,422,199[e]
July 1960	1,379,441	179,641	1,559,082[f]

Sources: [a] *Rudé právo*, November 20, 1948; [b] *Rudé právo*, May 27, 1949; [c] *Rudé právo*, February 27, 1951; [d] *Rudé právo*, June 12, 1954; [e] *Rudé právo*, June 19, 1958; [f] *Rudé právo*, July 8, 1960.

Despite the fact that Party membership had been reduced by one million from the all-time high of over two and one-half million which it had reached in the fall of 1948, its one and one-half million members and candidates continue to make it far too large by communist standards. While the Soviet Communist Party embraces some 4 percent of the total population, almost 12 percent of the Czechoslovak people belong to the KSČ. No other Communist Party in the world comes anywhere near that ratio. Why has the Party leadership thus

[6] See directives of the Central Secretariat of the Party of November 1949, *Pravda*, January 10, 1950; also, *Rudé právo*, April 26, 1952, calling for a "week of order during which cards are to be recalled and checked."

far had so little success in correcting a situation which most definitely is at variance with Leninist conception of an elite party? Why did all those purges undertaken in the course of the ten years separating the communist coup from the Eleventh Party Congress fail to reduce the Party's inflated size?

The answer seems to be that the Party is permeated by opportunists who cling to it as tenaciously as ticks hold to the animals on which they feed. By 1953, Party members from prewar days represented only a meager 1.5 percent of the total membership, while 91 percent were postwar entries and another 7.5 percent were added through the incorporation of the Social Democrats in 1948.[7] Most of these "mayflowers," so dubbed because they joined the Party after May 1945, sought Party membership essentially for opportunistic reasons. Since there are thus only about one to two Old Guard Communists for each one hundred mayflowers, and most of them are badly needed for more important functions, the postwar Communists have assumed control of most of the Party's primary units and local organizations. Consequently, the screening processes of the Party's rank and file have been administered mostly by those against whom they are primarily directed. Those chosen to sit on the screening commissions more often than not have been the same opportunists who were supposed to be eliminated. Indeed, many of the would-be purgers were and are no better than those they were supposed to purge, and they are keenly aware of the fact that their turn to be purged might come next. Hence, they have behaved as leniently as they could, unmasking as few unworthy members as possible and resorting to hand-in-glove collusion with other fellow-opportunists.

RULES AND POLICIES OF ADMISSION

While the purge aims at reducing the size of the Party by ejecting those found unworthy of membership, provisions have had to be made to bring about stricter control over the admission of new members. As a beginning step in that direction the admission of new members was suspended altogether in the fall of 1948. After the Ninth Party Congress in May 1949 this suspension was lifted with the proviso that, until further notice, only applicants from the ranks of the working class would be eligible, and from among them no one would be accepted but shockworkers who had been exceeding their

[7] B. Kohler's article in *Za trvalý mír, za lidovou demokracii; Zpráva o Československu,* IV, 9, p. 3.

norms of production for at least three consecutive months.[8] Meanwhile, new and stricter admission rules were prepared and approved by the Party's Central Committee in February 1951.[9] Under these rules, closely patterned after the Soviet model and only slightly amended by the All-State Party Conference in December 1952, Party membership has been opened to "every working citizen of Czechoslovakia [over eighteen years of age] who does not exploit any one else's labor, recognizes the Party's program and statutes, actively supports their realization, works in one of the Party's organizations, and fulfills all Party decisions."[10] Each applicant must fill in a form packed with searching questions and submit his detailed personal history. The application must be countersigned and recommended by two guarantors with at least two years of good standing as Party members. These guarantors "bear responsibility for the trustworthiness of their recommendations." The application is considered by the executive committee of the primary organization at the applicant's working or dwelling place. A recommendation is then made and the plenary session of the organization passes on the application after having heard the applicant tell them about his life and the reasons which prompted him to apply for admission. To be valid, the resolution of the primary organization must be affirmed by the Party's district or city executive committee. Stiffer requirements are prescribed for former members of other parties who must be recommended by five Party members with at least four years' membership.[11] After fulfilling successfully all these conditions the applicant becomes first a candidate for membership for one year during which time he may not vote, may not be elected to the executive committee, or sent as a delegate to Party conferences. This probationary period is used to make sure that the candidate would make a worthy member. If he passes this prolonged test with flying colors, he then goes once again through the same complex process of admission with all the paraphernalia of guarantors and checks. If everything is in order, he is then issued the card of a full Party member.

With the adoption of the new rules, admissions to membership which had been suspended pending the 1950 screening were resumed. However, the expected onrush of the acceptable kind of membership-

---

[8] *Lidové noviny*, May 27, 1949.
[9] *Rudé právo*, April 13, 1951.
[10] *ibid.*, November 2, 1952; *Pravda*, December 20, 1952.
[11] The requirement that the admission of former members of other parties must be approved by the Party's Central Committee was rescinded in 1956.

seekers failed to materialize. So disappointing was the response of those whose membership the Party desired, namely the workers, members of collective farms, and technicians, that the leaders ordered Party organizers actively to seek out potential candidates for membership and persuade them to join. "Party organizations may not and must not leave . . . admission to the Party to chance or let it proceed automatically. The committee of the primary unit and the plenary session are directly to designate the workers and technicians of the plant, the peasant members of the JZD [the Czechoslovak equivalent of collective farms] and the best people among the intelligentsia . . . whom we want in the Party. The committee will assign one or more comrades to prepare them for admission by systematically discussing with them political events, having them read Party newspapers and literature, recommending attendance at political lectures, etc. . . . "[12] Similar thinly veiled suggestions that the "right people" were not merely to be asked but should be *told* to join continued to appear and reappear in succeeding years, bearing witness to the lax interest in Party membership.[13] All in all, only 83,154 new members joined the Party in the five years separating the Ninth and Tenth Party Congresses.[14] The absence of any corresponding figures in the annals of the Eleventh Party Congress of 1958 suggests that there must have been nothing to boast about in that respect between 1954 and 1958. The situation seems to have somewhat improved in 1958-1960. As reported by *Život strany* (No. 14, p. 890) in July 1960, 218,407 new Party candidates were admitted in the years 1958, 1959, and the first quarter of 1960.

Several reasons account for this unexpected switch from former eagerness to subsequent reluctance to secure title to the membership card of the KSČ, despite the fact that it opens the gate to personal advancement for its holder. One such reason lies in the persistent hopes of an early change, possibly of outright liberation. Although such hopes have dimmed somewhat over the years, particularly after the West's inertia at the time of the Hungarian uprising and the recent Soviet successes with the sputniks, they are still very much alive. With

[12] *Rudé právo*, April 13, 1951.

[13] See, for instance, Novotný's speech to the Central Committee in December 1953, *Rudé právo*, December 6, 1953; Kopecký's speech in the Central Political School of the KSČ, *Rudé právo*, July 12, 1953; also, *Rudé právo*, June 15, September 11, and October 23, 1952, and May 18, 1953. *Život strany*, the Party's main magazine for Party affairs, has been replete with such admonitions year after year.

[14] *Rudé právo*, June 12, 1954.

people who have seen so many regimes come and go, such aspirations are hydra-headed and one learns to accept disappointment. The depth of such beliefs, and their naïveté, was illustrated some years ago. A rumor began to circulate that the Russians would reenter Czechoslovakia whereupon the Americans would march into those parts of the country which they had liberated in. 1945. This wild rumor was enough to induce many more vacationers than usual to spend their furlough in the area supposed to be reoccupied by the Americans. The point is obvious: such people still hope for a post-communist order. Feeling that way, why would they, for a few transient benefits of Party membership, want to act, not only against their own moral code, but also against their future interests?

Another factor dissuading people from seeking admission stems from the various unpalatable duties which the Party imposes on its members. The Party Statutes demand that they must be exemplary workers showing others how to work. "The sons and daughters of the KSČ march in the first rows of fighters for the new forms of work, for the adoption of progressive Soviet methods, for the development of socialist competition."[15] Thus they must be first to volunteer for additional work, to propose and participate in special work shifts in honor of the October Revolution, or to express their resolute protests against "American imperialism." They must display their high level of communist consciousness by spending part of their vacations to help out in the coal mines or in the fields at the peak of the harvesting season. They must incur the wrath of their fellow-workers by seeking to persuade them of the desirability of such distasteful features of Party policy as the need to strengthen the work norms or to delay the promised reduction of working hours. They are directed to spy on others. They must spend long hours of their free time attending innumerable boring meetings and classes of Party schooling. They must study the classics of Marxism-Leninism and read the tedious Party press so that they can keep abreast of any changes in Party policy or in interpretation of Marxism-Leninism the day may bring.

In view of the host of exacting duties which one must assume in joining the Party, the benefits of Party membership seem rather bleak by comparison, especially to those who harbor no strong political ambitions. A competent worker, farmer, scientist, or technician knows that the regime needs him, will reward him for good work, and pay him the bonus for exceeding the norm (the planned output),

[15] *ibid.,* November 12, 1952.

or for making a helpful invention, whether he is a Party member or not. On the other hand, should he be found, justly or unjustly, neglectful of his duties, the penalty would be heavier if he were a Communist, as the Party tends to deal more sternly with those who violate its trust. The principal groups actively seeking admission, therefore, are office-seekers and government officials who hope that the red star on their lapel will bolster their chances of appointment or promotion, and that it might perhaps even help them to avoid the dreaded misfortune of being transferred some day to "productive work" in factories or mines.

While dealing with the question and problems of admission, another significant change in membership policy should be mentioned, namely, the removal of the bar on admission of Germans. That such a bar had existed at all may come as a surprise to those who are aware of the lofty position which proletarian internationalism holds in the Marxist-Leninist ideology. The fact that the Germans of Czechoslovakia were ineligible for Party membership from 1945 to 1950 illustrates how even the most fundamental tenets of doctrine can be temporarily set aside when so demanded by Party strategy. In an endeavor to exploit the bitter anti-German feelings of the Czechoslovak people caused by six years of Nazi oppression, the KSČ developed a highly nationalistic attitude, and the Party which used to have a sizable proportion of Germans among its members in prewar Czechoslovakia, became in 1945 the most anti-German of all Czechoslovak parties. It backed most vociferously the deportation of all Sudeten Germans and rushed for confiscation of their property which it then used for its spoils system to reward its supporters and dangle as bait before those who hesitated. Its agents in the communist-controlled Ministry of the Interior and in the police were responsible for most of the cases of extreme harshness which occurred in the course of the transfer. From my position as Secretary to the President of Czechoslovakia I could personally observe the callous behavior of the communist Minister of the Interior who, acting on Party instructions, simply ignored the many urgent requests for a more lenient attitude addressed to him by and on behalf of Dr. Beneš. It was in line with this German-baiting strategy that the Party leadership decided not to admit any Germans and to consider as extinct the membership of those who had held it before the War, except for a few cases of Sudeten German Communists who had been abroad during the War.

When Soviet Russia later found it profitable with the quickening crescendo of the cold war to court the Germans, Czechoslovak Communists had to fall into line. They began to talk officially about a "reborn, denazified, truly democratic, and peace-loving Germany of the East," contrasting it with the "Nazi-infested Germany of the West, whose governing circles served as lackeys of American imperialism." An exchange of high-level delegations took place, with East German Premier Grotewohl paying an official visit to Praha, and Gottwald reciprocating with a visit to Berlin. Under these circumstances the anti-German ban had to be abandoned, and since 1951 Germans have again become eligible for Party membership. In spite of its careful preparation by the Party press the change in admission policy gravely dismayed many Party members and the leadership had to launch a whole campaign of "persuasion" to allay the doubts of members.[16] "The committees of the organizations shall make sure to explain to members and workers," the Party directives read, "why they [the Germans] are admitted into the Party, stressing that our Party is permeated by the spirit of proletarian internationalism, that international solidarity of the workers is in no contradiction to, but in close connection with, true patriotism."[17]

SOCIAL STRUCTURE

The chief purpose of the changes which the Party leadership made in admission rules and policies was to secure a better social structure for the Party. "Correct class composition" is to communist parties what complexion is to a movie star. As she goes to no end of trouble to improve her complexion and uses makeup to conceal the natural deficiencies of her looks, so the communist parties strive for better social composition in their membership and, if need be, apply rouge to embellish the reality. To qualify as the vanguard of the working class the communist parties believe that their membership ought to consist of as high a ratio of production workers as possible. On the other hand, the iron logic of their elitism and, after they had overthrown capitalism, their nature as an instrument of power, forced them to absorb a high proportion of administrative and managerial personnel on all political and economic levels. As these are mostly recruited from among the intelligentsia, the proportion of manual

[16] *ibid.*, March 1, 1950, and May 7, 8, and 9, 1950.
[17] *Funkcionář*, May 11, 1951.

32

workers—the typical specimen of the proletariat—tends to decrease and that of the white-collar group to increase. However, "A party perishes," teaches the *Short Course of the History of the Communist Party of the Soviet Union,* the obligatory reading for all Communists the world over, "if it shuts itself up in its narrow party shell, if it severs itself from the masses, if it allows itself to be covered with bureaucratic rot."[18] To prevent that disaster from happening the communist parties are supposed to invigorate themselves by replenishing their ranks with "the best sons and daughters of the proletariat."

As a result of its open-door recruitment policy in the early part of 1948, the KSČ grossly violated this Leninist-Stalinist precept. While workers and custodial personnel constituted 57 percent of the Party prior to the February coup, their proportion sank to 45 percent by the time of the Ninth Congress in May 1949.[19] On the other hand, the ratio of white-collar employees rose from 8.5 to 15.5 percent and that of small workshop owners from 4 to 5.5 percent. To correct this unfavorable class composition several measures were adopted in 1948-1949. A great many Party members of nonworker origin were demoted to the status of candidacy. The waiting period was fixed at one year for workers with at least two years of work in production, but at two years for other candidates.[20] In converting candidates to membership, Party organs were ordered to apply stricter criteria to nonworkers than to workers. As mentioned earlier, the Ninth Party Congress issued a ban on admissions except for selected manual workers. Even when general admissions were resumed again in 1951, strict instructions were issued to concentrate on recruitment of manual workers and small peasants, and to limit admission from among the ranks of intelligentsia mainly to technicians. Some of the Party's district committees went so far as "directly to prescribe the number of men, women, industrial workers, farmers, and youth to 25 years of age who should be admitted to membership."[21] According to the Party directives of 1959 workers-at-the-bench are to constitute at least 60 percent of those admitted to Party candidacy and collective farmers at least 20 percent.[22]

---

[18] English edition of 1939, p. 362.

[19] Slanský's speech to the Congress, *Lidové noviny,* May 27, 1949.

[20] A similar privilege was conferred in 1958 on members of collective farms. In 1960 the candidacy was set at one year for "all categories of the working people." *Rudé právo,* July 8, 1960.

[21] *Rudé právo,* November 18, 1953.

[22] *Život strany,* No. 12 (1959), p. 708.

How successful have been these persistent efforts to improve the Party's social composition and make it more proletarian? Judging by the stubborn reticence concerning changes in the Party's social structure since 1949, the results must have been far from satisfactory. Unlike his predecessor at the Ninth Congress of 1949, meanwhile hanged as a Titoist traitor, the new First Secretary of the Party's Central Committee, Antonín Novotný, failed to include in his long report to the Tenth Congress, held in 1954, any specific figures on this matter.[23] Instead, using a stratagem familiar in the Soviet Union, he resorted to a hazy statement that 60 percent of the Party members were "workers by original occupation." The same deceptive device was used again in 1958 when the Eleventh Party Congress was informed that "almost 61 percent of members and candidates are workers by original occupation."[24] But there is a great difference between "workers by original occupation" and actual workers in production, "workers-at-the-bench." As long as the Soviet Party cared to publish data on these matters, the two categories had always differed by a full one-third or more.[25] Although no over-all data are available in the case of Czechoslovakia to allow a dependable estimate as to how many of that 60 or 61 percent of workers by original occupation are actual workers-at-the-bench, the leadership's silence itself betrays that the gap between the two categories must be substantial.

A striking illustration thereof was supplied by the figures on the social composition of the voting delegates to the Eleventh Party Congress. As proudly announced by the Verification Commission of the Congress, 77.3 percent of the delegates were workers by original occupation, which further reflected, in the Commission's words, the fact that the KSČ was indeed "a party of the working class."[26] But in the same breath the Commission reported that there were 354 workers and foremen directly employed in industry, construction, and transportation among the 1,323 voting delegates. Translated into percentages this means that only 25 percent of the delegates were actually workers-at-the-bench as compared to over 77 percent of workers by original occupation. A similar ratio was conceded by the report of the Credentials Commission of the Party's National Conference in July

---

[23] *Rudé právo*, June 12, 1954.
[24] Report of the Verification Commission, *Rudé právo*, June 22, 1958.
[25] See table in Julian Towster, *Political Power in the USSR*, New York, 1948, p. 317.
[26] *Rudé právo*, June 22, 1958.

1960 (published in *Život strany,* No. 14, p. 890) concerning the membership of regional and district committees of the Party. While 74.6 percent of regional committeemen were said to be "of worker origin," only 21.8 percent were reported to be "workers." Corresponding figures for district committees were 78 and 17.5 percent, respectively. While these ratios can by no means be applied to the Party membership as a whole, they do indicate that the two categories are vastly different.

The Party's continuous failure to secure a correct class composition of its membership is further corroborated by the frequent recurrence of complaints about the low membership percentages of workers, the meager attention paid to "the social background of candidates," "the preparation of best workers in industry and agriculture for admission into the Party," and similar neglect.[27] By Novotný's own admission at the Tenth Congress no more than 56.2 percent of those who became members since the Ninth Congress of 1949 were workers.[28] Translated into absolute figures this amounts to an increment of a meager 46,702 workers in five years of hectic recruiting efforts! Another confirmation of the unsatisfactory social composition of the Party was supplied by the session of the Party's Central Committee which concerned itself at length with this thorny topic in June 1959. Although it failed once again to reveal over-all percentages of Party membership along occupational lines, the Central Committee bewailed the excessive admission of administrative personnel, pensioners, and housewives, and conceded that "only a little over 10 percent of the construction workers were members or candidates of the Party."[29] The Party's effort to recruit more workers seems to have been somewhat more successful in the last few years. As reported in *Život strany* (No. 14, p. 890) in July 1960, 55 percent of the 218,407 candidates admitted in 1958, 1959, and the first quarter of 1960 were workers.

Similar difficulties developed in connection with the attempts to attract and keep more members from among the small peasantry. Following to the letter Lenin's advocacy of an alliance of workers

[27] *ibid.,* February 7 and August 17, 1952, December 6, 1953; *Pravda,* November 17, 1953; Novotný's report to the Eleventh Congress, *Rudé právo,* June 19, 1958; Jan Večeřa, *Za další upevňování základních organisací strany* (For a Further Strengthening of the Party's Primary Units), Praha, 1957, p. 8; and recurrent complaints in *Život strany.*

[28] *Rudé právo,* June 12, 1954.

[29] *Život strany,* No. 12 (1959), p. 708.

with the poorer segments of the peasant population, the KSČ leaders have been striving hard to raise the membership ratio of "working peasants." The extreme secretiveness which the Party maintains concerning peasant representation indicates, however, that its efforts must have been far from successful. In his reports on the state of Party membership to the Tenth and Eleventh Party Congresses, Novotný failed altogether to give any figures, absolute or percentile, on this intriguing matter. While he mentioned in 1954 that 68 percent of "the total number of farmers organized in the Party" were members of the JZD, he carefully refrained from saying what the total number was.[30] On various occasions, however, the Party press has been more communicative. "The weakest link is the admission of candidates from the ranks of small farmers," lamented *Rudé právo* on October 23, 1952, listing a number of districts which failed to gain more than one peasant candidate in the course of the whole year. Of the 4,475 candidates admitted in 1958 in one of the richest agricultural regions of Czechoslovakia only 386 were collective farmers.[31] As a result, 98 of the region's 731 rural organizations of the Party did not have a single farmer on their membership rosters, 71 had only one farmer each, and 75 only two each. Reporting this sorry state of affairs, *Rudé právo* stated that "a similar situation existed certainly in the other regions as well."[32] In another highly agricultural region in middle Moravia only 38 collective farmers joined the Party in two and one-half years out of 7,000 collective farmers living in the region.[33]

Similar complaints have been aired on a number of other occasions.[34] This is also why the term of Party candidacy for collective farmers with two years of collective farm work was reduced from two years to one in 1958.[35] The low ratio of peasants among the delegates to the Tenth and Eleventh Party Congresses points in the same direction, although the selection of congressional delegates does not reflect accurately the composition of the total membership. Lumped together with "other workers in agriculture," a designation covering Party supervisors and other bureaucrats in charge of agriculture, peasants composed only 7.8 percent of the total number of

[30] *Rudé právo*, June 12, 1954.
[31] *Život strany*, No. 7 (April 1959), p. 409.
[32] *Rudé právo*, October 16, 1959, and September 11, 1959.
[33] *Život strany*, No. 15 (August 1959), p. 956.
[34] *Rudé právo*, February 7, 1952 and December 6, 1953; *Pravda*, November 17, 1953; Večeřa, *op.cit.*, p. 8; *Život strany*, No. 24 (December 1959), p. 1490.
[35] *Rudé právo*, June 22, 1958.

delegates at the Tenth Congress, while 72 percent were styled as workers and over 14 percent as white-collar personnel.[36]

As for the Eleventh Party Congress, official figures show that 225 of the 1,323 voting delegates "worked in agricultural production."[37] Of these 190, i.e., a little over 14 percent of the total number of the delegates, were listed as collective farm members and 35 percent as working on state farms and machine-tractor stations. Again, however, there is no way of saying how many of these delegates from the agricultural sector were actual dirt farmers and how many were farm directors and other administrative personnel who are mostly city people assigned to supervise the unreliable peasant element and are not peasant any more than the personnel of meteorological stations in the Arctic can call themselves Eskimos. Only one thing seems to be certain: that there was no independent farmer among the voting delegates to the Eleventh Congress, as all those reported as representing agricultural production were either collective farmers or employees of state farms and machine-tractor stations.

YOUTH

Another major concern of communist parties relating to membership composition has traditionally been the desire to keep the Party virile and youthful by steady injections of young blood. That part of the generation which had reached maturity under non-communist rule is mistrusted. The Party's future is seen in the younger groups reaching adulthood under communism who are fully exposed to the monopolized impact of communist indoctrination and thus are supposed to constitute a superior material from which to weave a stronger Party fabric.

Intent upon a continuous rejuvenation of Party ranks as the best guarantee of its future, the KSČ, upon seizing power, promptly moved to emulate the Soviet model in setting up youth organizations designed to serve as a rich reservoir from which the Party would eventually draw the largest portion of its membership. As in Soviet Russia the Pioneer movement was organized to attract school children between the ages of nine and fourteen years to provide a broad undergrowth from which to select the most suitable boys and girls for the second and far more important stage of political conditioning, the

[36] *ibid.*, June 16, 1954; also, *Tribuna*, vi (September-October 1954), pp. 9ff.
[37] *Rudé právo*, June 22, 1958.

ČSM, Czechoslovak Youth Union. Corresponding to the Soviet *Komsomol,* the ČSM is a mass organization consisting of a pyramid whose foundation is some 20,000 basic units and whose apex is a congress of delegates meeting at intervals of several years and electing a central committee as its main central organ. Like its Soviet counterpart, the ČSM is tightly controlled and operated by the KSČ whose auxiliary it really is.

When it was founded in 1949-1950, over one million Czechoslovak youngsters between the ages of fourteen and twenty-six, i.e., almost half of the eligible youth, were "persuaded" to join; and it looked as if the Party had got itself a goose that would lay golden eggs in the form of a steady stream of zealous and well-indoctrinated candidates for Party membership. But it soon appeared that the goose was far less productive than expected. Stagnation in membership as well as in spirit and activities became the most pronounced characteristic of the much-pampered institution. Since the formal establishment of ČSM in 1950, its number of members has remained stationary. Despite the Party's frantic endeavors to swell ČSM ranks by incessant recruitment drives, the membership rose only from 1,055,000 to 1,116,428 in 1955, and amounted to 1,112,000 at the time of the Eleventh Party Congress in June 1958.[38] "In spite of all its efforts," deplored *Mladá fronta,* the Union's daily, on April 27, 1956, "the Youth Union succeeded neither in attracting into its ranks the majority of young people nor in exercising decisive influence upon the youth outside the Union." The relative relaxation of controls in the post-Stalin era caused many of the basic units of the Union to fade away or lapse into utter passivity, especially in rural areas. As Novotný conceded in 1956, there were no organizations of the Youth Union in as many as 4,500 villages.[39] That was also when many ČSM members gained courage to spell out the reasons for their adverse attitudes and get publicity for what they had to say. *Mladá fronta* itself took the unprecedented step of publishing a scathing criticism of the ČSM from the pen of one of the organization's members, a high school girl. "I am completely indifferent to the ČSM," the girl wrote. "Without taking the slightest interest I vote each year for the new committee and listen with silent amusement to their new plan, the evaluation of the work of the previous committee, the thanks for the vote of confidence—but I do not expect anything at all to come out of

[38] M. Vecker's report, *Rudé právo,* June 22, 1958.
[39] *Rudé právo,* June 12, 1956.

all this . . . . The Youth Union has no attraction for me, no appeal. It is not youthful, but old and weary. It is for old grandmas and grandpas who want more tranquility than I. Something is lacking in the Union which I myself cannot define . . . ." Following the publication of this letter *Mladá fronta* invited its readers to contribute to a daily column which it started under the title "What Does the ČSM Mean to Me?" The gist of the answers was simple and unanimous: The Youth Union was dying of intolerable boredom and its name ought to be changed to Tedium, Incorporated.[40] Instead of generating enthusiasm among the youngsters for the new system, instead of making them more receptive to the communist creed and conditioning the best of them for admission to the Party, their voluntary-compulsory membership in the Youth Union only made them more resentful of communist regimentation.[41] What continued to keep most of them in the Union was primarily their realization that they might otherwise endanger advancement in their jobs or jeopardize their chances of admission to institutions of higher learning.[42] "We do not seek to conceal," admitted the First Secretary of the ČSM at the Eleventh Party Congress in 1958, the fact that there are "those who are not worthy of ČSM membership, particularly those who join the Union to obtain advantages, [who join it] essentially for opportunistic reasons, as occurs, for instance, in schools. Does a member who knows of the ČSM only when it is a question of admission to a college or assignment to work belong in the Union?"[43]

Unavoidably, such a situation could not remain without adverse effects on the Party's efforts at rejuvenating its ranks by the influx of dedicated youthful Communists. What the KSČ has been getting via the Youth Union is mostly young opportunists ready to buy personal advantages by superficial conformism but cured of illusions which they might have held previously about the nature of communism. While the addition of an adequate number of young opportunists might in due time make the Party younger in the physical sense, it certainly cannot rejuvenate it in spirit. Whether or not any physical rejuvenescence has as yet been attained cannot be deter-

[40] For details see *News from behind the Iron Curtain*, 4, 6 (1955), pp. 25ff. Hereafter cited as *News;* also, *Československý přehled,* IV, 7-8 (1957), pp. 39ff.; *Mladá fronta,* October 14, 19, and November 4, 1958.

[41] The compulsory character of membership in a great many cases was admitted by *Mladá fronta,* May 30, 1956.

[42] About the continued disaffection of the members of the Union see *Tvorba,* April 25, 1956, *Mladá fronta,* June 19, 1957, and August 21, 1960.

[43] Vecker's report, *Rudé právo,* June 22, 1958.

mined because of the dearth of published data. At the Ninth Party Congress in May 1949 the percentage of Party members below twenty-five years of age was said to be 14.5 percent. No figures to that effect were revealed at either the Tenth of the Eleventh Party Congress. Such partial data as could be gleaned from various press articles indicate that the percentile share of persons under twenty-five among the newly admitted Party candidates is considerably higher than that of other age groups. Thus 51.2 percent of those granted the status of candidacy between the Ninth and Tenth Congresses were below twenty-five and 29 percent were between twenty-five and thirty-five.[44] However, since no announcements are made about the age of those who simultaneously cease to be members or candidates, the net results cannot be determined. That the Party's hope of gaining in the Youth Union a rich reservoir of Party recruits has thus far fallen short of expectations has been confirmed recently by *Rudé právo:* "It is necessary to point out that the number of Party members in the organizations of the Youth Union has been declining substantially from year to year. Of the total membership of the Youth Union only 5 percent are Party members."[45] That would put the number of young people who belong simultaneously to the Youth Union and the Party at some 55,000, i.e., only about 4 percent of Party membership. Thus, twelve years after its seizure of power, the KSČ continues to have little attraction for the young generation, despite the many offices and prebends it has to offer to its faithful. As Novotný told the Eleventh Party Congress, "The analysis of the age structure of the Party and its important tasks among the youth stress most urgently the need of enrolling in the Party a far larger number of active young people."[46]

WOMEN

A similar lack of recent over-all data prevails with respect to the ratio of women in Party membership. By the time of the Ninth Party Congress in 1949, as many as 33 percent of all Party members were women, half of them housewives.[47] But no breakdown of Party membership by sex was included in reports to the Tenth and Eleventh Party Congresses. The lower representation of women among the delegates, 13.3 and 14 percent respectively in 1954 and 1958, while

[44] *Rudé právo,* June 12, 1954.
[45] *ibid.,* June 20, 1957.
[46] *ibid.,* June 19, 1958; also, *Život strany,* No. 12 (1959), pp. 707ff.
[47] *Lidové noviny,* May 27, 1949.

clearly indicative of the weaker political influence of women under communism, cannot serve as a basis for any computation because Party delegates are by no means chosen in direct ratio to social origin, age, or sex, and women as a group are habitually underrepresented in Party Congresses.

ETHNIC MINORITIES

Finally, a few words should be said about the ethnic composition of the Party. In postwar Czechoslovakia the Czechs and the Slovaks are officially considered as two separate nations living together in a common state. Moreover, the illogical and unsymmetrical political arrangement which allows the Slovaks special autonomous organs of government while none are available for the Czechs extends also to the Party system so that there exists a Communist Party of Slovakia as a special subdivision of the KSČ with no equivalent on the Czech side. In view of this setup, as well as of the recent history of troubles between the Czechs and the Slovaks, it is of some interest to see how the Czech-Slovak relationship is expressed in terms of Party membership.

Upon their assumption of power in 1948 the Communists were considerably stronger in the Czech provinces than in Slovakia. While over 40 percent of the Czechs cast their ballots for the Communist Party in the 1946 elections, the Party was the choice of only a little over 30 percent of the voters in Slovakia.[48] Of the 2,311,066 members and candidates of the KSČ in 1949 only 236,432 were from Slovakia, i.e., slightly over 10 percent, although more than one-quarter of Czechoslovakia's population lived in that area. Also, the Party's appeal to the youth was far less effective in Slovakia than in the rest of the country. While the over-all percentages of Party members below twenty-five years of age in 1949 was 14.5, the corresponding figure for Slovakia was only 9.7.[49] The ensuing years altered only slightly this disparity in communist numerical strength in the two parts of Czechoslovakia. Of the delegates to the Tenth Congress of the KSČ in 1954, only 10.2 percent were Slovaks.[50] Reporting to the Eleventh Congress of the Slovak Communist Party in April 1955, its First Secretary, K. Bacílek, announced that the Party had 191,690 members, which amounted to about 13 percent of the total member-

---

[48] See table in William Diamond, *op.cit.*, p. 239.
[49] *Rudé právo*, May 27, 1950.
[50] *ibid.*, June 16, 1954 (Bacílek's report).

ship. By 1958 the Slovak membership in the KSČ climbed to 14 percent.[51] But this is still far below the 28 percent Slovak share in the total population of Czechoslovakia.

The reasons for the weaker standing of the Party in Slovakia than in the Czech provinces are easy to understand. Slovakia suffered more heavily at the hands of the Red Army than did Czech provinces. Slovak Catholicism goes deeper and is more conservative than the Czech variety. Despite a recent upsurge in its industrialization, Slovakia remains more agrarian than the Czech areas and has therefore a smaller ratio of industrial workers. Much less confiscated property was available for distribution in Slovakia than in the Czech provinces and thus there was much less reason to be thankful for gifts from the communist donors. The Slovaks have always resented "Praha centralism," no matter who ruled from Praha; and that was bound to militate even more so against the present rulers whose democratic centralism dwarfs whatever centralizing tendencies there had been in pre-Munich Czechoslovakia. The fact that the Communists had initially supported Slovak autonomistic demands in 1945, then reversed themselves sharply and reduced the Slovak autonomy to an empty shell, further added to Slovak bitterness. The interplay of these political, economic, and psychological factors has made the Slovaks somewhat more immune to communism than their Czech brothers, and this impedes Party recruitment in Slovakia even beyond the difficulties encountered in the Czech provinces.

Though the expulsion of the Sudeten Germans has made postwar Czechoslovakia nationally much more homogeneous, national minorities were not completely eliminated. There are some 415,000 Hungarians (about 3.1 percent of the population), 76,000 Ruthenians (0.5 percent), a remnant of some 163,000 Germans (1.2 percent) and some 79,000 Poles (0.6 percent).[52] How are these national minorities represented in the KSČ? As the KSČ does not release any figures on the ethnic composition of Party membership, this question cannot be answered. However, information is available on the nationality of delegates to the Tenth Party Congress, of whom 0.9 percent were Hungarian, 0.6 percent Ruthenian, 0.2 percent Polish, and 0.1 percent German.[53] These figures do not reflect the exact membership proportions of the said groups. Nevertheless, they do suggest

[51] Based on the report of the Verification Commission at the Eleventh Party Congress in 1958, *Rudé právo*, June 22, 1958.

[52] *Ročenka*, Praha, 1960, p. 58.

[53] *Rudé právo*, June 16, 1954.

the proportional share of minority ethnic groups in Party membership is well below the average. Relating the percentages of Party delegates to the percentages of total population one may further advance a conjecture that, of all these ethnic groups, Ruthenians have relatively the highest ratio of Party membership while Germans have the lowest, closely followed by Hungarians. That would correspond also to the prevalent attitude in Czechoslovakia, which looks upon Ruthenians as good Slav brothers who can be trusted more than Germans or Hungarians. By 1958 the share of ethnic minorities evidently sank still lower. As announced at the Eleventh Party Congress, the delegates of Ukrainian, Polish, German, and Hungarian nationality constituted together a mere 1.4 percent of the total number of voting delegates as against 1.8 percent in 1954.[54]

[54] Report of the Verification Commission, *Rudé právo,* June 22, 1958. The split among individual nationalities was not given in 1958, though it was given in 1954.

CHAPTER III
PARTY ORGANIZATION

THE communist parties' obsession with correct class composition is matched by their constant preoccupation with matters of organization. "Give us an organization of revolutionaries," Lenin wrote in 1902, "and we shall overturn the whole of Russia."[1] His life's work shows indeed that he concentrated as much on the excellence of organization as on the need for dedicated revolutionaries. This organizational perfectionism becomes even more imperative whenever the Party is transformed from a weapon of revolution into an instrument of power. The new duties and opportunities accruing to it after the overthrow of capitalism in each of the satellite countries brought with them new risks and temptations. Such dangers as "opportunistic pollution," "bureaucratic rot," abuse of authority, and complacency tended to deepen and multiply after the "proletarian" victory. "The history of the Party further teaches us that a party cannot perform its role as a leader of the working class if, carried away by success, it begins to grow conceited [and] ceases to observe the defects in its work . . . ," warns the *Short Course*. "A Party perishes . . . if it gives way to self-complacency and vainglory and if it rests on its laurels."[2] Furthermore, the Party's new role as supreme ruler necessitated both a substantial enlargement of Party apparatus and a constant streamlining of its machinery so that it might cope with perennial and increasingly complex governmental problems.

The Czechoslovak Communist Party could not escape such problems and dangers any more than its sister parties in the Soviet Union and elsewhere behind the Iron Curtain. To meet them, it too felt compelled to adapt its machinery and to refurbish and even amend its organizational philosophy. In doing so, the KSČ followed quite closely the Soviet model. Whenever a change occurred in the organizational pattern of the Soviet Party, Czechoslovak Communists un-

[1] *Chto Delat, Sochinenyia,* 3rd ed., Moscow, 1935, IV, p. 458.
[2] *History of the Communist Party of the Soviet Union (Short Course),* Moscow, 1939, p. 361.

dertook similar alterations. However, it seems that this imitative behavior of Czechoslovak Communists has been motivated more by considerations of personal security than by a genuine belief in the intrinsic value of Soviet organizational precepts and practices. To "do as the Soviet comrades do" has been and still is the best possible protection in case something goes wrong.

ADAPTATIONS AFTER THE SOVIET IMAGE

Thus the organizational pattern of the KSČ has undergone since 1948 a gradual adaptation along Soviet lines. The KSČ entered the era of the dictatorship of the proletariat with a constitution which differed in several ways from that governing the Soviet Communist Party. Instead of the monolithic Stalinist arrangement of first secretaries as leading Party functionaries on all levels, the KSČ had rather a dichotomous system headed by two officers, the Chairman and the Secretary. At all levels in the pyramid of the Party organs the usual powers and duties of the Soviet Party secretaries were shared by these two officers, the Chairman being the more important of the two. The Party's strongest man, Klement Gottwald, was Party Chairman while Rudolf Slánský, the number-two man, was Secretary General. Similarly, in the lower Party organizations the chairmanship was habitually held by the local Party leader with the secretary regarded as second best. Unlike the Soviet Party, the KSČ thus carried over into the fifties the original bolshevist pattern of Lenin's days when the highest leader did not hold the Party's top Secretaryship and when the Central Secretariat lacked the authority which it subsequently gained under Stalin's rule.

Nor was the status of the Chairman of the KSČ in any way comparable to the exalted position of the Secretary General of the Soviet Party. Although he was elected by the Party Congress rather than by the Central Committee, the Chairman wielded no special powers of any major importance, whether by virtue of Party Statutes or through their application in actual practice. He presided over the Presidium of the Central Committee which, like the Soviet Politbureau, was the conclave of the highest-ranking leaders. But he was only *primus inter pares* and could neither force his opinion on the others nor overrule them.

Yet another notable departure from the Soviet prototype existed at the very base of the organizational pyramid. While the foundation of the Soviet Party consisted of primary units established in factories, offices, collective farms, and other places where people work, the lowest Party units in Czechoslovakia were local organizations with membership determined by the place of residence rather than by the place of work. Even at the time of the Ninth Party Congress in May 1949, i.e., fifteen months after the February coup, local organizations of a strictly territorial type constituted over 70 percent of the Party's basic units.[3]

It was a foregone conclusion that such deviations from the organizational pattern of the mother party could not last long. What could be condoned on grounds of expediency at the stage of "the overgrowth of the national revolution into the socialist revolution," could no longer be tolerated once the dictatorship of the proletariat was firmly established. The initial step in that direction was taken in September 1951. The first major purge of high Party functionaries was then in full swing and Gottwald's group, which had been steadily gaining ground since the February coup, could thus accomplish two objectives: to remodel the Party's constitution and to profit by the occasion to entrench themselves more firmly in power. Acting in direct violation of the Party Statutes reserving such matters for the Party Congress, the Central Committee decreed a reorganization of the central Party organs along Soviet lines. The function of the Secretary General was merged with that of the Party Chairman. A Political Secretariat, composed of the seven highest-ranking Party leaders, was created "for the daily direction of the Party's political affairs" and given a new Organizational Secretariat of several elected secretaries as its subordinate auxiliary.[4]

The similarity of the new arrangement to the Soviet model is clearly apparent. The new seven-man Political Secretariat was an obvious replica of the Soviet Politbureau, while the Organizational Secretariat was a "kissing cousin" of the Soviet Orgbureau and Central Secretariat. The fusion of the two highest positions, the Party Chairmanship and General Secretaryship, also bore a strong resemblance to the Kremlin pattern. So did the substantial increase in the authority of the Party's topmost incumbent, Klement Gottwald, whose new status within the KSČ organization came fairly close to that of Stalin within the Communist Party of the Soviet Union. He now held the combined powers of Party Chairman and Secretary General.

---

[3] Novotný's report to the Tenth Party Congress, *Rudé právo,* June 12, 1954.
[4] *Rudé právo,* September 8, 1951. In December 1951, the membership of the Political Secretariat was increased to eight.

He headed both the Political and Organizational Secretariats, which gave him a definite advantage over his colleagues in the everyday operational control of Party affairs. The adaptation was completed in the ensuing session of the Central Committee in December 1951, when a new Commission of Party Control was set up to serve, as did its Soviet namesake, in the capacity of disciplinary arm of the Central Committee.[5]

By the end of 1951 the central organs of the KSČ were thus recast in strict conformity with the Soviet model. The only difference of any consequence was the continued existence of the Presidium of the Central Committee for which there was no equivalent in the Soviet system. But the 1951 transfer of the daily direction of the Party's political affairs to the Political Secretariat pushed the Presidium into political semiobscurity and paved the way for its extinction within the next three years.

The next step in the sovietization of the KSČ organization came in December 1952, when a National Party Conference convened to enact new Party Statutes. Since the Soviet mother Party adopted new Party rules at its Nineteenth Congress in October 1952, its obedient child could not act otherwise. "It is understandable," said Gottwald in his report on that "historic Congress" upon his return from Moscow, "that the draft of the new Statutes of our Party is based on the new Statutes of the Communist Party of the Soviet Union adopted by its Nineteenth Congress . . . . It is a fact that we have much to learn from our Soviet comrades even in matters of the Party's construction, organization, and work . . . ."[6]

In spite of these words of praise for the Soviet system, Gottwald's "creative application of the results of the Nineteenth Congress" led to only one notable alteration of the central organs and that was the careful omission of any mention of the Party Chairman. Though Gottwald continued even thereafter to be tacitly considered Party Chairman, the Statutes were drafted with the anticipation that he would be the last bearer of that august title. Indeed, the title died with him shortly thereafter in March 1953. His successor as President of the Republic and number-one Party man at the time, Antonín Zápotocký, was not awarded any specific Party title and was referred to solely as "member of the Political Secretariat." The direction of the work of the Organizational Secretariat was entrusted to another

---

[5] *ibid.,* December 8, 1951.
[6] *ibid.,* October 24, 1952.

member of the Secretariat, Antonín Novotný.[7] The matter was then regularized in September 1953 when, following N. S. Khrushchëv's formal election as First Secretary of the Central Committee of the Soviet Party, Novotný was chosen to fill the same position within the KSČ.[8]

A similar fate met the chairmanship on regional, district, and city levels. In line with Soviet practice and in order to consolidate operative leadership, the new Party Statutes of 1952 replaced the chairmen, who had been elected by the respective Party conferences, by "leading" secretaries. Chosen by the executive committees of the respective Party organizations, these secretaries had to be approved by the committee of the next highest Party level. The only chairmanships retained by the Statutes were those in local and primary units. But instead of being elected, as previously, by plenary sessions of these units, they were henceforth chosen by their executive committees from among their members. Furthermore, since the parallel positions of secretaries in these units were simultaneously eliminated, the said chairmen served for all practical purposes as secretaries, with the title of chairmen appended merely as a consolation prize.

But the main feature of the 1952 reorganization was the resolute drive to replace the existing system of local organizations based on residence with primary units established directly in places of work. "The foundations of the Communist Party must be in production, in the places of work," argued *Rudé právo*. While the system of local organizations may have been adequate for Social Democrats, "for whom the highest struggle was the election," it could not be enough for the Communist Party "which has higher goals . . . . From the beginning Lenin and Stalin built a revolutionary party in Russia so that its foundations lay in production . . . ."[9] In pursuance of the prescribed territorial-productive principle the base of the organizational pyramid was completely rebuilt in 1953. Local residence-based organizations in urban areas were abolished and their membership transferred to primary units in factories, business enterprises, offices, and other places of their employment. People in retirement were even assigned to primary units of their former work sites and housewives to those set up in their husbands' places of work. Occasionally, the furor of reassignment went far beyond the Party's

[7] *ibid.*, March 22, 1953.
[8] *ibid.*, September 14, 1953.
[9] *ibid.*, November 9, 1952.

original intentions, as the overzealous reorganizers kept assigning until some factory units had a majority of members who did not actually work there.[10] When the reorganization was over, what was left in the urban areas was a relatively small number of street organizations to hold under Party aegis those members who did not belong or could not reasonably be transferred to production units. By the time of the Tenth Party Congress in 1954 there were 29,933 production units comprising 67.2 percent of the total number of basic Party organizations as against 1,006 street organizations (2.2 percent) and the corresponding figures were 31,343 working-place units as against 1,643 street organizations as of January 1, 1960.[11]

The remaining 30.6 percent consisted of 13,623 village organizations. While the territorial-productive principle was drastically applied to urban settlements, the policy was to retain the original territorial principle in rural areas, at least until such time as the bulk of the rural economy was fully collectivized. With the precarious ideological hold of the Party over the peasantry and the dearth of staunch Communists in rural areas, it was deemed strategically more advantageous to have only one Party organization per village, open to both collective and individual farmers. Since many peasant Party members were doing all they could to delay collectivization in their area, any other course might have created a highly embarrassing situation where an undernourished and anemic collective farm unit would have contrasted sadly with a vigorous Party unit of individual farmers, hoping that they could obstruct collectivization more effectively from under the Party's banner.

With the adoption of the new Statutes in 1952 and the resolute reorganization carried out on their basis in 1953, the sovietization of the whole apparatus of the KSČ was brought to its virtual completion. The slight variation in the respective central Party organs of the two countries, resulting from the retention of the waning Presidium as an intermediate organ between the Political Secretariat and the Central Committee's plenum in the KSČ, disappeared in 1954 when the Tenth Party Congress decreed that the Presidium be abolished. Simultaneously, the Political Secretariat was renamed the Political Bureau and the Organizational Secretariat shortened to the Secretariat.[12]

[10] *ibid.*, November 9, 1952, January 16, 1953.
[11] *ibid.*, June 12, 1954, and *Život strany*, No. 14 (1960), p. 890.
[12] *Rudé právo*, June 16, 1954.

Thus, except for the different names of the two highest organs, the Presidium in the USSR and the Political Bureau in Czechoslovakia, there is now a complete identity in central organs. As for the lower organs, the only disparity of any substance which still remains lies in the continued Czechoslovak use of the afore-mentioned territorial principle for Party organization in rural areas. However, far from being a heretical deviation, this specific departure from the Soviet pattern is a legitimate Leninist device approved by the Kremlin for the period of the "transformation of the village to socialism." Once this transformation is completed and agricultural production fully collectivized, the territorial-productive principle will be introduced in rural areas. In fact, the initial steps in this direction have already been taken. A resolution of the Party's Central Committee of December 30, 1957, ordered the establishment of primary Party units in collective farms located in predominantly industrial areas as well as in those agricultural areas where an overwhelming majority of JZD members were Communists. However, as bared by *Život strany* (No. 13, p. 794) in July 1960, only 872 collective farm units were set up as of January 1, 1960, as against 13,191 village Party organizations based on residence.

While the vital need of the KSČ leaders to keep in the good graces of the Kremlin was the main motive force behind most of these rearrangements, there were several other reasons. Besides releasing several tens of thousands of badly needed functionaries for other Party work, the elimination of the "unhealthy dualism" of the Party command through the fusion of the separate functions of chairman and secretary established more clearly the lines of authority and heightened personal responsibility of the leading secretaries. The requirement that the choice of Party secretaries be subject to higher approval helped to tighten still further the reins of control by the superiors throughout the organizational pyramid. So did the transfer of the right to choose secretaries and bureaus from plenary sessions or conferences to the much smaller executive committees. The shift from the territorial to territorial-productive principle for the lowest Party units not only simplified the supervision of the Party's rank and file, but also served to strengthen labor discipline and to help boost the output.

THE PRESENT SYSTEM

Since the "rich experience of the Communist Party of the Soviet Union," acknowledged in the very First Article of the Statutes, has served the Czechoslovak Communists as their guiding light, it is hardly surprising that the present organizational structure amounts to a small but faithful reproduction of the Soviet original. Also, like her Soviet mother, the Czechoslovak daughter is a being of two widely different faces. The theoretical face, as outlined by the formal phraseology of Party Statutes, radiates broad and serene democracy, while the practical face displays the stern features of oligarchical totalitarianism.

Central Party Organs

According to Party Statutes the supreme organ of the KSČ is the Party Congress which is to meet every four years on the call issued by the Central Committee. An extraordinary congress may be convened on the initiative of the Central Committee and must be convened when demanded by at least one-third of the whole membership of the Party. The powers of the Congress are threefold: (a) It approves the reports of the Central Committee, the Central Auditing Commission and other central organs. (b) It determines the fundamental line of Party policy and tactics, and approves the Party program and statutes. (c) It elects a Central Committee and a Central Auditing Commission and determines their composition.

However, as Shakespeare said, "Thoughts are but dreams till their effects be tried." Three Party Congresses have taken place since the February coup, in 1949, 1954, and 1958, and all three have been assemblies of yes men, greeting with "thunderous ovations" the reports of Party leaders, electing and reelecting unanimously whomever the leaders had proposed, and approving without one vote of dissent the preordained results laid before them. Invariably, it would be resolved that the report of the main Party leader or leaders be considered "as the directives for further work" of the Party. No counterproposals, spontaneous debates, or embarrassing questions have ever marred the smooth harmony permeating the thirteen to fourteen hundred delegates usually sent to these congresses. In brief, since the communist seizure of power the congresses of the KSČ have become a carbon copy of their Soviet equivalent.[13] They sharply contrast with the Party's prewar congresses which abounded in lively exchanges of views and tough factional and ideological battles. Even the Eighth

---

[13] For further information on Party Congresses see *Rudé právo,* May 26-29, 1949, June 12-17, 1954; *Lidové noviny,* May 31, 1949; *Rudé právo,* June 19-23, 1958.

Congress of 1946, though much more conformist than its predecessors, was a debaters' paradise compared to the stifling uniformity of its successors.

The only time when the Party Congress might have become a forum for a genuine debate and a critical opposition might have made itself heard was just after the Twentieth Congress of the Communist Party of the Soviet Union in 1956. Khrushchëv's famous speech demolishing the Stalin myth made such a tremendous impression on many Party members and stirred up such hopes of forthcoming major changes that as many as 235 Party organizations dared to voice a demand that an extraordinary Party Congress be convened.[14] Such demands, allegedly made "under the influence of vague notions and various incorrect opinions," were scornfully rejected by the Party leaders and their initiators were pressed to reconsider. Thus Novotný could report to the National Party Conference which met in June 1956 that "a considerable proportion of these organizations became aware of the groundlessness of this demand and withdrew it."[15] By then the Party leaders had already managed to ward off the direct threat of the oppositional *élan* triggered by Khrushchëv's anti-Stalin pronouncement and to force it underground.

A similar spectacle of drab conformity is offered by national Party conferences which may be called by the Central Committee "to discuss urgent matters of Party policy" between the congresses. Even by the terms of the Statutes the National Conference is a powerless institution. All that it is authorized to do is to pass resolutions which are binding only if they are approved by the Central Committee and to replace up to one-fifth of the Central Committee's members. The impotence of the conferences has been amply corroborated by actual practice. Three such conferences were convened between 1948 and 1960. The first met in 1952 to adopt the present Party Statutes; the second was summoned in 1956 to consider the directives for the Second Five-Year Plan and the "situation and the tasks of the Party"; the third was convoked in 1960 to discuss a new Czechoslovak constitution and to approve the Third Five-Year Plan.

The 528 voting delegates attending the 1952 conference unanimously ratified the new Statutes as well as all the replacements of unworthy Central Committee members and alternates laid before

[14] Novotný's speech at the National Party Conference, *Rudé právo*, June 12, 1956.
[15] *ibid.*

them. The sixty-three delegates who were allowed to take the floor in the debate vied with one another in singing hosannas to Gottwald's leadership, in spitting fire against the purged "traitors" of Slánský's "conspiratorial center," and in mixing public breast-beating and self-critical humility. By a unanimous vote the delegates ruled that Gottwald's report should "become the directives for further Party work."[16]

The 1956 National Conference was of a similar nature. Although it met at the height of the post-Stalin "thaw" its proceedings belied the absence of Stalin's portrait which formerly was an indispensable requisite of such Party assemblies. Again, self-adulation and unanimity were the main ingredients of the Conference's fare. Party leaders indulged in self-righteous justification of their past policies, ably seconded by their henchmen who alone were allowed to take part in the debate. While there were more thrusts than usual against the "hidden enemies attacking the general line of the Party," the holders of "superficial and formalist conception of socialist democratization," "anarchistic attitudes," and "petty-bourgeois views" were given no opportunity whatsoever to raise their voices in the conference hall. All that had to be resolved was approved without dissent and Novotný's report became the directive of further work, as had Gottwald's four years previously.[17]

The same conformity and unanimity characterized the proceedings of the National Party Conference which met in July 1960. The thirty-three delegates who took part in the discussion had nothing but praise for everything that had been laid before them. As the official communiqués put it, the delegates were "in complete agreement with the Central Committee's assessment of the international situation and fully approved the attitude adopted by the Party's delegation at the meeting of the representatives of the communist and workers' parties at Bucharest." Novotný's report, the final version of the new constitution, the directives for the Third Five-Year Plan, and all other business of the conference was approved "with complete unanimity" and "long-lasting enthusiastic applause."[18]

If the Party Statutes were a true reflection of reality, the most important Party organ between the congressional sessions would be the Central Committee. It "directs the whole work of the Party; represents the Party in its relations with other parties, organizations, and

[16] *Rudé právo,* December 17-19, 1952.

[17] *ibid.,* June 12 and 13, 1956; also, *Československý přehled,* iii, 6 (1956), pp. 11ff.

[18] *Rudé právo,* July 6, 7, and 8, 1960.

institutions; organizes and directs various Party institutions; approves the Party's representatives in the government, the [Slovak] Board of Commissioners, the National Assembly, [and] the Slovak National Council; appoints the main editors of central press organs functioning under its control and confirms the leading secretaries of regional Party organizations; distributes the manpower and resources of the Party, determines the membership dues, and administers the central fund." It "directs the work of the central state agencies, the National Front, and public organizations through Party groups within these agencies and organizations." It convenes the Party Congress, prepares its agenda, and determines its basis of representation and the manner in which the delegates are to be elected. It also calls the sessions of the National Conference and confirms its resolutions. It elects the Political Bureau, the Central Secretariat, and the Commission of Party Control, and has the right to create political sections and appoint "Party organizers of the Central Committee for individual sectors of socialist construction which are of particular importance for national economy and the whole country."

This towering position assigned to the Central Committee by the above provisions, copied almost verbatim from Soviet Party rules, shrinks to much more modest proportions if measured by the yardstick of cold facts. The progressive eclipse which the Central Committee has suffered under the dictatorship of the proletariat is a living example of the withering away of intra-Party democracy under the scorching heat of Leninist-Stalinist totalitarianism. Prior to World War II the Central Committee was a very important organ, although the militant nature of the KSČ and its status as national section of the Communist International necessarily impaired its inner freedoms. When the Party was reestablished after the War, it was the Presidium of the Central Committee that emerged as both the main directorate of Party strategy and its chief policy-maker. Although the Central Committee as a whole lost much of its prewar authority, it still was not altogether devoid of political significance and occasionally indulged in genuine though cautious criticism. With the coup of 1948 its final demise began and was consummated in the Great Purge of 1950-1951.

As no records of the Central Committee's proceedings are published, conclusions as to its relative standing within the Party hierarchy must be based mostly on circumstantial evidence. All the data thus obtained leave little doubt that this once prominent body has been reduced to a rubber-stamp assembly ever ready to underwrite whatever is laid before it by the Party leaders. That is definitely the impression one gains from the perusal of reports on the Central Committee's meetings published in the Party press and that is also the verdict of whatever off-the-record information is available from communist sources.[19] Perhaps the most blatant illustration of the sycophantic nature and behavior of the Central Committee was offered by its attitude toward the Party's Central Secretary, Rudolf Slánský. On May 17, 1951, Slánský delivered the keynote address at the session of the ninety-seven-man Central Committee on the solemn occasion of the Party's Thirtieth Anniversary. His speech was interrupted as many as nineteen times by "stormy," "enthusiastic," and "longstanding applause."[20] Yet, less than four months later, that same Central Committee approved "unanimously and with enthusiastic agreement" Slánský's removal from the Secretaryship.[21] Another three months thereafter it displayed the same unanimity in ordering Slánský's expulsion from the Party.[22]

The prostration of the Central Committee vacated the highest position of Party hierarchy first for its Presidium and then for its Political Bureau, with the latter firmly assuming the reins of actual leadership upon its creation in 1951. Both in its composition and in its powers the Bureau corresponds to the Soviet Party's Presidium. Admission to this inner sanctum is reserved solely for a few topmost leaders. Only about a dozen Czechoslovak Communists have thus far been found worthy of the honor, and the Bureau's complete roll as of 1960 amounted to ten full members and three alternates, the last-named serving in a consultative capacity.[23] Like its Soviet equivalent, the Bureau is self-perpetuating. The candidates are handpicked by the Politbureaucrats themselves, and once so chosen, they are certain to be elected by the Central Committee. The Bureau's powers know virtually no limits beyond those imposed on them by the Kremlin. The authority of this narrow oligarchy, which a laconic phrase in the

[19] *Rudé právo*, March 1, 1950; *Pravda*, March 3, 1950; *Rudé právo*, March 30, 1956, June 30, 1955, September 8, 1956, September 14, 1953, December 8, 1951, February 27, 1951, May 18, 1951.

[20] *Lidové noviny*, May 17, 1951.

[21] *Rudé právo*, September 8, 1951.

[22] *ibid.*, December 8, 1951.

[23] Full members: Karol Bacílek, Rudolf Barák, Pavol David, Jaromír Dolanský, Zdeněk Fierlinger, Jiří Hendrych, Václav Kopecký, Antonín Novotný, Otakar Šimůnek, Viliam Široký. Alternate members (candidates): Jan Hlína, Ludmila Jankovcová, Rudolf Strechaj.

Party Statutes entrusts with "the direction of the Party's work between the sessions of the Central Committee," encompasses both Party and State affairs. As the leading organ of the dictatorship of the proletariat the Bureau is the only real policy-maker in the country. It relegates all other Party and government agencies to the role of mere executors of its supreme will. Meeting at least once a week, and unimpeded by any considerations of the rule of law, separation of powers, or any other such inhibitions, it makes all major (and often even minor) decisions and supervises their execution in every conceivable field, ranging from foreign policy, defense, and economic planning to the sanctioning of wages and work norms, distinctions between the "rich" and the "middle" peasants, or factory physicians' leniency toward workers suspected of simulating sickness.

The right arm of the Political Bureau in the performance of its truly Herculean tasks of supreme totalitarian control is the Central Secretariat. As is the case with the Political Bureau, the Central Secretariat of the KSČ is a small alter ego of the Secretariat of the Central Committee of the Soviet Party. It is headed by a First Secretary elected by the plenum of the Central Committee, together with several other members of the Secretariat who act as his deputies.[24] In reality, however, all these secretaries are chosen by the Political Bureau and their election by the Central Committee is a mere formality. The Secretariat is subdivided into sections closely patterned after the Soviet model and even bearing names identical to their Soviet equivalents. Each section is assigned a specific function or area of operations and is staffed by dependable Party members employed on a full-time basis.

Sharply contrasting with these many similarities of the Central Secretariat of the KSČ with its Soviet namesake is the marked difference in their statuses. In Stalin's era the Secretariat of the Central Committee of the Soviet Party was far from subordinate, either to the Central Committee or to the *Politbyro*. As an organ primarily responsible for carrying out Stalin's orders and thus deriving its authority to act directly from the Soviet Dictator, the Secretariat was often more important than the *Politbyro* itself. A somewhat similar situation developed as a result of Khrushchëv's practice, meanwhile changed in

[24] The following were elected to the Secretariat at the close of the Eleventh Party Congress in 1958: Antonín Novotný, Oldřich Černík, Jiří Hendrych, Bruno Kohler, Vratislav Krutina, Vladimír Koucký, Antonín Krček, František Zupka. *Rudé právo*, June 22, 1958. In July 1960, Alexander Dubček was added to the Secretariat. *Rudé Právo*, July 12, 1960.

1960, of making most Presidium members also secretaries of the Central Committee. As long as they voted together this secretarial nucleus commended a safe majority on the Party's Presidium, which thus placed the Secretariat above the Presidium in terms of actual power.

This cannot be said, however, of the Central Secretariat of the KSČ. Although it has always been an important institution, it has so far been held well below the Political Bureau. The only instance of an attempt to build it into an independent center of power occurred in the first three years after the February coup of 1948, when the Secretariat was headed by Gottwald's main rival, Rudolf Slánský. Indeed, Gottwald's bill of indictment against the subsequently ousted Secretary General included a charge that the Central Secretariat "sought to play the role of the leading Party organ" and that it became accustomed to interfering directly with the work of ministries and other agencies "over the heads and without the knowledge of responsible comrades."[25] Of all the fantastic crimes allegedly committed by Slánský, ranging from plans to restore capitalism to a plot to shorten the life of Klement Gottwald, Slánský's abuse of the Secretariat is probably the only charge which can be given credence. Gottwald and Slánský had been at loggerheads for some time and it was understandable that Slánský would wish to buttress his position by enhancing the authority of the organ which he headed. Whatever Slánský's ultimate intentions may have been, they came to naught with his liquidation. Gottwald, who succeeded Slánský as head of the Central Secretariat, had neither any interest in elevating its status nor any need to do so. With Slánský's ouster, he became the uncontested Party leader. In his capacity as Party Chairman he presided over the Presidium as well as the Political Secretariat which was packed with his henchmen. As President of the Republic he held a position of such traditional prestige that he was virtually beyond challenge by any of his Party colleagues. When Gottwald died in March 1953 Antonín Zápotocký, then definitely the next highest-ranking Communist after Gottwald, inherited the Republic's Presidency but not the leadership of the Central Secretariat which was entrusted to Antonín Novotný, a relative newcomer to the ranks of topmost Party

[25] A confidential circular letter on the session of the Central Committee on September 6, 1951, *Zpráva o Československu*, II, 11 (1951), pp. 7ff.; also, Kopecký's explanation in an editorial in *Rudé právo*, September 8, 1951; and Gottwald's report to the Central Committee on December 6, 1951, *Rudé právo*, December 8, 1951.

leaders. Novotný made good use of his position to feather his own political nest, but insofar as is known, made no attempt to convert it into anything more important than it had been in Gottwald's days.

To complete our review of Party organization on the central level, brief mention should be made of the Central Auditing Commission and the Commission of Party Control. Both of these are of minor political importance. The former, elected by the Party Congress, checks the accounts of Party organizations and enterprises. The latter is set up by the Central Committee to hear appeals of Party members and candidates against disciplinary decisions of lower Party organs and to investigate complaints assigned to it by the Central Committee.

Intermediate Party Organs

Connecting the apex of the organizational pyramid with its broad base of primary units are two or three successive tiers of territorially graduated organs corresponding to the respective subdivisions of state administration. The highest layer immediately below the national organs consists of regional organizations, each of which is in turn broken into district organizations and a coordinate city organization for the regional capital. With the consent of the Party's Central Committee the city organization in larger regional capitals may be further subdivided into precinct organizations.

The basic organ of the regional organization is a regional conference of delegates chosen in district and city conferences, which meets every two years to approve reports of its executive organs, to elect a regional committee of thirty-three to forty-three members and an auditing commission, and to discuss matters pertaining to Party work in the region. The regional committee which is to meet at least once every six weeks is assigned a truly impressive array of duties by the Party Statutes. It "secures the firm fulfillment of the Party's directives, the development of criticism and self-criticism, and the education of Communists in the spirit of an uncompromising attitude toward disorders; directs the study of Marxism-Leninism by members and candidates of the Party; organizes communist education of the workers; directs and controls the work of the district and city Party organizations and confirms the leading secretaries of district and city committees; establishes regional Party schools; subject to the approval of the Central Committee of the Communist Party of Czechoslovakia, appoints the editor-in-chief of the regional paper; proposes candidates to regional people's committees [organs of regional government], the National Assembly, and to the Slovak National Council in Slovakia; directs the work of the Communists in the regional people's committee and in the regional organs of the mass organizations; distributes the Party personnel and funds in the region and administers the regional treasury and Party economy; informs systematically the Party's Central Committee and sends the Central Committee a report on its activities at prescribed dates." Finally, it elects a bureau of nine to eleven persons as well as a leading secretary and two to three secretaries of the regional committee who must be approved by the Central Committee. This bureau meets at least once a week and "directs all the work of the regional organization between the sessions of the regional committee." It creates a secretariat for "discussion of current affairs, control of the fulfillment of Party decisions, and direction of the apparatus of the regional committee."

Except for minor variations, the organs of district and city Party organizations are duplicates of synonymous organs on the regional level and their scope of authority is a smaller-scale paraphrase of the regional arrangement. The committees and bureaus are somewhat smaller than their regional equivalents. And, of course, the regional committee replaces the Central Committee wherever higher approval is prescribed. On the other hand, the district, city, and precinct committees have the primary duty of directing and controlling the primary organizations and keeping the members' records, and they have as well the specific authority to approve or disapprove the primary unit's decision conferring Party membership or expelling a member from Party ranks.

While they serve in that capacity, secretaries and bureau members of the regional, district, and city committees are released from their regular employment and work full time on Party affairs under the over-all control of the leading secretaries who correspond to the first secretaries of the Soviet intermediate Party organs. The individual bureau members usually act as chiefs of various departments in which the machinery and the work of the intermediate organizations are subdivided, such as agitation and propaganda, agriculture, industry, trade and banking. Serving below the chiefs of departments are a number of reporters and trustees appointed by the respective committees for specific areas of work. The balance of the committee apparatus is made up of salaried full-time employees.

A crucial task of the intermediate levels of the Party hierarchy is to establish and maintain solid links of connection and supervision with the base of the organizational pyramid, the primary units and their membership. Logically as well as by Party Statutes this is first and foremost the responsibility of the lowest echelons of the intermediate Party apparatus, the district and city committees, acting with the aid of precinct and local committees wherever such are established. Since it is recognized that this key sector of organizational and ideological work cannot be disposed of satisfactorily by dispatching circulars from Party headquarters, the institution of ambulatory instructors has been copied from the Soviet guidebook.[26] Each of these itinerant peddlers of communism is assigned a number of primary units which he is to oversee and guide. He attends their meetings and meets regularly with their functionaries whom he instructs in the proper handling of Party affairs, oftentime dictating what should or should not be done.[27] He checks compliance with Party resolutions and directives. He seeks to gather information about the moods and attitudes of the members and keeps an eye both on those showing promise and those of doubtful loyalty. He thus acts also as a valuable informer whose evaluation is included in the all-important cadre report, the confidential file kept on each Party member.

The work done by Party instructors is further supplemented in each area by hosts of Party agitators, propagandists, and activists whose training is a primary responsibility of district and city committees and who operate mostly on a part-time basis.[28] Gathered in groups of Party activists, they are supposed "to acquaint Party ranks with the committees' directives and resolutions, to strengthen contacts with primary units and to improve the ability of the whole district and regional organization to act."[29] They also play an important role in fostering the cause of communism among non-Party masses.

The regional and district or city organizations are the main intermediate tiers of the organizational pyramid, and they are the only ones in most areas. However, a third layer of intermediate organs is provided in cities, in large communities which have the character of a city either because of their industrial importance or the size of their

[26] *Lidové noviny,* May 27, 1949; *Rudé právo,* July 18, 1953; *Funkcionář,* IV, 22, p. 1137.
[27] *Rudé právo,* August 2, 1953.
[28] *Rudé právo,* August 11 and 17, 1952, July 16, 1953, and December 15, 1953.
[29] *Rudé právo,* October 16, 1953.

population or Party membership, and in rural settlements having more than one primary unit. In such communities a joint local committee is elected by a plenary session of all the primary units or by a conference of delegates. The committee in its turn elects a chairman who actually serves (since 1953) as secretary. The main function of these local committees is to propose candidates to the organs of local government, direct their work, and serve as the local arm of the district Party organs in the area.

As can be seen from this outline of the intermediate Party organs, the designation of "the highest organs" given by the Statutes to Party conferences on the respective levels is as much of a misnomer as calling the National Party Congress the highest organ of the KSČ. The decisive organs on both the regional and the district or city levels are the Party secretaries who, though formally elected by the respective committees, are actually handpicked by higher Party leaders. In practice, the Party's Political Bureau, acting mostly upon the recommendation of the First Secretary of the Central Committee, chooses the candidates for regional secretaryships. The regional secretaries in turn are primarily responsible for seeing to it that the "right" comrades are selected for the district and city secretaryships. Although the choice of chairmen-turned-secretaries of local Party committees is not formally subject to higher approval, the district secretaries are expected to do all they can to prevent "unworthy" comrades from "worming" themselves into such positions. Should it happen that an incumbent of these leading executive positions forfeits the trust of the leaders, the absence of express provisions reserving the right of removal by higher organs does not seem to create any problem. As is borne out by many instances of such removals, the respective committees can always be made to replace undesirable functionaries by others.

Thus, in line with the Soviet pattern, it is this all-embracing network of first secretaries that constitutes the backbone of the entire system. Like the Soviet *obkom, gorgkom,* and *raikom* secretaries, they are the key political figures on all territorial levels. They are the nabobs of the communist system engaged full time in directing and controlling, on behalf of their superiors and under their watchful supervision, not only the Party apparatus but also the machinery of government in the area assigned to their jurisdiction. As *Rudé právo* put it, "Control within the Party from top to bottom, in central organs, in regional and district committees, and in primary units is just

as important as it is in the people's committees, in the state apparatus, in economy, and in the mass organizations . . . ."[30] While the
channels of authority begin at the apex of the pyramid and from
there spread down over the successive secretarial layers like a broadening waterfall descending over several graduated levels, the real lines
of responsibility go in the opposite direction. In theory, the secretaries
and the bureaus are responsible to their committees and these in their
turn answer for their activities to the respective Party conferences.
But the practice of democratic centralism reduces this kind of accountability to mere formality and replaces it by much stronger lines
of responsibility running upward from the chairman-secretary and the
committee of the local organization over the district secretaries and
their aides to the regional Party leaders who are in turn responsible to
the central Party organs.

Nor are the intermediate organs the only agents of direct control
on their respective levels. Using its right to appoint Party organizers
"for individual sectors of socialist construction," the Central Committee sets up its own independent watchdogs wherever it may wish
to do so, and thus extends its parallel controls at will into the spheres
assigned to the supervision of lower Party organs. Although these
Party organizers do not formally superintend the lower Party organs
that operate concurrently in the same establishments, the very fact
that they derive their authority from the Party's Central Committee
and report to it on shortcomings which they may find enhances their
prestige and makes acceptance of any advice they offer to the lower
organs well-nigh mandatory.

Primary Party Units

The base of the organizational pyramid is formed by over 47,000
primary units which "connect the masses of workers, working peasants,
and intelligentsia with the leading organs of the Party." Since the
1952 reorganization most of these units are organized, in deference
to the territorial-productive principle, directly in the places of the
members' work, in factories, workshops, business establishments, state
farms, machine-tractor stations, offices, and educational institutions,
as well as in railway junctions and highway maintenance units.[31]
Similarly, primary units are established in the Armed Forces. But the
latter are, like their Soviet equivalents, exempt from regular Party

[30] *ibid.*, November 9, 1951.
[31] *Funkcionář,* March 20, 1953.

hierarchy and are operated separately according to special directives of the Party's Central Committee which supervises them through the Main Political Administration of the Armed Forces. Units based on a strictly territorial principle exist today only in rural communities, while a small number of about fifteen hundred so-called street organizations continue to operate in the cities to take care of those Party members who could not be transferred to production units. With a few exceptions, the rules governing the organizations and the duties of the primary units are an almost literal translation of corresponding Soviet Party regulations. A minimum of three members is prescribed and the establishment of the unit must be approved by the district or city Party committee. Candidate groups led by a Party member may be created wherever there are less than three members. In large factories or offices, where there is a greater number of Party members and candidates, separate primary units are set up in individual workshops, divisions or sections with the approval of the regional Party committee.[32] Primary units with more than one hundred members and candidates may be similarly subdivided into individual sectional units. The members of a primary or sectional unit may be further split up by sectors of work or production processes into Party groups.

The functions and duties of the primary units are quite exacting. Their definition, which reads like a leaf from Soviet Party rules, may be summarized as follows:

a. Agitational and organizational work among the masses for the realization of Party slogans and resolutions and for the direction of local press (factory periodicals, newspapers to be pasted on walls, etc.).

b. Recruitment of new members for the Party and their political training.

c. Organization of political education of Party members and candidates so that they acquire the minimum knowledge of Marxism-Leninism.

d. Mobilization of workers in factories, offices, institutions, state farms, machine-tractor stations, villages, etc., for the fulfillment of the plan, for the strengthening of labor and state discipline, for the development of socialist competition and the shockworkers' movement.

[32] Until 1958 the creation of separate primary units in individual workshops was allowed only when the total number of Party members and candidates in the respective factory or office exceeded 300. *Rudé právo*, June 22, 1958. See also Jan Večera, *Za další upevňování základních organisací strany* (For a Further Strengthening of the Party's Primary Units), Praha, 1957, p. 19.

e. Right to control the activities of management in production and trade enterprises as well as on state farms and machine-tractor stations by pointing out management's shortcomings and assisting in their elimination, but exclusive of the right to replace the plant management.[33]

f. Duty to point out shortcomings in the work of ministries and other central departments as well as in agencies of local administration and to send their comments to proper Party authorities.[34]

g. Struggle against disorders and uneconomical operations in enterprises, offices, state farms, etc., and daily concern for the improvement of the cultural and living conditions of the workers, working peasants, and the intelligentsia.

h. Development of criticism and self-criticism, and education of Communists in the spirit of an uncompromising attitude toward shortcomings.

i. Helping Party members and candidates charged with public functions or with work in non-Party organizations to fulfill their duties in an exemplary fashion and seeing to it that they account for their work to the Party organs.

j. Active participation in national economic and political life.

k. Approval of candidates to the local people's committees in rural communities and direction of their work.

The highest organ of the primary unit called upon by the Party Statutes to take care of these overwhelming tasks is the plenary session of its members. Its monthly meetings, attendance at which is the "basic duty of every Party member," are supposed to discuss regularly these tasks and to "determine the manner in which they are to be implemented." However, as in the case of the intermediate organs, the real burden lies on the shoulders of the three- to eleven-man committees elected by the annual plenary sessions of all primary and sectional units with more than five members, or the single trustee chosen in units with up to five members. Meeting at least once a week under a chairman whom they elect, these committees, which are the Czecho-

---

[33] A suggestion was made in 1958 that the primary units be given the right to "inquire into and suspend any wrong and socially harmful decisions" of the management of economic enterprises (*Rudé právo*, May 21, 1958). But the suggestion was turned down at the Eleventh Party Congress on the ground that "such a change in the Party rules could lead in its consequences to an administrative method of work on the part of the Party organizations . . . . " (*Rudé právo*, June 22, 1958.) Evidently, the Party leaders feared the manner in which such a right might have been taken advantage of by the Party's rank and file.

[34] Added by the Tenth Congress.

slovak counterparts of the bureaus in the Soviet primary units, "direct the entire work of the Party organization." Each committee member is assigned a specific function for which he is personally responsible. The chairman, who is in fact the committee's first secretary, serves as coordinator and over-all controller. He is the most important single person in the primary unit, although he tends to lack the ascendancy characteristic of the first secretaries of the primary Party units in the Soviet Union. Unlike his Soviet equivalent, he is not subject to formal approval by higher Party authorities, except in primary units established in ministries and other central offices, in which case he must be confirmed by the Party's Central Committee. As revealed by some of the escapees and confirmed by occasional criticisms in the communist press, there are instances when the chairman becomes the virtual boss of the primary unit. But this is due mostly to the lethargy of other committee members who shirk their disagreeable duties and gladly allow them to devolve on the chairman. Since higher Party directives have to be taken care of and the chairman is primarily responsible, he disposes of the matter personally, often on paper only, and supplies the supervisory organs with the customary report that the directives have been implemented. Quite frequently, he is urged to behave this way by the instructors or other functionaries of the district organization so that they can in turn report to their superiors that their orders have been carried out.[35]

Clustered around the leading organs of the primary units are a multitude of auxiliary functionaries operating under their directives and supervision. Probably the most important among them are the "leaders of the Party groups." Besides collecting membership dues they are responsible for the work of the groups entrusted to their control. In this ominous capacity they have replaced the ill-famed "tenners," so called because each of them was in charge of ten Party members. As directed in a confidential circular of the Party's Central Secretariat of 1951, the tenners were to exercise continuous control over their respective groups. They were to keep tab on the members' attitudes, on what they read, whom they met, and whether or not they listened to foreign broadcasts. They were to check regularly the members' attendance at work and their working morale. They were to see to it that the members' children were supplied with Party literature and to ascertain whether parents required their children to read the supplied materials. They were to report their findings each Satur-

[35] *Rudé právo,* August 2, 1953.

day to the local Party chairman.[36] Undoubtedly, the duties of their successors, the Party group leaders, are essentially the same. Moreover, since they work in the same place as the objects of their control, they are deemed to be in a position to do an even better job than the tenners, especially in bolstering socialist discipline and overfulfillment of production goals.[37]

The shift to the territorial-productive principle and the substitution of factory group leaders for the tenners was not, however, allowed to do away with the Party's residential controls. Rather, in accordance with the directive of the Party's Political Secretariat on the reorganization of street organizations, their supervisory functions were taken over by "Party agitators."[38] "Appointed for every house or, in smaller towns, for a street or block of houses," they should "help the workers living in their precinct to understand correctly the Party's policy and to be informed correctly and truthfully of internal developments."[39]

Party Organs in Slovakia

While the organizational pattern described in this chapter applies to the whole of Czechoslovakia, an additional layer is interposed between the central and intermediate Party organs in Slovakia. As mentioned in Chapter I, the KSČ emerged from the war years with a younger sister in the form of a separate Communist Party in Slovakia. Conceived as it had been solely in response to tactical needs of a temporary nature (to assure Communists of larger representation in the government and to enable them better to exploit the rampant Slovak nationalism), the Slovak Party dropped its "independent" status after the February coup, when the erstwhile needs were no longer there. In September 1948 the Party was solemnly reunited with the elder sister. However, partly as a concession to Slovak feelings and partly in deference to the Soviet-style nationality policy, the Slovak Party was allowed to retain at least some of its identity within the firm embrace of the KSČ.

The regional organizations in Slovakia constitute "a territorial organization of the Communist Party of Czechoslovakia in Slovakia" which is designated by Party Statutes as the "Communist Party of

---

[36] For a summary of the circular, see Pavel Berka's article in *Československý přehled,* III, 1 (1956), pp. 13-14.

[37] *Rudé právo,* January 22, 1953.

[38] *ibid.,* January 20, 1953.

[39] *ibid.*

Slovakia," the KSS. Its highest organ is a Congress of the KSS which meets every four years (two years until 1960) to hear and approve the report of its Central Committee, discuss the tasks of the Party in Slovakia, and elect a Central Committee and an Auditing Commission. The Central Committee in turn creates a Bureau "for the direction of political-organizational work between the sessions of the Central Committee," a Secretariat "for current work, mainly for organizing control of fulfillment of Party resolutions and for selection of cadres" and a Commission of Party Control for disciplinary matters.

In their formal setup these organs of the KSS look like a duplicate of the central organs of the KSČ. But in terms of actual powers they are quite different. The Party Statutes themselves document the subordinate character of the Slovak organs. Resolutions of the Congress and the Central Committee of the KSČ are binding for the Slovak Party. Its own Congress can be convened only "in agreement with the Central Committee of the Communist Party of Czechoslovakia." Unlike their Czechoslovak comrades, the Slovaks have no right to determine the fundamental lines of Party policy and tactics, not even for Slovakia, or to adopt Party programs and statutes. The Central Committee of the Slovak Party "carries out the resolutions of the Central Committee of the Communist Party of Czechoslovakia" and "settles political and organizational matters of the Party in agreement with the Central Committee of the KSČ," to whom it must also send periodic activity reports. It appoints on its own neither the Party's representatives to the Board of Commissioners (meanwhile abolished) and the Slovak National Council (the organs of the Slovak Autonomous Government) nor those to "higher Party and public functions," but may only nominate suitable candidates for such offices to the Central Committee of the KSČ, which alone makes the final decision.

The statutory inferiority of the Slovak Party organs is amply corroborated by actual developments. While its Congress has been meeting regularly every two years since the adoption of the new Statutes in 1952, its proceedings have always been marked by complete subservience toward the KSČ leadership and by parrot-like repetition of the tunes already struck in Praha.[40] Insofar as one can judge by limited information on the matter, the sessions of the Central Committee of the KSS, of its Presidium, and of the Bureau that succeeded it display similar characteristics.

[40] On the Tenth Congress see *Pravda,* June 14 and 16, 1953.

CHAPTER IV

THE PARTY'S OPERATIONAL CODE
IN THEORY AND PRACTICE

WITHIN the Marxist-Leninist ideological armory high priority is assigned to principles governing the interrelationship between Party organs and individual Party members. Elaborated primarily by Lenin, this operational code seeks to reconcile the precepts of inner democracy with the paramount needs of iron discipline and autocratic leadership. Thus, unwittingly, Lenin built into the chosen Party a Jekyll-Hyde complex with the good Dr. Jekyll steadily losing ground to the evil Mr. Hyde. In due time the high-minded principles of "inner-Party democracy" shared the fate that has befallen so many other tenets of Marxism-Leninism. Their substance had been corroded by the destructive acid of totalitarianism.

The Czechoslovak Communists have been as imitative of the Soviet Party in the adoption of their operational code as in the arrangement of their Party's organizational structure. The time-honored Leninist precepts of "democratic centralism," "free and businesslike discussion," "criticism and self-criticism," and "the observance of Party and state discipline" were enthroned as supreme deities guiding the Party's behavior. The chapter of the KSČ Statutes dealing with the duties of Party members was taken bodily from the Soviet Party rules. When the post-Stalin condemnation of the "cult of the individual" elevated the "Leninist principle of collective leadership" in Soviet Russia, Czechoslovak Communists at their Tenth Party Congress in 1954 promptly inserted a like section in their Party Statutes. Also, the KSČ inherited from the Soviets the sharp contrast between theoretical concepts and their application in actual practice.

INNER-PARTY DEMOCRACY

According to its Statutes, the foundation of the Party's internal life is "inner-Party democracy" and its cornerstone is "democratic centralism." "Lenin's and Stalin's bolshevik principle of democratic centralism," said Gottwald, "offers a reliable guidance on how to build the Party and how to shape the mutual relationship of its organs on all levels."[1] Copying Soviet rules, the KSČ Statutes refer to it as "the guiding principle of the organizational structure of the Party" and use an exact translation of the Russian formula to spell out its four basic points: (a) election of leading Party organs, from the lowest to the highest; (b) periodic accountability of elected organs to the organizations which elected them; (c) strict Party discipline and subordination of the minority to the majority; (d) the unconditionally binding character of the decisions of higher organs on lower organs.

At face value, these four elements of democratic centralism are compatible with the concepts of democracy. In theory, their use would not impair the democratic character of the Party embracing them. But, in adopting the Soviet formula, communist leaders of Czechoslovakia absorbed simultaneously the body of dictatorial usages and practices that have grown around it in its native Russian habitat and distorted the formula's original meaning. Consequently, the gap between the theory and the practice of democratic centralism is almost as wide in Czechoslovakia as it is in the country of its origin. This can be illustrated by taking the four basic ingredients of democratic centralism and comparing their democratic phraseology with actual Party conditions.

In accordance with the first principle, Party Statutes provide for periodic elections of leading Party organs from bottom to top. Indeed, the prescribed time schedules of these elections have been scrupulously followed. At stipulated times Party conferences or congresses on different levels meet to choose the delegates to the next higher organs and to select their own executive committees. These committees in turn create their own bureaus and choose their own secretaries. However, in most instances, these outward trappings are deceiving. The key officers at all intermediate Party levels are the Party secretaries and the Statutes themselves disclose that their selection is subject to higher confirmation. Although this statutory limitation does not apply to the choice of other Party functionaries, the evidence clearly indicates that the higher Party organs can always bar the election or cause the removal of anyone of whom they disapprove. Such removals by higher fiat have occurred quite frequently, especially in connection with major purges. There also exists a complementary rule of democratic centralism, unmentioned by Party

[1] *Rudé právo,* December 8, 1951.

Statutes, which makes the various Party secretaries primarily responsible for the selection and placement of the cadres under their jurisdiction. By implication this includes the functionaries of Party organs. District and city Party committees, acting mainly through their instructors, manipulate the elections of functionaries in the primary units and local Party committees. As *Rudé právo* stressed, "It is up to them to guide correctly the choice and election of the new committees . . . . It is their duty . . . to send an experienced member of the Party *aktiv* to give the comrades good advice . . . ."[2]

Similar kinds of advice are tendered by the regional Party bureaus as to the choice of candidates for district and city Party offices, and it is most inadvisable to leave such advice unheeded. The prospective functionaries of regional Party organizations and of the central offices of the Slovak Communist Party are in their turn cleared by the Party's Central Secretariat acting with the approval of the Political Bureau. The Central Secretariat's "gross mistakes in the selection and distribution of higher cadres in the Party apparatus" were, in fact, the main cause of Rudolf Slánský's removal from the position of Central Secretary in September 1951.[3] Finally, at the very apex of the hierarchy, the admission of new members to the central Party organs is within the exclusive authority of the Political Bureau, the Party Statutes notwithstanding. It is this small group of top Party leaders who actually decide who will be allowed to sit in the Central Committee, and the Central Committee invariably gives the leaders' choice its unanimous assent. When the need arises to deprive anyone of Central Committee membership, it is again the Political Bureau who secures the member's resignation. The Political Bureau itself is, as mentioned in the previous chapter, a self-perpetuating body that chooses its new members by cooption. Except for death in office, membership in the supreme Party conclave is lost by enforced resignation. While two members of the Political Bureau have died in office, two have lost membership dishonorably: Rudolf Slánský, who paid with his life, and Alexei Čepička, who managed to cling to life in the Malenkov-Molotov-Kaganovich fashion.

Hence, elections of Party organs, conducted with studied regularity under the guise of democratic centralism, have been essentially rubber-stamp acclamations registering dutiful approval of slates of uncon-

---

[2] *ibid.*, February 18, 1953.
[3] See a confidential circular on the session of the Central Committee in September 1951, *Zpráva o Československu,* II, 11 (1951), p. 7.

tested candidates approved by higher Party authorities. Nevertheless, at lower echelons of the Party, there have been a few occasions in which the officially approved candidates did not secure a majority and therefore had to be replaced. In 1949 Slánský told the Ninth Party Congress that several district Party conferences failed to elect some of the recommended committee members, including even a few district Party chairmen and secretaries.[4] Similar instances, mostly on local levels, were reported in the early post-Stalin era. This is why Party leaders have thus far not dared to trust the rank and file even with such a minor concession as the secret ballot, although such a right is enjoyed by Soviet Party members and is available in general elections in Czechoslovakia. When the present Statutes were adopted in 1952 the absence of the secret ballot was explained by the fact that Soviet Party rules introduced the secret ballot only "after the full liquidation of the exploiting classes and after the complete collectivization of the village."[5] While a similar justification was advanced against renewed requests for the introduction of the secret ballot at the National Party Conference in 1956, the Party spokesmen let the real reason slip out: "Experience has shown that by instituting such secret ballots a number of organizations could be misused to elect candidates who offer no guarantee that they would fight for the correct policy of the Party."[6]

What has been said of elections holds true also of the second element of democratic centralism, the accountability of elected organs to their electors. Again, reports of the work performed have been rendered with almost monotonous regularity by the appropriate Party functionaries, from the Party's First Secretary to the trustees and group leaders of primary units. Occasionally, accounts of lesser functionaries encounter adverse comments or disagreeable questions from the more inquisitive or courageous members of the Party, especially in the lowest Party units. But mostly the reports are passed without dissent by plenums of members hoping merely to get through with the dreary business as quickly as possible, and knowing that they could change nothing and would only harm themselves should they be unduly critical. This has been especially true of reports from highest Party leaders which seem to be beyond even the mildest criticism. As shown in the preceding chapter, they have been in-

---

[4] *Lidové noviny,* May 27, 1949.
[5] Široký's address at the National Party Conference in December 1952.
[6] *News,* 5, 8 (1956), p. 21.

variably approved in their entirety with "enthusiastic unanimity" and made into binding directives. If a Party member "is possessed of a sound class instinct," warned no less a Communist than Gottwald himself, "and if in addition he is equipped with a minimum ability to apply this doctrine to a given situation . . . then he will never hesitate to defend and carry out the decisions of the leading Party organs even though they may not have been able to consult him in advance."[7] Who, then, would run the risk of being caught lacking such an important proletarian requisite as the "sound class instinct"?

A similar transformation has occurred in the third basic principle of democratic centralism which calls for the subordination of the minority to the majority. Since the present totalitarian practice of Marxism-Leninism knows no minority and majority in the customary political sense, the above clause is meaningless by Western standards. All Party policies are decided by the small conclave of Party leaders sitting in the Political Bureau and acting under the supreme guidance of the Kremlin. Their decisions are unchallengeable. Formation of any factions whatsoever constitutes a crime against the Party's "unity of will and action." To be at odds with the leadership's decision on anything but trivial details amounts to deviationism punishable by demotion, expulsion, or worse. As *Rudé právo* said after Slánský's ouster in 1951: " . . . one cannot talk of a unified organization without the existence of an authoritative center . . . to whose directives the whole Party must be subordinated . . . . Centralism would have no sense without a strict, iron discipline, as only iron discipline assures unity of will and action . . . ."[8] While the Party rule speaks of the subordination of the minority to the majority, in reality it ought to read: subordination of the whole Party to its Political Bureau.

It is only in the fourth and last ingredient of democratic centralism that there is some relation between theory and practice: namely, in the rule that the decisions of higher organs are unconditionally binding on lower organs. As a platoon or company must obey unquestioningly the orders of its superior officers and they in turn must behave in the same way toward the higher command, so must the regimented cohorts of the KSČ follow the orders of their Party generals,

---

[7] *Rudé právo,* December 8, 1951.

[8] December 12, 1951. See also an article on the "Leninist Concept of Inner-Party Democracy" in *Život strany,* No. 23 (1959), pp. 1407ff.

lieutenants, or corporals, no matter how much they may disagree with them. But even in this crucial matter, practice can be reconciled with theory only if one ignores Section 23 of the Party Statutes which says that "the highest leading organ of each Party organization is the plenary meeting of members (for primary organizations), the conference (for the district, city, and regional organizations), and the congress (for the Communist Party of Slovakia and for the Communist Party of Czechoslovakia)." Since totalitarian practice robbed these "highest leading organs" of their actual powers of decision-making, the provision for the "unconditionally binding character" of higher decisions applies in reality only to the rulings made by the bureaus and committees. Consequently, it has a much narrower meaning than its wording would suggest.

In addition to democratic centralism, inner-Party democracy is allegedly manifested by "the inalienable right of free and business-like discussion of Party policy" guaranteed to each Party member by the Statutes. Lest a misunderstanding arise, the Statutes, translating once again from the Soviet original, hasten to add that "inner-Party democracy must be applied in such a way that it cannot lead to attempts by a small minority to force its will upon the great majority of the Party, to spread hostile alien ideology and arguments, to form factional groupings which break Party unity or shake the firmness and strength of the working class."

With its arteries narrowed by such autocratic sediments it is not surprising that "free and businesslike discussion" has been suffering from chronic anemia. Not that enough words are not spoken. In the meetings of communist assemblies, especially those on higher levels of the Party pyramid, high-sounding rhetoric flows as richly as vodka at a Kremlin banquet, and as many as several dozens of Party members may take part in the debate which follows the long-winded reports and pep talks from Party leaders. But all that the debaters ordinarily do is to rehash the themes already developed by the leaders, praise their Leninist wisdom, and thunder against real or imaginary enemies and doubters. Meticulous care is taken to keep any discussion strictly within the limits allowed by Party leaders and blame is allocated only to those below or to predetermined scapegoats. Advocacy of alternative policies is not tolerated and any direct challenge to the Party command would be construed not merely as a *lèse majesté* but as high treason. Published reports of the KSČ proceedings as well as oral testimony of those who have taken part in these weird rituals amply document the depth to which free and businesslike discussion has sunk in the era of the dictatorship of the proletariat.

While Party leaders frown at any debate which casts the slightest aspersion upon them or questions the official Party line, they invite and encourage criticism of others. One of the major duties that the Statutes impose on Party members is to develop "criticism from below, to reveal shortcomings in the work and to strive for their elimination, to fight against ostentatious self-satisfaction and against being intoxicated by success." By insisting on "the ventilation of Party organizations by the good wind of criticism," the leaders seek to attain several purposes.[9] They uncover shortcomings, inefficiency, corruption, and other malpractices in the Party system and operations, and are thus in a better position to correct them. They gain additional insight into the conduct of various lower functionaries, among both the critics and the criticized. By removing or otherwise disciplining those shown as inept, venal, or overbearing, the leaders can in one stroke rid the Party of undesirables and display in a dramatic fashion their own responsiveness to the sentiments of the Party's rank and file. In so doing they also divert attention from their own misdeeds and provide a safety valve for releasing pent-up anger. Simultaneously, they can spot those who deserve promotion for "constructive" criticism as well as those who may have inadvertently revealed "negativist" or "nihilistic" tendencies and ought therefore to have their wings clipped. Last but not least, listening to critical voices on various Party levels enables the leaders to gauge "public opinion" within Party ranks.

Considering these important functions of "criticism from below" it is easy to understand why Party Statutes call the "suppression of criticism a heavy evil" and why Party leaders never tire of stressing the need of "constructive" criticism.[10] On the other hand, it is equally understandable why most lower functionaries take a dim view of the whole matter. Pressed hard from above, they have to get things done. Since so much of the Party business is anything but pleasant, this is hardly likely to endear them to the rank and file. Yet, when something goes wrong, it is against them that the wrath of their subordinates turns first. Generally, they will be backed by their superiors. But when criticism reveals an especially high level of discontent the

---

[9] Gottwald's address to the Central Committee, *Rudé právo*, March 1, 1950.

[10] For examples of such exhortations see *Rudé právo*, March 1, 1950, February 20, 1954, and April 15, 1954.

generals may prefer sacrificing their sergeants and lieutenants by accusing them of excesses of zeal or abuse of authority. Aware of such risks, the lower functionaries have developed an extreme sensitivity to any kind of criticism, constructive or otherwise. "The responsible regional and some district functionaries suppressed criticism by Party members," the Ninth Party Congress was told by the Party's Secretary General. "They intimidated such Party members, threatened them, directed the SNB [police] organs to collect materials against the critics, and had them subjected to examination by the organs of state security."[11] Four years later *Rudé právo* was still complaining that "leading functionaries have not yet disappeared who . . . consider criticism from below as an attempt to undermine their authority [and who] resort to the concealment of mistakes and suppression of criticism for fear of being discredited . . . ."[12] And in 1959 *Život strany* lashed out at the "Party functionaries who recognize the usefulness of criticism and initiative from below in general terms, but at the same time find it hard to tolerate better proposals and suggestions advanced by the rank and file."[13]

A mandatory concomitant of criticism is *sebekritika,* or self-criticism. Without self-criticism, said Stalin, "It is impossible to educate correctly the Party, the class, and the masses. Without the correct education of the Party, the class, and the masses there is no bolshevism." As in the case of its Soviet counterpart, *samokritika,* probably none of the ingredients of inner-Party democracy is more ritualistic than the KSČ's insistence on *sebekritika.* Behaving much in the manner of the medieval flagellants who sought to atone for their sins by whipping themselves in public, members of the modern Leninist sect purge themselves from their sins against the Marxist-Leninist dogma by periodic public confessions of errors and weaknesses. When the time comes to indulge in this ritual, Party functionaries one after the other recount the litanies of their real or imaginary inadequacies, promise to do better, and often sign socialist pledges with specific commitments. However, the self-critics endeavor to make their self-flagellation as painless as possible. They much prefer to put on public display only their minor errors and try to by-pass those misdeeds which might bring them into serious trouble.

The most macabre manifestations of communist self-criticism, and

---

[11] *Lidové noviny,* May 27, 1949.
[12] *Rudé právo,* August 5, 1953.
[13] *Život strany,* No. 23 (1959), pp. 1422ff.

the ones most repugnant to Western observers, are the self-accusations exacted from the Party members tried by communist courts. An especially sickening spectacle of this type of self-criticism was offered by the monster trial against Slánský, Clementis, and their alleged collaborators in November 1951. The accused not only confessed to all their "crimes," most of which they had never committed, but asked the Court to give them a death sentence so that their fate might discourage others from committing similar crimes. One of them, André Simone, pleaded: "I have been a writer and a beautiful saying refers to writers as architects of the people's souls. What sort of architect have I been—I who have poisoned the souls? Such an architect of the souls belongs on the gallows. The only good service I can still render is to serve as a warning to all those who by their origin, temperament, or other characteristics are in danger of following the same path to hell. The stiffer the penalty, the more effective will the warning be."[14]

Having reviewed the main ingredients of inner-Party democracy, let us turn to the question of whether there has been any discernible trend in this field since 1948. Has there been an improvement, or a deterioration, or has it remained about the same in the course of years? Is there more or less democracy within the KSČ today than when the Party seized power in 1948?

To answer this question, the period since 1948 must be divided into two parts separated by Stalin's death in 1953. While it is common knowledge that the communist coup of 1948 dealt a fatal blow to Czechoslovak freedom, it had equally serious effects on inner-Party democracy. Although dictatorial practices were on the ascendancy within the Party even prior to 1948, the necessity to expand in the relatively competitive political market of 1945-1948 inevitably placed certain restraints on the leaders' authoritarian tendencies. Some particles of democracy were bound to rub off on the Party from its living in close quarters with its democratic rivals. But with the Party's seizure of a monopoly of power this came to an end. The establishment of the dictatorship of the proletariat could not leave its instrument unaffected. The fear, bitterness, and lust for revenge caused by the purges, which were soon to follow the February triumph, created the worst possible climate for the growth of inner-Party democracy. So did the well-known Stalinist teaching on "sharpening of the class struggle" during the construction of socialist society. Nor could the

[14] *Práce,* November 23, 1952.

many Party members, whose erstwhile rosy vistas of life under communism were rudely shaken by the decidedly less rosy realities, be allowed to shatter the disciplined unity of the Party by using inner-Party democracy for spreading their disillusionment. Rock bottom was hit during the Greek Purge of 1950-1951 when the witchhunt for "cosmopolites," "titoist traitors," and other "agents of Western imperialism" reached its climax.

After the passing of Stalin, which was closely followed by the death of Czechoslovakia's own "little Stalin," Klement Gottwald, there were several months of suspense. What would come next? The grand question hung unspoken from Party members' lips and beamed from their expectant eyes, while the Party chieftains and their henchmen went stiffly and nervously about their routine business in the customary Stalinist fashion. But when the post-Stalin thaw began in Russia and neighboring Hungary, it spread quickly into the ranks of the KSČ, despite the icy reception of Party leaders who were deeply worried about adverse consequences. Matters were made more difficult by Khrushchëv's reconciliation with Tito in 1955 and still more by the explosion of the Stalin myth at the Twentieth Congress of the Soviet Party in 1956 and Khrushchëv's announcement of the "different-roads-to-socialism" doctrine. Resuscitated by these potent injections, a new and surprisingly vigorous inner-Party democracy soon appeared. Slowly and hesitantly at first, but then with increasing frequency and strength, critical voices made themselves heard. Party members displayed increasing "signs of ideological instability," "succumbing to illusions of tolerant liberalism" and "an incorrect conception of freedom under socialism."[15] It was at this time also that demands were made for the convocation of an extraordinary Party Congress and for the adoption of secret balloting for Party elections.

The extent to which inner-Party democracy managed to loosen the strait jacket into which it had been forced in the Stalinist era was revealed by the Party's First Secretary. His report to the National Party Conference in June 1956 bristled with recurrent references to comrades "attacking the general line of the Party and resorting to numerous other abuses of their inalienable right of free and businesslike discussion" guaranteed to them by the Party Statutes.[16] Such abuses of free and businesslike discussion could not be tolerated for

---

[15] J. Hendrych in *Život strany*, February 5, 1956.
[16] *Rudé právo*, June 12, 1956. The problems which these and other post-Stalin developments have posed for the Party leaders are discussed in Chapter vi.

long and Novotný's keynote speech signaled the start of a resolute back-to-orthodoxy counteroffensive. The screws of Party discipline began to be tightened again and a holy war was declared on the "revisionists," as the Party leaders now call those who want to liberalize the Party. Aided by the forcible suppression of the Hungarian uprising and by the swing toward neo-Stalinism which developed in the Soviet Party in 1957-1958, Party leaders succeeded in stemming the tide and undercutting a great many of the gains which inner-Party democracy had scored in the preceding years. However, they have thus far failed to push it into the dark hole where they kept it hidden in the days of Stalin. At present, inner-Party democracy seems to stand roughly halfway between its lowest point of the early fifties, when it virtually did not exist, and its high of the first months after the Twentieth Congress of the Soviet Party in 1956.

It should be added that the practice of inner-Party democracy has varied rather considerably from one layer of the organizational pyramid to the other. Naturally, it has been least restricted at the very top, in the Party's Political Bureau, where exchanges of arguments have been relatively free.[17] But the main locale of whatever genuine discussion and criticism there have been lies in the primary units and local Party conferences. The base of the pyramid seems thus to be the soft underbelly of the Party system and its least disciplined part. Contrariwise, the intermediate layers, the regional and district organizations, are those where Party discipline has customarily been highest and inner-Party democracy lowest.

Collective Leadership versus the Cult of the Individual

Another basic rule of the Party's operational code is the principle of collective leadership. "Collective leadership is an integral component of inner-Party democracy," say the Party Statutes. "It is the supreme principle in discussion and decisions in all Party organs from the Central Committee down to the primary organizations. The application of the principle of collective leadership offers the strongest guarantee of the correctness of adopted resolutions and ensures a broad initiative of the Party masses. The principle of collective leadership does not weaken personal responsibility. The cult of personalities is in conflict with the principles of the Marxist-Leninist Party."

[17] See Chapter v.

To understand the proper meaning of this provision it is necessary to review briefly the developments which led to its insertion in the Party Statutes in 1954.

Until Stalin's death the KSČ was second to none in the deification of the Soviet Dictator who had in fact become the supreme ruler over Czechoslovakia after the communist coup of 1948. Knowing that unflinching personal fealty to Stalin, or a successful pretense of such, was a condition *sine qua non* for holding any Party and government function, the Czechoslovak communist leaders from Gottwald down vied with one another in idolatory of the ever-suspicious tyrant. No communist functionary dared to open his mouth without paying rich adulatory tribute to the "Great Stalin," the "Teacher of the working people of the whole world," and "the greatest man of the present time."[18] After 1948 the cult of the individual grew up around Klement Gottwald, although it remained at a respectable distance from the treatment reserved for Stalin. Between 1948 and 1953 sycophantic references to Gottwald became a standard item in the concluding formula of all major speeches by his colleagues. As in the case of Stalin, Gottwald's name was usually adorned with various flowery epithets, such as "the best disciple of Stalin," "the heart and the brain of our Party," "the Great Teacher of our new science of history."[19] Articles glorifying Gottwald were included in school textbooks. His portraits were displayed in Party halls and public offices. Many more streets, squares, and factories were named after Gottwald than after any other Czechoslovak Communist. Much like Stalin's ukases, Gottwald's pronouncements began to be treated as binding commands subject to no criticism or dissent. Some of the communist amanuenses even began to differentiate among several types of Communists and came to the conclusion that the "Gottwaldian type" was definitely the best of the species. While Gottwald's glorification never reached Soviet proportions and though Gottwald never quite attained the one-man rule of Stalin, he came fairly close to it and after the purge of Slánský in 1951 became an uncontested *primus* without *pares*.

At the time of Stalin's death in March 1953 Czechoslovakia was thus addicted to the cult of the individual more than any other Soviet satellite, and the abrupt reversal of the trend in the Soviet Union

[18] For a few examples of Stalin's glorification in Czechoslovakia see *Rudé právo,* December 21, 1949; *Tvorba,* December 20, 1951; *Rudé právo,* December 14, 1951.

[19] *Rudé právo,* May 17, 1951, and February 8, 1952; Jan Pachta, *Gottwald a naše dějiny* (Gottwald and Our History), Praha, 1948.

following the Dictator's death would undoubtedly have created a serious problem for Klement Gottwald. The Soviet substitution of the new deity of collective leadership for the one-man rule of Stalin's days and the resolute condemnation of the "pernicious cult of the individual" would certainly have knocked the pedestal from under the feet of Gottwald. His timely death, which followed, as if by a stroke of destiny, by only a few days that of the man who had made him governor of Czechoslovakia, deprived the public of a highly interesting spectacle and solved for the KSČ a very delicate problem. With the Czechoslovak incarnation of the cult of the individual gone, all Gottwald's heirs had to do was to jump on the new Soviet band wagon of collective leadership. In sharp contrast to previous practices, Stalin's name now virtually ceased to be mentioned, except in a strictly historical connection, and no occasion was wasted to extol the virtues of collectivity as "the highest principle of Party leadership." When the Tenth Party Congress placed the newly vindicated principle in the amended Party Statutes of 1954 it was only a logical outcome of this development.

While the Czechoslovak Party leaders gladly deferred to collective leadership they did not relish the idea of any major downgrading of Stalin. To deserve their high positions they had been forced to cater to Stalin's every whim, often disregarding the vital interests of their own people and purging thousands, including many high-ranking Party members. They had stressed Stalinism as the only way to build socialism in Czechoslovakia and had ruthlessly disposed of those who thought otherwise. In these respects the top hierarchy of the KSČ could be considered as arch-Stalinist. Hence, their personal interests would have been served best if the dead Stalin, who could no longer harm them, had been allowed to retain his position alongside Lenin and Marx. That is why they welcomed with open arms, and readily joined in, the Soviet vindicatory trend of 1954 and 1955 which restored Stalin to the status of "the great continuer of Lenin's cause." When Khrushchëv himself began to defer to Stalin's theses and used them in February 1955 to brand Malenkov as a "right-wing deviationist," Zápotocký and his associates felt that they could at last catch up on the many sleepless nights caused by the grave uncertainties of the first post-Stalin months.

One can, therefore, imagine what a shock it was for them when Khrushchëv quite unexpectedly launched his devastating attack against Stalin at the close of the Twentieth Congress of the Soviet Party in February 1956. Already plagued by a growing disaffection among the workers, the sullen resistance of the peasantry, rising ferment among students and intellectuals, and smoldering discontent of the Party's rank and file, Party leaders had ample reason to be alarmed by the potentialities released by this stupefying twist. They realized better than the Soviet iconoclasts what an encouragement this would be not only for non-communists but also for the majority of their own Party members who could never stomach their leaders' subservience to the Kremlin.

Haunted by such fears, Party leaders decided to divulge the new line slowly and in a greatly diluted form. In its long release on the results and lessons of the Twentieth Congress, expressing the official attitude of the Czechoslovak Party leadership, the Czechoslovak Press Agency embarked upon the touchy issue by stressing that "it is necessary to see the positive role which Stalin played in the period after the death of Lenin when he, together with a majority of the Party and other pupils of Lenin, defended Leninism in the struggle against the Trotskyites and other enemies of Lenin." It went on to credit Stalin with "the historical merits" of having "resolutely frustrated the attempts of enemies who tried to destroy the Party and the Soviet State." Only after having thus cushioned the impact of the criticism which was to follow did the report state that "in the latter period of his activities Stalin committed many mistakes" and that "shortcomings appeared in his work, such as in the principle of collective leadership."[20]

Czechoslovak Communists were even more cautious in applying the "results and lessons" of the Congress to Gottwald. Dealing with the "cult of Gottwald" at the meeting of the Party's Central Committee in March 1956, Novotný all but exonerated the dead leader and blamed instead the entire Central Committee for having created a false atmosphere of untouchability around the otherwise modest Gottwald, imitating thus the system of personal adulation introduced in Russia by Stalin. While leaving the memory of Gottwald alone, the ax fell on Gottwald's son-in-law, Alexei Čepička, First Deputy Premier, Minister of Defense, and member of the Party's Political Bureau. In April 1956 Čepička was relieved of all his Party and government functions and was expelled from the Central Committee. Thus he became the first and so far the only really prominent victim of the reappraisal of Stalinism in Czechoslovakia.[21]

The cautious stand of the Czechoslovak communist leaders on

---

[20] *News*, 5, 4 (1956), p. 46.
[21] *Rudé právo,* April 10. 1956.

the intricate matter of de-stalinization paid dividends. Not only did it help them to weather the storm unleashed in Eastern Europe by the destruction of the Stalin myth, but it saved them the trouble and the inconvenience of yet another sharp about-face when Khrushchëv, under the impact of the Polish and Hungarian revolts, began to refer to Stalin as a "model Bolshevik" and "great Marxist." Since they had disliked the excessive downgrading of Stalin in the first place, the KSČ leaders most eagerly seized on the new Soviet trend.

In the beginning the new reassessment took a cautionary tone. "The condemnation of the cult of the individual does not mean that the Party line has changed," warned Kopecký, addressing the National Party Conference in July 1956. But the tone sharpened substantially after the Polish and Hungarian revolts. "The ambiguous word 'de-stalinization' stands only for the idea of weakening and giving way to the forces of reaction," cautioned *Rudé právo* on January 29, 1957. "It serves as a hiding place for two other very evident ideas—the loosening of friendship and the betrayal of the alliance with the Soviet Union." And the paper further warned that those "who beat the drum of de-stalinization and so-called national communism follow the official tune composed and conducted by the American State Department." The wreath which Zápotocký laid on Stalin's tomb in the Lenin-Stalin Mausoleum during the January 1957 visit of Czechoslovak Party leaders in Moscow was significantly inscribed: "To the Great Leader of Socialism—J. V. Stalin." The current pro-Stalin line was well summarized in the report delivered in June 1957 at the plenary session of the Party's Central Committee by its Secretary, Jiří Hendrych: "We shall defend the great revolutionary merits of Stalin and his important contribution to the development of our country."[22]

This is where the issue of collective leadership versus the cult of the individual stands officially today. Stalin is once again reestablished in his role as the foremost collaborator of Lenin and liberator of Czechoslovakia, but the excessive incense-burning of earlier days has not returned and eulogies are reserved for special occasions only. The Generalissimo's huge statue on Letná Hill in Praha and other such monuments have remained. But most of the movable relics of Stalin's glory, such as pictures and books, have disappeared even from the Party's assembly halls. The "modest" Gottwald continues to lie in state in the Mausoleum on Žižkov Hill in Praha and is dutifully

[22] *ibid.*, June 19, 1957.

commemorated on proper occasions as the Republic's "first worker President" and the most prominent historical figure of the Czecho-slovak communism. A statue in his honor was solemnly unveiled in 1956 in the town of his birth and the commemoration of his 60th birthday was quite ostentatious. At the same time, the "Leninist principle of collective leadership" is referred to repeatedly, while the "cult of the individual" comes in for occasional criticism and lower Party functionaries are on occasion publicly reprimanded for indulging in this vice.

PARTY SCHOOLING

A very important part of internal Party operations is the political education of Party members and candidates. "Increasing his political awareness and mastering the fundamentals of Marxism-Leninism" is one of the most essential duties imposed upon a Party member by the Party Statutes; and the obligation to direct, organize, and control the political education of members and their study of Marxism-Leninism is among the basic functions assigned to Party organizations on all intermediate and primary levels. The reasons why communist leaders are so greatly concerned with the ideological orientation of Party members are quite clear. In the end, the fate of communism will be decided by the success or failure to create a new type of "communistic man," a man who will genuinely believe that communism gives him a better deal than Western democracy. But to have any chance of success in the mass production of this new species, the "vanguard of the proletariat" must be remodeled first.

Soon after they seized power the KSČ leaders began to work systematically at this all-important task. In November 1949 they launched with great fanfare a new program of Party schooling which has since been the Party's main institution for systematic ideological training and political indoctrination. As it has developed over the years, the system of Party schooling offers several types of classes meeting once a week in four-hour periods from October to the end of May and graduated according to the "ideological maturity" required for admission.[23] There are basic courses on fundamentals of Marxism-Leninism, socialist economics, history and structure of the

[23] For a description of the system of Party schooling see *Rok stranického školení* (Year of Party Schooling), an annual publication of the Propaganda and Agitation Department of the Central Committee of the KSČ, containing detailed curricula and other directives; also various articles on the progress of Party schooling in *Život strany*.

Communist Parties of Czechoslovakia and the Soviet Union, and current affairs. There are Evening Schools of Marxism-Leninism to offer advanced courses primarily for Party functionaries and other advanced students as well as various seminars for further training of propagandists and agitators. Since 1953 special higher evening schools, named "Evening Universities of Marxism-Leninism," have been set up in the four largest cities, Praha, Brno, Ostrava, and Bratislava, to offer a still more advanced teaching of the "science of sciences." Finally, at the top of the whole system, there has been since 1953 a Party University where the cream of the communist elite is sub-jected to three years of intensive study containing all that a graduate Marxist-Leninist is supposed to master.[24] Although it is a *Party* school established by a resolution of the KSČ's Central Committee and de-signed to train future Party leaders, a government ordinance gave it the status of a regular university and its graduates the rights and duties of graduates of other universities.[25] Since 1958 even a Doctorate of Communist Science is being offered. It is awarded by the Institute of Social Sciences attached to the Party's Central Committee.[26]

Provision is also made within the framework of Party schooling for what is called an "independent study of Marxism-Leninism." It is intended for "ideologically mature Party functionaries who have progressed in their Marxist-Leninist self-education so far that they can further deepen and broaden their knowledge through independent studies."[27] The arrangement of these independent studies somewhat resembles an American college reading course. Each participant com-mits himself to study a certain number of books, especially such communist classics as Lenin's works, and to prepare lecture themes and papers on the basis of the materials thus studied. The students are divided into smaller groups of ten or so, and each group is super-vised by a consultant appointed by the regional Party committee who serves as a tutor.

The entire system of Party schooling is under the over-all super-vision of the Party's Central Committee acting mainly through its Department of Propaganda and Agitation. The latter sets the types of courses, prescribes their curricula and themes of study, and de-termines the methods of organization and instruction. But except for the Party University, which is attached to the Central Committee,

[24] *Pod zástavou socialismu,* 2, 7 (April 1953); *Rudé právo,* September 2, 1953.
[25] Government ordinance No. 97 of November 27, 1953.
[26] Law No. 70 of December 19, 1957.
[27] *Rudé právo,* September 16, 1957.

the actual operation of Party schooling is in the hands of the Party's regional and district committees working in close cooperation with lower Party organizations in the respective regions and districts. General supervision is maintained by the departments of agitation and propaganda *agitprops* of the regional and district Party secretariats. They are aided in their work by the advisory and study offices of Marxism-Leninism. It is the duty of the *agitprops* to make all the practical arrangements, assign students to respective courses and classes, secure an adequate number of qualified teachers from among suitable functionaries and propagandists, to prepare them for their tasks in summer schools and, most important, to check regularly on the content and quality of instruction. The responsibility of supplying students and the burden of persuading them of the beneficence of Party schooling lies with the primary organizations.

According to Party resolutions, members' participation in the Party schooling is voluntary. But as it is with many things so styled under totalitarian communism, it is rather a matter of volunteering —or else. "The directives of the Political Secretariat of the Central Committee of the KSČ which speak of voluntary participation in the Year of Party schooling have not been understood correctly in all the districts," a Party press release said. "The voluntary character has not been meant in the sense that the comrades do not have to join the schooling, but that their request should be taken into account in considering their assignment to either the lower or the higher grade of the schooling according to their ideological and political maturity."[28]

In terms of registration for the courses Party leaders can be well pleased, although they occasionally give vent to criticism on that count. According to Party announcements, 51 percent of all Party members registered for the first year of schooling (1949-1950) and 55 percent for the second year (1950-1951).[29] On the basis of these figures for the initial years of schooling one can reasonably assume that practically all Party members and candidates must have by now gone through one or more of the courses. However, as indicated by repeated complaints of the communist press and confirmed by reports of escaped participants of the schooling system, the students' actual attendance has been far from exemplary and the cutting of classes under flimsy pretexts or no pretext at all has been widespread. Habitually, the attendance with which the school year starts gradually

[28] *Rovnost,* September 23, 1952; also, *Rok stranického školení.*
[29] *Rudé právo,* February 27, 1952.

melts. "At the beginning of the Second Year of Party schooling we had three evening classes attended by forty-three comrades," read a report from a Party school in central Slovakia filed toward the close of the school year. "Today we have only one evening class with ten students."[30] Again, one year later, *Rudé právo* reported areas where Party schooling was virtually dormant for a good part of the school year: "Comrades just wave their hands and say, 'Either the teacher does not come, or so few students appear that schooling is postponed.' And it is so postponed from one month to another."[31]

Such instances of lax participation, which have been anything but rare, have been fought with what Party leaders cryptically call "organizational measures" and "broad use of the methods of persuasion." When a Party member leaves general exhortations unheeded and persists in violating his membership duties by either failing to enroll or by recurrent absenteeism from classes, his Party superiors have a hard talk with the culprit. After they have explained to him the disagreeable consequences which such an attitude might have for him, the member usually sees what an improved knowledge of Marxism-Leninism would mean for his "socialist tomorrow" and "voluntarily" mends his ways.[32] The trouble is that in some instances the would-be persuaders themselves also seek to evade their duty to attend Party schooling.[33]

While this kind of persuasion has been fairly effective in obtaining the desired volume of registration and in bolstering attendance, it can hardly be instrumental in turning out genuine communist converts. Faced with a Hobson's choice, Party members and candidates sit through the required courses, taking a nap in class, or playing hooky whenever it is safe to do so. They study the absolute minimum necessary to avoid being flunked and memorize a few familiar quotations to show that they are acquainted with such classics of Marxism-Leninism as Lenin, Stalin, and Gottwald. "The main weakness was in the answers to questions on dialectical and historical materialism," bewailed a communist analysis of final examinations in Party evening schools in July 1954.[34] It scored "many other deficiencies in the ideological level of the students" and cited examples of glaring lack of comprehension of such crucial ideological matters as "the role of

---

[30] *ibid.*, June 14, 1951, February 24, 1953.
[31] *ibid.*, August 14, 1952.
[32] For examples see *Rudé právo,* September 22, 1952.
[33] *ibid.*, April 15, 1953.
[34] *Rovnost,* July 6, 1954.

the masses and individuals in history" or Lenin's teaching on agriculture.[35] Some of the students acquire high versatility in the "quotation-mania" and can produce a fitting Marxist-Leninist quotation in the manner of magicians pulling rabbits from their hats. But it seems that relatively few of this captive audience become true and loyal followers of the communist creed.

During the early years of Party schooling a convenient scapegoat for this failure "to arm the Communists ideologically for the struggle against bourgeois survivals" was found in the "Slánský gang." "The causes of these serious shortcomings in Party schooling and the whole front of our ideological struggle lies first and foremost in the sabotage by the gang of Slánský and his associates," explained the Party's Political Secretariat in May 1952. "They endeavored to dull the sharp edge of the Marxist-Leninist theory . . . they distorted the teaching of Marxism-Leninism, strove for its revision, attempted to deprive it of its revolutionary content. They thus wished to deaden the ideological life in our Party, to break its ability to act and its unity . . . . They strove to tear the Party's educational work away from everyday policy, from the burning tasks of the day, from the questions of our construction, and to sidetrack Party education to idle and dry Talmudistic philosophizing and memorizing of dogmas."[36]

Much of the blame has also been laid at the teachers' door. Over the years of Party schooling there have been recurrent attacks on teachers "contaminated by social democratism," "vacillating and succumbing to petty-bourgeois influence." They have been reprimanded for "failing to correct" mistaken opinions of the students on the most fundamental articles of Marxist-Leninist faith, for negligence in the preparation and delivery of lectures, for indulging in "academic debates on abstract themes" rather than equipping students with ideological weapons with which to fight against "nationalist, social democratic, and other deviations."[37] Even outright cases of sabotage have occurred such as that of a teacher who "praised America and said that, on the whole, the Soviet Union was alien to us," or of a similar specimen who defended the *kulaks* and even boasted of it publicly "with brazen laughter."[38] Fault has been found with the lecturers for

[35] *ibid.*, September 23, 1952.

[36] *Rudé právo*, May 19, 1952.

[37] *Rudé právo*, September 15, 1951, *Funkcionář*, March 5, 1951; *Literární noviny*, December 10, 1955; *Rudé právo*, February 24, 1953; *Rok stranického školení;* and recurrent criticism in *Život strany* over the years.

[38] *Rovnost*, September 23, 1952; *Rudé právo*, December 1, 1952.

"an uneconomical use of Party literature" through negligent distribution of brochures prepared for the Party schooling which were left collecting dust on the shelves rather than being distributed among the pupils.[39] Obviously, it has proved impossible to recruit an adequate number of teachers who would meet the triple test of being dependable Communists, well-acquainted with the material on which they were to lecture, and capable of presenting them in an interesting and appealing fashion. That this is so should cause little surprise. A lecturership in the Party schools is one of the least desirable positions in the communist system. Not many people relish expounding dry doctrines, which they often do not themselves believe, to captive audiences that consider it all an unnecessary nuisance.

But the basic flaw of Party schooling lies neither in the "ravages caused by the Slánský gang" nor in the inadequacy of the teachers. It lies in the subject itself. A theory that is wrong in its basic suppositions and is belied by the facts which its students encounter daily cannot be taught successfully, no matter how brilliant its exposition. The post-Stalin thaw has made matters even worse. Its relative relaxation has encouraged the students to ask critical questions, which they had previously kept for themselves, and the teachers to be more outspoken and more sincere in their answers. Khrushchëv's ideological prestidigitations at the Twentieth Congress were enough to confuse and lead astray even seasoned Party members, let alone Party novices freshly graduated from Party schools. The dilemma was well put by the Slovak *Pravda*: "Some comrades who succeeded in previous years in acquiring a certain knowledge of Marxism-Leninism from the Party schooling have begun to doubt after the Twentieth Congress' crushing criticism of the cult of the individual and the revelation of the serious mistakes by J. V. Stalin. They say: 'Why did I study? What should I believe now from what I have learned? What remains valid?' "[40]

Thus the ten years of Party schooling bear out a statement made in 1952 by the Nestor of Czechoslovak Communists, Zdeněk Nejedlý: "It is far easier to supply new techniques than new brains. We are gaining this conviction from our daily practice."

SUBSERVIENCE TO THE KREMLIN

Difficult as it is, the "supplying of new brains" is made much harder by the Party's subservience to the Kremlin. No principle of

---

[39] *Pravda*, April 22, 1951.
[40] *ibid.*, May 1, 1956.

the Party's operational code has been followed more closely and none has withstood better the turbulent vicissitudes of recent years. The Soviet Union is mentioned three times in the five sentences that constitute the First Section of the Party Statutes. The Party builds socialism in Czechoslovakia "with the aid of the Soviet Union"; it is to be guided by "the rich experience of the Communist Party of the Soviet Union"; and it educates the working class "in loyalty and friendship to the Soviet Union." These solemn assurances of the Party's constitution have been outdone in actual practice. Since enough evidence has already been presented in this and foregoing chapters on the KSČ's imitation of the Soviet model, only a few illustrations need be added to complete the picture and to sketch more recent trends.

This subservience had its high point in the Stalinist era when an unapproved departure from Soviet pattern was the worst of heresies. "Mean vilification of the Soviet Union," "expression of unfavorable opinions of the conditions in the USSR," "adoption of a sharply hateful attitude toward the USSR," "attempts to prove that development toward socialism must proceed in Czechoslovakia along another path than in the Soviet Union," "sabotaging the application of the experience of the All-Union Communist Party"—these were among the worst of the alleged crimes that brought Slánský and most of his fellow-conspirators to the gallows in 1952.[41] There is reason to believe that the Great Purge itself was motivated mainly, if not solely, by the desperate need of Gottwald and his associates to prove their loyalty to Stalin. By offering the supreme sacrifice to the Soviet Moloch they hoped to allay his suspicions, retain his trust, and avert bloodletting from themselves.[42] Innumerable less tragic examples could be cited to document the master-servant relationship between the Soviet Party and the KSČ leadership in even trivial matters.

While blood-letting ceased to be its highest expression by 1953, subservience toward the Kremlin was not diminished after the death of Stalin. At first sight, a few developments might have been mistaken for signs of the daughter's diminished dependence on the mother Party. The most striking of them has been the trend, apparent since the latter part of 1955, toward toning down the previous excessive praise of everything Soviet. "There are people in our country who, for God knows what reasons, describe Soviet citizens as people who

[41] *Rudé právo,* February 27, 1951.
[42] This is discussed more fully in Chapter v.

can do everything, and do it to perfection by a simple wave of hand," wrote the editor-in-chief of *Dikobraz*, the main Czechoslovak humor magazine, in September 1955.[43] People have even been scolded for "embarrassing Soviet people by their exaggerated admiration of certain things in the USSR, even though the Soviet comrades know very well that the same things in our country are at least as good."[44] But this new fashion has been unmistakably Moscow-made and followed the exhortations by Khrushchëv, Mikoyan, and other Soviet leaders that the Soviet people should pay more attention to the achievements of other nations, especially of the people's democracies, and learn from their experience. Besides, it was well-suited to the post-Stalin line of professed modesty and tolerance which has been refreshing even if not perfectly consistent.

Be that as it may, a cool analysis of communist behavior and pronouncements since 1953 clearly indicates that the master-servant relationship of the Stalin days has changed only in form, not substance. "The relation to the Soviet Union was and is a touchstone of loyalty and devotion to the idea of socialism for every Marxist party and for each and every of its functionaries," wrote Zápotocký in November 1953.[45] The actions which the Czechoslovak rulers have taken in the post-Stalin era, and especially their timing, reveal that in each and every instance they have acted in pursuance of Soviet guidance. Whether it was their cautious adoption of Malenkov's economic "New Course," the alternation of concessions and retrenchments on the home front, the invocation of the "Geneva" or "Camp David" spirit, and participation in the post-Stalin permutations of smiles and rocket-rattling foreign policy, the praise of collective leadership, or the purge of the Molotov-Malenkov-Kaganovich anti-Party group, the KSČ leaders saw to it that they remained within the bounds prescribed by the Kremlin. Despite their serious misgivings and against their better judgment, they followed the Soviet course even in matters which were most disagreeable and most likely to cause them trouble, such as the reversal on Tito, the downgrading of Stalin, the admission of guilt for past police excesses, and the amnesty for the surviving victims of the Slánský-Clementis trial.

This sycophancy has become even more pronounced and certainly more vociferous in the wake of the Polish and Hungarian revolts.

[43] *News,* 5, 2 (1956), p. 41.
[44] *ibid.*
[45] *Rudé právo,* November 7, 1953.

Public adulation of the Soviet Union came once again into fashion after the momentary spell of modesty that followed Stalin's death. "For the peoples of Czechoslovakia friendship with the Soviet Union is most fundamental," said Zápotocký when he reached Soviet soil in January 1957, responding within twenty-four hours to the summons of the Soviet rulers to discuss with them "matters of interest to the two countries." In a toast at a banquet given on the same occasion Voroshilov declared the Czechoslovak Communists to be "the best, the closest, and the dearest friends" of the Bolsheviks. The joint Soviet-Czechoslovak declaration issued at the conclusion of the visit amounted to a virtual fealty oath of a vassal to his king.[46] Similar tributes to the Kremlin followed on every suitable occasion, notably at the Slovak Party Congress in April 1957, in the Central Committee session of June 1957 and, most of all, during Khrushchëv's visit to Czechoslovakia in July 1957. The Soviet Party leader could rightly declare, as he did on July 11, 1957, while addressing the workers at the huge ČKD–Stalingrad Works in Praha: "We are leaving you with the conviction that the cause of Leninism in Czechoslovakia is in good hands."[47] Similarly, the KSČ leaders followed a straight Moscowite line in the Moscow-Peking ideological debate of 1960.

What is the explanation of this continuing subservience of the Czechoslovak communist leaders to the Kremlin? After all, the rigid link and the tight grip of Stalinism are gone. Tito's course of independent communism has been dramatically vindicated and the Soviet road to socialism need no longer be strictly followed. Because of the nuclear stalemate a head-on collision between the Soviet and non-Soviet worlds seems to be more remote than ever. Despite recurrent sabre-rattling, "fraternization," "cultural exchanges" and trading with the West continue to be stressed as prominent tools with which to defeat "decaying" capitalism. Such factors ought to have operated to lessen Moscow's hold on the Czechoslovak Party.

Paradoxically, the primary reason lies in the inner weakness of the Czechoslovak Party leadership. The weaker the leaders are vis-à-vis the body of the Party membership, the more they must lean on the Soviet Party. By their behavior under Stalin's rule, they had made themselves heartily disliked by their one-time supporters and the group of their loyal followers kept dwindling. The developments that had taken place throughout the Soviet-controlled world after Stalin's

[46] *ibid.*, January 29, 1957.
[47] *East Europe*, 6, 9 (1957), p. 41.

death sparked strong hopes of impending change among its would-be reformers, hopes that, if realized, would ultimately lead to the elimination of the present Party leadership. The Polish and Hungarian revolts in particular appeared to the Czechoslovak leaders as an ominous writing on the wall. They realized only too well what might have happened in Czechoslovakia had not Soviet armed intervention in Hungary prevented the rout of communism in Hungary. Under such circumstances, the instinct of self-preservation itself makes them cling tenaciously to the Soviet coattails and to do everything to deserve the Kremlin's protection without which they themselves would be doomed.

THE PARTY MEMBER'S DUTIES: A MODEL COMMUNIST

Having considered the basic principles, written and unwritten, of the Party's operational code, it is appropriate to scrutinize briefly the main duties it imposes on Party members. What does the KSČ want a model Communist to be and to do? How does the average Party members of flesh and blood measure up to the ideal prescribed by the Party Statutes?

As mentioned earlier, the weighty catalogue of membership duties listed in the 1952 Party Statutes was copied from Soviet Party rules. Therefore, the Czechoslovak Party member is supposed to behave in exactly the same manner as his Soviet equivalent. Paraphrased in a much contracted form, the Statutes expect each and every member to guard the unity of the Party; to be an active fighter for the fulfillment of Party decisions; to be an example to others in his work; to guard and strengthen public socialist property; to strengthen the contacts with the masses and to explain to non-Party masses the meaning of Party policy; to increase his own political awareness and his knowledge of Marxism-Leninism; to observe Party and state discipline; to develop self-criticism and criticism; to report shortcomings in work; to be truthful and honest before the Party and not to permit concealment and distortion of truth; to keep Party and state secrets and display political vigilance; to carry out without fail Party directives on the correct selection of cadres on the basis of their political and working qualification without regard to personal loyalties, local ties, or kinship.

Together, these mandates amount to a big order that only few of the very best Party members can fill. To qualify as a model Communist of this kind the member would have to combine in one and the same person the characteristics of a born conformist, fanatical vigilante, unscrupulous denouncer, apostle of selfless dedication, robot devoid of feelings of true love or friendship, and indefatigable eager beaver. Besides being equipped with a supple backbone, he would have to develop a knack for discerning safely the dim boundary separating desirable criticism from insubordination. On top of all this he would have to be endowed with a sort of sixth sense that wou[l]d enable him to scent in advance the future shifts in the Party's offi[cial] line and thus to avoid the ever-lurking pitfalls of deviationism.

While the performance of some membership duties comes easily and naturally to a model Communist accustomed to serve as a cog in a well-lubricated Party machine, the discharge of others is sometimes trying even for the most hardened and loyal Party members. To be "an active fighter for the fulfillment of Party decisions" sounds simple enough—until one realizes what some of these decisions ordain. How can a Communist who happens to be chairman of a collective farm display socialist zeal in carrying out the Party decision that the *kulaks,* who have "wormed" their way into the collective farms, be ejected? Knowing that these "vicious class enemies" are his best and most experienced hands and that without them the farm under his charge would find it even more difficult to meet government delivery quotas, the active fulfillment of Party orders puts him into a most difficult situation. Or how eager can even a devout Party functionary be to actively implement Party resolutions asking for criticism from below or censoring the cult of the individual when the very fact of his unswerving insistence on the proper fulfillment of higher instructions may have made him the prime target of such criticism? More likely he will feel a strong urge to adopt that "passive and formal attitude" which the Party Statutes proscribe as "incompatible with Party membership."[48]

No less exacting is the model Communist's duty to serve as "an example at work." The disagreeable implications of this duty have already been mentioned in Chapter II as a major factor dissuading people from seeking admission into the Party and they need not be discussed further here.

Another cluster of tasks, highly unpalatable even for the ideal Communist, arises from his duty to strengthen contacts with the masses and explain to them the Party's policies. No postulates of

[48] For example, of these difficulties see *Rudé právo,* August 8, 14, and 30, 1952; *Rovnost,* October 25, 1952.

communist strategy has been stressed more than the paramount need of maintaining the closest possible connections with the masses. Using Stalin's well-known parallel between the Party and the legendary Greek hero Antaeus, who was invincible as long as he touched earth, the *Short Course* concludes by stressing connections with the masses as "the clue to the invincibility of the bolshevik leadership." Should they ever lose such contact, the Communists would "lose all their strength and become mere ciphers." Loyal to this Leninist-Stalinist legacy and keenly aware of the disaffection of the Czechoslovak masses toward the communist cause, the KSČ leaders place an especially heavy emphasis on this particular aspect of Party activities. No opportunity has been wasted to remind Party members of this vital part of their work.

In the fulfillment of this duty Party members are to mix with the crowds, join non-Party mass and other organizations, enter into conversations with their fellow-workers, organize debates in apartment houses and other appropriate places, and seek every suitable opportunity to propagate the Party line and to counter adverse opinions. Whenever a disagreeable Party decision must be forced upon non-Party masses, Party members are mobilized to perform the thankless task of making the masses "understand and accept it." It takes little imagination to picture how warmly a peasant will receive communist agitators who visit him to expound the tremendous advantages he will gain by handing over his land, cattle, and agricultural machinery to the Unified Agricultural Cooperative. And one can visualize with equal ease the quandary of a comrade seeking to justify the currency reform to those whose savings have been virtually obliterated by that reform. Small wonder that many Party members "are helpless when confronted with the dirty and mendacious propaganda of the enemy," and that "they behave as if they have lost their class consciousness, as if they have lost their perspective and revolutionary *élan*," or that they substitute "quotation-mania" and "parrot-like repetition" of sterile formulae for forceful arguments of their own.[49]

Perhaps the most sinister of the many burdens the ideal Party member has to carry is his duty to keep the leading Party organs informed of any shortcomings he discovers regardless of persons involved. What this euphemistically styled rule actually requires him to do is to serve as a round-the-clock spy and informer. None of his duties is fraught with greater risks. The better he fulfills it the more

[49] *Rudé právo,* November 9, 1951, and December 6, 1953.

hated he is by those around him. Feeling endangered by his activities, his associates will use every opportunity to get rid of him in one way or another. But should he neglect the denouncer's role and be caught at it by another informer, he would be strictly punished as a "violator of the Party's will." Moreover, there is always the chance that successful denunciation of a superior may help the denouncer's promotion. Thus the member is subjected to strong temptations pulling him in opposite directions. Also, as interpreted by Party leaders and pressed home by communist indoctrination, the clause "regardless of persons involved" implies the duty to inform, if need be, on members of one's own family.

That Party leaders earnestly mean this repugnant aspect of the duty was revealed in the most drastic manner during the Slánský trial. In a letter addressed to the President of the State Court, the wife of Artur London, one of the accused, denounced her own husband as a "traitor to his Party and his country," declared herself to be "happy that the treacherous gang had been unmasked and rendered harmless" and asked "for a just punishment for the traitors."[50] Even more shattering was the letter which the son of another of the alleged collaborators of Slánský, Ludvík Frejka, addressed to the presiding judge: "Dear comrade, I demand the heaviest penalty, the penalty of death, for my father. Only now do I see that this creature, whom one cannot call a man because he did not have the slightest feeling and human dignity, was my greatest and vilest enemy . . . . Hatred toward my father will always strengthen me in my struggle for the communist future of our people. I request that this letter be placed before my father and that, if the occasion permits, I may tell him all this myself."[51] Whether the hands that wrote these two ghastly documents were guided by genuine belief, by fear, or by a desperate feeling of self-preservation, or whether the letters were a result of police extortion, is not known. But their publication in the Party's main daily allows for no mistake as to the interpretation of membership duties by the Party leaders. Fortunately, these are only isolated cases and it seems that even model Communists mostly have within them a residuum of bourgeois morality that makes them shudder at the thought of denouncing their own families.

The failure of Party leaders to gain precedence for Party loyalty over family attachments and close personal affiliations has had an

---

[50] *ibid.*, November 24, 1952.
[51] *ibid.*, November 25, 1952.

adverse effect on the hallowed duty to select cadres solely on the basis of their political and professional qualifications. Reports from non-communist sources as well as information obtained from communist defectors are at one in their emphatic assertions that never before have nepotism and personal favoritism flourished as they do under the rule of communism. That is indirectly but amply confirmed by repeated public attacks by Party leaders and their press on dishonest Party members who select cadres for important positions "on the basis of personal acquaintance" and who "sacrifice the interest of the cause to relations of friendship and kinship."[52] Judging by such overwhelming evidence from many different sources one definitely gets the impression that, when it comes to obtaining privileges, the Party membership card serves only as a general admission ticket which must be supplemented by the special ticket of close personal ties to assure the entrant a "reserved seat."

That this is so is an inevitable result of totalitarian dictatorship. With the pulverization of all truly non-communist organized groupings and the saturation of all non-Party groups still allowed to function by Party and police spies, the only dependable ties that have withstood the onslaught are the bonds of family and kinship and the mutual trust of well-tested personal friendship. They have thus become the logical nuclei of mutual protection against the multiple dangers lying in wait behind every bush in the communist jungle. "One hand washes the other," says a Czech proverb. Placing a relative or a good friend in a position of authority is the best way to feather one's own nest and enhance one's own security. Such interlocking mutual-aid pacts permeate the Party from top to bottom, converting it into a conglomeration of innumerable cliques. Such a practice, coupled with the absence of any really fearless criticism, provides numerous opportunities for the appointment of incompetents and the use of false pretenses. Falsehood, like dry rot, flourishes even more as air and light are excluded.

[52] *ibid.*, August 5, 1952; *Život strany,* No. 22 (November 1959), pp. 1380ff. See also Chapters x and xviii.

CHAPTER V

THE RULING OLIGARCHS

As THE PRECEDING pages have shown, the exercise of all power in Czechoslovakia is concentrated in the hands of the Political Bureau of the Party's Central Committee. Since this is so, no analysis of the communist regime in Czechoslovakia would be complete without an inquiry into the conditions prevailing within this ruling oligarchy. What type of people are they? What are their background and their mentality? How solid are their communist beliefs? Are they really as convinced of the superiority of the Soviet way as their public utterances seem to indicate? What are their mutual relationships and their relative standing within the junta? Is there any evidence of clique-forming? Is there a tendency toward a one-man rule as has reappeared on the Soviet scene with Khrushchëv's spectacular rise on the Soviet stage?

Without doubt, these are important questions. But they are exceedingly difficult to answer. As in all totalitarian dictatorships, whatever pertains to the pinnacle of power is shrouded in a veil of secrecy. The Politbureau meetings are strictly executive sessions held in complete privacy. No reports of proceedings are published, and painstaking care is used to prevent leakage of any information on possible clashes of opinion or dissent in voting. Whenever results of the Politbureau's deliberations are announced, they are invariably presented as having matured quickly and painlessly in harmonious teamwork. Nor have any defectors from the ranks of the Czechoslovak Politbureau or the circle of their most intimate collaborators thus far reached the Free World to supply direct information on how the actual working processes within the Party's topmost organ and personal relationships among its members compare with the official claims of cooperative monolithism. Hence, the conclusions arrived at in this chapter must be based mainly on circumstantial evidence supplied by those who held positions in the official retinues of some of the ruling oligarchs and could thus catch at least occasional glimpses of the Politbureau's well-kept secrets.

Any attempt at political portraiture of the ruling oligarchy must

necessarily begin with the Big Three, Gottwald, Slánský, and Zápotocký. Although they are no longer alive, they held key positions
at the most crucial junctures in the Party's history and set precedents
for their successors.

KLEMENT GOTTWALD, THE "HEART AND THE BRAIN" OF THE PARTY

Klement Gottwald was the most important of the trio, and the
one and only Czechoslovak Communist who had almost attained
one-man rule.[1] His rise to prominence began in 1925 when at the
age of twenty-nine he was elected to the Party's Central Committee.
He soon became the leader of the Committee's left wing, dubbed the
"Karlín boys," a group which hotly opposed the passivity of the
Bolen-Jílek reformist majority and clamored for more forceful revolutionary action. But when the Red Day demonstration ordered by
the Party leadership at the radicals' behest proved to be a colossal
flop, Gottwald readily pinned the blame on the Bolen-Jílek group
whom he accused of having "lost connections with the masses."[2] As
the main spokesman of the Party's left wing at the Sixth Congress of
the Comintern, which followed on the heels of the Red Day fiasco,
Gottwald gained the Kremlin's support, was elected to the Comintern's Executive and entrusted with the leadership of the KSČ. It
was this ostentatious approval by the Moscow bosses that paved the
way for Gottwald's election to the number-one Party position, that of
Secretary General, at the Fifth Party Congress in 1929. After that
period he managed to cling to the exalted status of Czechoslovakia's
highest-ranking Communist through thick and thin until his death
in March 1953.

Although he was deeply indebted to the Kremlin for all his triumphs, from the 1929 election as the Party's Secretary General to
his ascendancy to the Republic's Presidency in 1948 and the victory
over Slánský in 1951, Gottwald had little liking for, and was devoid
of any illusions about, his Soviet creators. As Paul Barton states in
his interesting analysis of the Slánský trial, Gottwald's attitude toward the "Muscovite pontiffs" was characterized by cynicism rather
than fanaticism.[3] "The imbeciles order us to . . . " was the introductory formula which he used, according to Barton, when laying

---

[1] On his background see also Schmidt, *op.cit.*, pp. 460ff.
[2] *Rudé právo*, February 5, 1949. See also Chapter I.
[3] Paul Barton, *Prague à l'heure de Moscou*, Paris, 1954, p. 111.

the Kremlin's directives before the narrow circle of Party leaders in the thirties.[4] Whether or not Gottwald had actually made use of such a formula, it is not difficult to believe that he had no illusions about his Soviet superiors. My own inquiry into this topic seems to indicate that Gottwald's feelings did not change in the postwar era, although he had to keep them carefully hidden under a thick layer of sycophantic pretense.

The six long years which Gottwald spent in communism's mecca during the Second World War could only harden his cynicism and kill whatever illusions may have lingered from youthful years. The poor-relative treatment which he experienced during the early part of his exile in Moscow could hardly make him like the Kremlin "imbeciles" more than he did in the thirties. More than ever he realized that they looked upon him merely as a tool which would be discarded if and when it had outlived its usefulness. Nor could his prolonged stay in Russia induce him to fall in love with the Soviet way of life. Although he had paid previous visits to Moscow, none of them gave him such an opportunity to observe how life in the promised land of communism really compared with what he had left behind him in "capitalist" Czechoslovakia. It is one thing to see life from the vantage point of a Comintern delegate, who is well cared for in the course of a short visit; but it is quite another experience to share for several years with the Kremlin's ordinary subjects their everyday life with all its drabness, restrictions, and privations. While Gottwald and his top-ranking associates were wise enough to keep their findings to themselves, some of their underlings complained privately about their disillusionment and even confided in unguarded moments that their chiefs felt much the same way.

This sobering experience contributed a good deal toward convincing Gottwald that the Soviet way was not quite so well suited for Czechoslovakia and that, while paying due homage to the Soviet example, the country ought to follow its own path toward socialism. Such attitudes came subsequently to the forefront on a number of occasions. In the years 1945-1947, Gottwald repeatedly stressed that the Soviet way was not suitable for Czechoslovakia; and he advocated a peaceful transition to socialism long before Khrushchëv's pronouncement on the "different roads toward socialism" at the Twentieth Congress of the Soviet Party in 1956.[5] True, such statements did not

---

[4] *ibid.*
[5] *Rudé právo,* September 27, 1946.

deviate from the general line of Soviet-approved propaganda of those years, which was designed to portray Communists as "patriotic social reformers" who harbored no thoughts of setting up a dictatorship of the proletariat. But the ardor with which Gottwald persisted in a theme which he knew to be condoned by the Soviets as a temporary strategem was not due solely to his desire to satisfy the Kremlin. The most striking proof of Gottwald's innermost beliefs about the inadvisability of wholesale sovietization of Czechoslovakia was supplied, however, by his decision to accept the Western invitation to the Paris conference on the Marshall Plan in July 1947. The circumstances under which Gottwald committed this heresy leave no doubt about his desire to let Czechoslovakia share in American aid. When the Czechoslovak Cabinet met under Gottwald's Presidency on July 4, 1947, to consider the Anglo-French invitation, the negative Soviet attitude to the whole idea was already known, although no instructions to that effect had as yet been sent to the sister parties. Hence, before allowing a vote to be taken on such a matter, a responsible Communist should first have sought the Kremlin's advice. Instead, Gottwald simply acted upon the assurance of the pro-western Foreign Minister, Jan Masaryk, that the Soviet chargé d'affaires in Praha "did not raise any objections."[6]

Gottwald's emphasis on the special Czechoslovak way toward socialism and his evident desire not to sever economic links with the West made a good impression on President Beneš. While he was aware of Gottwald's vital need to remain on good terms with the Kremlin, Dr. Beneš felt that Gottwald's dislike of orthodoxism and his relatively high level of practical common sense would cause him to avoid extreme solutions as much as possible. In contrasting Gottwald with his predecessor in the Premiership, Zdeněk Fierlinger, the fellow-traveling Socialist, Dr. Beneš once told me: "It is tough to bargain with Gottwald. But when we reach an agreement I know that he will do what he has promised." Eventually, Beneš was bitterly disappointed in his expectations when Gottwald forced him into submission to the communist *Diktat* in February 1948.

Yet Beneš was not altogether wrong about Gottwald. Had Gottwald not been pressed so hard by Stalin, he might have justified Beneš's hopes. But the heresy which he committed by accepting the Marshall Plan invitation without clearing the matter first with the Kremlin enraged the Soviet Dictator and caused Gottwald to fall into

[6] *Ripka, op.cit.,* p. 47.

disgrace.[7] Persistent rumors to that effect began to circulate in Czechoslovakia and in the other people's democracies soon after the Marshall Plan incident. As reported later by the ex-editor of the London Daily Worker, Douglas Hyde, Tito spoke of Gottwald's disgrace quite openly in the summer of 1947.[8] Gottwald was not included in the Czechoslovak communist delegation to the constituent meeting of the Cominform in September 1947. Andrei Zhdanov, who addressed the meeting on behalf of the Soviet Party, must also have had Gottwald in mind when he sternly rebuked "certain comrades" who thought that the dissolution of the Comintern had meant a severance of connections with the other communist parties.

Had Tito broken out of the Kremlin fold at that time, rather than in 1948, and shown thereby that a Communist could oppose Stalin and get away with it, Gottwald, who was then really a national Communist at heart, might well have displayed more resistance to the Kremlin at that crucial juncture of events. Although he lacked Tito's dash and prowess, he might have considered such a course safer than throwing himself completely on the mercy of a man of whose mercilessness he was well aware. After all, Beneš was still on hand, ready to prod him in that worthwhile direction and to extend him a helping hand. Unfortunately, Tito's spectacular exploit was yet to come, and in the summer and fall of 1947 it all looked as though a Communist who refused to dance to Stalin's tune was committing political suicide. Thus, the only path which Gottwald's calculating mind saw open to him was the customary communist Canossa path: to prostrate himself before Stalin and thus regain his graces. In this Gottwald succeeded beyond his wildest dreams. When he left for a vacation trip to Crimea in the summer of 1948, after having replaced Beneš as President of Czechoslovakia, rumors began to circulate even among the high Party members that Gottwald would not return.[9] However, what was supposed to be his swan song became a sensational rehabilitation. Somehow, Gottwald managed during his prolonged stay in Russia to persuade Stalin that he was better suited than anyone else for the role of Soviet governor in Czechoslovakia. How he accomplished this feat has never been revealed. Most prob-

---

[7] See Chapter i for details.
[8] Douglas Hyde, *I Believed,* London, 1952, p. 221.
[9] Zápotocký subsequently confirmed these rumors in his speech in the National Assembly on October 7, 1948. Antonín Zápotocký, *Revoluční odborové hnutí po únoru 1948* (The Revolutionary Trade Union Movement after February 1948), Praha, 1952, p. 221.

ably, Stalin, who was a connoisseur of the frailties of human nature, came to the conclusion that Gottwald had learned his lesson. He knew also that after the 1948 February coup and the forcible overthrow of Beneš with Soviet backing, Gottwald was no longer in a position to give him further trouble. Indeed, from that time until his death in 1953 Gottwald continued to behave like a marionette acting in response to the strings pulled by the Kremlin.

RUDOLF SLÁNSKÝ, THE "VILLAINOUS COSMOPOLITE"

Gottwald's rehabilitation spelled trouble and eventual tragedy for his leading rival, the Jewish-born Rudolf Slánský. That it should have been so is one of the strange twists of fortune which sometimes occur in the undercover machinations of totalitarian communism. No member of the KSČ was more persistent in following the Moscow line and none symbolized subservience to the Kremlin better than Slánský. Together with Gottwald he had belonged to the Party's left-wing "Karlín boys" of the twenties. He spent the war years in exile in Moscow and was secretly dispatched, as the Party's leading agent, to Czechoslovakia in 1944. While Gottwald committed the grave error of agreeing to Czechoslovakian participation in the Marshall Plan consultations in July 1947 Slánský's star rose even higher. He was chosen to lead the Czechoslovak delegation to the constituent meeting of the Cominform and became the main representative of the KSČ on the new Communist International. After the February coup of 1948 Slánský felt stronger than ever. In an oblique attack on Gottwald's policy he began to insinuate that the Party should have seized power immediately after the War instead of wasting time by compromising with the bourgeois elements. He took advantage of his function as the head of the Party's Central Secretariat to place his henchmen in important Party and government positions.[10] That was also when his Secretariat "sought to play the role of the leading Party organ" and place itself above the "responsible comrades" in the ministries and other government agencies.[11]

However, Gottwald's amazing political recovery after his sojourn in the Crimea in the summer of 1948 was a hard blow for Slánský's ambitions. In the session of the Central Committee in November 1948 the Party's Secretary General had to listen rather dejectedly and without any rejoinder to Gottwald's resolute counterattack on the

[10] *Zpráva o Československu*, II, 11 (1951), pp. 7ff.
[11] *ibid.*

"pseudo-Marxists" who did not like the Party's policy before 1948.[12] From then on Slánský made no major address without meekly deferring to Gottwald's leadership.[13] Nevertheless, having cut down Slánský's stature to more bearable proportions, Gottwald did not show any signs of pressing home his victory over his tight-lipped doctrinaire rival. In December 1949 Slánský was assigned the high honor of delivering the eulogy of Stalin on the Dictator's seventieth birthday in a special solemn session of the Central Committee.[14] In April 1951 the Cominform Journal, *For the Lasting Peace, for a People's Democracy,* published his article in which he attacked Western imperialists and extolled "Stalin's genius."[15] Upon the occasion of his fiftieth birthday on July 31, 1951, Slánský was awarded the Order of Socialism and received a hearty congratulatory telegram from the Party's Central Committee, signed by Gottwald and Zápotocký.[16] Another leading Czechoslovak Communist, Václav Kopecký, member of the Party's Presidium, Minister of Information, and a staunch Stalinist wrote a highly laudatory article for *Rudé právo* wherein he described Slánský as "a close and faithful collaborator of Klement Gottwald," "a devoted and fiery fighter under the banner of Lenin and Stalin" and "an outstanding example of a communist revolutionary."[17] On August 17, 1951, the aircraft factory of Letov was renamed the Rudolf Slánský Aircraft Works because the workers "wished thus to express their gratitude and love to comrade Slánský . . . the closest collaborator of comrade Gottwald."[18]

Only one sour note marred this burst of panegyrics around Slánský's fiftieth birthday, but its ominous meaning could not have been lost on the Party's Central Secretary. While he had received glowing congratulations from his own Party and from the satellite sisters, none came from the Soviet Party and there was no mention of Slánský's jubilee in the Soviet press. The significance of this unusual Soviet silence was disclosed in the session of the Central Committee of the KSČ on September 6, 1951, when Slánský was blamed

[12] Klement Gottwald, *Od února na cestě k socialismu* (From February on the Road to Socialism), Praha, 1948, p. 15.

[13] See his speech at the Ninth Party Congress, *Lidové noviny,* May 27, 1949; his speech of May 17, 1951, where he mentioned Gottwald twenty-two times. Barton, *op.cit.,* p. 157.

[14] *Lidové noviny,* December 21, 1949.

[15] Reprinted also in *Rudé právo.*

[16] *Rudé právo,* July 31, 1951.

[17] *ibid.*

[18] *Rudé právo,* August 18, 1951.

for mistakes in selecting Party cadres and for undue interference with various government agencies.[19] Although these charges cost him the headship of the Central Secretariat, Slánský was allowed to retain his status as a high-ranking Communist in good standing. Not only was he moved up to the position of Deputy Premier, but he remained on the Party's highest organ, the Political Secretariat, and was still preceded in the official listing only by Gottwald, Zápotocký, and Široký.

For a short while it looked as though Slánský's removal from the Central Secretariat of the Party had settled the whole affair. In November 1951 Slánský's selected works were published under the title *For the Victory of Socialism* and hailed by *Rudé právo* as "a further important help for the study of the history of our Party and for the improvement of the ideological level of its members." However, less than two weeks thereafter an official government communiqué announced that "hitherto unknown circumstances have recently been established which prove that Rudolf Slánský has been guilty of active anti-state activities" and that "he has been detained for purposes of investigation."[20] One year later, after having confessed all the crimes of which he had been accused, Slánský was sentenced to death and was hanged with ten of his alleged collaborators.

The story of Slánský's fall leaves a definite impression that the primary responsibility for the Great Purge and for the ultimate physical liquidation of Slánský and of his alleged associates must be placed on the shoulders of the Kremlin. Why would Gottwald and the whole Party leadership have conferred the highest communist decoration on Slánský and eulogized him on the occasion of his fiftieth birthday if they had intended to downgrade him within the next six weeks? Such a die-hard Stalinist and archopportunist as Kopecký, in particular, would never have written his laudatory article had he had the slightest inkling of Slánský's imminent fate. Nor would Gottwald and his associates have allowed the publication of Slánský's selected works if they had been planning to get the author arrested for treasonable activities within less than two weeks. To be sure, Gottwald sought to explain the two stages in Slánský's fall by claiming that, originally, Slánský was believed to have acted "without deliberate, malicious intent," but that "new revelations" proved subsequently his "leading part in the conspiracy against the Party and the

---

[19] *ibid.*, September 8, 1951.
[20] *Rudé právo,* November 28, 1951.

State."[21] Such allegations, however, seem to be at odds with the established facts. The most prominent of Slánský's alleged associates, Clementis, Šling, and Švermová, had been arrested and had confessed their crimes in 1950 and early 1951. It is unbelievable that they confessed everything about themselves and at the same time managed to conceal the part played by their alleged leader. Furthermore, Slánský and his alleged fellow-conspirators were supposed to have been perpetrating their evil deeds over a long time, some of them as far back as prewar days. But it is unthinkable that these wrongdoings would have remained undetected for so long in such an elaborate system of multiple checks.

Thus the only plausible explanation seems to be that the Kremlin rather than the KSČ leadership was instrumental in bringing about the Great Purge and provided the relentless drive that pushed it to its macabre climax. Although Gottwald and his associates grew quite cynical, and the use of coercion and subterfuge became their daily bread, they were not a group of sadists delighting in the physical destruction of their fellow-comrades. While they did want to get the better of their rivals, they would have preferred disposing of them by mere downgrading. But, to the great misfortune of the purged victims, they were not in a position to decide, but had to do whatever was necessary to satisfy Stalin. Purging and bloodletting were indispensable disciplinary measures of the Stalinist system and its major therapeutical methods when something went wrong. Therefore, the application of the "rich experience of the Communist Party of the Soviet Union," to which the Czechoslovak Communists were committed, was bound to lead to similar processes in stalinized Czechoslovakia as soon as conditions therefor had matured.

Such a situation developed in Czechoslovakia in 1949 and 1950. The food situation worsened while the process of collectivization and industrialization was being accelerated. Workers' sullen resistance to ever-increasing norms of production was stiffening. The deliveries of important items for Russia fell more and more behind schedule. Soviet impatience and pressure grew and resulted at one time even in a halt of the badly needed Soviet deliveries of grain. As the communist system as such can never be wrong, failures must be blamed on "traitors" and "saboteurs" who had infiltrated the Party and who must be ferreted out and liquidated. First, some lesser digni-

[21] Speaking to the Central Committee on December 6, 1951. *Rudé právo,* December 8, 1951.

taries are sacrificed and made to confess. Their confessions either involve or are made to involve some of their superiors. And so the ominous purgative spiral rises and rises until it hits the very top. Under these circumstances, all scruples or considerations of personal friendship are cast aside and one's own security is all that matters. Finding a convenient scapegoat, heaping abuse on his head, and deferring to the supreme purger become the only hope of surviving the storm.

Why Slánský was chosen as the main villain rather than Gottwald or Zápotocký, who were both more nationalistic than Slánský and whose past had been more "deviationist," can only be surmised.

One conjecture which seems to have much credibility is that Slánský's eclipse and ultimate fall were caused mainly by the fall of Andrei Zhdanov.[22] Indeed, the death of Zhdanov led to a ruthless elimination of a number of his protégés from the Soviet Party apparatus. While it is difficult to prove that Slánský was Zhdanov's protégé, the two had been in frequent contact in Cominform affairs. Since Slánský was also the KSČ's main representative in the Cominform, he was probably closer to the Soviet Cominform boss than any other high-ranking Czechoslovak Communist. One may also note that the sudden rehabilitation of Klement Gottwald coincided with Zhdanov's eclipse in the summer of 1948.

Another theory attaches considerable importance to Slánský's Jewish origin.[23] Eleven of the fourteen high Communists who stood on trial were Jews. In his accusation of the Slánský group Gottwald declared that they "had not sprung from the roots of our country and our Party" and that they mostly belonged to "those types whom I called cosmopolites . . . ."[24] Zápotocký referred unmistakably to Slánský's race when, talking about "those who conspire against the Republic," he stressed that "we shall brook no interference in our internal affairs by foreign influences whether it be Washington, or London, Rome, or *Jerusalem.*"[25] The communist Minister of Justice clearly distinguished between Slánský and Šling (both Jews) whom he called "cosmopolites" and the non-Jewish defendants, Husák,

[22] Blažej Vilím, former Secretary General of the Social Democratic Party in the article "The Victim of Zhdanov," *Features and News from behind the Iron Curtain,* a publication of the Czechoslovak Information Center in London, II, No. 45.

[23] For instance, see Barton, *op.cit.,* especially pp. 90-102.

[24] *Zpráva o Československu,* II, 11 (1951), p. 7.

[25] *Rudé právo,* December 19, 1951. Italics added.

Clementis and Novomeský, whom he labeled as "bourgeois national-ists."[26] The trial itself was full of sorties against Zionists.[27] While it could hardly be said that Slánský was thrown to the wolves *because* of his race, his Jewish origin did not do him any good. In spite of his public pronouncements against anti-Semitism, Stalin never shed his instinctive mistrust of the Jews. Nor did the Czechoslovak man-in-the-street lose altogether his slight anti-Jewish bias of earlier days. It was therefore convenient to be able to shift most of the blame for various shortcomings and blunders onto "alien" elements whose true loyalty lay elsewhere and, by the same token, to exonerate the "true native sons of the people," such as Gottwald.

Antonín Zápotocký, the Reconstructed Right-winger

Unlike the other two members of the Party's topmost trio, An-tonín Zápotocký belonged before the War to the Party's right wing. Having joined the newly established Communist Party at the mature age of thirty-six after twenty years of activity in the Social Demo-cratic Party which his father had helped to found, this one-time stone mason was too practical-minded to fall for some of the most extremist tenets of pure Leninism. Although he was one of the founders of the KSČ and became its Secretary General in 1922, his rightist leanings weakened his position when the more radical Karlín group eventually gained the upperhand in the Party. However, unlike the other "right-wing opportunists," he managed to squeeze through and get himself elected to the new Party leadership headed by Gottwald which was brought to power by the crucial Fifth Party Congress in 1929. In the same year he was elected Secretary General of the Communist Trade Unions and served in that capacity until 1939. He was also member of Parliament for the KSČ in prewar days. After the Nazi seizure of Czechoslovakia he was caught by the Nazi guards when attempting to cross the border into Poland and was interned until the end of the War.

Strangely enough, it was not his Party position but his long years of prominence in organized labor which were the main sinews of his political strength and netted him eventually the number-one position in the Party and the Presidency of the Republic after Gott-wald's death. When he returned with the aura of a martyr from the

[26] *News*, I, 3, p. 4.
[27] *Rudé právo*, February 28, March 4, October 26, 1952.

Sachsenhausen concentration camp in 1945, he was a logical choice for Chairman of the Revolutionary Trade Union Movement (ROH) which gathered under its wing the whole of Czechoslovakia's organized labor irrespective of Party affiliations. The crucial role assigned to the ROH, which had meanwhile been fully converted to a major weapon of communist revolution, during the February coup of 1948 catapulted Zápotocký to a position of leadership which almost equalled that of Gottwald. The brilliance with which he maneuvered his ROH cohorts in the decisive days of the struggle must have substantially enhanced the Kremlin's opinion of the one-time social democratic regional secretary. The reward came quickly. When Gottwald became President of the Republic after Dr. Beneš's resignation in June 1948, Zápotocký succeeded Gottwald as Prime Minister. After Gottwald's death in March 1953 he stepped once again into his predecessor's shoes and was elected President of the Republic in spite of general expectations that this office would die with its incumbent.

Zápotocký's main asset was his skill in handling people. His long years of experience among social democratic workers and his innate shrewdness and good sense of humor enabled him more than any other member of the ruling junta to find the right approach to the common man. His blunt manner of speaking and readiness to concede a point here and there made him appear humbler and more sincere than he really was. As reported by Pavel Korbel, who had served under him and under Gottwald, Zápotocký showed much more personal interest in his subordinates than did Gottwald.[28] He placed less emphasis than most of his Party colleagues on mere Party membership and more on professional qualification in choosing people for positions in the government and in the country's economy. He even rebuked publicly the Party's cadres commissions in April 1949 for their belief that it was good policy to entrust important positions solely to Party members.[29]

He was known also to have opposed some of the more extreme measures, such as the draft law on forced labor camps which he laid before the National Assembly only after he had been outvoted by his Party colleagues.[30] On a number of occasions he spoke out in Cabinet meetings against an uncritical imitation of Soviet measures.[31]

[28] *New Leader,* April 17, 1953, pp. 9ff.
[29] Antonín Zápotocký, *op.cit.,* pp. 326ff.
[30] Barton, *op.cit.,* p. 189; Korbel, *op.cit.,* p. 11.
[31] Korbel, *op.cit.*

Such attitudes made Zápotocký distinctly more popular or, to be more accurate, less unpopular than any other member of the Party's Politbureau.

On the other hand Zápotocký yielded to none of his colleagues in opportunistic adaptability. Having sustained so many attacks for right-wing tendencies, he learned that the safest way of survival was to repent promptly and to do as he was told by the Soviet chiefs, no matter what his own thoughts or feelings might be. To bend rather than to break became his time-tested motto. "After long years of personal experience," he said in 1945, looking back on his long and durable political career, "I can assure you that often I gain more by submitting to a decision, even though I may consider it as unjust, than by obstinately protesting against it."[32] This one revealing sentence sums up accurately his life philosophy of inveterate conformism. It was this attitude rather than any conviction of the excellence of the Soviet methods that made him bow to the Kremlin's every directive and swallow with relative ease every humiliation.

Typical of his mentality and behavior was a sad event which gave Zápotocký his first taste of Soviet liberation.[33] Upon being freed from the concentration camp toward the close of the Second World War a group of men and women that included Antonín Zápotocký was subjected to the shock of rough treatment at the hands of the Red Army. To protest such indignities the group voted to send a two-man delegation composed of Zápotocký and Dolanský to lodge a complaint with the Red Army Commander, hoping that the word of so prominent a Communist as Zápotocký would carry weight with the Red Army. Although the Soviet military headquarters were nearby, it was many hours before the delegation finally returned in a state of utter dejection. As it turned out, the portly Red Army Commander received the delegation in quite a congenial mood. He nodded pensive approval as Zápotocký explained his meritorious Party record and complained about the behavior of the Red Army. Whereupon he called for his sergeant and ordered him to use Zápotocký and Dolanský to unload a truck of ammunition.

Although he never again had to unload ammunition for Red Army commanders, Zápotocký nonetheless continued to serve as the

---

[32] Antonín Zápotocký, *Po staru se žít nedá* (One Cannot Live in the Old Way), Praha, 1947; Barton, *op.cit.*, p. 127.

[33] Ivan Herben in *Československý přehled*, III, 11 (1956), pp. 17-18.

Kremlin's handy man until his death in 1957. Undoubtedly, there were moments when he disliked extremely what he had to do. But his opportunism always won the upper hand over his remorse.

OTHER POLITBUREAUISTS

With the Big Three gone, only two Old Guard Communists remained on the Politbureau by 1960 among those nationally known in prewar days: Jaromír Dolanský and Václav Kopecký. Except for their Party allegiance, they are as opposite as two men can be.

Dolanský, a graduate of Praha's Charles University, is a well-mannered intellectual interested chiefly in economic and financial affairs. In his youth he belonged to Thomas Masaryk's Realist Party —not a very commendable background for a Leninist Communist. He joined the KSČ at its inception in 1921 and became Secretary of its Parliamentary Club in 1928. Like Zápotocký, he was caught by the Nazis while attempting to escape to Poland in 1939 and was held incommunicado for the duration of the War. Upon his liberation he spent several months in Moscow where he undoubtedly received Stalinist briefing before returning to Czechoslovakia. His background and his personality did not make him well suited for dynamic leadership and that is why he has always worked mainly behind the stage. Although he is a devout Marxist, he is more sensible about it then most of his Politbureau colleagues. As First Deputy Premier charged with over-all supervision of the country's economy, he probably seeks, in the inconspicuous manner typical of him, to do away with as much nonsense as he possibly can without endangering his position. But his overcautious mind has always counseled him to stay well within the bounds prescribed by the Kremlin and to follow the Moscow line in any of his relatively few major public statements.[34]

While Dolanský definitely belongs to the category of "cultured" Communists, there is little that can be called cultural about Václav Kopecký, one of the leading quadrumvirate of Czechoslovakia communist leaders who spent the war years in Moscow. He is a rabble-rousing demagogue yielding to none in subservience to the Kremlin. While all the Kremlin's lieutenants in Czechoslovakia have been conditioned to react to Soviet shifts as weathervanes turn after the changing winds, none of them can do so with more alacrity than Kopecký. That was the main reason, apart from his journalistic work before

---

[34] For instance, see *Rudé právo,* February 27, 1952, reporting his speech on the Fourth Anniversary of the communist coup.

the War, why this unregenerated Stalinist was chosen to be the czar over Czechoslovak culture and that is why he kept that role, from his vantage position as Politbureau member and Deputy Premier, in the post-Stalin era.

Just as ruthless as Kopecký, and almost equal to him in versatility and transmutative abilities, are two members of the Slovak communist Old Guard, Viliam Široký and Karol Bacílek. Both of them held fairly high positions in the Slovak branch of the Party before the War, but neither was known well enough outside the Party circles to become a public figure, even though Široký was member of Parliament since 1935. Both took an active lead in organizing an illegal communist movement in Slovakia after the Party had been outlawed in 1938-1939.

Široký was arrested in 1940 for his activities and held in jail until 1945. During his trial he drew a peculiar parallel between the Slovak Communist Party and the semi-Fascist Slovak People's Party, whose regime put him on trial. He argued that both parties pursued the same goal, except that the latter counted on Berlin while he relied on Moscow. Typical of his versatility were the directives which he had sent his Slovak comrades from the Bratislava prison in 1942. He was then against the slogan "For a Soviet Slovakia" because "every conception had its time" and "in the present day of quick unfolding of international events . . . one phase may speedily shift into another." The Party must therefore be prepared "to quickly change its slogans, its demands, and its tactics."[35] After his release from prison he promptly resumed the leadership of the Slovak Communist Party which was then formally separate from the Czechoslovak Party, and became Deputy Premier. Upon Zápotocký's accession to the Republic's Presidency he moved up to the position of Premier which he has held since.

Bacílek was more fortunate during the war insofar as he managed to slip across the border and get to the Soviet Union where he reportedly served in the Red Army. He was sent secretly to Slovakia in 1944 and took part in the preparations of the Slovak anti-German uprising of that year. His rise to national prominence came in May 1949 when he became a member of the Party's Presidium. In September 1951 he was promoted from ordinary Central Committee membership directly to the Party's Political Secretariat. He thus bypassed more than a dozen comrades who had seniority over him.

[35] *Za svobodu,* p. 198.

These included such prominent figures as Kopecký, who joined the pinnacle of power only three months thereafter, V. Kopřiva, Minister of State Security, V. Nosek, Minister of the Interior, and the "Red Grandpa," Z. Nejedlý. Simultaneously, Bacílek was made Minister of State Control, and a few months later replaced Kopřiva as Minister of State Security and thus became the number-one police chief in the nation. In February 1953 he became Deputy Premier, but resigned in September 1953 in order to devote full-time attention to the Slovak Party affairs as the First Secretary of the Slovak Communist Party.

Even more spectacular than Bacílek's was the truly meteoric rise of the one-time mechanic, Antonín Novotný, the number-one Czechoslovak Communist of today. Although he joined the Party at the age of seventeen in the year of its foundation, 1921, the highest position he had attained prior to the war was a relatively modest regional secretaryship. He was arrested by the Gestapo in 1941 and spent the rest of the War in the Nazi concentration camp of Mauthausen. In 1946 he was elected to the Party's Central Committee. It was the downgrading of Slánský that put him on the path to success. He was listed as first among the Central Committee secretaries elected in September 1951 to serve under Gottwald in the Organizational Secretariat. In December of the same year he was promoted to full membership in the Political Secretariat and in the Presidium. He thus became the only Communist, apart from Gottwald, who sat both in the Political and in the Organizational Secretariat. After Gottwald's death he, rather than Zápotocký, was chosen to head the Party's Central Secretariat. When Khrushchëv was formally named First Secretary of the Central Committee of the Soviet Party, the same title was conferred in September 1953 on Novotný. Since that time he has been the Party's main spokesman and has delivered all the main reports at the Central Committee's meetings as well as at Party congresses and conferences. His primacy within the Party hierarchy was established when he added the Republic's Presidency to his function of the Party's First Secretary upon Zápotocký's death in 1957 and thus merged the highest Party and government offices in his hands.

Novotný is a typical *apparatchik* who has gained his present status chiefly by his secretarial abilities and by cleverly hitching his wagon always to the winning side. He is obviously considered *persona gratissima* by Khrushchëv, who displayed his appreciation of Novotný during his visit to Czechoslovakia in 1957. In all probability Khrushchëv's trust in Novotný is quite justified. His whole career shows

Novotný as a well-disciplined Party man, who never steps out of line and always adheres to the letter to higher directives. Since his assumption of the First Secretariat his statements and activities have unfailingly reflected the Soviet line. As he had previously operated behind the scenes as a sort of grey eminence and had played no prominent part in earlier Party struggles, he lacks even the limited popular appeal which his predecessors enjoyed among some segments of the Party's rank and file. Nor does he have any of Zápotocký's or Gottwald's dynamism; and his uninspiring personality is unlikely to become a rallying point for anything but a narrow stratum of equally uninspiring *apparatchiks*. Thus Novotný is admirably suited for the role of Kremlin's chief lieutenant in Czechoslovakia.

Zdeněk Fierlinger, who was added to the Politbureau's roster in 1954, is the only former Social Democrat among the full members of the highest Party organ. His promotion was well merited. He was once dubbed "quislinger" for his betrayal of democratic socialism in favor of communist totalitarianism and he figured among the main gravediggers of Czechoslovak democracy. It was primarily his personal ambition that turned him into Czechoslovakia's Benedict Arnold. While serving as Czechoslovakian Ambassador to Moscow during the war, he came to the conclusion that Soviet Russia would be in a position to dominate Central Europe. Hence, he felt that his personal fortunes would be better served if he attached himself to Gottwald. His pro-communism was further buttressed by his obstinate belief in the virtues of wholesale socialization.

In sharp contrast to the aging Fierlinger, Rudolf Barák, who was admitted to the Party's highest conclave together with Fierlinger in 1954, is a representative of the rising younger communist generation. At the time of the Ninth Party Congress in 1949 he was a virtual nonentity. As late as December 1952, he was not considered prominent enough to sit on the Party's Central Committee, and the Party Conference that met in that month elected him only to be a Central Committee candidate. Yet in the governmental reshuffle following Gottwald's death in March 1953 he emerged as a Deputy Premier. When the number of deputy premiers was reduced in September 1953 he landed the important office of Minister of the Interior which included the duties of the abolished Ministry of State Security. The Tenth Congress of June 1954 elevated him to full membership in the Central Committee and, in a manner unprecedented in the annals of the Party, he was immediately moved up to full membership in the Political Bureau. Because he is a newcomer to the national political scene and the topmost Party organs, not much dependable evidence on his temperament and real beliefs could as yet be gathered. His public pronouncements have all conformed strictly to the prescribed lines.

Of the three newcomers who were elevated to full membership in the Politbureau in 1958, the best known to students of Czechoslovak communism is undoubtedly Jiří Hendrych. He is an all-out *apparatchik* in Novotný's fashion and a rigid neo-Stalinist. He appeared on the roster of the Party's Central Committee in 1946 and was elected member of Parliament after the 1948 coup. In 1949 he became deputy chief of the important section of culture and propaganda of the Central Secretariat. In 1951 he was elevated to one of the secretaryships of the Central Committee and became a member of its Organizational Secretariat. Although temporarily dropped from the Secretariat in 1952, perhaps in connection with the liquidation of Slánský, he regained his position there in 1954. But his rise to real prominence came mainly in 1956-1957 when he revealed himself to be among the most resolute advocates of a stiff Party line and ideological orthodoxy. It was this determined antirevisionist stand that brought him his last promotion to the highest Party conclave.

Much less nationally known in Czechoslovakia than Hendrych is Pavol David, the third Slovak to be given a place on the Party's Political Bureau. Although he has served as Deputy in the National Assembly since 1948, his real work seems to have been confined to Party affairs in Slovakia where he began to rise in stature in the early fifties. Having been elected to the Central Committee of the Slovak Communist Party in 1950, he was made one of its secretaries and a member of the Slovak Party's Political Bureau in 1953. Only at the Tenth Congress of the KSČ in 1954 did he qualify for full membership in the KSČ's Central Committee. His relatively few public utterances have fully conformed to the current Party line and he has recently become one of the most ferocious critics of Slovak "bourgeois nationalism."

Unlike Hendrych and David, who earned their promotion primarily through their work in the Party apparatus, Otakar Šimůnek, an Engineering School graduate, never held any Party position of note until he suddenly emerged as a member of the Party's Central Committee and an alternate member of its Politbureau at the Tenth Congress in 1954. Prior to that he was Minister of Chemical Industry and, since July 1954, Chairman of the State Planning Office (re-named the State Planning Commission in 1959), the Czechoslovak equivalent of the Soviet *Gosplan*. He is the first representative of the technical intelligentsia to reach the summit of the KSČ hierarchy. Evidently, he owes his amazing rise mostly to his achievements in the field of industrial management and economic planning.

THE POLITBUREAUISTS' RELATIVE STRENGTHS AND MUTUAL RELATIONS

While all ten full members who constitute the Political Bureau as of 1960 are formally equal, some of them, to use Orwell's famous expression, are more equal than others. Until Czechoslovakia changed to the post-Stalin Soviet method of listing the Party chieftains in alphabetical order, the ranking of the Politbureau members could be easily determined. Invariably, their names appeared in the same order on every official announcement as a reflection of their relative prominence. This order also appeared on documents bearing their signatures as well as on released photographs of their attendance at Party and government festivities. At the time of Gottwald's death in 1953 the order was as follows: Zápotocký, Široký, Dolanský, Bacílek, Čepička (meanwhile demoted), Kopecký, and Novotný.[36] Fierlinger, who was not then a Politbureau member followed next and Barák was still further behind.[37]

With the change to an alphabetical listing, this useful keyhole into the Politbureau's kitchen was plugged, and students of this matter must fall back on other evidence. As to the present number-one position there can be no question whatsoever. The strongest of the Polit-bureau members is, without doubt, Antonín Novotný. As the Party's First Secretary he prepares the agenda for the meetings of the Polit-bureau and the Central Committee, delivers the main reports, rec-ommends measures to be taken, and supervises the carrying out of whatever resolutions are adopted. As President of the Republic he holds the highest executive office, an office traditionally occupied by the country's leading political personage. However, he has not yet come anywhere close to a one-man rule or even attained the level of authority enjoyed by Gottwald in the last years of his rule.

Nor does there seem to be much doubt that Zdeněk Fierlinger is

---

[36] See, for instance, *Rudé právo*, March 17 and 20, 1953.

[37] See also the order in which deputy premiers signed laws, *Sbírka zákonů* (Collection of the Laws), 1953.

politically the weakest of the lot. Although he has at last been given a coveted seat on the Political Bureau, he has by now been eased out of all executive functions and assigned the decorative position of Chairman of the National Assembly. The voice of the Socialist-turned-Communist, who is also the oldest of all the Politbureau members, weighs probably less than anyone else's.

The relative positions of the other Politbureau members are not so clear. An analysis of their respective responsibilities, the importance of speeches which they deliver, and other circumstantial evidence of this kind permits three conjectures: (1) Široký still continues to be slightly ahead of his colleagues in authority despite his failure to move up from the Premiership to the Presidency as his two communist predecessors had done. (2) The voice of Dolánský still has probably a little more weight in the Politbureau's deliberations than those of more recent comers, especially in economic affairs. (3) Jiří Hendrych, the only other member of the Politbureau besides Novotný to hold simultaneous membership in the Party's Central Secretariat, seems to be forging strongly ahead. He has already become the Party's main spokesman on ideology and appears, if all goes as usual, to stand the best chance of becoming number-two man of the Party.

Even scarcer are the clues which allow insight into clique-forming within the Politbureau. A tendency toward clique-forming is present in any party system, and it finds an especially congenial climate in a totalitarian oligarchy. But no secrets are more closely guarded than those pertaining to the personal ties and rivalries within the ruling oligarchy. Not until a close associate defects or a Politbureau member is purged does the curtain rise for a moment to allow a quick glimpse of what goes behind it. Apart from the rather one-sided or distorted picture provided on such rare occasions, one has to rely mostly on clues provided by the Politbureauists' past associations and conflicts. However, even this approach fails to reveal any stable subgroupings within the Politbureau as seen in 1960. Unlike his counterparts in Russia, none of the present Politbureau members owes his promotion to any particular colleague. Hence, there are no protégés who would feel the necessity of staying in the good graces of their protectors and of constituting a narrower coterie around him. Nor would it be in Moscow's interest to allow the rise of any strong man or any closely knit personal alliance within the ruling bodies of satellite communist parties. They can be handled more easily if they consist of mutually uncommitted equals. On the other hand, the men in the Czechoslovak Party's Political Bureau have no desire to upset their own applecart by internecine warfare. They are glad that the nightmarish era of Stalinism and the Great Purges is behind them. They feel that the safest way of avoiding such terrible risks is to refrain from tampering unduly with the *status quo* and pushing their own ambitions too far. Lively memories of the dangers from above, coupled with fear of ever-lurking dangers from below, cause them to stick together rather than to fall apart into smaller cliques. Not wanting to hang separately, they hang together. Only a revival of old-fashioned Stalinism in Russia or some near-cataclysmic developments in Czechoslovakia would alter the situation.

These considerations account also for the stability of the Politbureau membership. While the personnel of the Soviet Party Presidium has been transformed beyond recognition in recent years so that only a few are left who served in Stalin's Politbureau, its Czechoslovak equivalent has been barely scratched and only one of its members (Čepička) has been demoted since Slánský's purge in 1951. The durable composition of the topmost Party council is all the more striking if it is contrasted with the tremendous turnover in the personnel of the Party's Central Committee between 1949 and 1954. Of the ninety-seven members of the Central Committee elected by the Ninth Party Congress in 1949 only thirty-four were reelected to the new eighty-four-men Central Committee chosen by the Tenth Congress in 1954; and of the thirty-two candidates of the Central Committee of 1949 only nine were reelected as candidates or full members of the Central Committee in 1954.[38] Even worse hit was the Central Committee's Secretariat. Of its seven members chosen in 1949 none figured on the Secretariat selected at the close of the Tenth Congress. Two had been executed, three purged, one had been demoted, and one had died.

Since 1954 the Central Committee membership has become more stable and sixty-three of the eighty-four members of the Central Committee chosen at the Tenth Congress in 1954 were reelected by the Eleventh Congress in 1958. Although the reelection of some of them may have been facilitated by the increase of Central Committee seats from eighty-four to ninety-seven, the main reason lay undoubtedly in the post-Stalin abstention from high-level purging. Similarly, four out of the five secretaries of the Central Committee retained their mem-

---

[38] The number of alternates of the Central Committee was reduced from thirty-two in 1949 to twenty-eight in 1954.

bership in the Central Secretariat in 1958. Only the ranks of the Central Committee candidates suffered a major reshuffle at the Eleventh Party Congress. Of the twenty-eight candidates elected in 1954 only eleven were kept in that capacity or promoted to the full membership of the Central Committee in 1958, despite the increase of the over-all number of Central Committee candidates from twenty-eight to fifty.[39]

THE POLITBUREAU'S INTERNAL WORKING PROCESSES

With the veil of secrecy tightly wrapped around the Politbureau sessions dependable information on its internal working processes is virtually unavailable. If one were to judge by public communist pronouncements, the Politbureau is a haven of harmony. Guided by the infallible precepts of the Marxist-Leninist creed, its ten members agree with consistent unanimity on even the most complex matters that confront them. That this highly idealized picture does not square with reality is obvious. Only a group of saints or angels could display such serene concord in the face of the tremendous and highly controversial problems crying for solution; and the Czechoslovak Communists are neither. The bitter feuds that have time and again broken through the outward façade of unity on corresponding supreme Party organs elsewhere in the communist world make it hard to believe that the Czechoslovak Politbureau can remain wholly unaffected by such dissensions. That this has not been so is confirmed by what little information has leaked out about the Politbureau's inner dealings. It indicates that disagreements have upon occasion arisen and intrigue has taken place. Such were, for example, Zápotocký's quarrel with Čepička over the labor camp laws, the rivalry between Gottwald and Slánský, or the mutual enmity between Slánský and Dolanský.

However, it may be conceded that there have probably been fewer controversies on matters of policy or tactics within the Czechoslovak Politbureau in the recent years than in the corresponding organs of most of the other communist countries. With no man of Tito's, Mao's, or Gomulka's stature among them, the men who constitute the present leading core of the KSČ are a group of sycophantic followers of the Kremlin whose very existence depends on Soviet support. Having no difficulty in agreeing to let themselves be guided by Soviet directives, they have little cause for dissension.

[39] For lists of names see *Rudé právo*, June 22, 1958.

CHAPTER VI
COMMUNISM'S PERNICIOUS ISMS

WITH THE ESTABLISHMENT of the dictatorship of the proletariat in 1948, the Party's "heroic era" came to an end and that of "socialist construction" began. Like their Soviet tutors and so many other revolutionaries before them, the Czechoslovak Communists were soon to discover that, far from lessening their worries, the seizure of power had only multiplied them. As Milton has said, "Who overcomes by force, hath overcome but half his foe."

What are, then, the major inner-Party problems and dilemmas that have confronted the KSČ since its conversion from a weapon of revolution to an instrument of power? Some of them have been mentioned in preceding chapters but the matter deserves a more systematic treatment. Nothing mirrors the true character of the KSČ better than an exploration and diagnosis of the ailments that continue to plague the Party's body politic in spite of all the remedies administered by its chief medicine men.

TITOISM

Of all the specters haunting the orthodox Leninist-Stalinists in the last years of the Stalin era none was exorcized more ferociously and fought more vigorously than Titoism. To be labeled a "Titoist" meant not only political disgrace but often criminal prosecution that could, and sometimes did, involve capital punishment. Untold thousands of Communists were demoted, purged, and liquidated throughout the satellite world for having been stricken by that black plague.

Initially, the leaders of Czechoslovak communism yielded ground to no one in the anti-Titoist crusade. After Tito had been denounced by the Cominform in 1948 they staged a nation-wide witchhunt for Titoists. Except possibly for Hungary and Albania, this persecution had been more widespread and more virulent in Czechoslovakia than in any other country within the Soviet orbit. Perhaps more than anywhere else Titoism was used as a convenient tool in settling personal rivalries in the uppermost crust of Party leadership, such as Gottwald versus Slánský and Široký versus Clementis. Rudolf Slánský, the

KSČ's Secretary General and the number-two Czechoslovak Communist was the highest-ranking satellite Communist executed as a "Titoist traitor." In addition to their desire to please Moscow, Gottwald and his associates were prodded in their anti-Titoist drive by their hearty dislike for Tito himself who had been derisively critical of them for their "temporizing with bourgeois elements" prior to 1948.

Therefore, it is hardly surprising that the abrupt Soviet reversal, dramatized by Khrushchëv's unprecedented pilgrimage to Belgrade and his apology to "Judas Tito" in the spring of 1955, shook the Czechoslovak rulers and caused them to drag their feet for many months before they fell grudgingly into the new Soviet line. As late as July 1955 Tito could rightly complain, in his speech in Karlovac, that the Czechoslovak Communists "find it difficult to admit their mistakes before their own people, as the dead cannot be resuscitated." Indeed, of all the satellite rulers, the Praha regime was the last one to adopt Khrushchëv's new line on Tito and to apologize obliquely for past mistakes. It was only on the eve of 1956 that Zápotocký cautiously touched upon the hot topic in his New Year's message, blaming it all on "misleading information and the diversionary activities of the enemy." He asked that the past in Yugoslav-Czechoslovak relations be blotted out, and sourly admitted that the "propaganda campaign which developed after the breach [in 1948] went at times too far."[1] While the so-called Titoists were being publicly rehabilitated to the South and to the North, all that the Praha regime did was to release from jail, in an almost clandestine fashion and without a word of apology, those members of the "Slánský-Clementis gang" who had been lucky enough to get away with prison sentences, and to concede that those accusations against Slánský and his accomplices that had been based on Titoism were false.[2] One of the leading Czech Communists, Rudolf Barák, went so far as to claim that it was Slánský who had fraudulently allowed Tito's name to be linked with his. According to Barák, Slánský had actually "welcomed the atmosphere created by the wrong accusations against the leading Yugoslav comrades!"[3]

How bitter was the pill which the Czechoslovak rulers felt obligated to swallow to please Khrushchëv is clearly apparent from their

---

[1] *Rudé právo,* January 2, 1956.
[2] *News,* 5, 5 (1956), p. 57.
[3] *ibid.,* 5, 8 (1956), p. 21.

subsequent behavior. While the relations between Yugoslavia and the USSR were improving, the Czechoslovak Communists came out dutifully with a few general gestures of friendship, exchanged some delegations, and even admitted past errors regarding Tito. This was especially so after the Twentieth Congress of the Soviet Party which, with its doctrine of "different roads toward socialism" and the explosion of the Stalin myth, seemed to vindicate Tito's stand.[4] On the other hand, when Soviet-Yugoslav relations took a turn for the worse, following the revolts in Poland and Hungary, the Czechoslovak Communists began to snipe at Tito again. Typical of their peevish attitude toward things Yugoslav was a publication of a map of Yugoslavia by the Czechoslovak Central Administration for Land Survey and Cartography. The descriptive text on the map spoke of "a revolution which has only partially succeeded"; of "so-called workers' councils"; of the "stagnating" Yugoslav economy developing in a "haphazard manner"; and of "certain bourgeois elements . . . which aim at the restoration of the bourgeois system."[5] However, uncertain as they were about the way matters would eventually turn out, the Praha regime preferred to paraphrase whatever the current Moscow line was at the time rather than develop too much initiative of its own.[6] Thus it obediently followed the Moscow example in not sending a Party delegation to attend the Congress of the Yugoslav Communist Party in April 1958; and the Czechoslovak Ambassador to Yugoslavia promptly abandoned his seat as observer when the signal was given by the Soviet Ambassador to leave the hall in protest against Rankovich's criticism of the stiffening Soviet attitude toward the Yugoslav Party.

This deliberate Soviet insult to Yugoslav comrades, the Chinese Communists' wanton anti-Tito tirades, and especially the elaborate condemnation of the Yugoslav position published in Moscow's *Kommunist*[7] convinced the Czechoslovak leaders that the official

---

[4] See speeches by Zápotocký, Novotný, and Barák at the National Party Conference in June 1956, *Rudé právo*, June 12, 1956, and *News*, 5, 8 (1956), pp. 15ff.

[5] *Kommunist* (Belgrade), January 10, 1958, *East Europe*, 7, 3 (1958), p. 31.

[6] For instance, *Rudé právo*, November 19, 1956, repeating Tass's criticism of Tito's attitude on Hungary; Novotný's criticism of Tito at the session of the Party's Central Committee in December 1956, *Rudé právo*, December 9, 1956; *Rudé právo*, March 8, 1957, reprinting a sharp rebuke of Popovic's speech taken from Moscow's *Pravda* of March 6, 1957.

[7] P. Fedoseyev and Others, "*O proyekte programmy Soyuza kommunistov Yugoslavii*" (On the Draft of the Program of the Yugoslav Communist League), *Kommunist* (Moscow), No. 6, 1958.

Marxist-Leninist line on Titoism had at last crystallized into a definitive shape. Rejoicing at this vindication of their initial reluctance to fraternize with Tito when it was fashionable again in 1955-1956, they wasted no time in jumping on the anti-Titoist band wagon. On May 8, 1958, an editorial in *Rudé právo* spelled out the regime's official stand that adhered more to the firm but relatively dispassionate Soviet attitude rather than to the vitriolic denunciation by the Chinese Communists.[8] The same resolute rejection of Titoism characterized the proceedings of the Slovak and Czechoslovak Party congresses meeting in May and June 1958, respectively. Delivering the main report to the KSČ's Congress, Novotný upheld the Cominform's anti-Yugoslav resolution of June 1948 (expelling the Yugoslav Party from the Cominform) as "correct in principle," while admitting mistakes in "the methods of its execution" and labeling as incorrect the Cominform's second anti-Yugoslav resolution of November 1949 (calling for an open revolt against Tito). But he rebuked in sharp terms "the un-Marxian attitude of the Yugoslav leaders" whom he accused of "distorting and falsifying" the Marxist-Leninist teaching "from opportunistic, nationalistic, and subjectivistic positions."[9] The "un-Marxist revisionist attitude proclaimed by the Yugoslav Communist League" was also scored in the resolution which was passed with habitual unanimity by the Congress before it adjourned.[10]

NATIONAL COMMUNISM

If Titoism were only what the literal construction of the word conveys, namely siding with Tito in his feud with Stalin, the Soviet Dictator's death and the ensuing reconciliation between Belgrade and Moscow, as long as it lasted, should have shelved the issue. However, it is common knowledge that "Titoism" was a misnomer that served as a convenient alias for what is generally known as "national communism." Hence, far from healing that insidious sickness within Marxism-Leninism, Stalin's death and decanonization, plus Khrushchëv's emphatic enunciation of the different roads toward socialism and his 1955-1956 concessions to Tito, have only aggravated it. All over the Soviet-controlled world national communism began to raise

---

[8] *Jen Min Jih Pao,* May 5, 1958, Russian translation in *Pravda* (Moscow), May 6, 1958.
[9] *Rudé právo,* June 19, 1958. For accusations leveled at Yugoslavia at the Slovak Party Congress of May 1958, see Pavel Berka's article in *Československý přehled,* v, 5 (1958), pp. 26ff.
[10] *Rudé právo,* June 23, 1958.

its head and press with increasing vigor against the weakened walls of Stalinist monolithism.

As could have been expected, the Czechoslovak Party was caught in the middle of this weird battle of attrition between the opposing forces of sovietism and national communism. If "national communism" means an adherence to the basic communist tenets, such as wholesale socialization and the dominance of the Party, coupled with a desire not to be subjected to interference and orders from the Kremlin, then it is obvious from what has been said in the preceding chapter that both Gottwald and Zápotocký qualified as potential national communists. To a lesser extent this is probably true of some of the present Czechoslovak oligarchs as well. Consequently, such men should have been pleased by the victories that the cause of national communism achieved with Yugoslavia's rehabilitation in 1955 and with Poland's 1956 October Revolution. However, having bet everything on the Kremlin card, they have come to the conclusion that they had already forfeited their chances of retaining power, should national communism prevail in Czechoslovakia. The close brush with death which communism experienced in Hungary strengthened them even more in the belief that their personal salvation lay only in their power of intimidation, which in turn depended primarily on the availability of Soviet military assistance in case of necessity.

Realizing that national communism presents almost as deadly a danger for them as anti-communism, KSČ leaders have singled it out as their chief domestic enemy and concentrated their heaviest barrage on it. Addressing the meeting of the Party's Central Committee in December 1956, Novotný denounced national communism as an ally of the imperialists who saw in it "some kind of first phase for the return to the old capitalist system." He rejected both the "incorrect views and moods" in Poland and Tito's distinction between Stalinists and non-Stalinists, and stated in no uncertain terms: "The Leninist example remains for us the only binding example which is being applied creatively in different historic and socio-economic conditions."[11] A few days later national communism was scored again and an unwavering friendship with the USSR, as a prerequisite for the victory of socialism, was stressed in a joint resolution prepared by a conference of delegates from the Central Committees of the Communist Parties of Czechoslovakia and East Germany.[12] Similar dire warnings,

[11] *East Europe*, 6, 2 (1957), p. 46.
[12] *Rudé právo*, December 21, 1956.

coupled with an ardent advocacy of closer ties with the Soviet Union, dominated the proceedings of the Twelfth Congress of the Communist Party of Slovakia held in Bratislava in April 1957, as well as the meeting of the Czechoslovak Party's Central Committee in June 1957.[13]

REVISIONISM

Since 1957 the term "revisionism" has also become fashionable for the designation of communism's main ideological ailment. Having been first applied to the anti-Stalinist Polish Communists who pressed for further advances on the reformist road initiated by Poland's 1956 October Revolution, this latest addition to the proscribed isms was placed officially on the Soviet index by the Moscow Socialist Commonwealth Manifesto signed by the Soviet and satellite Communists on the occasion of the Fortieth Anniversary of the Bolshevik Revolution.[14] While this concept is actually borrowed from the attic of the Marxian past and only dusted off and refurbished for its present use, this old-new label is a more fitting description of the present communist malaise than is either Titoism or national communism. What the revisionists want is a full-scale revision of Marxism-Leninism that would cut out its totalitarian core, release it from Soviet bondage, and convert it into a more benign form only slightly differentiated from Western European socialism.[15]

"Present-day revisionism seeks to smear the great teachings of Marxism-Leninism, declares that they are 'outmoded' and that they have allegedly lost their significance for special progress," reads the angry definition of revisionism contained in the Socialist Commonwealth Manifesto. "The revisionists try to destroy the revolutionary spirit of Marxism-Leninism, to undermine the faith of the working people in socialism. They deny the historic necessity for a proletarian revolution and the dictatorship of the proletariat during the period of transition from capitalism to socialism, deny the leading role of the Marxist–Leninist Party, reject the principles of proletarian internationalism, call for the rejection of the Leninist principles of Party organization, and above all, of democratic centralism, and demand

[13] Especially, speeches by Novotný and Bacílek, *Pravda,* April 27 and 28, 1957; *Rudé právo,* June 19, 1957.

[14] *Pravda* and *Izvestia,* November 22, 1957. English text in the *Current Digest of Soviet Press,* IX, 47 (1958), pp. 5-6.

[15] See Edward Taborsky, "The Reluctant Satellites," in J. S. Roucek's *Modern Ideologies,* New York, 1961.

that the Communist Party be transformed from a militant revolutionary organization into some kind of debating society."

Communist proclamations must, of course, be taken with a big grain of salt. But it seems that, for once, the Manifesto's description of these hair-raising heresies is very close to the truth as borne out by the mighty torrent of revisionist thought that has managed to break through the floodgates of communist censorship and fight its way into the Party-controlled press, especially in revisionism's main arena, Gomulka's Poland.

Although Czechoslovak revisionism has never assumed as explosive a character as its tougher counterpart in Poland and Hungary, it has not been less far-reaching in its postulates. Its high tide came in the spring and summer of 1956. Encouraged by Khrushchëv's demolition of the Stalin myth, the inner-Party opposition, which had been restless ever since the announcement of Malenkov's New Course in 1953, moved to a full-fledged offensive against Party leaders. Besides being confirmed by a number of reports coming from Czechoslovakia at that time, as well as by the increased concern apparent from the communist press, the ferment into which the flare-up of revisionism brought the Czechoslovak Party was amply revealed by the proceedings of the National Party Conference held on June 11-14, 1956. In his report to the Conference Novotný flayed "reformist illusions about harmony and reconciliation of class interests"; voices "demanding freedom for bourgeois and anti-socialist propaganda"; views "reflecting the petty-bourgeois criticism of Party policy"; attempts to "smuggle" into the Party views "calling under the pretext of 'freedom' for a return of pre-February conditions," i.e., those existing before the communist coup of 1948.[16] Citing a shocking illustration of misbehavior, he admitted that during the session of the Party's Central Committee in March 1956 some of the ideological workers began to doubt even "the very foundations of Marxism-Leninism." Other speakers at the Conference spoke in much the same vein.

Faced with an open, though unarmed, revolt within the Party and a smoldering disaffection without, the Party leadership felt that the only way they could keep control of the situation was to tighten the reins once again. Against their own convictions and with grave misgivings they had tried the post-Stalin, Moscow-sponsored softer line, and it had not worked. In that respect they had certainly as-

[16] *Rudé právo,* June 12, 1956.

sessed the situation more realistically and were more alive to the risks involved in such flirtations with freedom than Khrushchëv. Hence, while continuing to pay lip service to the "lessons of the Twentieth Congress," they began again to crack the whip more vehemently. This swing toward neo-Stalinism began in Czechoslovakia months before the revolts in Poland and Hungary exposed the futility of any hopes that the disillusioned masses behind the Iron Curtain could be bribed into acceptance of the Marxist-Leninist rule by a few minor concessions. Kindly official invitations that people "throw away their fears" and embark on "courageous criticism of shortcomings," characteristic of the months following the Twentieth Congress, were replaced by renewed attacks against "the internal enemy" who "has not by far given up his anti-state and antipopular activity" and by stern rejection of "all liberalistic tendencies," "demands for 'freedom' to spread bourgeois ideologies and an underrating of the state apparatus and of the guiding role of the Party in all spheres of life."[17] Strong emphasis began again to be laid on "the role of the state security organs as guardians of socialist achievements of the people."[18]

The suppression of the Hungarian uprising and the gradual restriction of earlier revisionist gains in Poland greatly aided the neo-Stalinist leaders of the KSČ to prevent the revisionist menace from getting out of hand. But it has done nothing to alleviate the sickness itself, let alone to put the patient on the road toward recovery. While the stiffening of the neo-Stalinist controls has closed the lips or stopped the pen of many a critic, it could change neither their thoughts nor their resolve to bring their designs to fruition if and when another chance presents itself. That the Party leadership is fully aware of the continued presence of the revisionist challenge has been clearly apparent in its mammoth antirevisionist campaign unfolded in 1957-1958. The keynote was sounded at the session of the Party's Central Committee in December 1957 where the struggle against revisionism was declared to be "the main task of the revolutionary workers' movement." The crusade spread over all the nation and no meeting, big or small, could adjourn without dutiful antirevisionist tirades. The communist scribes were ordered to keep the Party's journals well supplied with belligerent materials designed to counteract the "vicious poison."[19]

[17] *ibid.*, July 11, 1956.
[18] *Československý přehled*, III, 7-8 (1956), p. 3.
[19] For instance, *Rudé právo*, January 1958; *Tvorba*, December 19 and 26, 1957; *Práce*, January 2, 1958; *Mladá fronta*, January 5, 1958.

Special attention was paid in this connection to Poland and Yugoslavia, the two mainsprings of revisionist thought in Eastern Europe. Gomulka's experiment, in particular, was watched with raised eyebrows by the Praha regime which was well aware of the highly contagious nature of such happenings in a next-door neighborhood. In an effort to prevent the contagion from spreading, the regime felt compelled for a while to seal off the Polish border as tightly as that between Czechoslovakia and Western Germany and to include the Polish radio stations in its jamming operations against the transmission of "Western imperialist propaganda." Since Gomulka's comeback the Czechoslovak Party spokesmen and their press have been sharply critical of each and every revisionist advance in Poland and applauded every reimposed neo-Stalinist restriction.[20] Meddling freely in Polish internal politics they have indulged in smearing such prominent figures of Polish revisionism as Kolakowski, Kott, Woroshylski, Wazyk, and occasionally censuring even Gomulka himself.[21]

The continued worries of Party leaders about the revisionist menace were also documented by the proceedings of the KSČ's Congress of 1958. Delivering the main report, Novotný once again denounced revisionism as the main danger of communism and congratulated the Party on having successfully repelled revisionist tendencies in its midst. But he poured cold water on any wishful thoughts that revisionism had been licked: "We have never believed that the danger of revisionism had been liquidated by the repulsion of its first wave. Many opportunistic elements have only hidden behind a pretense of silence and duplicity."[22] The resolution adopted by the Congress pledged a resolute struggle against "revisionism which attacks the fundamental principles of Marxism-Leninism and tries to break the unity of the revolutionary communist movement."[23]

The revisionist dilemma is further complicated by the communist inability to pin on revisionism the favorite label of "bourgeois origin." Not that communist leaders have not tried. Following the Soviet cliché, the Praha regime's propagandists have been burning the midnight oil in a strenuous effort to portray revisionism as a creation of

---

[20] *Rudé právo*, December 9 and 11, 1956, and January 9, 1958; *Tvorba*, December 19, 1957; *Mladá fronta*, November 28, 1957; also, Hendrych's attack on "petty-bourgeois radicalism" in Poland in the December 1956 session of the Party's Central Committee, *Rudé právo*, December 14, 1956.

[21] *Rudé právo*, December 23, 1957, and January 9, 1958.

[22] *ibid.*, June 19, 1958.

[23] *ibid.*, June 23, 1958.

"American imperialism" and as a "class weapon of the bourgeoisie in its struggle against the working class."[24] In his address to the Eleventh Party Congress Novotný designated revisionism as "an expression of survivals and influences of bourgeois and petty-bourgeois thinking in our own ranks."[25] But these verbal acrobatics have been prompted by the desire to keep in line with the Soviets rather than by any hope that such assertions would be accepted at their face value. For the ranks of the revisionists consist of men of long-standing and meritorious service to the communist cause. Moreover, they, rather than their neo-Stalinist mentors, are endowed with that ideological zeal and spirit of sacrifice that characterized the earlier disciples of the communist creed when allegiance to the teaching of Karl Marx meant privation and suffering instead of the executive's swivel chairs bestowed upon today's orthodox Communists with clean cadre reports. That is what makes this fratricidal struggle between the two categories of Communists so complicated for the present holders of power. "The fight against revisionism is a complicated matter," lamented *Rudé právo* on January 9, 1958, "because revisionism appears misleadingly under the title of creative development of Marxism while its ideas are formed with particular care in the people's democratic countries where the revisionists cannot take the anti-Party line quite openly . . . . It must also be taken into consideration that the revisionists very often do not attack directly and openly the basic theses of Marxism-Leninism, but concentrate on questions of practical politics."

Fortunately, however, for the KSČ leaders, the revisionist threat is lessened, at least for the present, by three rather important limiting factors.

First, the Czechoslovak revisionist camp is sorely lacking in forceful leadership. Among its adherents there is no one anywhere near the caliber of a Gomulka or even a Nagy. The one man who could have met some of these requirements of leadership was Vlado Clementis who alone among the Czechoslovak communist elite had the courage to think aloud and to stand up for some of his ideas, at least within the Party's conclave. But it is unlikely that this Slovak intellectual would have had a strong enough appeal to the Czech industrial workers, even had he survived the Stalinist purges. The significance of this lack of suitable revisionist leadership should not, of course,

---

[24] *ibid.*, January 9, 1958.
[25] *ibid.*, June 19, 1958.

be exaggerated. Revolutions of this type start more often than not without a pronounced leader who emerges only subsequently in the course of the revolution. In Hungary, for instance, Imre Nagy did not actually lead but was rather pushed into leadership by quickly unfolding events. Undoubtedly, however, the availability of a proper leader at the crucial stage of developments in October and November 1956 might have made a difference. This is particularly so because of the rather unfortunate Czech habit of waiting for a signal from above and depending too much on the leader, a habit which had developed most pronouncedly during the Masaryk-Beneš era.

Second, in additon to this excessive reliance on the leader in time of crisis, there are some other national characteristics, political traditions, and behavioral patterns which have dulled the sharpness of the revisionist challenge. Among the major traits of the Czechoslovak mentality are a down-to-earth realism, a mistrust of doctrinaire shibboleths, an overdose of caution, a dislike for doubtful risks, and a lack of romantic heroism. When confronted with what he thinks to be a superior power, the average Czech resorts to devious maneuvering, covered up by a pretense of submission, rather than to an outright frontal opposition. He prefers to bend and preserve his strength rather than break in a gesture of bold defiance. He is ready to rise and fight for his cause and conviction as much as any one else, but, unlike his fanatical Hussite ancestors, he is ready to do so only if he sees a realistic chance of success. That is why he took up arms against the Nazis in September 1944 in Slovakia after the Red Army had reached the Carpathian Mountains, and again in May 1945 in Praha, hoping in both instances for quickly forthcoming aid from the Russians and Americans, respectively. That he did not do the same on the occasion of the Hungarian uprising was because he did not believe that the Soviets would allow the Hungarians to get away with it. While this attitude characterizes the nation as a whole, it also applies to a considerable extent to the revisionist faction of the KSČ.

Finally, the realism characteristic of the typical Czech mentality affects the revisionist cause in yet another way. It makes it difficult to uphold a proper level of doctrinal firmness and ideological zeal for a prolonged period, even among those who joined the Party because of their belief in the virtues of communism. When the initial intoxication evaporates, the former believer in communism either quits in disgust or, more commonly, sticks to his Party membership out of sheer personal opportunism. But opportunists and mere ritualists hardly ever become reformers. Hence, the truly devout revisionist, ready to grapple bare-handed with superior forces to avenge betrayal of a sincere faith and to redeem the purity of an original belief, is rarer in Czechoslovakia than most anywhere behind the Iron Curtain. This accounts probably for the fact that those who raised critical voices in Czechoslovakia in the crucial year 1956 were mostly non-communists and an admixture of those communists who misread the theses of the Twentieth Congress. In contrast to the Poles and the Hungarians, true Communists in Czechoslovakia, for the most part, kept clear of the oppositional side of the melee. They definitely did not rise to the leading role in the manner of their fellow-revisionists in Poland and Hungary. This might at first glance be mistaken for loyalty to the doctrine, but in reality it is a symptom of Czechoslovak communism's sterility and ideological stagnation. This was well characterized by an escapee student from Czechoslovakia: "The religious reformation was successful only where a live religious belief existed, but failed wherever church membership became only a lifeless tradition. In the same manner the communistic reformation could attain success only where Communists themselves think critically of communism and see in it a living program."[26]

All this is not intended to create the impression that Czechoslovak revisionism is reduced to impotence. It can and does create a weighty problem within the Party. It does so, however, primarily because it enjoys the silent backing of the country's latent anti-communist forces, the majority of whom consider the revisionist platform to be the only practicable solution in the present balance of power on the world scale and within the communist orbit. That is why, on the other hand, such a revisionist alternative could hardly be of a long duration in Czechoslovakia unless it were kept in power by Soviet support in much the same manner as is the present Praha regime. Without such backing it would soon be overwhelmed by the forces of anti-communism.

BOURGEOIS NATIONALISM

While revisionism is new wine in an old bottle, both container and contents are old when it comes to bourgeois nationalism. Of all the condemned isms, none has been attacked over a longer span of time. Yet none has been more durable. Obviously, not even the dec-

---

[26] *Československý přehled,* IV, 2 (1957), p. 30.

ades of continuous indoctrination in the virtues of proletarian internationalism could fully vanquish nationalistic inclinations within the "vanguard of the proletariat" itself.

Although frequently used, the term "bourgeois nationalism" has never been adequately defined and its practical application has been very broad. Judging by Soviet usage, its main ingredients seem to be an excessive consciousness of belonging to a given ethnic group and an undue insistence on local self-government. In the Soviet Union the label has mostly been attached to members of non-Russian nationalities and much less to Russians found guilty of "Russian chauvinism." Insofar as the vice is committed by a Party member, the conception of bourgeois nationalism strongly resembles that of national communism. Although placed in circulation by opposite camps—"bourgeois nationalism" by the Bolsheviks and "national communism" by the West—the two terms differ from one another little more than Tweedledee from Tweedledum. In fact, the communist rulers definitely prefer the label "bourgeois nationalism" which has been broadened to include instances of deviationism that have little in common with nationalistic feelings. Since the introduction of the old-new formula of revisionism as a more general catchall for various communist heresies, the tendency has recently developed to construct bourgeois nationalism somewhat more restrictively.

This is clearly demonstrated by Czechoslovak practice. While the designation of "bourgeois nationalism" is still used rather loosely and casuistically, it is now generally reserved for those whose real or alleged misbehavior stems primarily from their ethnic appurtenance or from sentiments of local patriotism. On the other hand, those who object to Soviet predominance principally on the ground that it is contrary to genuine proletarian internationalism are now most often included among the revisionists, even though an accusation of bourgeois nationalism or some other bad ism may be thrown in for good measure.

Though Czech Party members are by no means immune to the bourgeois nationalistic heresy, its most fertile ground is among the Slovaks. "One of the weakest sectors of our ideological struggle is the struggle against bourgeois nationalism," bewailed the Slovak *Pravda* on December 14, 1956. The growing concern of the Party leadership about the spread of the heresy among Slovak Party members is documented by the increasing criticism to which the Slovak branch has been subjected in the past years. No occasion has been missed to remind the Party membership of the danger and the wickedness of bourgeois nationalism and of the urgent need to wage a merciless battle on this archenemy of proletarian internationalism. "Bourgeois nationalism is a poison," said Bacílek, delivering the opening speech at the Twelfth Congress of the Slovak Party in April 1957.[27]

Why the Slovak branch of the KSČ is especially vulnerable in this respect is easy to understand. Traditional Slovak nationalism is too deeply rooted in the heart of many a devout Slovak Communist to be discarded merely upon higher orders. Even such high-ranking Party men as Clementis, Husák, and Novomeský (subsequently purged for bourgeois nationalism and Titoism) firmly believed that there was no contradiction between their loyalty to communism and to Slovak patriotism. I have never encountered a more forceful, more fiery, or more enthusiastic advocate of the Slovak national cause than Laco Novomeský, the prominent Slovak communist writer whom the Party sent to London in 1944 for the specific purpose of persuading Beneš to yield to Slovak nationalistic demands. Always directed against those who wielded authority in Czechoslovakia's capital, the historic Slovak aversion to and suspicion of Praha centralism necessarily turned against the KSČ leadership. Thus it was bound to enhance nationalistic and autonomistic leanings among Slovak Party members. Last but not least, KSČ's abrupt abandonment of its earlier vigorous support of Slovak nationalistic postulates when tactical needs no longer demanded it after the February coup of 1948, deeply and permanently undermined the loyalty of the many Slovak Communists who had taken the KSČ's original stand in earnest. That is why it is difficult to believe Bacílek's assertions that a good deal of bourgeois nationalism within the Party was to be blamed on the officials of the "former Republic and of the Slovak Fascist State" who, "posing as workers," have joined the Party.[28]

Finally, it is significant, although not at all surprising, that bourgeois nationalism has found fertile ground among Party members of Hungarian descent. Addressing the Slovak Party's Eleventh Congress in April 1955, Bacílek complained that "some of our citizens of Hungarian nationality, and they comprise also some members and functionaries of our Party, forget that the Czechoslovak Republic is

[27] *Pravda*, April 27, 1957.
[28] *East Europe*, 7, 3 (1958), p. 43.

their fatherland and that the Central Committee of the KSČ determines policy for the Hungarian comrades as well . . . ."[29]

Thus, far from diminishing, bourgeois nationalism has been gaining strength under the thin veneer of proletarian internationalism. As in the Soviet Union, it has developed especially among members of ethnic minorities. Once again, living evidence suggests that Marxism-Leninism lacks the capability of becoming a substitute for the intangible bonds of nationality.

RELIGIOUS OBSCURANTISM

One of the strangest paradoxes one encounters in studying inner-Party problems confronting KSČ leaders is the fact that there are still Party members who not only believe in God but even retain their formal church affiliations. Since Marxist-Leninist teaching is militantly atheist and seeks to impose a rigid monopoly of its own creed upon its followers, one should have thought that, upon joining the so-called vanguard of the proletariat, each Party member would as a matter of course have severed whatever religious links he might have had. Those taking Marxism-Leninism seriously should do so because of genuine atheist beliefs. Those joining the Party for opportunistic reasons could be expected to turn their backs on the church in order to better camouflage their true convictions. While this is obviously very much so in Soviet Russia, it is still far from being a uniformly observable rule of behavior in Czechoslovakia.

As revealed by interviewed escapees as well as by periodic complaints in the Party press, there are Party members who "forget" to withdraw from church membership.[30] Whether or not formally affiliated, some Party members occasionally attend church services, especially at Christmas and Easter time. When detected by Party watchdogs in such illicit behavior, they often attempt to justify their conduct by an alleged desire to check whether the pulpit is used for anti-Party purposes. Instances where the father cancels his church membership prior to becoming a Party member but allows his children to go to church are fairly frequent. Also, even Party members without church affiliation far too often compromise the Party's atheist stand and abet religious "superstitions" by using the minister's services

[29] *Pravda*, April 24, 1955.
[30] *ibid.*, November 15, 1955; also, for a discussion on religion in *Mladá fronta* in the months of July and August 1957, see *Československý přehled*, IV, 9 (1957), pp. 11ff.

in ceremonies of baptism, marriage, and funeral.[31] Thus there are still "some Party members who even endeavor to create a basis for accommodating religious survivals with the newest discoveries science . . . ."[32]

Party leaders take a very dim view of this "religious obscurantism" within the Party's own ranks and try hard to extirpate it. With monotonous regularity various Party magazines run articles on the harmfulness of religious "superstitions" and their incompatibility with Marxism-Leninism. Party schooling devotes much attention to the "scientific" refutation of belief in the existence of God. Occasionally, satire and ridicule are resorted to, both in words and pictures. Outright expulsion from the Party is also used when other methods fail. However, these ultimate measures have thus far been applied only in extreme cases. The comparative lenience toward Party members addicted to religious obscurantism was explained in an interesting fashion by *Rudé právo* on October 10, 1954: "The Communist Party . . . takes into its ranks the most active builders of socialism. It cannot ask them to become mature Marxists all at once. That is why we do not expel from the Party those comrades who have not yet freed themselves of religious prejudices, but on the contrary we help them to shake off such prejudices."

SOCIAL DEMOCRATISM

Yet another widespread ism that does much harm to the Party is social democratism, sometimes also dubbed "social democratic sectarianism," "social democratic opportunism" or "anarcho-syndicalism." Although it is now implied in the broader concept of revisionism, the expression "social democratism" continues occasionally to be used independently of the latter. Furthermore, it has a specific flavor of its own in present-day communist usage. A Czech communist theoretician describes social democratism as "a form of bourgeois ideology adapted to disorient the working class so that, under the false pretense of a struggle for the betterment of its position, it may be disarmed ideologically and politically and made a helpless object of capitalist exploitation."[33] A far better insight into the substance of social democratism is yielded by a study of actual cases

---

[31] See, for instance, *Život strany,* No. 9 (1959), p. 571.
[32] *Pravda,* November 15, 1955; also, *Rudé právo,* November 9, 1958.
[33] V. Pachman in *Politická Ekonomie,* October 4, 1954.

of those accused of the heresy. It reveals that the main elements of social democratism, all of them heartily disliked by the Party leadership, are the following basic beliefs or grievances: (a) that the present economic system of Czechoslovakia is state capitalism rather than socialism; (b) that, contrary to earlier communist promises, workers have no say in the management of nationalized enterprises; (c) that trade unions should plead for the rights of workers instead of being a pliable tool in the enforcement of "socialist labor discipline"; (d) that there ought to be free collective bargaining and at least a tacit acceptance of the strike as a last line of workers' defense; (e) that the differentiation of wages and bonuses should not be so sharp.[34]

Pointed like a dagger at the very heart of the Marxist-Leninist economic system, social democratism is dangerous indeed, and has been an object of recurrent attacks by Party leaders for years. But fighting it is made more difficult by the fact that its main habitat is among the industrial proletariat, the supposed backbone of communism, and that its most efficient carriers can be found among long-standing Party members who can remember when "social democratism" was one of the Party's leading battle slogans. Under such conditions the all-too-much-abused epithet of "bourgeois" or "reactionary" has a hollow ring. So has the supposedly odious designation of such highly desirable workers' aims as *rovnostářství*, the Czech equivalent for Soviet *urovnilovka*, i.e., the "leveling off" of wage disparities. Fed by the workers' disillusionment over the disparity between the Party's rosy promises of better life and the grim realities of the day, social democratism is as hard to kill as the mythical Lernean Hydra. As Bacílek said, addressing the Central Committee of the Slovak Communist Party on December 18, 1953, "Bourgeois national ideologies, religious obscurantism, and also social democratism are those prejudices that remain the longest in the minds of the people and are the most difficult to conquer."

MASARYKISM

While all the isms thus far mentioned occur in varying degrees in all parts of the Soviet orbit, there is one particular ism that applies to Czechoslovakia alone. It is Masarykism, the loyalty to

[34] *Nová svoboda,* October 7, 1954, *Práce,* October 21, 1954, *Rudé právo,* September 19, 1954.

the political legacy of the philosopher-statesman Thomas G. Masaryk, the founder of democratic Czechoslovakia and the country's first President. The awesome dilemma which the memory of Thomas Masaryk, who had become a symbol of democracy for all Czechs, poses for the KSČ leaders, was stated with concise clarity in an article published at the height of the anti-Masaryk campaign in 1953: "A halo was purposely created around the 'Masaryk' Republic, which was a bourgeois state of industrialists and landlords. This legend depicted Masaryk as a 'humanitarian standing above classes,' a 'philosopher and statesman standing above all parties,' a 'liberator of the nation,' and the 'workingmen's friend.' The exiled traitors now in the service of Western imperialists are still trying to keep up this legend and are even attempting to magnify it . . . ."[35] Although Masarykism is far more than just an inner-Party issue, it presents an especially delicate problem within the Party's rank and file. Many workers still recall with affection the venerable President whom they knew to have been their friend.[36] Despite the attempts of Party leaders to distort the truth they are well aware of Masaryk's humble and truly proletarian origin. And his ideals of humanitarian democracy and social justice for all are bound to appeal strongly to Party members disappoined by the gospel of dialectical materialism and searching for a better alternative.

Confronted with a problem of this magnitude, Party leaders could not remain neutral or by-pass the issue. The precepts of Leninist strategy left only two ways open to them. They could attempt to appropriate Masaryk's memory for the Party by proclaiming Masaryk a precursor of communism and by posing as his real successors engaged in broadening and deepening his political legacy. Or they could reject him as a bogus reformer trying to save capitalism under the pretense of concern for the people's needs. Successively, they experimented with both.

Aware of the tremendous asset that would accrue to the Party if Thomas Masaryk could be posthumously claimed as a sort of "non-Party Bolshevik," the KSČ leadership tried first the appropriative process. Between 1945 and 1948, and for a short while even after the February coup of 1948, the spokesmen of the Party praised Masaryk as an outstanding defender of social progress, justice, and liberty. On the ninety-eighth anniversary of Masaryk's birth on March 7, 1948,

---

[35] *Svět práce,* April 23, 1953.
[36] "Today we still encounter the opinion that Masaryk was 'a friend of the workers,'" wrote *Rudé právo* on May 28, 1954.

two weeks after the establishment of the communist "dictatorship of the proletariat," Nejedlý wrote a eulogy of Masaryk wherein he hailed "Masaryk's heritage" and spoke of the people's democratic regime as "Masarykist."[37] Gottwald himself paid an official visit to Thomas Masaryk's grave at Lány. Nor can it be said that this was a Machiavellian attitude dictated solely by considerations of Party tactics. Although they had been critical of Thomas Masaryk during his lifetime, KSČ leaders had a sound respect for him and his high principles. "I gazed at Masaryk . . . with admiration," wrote Nejedlý on the occasion of Masaryk's death in 1937. "How far ahead of his time he was . . . . Professor, philosopher, ideologist who spoke by deeds . . . . How great he was . . . a unique phenomenon and example."[38] Had they been able to get away with their stratagem, KSČ leaders could have served the goals of Marxism-Leninism well without doing too much violence to their conscience.

However, these efforts to draft Masaryk for the cause of communism were soon abandoned and for a while he was officially ignored. It looked as though the Communists would try, to use Orwell's dictum, to annihilate Masaryk in the past as well as in the future by a conspiracy of silence. But the silence ended toward the close of 1950 and a campaign of gradual denigration began. The first major step toward the reappraisal of Masaryk's role was taken on the occasion of the one-hundredth anniversary of his birth in March 1950. While credit was still given to Masaryk for his struggle "for freedom of thought and his interest in man," he was condemned for his "program of reformism, attempt to lead the workers away from the revolutionary theory, effort to disorient the workers' movement, and to deprive it of the compass of Marxism."[39] Nonetheless, Masaryk was still considered enough of a *persona grata* that a wreath was placed on his grave by the communist Premier of Czechoslovakia, Antonín Zápotocký, and an official governmental delegation including one Deputy Premier, the Minister of Defense, the Chairman of the National Assembly, and the Mayor of Praha.

Yet, by December 1950, Masaryk was declared to be an "enemy of socialism and a pillar of bourgeoisie."[40] From then on he has been

---

[37] Richard Hunt, "The Denigration of Masaryk," *Yale Review,* 43, 3 (March 1954), p. 419.

[38] *News,* 2, 7 (1953), p. 9.

[39] Editorial in *Tvorba,* March 6, 1950; *Lidové noviny,* March 7, 1950; and *Rudé právo,* March 7, 1950.

[40] *Tvorba,* December 6, 1950.

a favorite target of communist vilification on every suitable occasion.[41] The anti-Masaryk campaign reached its climax in the spring of 1953 when vituperative press articles were provided with additional fuel through a three-hundred page defamatory publication entitled *Documents on the Anti-Popular and Anti-National Policy of T. G. Masaryk*.[42] Although the frequency of anti-Masaryk tirades has lessened in the ensuing years, their intensity has not diminished. In 1954 the offensive was continued not only in the periodical press, but also in a new collection of *Documents on the Anti-Soviet Intrigues of the Czechoslovak Reactionary Circles*[43] and V. Král's book on *Masaryk's and Beneš's Counter-Revolutionary Policy against the Soviets*.[44] Similar attacks have been recurring in the Czechoslovak press and radio ever since.[45] And in 1959 three additional volumes were published: *T. G. Masaryk and the Czech Politics,* from the pen of J. Křížek who had written in 1955 a book on T. G. Masaryk's alleged struggle against the revolutionary workers' movement prior to the World Imperialist War; *T. G. Masaryk and the Russian Revolution,* by Theodore Syllaba; and *Masaryk and Pre-Revolutionary Russia,* by Julius Dolanský.

Why have the Czechoslovak communist leaders given up their earlier positive attitude toward Masaryk? Having decided to drop their appropriative process and adopt a critical but relatively moderate attitude toward him in 1949-1950, why have they gone over to the savage abuse of 1952-1953?

The reversal from praise to the mild criticism of 1949 was a logical result of changed circumstances. Having seized and consolidated their power, KSČ leaders no longer felt the tactical need of posing as Masaryk's heirs. On the contrary, the more disillusioned the Party's rank and file grew about the leadership's policies, the more dangerous it was to pay even lip service to Masaryk's memory. For it invited comparison between the communist "people's democracy" and the humanitarian democracy of Thomas Masaryk, a comparison from which the former was bound to emerge as a poor second. More-

---

[41] For a few examples see *Tvorba,* February 22, May 10, and December 20, 1951; *Rudé právo,* April 10, 1951; *Lidové noviny,* September 9, 1951; *Mladá fronta,* August 19, 1951; and January 27, 1953; *Rovnost,* October 25, 1952.

[42] *Literární noviny,* February 1, 1953; *Rudé právo,* April 27, May 8, and December 6, 1953; *Svět práce,* April 23, 1953; *Mladá fronta,* January 27, 1953; *Zpráva o Československu,* IV, 5 (May 1953), pp. 24-25.

[43] *Dokumenty o protisovětských piklech československé reakce,* Praha, 1954.

[44] *O Masarykově a Benešově kontrarevoluční protisovětské politice,* Praha, 1953.

[45] For instance, *Československý přehled,* IV, 9 (September 1957), pp. 9-10.

over, since his opposition to communism was too well known, any attempt to pass Masaryk for a pro-communist had little chance of success. Thus the leadership's well-founded worries over the members' ideological laxness unavoidably led to the rejection of Masaryk and his philosophy.

But the switch from the comparatively moderate censure of 1949-1950 to the defamation which was soon to follow was undoubtedly due to the cogent desire of the KSČ leaders to deserve the trust of the Kremlin by a display of adequate Marxist-Leninist orthodoxy. As far as they were concerned, such men as Gottwald, Zápotocký, Dolanský, Nejedlý, or most of the other communist hierarchs would have been satisfied with the first stage of Masaryk's downgrading. As they had on the occasion of Masaryk's Centenary in 1950, they would have wished to continue to give Masaryk his due as an enlightened bourgeois statesman while censuring him for his anti-Marxism and for his failure to grasp the meaning of the October Revolution. They knew how hallowed the memory of Masaryk was to most Czechs and even many Party members. Had they had a choice, they would have probably tried subtler methods to dislodge that memory rather than resort to spiteful abuse which could only defeat its purpose. As in so many other respects, their dependence on the Kremlin had pushed the KSČ leaders to an extreme to which they did not originally intend to go.

Considering the magnitude of the anti-Masaryk campaign, its results thus far seem to have been meager indeed. Streets and other places named after Masaryk have been rechristened and the numerous statues of the Republic's Founding Father have been removed, not without angry but fruitless local protests and demonstrations. His books are on the index and may be lent by special permit only to those engaged in the Party-approved task of destroying "the Masaryk legend." However, according to reports coming from Czechoslovakia and interviews with escapees, Thomas Masaryk continues to be loved and respected. Although dead for more than twenty years, he is by far the most popular personage even among ordinary Party members. Typical of the attitude of many Czechoslovak Communists is the following incident reported by the Party press in 1952 in the midst of the ferocious anti-Masaryk campaign: "Thus, for instance, on March 7 of this year the chairman of the local people's committee in Brněnec and a member of the Communist Party of Czechoslovakia opened the meeting of the plenum by remembering the greatest man

139

in the history of the Czech nation, Thomas Garrigue Masaryk. The other Communists kept silent. This is a typical example of the lack of fighting spirit against enemy ideology . . . ."[46]

OTHER HARMFUL ISMS

Besides the major isms discussed on the preceding pages a host of other minor ones figure on the KSČ's index. They have all been coined in Moscow and the Czechoslovak rulers have simply incorporated them in their vocabulary without bothering too much whether or not such ideological heresies actually are common enough in Czechoslovakia to warrant the use of such terms.

Among the deadliest of such isms in the last stage of the Stalinist era was cosmopolitanism. "Cosmopolitanism means world citizenship," said Kopecký, defining the term in his address before an ideological conference in February 1952. "We know that this conception, which implies the deadening of one's relationship to the native land, to one's own people, and the acceptance of the mentality of nonnational world community, originated as an ideological product of the capitalist development . . . . It is to the interest of the bourgeoisie that the nations which it wishes to subdue possess the weakest possible national consciousness, that they be devoid of warm national and patriotic feeling, that they be ready to accept foreign capitalist influences, alien thought and alien mores, that they feel 'cosmopolitan' and inclined therefore to subject themselves to foreign rule."[47]

Coupled with "Zionism," this label was primarily applied to Communists of the Jewish race, whose sympathies supposedly gravitated more toward the West and Judaism than toward native communism. This outburst of anti-Semitism in a new garb reached its highest pitch in Czechoslovakia at the time of Slánský's arrest and trial in 1951-1952.[48] However, since cosmopolitanism and Zionism were artificial whipping boys created solely for the sake of doing as the Kremlin was doing, the two isms were put into cold storage with the change of atmosphere in the post-Stalin era.

On the other hand, post-Stalin developments have reactivated the struggle against the perennial problem of dogmatism and sectarianism, occasionally also called "Talmudism." Scored periodically during the Stalin era, the doctrinal rigidity implied by these terms became more burdensome when the need arose, after Stalin's death,

---

[46] *Rovnost,* October 25, 1952.
[47] *Rudé právo,* February 28, 1952.
[48] See Chapter v.

to streamline the communist system. "Dogmatism and sectarianism hinder the development of Marxist-Leninist theory and its creative application in changing conditions," says the Socialist Commonwealth Manifesto of November 1957. "They replace the study of the concrete situation with merely 'quoting the classics and sticking to books' and lead to the isolation of the Party from the masses." In condemning dogmatism, the Manifesto has made it clear, however, that it is to be considered as a lesser danger than revisionism, and has left it for each Communist Party to decide "which danger threatens it more at a given time . . . ."[49]

The neo-Stalinist leaders of the KSČ have had no difficulty in determining which of the two dangers to consider more serious. While concentrating their fire on revisionism they have been rather lax in combating dogmatism. Occasionally, the latter evil has been mentioned, but mostly in an inconspicuous fashion and with obvious lack of zest. Having just passed through an agonizing experience triggered by Soviet tampering with communist dogma, Praha rulers abhor doctrinal changes and adaptations. Fearful lest they might stir up the hornet's nest again if they relax their rigidity, they feel compelled to adhere to dogmatism rather than to fight it. Thus, in Czechoslovakia, dogmatism represents a dilemma which is rather different from other harmful isms. The latter ills are contracted mostly by communism's foot soldiers, the Party's rank and file. Dogmatism, on the other hand, is a sickness that mainly attacks communism's officers' corps, the KSČ leadership and their lieutenants.

Still other isms that the Party shepherds find threatening their flocks are "anarchism," "nihilism," "fractionalism," "parrot-ism," "dilettantism," "ritualism," "schematism," "intellectualism," "pettybourgeois extremism," "alibiism," "liquidationism," and "capitulationism." Besides being self-explanatory, these expressions do not add anything of substance to the previously mentioned list. Their main purpose seems to be rather to enrich the vocabulary of abuse that the leaders can hurl against the lax Party membership or to lend more variety to the obligatory rituals of periodic self-criticism. Hence, their analysis can be dispensed with.

THE DIAGNOSIS

At first glance this long list of "pernicious isms" creates the impression that the Party is ridden by a multitude of illnesses. However, a closer examination shows that most of these isms are only varied

[49] *Pravda* and *Izvestia,* November 22, 1957.

manifestations of the one and the same, but very serious, illness that could perhaps best be called corrosion of faith. Although the absence of free elections and of any impartial public opinion polls makes a full proof impossible, all the evidence gathered in this book clearly indicates that faith in Marxism-Leninism has been on the decline in Czechoslovakia ever since the establishment of the dictatorship of the proletariat in 1948. Disappointed by the harsh realities falling so far short of the earlier promises many of Marx's and Lenin's loyal disciples have turned their backs on the ideological ware peddled to them under the Marxist-Leninist label. Some of them quit the Party in disgust or allowed their membership to lapse through the more convenient and less risky device of nonpayment of dues. Others were expelled or stricken from the Party rolls for anti-Party activities or negligence in the performance of membership duties. But most of those who refrained from being too outspoken have kept their Party membership, either from sheer opportunism or because they hope that some day they might be able to purge its teaching and its practice of what they consider to be the elements of corruption brought into it by their leaders.

It is this last-mentioned group that is the most active carrier of the ideological sickness and the most effective corrosive agent of Marxist-Leninist totalitarianism, no matter what isms may be pinned on them. These are the men who advocate class peace and believe in the "reactionary utopia" in which the National Front could fulfill its mission without the leadership of the Communist Party.[50] They are the voices recommending that "Marxism must be improved by injections of neo-Kantism, positivism, or other idealistic tendencies."[51] They are the "black sheep" who have dared, as Yugoslavia's Djilas has, to suggest the establishment of an oppositional party and who make provocative motions that all the cadre questionnaires "be brought to St. Wenceslaus square [Praha's Times Square] and burnt as the highlight of a true popular festival."[52]

Thus the average flesh-and-blood Party member falls far short of the model Communist in the picture-book of the Party Statutes. Though he bows to the orders of the Party and participates in the customary rituals, he does so only because he must. He is either an opportunist, whose belief in the virtues of communism is only skin-

[50] Editorial in *Rudé právo*, November 30, 1955.
[51] Karel Kosík in *Literární noviny*, January 7, 1956.
[52] Pavel Berka's article in *Československý přehled*, III, 6 (1956), p. 12.

deep, or a revisionist who dislikes the Party leaders for what they did to the idealized picture of communism that he once had. His general attitude and behavior are well illustrated by the following fictional conversation between a communist guide and a foreign visitor to whom he was showing the famous St. Vitus Cathedral in Praha. "Are you a Catholic?" asked the guide, noting the visitor's genuine interest in the church. "By faith only, not by way of life," the visitor confessed. When the visit was over the foreigner, impressed by the guide's expert explanation of the Cathedral's history, could not resist asking him: "Are you really a Communist?" "By way of life only, not by faith."

CHAPTER VII
THE NATIONAL FRONT PARTNERS

It is axiomatic that the student of communist systems must watch with special care for semantic extravagances, which the jargon of communism abounds in. No matter what he may be exploring, his primary task is to cut through the ornamental phraseology and get to the essence. Nowhere is this axiom more valid than in the study of the non-communist parties that are still allowed to vegetate in today's Czechoslovakia. The very use of the word "party" to designate these groupings with no will power of their own is a gross distortion. If "political parties" means "voluntary associations of people adhering to a common political program and seeking power for the purpose of putting such a program into effect," then the Czechoslovak non-communist parties of today are not parties at all. They have no programs of their own and their avowed purpose is to wait on the Communist Party, hail its leadership, and act as its handymen in the realization of its Marxist-Leninist goals.

The Regenerated National Front

The conversion of the Czechoslovak non-communist parties from KSČ's competitors to its servants was carried out with a speed and suddenness that make Lenin's movement against the opponents of bolshevism in 1917-1918 appear slow by comparison. Making full use of their political prerogatives, the ministers of three of the four non-communist parties represented in the Cabinet of the National Front resigned on February 20, 1948, in defiance of Gottwald's malpractices and in the hope that their action would prompt an earlier general election which would strengthen them and weaken the KSČ. A few days later they were on the run or under arrest, denounced as traitors not only by the Communists but also by the "regenerated" leadership of their own parties installed practically overnight by Gottwald's henchmen.[1] Headquarters and press organs of all the non-

[1] On how it happened see Hubert Ripka, *Le Coup de Prague,* Paris, 1949, pp. 241ff.

communist parties, including the Social Democrats, were seized by the communist-controlled police and handed over to hand-picked fellow-travelers. Action Committees of the Regenerated National Front were set up throughout the country and began at once to purge all governmental and party organs of unreliable elements of the non-communist parties. Assumption of any function in them was made conditional upon clearance by the proper Action Committee.

Having reduced them to impotence and made sure that they are now headed by dependable puppets, the KSČ has thus far shown no intention of administering a liquidating *coup de grâce* to these relics of pre-communist days. The only party that has gone out of existence is the Social Democratic Party, which responded to "the elemental workingman's longing for unity" by allowing itself to be swallowed up by the KSČ in April 1948.[2] However, this was treated as a long-overdue patching-up of the split of 1920-1921 and as the return of an erring son to the paternal embrace of true Marxism, while the non-Marxist parties have continued their separate existence under the dictatorship of the proletariat. They have even been permitted to retain their pre-1948 names and newspapers, save for the Slovak Democratic Party whose emasculated post-coup body was given a new name, the Slovak Renaissance Party.

MEMBERSHIP AND ORGANIZATION

Very little information is available about the membership and organization of the non-communist parties, and it would appear that the KSČ and the parties themselves are bent on keeping such data secret. The probable reason for this secretiveness is the pitiful situation in which the non-communist parties find themselves in the communist system, a situation that hardly offers a propitious topic for propaganda.

No membership figures have ever been announced by any of the four existing non-communist parties and indirect sources give only a rough estimate of their size. Some 12,000 to 13,000 members are credited to each of the two parties operating in Czech lands, the Czechoslovak Socialist Party and the People's Party.[3] Of the two non-communist parties existing in Slovakia, one, the Slovak Freedom Party, is so small that, unlike the other three, it has been given no seat on either the Council of Ministers or the Slovak Board of Com-

---

[2] *Právo lidu*, April 18, 1948.
[3] *Československý přehled*, IV, 3 (1957), pp. 12ff.

missioners, the pre-1960 Slovak regional executive. Another clear sign of its smallness is the fact that it publishes only a weekly paper, *Sloboda,* while each of the other three has its own daily. The other Slovak party, the Slovak Renaissance Party, is larger than its tiny Slovak sister, but undoubtedly smaller than either one of the Czech cousins. This can be inferred from its smaller representation on the Council of Ministers where it had until July 1960 only one seat as compared to two such seats for each of the two Czech parties, as well as from the much smaller number of deputies it has been allowed in the National Assembly.[4] Also, the small circulation of its daily paper, *L'ud,* listed as 5,000 copies, permits a conjecture that the Party's membership is not likely to be too far from that figure.

Thus, even if all the members of the present non-communist parties are added together and allowance is made for a margin of error, the total would still be well below 50,000. This is only a small fraction of the membership of these parties which, prior to the communist coup, ran into many hundreds of thousands.[5] In part, this great decrease in membership is the intended consequence of the purging undertaken by the communist-controlled Action Committees. Neither the communist rulers nor their fellow-traveling servants wished to retain within the regenerated parties strong-willed party regulars who would have done all they could to impede their parties' satellization. On the other hand, most of the members quit of their own will in protest against the perversion of their parties' purposes.

These pitifully low membership figures have been causing concern not only to the fellow-traveling leaders of the non-communist parties, but to the KSČ leaders as well. Although the latter were and are in no way interested in maintaining the membership of non-communist parties on pre-coup levels, neither do they want them to melt away, at least not yet. At the current stage of "socialist construction" these satellite parties perform a useful function as transmission belts for KSČ decisions, and it is, therefore, in the best interest of communism to keep them in operation. That is why the non-communist parties were instructed toward the end of 1949 to increase their membership.[6] Typical of the KSČ's solicitude in this respect was its behavior in 1953 when the non-communist parties almost fell apart because

---

[4] See below. In the reshuffle which took place in July 1960 the Slovak Renaissance Party lost its representation in the Cabinet altogether; and the Czech Socialist Party and the People's Party were allowed to retain one seat each.

[5] Exact figures are unavailable.

[6] Ivan Gadourek, *The Political Control of Czechoslovakia,* Leiden, 1953, p. 59.

of the large-scale exodus of their members, enraged by their leaders' support of the ruthless "currency reform" of June 1953. Communist supervisors at that time took the unprecedented step of forbidding the organs of the Czechoslovak Socialist Party, where the danger of disintegration was gravest, to strike from the party rolls any members, even those who did not pay their dues or shirked such civic duties as volunteering for working brigades.[7]

Just as data on the size of the non-communist party membership are scanty, so are those on its social structure very sketchy. The information supplied by escapee members of non-communist parties suggests that they continue to draw their tiny followings mostly from the same social strata as in pre-communist days. The members of the Czechoslovak Socialist Party are mostly recruited from former urban middle-class groups and white-collar workers. The People's Party continues to be typically Catholic and predominantly agrarian. The Slovak Renaissance Party obtains the bulk of its meager retinue from the Slovak peasant population and some of the small-town intelligentsia, both Catholic and Protestant. The dwarfish Slovak Freedom Party is supposedly Catholic.

Czechoslovak underground sources indicate that the regenerated non-communist parties are composed largely of old party members from pre-coup days. It seems that, guided by the typical Czech sense of practicality, some of the party regulars, who managed to evade the purging hand of the Action Committees, have decided to save what they could from the ruins. Behaving much in the manner characteristic of the good soldier Schweik of Jaroslav Hašek's famed novel, they have put up a façade of pretended loyalty and feigned eagerness for the "people's democracy," while pursuing their own unpretentious ends as much as they can. At least they feel they have established a legitimate pretext for meeting regularly with some of their old friends, thereby holding together a scattered cluster of organizations that could be quickly reconverted into anti-communist nuclei ready to spring into action should the situation change. It has been impossible to prevent infiltration into the groups by communist spies and informers, but most of these are known and the party old-timers can beware of them as well as keep a check on them for the future settling of accounts which most old party members firmly anticipate.

The members' attitude is well illustrated by the following descrip-

[7] *Československý přehled,* IV, 3 (March 1957), p. 13.

tion of a typical non-communist party meeting, given by an escapee functionary:

"As reporter of the city committee of my party I had to take part in the meeting of one of our district organizations. About sixty persons were present. The presiding secretary of the district organization welcomed me in a very friendly fashion, but told me in the same friendly manner: 'If you want to chatter here about the same nonsense that we must listen to daily on the Praha radio, then you had better leave. Nobody here is interested in that.' When I informed him that I had no intention whatsoever of delivering a speech . . . it was received with a general satisfaction. We then chatted throughout the meeting about problems of food supplies and about how Communists were running into difficulties . . . ."[8]

The organizational structure of non-communist parties resembles that of the KSČ. Each is organized into four tiers—local, district, regional, and central—and at each level there is a plenary meeting or conference of delegates which elects an executive committee. These committees in turn select their chairmen, secretaries, bureaus, or presidiums. The main working organs are the presidiums on the top and the secretariats on central, regional, and district levels. The executive committees meet from time to time to rubber-stamp what has been done and to approve nominations laid before them. The national party conferences are summoned occasionally and dispose of their meager business with customary unanimity. However, party congresses, which are supposed to be the highest party organs, have not been heard of. It seems that the leaders of non-communist parties prefer to hold conferences of regional or district party delegates rather than bother with the convocation of regular congresses. Occasionally, they also call motley sessions of central executive committees, including party representatives in the National Assembly and functionaries of lower party secretariats.

A notable difference from the organizational pattern of the KSČ is the absence of primary units in factories and other places of work. The non-communist parties do not apply the territorial-productive principle but instead conduct their operations on the lowest level through local organizations created on a territorial basis. Since the over-all membership is so low and is certain to include only a negligible number of industrial workers, the establishment of primary units is well-nigh impossible. Furthermore, it may be doubted that

[8] *ibid.,* I, 6 (August 1954), p. 30.

the Communists would welcome the existence of units from other parties in such a psychologically sensitive locale as the production plant. Nor can the network of local organizations of non-communist parties be very dense. Most probably the basic organs responsible for local operations are the district party secretariats.

Another characteristic feature of the regenerated parties, in view of their small membership, is the high ratio of functionaries to ordinary party members. In fact, the non-communist parties began their satellite careers after the coup of February 1948 as bare skeleton crews of functionaries checked and cleared by the Action Committees. Even after their membership basis had been broadened the heavy overload of functionaries remained. It cannot be otherwise if one operates a four-tier organizational pyramid for only a few thousand members. Moreover, the communist concept of the National Front makes it imperative to assign members of non-communist parties to many functions on all levels of the people's committees and in the people's courts. Hence, the conclusion is inescapable that most of the non-communist party members hold party or other public functions and that an ordinary rank-and-file member without any such function must be a rare figure.

THE LEADERSHIP

The real control of the non-communist parties rests with the chiefs of the KSČ. As stated in an authoritative communist study of the problems of the people's democracy, "The leading role of the communist parties lies primarily in the fact that they work out the political line which constitutes the basis for the activity of the whole mechanism of the people's democratic state, *the other political parties,* and mass organizations."[9] A Czechoslovak college textbook on the theory of the State puts it even more bluntly: ["With the establishment of the people's democracy] the leadership of the Communist Party becomes absolute. This is in no way affected by the fact that the system of several political parties has thus far been preserved. The other political parties do not any longer carry out any particular political line of their own, but take over the general line of socialist construction as determined by the communist parties."[10]

[9] J. Houska and K. Kára, *Otázky lidové demokracie* (Questions of the People's Democracy), Praha, 1955, p. 229. Italics added.
[10] Radim Foustka *et al., Doplňková skripta z theorie státu a práva* (Supplementary Scripts on the Theory of the State and the Law), Praha, 1954, p. 141.

This subjection to the KSČ is openly conceded by the spokesmen of the satellite parties themselves. "Under the leadership of the Communist Party of Czechoslovakia our country grows, strengthens, and develops economically and culturally," read a sycophantic telegram sent by the Chairman and Secretary General of the Czechoslovak Socialist Party to the KSČ on the latter's thirtieth anniversary in 1951. "Today, thanks to the Communist Party of Czechoslovakia, the Czech and Slovak peoples march in the forefront of progressive mankind . . . . The members of the Czechoslovak Socialist Party will express their thanks to the Communist Party of Czechoslovakia by working even harder in order to contribute, under its leadership, to an accelerated construction of socialism in our fatherland, to the strengthening of the Czechoslovak front of peace, and to the deepening of our friendship for the Great Stalin."[11] Similar subservience has been displayed year after year on every suitable occasion by all of the regenerated parties.[12] The greetings which the heads of all four parties delivered in person to the Eleventh Congress of the KSČ in 1958 indulged in the same kind of incense-burning and humble recognition of communist leadership, coupled with customary promises that the members of the four parties "will fulfill with enthusiasm and love all the tasks which will be assigned by the historical Eleventh Congress of the Communist Party of Czechoslovakia."[13]

In full conformity with this master-servant relationship, the "historic decisions and documents" of the Central Committee and other central organs of the KSČ have been the perennial central theme of "discussion" and "enthusiastic approval" in the sessions of the presidiums and central committees of the non-communist parties.[14] Year after year pronouncements of the KSČ leaders have been adopted by the leading organs of each of the non-communist parties as "directives for further work of the party in all its organizational

[11] *Svobodné slovo,* May 17, 1951.

[12] See, for instance, *Svobodné slovo,* February 28 and April 25, 1951, January 6 and February 10, 1953, and April 15, 1960; *Lidová demokracie,* February 13, 1951, August 30, 1956, June 25, 1957, and April 17 and 20, 1960; *L'ud,* April 14, 1953; *Rudé právo,* June 15, 1952, and January 11, 1953; Josef Plojhar, *Vítězný únor a československá strana lidová* (The Victorious February and the Czechoslovak People's Party), Praha, 1958; *O úloze bývalé národně socialistické strany* (On The Role of the Former National Socialist Party), Praha, 1959.

[13] *Rudé právo,* June 19, 1958.

[14] *Lidová demokracie,* June 25, 1957, and October 20, 1959; also, *Československá strana lidová. Pro vítězství míru: úkoly funkcionářů československé strany lidové po X. sjezdu KSČ* (Czechoslovak People's Party. For the Victory of Peace: The Tasks of the Functionaries of the Czechoslovak People's Party after the Tenth Congress of the KSČ), Praha, 1954.

units."[15] The agenda of their presidiums and central committees has included such items as preparations for the "joyful" commemoration of the Republic's liberation by the Red Army, the "Great October Socialist Revolution," and other communist red-letter days, together with commendation of party members who have excelled in the working brigades and collections of scrap materials organized in honor of Stalin's birthday, the anniversary of the Red Army, or similar festive occasions.[16] Fiery protests have been raised against such "attacks on civic freedoms" as the outlawing of the Communist Party in West Germany, the ouster of the World Peace Council from Paris, American "espionage," or "Vatican intrigues" while ringing applause has been bestowed on each and every communist-supported cause and action.[17] As long as Stalin and Gottwald lived, their writings were a compulsory subject of study for all non-communist party functionaries and no opportunity was wasted to swear loyalty and love to Gottwald and to "the best friend of our people and of the workers of the whole world, J. V. Stalin."[18] After Gottwald's death, allegiance was shifted to the new KSČ leadership, although the accompanying panegyrics were toned down in deference to the post-Stalin emphasis on "collective leadership."

Nor has communist guidance been limited to matters of policy and ideology. Ever since the coup of 1948, the KSČ has acted as a self-appointed supreme arbiter even in the purely internal affairs of its non-communist partners in the "regenerated" National Front. For obvious reasons, primary attention has been paid to personnel matters. The leaders and all the main functionaries of the non-communist parties are hand-picked by the KSČ and keep their position only so long as they enjoy its confidence. Since it is in communist interest to provide their transmission belts with a respectable front, the eye-catching top positions have been assigned to persons who had some standing within the respective parties prior to the coup. Although none of the men chosen as chairmen, vice-chairmen, and general secretaries of the three main non-communist parties belonged to the very first line of leadership in pre-communist days, they have been

---

[15] *Svobodné slovo,* February 28, 1951.

[16] *ibid.,* April 25, 1951, November 23, 1958.

[17] *Lidová demokracie,* September 25, October 13 and 14, 1953, August 30, 1956; *Svobodné slovo,* April 25, 1951.

[18] *Rudé právo,* June 15, 1952; see also *Svobodné slovo,* April 25, 1951, November 1, 1951, and January 6, 1953; *L'ud,* December 5, 1952; Emanuel Šlechta, *Klement Gottwald,* Praha, 1954, a sycophantic booklet by the fellow-traveling leader of the Czechoslovak Socialist Party until his death in 1960.

party regulars of some prominence and are rather well-known among the parties' rank and file. That is also the reason why, with the exception of the purged Chairman of the Slovak Renaissance Party, J. Ševčík, they have been kept in their positions year after year. Their durability is probably due as much to their pliability as to the fact that the number of available fellow-travelers who had held party positions of some note in pre-communist days has been steadily shrinking. While non-communist parties are left more discretion in the selection of their lesser functionaries, the communist secretariats on all organizational levels have a veto power against any choice that is not deemed in the KSČ's interest.

Similar powers of control are exercised over the nominations of non-communist party candidates for all public offices and elective functions, such as seats in the National Assembly, on the various people's committees, and judicial bodies. Not once since the 1948 coup have the non-communist parties been allowed to run their own candidates on a competitive basis. As long as the system of large electoral districts was used, they were simply assigned a number of places on the joint slate of candidates of the National Front so that the voters would not be embarrassed at having to decide between two or more such lists. Under the present system of single-member constituencies they are similarly asigned certain electoral districts so that the number of seats which they can thus gain is determined by the KSČ. Since all candidates run under the label of the National Front and their party affiliation is not always known, it is impossible to ascertain accurately the ratios of elective offices that have been reserved for non-communist parties. Of the 300 deputies of the National Assembly elected in the first post-coup parliamentary elections in May 1948 twenty-four could be identified as members of the Czechoslovak Socialist Party, twenty-four as members of the People's Party, eight as belonging to the Slovak Renaissance Party, and five to the Slovak Freedom Party.[19] In the National Assembly elected in 1954 the Czechoslovak Socialist Party had nineteen deputies, the People's Party twenty, the Slovak Renaissance Party five and the Slovak Freedom Party three, as against 226 communist and 55 "nonparty" deputies out of a total number of 368.[20] The corresponding figures for the 300-man National Assembly elected in June 1960 were 15 seats for

[19] *Československý přehled,* IV, 3 (1957), pp. 12ff.
[20] Bedřich Rattinger, *Nejvyšší státní orgány lidově demokratického Československa* (The Highest State Organs of People's Democratic Czechoslovakia), Praha, 1957, p. 29.

the Czechoslovak Socialist Party, 16 seats for the People's Party, 4 for the Slovak Renaissance Party, and 2 for the Slovak Freedom Party.[21] All these data fully corroborate the shabby treatment that the four regenerated parties, which had polled almost 49 percent of the popular vote in the elections of 1946, have suffered at the hands of their communist partners.

Formally, communist guidance and supervisory activities are carried out through the National Front in which the KSČ is but one of the five constituent parties. In practice, however, the committees of the National Front on all levels are dominated by the KSČ as completely as if they were its own subdivisions, which they are for all practical purposes. As reported by those who sat on those committees, the recommendations made by the KSČ's representatives are considered as binding commands which no delegate of the other parties dares to challenge or even question. Thus the "unanimous resolutions of the National Front" are, in fact, communist orders in disguise. "The National Front as a system of political parties and mass organizations, whose important characteristic is the exclusive leadership of the KSČ, is a substantial part of the system of the dictatorship of the proletariat at the present developmental stage of our people's democracy."[22]

The Operational Pattern

This subservience of non-communist parties colors their whole pattern of operations. Its most typical feature is sluggishness and lack of initiative. As a private learns that it is better to await the sergeant's command than to volunteer, so do the organs and members of non-communist parties wait for express instructions from their superiors before tackling any task. In implementing such instructions they do only the minimum that is necessary to keep them out of trouble. They fulfill the directives much better on paper than in actual field work. "Passing the buck" and "eye-washing" are among their most favorite operational devices. Energetic pursuance of prescribed goals seems to be the monopoly of ambitious fellow-travelers on the top and professional overseers planted throughout the structure of the non-communist parties by their communist chiefs.

Their inner-party operations are a somewhat fuzzy copy of the communist model. The relationship between their various organs is

---

[21] *Volksbote* (Munich), June 25, 1960.
[22] J. Houska and K. Kára, *op.cit.*, p. 210.

regulated by a rather diluted version of democratic centralism. As in the case of the KSČ, emphasis is on subordination to party superiors and on the binding character of higher decisions. However, unlike their communist equivalents, the lower units of the non-communist parties have to serve under two chiefs: their own party superiors and also the KSČ's secretariats operating on the same hierarchical levels. Fortunately for them, discrepancy in the respective orders of these two sets of chiefs is likely to occur only on rarest occasions; and if it does, they know that the directive of the KSČ is the one to be given precedence.

Inner-party democracy, which is supposed to permeate the non-communist parties as it does the KSČ, is as inoperative within the former as it is within the latter. In a sense there is probably even less democracy within them. It is a psychological fact that, to prove himself, a fellow-traveler feels the urge to emulate his model by becoming more rigid and "more papal than the Pope himself." Also, the relatively substantial amount of free discussion that exists, especially since Stalin's death, on the topmost level of the KSČ, in its presidium, is denied the corresponding organs of the non-communist parties. Owing their precarious existence to the KSČ and being infested with its spies, the presidiums and central secretariats of the non-communist parties simply cannot afford such a dangerous luxury.

Like the KSČ, non-communist parties are responsible for the proper indoctrination of their members and have the duty to organize party schooling for that purpose. However, their system of schooling is far less elaborate than its communist counterpart. Every year there is a "basic political seminar," consisting of a few lectures on prescribed socialist topics held in lower party units, and special centers set up for that purpose.[23] These lectures are delivered by higher party functionaries and by lecturers trained for the purpose in special courses. Various other political seminars of short duration are held from time to time for more mature members and functionaries.[24] Individual study is also prescribed for senior members, but there does not seem to be much extensive supervisory machinery as there is for similar studies by KSČ members. The topmost level of schooling in non-communist parties is provided by the Central Political Schools. Located in scenic country settings, they offer periodic seminars at-

---

[23] *Svobodné slovo,* November 1, 1951, and January 6, 1953.

[24] *L'ud,* December 5, 1952; *Svobodné slovo,* November 1, 1951, January 6, 1953, and September 18, 1959.

tended by members of the respective parties' presidiums, their M. P.'s, and other high party functionaries. Some of these seminars last as long as two weeks, but usually they are week-end affairs.[25]

The themes and topics dealt with in the various types of party schooling leave no doubt as to their origin or purpose. For instance, the basic political seminar of the Czechoslovak Socialist Party for 1951-1952 consisted of four lectures with the following self-explanatory titles: (1) Victory of socialism in the USSR; (2) Socialism and patriotism; (3) Construction of our economy; (4) The world struggle for peace and socialism.[26] Individual members were supposed to concentrate, in the same school year, on the writings of Klement Gottwald. The main subject matter considered in higher seminars in 1952-1953 was the material of the Nineteenth Congress of the Communist Party of the Soviet Union "and especially the newest, ingenious work of Generalissimo Stalin, *The Economic Problems of Socialism in the USSR*."[27] A summer seminar held in July 1953 for the members of the Presidium of the Czechoslovak Socialist Party, its deputies, and the chairmen of the Party's regional organizations, was devoted mainly to "the evaluation of the life and work of T. G. Masaryk in the light of recently published documents on his antinational and antipopular policies."[28] Another seminar convened in September 1959 discussed "the antisocial policy of the former [Czechoslovak Socialist] Party from its foundation until the Second World War."[29]

Similar conformity characterizes the few periodicals that the non-communist parties are allowed to publish. Whether it is the Czechoslovak Socialist Party's daily *Svobodné slovo* or its weekly ideological magazine *Socialistický směr,* the People's Party's daily *Lidová demokracie,* the Slovak Renaissance Party's *Ľud,* or the Slovak Freedom Party's weekly *Sloboda,* politically they all speak the same language, that of the KSČ. Only in the days of ferment in the wake of the Twentieth Congress of the Soviet Party did some of them venture for a short time to give room to mildly critical voices.[30] This was particularly true of the coverage of the criticism-filled proceedings of the National Congress of Czechoslovak Writers in April 1956.[31] Nevertheless, in spite of their political conformity, two of the non-

[25] *Lidová demokracie,* September 16, 1951, and June 24, 1952; *Svobodné slovo,* September 4, 1951, and January 6, 1953; *Ľud,* December 5, 1952.

[26] *Svobodné slovo,* November 1, 1951.

[27] *Ľud,* December 5, 1952; also, *Svobodné slovo,* January 6, 1953.

[28] *Svobodné slovo,* July 14, 1953.

[29] *ibid.,* September 18, 1959.

[30] *Ľud,* April 18, 1956; *Svobodné slovo,* April 22, 1956.

[31] *Svobodné slovo,* April 25 and 27, 1956; *Lidová demokracie,* April 30, 1956.

communist party papers, *Svobodné slovo* and *Lidová demokracie,* have daily circulations of 120,000, which is about ten times the estimated number of each party's membership. There are two reasons for this sizable circulation: first, the papers are bought, through force of habit, by many former members of these parties who either failed to be cleared for membership after the communist coup or did not want to join the post-coup caricatures of their former parties; and, second, the two papers carry more news on sports and nonpolitical variety items than their communist equivalents, which makes them at least slightly more palatable to the general reader than the stern official Communist Party papers.

In one respect, the drafting of their party platforms, the operations of non-communist parties are simplicity itself. Since their political motto is that what is good for the Communist Party is good for them and for the nation, their leaders have little trouble devising party objectives, formulating basic political principles, and putting them into proper verbal setting. They simply reach for the proceedings of the latest session of the Central Committee of the KSČ, mix in a few paragraphs of their own, carefully patterned after some recent editorials of *Rudé právo* and other communist periodicals, and present this twice predigested Red goulash to the plenary sessions of their presidiums or central executive committees. After a discussion in which the discussants vie with one another in a public display of gratitude for the wise leadership of the Communist Party, the session accepts unanimously their leaders' statement as "a binding directive for the work of all the functionaries and members of the party, as the fundamental political and ideological line for further work."[32]

THE RAISON D'ETRE

Since the regenerated parties may not develop any programs of their own, let alone compete with the KSČ for political power, they constitute no threat to communist leadership under present circumstances. However, the very presence of parties other than the Communist in a country governed under the Marxist-Leninist concept of the dictatorship of the proletariat invites the question why these parties are allowed to exist at all. After all, even in their present mutilated form, they remain one of the very few institutional links with the pre-communist past. Two of them, the Czechoslovak Socialist Party and the People's Party, have played a prominent role under

[32] *Lidová demokracie,* June 25, 1957.

substantially the same names not only during the twilight of freedom in 1945-1948, but also in the Masaryk Republic which the Communists seek so persistently to smear. Both had been among communism's staunchest opponents. Moreover, one of them still carries the word "socialist" in its name and thus offers, at least nominally, an alternative to the socialism represented by the KSČ, a phenomenon which is not duplicated anywhere else within the Soviet orbit. From the point of view of strict Marxist-Leninist logic such parties have no place in a system ruled in the name of Lenin. Their continued retention seems to be motivated mainly by two reasons, one of a theoretical and one of a practical nature.

The theoretical justification of this anomaly rests on the postwar amendment of the original Leninist teaching on the transition from capitalism to communism. While previously this transition had been viewed in terms of two successive stages of socialism and pure communism, another stage, or substage, has been added after World War II: that of a "people's democracy" as a preliminary to the Soviet-type socialist stage. One of the distinguishing features of this "people's democratic" stage of "socialist construction" seems to be that noncommunist puppet parties may be permitted to function. This doctrinal innovation was made to measure for the Czechoslovak Communists whose theory of the February revolution rests upon the assertion that only small groups of treacherous leaders of the other parties conspired against Gottwald's legitimate government, while the majority of their rank and file stood with the Communists on the side of the people. Hence, the correct policy was not to liquidate the noncommunist parties, but to "regenerate" them and to replace their "wicked reactionary leaders" by those who were prepared to abide by the "will of the people."

On the practical side, the KSČ leaders hope that at least some of their subjects may be beguiled by the ostentatious spectacle of several non-communist parties collaborating with their communist partners. The partnership with the Catholic People's Party, led by the "patriotic priest" Plojhar, is used to prove how untrue are the accusations that the Communists persecute religion. The so-called documentary evidence about Masaryk's and Beneš's antipopular activities is deemed to be more persuasive when such opinions are voiced by the leaders of Beneš's former party.[33] Similarly, the KSČ leaders con-

---

[33] See the discussion on V. Široký's report to the National Assembly in April 1953, *Československý přehled*, IV, 4 (1957), p. 7.

sider it more tactical if the leading spokesmen of the non-communist parties themselves, rather than the Communists, attack the treacherous former leaders of their own parties who have escaped to the West and work to convert Czechoslovakia "into an economic-military base for the struggle of Western imperialism against socialism and peace . . . ."[34] Also, it is in the best interest of the KSČ if members of non-communist parties take part in such "building tasks" as inducing peasants to join the collective farms and workers to participate in socialist contests, volunteering for working brigades, making people join the Union of Soviet–Czechoslovak Friendship or enroll in courses in the Russian language.[35]

Thus there are a number of ways in which KSČ leaders can and do use non-communist parties in the furtherance of the communist cause and to "draw the more backward strata of the petty bourgeoisie into the construction of socialism."[36] They are well aware of the fact that they cannot convince older members of these parties that pulling chestnuts out of the fire for the Communists is their parties' proper vocation, but they hope that they may befuddle some who are too young to have had party experience in pre-communist days. Some reports from Czechoslovakia indicate that the communist leaders have not been altogether without success in that respect, at least in the negative sense of eliciting an impression that this is how parties normally behave.[37]

PROBLEMS AND PROSPECTS

Although the regenerated parties have been operating with apparent smoothness under the patronizing wing and watchful eye of the KSČ, they have had their share of difficulties. As auxiliaries of the KSČ they could not remain unaffected by the dilemmas plaguing their mentor, and they have been suffering from many of the same troubles afflicting the KSČ. Many of the notorious villains that have infiltrated the KSČ, such as bourgeois nationalism, Masarykism, religious obscurantism, and other "pernicious manifestations of petty-bourgeois ideologies" have obviously found a congenial field of operations within the bodies politic of its National Front partners. Like

[34] *Rudé právo,* February 24, 1951; also, *Lidová demokracie,* February 13, 1951, *Rudé právo,* April 18, 1953.
[35] *Lidová demokracie,* October 20 and May 19, 1953; *L'ud,* July 5, 1951; *Svobodné slovo,* October 6, 1953; *Literární noviny,* November 7, 1953.
[36] Radim Foustka, *op.cit.,* p. 141.
[37] *Československý přehled,* IV, 3 (1957), pp. 13-14.

their colleagues of the KSČ, the members of the non-communist parties have been neglecting party schooling, shirking attendance in Russian language courses and participation in the Union of Soviet–Czechoslovak Friendship, evading their "voluntary" duties in working brigades and *aktivs,* and displaying laxity in self-criticism, class struggle, and anti-*kulak* activities.[38]

The situation grew worse after Stalin's death. The cultivation of the "Geneva spirit," the destruction of the Stalin myth, the thesis of "different roads toward socialism," and other spectacular shifts of the post-Stalin era naturally have led many non-communist party members to believe that the time has come when their parties should regain at least a part of their erstwhile independence. While their leaders, fearful of what any such change would do to their personal fortunes, continued as servile as usual, signs of ferment have begun to appear among the parties' rank and file. Some of their members have come to believe that the National Front could fulfill its mission without the leadership of the Communist Party and to play with an idea, based upon "an incorrect interpretation of developments in other people's democracies," of replacing the National Front by "a coalition of parties."[39] The over-all temper of the ordinary members of non-communist parties has been well characterized by the following report from Czechoslovakia: "On the whole, one can say that perhaps 95 percent of the party are against the regime, even those who have functions in the people's committees. Mostly, these members do not feel like new, but like old party members. The remaining 5 percent of the membership are people who have been sent into the party either by the National Front to assume leading positions or those who have sold themselves out to the regime."[40]

Evidently, the regenerated parties have not turned out according to communist expectations. They carry out, under strict communist supervision, the functions for which they have been allowed to exist, but they do so half-heartedly and as inefficiently as circumstances permit. While their functionaries publicly profess loyalty to the KSČ and the Kremlin, most of the membership would turn against the communist rulers the moment they could see a realistic chance of success. In that respect they are tacit allies of communism's own revisionists. Nor can the KSČ rulers place too much trust in the

---

[38] *Lidová demokracie,* May 19, 1953.
[39] *Rudé právo,* November 30, 1955, and March 19, 1957.
[40] *Československý přehled,* IV, 3 (1957), p. 13.

leaders of non-communist parties, no matter how obsequiously they may behave. I personally knew some of them prior to their "regeneration" and learned about the mentality of others from those who knew them well. On this basis I can say that none of those who have assumed the leadership of non-communist parties following the February coup of 1948 have rallied behind the communist cause because of inner convictions. They have become fellow-travelers out of sheer personal opportunism, mixed here and there with a tiny dose of wishful and self-righteous belief that they are saving what can be saved. When they embarked on the sinuous road of collaborationism with the Communists in 1948, and in some instances even earlier than that, they did not anticipate how far they would have to go. They did not realize that the KSČ leaders, pressed in their turn by the Kremlin, would never be satisfied until they had reduced their collaborators to a state of total abjectness and made them, as Shakespeare's dictum goes, hold the candle to their shames. By now they have sunk too deeply in the mire to cherish any hope that a defeat of communism would not bury them under the debris. With their personal fortunes tied so inextricably to the continued existence of communist rule, they have little choice but to go on dragging the communist chariot. On that account their masters need have no worries so long as they hold the reins firmly in their hands. But should the communist regime begin to totter, such fellow-travelers might well seek to save their skins by changing sides. Who betrays once finds it easy to betray again.

Thus the triple relationship of the KSČ, regenerated non-communist party leaders, and their members is a grand scheme of multiple pretense. The rank and file of the non-communist parties pretend loyalty to their party leaders, to the KSČ, and to the Soviets, while in reality they dislike them all. The leaders of the KSČ and of the non-communist parties feign to accept this bogus loyalty for real, although they know better. The regenerated leaders of non-communist parties in turn sham devotion to communism in front of the KSČ superiors as well as before their own party members, both of whom behave as if they took such simulations at their face value. And the whole show is performed again and again before a captive audience of the whole nation which pretends to believe that what the actors say and do stems from their genuine convictions. It all resembles Hans Christian Andersen's famous fairy tale about the Emperor who walked naked through the streets while his subjects pretended to see him dressed and to admire his nonexistent costume, except that the innocent child who shattered the pretense in the fairy tale is not allowed to spoil the tragicomic spectacle in Czechoslovakia.

This being so, one might wonder how much longer this fantastic pretense will be continued. From what has been said above on the *raison d'être* of non-communist parties, it is clear that they are intended to be only temporary devices which will be eliminated when no longer needed. Since the pace of the construction of socialism has been notably accelerated in recent years and its impending completion has been proclaimed, it would seem that the non-communist parties will soon be approaching their end and will share the fate that has befallen their fellow-traveling sisters throughout most of the Soviet orbit.[41] The amended electoral law of 1960 has already dropped any mention of the non-communist parties from its new definition of the National Front. The previous electoral law of 1954 listed the Czechoslovak Socialist Party, the Czechoslovak People's Party, the Slovak Renaissance Party, and the Freedom Party as constituent parts of the National Front. On the other hand, the new law refers to the National Front only as a grouping "associating, under the leadership of the Communist Party of Czechoslovakia, the social organizations of the working people."[42] Although the new formula is broad enough to accommodate non-communist parties, it need not be changed one iota once the KSČ leaders decide to administer to their non-communist National Front partners the eventual *coup de grâce*.

The only thing that could avert this inglorious end would be a radical change of circumstances, such as that which took place in the first days of the abortive Hungarian uprising of 1956 or in Poland in the months following that country's October Revolution. Should such a situation develop, and not be upset by a Soviet intervention, there can be little doubt that the first thing the rank and file of the non-communist parties would want to do would be to get rid of their unworthy leaders and open their parties' ranks to ex-members left outside after 1948 and to the new blood needed to rejuvenate them. The process of "un-regeneration" would thus set in without delay and, unless checked by superior forces of renewed coercion, would quickly tip the scales in favor of the non-communist parties.

[41] See Novotný's speech at the Eleventh Party Congress, *Rudé právo,* June 19, 1958.

[42] See Section 21 of Law No. 37 of April 9, 1960.

PART TWO

THE TRANSMISSION BELTS OF
FORMAL GOVERNMENT

CHAPTER VIII

THE CONSTITUTIONAL FRAMEWORK

Two CONSTITUTIONS were enacted by the communist regime of Czechoslovakia within the period covered in the present volume: the Ninth-of-May Constitution of 1948 and the new Soviet-type Constitution of 1960. The constitutions of communist-dominated countries are, of course, anything but binding fundamental laws in the Western sense. Nevertheless, the difference between the two documents symbolizes well the extent to which Czechoslovakia's political institutions have been sovietized in the course of the twelve years that separate the Ninth-of-May Constitution from its 1960 successor.

CONSTITUTIONALISM—COMMUNIST STYLE

Whenever constitutions of dictatorial systems are considered, especially those of totalitarian communism, the student invariably is forced to ask why the rulers care to have any written constitution at all. Their power is absolute. All decisions of any importance are made within the supreme Party conclave and its underlings are in control of everything in every part of the country and in every segment of life. Why, then, do they bother with the formality of a fundamental law? Why do they insist on limiting their own powers, even though only nominally, by elaborate systems of constitutional prescriptions and restrictions that are protected legally—as in non-communist constitutions—against easy amendment?

The reasons underlying the Czechoslovak communist philosophy of constitutionalism are much the same as in the Soviet Union and in other people's democracies. It is one of the basic maxims of Marxist-Leninist teaching on the relations between the Party and the State that the Party makes policy, that it guides and controls but does not directly carry out its decisions.[1] For that purpose the Party maintains a machinery of government separate from the Party apparatus

---

[1] *Vsesoiuznaia Kommunisticheskaia Partia (b) v rezoliutsiakh i resheniakh s'ezdov, konferentsii i plenumov Ts. K. 1898-1935* (The All-Union Communist Party [B] in Resolutions and Decisions of the Congresses, Conferences, and Plenums of the C.C. 1898-1935), Moscow, 1936, I, pp. 314-315.

and continues to maintain it until the State "withers away." Thus a constitution performs a useful function in formalizing the complex system of levers and transmission belts through which the dictatorship of the proletariat operates. Similarly, it suits the favorite communist will-of-the-people machinations. No political system misuses the concept of popular sovereignty more than the regime of Marxism-Leninism, and its Czechoslovak variety is no exception to the rule. "The people are the master in this country. The people, liberated politically, socially, and economically, attain thus through the new Constitution a permanent guarantee of their full and real freedom." "In the Czechoslovak Republic the people are the only sovereign and the Constitution has no other sense but to uphold the fullest sovereignty of the people in all spheres of social life." "The new Constitution guarantees that the will of the people will henceforth be the law in our country."[2] So spoke the three communist front-benchers, including Gottwald himself, when they recommended the adoption of the Ninth-of-May Constitution. Both the Ninth-of-May Constitution and the new Constitution of 1960 are replete with references to the "people." As in the American Constitution, the introductory "We-the-People" formula is used and "the people" or "the working people" are designated as the sole source of all power. The effort to create an illusion that the Communists alone are the true servants of the people worthy of complete confidence is probably the main reason for having a constitution.

By the same token, the existence of a fundamental law, dressed up in polished juristic forms and interspersed with echoes of the democratic past, is designed to conjure up the aura of legitimacy which the communist rulers of Czechoslovakia seem to covet more than their colleagues elsewhere behind the Iron Curtain. That was especially so in 1948 when, desiring to break with the past as painlessly as possible, they went head-over-heels in their endeavor to present themselves to the public as the incarnation of the best in Czechoslovakia's political past.

Nor were the desire and the need to attain the smoothest possible transition to the new era of the dictatorship of the proletariat the sole communist motivation. The Czechoslovak Communists have never been as bitter an enemy of Western parliamentarism as Lenin had been. Gottwald and his associates aimed at the heart of Czechoslovak

---

[2] *Ústava devátého května* (The Ninth-of-May Constitution), Praha, 1948, pp. 15, 18-19, 23.

democracy and, without its destruction, their victory could not have been attained. But they were in no way prejudiced against the retention of modern parliamentarism's outward forms with which they became familiar through years of experience in the country's parliamentary institutions both prior to and after World War II.

THE NINTH-OF-MAY CONSTITUTION

Guided by such mixed constitutional concepts the communist constitution-makers produced in their first Constitution of 1948 a unique specimen *sui generis* which had no equal within the Soviet-controlled orbit. It was an elaborate hybrid, a combination of Western parliamentarism with sovietism. This was stated by the Communists themselves. "Our new Constitution will contain two component parts," explained the official commentary. "The older one is taken over from the first Constitution [of 1920] insofar as its provisions meet present conditions. The other part is quite new and is based on the achievements of the national and democratic revolution of 1944 and 1945."[3] These two mutually uncongenital elements, the leftovers of the Western democratic past and the new transplants from the East, vied with each other on many pages of the Ninth-of-May Constitution.

The Western Elements

The Western elements came to the forefront mainly in the retention of the parliamentary form of government; in the relative leniency of its economic clauses; and in some of the provisions in the field of civil rights and the judiciary.

THE RETENTION OF THE PARLIAMENTARY SYSTEM. No part of the Ninth-of-May Constitution showed less dependence on the Soviet model than that dealing with the legislative and executive branches of government. It did not adopt the Soviet pattern of a plural chief executive, which conferred upon the legislature the right to appoint and remove ministers and abolished the executive prerogative of parliamentary dissolution. On the contrary, the people's democratic Czechoslovakia of 1948-1960 retained in her Ninth-of-May Constitution all the features of the classical parliamentary system that had been enacted, after the Western European fashion, by the "bourgeois" Constitution of 1920. The only change of any substance which

---

[3] *ibid.*, p. 104.

the Communists made in the executive-legislative system of pre-communist days was the abolition of the senate and the creation of a unicameral legislature. But the latter was not a specifically communistic postulate. There was general belief in Czechoslovakia after the War that two chambers, which would be politically almost identical, were an unnecessary luxury. Thus, unlike Moscow's other satellites (except East Germany), communist Czechoslovakia continued to provide in her constitutional system for a single President of the Republic clothed with all the usual rights and prerogatives of a Head of State listed in most Western constitutions. She also preserved the typical parliamentary principle of political nonresponsibility of the Head of State, as well as the ministerial countersignature and the responsibility of the Cabinet for presidential acts.

This political rarity was all the more striking if viewed against the general trend of constitutional developments in the Soviet orbit. Yugoslavia, Albania, and Bulgaria adopted the usual type of people's democratic constitutions after the Soviet fashion from the very start: that is, as soon as they had been liberated and had drafted their very first postwar constitutions in the years 1945-1947. Rumania followed the line when her conversion to a full-fledged People's Democracy was completed by the dethronement of King Michael in 1948. Hungary scrapped her 1946 Constitution in 1949 and adopted a new one patterned after the constitutions of the Balkan group. Poland followed suit in 1952 and replaced her Little Constitution of 1947, which had preserved large parts of the Polish Constitution of 1921, by a new fundamental law which closely resembles the Balkan prototype. In a contrary manner, the "Judas" Tito has restored individual Presidency in Yugoslavia following his split with Stalin, and thus has put an even worse stigma on that bourgeois institution in the eyes of orthodox Communists.

Considering these developments, one would have assumed that it would not be long before Czechoslovakia had to join the rest of the satellite family and discard the Ninth-of-May Constitution in favor of one which would be more people's democratic and would do away with the remnants of bourgeois-capitalist influences. In fact, indications came from Czechoslovakia on several occasions that such a change was being contemplated. According to one such report in 1949 some members of the Party's legal commission expressed the opinion that Czechoslovakia ought not to wait until the suggestion came from the Cominform, but should remodel her Constitution on her own initiative.[4] The commission reportedly intended to bring the matter before the Party leaders, but nothing happened. Neither the Hungarian nor the Polish example prompted the Czechoslovak rulers to redesign their constitutional system after the prevalent satellite pattern.

It was generally believed that the Czechoslovak failure to follow the pattern in this respect had something to do with Gottwald. The first communist President of Czechoslovakia was known to be deeply in love with the presidential office. Much more important, the combination of number-one Party position with the traditional prestige of the Republic's Presidency represented a highly valuable political asset of which Gottwald was well aware. Moreover, the Czechoslovak situation was further complicated by the fact that the two highest governmental offices, the Presidency of the Republic and the Premiership, were held by the two top men of the Party, Gottwald and Zápotocký, respectively. When Hungary abolished the Presidency, no problem could arise as to what to do with its incumbent, the fellow-traveling Social Democrat Szakasits, who had no political importance. Similarly, when Poland followed suit in 1952, it was relatively simple to ease out another fellow-traveling former Social Democrat, Cyrankiewicz, from the Premiership to make room for the Party's leader, Bierut, who lost his presidential office in the reorganization. But Zápotocký was neither Szakasits nor Cyrankiewicz. He was the co-founder of the KSČ and the native Communist who had probably contributed most to the success of the communist coup in 1948. After the purge of Rudolf Slánský in 1951 he rose to the number-two position in the Party. Hence, the question of what to do with Zápotocký should Gottwald move from the abolished Presidency to the Premiership would have been more complicated than either the Hungarian or the Polish reshuffle.

Gottwald's death in March 1953 solved this dilemma and offered a unique opportunity for the long overdue constitutional change. However, contrary to all expectations, the opportunity was allowed to slip by. Within one week after Gottwald's death Antonín Zápotocký was elected to succeed him as President of Czechoslovakia. Obviously, Zápotocký could not resist the temptation of moving "up the hill" to the historic quarters of the Kings of Bohemia and Presidents of Czechoslovakia. That he could have done this was due to a double stroke of fortune. Not only did he manage to outlive his predecessor,

---

[4] See *Zpráva o Československu*, III, 2 (1952), p. 19.

although he was years older than Gottwald, but fate played into his hand when the death of Gottwald followed the death of Joseph Stalin. Had Gottwald passed away while Stalin was still alive, the Soviet Dictator might have used the occasion to prevail upon Czechoslovak Communists to eliminate that bourgeois office and thus bring the Czechoslovak political system more closely into line with that of the other satellites. Stalin's death turned the whole attention of his heirs for a while to their own internal problems and bade them exercise caution and restraint in dealing with the satellites. Prudence itself counseled against any drastic changes in those uncertain days following Stalin's death. Capitalizing on this double stroke of fortune, Zápotocký attained the unexpected. He became the second communist President of Czechoslovakia.

Still, the general belief continued to persist that this was to be an exceptional arrangement made for Zápotocký and that he was going to be the last of the presidential species in Czechoslovakia. Once again, however, such expectations proved to be false. When Zápotocký died in November 1957, yet another first-rate opportunity for the abandonment of the parliamentary system was by-passed and a third "worker" President of Czechoslovakia was elected in the person of the Party's First Secretary, Antonín Novotný.

Thus the single-head Presidency and the parliamentary system displayed an amazing durability in communist Czechoslovakia and survived all the persistent rumors predicting their impending doom. With the succession of three communist presidents it would seem that a certain constitutional tradition developed which the communist rulers of Czechoslovakia were eager to preserve in spite of its uniqueness within the family of Soviet satellites. Held formerly by such giants as Thomas Masaryk and Eduard Beneš, the Presidency had acquired in Czechoslovakia a stature and a value, both symbolic and political, beyond and above those accruing to similar institutions in other parliamentary regimes. Hence, while heaping abuse on the heads of Masaryk and Beneš, the KSČ was anxious to appropriate for itself the prestige that had surrounded the Presidency in earlier days.

OTHER DEVIATIONS FROM THE SOVIET PATTERN. While the formal retention of the parliamentary system was the most striking Western element in the Ninth-of-May Constitution, there were several other notable departures from the Soviet pattern. In the chapter on civil rights, protection was provided against arbitrary arrest by a prescription that "a written warrant granted by a judge" must be served "at the time of the arrest or, if this is not possible, within 48 hours thereafter." The press could not be subjected to preliminary censorship "as a rule." Although the right "to be without denomination" was specifically protected along with public and private profession of religious worship, any mention of "antireligious propaganda" after the fashion of the Soviet Constitution was carefully avoided. Unlike the Soviet fundamental law and its satellite equivalents, protection of private ownership was also listed, although in communist philosophy rights pertaining to private property figure well below such other citizens' rights as the right to work, education, and equality. Moreover, in allowing expropriation "only on the basis of the law and upon payment of compensation, except in cases where the law shall prescribe that no compensation be given," the Ninth-of-May Constitution paraphrased almost verbatim a similar provision of the bourgeois Constitution of 1920. Such use of libertarian phraseology of the twenties was apparent throughout the whole chapter on civil rights.

Nominal reflections of the democratic past appeared also in the chapter on the judiciary, which contained a number of provisions that were absent in the Soviet and other people's democratic constitutions. It began with the restatement of the classical maxim of the democratic judicial systems that "no one shall be withheld from his lawful judge." In line with the time-honored doctrine of the separation of powers it stipulated that "the judiciary shall in all instances be separated from the administration." It protected civilians from being subjected to the authority of military courts by limiting such extension of military jurisdiction only to "time of war or national emergency, and only in respect of acts committed in such a time." It buttressed the principle of judicial independence by prescribing, as had its democratic predecessor, that judges "shall always be appointed permanently" and that they "may be transferred, dismissed, or pensioned against their will only in cases of a reorganization of the judiciary for a limited period prescribed by law, or by virtue of a valid disciplinary finding." It recognized the principle that the State and the judge were liable "in respect of damages arising out of a violation of the law committed by the judge in the discharge of his office."

Finally, a few but rather spectacular deviations from the Soviet model appeared in the chapter on national economy, although that was the field most likely to be patterned after the Soviet model. In contrast to its Soviet counterpart, the Ninth-of-May Constitution permitted private ownership of land up to fifty hectares, which was not strictly small-holding under Czechoslovak conditions. Similarly, it allowed even "the means and instruments of production" to be in private ownership of individual producers and guaranteed private ownership of "small and medium enterprises of up to fifty employees." Thus it implicitly sanctioned private employment of labor, which falls under the odious heading of exploitation of man by man in the communist dictionary.

The Eastern Elements

The Eastern elements of the Ninth-of-May Constitution came to the fore mainly in the political Declaration that served as its preamble and in the chapter on the economic system and local government. But they penetrated also into other parts of the Constitution, especially those dealing with civil rights and the judiciary.

CONSTITUTIONALIZATION OF HISTORICAL DISTORTIONS. Nowhere in the Ninth-of-May Constitution were the Eastern elements more numerous than in its preamble; and nowhere was historical truth more distorted to show that all good things were coming Czechoslovakia's way from the East. It was the Great October Socialist Revolution that "inspired" the Czechs and the Slovaks to create an independent Czechoslovakia in 1918. It was "the great example of the revolutionary struggle of the Russian workers and peasants" that made them "long for a better social order, for socialism," but this "progressive endeavor . . . was brought to naught by the numerically weak section of capitalists and landowners." Again, in 1938 it was the Czechoslovak bourgeoisie that "allied itself in the time of greatest peril with the enemy against the people and thus enabled world imperialism to settle its differences, albeit temporarily, at the expense of both our nations [Czechs and Slovaks] by the shameful Munich Pact." The struggle for liberation was won in 1945 "with the aid of the Allies, above all the great Slav Power, the Union of Soviet Socialist Republics" and "brought to a victorious conclusion in the liberation of Praha by the Red Army." Naturally, the February coup of 1948 was portrayed as a democratic revolution won against the evil endeavors of domestic and foreign reaction and as "a continuation of the progressive and humanitarian tradition of our history."

In their genuflections toward the East the communist constitution-makers even reached deep into the Middle Ages. Alluding to the earliest endeavors of the Greek missionaries Constantine and Methodius to introduce Christianity into the area, they stressed the point that the Czechs and Slovaks "jointly accepted from the East the highest achievement of the culture of that era—Christianity." But they conveniently forgot that the efforts of the two brothers were soon to yield to the work of Christian missionaries from the Southwest. They also drew into the picture the reformist Hussite movement of the fifteenth century, laying a rather excessive and one-sided emphasis on its "ideals of liberty of thought, government of the people, and social justice" as if its mainspring and *raison d'être* had not been the quest for the purity of the church and deeper religious fervor.

THE ECONOMIC SYSTEM. That the economic clauses of the Ninth-of-May Constitution bore a definite Moscow-made label was perfectly natural. The nationalization of all major economic enterprises had already been sanctioned by both the Communists and the majority of non-communists in 1945 and undoubtedly responded at that time to the predominant will of the Czechoslovak people. It had been carried out prior to the adoption of the Ninth-of-May Constitution. Hence, when it came to the constitutional anchoring of the new system, it was only logical to look for guidance to the country which had had the longest experience with a socialist economy. Like its Soviet model, the Ninth-of-May Constitution denoted three types of ownership: national (State), cooperative, and private. It enumerated the categories of means of production that were exclusively within national ownership, but left the door open for nationalization in other fields as well. However, unlike the Stalin Constitution, it failed to list land as an exclusive state property. It provided for an all-embracing Uniform Economic Plan through which the government directed all economic activity and imposed on all persons and bodies corporate the duty to adapt their economic activities to the Plan. Laying the constitutional groundwork for innumerable prosecutions for violations of the sacrosanct Economic Plan, it made it "the duty of every one who is allotted any task whatever in the operation and implementation of the Uniform Economic Plan to carry out the said tasks conscientiously and economically to the best of his personal and economic capacity."

THE LOCAL SOVIETS. Another major Eastern import was the provisions concerning the people's committees. Devised by Gottwald and his associates in the latter part of the War as replicas of the soviets of the USSR, they were forced upon the reluctant Beneš who signed the decree providing for their establishment while he was still in

London in 1944. The people's committees, like the Russian soviets of 1917, were under communist control and played a prominent part during the vital first stage of the communist conquest of Czechoslovakia in 1945. They became general organs of public administration on all levels of local government and were affirmed as such by the Ninth-of-May Constitution. More than any other people's democratic institution they were supposed to evoke the illusion of broad self-government, and the constitutional phraseology that enveloped them was couched with that primary purpose in mind. "In discharging their tasks," the Constitution asserted, "the people's committees shall lean on the direct participation and initiative of the people and shall be subject to the control of the people." In their oath of office all members of the people's committees had to pledge their loyalty to the people. They were also held "accountable to the people for their activity" and an Act was promised to prescribe "the manner in which the people shall exercise this control and carry into effect the said responsibility." On the other hand, while talking of "effective decentralization of the entire public administration," the Ninth-of-May Constitution provided for a stiff subordination of the people's committees to superior organs. It copied its Soviet model in decreeing that "a people's committee of a lower instance shall be subordinated to a people's committee of a higher instance," and all of them "shall be subordinated to the organs of governmental and executive power, in particular the Ministry of the Interior." Also, it left all the people's committees completely at the mercy of the central government by stating that "a people's committee may be dissolved, in particular where it does not discharge its duties or where its activity endangers the proper operation of the public administration."

DILUTION OF THE BILL OF RIGHTS. The Bill of Rights of the Ninth-of-May Constitution was heavily loaded with Soviet-style additions and exclusions, although, more often than not, it used the democratic wording of the 1920 Constitution. In line with the Soviet example, political rights were supplemented with social rights, such as the right to work, to leisure, to just remuneration for work, and to protection of health. While the inclusion of these social rights in the Constitution proper was generally welcomed by the populace, that could not be said of other Eastern admixtures which took the heart out of most of the freedoms so solemnly guaranteed by the Constitution. While arrest could occur only upon warrant issued by a judge, the only protection offered a person taken into custody by a public functionary was that the detained person was to be brought within 48 hours before "such authority as may be competent, according to the nature of the case, to deal with it further." Warrants authorizing searches were to be issued not only by a judge but also by other "competent authority." The constitutional guarantee of freedom of the press was virtually nullified by a provision that left the state to decide who should publish periodicals, and under what conditions, as well as to determine "the manner of the planned direction of the issue and distribution of nonperiodical publications." Nor was the situation made any better by the monopoly conferred upon the State in the field of motion pictures, television, and broadcasting. Save for the rather insignificant right to petition, the exercise of civil rights was subject to further definition or regulation by the laws to be issued. Thus the Ninth-of-May Constitution created in its Bill of Rights only a bare skeleton and left it to the communist-dominated National Assembly to decide how much muscle and sinew were to be added to make it operative.

The communist constitution-makers added to the Bill of Rights five sections dealing with the fundamental duties of the citizen toward the State and the Community. They made it a constitutional duty of every citizen not only to be loyal to the Republic, to uphold the Constitution, and obey any call to the defense of the State, but also to "observe in all his actions the interests of the State," "to assist in the maintenance and furtherance of national property and to guard against its being diminished or damaged." They balanced the right to work with a duty to work and "to contribute by his work to the common weal." And they left the door wide open for the imposition of other personal duties by stating that "public authority may demand personal services only on the basis of the law."

Finally, lest the Bill of Rights be misunderstood, they added to it an ominous, broadly phrased warning that "statements and acts that constitute a threat to the independence, entirety, and unity of the State, the Constitution, the Republican form of government, and the People's Democratic Order are punishable according to law" and that "the misuse of civil rights and liberties to such ends is inadmissible." As if all this were not enough, they provided, in a clause so elastic that it could be stretched ad libitum, for a further restriction of citizens' rights and liberties in time of war and "when events occur that threaten in increased measure the independence, entirety, and unity of the State, the Constitution, the Republican form of government, and the People's Democratic Order, or public law and order."

OTHER TRANSPLANTS FROM THE EAST. There were other Soviet derivatives scattered through the Ninth-of-May Constitution. It adopted the system of lay assessors to sit, with equal vote, with professional judges and established grounds for their recall. Going even beyond the Soviet constitutional pattern, it imposed on all judges the obligation to abide not only by laws but also by government ordinances, and thus did away with one of the key functions of a democratic judiciary, the judge's right to lay aside rulings of executive authority that did not accord with legislative enactments. As in the Soviet system, the binding interpretation of the laws and the decision as to whether an Act was contrary to the Constitution were vested in the Presidium of the National Assembly. Also, the Ninth-of-May Constitution established a state monopoly in the field of education by decreeing that "all schools shall be state schools" and by conferring upon the State the supreme direction and supervision of all education and instruction.

Eastern Interpretation Behind a Western Façade

Thus the Ninth-of-May Constitution was a Janus-like creature with one face turned toward the East and the other looking nostalgically to the West. Considering the circumstances under which it was adopted, it was a remarkably moderate document. Having just overcome their opponents and acquired absolute power within the country, the communist leaders could have promulgated a full-fledged Soviet-style constitution. Instead, for the reasons mentioned above, they displayed an unusual restraint and created a fundamental law in which the Western elements clearly predominated over the transplants from the East. While there were loopholes that vitiated the value of many of the Constitution's guarantees, especially in the field of civil rights, there were relatively few positive provisions that could be said to infringe *per se* upon the basic principles of democratic rule. Indeed, had the KSČ's monopoly of power been broken and genuine noncommunist parties taken over the reins of government while the Ninth-of May Constitution was in force, not too many changes would have been needed to make it serve reasonably well as the fundamental law of a new democracy.

The worst violation of democracy was in the over-all intent of the Ninth-of-May Constitution, in its interpretation, and in the way in which it was applied by the communist leaders, rather than in the letter of the Constitution. The spirit in which the Constitution was to be understood and applied was revealed by Gottwald himself on the very day of its adoption. "The choice of the ninth of May, 1948, for the adoption of the new Constitution by the Constituent Assembly is not a mere coincidence," he said addressing the Assembly. "Today it is three years since the famous Soviet army completed the defeat of Hitlerite Germany and liberated Praha from the German occupants. There is a *deep inner connection* between that great liberating action of the Soviet army and our new Constitution."[5] The ominous emphasis on the significance of that day, which symbolizes Czechoslovakia's inclusion in the Soviet orbit, was also a clear indication of the manner in which the Ninth-of-May Constitution was to be used. So was the notice served by the official commentary to the Constitution that its introductory Declaration, replete with incense-burning to the East and with gross distortions of historical truth, was to be "the most important tool of the new Constitution's interpretation."[6]

THE NEW SOCIALIST CONSTITUTION OF 1960

Despite the perennial rumors predicting its impending end, the Ninth-of-May Constitution remained in force for more than twelve years. It was not until the fall of 1959 that the KSČ leaders decided to replace it with a new fundamental law.[7] On April 19, 1960, the draft of the new Constitution was published as a special supplement to the Party's daily, *Rudé právo,* as well as other dailies. After a "nation-wide discussion" it was approved without dissent by a national Party conference, summoned for that purpose in July 1960, and passed with the customary unanimity by the National Assembly on July 11, 1960.[8]

The basic reason for the replacement of the Ninth-of-May Constitution with the new "socialist" Constitution of 1960 stems from the regime's claim of a "virtual completion of socialist construction" in Czechoslovakia. "Socialism has won in our country," proclaims the preamble to the new Constitution. "We have entered upon a new stage of our history and determined to proceed to new and higher goals. In completing the socialist construction we are moving on toward the construction of a mature socialist society and gathering forces for

---

[5] *Ústava devátého května,* p. 22. Italics added.
[6] *ibid.,* p. 115.
[7] *Rudé právo,* November 5, 1959.
[8] Constitutional law No. 100 of July 11, 1960, and *Rudé právo,* July 12 and 13, 1960.

the transition to communism." In line with the communist concept of the nature and the role of the Constitution, such a shift from one developmental stage to another calls for a corresponding change in the formal constitutional framework. As explained by a member of the commission for the preparation of the new Constitution, "We do not consider the Constitution to be a declaration of principles that stand above time and space. We consider it a document closely related to the life of society and to its stage of development."[9]

In the twelve years of communist control totalitarian reality had indeed outgrown the comparatively moderate clauses of the Ninth-of-May Constitution. By 1958-1960 many of its provisions were so much at variance with actual conditions of life under the dictatorship of the proletariat that something had to be done about it. Otherwise, the Constitution would have become an object of disrespect and ridicule even among the Party's faithful and would have lost all its indoctrination value. Thus a pressing practical necessity combined with theoretical motivation in favor of constitutional change. Finally, there had been for some time a growing feeling among Party chieftains and their lieutenants that the Ninth-of-May Constitution was so badly out of step with the general constitutional pattern prevalent within the Soviet orbit that remedial measures were imperative.

Thus the decision made in 1959 to prepare a new constitution was by no means unexpected. Nor was there the slightest doubt that it would gravitate considerably more toward the Soviet model than did its 1948 predecessor. The only question was whether it would go Soviet all the way, or whether it would preserve certain peculiarities of its native habitat. As it has turned out, the new 1960 Constitution of Czechoslovakia cannot properly be designated as a replica or a mere imitation of the present Constitution of the USSR. While it goes well beyond the Ninth-of-May Constitution in absorbing additional Soviet elements, it still retains, though devoid of real substance, a modicum of Western parliamentarism. On the other hand, it incorporates several Leninist concepts which do not appear even in the Constitution of the USSR.

Incorporation of Marxist-Leninist Concepts

Probably the most conspicuous innovation is the above-mentioned inclusion in the 1960 Constitution of certain Marxist-Leninist con-

[9] Pavel Peška in *Zemědělské noviny,* April 13, 1960.

cepts that were kept out from the Ninth-of-May Constitution. Like the fundamental law of the USSR, the new Czechoslovak Constitution proclaims "the vanguard of the working class," the Communist Party of Czechoslovakia, to be "the leading force in society and in the State." It refers three times to "the scientific world outlook of Marxism-Leninism" which is supposed to guide all education and all cultural policies, and to govern "the direction of society and the planning of its further development." The well-known Leninist precept of democratic centralism, mentioned twice in the Constitution's first section, has also been made a formal part of Czechoslovak constitutional law as a supreme canon of the direction of the State and society.

Similarly, the new Constitution embodies several notorious devices of present-day communist propaganda and strategy of peaceful co-existence. Its very first article proclaims proudly Czechoslovakia's membership in the world socialist system and her comradely cooperation with the USSR and other socialist countries, based on "mutual comradely help and the international socialist division of labor." It lists the preservation of a lasting peace in the entire world and friendly relations with all nations as the main objectives of Czechoslovakia's foreign policy. Furthermore, the preamble of the 1960 Constitution declares the country's adherence to the Khrushchëv-sponsored competition-of-ideas tactics when it promises that Czechoslovakia "will help in persuading all nations of the advantages of socialism as the only way leading to the welfare of all mankind." In yet another such propaganda gesture the Constitution solemnly offers "the right of asylum to foreign nationals persecuted for their defense of the interests of working people, or for their participation in the national liberation struggle, in scientific and artistic work, or in activities in defense of peace."

But most noteworthy in terms of communist constitution-making is the inclusion in the new Constitution of several Marxist-Leninist axioms relative to the transition from socialism to communism. Besides being mentioned in the preamble, the "gradual transition to communism" is restated as the chief goal of state policy in the body of the Constitution itself. In so doing, the Constitution incorporates, and thus converts into constitutional mandates, the prerequisites that official interpreters of Marxism from Marx to Khrushchëv have laid down as a condition *sine qua non* for the advent of the communist millenium. It refers to the "overcoming of the substantial differences between physical and mental work, and between town and country." It stresses the necessity of an "all-round development of production on the basis of an incessant progress of science and technology and an increase in the productivity of labor." It contains even an assertion that "some of the tasks of the state organs are gradually being transferred to social organizations." Thus it echoes the very latest Soviet reinterpretation of the "withering away of the State" which is now visualized by Khrushchëv simply as a gradual transfer of state functions to the "social organizations of the people."[10]

Rewriting of Economic Clauses

The virtual completion of socialization necessitated a drastic rewriting of the economic clauses of the Ninth-of-May Constitution. After the Soviet fashion, and in compliance with the Marxist-Leninist concept of economic materialism, new provisions relative to the economic system and to ownership have been inserted in the first article of the 1960 Constitution dealing with the foundations of the communist society. Their substance has been taken over from corresponding clauses of the Soviet Constitution. Such relics found in the Ninth-of-May Constitution as the guarantee of private ownership of small and medium enterprises up to 50 employees and landholdings up to 50 hectares, have been omitted as a matter of course. As in the Soviet Constitution, only "small private economy based on one's own work and precluding exploitation of the labor of others" is henceforth permitted. Exploitation of man by man is likewise proclaimed as having been abolished. Unified Agricultural Cooperatives, the Czechoslovak version of the Soviet *kolkhozes,* are specifically mentioned in the Constitution itself and promised complete state support. The concept of all-embracing economic planning is spelled out somewhat more fully than in the Ninth-of-May Constitution and democratic centralism is prescribed as the guiding operational principle of the entire economic system.

The only noteworthy deviations from the Soviet pattern insofar as the economic system is concerned deal with land ownership and household plots. Unlike the Soviet Constitution, the new fundamental law of Czechoslovakia does not list land among the means reserved for exclusive state ownership. It thereby indirectly sanctions

---

[10] See Khrushchëv's speech to the Twenty-First Congress of the Soviet Communist Party, *Pravda,* January 28, 1959.

private ownership of land, and this is probably the most un-Leninist of the several Czechoslovak departures from the Soviet constitutional pattern. Similarly, the 1960 Constitution does not mention the household plots left to collective farmers for their personal use. The omission stems logically from the fact that communist Czechoslovakia has not yet disallowed private ownership of land. But it may well be that the Czechoslovak constitution-makers have been already looking ahead toward the eventual abolition of the household plots, which is yet another avowed prerequisite of the ultimate stage of pure communism.

Further Sovietization of the Bill of Rights

The process of sovietization of civil rights, begun in 1948, was completed in the Constitution of 1960. While the civil-rights clauses of the Ninth-of-May Constitution sounded like a distant echo of the democratic past, their 1960 version carries an unmistakable made-in-Moscow trade-mark. Like its Soviet model, the Czechoslovak Bill of Rights of 1960 emphasizes economic and social rights, such as the rights to work, leisure, health care, and education, and de-emphasizes civil rights proper. It lists first, and elevates thus above all the others, the duty and the right to work: "In a society of working people an individual can attain the fullest development of his capabilities and the realization of his legitimate interests only through active participation in the development of the entire society, particularly through an appropriate share in social work. Therefore, work for the benefit of the whole is the foremost duty and the right to work the foremost right of every citizen."

Similarly, in guaranteeing basic political freedoms of speech and assembly, the 1960 Constitution adopts the Soviet stratagem of hemming them in by the notorious phrase "in conformity with the interests of the working people." Also, in contrast to its 1948 predecessor, it no longer contains specific guarantees of freedom of association, creative work, and scientific research. Nor does it include the limited habeas corpus provision found in the Ninth-of-May Constitution.

Furthermore, the entire 1960 Bill of Rights is riddled with various restrictive clauses which nullify whatever value the constitutional guarantees of citizens' civil rights may have. Among the manifold duties it imposes upon the Czechoslovak citizens are such obligations as "to observe in all their activities the interests of the socialist State and the society of working people"; to "protect and strengthen socialist property as the untouchable basis of the socialist system"; to "abide by the rules of socialist life."

This strong emphasis on citizens' duties toward society is, of course, the logical outgrowth of the communist concept of the subordination of individual to collective interests. The Czechoslovak constitution-makers stood on a solid ideological ground when they placed a basic clause to that effect at the very head of their new Bill of Rights: "In a society of the working people, where exploitation of man by man is abolished, the development and the interests of each member of the society are in harmony with the development and the interests of the society as a whole." Besides being good Marxism-Leninism, the clause is meant also to serve as an additional limitation of individual rights. As explained by a member of the commission for the preparation of the 1960 Constitution, the said clause "gives a directive for the interpretation of the various provisions regarding the citizens' rights and duties in case someone would want to misuse his right contrary to the interests of the whole and to the detriment of the society."[11]

Institutional Changes

Finally, the 1960 Constitution emulates the Soviet example by redefining the functions of the highest state organs and ridding itself, in Novotný's words, "of all the remnants of the liberalistic, pseudodemocratic principle of the separation of powers."[12] Since these institutional changes will be considered in the ensuing chapters, only a few basic features will be mentioned in the present chapter to illustrate the new constitutional trends.

Thus the National Assembly has been promoted from the highest organ of legislative power, which it was under the Ninth-of-May Constitution, to the highest organ of state power. It has become the supreme guardian of the Constitution and its powers have been redefined in language patterned after the Soviet Constitution of 1936. A similar refashioning after the Soviet image has taken place in the field of the judiciary. As does the Constitution of the USSR, the new Czechoslovak fundamental law lumps together in one and the same chapter the courts and the prosecuting branch, the procuracy. It even improves on the Soviet model, for it defines the role

---

[11] Jan Moural in *Práce,* April 26, 1960.
[12] Novotný's report to the Central Committee, *Rudé právo,* April 16, 1960.

of the courts and the procuracy in impeccable Marxist-Leninist terms. Besides assigning these two watchdogs of "socialist legality" the duty to "protect the socialist state, its social system, and the rights and legitimate interests of the citizens and organizations of the working people," it directs them simultaneously to educate citizens in "loyalty to the cause of socialism" and "honorable implementation of their duties to the State and society." Also, it does away with the few deviations from the Soviet pattern which existed in the Czechoslovak judicial system prior to 1960.

On the other hand, the 1960 Constitution still retains the "bourgeois" institution of the single-head Presidency of the Republic, although downgrading its constitutional status. The President is referred to as a "representative of state power" and ranks constitutionally below the National Assembly to which he is also made responsible for the exercise of his presidential function. Nor does the President have any longer the rights to dissolve the National Assembly or veto its laws, both of which he enjoyed under the Ninth-of-May Constitution. Nevertheless a unique opportunity for doing away with the office, a conspicuous leftover of the democratic past, was once again allowed to slip by. This very fact points to the validity of the psychological and political reasons for retaining the Presidency which have been advanced on the preceding pages. The powerful impact of the pre-communist presidential tradition was openly conceded by Novotný himself. Seeking to justify the continuation of such an anomaly at so advanced a stage of the socialist construction, the Party's First Secretary and the Republic's President explained that the Presidency "became a characteristic trait of the Czechoslovak State in the eyes of the working people" and that "it had its great importance also from the international-political standpoint."[13]

Thus the new Constitution of the Czechoslovak Socialist Republic, as Czechoslovakia has now been renamed, and the manner in which it contrasts with the Ninth-of-May Constitution of 1948 reflect with considerable accuracy the extent to which Czechoslovakia's body politic has been sovietized in the twelve years that separate the two fundamental laws. While a few concessions continue to be made, even as late as 1960, to the tenacious traditions of the country's parliamentary past, the new Constitution is saturated with concepts and derivatives borrowed from Soviet commu-

[13] *ibid.* See also *Život strany,* No. 13 (1960), pp. 880ff.

nism. The pseudolibertarian phraseology of 1948 has vacated the field to the current jargon of Marxism-Leninism. At the same time, by embodying in its clauses the basic communist dicta pertaining to the transition from socialism to communism, the 1960 Czechoslovak Constitution has become, from the communist viewpoint, the most advanced fundamental law of the communist orbit, and has in that respect overtaken even its Soviet model.

CHAPTER IX

THE EXECUTIVE TRANSMISSION BELT—I

THEORETICAL BASIS AND ORGANIZATION

THE SUPREME reins of government over the "people's democratic" Czechoslovakia are in the hands of the KSČ. However, by long-standing communist precept, the Party is not supposed to act as its own administrator in the affairs of State. "The functions of the Party collectives must on no account be confused with the functions of the state organs," cautions a resolution adopted at the Eighth Congress of the Soviet Communist Party in 1919. "Such confusion would produce fatal results . . . . The Party must carry out its decisions through the soviet organs . . . . The Party should endeavor to guide the activities of the soviets, not to supplant them."[1] The need of a "precise demarcation" between the work of the Party and the state organs was emphasized at other Party congresses.[2]

These Soviet pronouncements laid a firm ideological foundation for the dichotomy of a *real* and a *formal* government that is characteristic of the countries subjected to the dictatorship of the proletariat. The Party is the exclusive policy-maker on all governmental levels and thus the country's *real* government. "In our state mechanism we apply the Leninist principle that political decisions of the ruling Communist Party, made by its leading organs, are binding in the political sense for the whole state," stresses a Czechoslovak government textbook.[3] But the actual execution of the Party's policies is entrusted to the agencies of *formal* government operating under the all-pervasive Party controls. "It is the substance of the Party leadership of the state apparatus that the Party determines the

[1] *Vsesoiuznaia Kommunisticheskaia Partia (b) v rezoliutsiakh i resheniakh s'ezdov, konferentsii i plenumov Ts. K. 1898-1935* (The All-Union Communist Party [B] in Resolutions and Decisions of the Congresses, Conferences, and Plenums of the C.C. 1898-1935), Moscow, 1936, I, pp. 314-315.

[2] *ibid.*, pp. 325, 425, 483, 485, 512; II, pp. 7-8.

[3] Bedřich Rattinger, *Nejvyšší státní orgány lidově demokratického Československa* (The Highest State Organs of the People's Democratic Czechoslovakia), Praha, 1957, p. 6.

line of state policy, but does not replace the state organs and does not directly exercise state power."[4] Evidently, this unequal dualism is to continue until the promised advent of pure communism when the "withering away" of the State should make government, as we know it, unnecessary.

In addition to the need of following the Soviet prescription there were other reasons which prompted Czechoslovak Communists to preserve an elaborate machinery of formal government and to limit the Party's role in state affairs to policy-making, guidance, and supervision. As mentioned earlier, they considered it rather politic in the first years of their rule to pose as the heirs of the best traditions of Thomas Masaryk's democracy, and the formal retention of the governmental framework of precommunist days fitted well into such tactics. Also, having gained broad experience with all the branches of government and having established themselves in force in the country's administration between 1945 and 1948, the Czechoslovak Communists were in an incomparably more advantageous position vis-à-vis the formal government in 1948 than Lenin had been in 1917. While Lenin had little use for political institutions available at the time of his seizure of power, the Czechoslovak communist leaders simply took over the governmental machinery of Beneš's Third Republic and used it as the executor of the Party's will. Finally, as discussed more fully in Chapter v, until Slánský's liquidation the Party-government dualism drew additional nourishment from the Gottwald-Slánský rivalry. Since Slánský's strength lay in his control over the Party apparatus, it served Gottwald's interest to clip his rival's wings by protecting the agencies of formal government, which he headed as President of the Republic, against excessive encroachments by Slánský's henchmen from the central Party apparatus.[5]

How was the formal government reorganized after the communist seizure of power in 1948? What changes were made in its structure and operational patterns in order to make it fulfill its new role as transmission belt for Party decisions? To what extent, if any, did the precommunist parliamentary institutions, retained by the Ninth-of-May Constitution and continued even in the new socialist Constitution of 1960, withstand the shattering impact of the

---

[4] *ibid.*, p. 13; also, Pavel Levit, *Správní právo, část obecná* (Administrative Law, General Part), Praha, 1954, p. 9.

[5] *Zpráva o Československu*, ii, 11 (1951), pp. 7ff.

dictatorship of the proletariat and the overwhelming pressures of sovietization to which they were thus exposed? Is anything left of the parliamentary and administrative practices of the past? How did the innovations imported from the East fare in an environment of a basically Western-orientated community? What are the major problems that the operation of such a hybrid system of government, composed of Eastern and Western elements, presents to the KSČ leadership?

In dealing with these and related issues it is proposed to examine in turn the three traditional branches of government. Although there is no room for any separation of powers in a system of totalitarian communism, the functional division between the legislative, executive, and judicial branches was formally preserved. The executive function will be considered first because it overshadows its legislative and judicial counterparts in communist Czechoslovakia as it does in all communist-controlled countries. The ensuing chapters will be concerned with the remaining two branches of formal government and with the organs of local administration.

THE PRESIDENCY

The most unusual feature of the executive arrangement in communist Czechoslovakia and the reasons therefor have been mentioned in the preceding chapter. Unlike the other countries of the Soviet orbit, Czechoslovakia continues to have a President of the Republic who is granted formal powers similar to those customarily enjoyed by the Heads of State in Western Europe.

Presidential Powers

Under the Ninth-of-May Constitution the President of Czechoslovakia was elected by the legislature for a seven-year term of office from which he could be removed only by parliamentary impeachment, and this solely on a charge of treason. He represented the State in foreign relations, negotiated and ratified international treaties, and received and appointed envoys. He summoned, adjourned, and had the right to dissolve the Parliament. He signed the laws and had the right of suspensive legislative veto. He submitted to the legislature messages on the state of the Republic and recommended to it such measures as he considered necessary and expedient. He appointed the Prime Minister and the members of the Cabinet, and assigned to them individual departments. He also appointed the highest government officials, judges, and university professors. He had the right to preside over the meetings of the Cabinet and to request from the Cabinet as a whole, or from individual ministers, oral or written reports. He was the supreme commander of the armed forces and appointed all higher Army and Air Force officers. He awarded decorations, proclaimed amnesties, and granted pardons.

However, any act of executive power performed by the President of the Republic had to be countersigned by a responsible member of the Cabinet. As the President was not held accountable in respect to the exercise of his office, political responsibility for presidential acts and pronouncements devolved on the Cabinet. Also, the Ninth-of-May Constitution retained the prewar dualism whereby all governmental and executive power, insofar as it was not reserved for the President, was vested in the Cabinet.

Thus, in terms of constitutional powers and prerogatives, the Czechoslovak Presidency under the dictatorship of the proletariat was a virtual duplicate of the Presidency of T. G. Masaryk's First Republic.[6] The only notable difference lay in the power of ministerial dismissal. Whereas formerly the President was given a legally (though not politically) unfettered right to dismiss members of the Cabinet, the Ninth-of-May Constitution granted him only the power to "recall the Cabinet *if it resigns,* as well as individual *resigning* members."[7] Although this change was rather interesting and significant from a formal, legalistic standpoint, it amounted to little in actual political practice. Under the well-established parliamentary usages of the First Republic ministers and cabinets used to resign as the result of a breakup of the governmental coalition or of inner-party difficulties, and not by presidential dismissal. Somewhat similarly, ministerial resignations under the dictatorship of the proletariat are secured within the Party's highest conclave.

While retaining the Presidency, the 1960 Constitution enacted a few changes designed to reconcile that bourgeois institution with the prevalent governmental pattern of the Soviet orbit. The President of the Republic is declared to be responsible to the National Assembly for the exercise of his function and he has no right to dissolve it or veto its laws. Since judges on all levels are now elected,

---

[6] On the Presidency under the First Republic see Eduard Táborský, *Czechoslovak Democracy at Work,* London, 1945, pp. 17ff., 111ff.

[7] Italics added.

the President has automatically lost his right to appoint them. Furthermore, his term of office has been reduced from seven to five years. On the other hand, the President's constitutional status has been somewhat enhanced. Presidential acts no longer require ministerial countersignature, the President is granted direct legislative initiative, and his right to recall the Cabinet and the individual ministers is no longer limited to instances when the Cabinet or the respective ministers resign.

That these changes have little practical meaning in a communist dictatorship where everything is decided by the Party is too obvious to require any further comment. However, the said changes would make but little difference even if the Constitution were a genuine "supreme law of the land" in the Western democratic sense. Even in pre-communist days the right to dissolve the legislature and to veto its laws was seldom used in Czechoslovakia, and hardly ever as the executive's political weapon against the legislature.[8] As for the newly decreed presidential responsibility to the National Assembly, the absence of any provision on the manner in which the legislative branch could enforce such a responsibility makes it evident that no such enforcement is contemplated. Indeed, presidential impeachment, the only way in which the President of the Republic could be removed from office under the Ninth-of-May Constitution, is no longer provided for in the Constitution of 1960.

In paraphrasing the Presidency provisions of the 1920 Constitution, which had in their turn been largely patterned after the constitutional system of the French Third Republic, the Ninth-of-May Constitution laid legal foundations for a weak, figurehead sort of Presidency. Were constitutional clauses applied as they read, the Cabinet and not the President would have become the chief executive, and the Prime Minister the most powerful single officer of the government. However, as had been the case under the First Republic, the Presidency managed to rise above the limitations imposed upon it by the communist constitution-makers, though for different reasons.

The high political status of the Czechoslovak Presidency of the twenties and thirties resulted from the tremendous prestige and outstanding personal qualities of the two democratic Presidents of Czechoslovakia, T. G. Masaryk and Eduard Beneš. Apart from a few ultranationalists and die-hard Communists, the whole Czecho-

[8] See Eduard Táborský, *op.cit.*, pp. 65-66, 68-69.

slovak people saw in T. G. Masaryk the founder of their new State and they felt a deep gratitude for what he had done. The people loved and respected him, and they had a profound trust in his political wisdom and moral integrity. All this gave the President-Liberator, as he came to be called, an enormous degree of authority far exceeding the narrow bounds of his constitutional prerogatives. A rather similar influence accrued to Beneš, T. G. Masaryk's chief collaborator during World War I and in the new Republic, whom Masaryk recommended as his successor when he resigned in 1935.[9]

When the Communists took over in 1948 the way was open for the deflation of the Presidency's status and its conversion into the ceremonial institution that would have been more suitable to both the language of the Constitution and the prevailing communist political concepts. All that was needed for that purpose was to fill the vacancy left by Beneš's resignation with a malleable political nonentity or some well-disciplined communist elder statesman. There were two all-too-willing prospects for such a reduced presidency. One of them was the number-one social democratic fellow-traveler, Zdeněk Fierlinger, and the other was the Zdeněk Nejedlý, aged professor of Praha and Moscow universities, whom the communist leaders seemed to have been grooming at one time for such a possibility. Had that happened and either of the two Zdeněks been kicked upstairs, the Czechoslovak Presidency would have been turned into a strictly honorary function such as the USSR's Chairmanship of the Presidium of the Supreme Soviet. However, to Fierlinger's and Nejedlý's regrets, the opportunity to downgrade the Presidency was not used and the vacant position was claimed by Gottwald himself. In so doing he set the precedent that has been followed in both of the presidential successions to date. On each occasion, the Presidency was passed on to the topmost Czechoslovak Communist of the time, Antonín Zápotocký in 1953 and Antonín Novotný in 1957.

The Three "Worker Presidents"

That Gottwald was the man to succeed Beneš, once it was decided to retain the Presidency under the system of the dictatorship of the proletariat, was perfectly natural. Since Thomas Masaryk and Eduard Beneš invested the office with so much prestige and made it the most influential political position in the country, it was quite logical that

---

[9] *ibid.*, pp. 111ff.; also, Emile Giraud, *Le pouvoir exécutif dans les démocraties d'Europe et d'Amérique,* Paris, 1938, pp. 270-271.

the top man of the KSČ should step into their shoes. Throughout all the years of Masaryk's and Beneš's Presidency the Czechoslovak man-in-the-street had looked at Hradčany Castle for guidance and leadership rather than to the Prime Minister and his Cabinet. Hence, it fitted the communist strategy of 1948 to entrust such a vantage point to a full-fledged communist leader rather than to a mere fellow-traveler. Since Gottwald had opposed Masaryk in presidential elections in pre-Munich Czechoslovakia, nothing could have symbolized better the completeness of the communist victory than Gottwald's accession to the Presidency after so many years of what had seemed hopeless effort. Also, because he had played his role as a moderate so well, Gottwald was more suited than ony other member of the Party hierarchy to move into Hradčany Castle. At a time when the Communists were taking such pains to claim that nothing was happening except that a few reactionary toes were being justly stepped on, it was politic to fill the Presidency with a Communist who seemed less radical than most of his high Party associates. By the same token, Gottwald's dislike of theorizing and his worker's background tended to make him more acceptable to some segments of the working class than would have been some of the more rabid doctrinaires among the Party leaders. Finally, and most importantly, Gottwald's appetite for the highest state office was whetted by his realization of the Presidency's value in the perennial jockeying for positions of strength within the Party.

When the KSČ leadership decided, upon Gottwald's death, that the Presidency should not be abolished, the choice of Antonín Zápotocký as successor was a foregone conclusion. Not only was he the number-two ranking Czechoslovak Communist and holder, as Premier of Czechoslovakia, of the number-two executive position, but he was the best known and the most popular member of the Party's dwindling prewar Old Guard. Of working-class origin, with no liking for excessive theorizing, and with commonsense and skill in handling people, he was more suited to the job than any one else among the Party leaders. As Široký said when he recommended the election of "Comrade Klement Gottwald's closest collaborator, Antonín Zápotocký," to the National Assembly: "Being the first worker to reside in the old Praha Castle, the historic monument of the glory and greatness of our fatherland, comrade Gottwald created a new presidential tradition: the tradition of a President who is an unshakeable fighter for, and completely devoted to, the cause of the working class and of socialism . . . . The functions of the President can be fulfilled only by a man who will continue this glorious Gottwaldian tradition."[10]

The choice of Antonín Novotný to succeed Zápotocký, upon the latter's death in November 1957, followed the pattern of conferring the office upon the highest-ranking Communist. Since his promotion to the First Secretaryship of the KSČ in 1953, Novotný's political star had been in steady ascent and in 1957 it outshone that of the ailing Zápotocký. Also, a communist tradition was adhered to in selecting a man of working-class origin for the highest state office. The "metal-worker" Novotný thus succeeded "the carpenter Gottwald and the mason Zápotocký."[11] On the other hand, precedent was broken in one significant respect: for the first time the Presidency was given to a man who had been unknown to the general public and had not belonged to the national leadership of the Party before the war. His elevation to the country's top executive office at the relatively young age of fifty-three thus symbolized the gradual eclipse of the Old Guard, and the rise in power and authority of the intermediate communist generation who had become Party members in prewar days, but gained prominence only after the coup of 1948. Also, in Novotný the Presidency for the first time got an incumbent who was an all-out *apparatchik* and nothing else.[12] That could not be said of either of his predecessors. Zápotocký's background bore within itself very little *apparatchikism,* as he was typically an able labor organizer and accomplished demagogue. Nor could Gottwald be labeled as a mere *apparatchik,* although his political past reveals plenty of work within the Party apparatus. He battled and fought for the Party's cause a good deal outside the Party apparatus, and his struggle with Slánský and the latter's Secretariat shows that he had to overcome and conquer the Party apparatus from without in order to reassert his leadership.

The Presidency and the Party

Since the Communist Party "alone is historically called upon to be the real executor of the dictatorship of the working class,"[13] the

---

[10] *Rudé právo,* March 23, 1953.
[11] *ibid.,* November 20, 1957.
[12] See Chapter v.
[13] The Resolution of the Twelfth Congress in 1925.

communist rule should have converted the Republic's Presidency into a mere transmission belt for Party decisions. To a very considerable extent that is what has happened in Czechoslovakia. During the few months of his Presidency after the coup of February 1948 Dr. Beneš was reduced to political impotence and held a virtual prisoner in his country seat at Sezimovo Ústí while the KSČ leaders ruled the country. His three successors, although formally elected by the Parliament, held office as appointees of the KSČ. While they swore in their constitutional oath of office to discharge their duties "in the spirit of the People's Democratic Order" and to abide by the Constitution and other laws, they knew that their higher duty was to follow the directives of the highest Party organs to which they were responsible. As stressed in a communist study of the highest state organs published under the auspices of the Communist Party University in 1957, "The President of the Republic was and is a member of the leading organs of the Communist Party of Czechoslovakia and of its collective leadership; [he] must, as fully responsible Party functionary, carry out the Party's policy in his high state function [and] follow the basic directives and principles of the Party . . . ."[14]

However, established traditions are hard to obliterate, especially when they can be bent to serve the ends of the new rulers. Once he had become President, Gottwald had every interest in preventing the office from being reduced to a mere appendage of the Party. Confronted with a formidable rival in the Party's Secretary General, Rudolf Slánský, he had cogent reason to uphold the authority of his presidential office while paying proper homage to the supremacy of the Party. It was perhaps symptomatic of his efforts in that direction that upon his accession to the Presidency he convened the meetings of the KSČ Presidium in Hradčany Castle rather than in the Party headquarters near Praha's *Prašná brána*.

Zápotocký in his turn had even more reasons to keep the Party from converting the Presidency into a mere tool. While Gottwald had, after Slánský's ouster, combined in his hands the office of the President and the direction of the Party's Central Secretariat, Zápotocký failed to inherit from Gottwald the latter function. Speaking on the Praha radio just one day after Zápotocký's election to the Presidency, Nejedlý bluntly declared that Zápotocký "could not become

[14] Rattinger, *op.cit.*, p. 68.

another Gottwald."[15] Hence, Zápotocký's major concern was to preserve as much of the President's prestige as possible. His frantic publicity-seeking after his election bears that out."[16]

With the election of Novotný the powers of the Party's Central Secretariat and of the Republic's Presidency were once again entrusted to one person. However, both the personal qualities of the new incumbent and the circumstances under which he moved up to Hradčany Castle were such as to suggest a decline in the political stature of the Presidency. A post-1948 upstart little known in prewar days, Novotný lacked the prestige and the aura of a fighter for workers' rights which his two predecessors acquired, rightly or wrongly, in precommunist days. Moreover, he acceded to the Presidency at a time when "collective leadership" became the slogan of the day and the "cult of the individual" a heresy. Hailing editorially Novotný's election and pointing out the "utmost significance that the supreme state office is now held jointly with the office of the First Secretary of the Communist Party of Czechoslovakia," *Rudé právo* served an unambiguous notice: "This clearly stresses the leading role played by the Communist Party, a fact recognized by all socialist and democratic forces in our country, by the Czech and Slovak working people, and by the entire National Front."[17] The same idea was re-emphasized during the "nation-wide discussion" of the new Constitution of 1960.[18] Novotný's behavior as President and all the circumstantial evidence that could be gathered on this matter indicates that, in the Novotný era, the Presidency came closer than ever to becoming an exalted branch office of the Party's Central Secretariat.

The Premiership, the Government Presidium, and the Cabinet

Next to the Republic's Presidency, three other institutions must be considered to obtain a well-rounded picture of the executive branch of government in communist Czechoslovakia: the Premiership, the Government Presidium, and the Cabinet (Council of Ministers). Of these three, the Premiership has displayed remarkable sta-

---

[15] *Zpráva o Československu*, IV, 3 (1953), p. 7.

[16] For examples of Zápotocký's buildup see *Rudé právo*, March 23, 24, April 10, 19, 20, 23, and 27, May 3, 10, and 30, June 3, 6, 12, 14, 20, 22, 23, 26, and 27, July 3, 4, 5, and 24, August 24, September 13 and 28, October 3, 4, and 9, 1953; *Svobodné slovo*, May 8, June 13 and 17, October 20, 1953.

[17] *Rudé právo*, November 20, 1957.

[18] *ibid.*, April 30, 1960.

bility in occupants and status. On the other hand, the relative standings of the Government Presidium and the Cabinet have been more uneven and their personnel less stable.

The Constitutional Position

As in the case of the Republic's Presidency, the provisions of the Ninth-of-May Constitution pertaining to the Premiership and the Cabinet were a slightly retouched paraphrase of the corresponding clauses of the Czechoslovak democratic Constitution of 1920. The Prime Minister, deputy prime ministers, and all the other members of the Cabinet were appointed by the Republic's President. Upon being so appointed the Cabinet had to present its program to the legislature and obtain its confidence. At all times the legislature had the power to unseat the Cabinet by a vote of no confidence or by rejecting the Cabinet's motion of confidence. The rather stiff conditions prescribed by the 1920 Constitution for the exercise of the legislative vote of no confidence were retained. A motion to that effect had to be signed by no less than on hundred representatives for presentation to the Presidium of the National Assembly, which was allowed a full eight days for its report on the motion. The presence of an absolute majority of all the members of the National Assembly and and an affirmative vote by an absolute majority of those present were required for the motion. The 1920 constitutional pattern also was preserved for the relationship between the Cabinet and the President, through the readoption of the principle of Cabinet responsibility for presidential acts, the requirement of ministerial countersignature, and executive dualism which left inherent executive powers to the Cabinet rather than to the President. Similarly, the authority to issue executive orders and regulations for the implementation of statutory enactments remained exclusively in the hands of the Council of Ministers.

There were only four departures from the "bourgeois" arrangements of 1920 worthy of note:

1. One of them has been considered above: unlike its predecessor, the Ninth-of-May Constitution failed to mention the President's right to dismiss the Prime Minister or the members of his Cabinet, for it spoke only of his authority to recall the Cabinet or individual Ministers *if they resigned.*

2. While the Cabinet itself was authorized under the 1920 Constitution to choose the deputy premier, the Ninth-of-May Constitution assigned this right to the President. Furthermore, it seems that post-

Stalin political practice deprived the Cabinet of the authority to appoint deputy ministers and added it to the list of presidential prerogatives. Since the Ninth-of-May Constitution did not deal with the matter, the choice of deputy ministers logically should have belonged within the authority of the Cabinet or the individual ministers. Indeed, until March 1951 the ministers used to appoint their own deputies. Thereafter the authority devolved on the Cabinet as a whole[19] and in March 1953 on the President of the Republic.[20] The reason for the last-mentioned devolution was obviously the desire to imitate the latest Soviet practice whereby deputy ministers in the post-Stalin reshuffle were appointed by the Head of State, the Presidium of the Supreme Soviet.

3. The Cabinet's collective responsibility was supplemented by individual political responsibility of Cabinet members. The pre-communist Parliament had no authority to unseat individual ministers. Had it wished to do so, it would have had to take up the issue with the Council of Ministers and defeat it by a formal vote of no confidence. In a contrary manner, the Ninth-of-May Constitution included a specific provision granting the National Assembly the right to "pass a vote of no confidence upon an individual member of the Cabinet" who then "shall be bound to tender his resignation into the hands of the President of the Republic." It is interesting to note that this is a reversion to the Czechoslovak provisional Constitution of 1919, which recognized both individual and collective responsibility in the manner of the French Third Republic.

4. Whereas the role of Prime Minister, as distinguished from other Cabinet members, was left undefined by the Constitution of 1920, the Ninth-of-May Constitution made an attempt to spell out more specifically the Premier's functions. Under its provisions the Prime Minister was to "direct the work of the Cabinet, summon and preside over its sittings, and determine the order of business." He also had authority to "coordinate the activity of all central departments and supervise the implementation of the government program."

However, none of these departures from the 1920 Constitution was of major importance and none of them detracted from the parliamentary character of the Czechoslovak cabinet system in so far as constitutional theory was concerned. Nor has any change of substance been made in this respect by the new Constitution of 1960.

[19] *Zpráva o Československu,* II, 3 (1951), p. 6.
[20] *Rudé právo,* March 26, 1953.

Since the President of the Republic is now directly responsible to the National Assembly, the Cabinet has automatically ceased to be accountable for presidential acts. The National Assembly's prerogative to vote the Cabinet out of office has been freed from the several limitations imposed on it by the Ninth-of-May Constitution. The provisions on ministerial impeachment have been dropped. Nor does the 1960 Constitution contain any specific clause outlining the duties of the Prime Minister. Rather, in deference to the collective leadership principle, it clothes the Cabinet as a whole with the authority to "unify, direct, and control the work of the individual ministries and other central agencies of the state administration." But all these are only minor adaptations that do not affect in any way the core of the previous constitutional arrangements.

The Premiership

Had the Ninth-of-May Constitution been really adhered to, the Premier would have been the strongest single executive officer in the country, and would have overshadowed the President in political power almost as much as the Prime Minister of Britain outshines the British Monarch. A trend in that direction developed after the war. When President Beneš returned home from his exile in 1945 the dominance of the Communist Party, backed to the hilt by Soviet influence, prevented him from regaining the authority which he had commanded in the First Republic.[21] Thus, for the first time in Czechoslovakia's history, the country's highest office sank to the level of the proverbially weak French Presidency of pre-De Gaulle era and the center of gravity shifted to the Chairmanship of the Cabinet. However, the beneficiary was not the then Premier, Zdeněk Fierlinger, but the KSČ's leader, Klement Gottwald, who preferred at that time to be only Deputy Premier and to operate from a less conspicuous position through a dependable fellow-traveler. When Gottwald assumed the Premiership in his own name, after the 1946 parliamentary elections in which the KSČ became the country's strongest party, the stage seemed well set for a strong Premiership that would relegate the Presidency to a secondary role.

Had Eduard Beneš been willing to become a pliable tool of Moscow, and to continue serving as the Republic's President under the

---

[21] Edward Taborsky, "The Triumph and Disaster of Eduard Benes," *Foreign Affairs*, July 1958, pp. 669ff.

dictatorship of the proletariat, such a tradition undoubtedly would have been established. As had occurred in the Soviet Union and in all the satellites, the Czechoslovak Premiership would have become the key function in the formal government. Dr. Beneš's abdication and Gottwald's accession to the Presidency nipped this development. Nevertheless, the Premiership continued to be a highly important executive position second only to the Presidency. A tradition developed whereby the office was reserved for the second or third most prominent Communist in the country, depending upon whether or not the Party's First Secretaryship was held jointly with the Republic's Presidency. When Zápotocký succeeded Gottwald in the Premiership in June 1948, he was already the uncontested number-three person in the communist hierarchy, preceded only by Gottwald and the then Secretary General of the Party, Rudolf Slánský. After Slánský's removal, Zápotocký moved up to number two. Similarly, when Široký took over the office following Zápotocký's promotion to the Presidency, he was second only to Zápotocký. Although he had since been by-passed by the Party's First Secretary, Antonín Novotný, Široký continued to be third in line until the death of Zápotocký in November 1957 when he automatically regained the number-two position behind Novotný who rose to the Presidency. Also, the importance of the Premiership could not but be enhanced by the durability of its occupants. None of them had been demoted, and, as illustrated by Gottwald and Zápotocký, the only exit thus far has been by way of promotion to the Presidency. Although Široký failed to be so promoted, he has served as Premier without interruption since March 1953, in spite of the post-Stalin shifts and vicissitudes that had befallen his counterparts in the Soviet Union and elsewhere in the Soviet orbit.

The custom of assigning the Premiership to the second or third highest-ranking Communist and the fact of the incumbents' durability have tended to bolster the Premier's position vis-à-vis his Cabinet. Constitutionally, the Prime Minister is hardly more than a *primus inter pares*. Although he summons and presides over the Cabinet's sessions, his vote is the equal of his Cabinet colleagues. Hence, the Prime Minister is formally precluded from doing anything of political consequence without the approval of a majority of his colleagues. But the practice of the dictatorship of the proletariat has shaped things rather differently. As the supreme rule in the country is in the hands of a narrow oligarchy of the topmost Party leaders, the Cabinet sessions are dominated by those of its members who are simultaneously members of the Party's Political Bureau. This is confirmed by the few higher ministerial employees who absconded and made their way to the West. Before any issue of importance is taken up by the Cabinet, these ruling oligarchs have already decided the matter in the Party's Politbureau. A few of them, including the Prime Minister, may have caucused on the matter with the President and reached a decision in a "smoke-filled room" in Hradčany Castle even prior to the Politbureau's meeting. Thus the Premier towers high above those of his Cabinet colleagues who are not members of the Party's Political Bureau, but he is at the same time only slightly more prominent than those who belong to the highest Party organ.

The Government Presidium

This inequality among individual Cabinet members was further enhanced in January 1953 when the Czechoslovak Communists superimposed a Government Presidium on the Cabinet. Composed of the Premier and his deputies, this communist creation was assigned the task of attending to the current work of the Cabinet between its sessions and directing and controlling the activities of the individual ministers.[22] The establishment of this super-Cabinet brought the Czechoslovak executive arrangement one step closer to the Soviet model. Both in its composition and its functions the Government Presidium was patterned after Stalin's "inner Cabinet," and it seems that the change was motivated mainly by a desire to please Moscow. That is also indicated by the fluctuation in its membership. As it was the Soviet practice in the last years of the Stalin era to have a substantial number of deputy premiers, the Czechoslovak Government Presidium was staffed with as many as nine deputy premiers when it was first established in January 1953. When the Soviet trend was reversed after Stalin's death, and the number of deputy premiers was sharply reduced from thirteen to five, the Czechoslovak Communists decided after a slight delay to cut the number of their deputy premiers accordingly.[23] They responded in the same manner to subsequent Soviet shifts, increasing and decreasing the size of their Government Presidium whenever a similar trend was noticed in Moscow. Similarly, they copied the post-Stalin Soviet differentiation between first deputy premiers and plain deputy premiers, and conferred the nobler title of

[22] Government ordinance No. 5 of January 31, 1953.
[23] Government ordinance No. 77 of September 11, 1953.

First Deputy Premier on the two most prominent among the deputy premiers, Jaromír Dolanský and Alexei Čepička.[24]

Although the Czechoslovak Cabinet continues formally to be a Cabinet of the regenerated National Front, its Presidium has been out of bounds for the non-communist partners. With the formal establishment of the Presidium in January 1953, the earlier custom of reserving one deputy premiership for the leader of one of the non-communist parties was discontinued. For a while it even looked as though the Government Presidium might become an exclusive club of the highest Party leaders. Except for Gottwald, who was not eligible because he was President of the Republic, all the members of the Party's Politbureau simultaneously became members of the the Government Presidium upon its establishment. However, the bar against admission of second-line communist leaders has been somewhat relaxed in the post-Stalin era, and occasionally ordinary members and even alternates of the Party's Central Committee have been given seats in the "inner Cabinet."[25]

The Cabinet and the Ministries

The dominant position of the President of the Republic, the heightened status of the Premier, and the creation of the Government Presidium as a super-Cabinet, has left the Council of Ministers in the fourth place on the executive scene. While both the 1948 and the 1960 Constitutions assigned the Cabinet a decisive executive role, actual practice has transformed it into a body of routine administrators subject to the directives of their Party superiors. The Cabinet ceased to be a supreme policy-maker the moment the Communists took over in February 1948. But its political eclipse deepened when the Government Presidium was reorganized in January 1953 and clothed with special supervisory powers over the Cabinet's work. Department heads began to be chosen more and more from among the lower echelons of the communist hierarchy. Oftentime deputy ministers moved up to succeed their chiefs who moved on to the Government Presidium. After the Eleventh Party Congress in June 1958 only two Politbureau members kept direct departmental duties:

[24] The practice of appointing *first* deputy premiers was abandoned in July 1960.

[25] When made deputy premiers in March 1953, Barák was only an alternate of the Central Committee and Beran was not even that. Similarly, Rudolf Strechaj, who became deputy premier in July 1960, held no position on the Party's Presidium.

Rudolf Barák as Minister of the Interior and Otakar Šimůnek as Chairman of the State Planning Office; and that has remained so in the new Cabinet appointed in July 1960. All the remaining department heads belong to the lower level of communist leadership. Some of them are so low in Party ranking that they do not appear among the alternates of the Central Committee; and a few are not even Party members. Besides enabling the members of the Government Presidium to concentrate more fully on their supervisory functions, this arrangement makes them less vulnerable without detracting from their powers of control. Since they have no direct responsibility for departmental operations they have a somewhat better chance of escaping criticism when trouble develops, and the blame can be laid more easily on the shoulders of the second-line communist leaders.

The number and functions of the ministries have been changed frequently. Beginning in February 1949, with the creation of a State Planning Office, an equivalent of the Soviet Gosplan, the communist rulers of Czechoslovakia have been adapting their country's administrative structure more and more to the Soviet model. Whenever the Soviets added new ministries or other agencies, Czechoslovakia did likewise. Whenever Soviet ministries were reduced in number and merged into larger units, so were they in communist Czechoslovakia.[26] The only instance worthy of mention when KSČ leaders failed to follow the Soviet lead in matters of ministerial reorganization occurred in connection with Khrushchëv's abolition of most of the Soviet economic ministries in 1957 and the more recent abolition of the ministries of State Control and Interior. Presumably, Czechoslovakia has not yet advanced to the higher Soviet stage that would warrant such a radical diminution of the central administrative machinery. Nevertheless, under the impact of Soviet developments, a much advertised decentralization campaign has been unfolded and has resulted in the transfer of certain ministerial functions to regional and lower administrative agencies.[27]

---

[26] These numerous organizational changes have been enacted by a long series of laws and government ordinances: laws No. 60 of February 22, 1949, No. 187 of July 14, 1949, No. 217 of October 14, 1949, and No. 41 of July 8, 1959; government ordinances Nos. 73 and 74 of September 7, 1951, No. 5 of January 31, 1953, No. 77 of September 11, 1953, No. 25 of May 28, 1955, No. 48 of October 14, 1955, No. 1 of January 20, 1956, No. 19 of June 16, 1956, No. 50 of July 31, 1957, No. 9 of March 14, 1958, Nos. 10, 11 and 12 of March 21, 1958, No. 34 of June 6, 1958, No. 53 of July 30, 1958, No. 60 of October 13, 1958, No. 3 of January 23, 1959, No. 44 of July 11, 1959, and No. 52/1960.
[27] See Chapter x.

The official explanations of the recurrent changes in the organizational pattern of the Czechoslovak central administration have been signally unconvincing. Giving the National Assembly the reason for the large-scale reorganization of October 1951, Zápotocký said: "In order to make the ministries more operative and more elastic, and to enable them to direct production properly and efficiently and to assume responsibility therefor, it has been necessary to subdivide production ministries into several agencies."[28] Similarly, another increase in the number of ministries decreed in January 1953 was explained by the argument that "Soviet experience had proved that it was better to have smaller, more active ministries with specific tasks rather than one ministry with a huge agenda."[29] It was even argued that the number of employees would decrease and administrative costs decline with the increase in the number of ministries![30] However, when the trend was reversed in September 1953 and the number of ministries was reduced, the official communiqué explained the change by the need for "the reduction in the cost of government apparatus, simplification of cooperation among individual sectors of state administration, and improvement of their directive activities."[31] Thus, whether the number of ministries went up or down, whether they were merged or split up, it was allegedly done for the same reasons.

Some of the changes were indeed motivated by the desire to streamline the administration and to improve its operations. Naturally enough, it was in the vital communist interest to secure the best possible machinery for the execution of the goals of socialist construction, especially in the economic field. This was so in the case of the first major reorganization in September 1951. The country's economy was then in poor shape, living standards were low, and dissatisfaction with the government's conduct of affairs was spreading. Worse still, Czechoslovakia's deliveries to the Soviet Union were lagging badly and Moscow did not conceal its displeasure. Something had to be done, especially in the field of heavy industry. By subdividing the top-heavy Ministry of Industry into several more manageable departments and simultaneously abolishing twenty-one national and ten Slovak directorates of nationalized production, the Czechoslovak rulers hoped to cut bureaucratic red tape and inject, as Zápotocký said, more elasticity

[28] *Rudé právo,* November 1, 1951.
[29] *Mladá fronta,* February 3, 1953.
[30] *ibid.*
[31] *Zpráva o Československu,* IV, 9 (1953), p. 5.

into the direction of that vital part of the country's economy. Similarly, the post-Stalin reduction in the number of ministries was undoubtedly intended to simplify the complexity of overgrown administrative apparatus and cut down on costs and personnel.

However, this cannot be said of most of other hurried and ill-conceived rearrangements. By 1951-1952 such men as Gottwald, Zápotocký, or Dolanský had enough administrative experience to know that a too frequent tampering with machinery is not conducive to administrative efficiency. Thus, as admitted by the KSČ spokesmen, the primary reason for most of the changes appears to have been no more or less than an endeavor to imitate the "Soviet experiences in successful government organization."[32] This was dictated not so much by a belief in the superiority of the Soviet ministerial system and its suitability for Czechoslovak conditions as by the realization that an imitation represented the least personal risk. When something went wrong, one could at least avoid the ominous and often fatal charge that one refused to learn from the "first socialist country" and possibly even committed sabotage by not applying the "rich Soviet experience." Also, frequent reorganizations seemed to create an impression that something was in fact being done to improve the functioning of the system.

While the number of ministries and their functions have been changed without respite, their internal organization has remained much as in pre-communist days. Each ministry is divided along functional lines into a number of sections headed by high-ranking career officials. The sections are similarly subdivided into smaller divisions. The Minister himself has a small secretariat of personal aides. About the only real innovation is the practice of appointing deputy ministers. The initial step in that direction was taken on communist initiative in 1945 when several state secretaries were appointed to serve as deputy ministers in various ministries. Seeking support of the Slovak nationalists, Gottwald justified the new practice by the need of equitable distribution of ministerial functions between the Czechs and the Slovaks. His other reason was to plant a Communist, Vlado Clementis, as second in command in the Ministry of Foreign Affairs and thus to keep a close watch over the popular non-communist Foreign Minister, Jan Masaryk.

[32] *Prague News Letter,* February 12, 1953; also, *Mladá fronta,* February 3, 1953. Even the names of the ministries, committees, and other central agencies have been taken over from the Soviet nomenclature.

After the communist seizure of power and the death of Masaryk both these reasons disappeared and the institution of state secretaries was dropped. Instead, the Soviet practice of surrounding the Minister with an array of deputies was adopted. Their main official function is to serve as the Minister's right hand men and to help him administer and supervise the various sectors of the ministry's work. But their unofficial mission is to keep an eye on the Minister's activities as well.

CHAPTER X

THE EXECUTIVE TRANSMISSION BELT—II

OPERATIONAL PATTERN

WHAT ARE the basic features of the communist executive's operational pattern? How has the dictatorship of the proletariat affected the inner functioning processes of the country's administration? How successful have the communist rulers of Czechoslovakia been in their efforts to refashion the administrative apparatus so that it will meet the all-important twin requirements of loyalty and efficiency?

THE PARTY'S ABSOLUTE COMMAND

However trite it may sound, the all-pervasive Party dominance must be mentioned once again, for it is the most important feature of the administrative operational pattern and its most fundamental principle. "The guidance of the State is in the hands of the Communist Party which does not share this guidance with anyone else," says an official university textbook on the theory of the State and law.[1] The Central Committee of the KSČ "directs the work of the central state organs," stress the Party Statutes; and this is the one administrative maxim that is immutable. No criticism enraged the communist rulers more than a suggestion made by a few critics, emboldened by Khrushchëv's condemnation of Stalin in 1956, that the Party ought to relax its tight administrative reins. As stated in the resolution of the Eleventh Party Congress in 1958, "the Central Committee of the KSČ is the center of all political, economic, and ideological work in the country."[2] Due to the narrow oligarchical system of the KSČ leadership, this applies really to the Central Committee's Political Bureau, which wields the actual authority, rather than to the Committee as a whole.

This dominance of the Party over the executive branch is secured

---

[1] Radim Foustka *et al.*, *Doplňková skripta z theorie státu a práva* (Supplementary Scripts on the Theory of the State and the Law), Praha, 1954, pp. 149-150.

[2] *Rudé právo*, June 23, 1958.

by placement of Party members in key administrative positions. As in the Soviet Union, most of the leading Czechoslovak Communists simultaneously hold top executive jobs. This is well illustrated by the distribution of the highest government functions among the KSČ leaders. As in 1960, the Party's First Secretary and number-one Czechoslovak Communist, Antonín Novotný, held the office of President of the Republic. The number-one Slovak Communist, Viliam Široký, served as Premier while the two highest-ranking members of the communist Old Guard, Jaromír Dolanský and Václav Kopecký, were Deputy Premiers. So were two other Politbureauists, Rudolf Barák and Oto Šimůnek, who headed at the same time the most important political and economic departments, the Ministry of the Interior and the State Planning Commission, respectively. Thus six of the ten full members of the Party's Politbureau manned the country's highest executive jobs and directly supervised the execution of Party directives which they themselves were issuing.

Consequently, the pattern of supreme administrative decision-making developed along the following lines: In Gottwald's days, in particular since Slánský's demise, such decisions were generally made at informal get-togethers of the inner circle of Party leaders held in Gottwald's presidential residence in Hradčany Castle. One member of this inner circle would be chosen to make the formal recommendation in the ensuing meeting of the Party's Politbureau and, if need be, in the Party's Presidium and/or Central Committee. Thereafter the matter would be formally acted upon by the Government Presidium and the Cabinet, and the appropriate minister would be assigned the duty of implementing it. Should misunderstanding develop in the Government Presidium or the Cabinet, the matter would be referred back to the Politbureau. Such a rare referral occurred, for instance, when Zápotocký, then Premier, did not see eye to eye with Čepička, who headed the Ministry of Justice, regarding a draft law on forced labor camps.[3] This general pattern continued after Gottwald's death, although the smoked-filled-room decisions in Hradčany Castle seem to have become less frequent.

Almost all other ministries and central offices are also headed by dependable Communists, mostly members and alternates of the Party's Central Committee. Only a few ministries of minor political significance are reserved for the leaders of the other parties of the National Front. Thus, at the beginning of 1960, the chief of the

[3] Paul Barton, *Prague à l'Heure de Moscou,* Paris, 1954, p. 189.

Catholic People's Party, the defrocked priest Josef Plojhar, held the position of Minister of Health, and its deputy chairman, A. Pospíšil, was Minister of Power and Water Conservation. Their equivalents in the Czech Socialist Party. Emanual Šlechta and Alois Neumann, headed the Ministries of Construction and Communications.[4] The chairman of the Slovak Renaissance Party, Josef Kyselý, who had been the only non-communist deputy premier until the creation of the Government Presidium in January 1953, served as chief of the unexciting Ministry of Local Economy from its creation in 1953 to its abolition in 1958 when he became chairman of the Governmental Committee for the Development of Agriculture, Forestry, and Water Conservation.[5] But the Party headquarters provide all the non-communist ministers with alert communist deputies to check on them.

Moreover, all agencies of central government are staffed predominantly with Party members who are directed by the Party Statutes to be "active fighters for the fulfillment of Party decisions" and "to report shortcomings in work." In each agency Party members and candidates belong to a tightly organized and rigidly disciplined Party primary unit bound by the statutory duty "to point out shortcomings in the work of ministries and other central departments." While a great many Party members seek to evade this disagreeable and sometimes dangerous task as much as they can, there are nevertheless enough opportunists and zealots on whom the Party leadership can count for these denunciatory chores. It is the basic rule of the Party's cadres policy to place the most dependable Communists in strategic positions throughout each ministry in order to have close check on the activities of all fellow-comrades and non-communists alike.

THE CONTROLS

These Party checks are supplemented by a number of other controlling devices fashioned after the Soviet model.

Police Controls

The least conspicuous of these devices is the police agency. This ubiquitous right arm of every dictatorial regime, which reaches into every corner of social life in communist Czechoslovakia, has its agents

---

[4] When the Ministry of Construction was replaced by the State Committee of Construction in 1956, Šlechta became its chairman. He died in 1960. See also Chapter VII, n. 4.

[5] Kyselý lost his cabinet position in the governmental reshuffle of July 1960 when he became one of the deputy chairmen of the new National Assembly.

planted in strategic positions throughout the administrative system. While a few of them are openly identified as such, most operate in the manner of undercover agents posing as regular employees of the agency which they are to monitor. They are supplemented by a network of informers who have the duty to report anything suspicious to the police agents to whom they are assigned. Though the police agency does not interfere directly with administrative operations, it is nevertheless an important and dreaded weapon of control. Due to the multitude of regulations and directives, and the communist tendency to impute evil intent even when none exists, matters that would call for minor disciplinary action in the non-communist administrative system occasionally trigger police measures in communist Czechoslovakia.

Personnel Divisions' Controls

Both the Party and the police cooperate closely with the departmental personnel divisions which have direct responsibility for employees' loyalty and efficiency. More than any other division these are staffed with die-hard Communists who can be depended on to apply ruthlessly the prescribed personnel policies. Working in close contact with and under the actual direction of the cadres section of the Party's Central Secretariat, they handle all matters of recruitment, promotion, transfer, and discipline. Since their recommendation plays such a crucial part in the employees' careers, the divisions of personnel are among the most important agencies of personnel controls.

The Ministry of State Control

Another awe-inspiring organ of supervision over the administration is the Ministry of State Control. It was set up in 1951 as a Czechoslovak equivalent of its Soviet namesake and its authority was further broadened in 1952.[6] As stated in a Czechoslovak college textbook of administrative law, the Ministry's main mission is "a struggle for economy, protection of socialist property against stealing and against the attacks of the class enemy, a struggle against marauders in the state and economic apparatus, a struggle for the maintenance of socialist legality in economic and financial affairs, a struggle against bureaucratism, a struggle for the observance of the prescribed number of employees."[7]

[6] Government ordinances No. 73 of September 7, 1951, and No. 38 of August 5, 1952. For the Ministry's Statute see No. 260/1952 of *Úřední list*.

[7] Pavel Levit, *Správní právo, část obecná* (Administrative Law, General Part), Praha, 1954, p. 152.

The fact that the Ministry's first head was Karol Bacílek, member of the Party's Politbureau, indicates the importance attached to the newly established Ministry, referred to as "the main link in the system of socialist economic control."[8] Although none of Bacílek's successors could boast of membership in the Political Bureau, they were all senior members of the Party's Central Committee and devout Party members of long standing.[9] The Ministry's continued importance is also underlined by the fact that it has been retained in Czechoslovakia even after its counterpart had been abolished in the Soviet Union. Evidently, the thesis of the "completion of socialism in a historically short period," announced at the April 1958 session of the Party's Central Committee and approved by the Eleventh Party Congress in June 1958 has made the retention of the Ministry more imperative than ever.[10]

The authority of the Ministry is outlined as follows:

1. It maintains strict control over the custody, receipts, and expenditures of state, cooperative, and other monetary funds and material values.

2. It checks on the execution of the laws, ordinances, and decisions of the government.

3. It gives its opinion on the report of the Finance Ministry on the fulfillment of the state budget.

4. It handles the complaints of the working people and takes appropriate measures.

To enable the Ministry to perform these important supervisory functions it has been granted the right to require from any Ministry, any central or other agency, cooperative or other organization any plans, documents, and explanations; to have access to all offices, stores, and other premises of such organizations; to issue binding directives with a view toward remedying any discovered defects; to impose disciplinary penalties and pecuniary compensation in case of neglect of duties; and to cause the guilty to be criminally prosecuted. And lest anyone think of hiding behind the duty to preserve state secrets, it is specifically decreed that such a duty may not be invoked against the organs of the Ministry of State Control.

The Ministry wasted no time getting to work. On September 7, 1951, the Cabinet passed the ordinance establishing it; and on Sep-

[8] Jurja Hromada, *Prehľad československých štátnych orgánov* (An Outline of Czechoslovak State Organs), Bratislava, 1955, p. 99.
[9] They were in succession: Jan Harus, Michal Bakula, and Josef Krosnář.
[10] *Rudé právo*, June 19 and 23, 1958.

tember 25, 1951, *Rudé právo* published a notice informing the public that the Ministry's "section for complaints" was ready to receive complaints "by mail, telephone, or through personal visits," and that it would remain open for such purposes daily from 8:00 a.m. to 6:00 p.m. as well as on Sunday morning. It also made it be known that "no complainant would suffer because of his good will to contribute toward the elimination of existing deficiencies." Dependable Party members were appointed as the Ministry's plenipotentiaries and regional commissioners assigned to keep year-round control over certain important enterprises. Special flying commissions of experts were also set up to aid the regular inspectors in complicated cases.[11]

Planning and Financial Controls

To this all-embracing and ever-present supervision by the Party, the police, and the Ministry of State Control must be added the planning and financial controls. The Uniform Economic Plan rules like a grim, impersonal deity over the fortunes and the fate of each and every agency and all of its employees. All government agencies and all their personnel have the supreme duty to do their best in furthering the Plan's goals. Those who do are rewarded and those who do not must suffer the adverse consequences of their neglect. The higher the official status of those who fail, the greater the responsibility and the stiffer the penalty, for the Uniform Economic Plan accepts no excuses. Acting as a stern executor of the "deity's" will, the Government Presidium and the Council of Ministers check regularly, with the help of the State Planning Commission, on progress in the fulfillment of the Plan. They cause the unworthy to be stricken with suitable penalties, whether that be a mere reprimand, demotion, or sharper reprisals administered through another watchdog of socialist legality, the public prosecutor.

As the state budget is above all a yearly financial expression of the Economic Plan, the financial and accounting controls are a complement of the planning controls. Each and every department of government is granted specific annual budgetary allocations and must operate strictly within these. Periodic checks are made by the Finance Ministry which has thus become another important agency of control. In 1952 a special Control and Revision Administration was created after Soviet fashion within the Finance Ministry "to strengthen the financial and budgetary discipline and to deepen the control over the

[11] See also *Hospodář*, November 22, 1951.

fulfillment of the state budget."[12] It was provided with a network of regional and district inspectors and vested with vast coercive powers much like those of the Ministry of State Control.[13]

The Procuracy's Controls

As shown in Chapter XII below, it was not until 1952 that the Czechoslovak Procuracy assumed the character of its Soviet model and developed thus from an organ of strictly judicial prosecution into the Party's general supervisor over the country's administration. "It is the function of the Procurator General to guard and strengthen socialist legality in the state administration. In particular, he brings to the attention of the organs of the state administration the defects he has found and initiates the examination of measures and decisions that are contrary to the legal order . . . ."[14] All the organs of the government are subject to these supervisory powers of the Procuracy, except the National Assembly and the Cabinet. In performing his role as watchdog over socialist legality in the state administration, the Procurator General and his subordinates may not, however, interfere directly with administrative operations, impose fines, or otherwise enforce their rulings. If a violation of socialist legality is uncovered, the Procuracy files a protest with the agency guilty of such a violation and, in case the latter does not correct the situation, with the next higher authority. In the last resort, a divergence of opinion between the Procurator General and a Ministry or another central office is settled by the Cabinet.

To enable the Procuracy to pursue its supervisory tasks without having to worry about whose toes it may step on, it has been set up as an independent central office subordinated to no other government agency but the National Assembly and thus in fact responsible only to the Party leadership. A communist college textbook characterizes it as follows:

"The Procuracy is organized in a strictly centralistic manner. The Procuracy's organs, i.e., the Procurator's deputies (regional and district procurators), all serve as organs of the Procurator General. All procurators are subordinate and responsible to the Procurator General. They are completely independent of the other organs of state power

---

[12] Law No. 86 of December 11, 1952; also, Hromada, *op.cit.*, p. 95; Pavel Levit, *Správní právo, část zvláštní* (Administrative Law, Special Part), Praha, 1956, p. 385.

[13] Hromada, *op.cit.*, p. 96; also, Government ordinance No. 30 of June 6, 1958.

[14] Levit, *Správní právo, část obecná*, p. 158.

and state administration, particularly the local ones. This insures a uniformity of legality and of its protection in the whole territory of the Republic. The general supervision by the Procuracy is directed from one center and is concentrated in the person of the Procurator General. All procurators act by his authorization and directives."[15]

Thus the Procuracy seems to be organizationally well fitted to supplement the controlling activities of the other supervisory agencies and even to supervise the administrative supervisors themselves. However, there is no way of saying how well it attends to this important function. While a good deal is known about the procurators' activities in matters of criminal prosecution, which are well-publicized, hardly any data are at hand regarding their work in the field of general supervision of the state administration. How many protests have been filed against officials exceeding their powers and violating laws and regulations? Unless such matters are considered serious enough to warrant criminal prosecution, they are mostly kept hidden from the public. Judging from such scanty information as is brought out about this matter by escapees, the Procuracy seems to have been rather inactive in that respect, especially with regard to the activities of central and regional administration. None of the escapees I have contacted could recall having heard of any protests filed by the Procuracy against ministerial or regional administration acts.

State Arbitration Controls

Communist textbooks and manuals mention also the organs of the State and Departmental Arbitration among the agencies engaged in the supervision of the state administration. Although their primary function is to settle economic disputes among national enterprises and thus to act as a sort of commercial tribunal,[16] in so doing the arbitrators necessarily gain knowledge of noncompliance with laws and regulations on the part of various administrators. While they are not authorized to resort to direct remedial action, it is their duty to "guard socialist legality and the planning and contractual discipline" by reporting such shortcomings to higher administrative authorities.[17] As the law stipulates, "the State Arbitration must notify the respective superior organs, and in necessary cases the Procurator General, of all the substantial violations of state, planning or contractual discipline, and other deficiencies in the work of the enterprises, organiza-

---

[15] *ibid.*
[16] In that capacity they are considered in Chapter xii below.
[17] Levit, *Správní právo, část obecná,* pp. 163-164.

tions, and establishments of the socialist sector and the organs of the state administration which have been revealed by the arbitration procedure."[18] The organs so notified must reply within thirty days and, in particular, express themselves regarding the suggestion of the State Arbitration as to how the deficiencies are to be removed and their recurrence prevented. If the State Arbitration organ considers such a reply as insufficient, it must insist that the measure which it has recommended be carried out.

The Kremlin's Controls

Finally, mention should be made of the Kremlin controls. To supervise their satellites the Soviet rulers use a variety of devices, such as oversized embassies and consular offices, sundry liaison missions, and a network of native confidants and undercover agents. But these devices cannot be considered as a part of the operational pattern of the Czechoslovak administration any more than the spying activities of Soviet agents can be regarded as a part of the administrative operations of non-communist countries. Nor did the Soviets attempt at any time to duplicate in Czechoslovakia the Polish experiment in planting a prominent Soviet Communist like Marshall Rokosowsky directly in the Czechoslovak Cabinet, although for a while rumors had been in circulation that Marshall Malinovsky was considered for such a position. At one time two former Soviet citizens did sit in the Czechoslovak Council of Ministers: Julius Maurer as Minister of Heavy Engineering and Alois Málek as Minister of Light Industry. But both are natives of Czechoslovakia and had spent the first thirty years of their lives in the country, emigrating to Russia in 1925-1926. Although they acquired Soviet citizenship and membership in the Soviet Communist Party, they never held prominent positions in the Soviet administration.[19] According to trustworthy reports from Czechoslovak underground sources Soviet citizens worked as advisers in some ministries during the Stalin era, especially in those of Defense and State Security. But they were relatively few and most of them have since returned to Russia.

CENTRALIZATION AND DECENTRALIZATION

Another prevalent trend in the organizational and operational pattern of the communist administration during the Stalin era was

---

[18] Government ordinances No. 47 of May 12, 1953, and No. 45 of September 21, 1954.

[19] Málek held a position in the textile industry of Kirghizia and was awarded several Soviet decorations. See *Rudé právo,* January 15, 1953.

the ever-tightening centralization. This was all the more conspicuous since the Czechoslovak Communists began their bid for power with an all-out advocacy of the broadest decentralization. As early as 1943 and 1944 they pressed President Beneš and his government in exile in London to agree to a sweeping reform of the whole structure of the Czechoslovak postwar administration, involving major grants of authority to various local government units.[20] They denounced the Czechoslovak Constitution of 1920 as extremely centralistic and insisted upon an almost dualistic arrangement of Czech-Slovak relations, including a special Diet with almost exclusive legislative powers in Slovakia as well as a special Slovak Board of Commissioners to head the Slovak administration. They were mainly responsible for including these postulates into the Košice Program of the first Czechoslovak government to be set up in the liberated Czechoslovak territory in 1945.[21] They continued to harp on these themes in much the same vein from 1945 to 1948, although they became much less enthusiastic about the Slovak self-government after the 1946 elections which resulted in a major victory in Slovakia for the anti-communist Slovak Democratic Party.

After the 1948 coup the previous emphasis on decentralization and Slovak autonomy was shelved. Here and there lip service continued to be paid to the general principle, but for all practical purposes decentralization was replaced by increasing centralization, pursued in the name of the Leninist-Stalinist democratic centralism. These centralizing tendencies, justified officially as being necessary for the successful construction of socialism, continued throughout the whole Stalinist era and were carried over into post-Stalin days.[22] The growing dissatisfaction with the work of the people's committees and their indulgence in "unhealthy manifestations of local patriotism" led in September 1953 and in March 1954 to the enactment of two new laws on the people's committees which amounted to a further tightening of central government's controls.[23]

However, the post-Stalin emphasis on less centralization in the Soviet Union, the growing economic difficulties, and the inability

---

[20] See Klement Gottwald, in *Cesta k svobodě* (The Road to Freedom), London, 1944, pp. 18ff.

[21] *Program prvé domácí vlády republiky* (The Program of the First Government of Czechs and Slovaks on Native Soil), Košice, 1945, Parts v and vi.

[22] Hromada, *op.cit.*, p. 26.

[23] *Rudé právo*, September 17, 1953. For a fuller discussion see Chapter xiii below.

of the top-heavy overbureaucratized administrative apparatus to obtain improvements induced the Czechoslovak rulers to take a chance with a few cautious steps toward decentralization. In the summer of 1954 the government modified somewhat the overcentralized system of regulations for agricultural production.[24] Issuing the Party directives to the National Party Conference in June 1956 the Party's First Secretary Antonín Novotný, spoke of "the decision to decentralize and simplify the state apparatus," scored excessive centralization in Slovakia and promised "a transfer of a substantial part of ministerial agenda to the [Slovak] commissioners" as well as an increase in the scope of authority of the people's committees.[25]

The government moved quickly to comply with this supreme Party ukase. Within less than two months the National Assembly passed a new constitutional law extending the powers of the Slovak regional organs.[26] The ministries began regretfully to divest themselves of some of their functions in favor of the people's committees. The Ministry of Health gave up its administration of pharmacies and some health resorts of local importance. The Ministry of Transport surrendered road maintenance and some other segments of its jurisdiction over the highways. The Ministry of Food Industry yielded matters relative to local supplies of consumer goods, the Ministry of Building Materials did the same in regard to building supplies to individual enterprises, and the Ministry of Internal Trade parted with the management of Restaurants. The Ministry of Education and Culture passed on to the people's committees the operation of motion picture theaters as well as the establishment and operation of schools and hiring of teachers, while the Ministry of Agriculture was relieved of the direct management of state farms, machine-tractor stations, and some agricultural schools. Similar transfers of agenda took place in the work of a number of other ministries.[27]

This first stage of decentralization, which went into effect in January 1957, was followed by another one aimed specifically at the industrial ministries. Taking due notice of Khrushchëv's thesis of economic decentralization, the Czechoslovak Communists decided to attack bureaucracy's stifling hold over industry by applying, in a diluted form, Khrushchëv's drastic remedy. In pursuance of a call

[24] *Rudé právo*, September 2, 1954.
[25] *ibid.*, June 12, 1956.
[26] See Chapter XIV.
[27] *Prague News Letter*, 12, 21, October 27, 1956, No. 25, December 22, 1956, and No. 24, December 8, 1956.

issued by the Party's Central Committee in September 1957, a sub-stantial decentralization was undertaken in the field of industrial pro-duction to become effective by April 1, 1958. While the Czechoslovak rulers did not follow the Soviet lead to the extreme of abolishing industrial ministries, they relieved them of much of their agenda, leaving them mainly in charge of general guidance while broadening the authority of individual plant management.[28] The "main admin-istrations," which served as supermanagers of various industries on the ministerial level, were abolished and most of their authority trans-ferred to individual enterprises or their trusts. As revealed in No-votný's report to the Eleventh Party Congress in June 1958, the apparatus of the economic ministries and central offices was thus reduced by 9,500 employees, i.e., one-third of their personnel.[29] An-other minor shift of agenda from a few ministries to local government authorities was effected in June 1958. Its most noteworthy feature was the transfer of the right to appoint the directors of the machine-tractor stations from the Ministry of Agriculture to the executive organs of the district people's committees.[30] Finally, decentralization was carried one step further in 1960 when additional agenda were transferred from ministries to the regional people's committees and some of the routine administrative business hitherto handled on re-gional level was assigned to the lower echelons of local government.[31]

Although a substantial slice of ministerial agenda devolved on lower organs as a result of the decentralization and simplification campaigns of 1959-1960, the whole system seems, by Western demo-cratic standards, rigidly centralized. If decentralization is to be under-stood as an enlargement of the powers of the local at the expense of the central authority, then the Czechoslovak rulers have barely scratched the surface of the problem. Much of what the ministries surrendered are trivial matters which should have never been adminis-tered on ministerial level. Giving up the direct management of res-taurants, pharmacies, or motion picture theaters hardly qualifies as a feat of decentralization. None of the key central controls of the Stalin era have been abandoned or softened in any way; rather the contrary is true. Nor can the idea of genuine decentralization of authority be benefited by the strong emphasis which the new Constitution of 1960 lays on democratic centralism. What the Communists call decentral-

---

[28] *ibid.*, 13, 21, October 26, 1957.
[29] *Rudé právo*, June 19, 1958.
[30] Government ordinance No. 34 of June 27, 1958.
[31] See *Rudé právo*, April 14, 1960.

ization is, therefore, primarily a deconcentration of certain activities designed to simplify the unwieldly ministerial apparatus, alleviate bureaucratic congestion at the center, and thus make ministerial guidance and supervision more effective for a better and faster "completion of socialism." It is a devolution of strictly defined duties rather than of discretionary powers, and as such it has little in common with the philosophy of decentralized authority as conceived by modern democracy.

MINISTERIAL MONOCRATISM

Communist concern for the maximum administrative efficiency counseled against the adoption of the collective principle for administrative purposes which had characterized the early years of the dictatorship of the proletariat in Russia. As explained in a recent Czechoslovak textbook on government, "Ministries which administer certain branches or sectors of the state administration are strictly monocratic organs wherein the ministers answer for all their acts," for only the monocratic principle "guarantees individual responsibility . . . and the possibility of faster and more elastic development."[32]

After the February coup of 1948 Action Committees of communist zealots sprang up in various ministries and became for a while self-styled *kollegia* purging the undesirables, deciding personnel policies, and even attempting to make other administrative decisions. But once the communist regime was firmly in the saddle, this came to an end and the monocratic principle prevailed. This could be done all the more easily since a strictly one-man management (*edinonachalie*) was solidly established in the Soviet system of administration at the time of Gottwald's seizure of power. Hence, the Czechoslovak rulers were acting in the best Stalinist tradition when they preserved the pre-communist monocratism in the operation of their transmission belts.

That does not mean that the collective principle is altogether absent from central administration. It applies to a few commissions that function on the central level of the administration, such as the State Commission for Academic Degrees. Furthermore, in each Ministry there exists a small board composed of the Minister and the leading officials of the Ministry, meeting more or less regularly to discuss the affairs of the department.[33] But the functions of this *kollegium*, fashioned after the Soviet *kollegia*, are strictly advisory. Whatever may

[32] Hromada, *op.cit.*, pp. 83 and 282.
[33] *ibid.*, p. 84; Levit, *Správní právo, část obecná*, p. 61.

be the opinion of the board's majority, the Minister's aye has it. Nor does there seem to be any formal arrangement, such as are theoretically available in the Soviet Union, authorizing the members of the *kollegium* to appeal against a Minister's decision with which they might not be in agreement.

MAJOR PROBLEMS: THE LERNEAN HYDRA OF BUREAUCRACY

As rulers everywhere, whether democratic, authoritarian or totalitarian, the Czechoslovak Communists impose two basic requirements on their system of executive transmission belts: loyalty and efficiency. Ever since their victory in February 1948 they have been working hard toward the attainment of these two goals, but have thus far fallen short of both.

The Issue of Loyalty

Understandably, loyalty has been a primary communist preoccupation. The administrative personnel which the communist leaders inherited upon their accession to power could not be trusted, and for good reasons. Although the KSČ enjoyed full freedom of political operations in prewar Czechoslovakia, Communists were ineligible for civil service, as were Fascists and Nazis. Save for an occasional Party member who managed to sneak through the anti-communist bar, the only Party members who could gain administrative experience prior to 1945 were the relatively few Communists who served in the offices of the Czechoslovak government-in-exile in Britain during World War II. Between 1945 and 1948 a substantial number of prewar civil servants joined the Party, especially in the ministries headed by communist chiefs. While such opportunistic recruits were welcome at a time when the Party was engaged in its abortive stratagem of gaining power in a "parliamentary" way, they could not be considered as suitable material from which a dependable administrative apparatus could be molded for the dictatorship of the proletariat. As a matter of fact, many of these bureaucratic turncoats were quite willing to trade their loyalty for a warm spot in the people's democratic officialdom, and they would have served the new masters with zeal and subservience. But the stigma of bourgeois origin and the opportunistic nature of their conversion made them unworthy of genuine Party trust. Thus the only people with administrative experience who were available in some quantity at the time of the communist coup, and whose loyalty was not in doubt were those prewar Communists who entered the civil service from 1945 to 1948.

Since the supply of dependable communist administrators was far too short to meet the truly voracious demands of the ever-growing government machinery, the communist rulers found it necessary, after the coup, to retain the services of vast numbers of employees of questionable loyalty and faulty "class profile." Being much more keenly aware than Lenin and his Bolsheviks of the intricacies and complexities of modern administration, they preferred the calculated risk of doubtful loyalty to that of administrative chaos. With his crude sense of practicality Gottwald used to justify the continued employment of such personifications of international capitalism as Eduard Outrata, former Director of the biggest Czechoslovak Armament Corporation: "He is a capitalist shark, but he does things rather well." And as mentioned elsewhere, Zápotocký rebuked the Party's cadres commissions in 1949 for their conviction that important positions should be entrusted only to Party members.[34]

While such an attitude helped to prevent administrative chaos following the February coup, it left the crucial issue of bureaucracy's loyalty toward the new regime wide open. Moreover, it made Gottwald, Zápotocký, and their associates vulnerable to Soviet criticism for tolerating "bourgeois elements" in high administrative posts. As the sovietization of Czechoslovakia began to gather momentum after the initial lull of 1948-1949 and the relentless Moscow-decreed drive toward higher production goals called for more and more scapegoats for failures and delays, the Czechoslovak rulers struck out against the "hidden class enemy" within the state administration. In a succession of purges most of the employees with bourgeois background have by now been weeded out from the central government organs and sent to work in mines and factories. Many of them fell victim to the first major transfer of 77,000 administrative employees into industrial production in 1951-1952. Those who survived or managed to find their way back into the administration after the storm subsided were caught in the thorough screening of political and class reliability to which all employees of ministries and central offices were subjected on the Central Committee's orders in the months preceding the Eleventh Party Congress. "It is impossible not to see," warned *Rudé právo* on January 25, 1958, in an effort to prod the purgers, "that

[34] Antonín Zápotocký, *Revoluční odborové hnutí po únoru 1948* (The Revolutionary Trade Union Movement after February 1948), Praha, 1952, pp. 326ff.

the defeated bourgeois class seeks to overcome its defeat . . . [by] infiltrating the organs of the proletarian State, hiding behind the cloak of professional ability, and taking advantage of the lack of vigilance and the conciliatory attitude of some Communists."[35] Yet another wholesale personnel screening of the entire state administration was undertaken in 1959. Decreed by the Party's Central Committee in connection with the slogan of "the completion of the socialist revolution" launched by the Eleventh Party Congress, the screening resulted in a removal from administrative ranks of tens of thousands of employees.[36] Nor can those "remnants of antagonistic classes" that weathered the latest purge hope but for a temporary reprieve. "Our Party will continue to strive for a state and economic apparatus of such a political and class profile as will guarantee a consistent execution of the will of the Party and the people," threatened Novotný in his speech to the Eleventh Congress heralding the accelerated drive toward the completion of the socialist revolution.[37]

Bureaucratic Hypertrophy

Besides seeking to rid the administration of employees of questionable loyalty and of a wrong class profile, these purges and transfers were also aimed at solving another major problem plaguing the communist rulers: the stifling hypertrophy of the bureaucratic apparatus. Indeed, there seems to be no harder nut to crack than the reduction of the overinflated ranks of communist administrators to more sensible proportions, and *keeping* them thus reduced. "The excessive inflation in our administrative apparatus is a burden from which, every one will agree, we must free ourselves," wrote *Rudé právo* on August 20, 1957, in one of its many articles devoted to this thorny problem. "However, experience has taught us that this is easier said than done . . . ." Addressing the Eleventh Congress, Novotný agreed: "Bureaucratism is alien to the proletarian State. But we are not Utopians believing that we shall destroy bureaucratism overnight by a decree or an ordinance."[38]

For all their efforts spent on that worthwhile objective since 1950 the Communist rulers can thus far boast only of rather meager results. Naturally, the potential victims fought their transfer to "productive

---

[35] *Rudé právo,* December 8, 1957, and Novotný's speech at the Eleventh Party Congress, *Rudé právo,* June 19, 1958.
[36] *Československý zpravodaj,* No. 285, March 9, 1960.
[37] *Rudé právo,* June 19, 1958.
[38] *ibid.*

work" tooth and nail. Nor were their communist superiors, many of whom had but little knowledge of administrative procedures, always pleased by the prospect of losing experienced personnel. Devious ways and means, including outright collusion, were resorted to in order to outwit the authorities.[39] Nonetheless, with considerable delay, the planned targets of personnel reduction were generally attained. But that was never the end of the story. Positions thus vacated were not eliminated but were refilled by Party members all too eager to trade the exalted worker's status for a more comfortable office chair. That is what had defeated the purpose of the 1951-1952 de-bureaucratization.[40]

Having learned their lesson, the communist rulers have lately adopted a new stratagem. When prescribing a reduction in personnel they simultaneously provide for the abolition of positions held by those who have been removed, and transfer a part of ministerial agenda downward to the people's committees and individual economic enterprises. They seek thus to make sure that the removed bureaucrats are not simply replaced with others possessed of better class origin. However, to judge by past experience, chances are very good that many of the officials dropped from central agencies will eventually land administrative jobs on lower echelons of the governmental hierarchy instead of "constructing socialism" on the production line. This is all the more likely as most factory managers are anything but overjoyed at the prospect of employing ex-bureaucrats and neither do the workers relish having them for fellow-workers.[41] As *Rudé právo* put it, "The question now is how many of the . . . dismissed administrative workers will strengthen the ranks of production and how many will, by various ways and means, again find cushy spots in offices . . . ."[42]

Thus the net gain scored against bureaucratism on the central level tends to be largely offset by its increase on the intermediate and lower levels of administration and by its inflation of the administrative machinery of individual enterprises.[43] The bureaucrats thrown out through the front door slip back through the basement entrance. Watching this perennial and somewhat pathetic struggle of communist rulers against the bureaucratic hydra which they themselves had helped to create one is almost inclined to consider as applicable

[39] *Rudé právo,* December 8 and 10, 1957, and February 29, 1960.
[40] See *Rudé právo's* belated explanation, August 20, 1957.
[41] See a complaint about such attitudes in *Rudé právo,* December 8, 1957.
[42] *Mladá fronta,* January 8, 1957.
[43] *Rudé právo,* August 20, 1957.

to Czechoslovakia a very fitting cartoon published in the Polish humor magazine *Szpilki*.[44] It portrays a multiheaded bureaucrat sitting behind a desk. The floor of the office is strewn with heads that had already been chopped off. A dejected Hercules, holding a big stick with which he had been mowing down the heads of that bureaucratic hydra, walks away, saying: "I give up."

Nevertheless, the communist Hercules's persistent mace-swinging did lower noticeably the overgrown ranks of central government employees and may have even achieved a slight state-wide reduction of the over-all number of bureaucrats, although the latter is by no means certain. According to the official *Czechoslovak Yearbook of Statistics*, the number of persons employed in "administration and the judiciary, banking and insurance, social organizations, and activities not listed elsewhere" fell from 269,000 in 1948 to 205,000 in 1958. On the other hand, the category of employees lumped together under the heading of "science and exploration, communal services, housing administration, health and social services, education, culture, enlightenment, and physical education" rose at the same time from 333,000 to 609,000.[45] Also, despite persistent communist efforts to transfer personnel from "nonproductive" to "productive" work, the number of persons engaged in "material production" and in "nonproductive branches" increased virtually by the same ratio of a little over 9 percent between 1954 and 1958.[46] Nor do official data warrant a conclusive answer to the question whether or not the bureaucratic element has been reduced in economic enterprises.[47]

Whatever the decrease in the bureaucrats' total, it is extremely doubtful whether any relief was gained from bureaucratism itself. As the Hungarian revisionist Gyula Hay had said, "In the pruning of bureaucracy, the most bureaucratic bureaucrat will survive . . . . Bureaucracy will be smaller, but as bureaucracy *per se* it will be more intense and more virulent . . . ."[48] That seems to have been the case

---

[44] July 7, 1957.

[45] *Ročenka*, 1959, p. 92.

[46] *ibid.*, p. 96.

[47] In industry proper the number of employees labeled as officials sank from 138,000 to 128,000 between 1953 and 1958; but the category listed as engineering-technical personnel, part of which also occupies bureaucratic swivel chairs, increased at the same time from 177,000 to 218,000 whereas the number of workers rose from 1,412,000 to 1,618,000. In construction the officials registered an increase from 9,000 to 20,000 between 1948 and 1958, engineering-technical personnel from 14,000 to 36,000 and workers from 171,000 to 257,000. All above data are from *Ročenka*, 1959, pp. 19, 21.

[48] *Irodalmi Ujsag*, October 6, 1956. Cited in *East Europe*, 7, 8 (1958), p. 16.

in Czechoslovakia. Since "class origin, political maturity, and devotion to the Party and the working class" have been prescribed as the decisive requirement for retention and replacement of government personnel, more and more civil servants are recruited from among die-hard Communists.[49] But no bureaucrat is more bureaucratic than a communist bureaucrat; for his rigid Marxist-Leninist orthodoxy and the initiative-stifling atmosphere of fear and suspicion in which he has to work magnify the vices of ordinary bureaucratism.

The Curse of Incompetence

Nor could the application of these "Leninist principles of selection" leave the efficiency of the the service unaffected. When considerations of professional qualification rate second to the class profile and civil servants with long years of experience are replaced by greenhorns with little practice in orderly administrative procedures, administrative efficiency must necessarily suffer. Few sides of life under communism are more amply documented than the low quality of the communist bureaucracy. I interviewed a number of escapees who had been in a position to compare the standards of the present bureaucrats with those of prewar days. Invariably and unhesitatingly, they considered the prewar civil service with all its deficiencies as having been far superior to its present communist equivalent. Reports from underground sources speak in the same vein. That these anti-communist quarters do not unduly exaggerate is confirmed by the incessant flow of criticism directed at the bureaucracy and its behavior by communist rulers themselves as well as by numerous cartoons and biting satires ridiculing bureaucratic deficiencies that appear continually in the Czechoslovak communist press.[50]

To remedy the situation and to secure a supply of better-trained personnel, the regime began to experiment in 1950 with various one-year and even six-month courses for the preparation of promising younger Communists of working-class origin for administrative positions. Among the agencies listed as having set up such snap courses were the Ministries of the Interior, Foreign Trade, Foreign Affairs, Finance, and Justice.[51] In pursuance of the same goal, state courses for the preparation of workers for colleges and universities were de-

---

[49] *Rudé právo,* January 25, 1958.

[50] For a few examples see *Rudé právo,* May 24, 1951, July 22, and December 8, 1957.

[51] *Práce,* October 1 and 15, 1950; *Lidové noviny,* October 11, 1950; *Hospodář,* June 8, 1950.

veloped for those who "come from worker and small peasant families, spent at least one year in production as workers or small peasants, proved to be the best workers, and showed their positive attitude to the people's democratic government by active participation in public life."[52] Suitable candidates between the ages of eighteen and twenty-eight were selected by communist-controlled trade union groups in factories and by communist-controlled Czechoslovak Youth Union in rural areas. Moreover, the whole school system was reorganized from top to bottom with a view toward securing as soon as feasible a steady stream of thoroughly indoctrinated "toiling intelligentsia.[53] Undoubtedly, in due time these communist efforts will result in an adequate supply of administrators who may have both the right class profile and desired professional ability. This ought to solve those problems which are caused by insufficient numbers of properly qualified personnel of working-class origin. But it will still leave them with those problems which have little to do with training and preparation but are inherent in the system of totalitarian communism as such.

Obezlichka and Lack of Initiative

One of these ills has been what the Czechoslovak Communists call *obezlichka,* a Russian word whose literal translation is "facelessness." It is, in essence, the tendency to evade personal responsibility. Although *obezlichka* pervades every sector of the communist system, it has found an especially profitable field of operation in the state administration. Knowing what disastrous consequences a wrong decision might have for him in a totalitarian system accepting no excuses for failures, a communist bureaucrat prefers very much to remain anonymous and spares no effort to shift the burden of responsibility on the other fellow. The result has been a continuous tug-of-war between superiors and subordinates as to who is to be held primarily responsible when something goes wrong. The communist rulers declared a merciless war on this *obezlichka* from the very beginning of their rule.[54] In the negative sense, they succeeded, for no decision can now be made or executed in communist Czechoslovakia without some "face" being held accountable for the result, be it good or be it bad.

However, by adopting the rigid Soviet precept of judging intentions and personal effort almost exclusively by their results, the KSČ

[52] *Rudé právo,* December 5, 1951; *Práce,* January 6, 1951. See also Chapter XIX below.
[53] See Chapter XIX for further discussion.
[54] *Rudé právo,* November 2, 1951.

leaders dealt a heavy blow to individual initiative. Even in prewar days Czechoslovak bureaucrats suffered from lack of initiative.[55] Yet they were daring initiators compared to their communist successors. The regime is well aware of it. While insisting on democratic central-ism as the basic operative principle of the state's administration, it recognizes the great importance of individual initiative.[56] But all its calls for more socialist initiative seem to find little response. Occasion-ally one or another employee comes up with a new idea of adminis-trative improvement, earns an official pat on the shoulder and an improver's bonus or even promotion. He may be cited publicly as "improver" or "innovator," meritorious titles conferred upon those who invent or improve a useful device or technique. But the majority of communist officialdom takes to individual initiative like a cat to water. They know that for every innovator or improver who gains reward and recognition there are many who reap the whirlwind, for failure of the best-intended experiment may all too easily be twisted into accusations of gross negligence or even sabotage. Hence, they pre-fer to cling to the established routines and follow to the letter instruc-tions of their superior, because that is the safest course in the long run.

The Spoils System of the Civil Service

Such caution is necessary since there is nothing in the communist administrative system that could vaguely resemble tenure or other arrangements that might protect employees against the whims of their chiefs.

In pre-Munich Czechoslovakia the two most pronounced features of the civil service system were a rigid classification of jobs according to educational standards and a security of tenure. All positions in the civil service were grouped into four classes and the required formal education was laid down by statute as a condition for appointment. A university degree was needed for any position in the highest (ad-ministrative) class, a senior high school diploma for the next class, etc. There was practically no way to be promoted from one class to another without first obtaining the respective school diploma. Once appointed, the civil servant enjoyed, after a three-year probationary period, full-fledged security of tenure.[57]

Between the end of the war and the communist coup of 1948 a number of appointments were made in disregard of these principles.

---

[55] Eduard Táborský, *Czechoslovak Democracy at Work*, London, 1945, p. 144.
[56] Hromada, *op.cit.*, pp. 26-27.
[57] E. Táborský, *op.cit.*, Chapter VIII.

But, on the whole, the rules still held. The communist seizure of power blew them to pieces. Communist Action Committees were established in all governmental agencies and usurped the authority to purge, demote, or promote whomever they pleased. Finally, in May 1950, the National Assembly passed a new law regulating the status of civil servants but left a good deal to be prescribed by executive order, which was subsequently issued on May 30, 1950.[58] The essence of the new civil service system as amended further in 1954 and 1956, may be briefly summed up as follows:[59]

The requirements of formal education for admission to the civil service have been dropped. Instead, the applicant is to be judged by four criteria: professional qualification, working experience, ability, and political maturity. Also, he preferably should have been employed in production "for an adequate time." The reason behind the last-named requirement is, according to *Rudé právo,* that no one should be a civil servant who could not first become acquainted with the life of the workers.[60] The number of civil servants and the salary system is determined, subject to the Cabinet's approval, by a government-appointed Systemization Commission on the basis of a manpower plan which is constantly adapted to the changing requirements of the national economy.

The rights and duties of civil servants are governed "by the same basic socialist principles as apply to other working people."[61] Civil servants must be "guardians of socialist legality" and pursue, in the performance of their duties, "above all the interest of the people's democratic state and of the working people."[62] They may be dismissed with or without notice whenever such a dismissal is in the interest of work discipline; and they may be transferred to other work, whether it be mining, factory work, or any other "productive" labor. They are rewarded according to the quality, quantity, and "social importance" of their work. Salary consists of basic pay, functional allowance, family benefits graduated according to the number of children, bonuses and premiums for special merits. Promotion is given on the basis of merit and the employee's "political growth."

As can be seen from this brief summary, security of tenure has been abolished, both in reality and in law, along with the other "rem-

---

[58] Law No. 66/1950 and government ordinance No. 120/1950.
[59] Government ordinance No. 17 of February 12, 1954, Presidium Decree No. 60 of December 13, 1956.
[60] *Rudé právo,* May 21, 1950.
[61] Levit, *Správní právo, část obecná,* p. 104.
[62] *ibid.,* pp. 109, 110.

nants of privileges typical of the bureaucracy of the bourgeois state apparatus."[63] There are virtually no objective requirements for admission since the earlier prerequisites of college and other degrees were eliminated without being replaced by entrance examinations such as exist in the United States or in Great Britain. An applicant may thus be appointed to any civil service class and may be promoted from one to another at the pleasure of his communist superiors. Such absence of the most elementary protection against arbitrary dismissal and unjust discrimination in matters of promotion cannot but gravely undermine the employees' morale. Although it is a system based supposedly on merit plus loyalty, in reality it is a novel version of the spoils system of the days when modern bureaucracy was in its infancy. But experience of modern government teaches that a truly able and efficient corps of administrators cannot be built on such rickety foundations. However much the rulers might seek to discourage it, such a system is bound to develop into a breeding-place of favoritism and corruption just as surely as a neglected swamp becomes infested with mosquitoes. That is what has happened in communist Czechoslovakia. Despite the sacrosanct Party duty of every Communist to disregard "personal loyalties, local ties, or kinship" in the selection of all cadres, the opposite is the rule. As borne out by a wealth of reports from non-communist sources and confirmed in an oblique manner by frequent complaints in the communist press, nepotism and cronyism thrive despite leader's efforts to eliminate such malpractices.[64]

The Reorganization Mania

Another major problem impairing administrative efficiency has been the incessant reorganization of the governmental machinery described in the preceding chapter. Anyone conversant with the working of modern administration knows that even a relatively modest transfer of agenda from one agency to another is far from being a simple affair, and that it takes some time to restore normal operations after such a transfer. Hence, any major agenda shifts should be undertaken only when they hold a very distinct promise of a substantial and lasting gain over the existing arrangement. It is more than doubtful that this was so with the afore-mentioned hectic merry-go-round of administrative reorganizations in communist Czechoslovakia. The continuous juggling of ministries, reapportionment of their functions, and their repeated splitting-up and merging were bound to play havoc

[63] *ibid.*, p. 104.
[64] See also Chapters XIII and XVII.

with the established administrative procedures, entangle customary lines of authority and channels of operations, and contribute substantially to bureaucratic red tape. That this is a fact is documented by information from escaped employees of the communist administration as well as from the senseless behavior of the communist reorganizers. Indeed, some of the newly created agencies were so ephemeral that they could have hardly settled down for business and established their filing system before they were ordered to close shop and hand their agenda back to the departments from which they had just been separated!

At first glance this reorganization mania seems to be a self-inflicted woe which could be easily eliminated if the communist rulers would simply cease reorganizing and would give their administrative apparatus a chance to get set and work out the proper practices. But this is hard to do under the Moscow-directed totalitarian communism which cannot admit that there might be any major flaws inherent in the Marxist-Leninist system. Hence, when wrongs develop, the communist rulers have to blame them on personal errors and sabotage, or on faulty functioning of the administrative transmission belts. Thus the reorganization mania seems to be almost as much an inseparable concomitant of Marxism-Leninism as are the purge, democratic centralism, and other similar precepts and devices.

Bureaucracy's Low Ideological Level

Finally, bureaucracy's low ideological level causes no small concern to communist leaders. With the successive elimination of employees tainted with bourgeois origin and their replacement by men with correct class profile and unblemished cadre reports, the ministries and other government agencies should now be filled with men whose loyalty to the cause of communism is beyond doubt and whose ideological zeal is beyond reproach. However, things have evidently not turned out that way. As disclosed by repeated lamentations of the communist press, the Czechoslovak bureaucrats, most of whom are Party members, have been rather remiss in that respect. Especially revealing of this ideological laxness on the ministerial front was a scathing criticism to which a whole Ministry (Agriculture) was subjected in *Rudé právo* in 1955.[65] The Party's main daily scored the "insufficient ideological activity" of the Ministry's communist employees and their neglect of Marxist-Leninist studies "which help

[65] *Rudé právo*, May 24, 1955.

to solve more fruitfully the practical tasks of the socialist construction." It found fault with the whole Party organization in the Ministry for its ideological complacency which resulted in its failure to cope resolutely with "various incorrect opinions distorting Party policy and affecting the Ministry's work." *Rudé právo* uncovered in the midst of the Ministry's administrators even advocates of such heresies as the idea that "the law of value was an unlimited regulator of agricultural production," that "it was absolutely unnecessary to plan small agricultural production," and that "it would be more useful to increase the prices, lower the purchasing [compulsory deliveries] quotas, and broaden the so-called free market . . . ." Similar complaints about ideological stagnation among administration personnel have been a fairly recurrent feature. Typical of the situation on the threshold of 1960 was a revealing editorial on the continued wrong selection of the cadres, published in *Rudé právo* on February 29, 1960. The paper scored repeated instances when persons of questionable loyalty had been entrusted with responsible government functions; and it listed the amazing fact that even some central agencies employed persons who had been denied loyalty clearance in the screening processes on lower administrative levels or in economic enterprises.

Thus it would seem that the determined communist effort to develop a new strain of bureaucrats combining superior administrative ability with utter devotion to the Party and high level of Marxist-Leninist consciousness has met with little success in the first twelve years of the dictatorship of the proletariat. Such exemplary communist administrators continue to exist mainly in communist political fiction, but are rare in real life. Rather, the prevailing type of communist bureaucrat is an individual whose paramount concern is to avoid the next purge or transfer into production. He is extremely sycophantic vis-à-vis his superiors and rather overbearing toward his subordinates. Worn down by continuous pressures from above, he strives to lapse into anonymity and pass the buck whenever confronted with disagreeable decisions, which is more often than not. He would rather sit at his desk writing circulars than work in the field, where he would have to take the trouble to make on-the-spot checks on the execution of higher directives to "face the masses." He has little use for the Marxist-Leninist ideology as such, but learns all that he is supposed to know in a system operated in its name.

CHAPTER XI
THE LEGISLATIVE RUBBER STAMP

No GOVERNMENTAL INSTITUTION better illustrates the profound gap between theory and practice in political systems based on the dictatorship of the proletariat than the communist legislatures. In constitutional theory they rule supreme. Not only do they enjoy the monopoly of legislative power, but they are masters of all the other central government agencies, which they create and abolish, and whose heads they appoint and remove. They alone have the exclusive authority to amend the constitutions on which their vast powers ostensibly rest and they are thus legally in absolute command over their own destinies as well as those of all other governmental organs. "From the constitutional viewpoint the leading position in the system of the highest state organs belongs to the National Assembly," states an official KSČ textbook on "the highest state organs."[1] Indeed, nowhere has the principle of legislative supremacy been carried further than behind the Iron Curtain; and the communist legislatures well deserve the lofty designation of "supreme organs of state power" applied to them by the Soviet bloc's constitutions. The well-known adage that a parliament can do anything except change a man into a woman—used to stress the dominant position of the British House of Commons—could fittingly be employed to underscore the towering constitutional status of its Soviet and people's democratic equivalents.

However, actual political practice tells a different story. It reveals communist legislatures to be Cinderellas whose feet failed to fit the lost shoe. In flagrant contrast to their tremendous constitutional prerogatives, legislative assemblies of the Soviet orbit have been reduced to mere rubber stamps for Party decisions which are fed to them at long intervals via the Party's executive transmission belt. The principle of legislative supremacy has thus been replaced in practice by that of

[1] Bedřich Rattinger, *Nejvyšší státní orgány lidově demokratického Československa* (The Highest State Organs of the People's Democratic Czechoslovakia), Praha, 1957, p. 6.

legislative inferiority which places communist legislatures well below the executive branch of the government.

Although the Czechoslovak National Assembly under the Ninth-of-May Constitution differed in some notable aspects from the Supreme Soviet of the USSR and even from the rest of the satellite legislatures, its political role fitted well the over-all communist pattern. While it bore more outward resemblance to Western European parliaments than any other legislature of the Soviet orbit, its political impotence was just as complete as that of its legislative sisters behind the Iron Curtain. What was left of the "pseudodemocratic survivals of the bourgeois past" has been taken care of in the constitutional change-over of 1960 from which the National Assembly has emerged as a virtual copy of the Soviet model.

PREWAR PARLIAMENTARISM

In order to evaluate the Czechoslovak legislature under the dictatorship of the proletariat it is necessary to consider briefly the legislative system of pre-communist days. A correct understanding of the weird *mésalliance* of Western parliamentarian usages with totalitarian substance that took place after the communist seizure of power is impossible without knowledge of the National Assembly's pre-communist past.

The prewar Czechoslovak legislature was a bicameral body with both its chambers elected the same way, except that the age requirement for voting and eligibility for the upper chamber, the Senate, was somewhat higher than for the lower house, the Chamber of Deputies.[2] Proportional representation was used, and though the term of office of senators was somewhat longer than that of deputies, both houses used to be dissolved at the same time. Consequently, the party complexion of both chambers was almost identical, which meant in practice that, in view of the strict system of party discipline existing in prewar Czechoslovakia, voting in the two houses ran along parallel lines. Since the Chamber of Deputies had the power to overthrow the Cabinet, and its three-fifths majority could always overrule an adverse vote of the Senate, it is obvious why the Senate came to be referred to as a "still-born child."

The executive-legislative relationship developed along the lines of the British Cabinet system. While the legislature never made use of its

[2] On the prewar Czechoslovak legislature see Eduard Táborský, *Czechoslovak Democracy at Work,* London, 1945, Chapter II.

power to overthrow the Cabinet, it was itself dissolved three times. Legislative primacy yielded in practice to executive supremacy, even though its political foundations were much shakier in Czechoslovakia than in Britain, due to the First Republic's multiparty system and the necessity of coalition governments.

Throughout the twenty years of its free existence the prewar Czechoslovak Parliament operated very much in the manner of legislative bodies of other European democracies. Broadly speaking, it combined certain features of French and British parliamentary practices. As in Britain, government-sponsored bills were almost certain to pass while opposition bills were invariably doomed to failure. The number and type of committees corresponded more to the French pattern, but their actual power over the bills was much weaker than in France and more nearly resembled English usage. Each party had a parliamentary club which shaped the party's legislative strategy and saw to it that party members in either house abided by party instructions.

Party discipline was enforced by a unique system the rigor of which far exceeded anything found in Western European democracies, Britain included. Before being placed on his party's electoral list each candidate had to append his signature to an undated undertaking that he was resigning from his seat. When and if he then quarreled with his party, its leaders simply provided the letter with a date and sent it to the clerk of the appropriate house. Though such procedure was in flagrant contradiction to an express constitutional provision prohibiting a member of Parliament from accepting instructions from any source, such undertakings were nevertheless held valid by the Electoral Court. Thus the Czechoslovak member of Parliament in prewar days was at all times bound by a straitjacket of rigid party discipline and any deviation from the party line could cost him his seat.

THE 1945-1948 INTERMEZZO

When Dr. Beneš's government returned to Czechoslovakia in 1945, legislative powers on the national level were at first exercised jointly by the President of the Republic and the Cabinet by way of presidential decrees. In October 1945 they were taken over by an indirectly elected Provisional National Assembly and after May 1946 by a popularly elected Constituent National Assembly which was vested with authority both to legislate and to draft and adopt a new constitution. These two legislatures of pre-communist days came into being in a rather irregular fashion.[3]

The first one was "elected" by provincial meetings of delegates chosen by local people's committees.[4] But actually all its three hundred deputies were handpicked by the leaders of the political parties of the National Front. Each of the six parties allowed to operate after the War nominated forty members and the remaining sixty seats were filled by "experts" representing various interest groups, such as the trade unions, cultural associations, and scientific groups. As the Communists were organized at that time in two separate parties, one for Czech lands and another for Slovakia, they obtained a total of eighty seats. Moreover, eighteen of the sixty experts subsequently joined the two communist parliamentary clubs. Thus the communist representation in the first postwar legislature was far bigger than that of any other party, amounting to almost one-third of the Assembly's total membership.

In May 1946 the Provisional National Assembly was replaced by the Constituent National Assembly elected, as the law put it, "on the basis of universal, equal, direct, and secret suffrage and in accordance with the principle of proportional representation."[5] It was a competitive election in which each party ran its own independent ticket, indeed one of the very few such elections held in Eastern Europe after the War. On the whole, it was a free election insofar as people with a reasonable amount of civic courage could vote for any one of the party ballots or cast a blank ticket. But there were several gross irregularities which impaired its fairness. Only the few officially permitted parties were allowed to participate. A substantial number of voters were excluded from the voters' registers under various pretexts, mostly those whom the Communists suspected of intentions to vote for non-communist parties.[6] There were widespread violations of the secrecy of voting. Communists organized campaigns for voting in public, urging factory workers to march with playing bands to the ballot boxes for

[3] A brief outline of the parliamentary system of 1945-1947 may be found in William Diamond, *Czechoslovakia between East and West*, London, 1947; also, Pavel Korbel's article in *Československý přehled*, II, 8 (1955), pp. 6ff.

[4] Government ordinance No. 48 of August 25, 1945, and constitutional decree of the President of the Republic No. 47 of August 25, 1945.

[5] Law No. 67 of April 11, 1946, and constitutional law No. 65 of April 11, 1946.

[6] This was possible because the local authorities who were in charge of the registration were mostly communist-dominated, as was the Ministry of the Interior that supervised the whole electoral process. See also Hubert Ripka, *Le Coup de Prague*, Paris, 1949, pp. 38-39.

collective voting in public. Since die-hard KSČ members were in control of most of the nationalized industries as well as in charge of the distribution of property confiscated from the Sudeten Germans and the allocation of fertilizers and agricultural tools, they were in a position to cause trouble for those who chose to cast the ballot in secret in spite of the communist insistence that no one should be ashamed to vote in public.[7]

Despite all these advantages, the Communists failed to achieve a majority that would enable them to do under the guise of parliamentary democracy what they had to do two years later by a revolutionary coup. Having polled 38 percent of the total vote, they became by far the strongest party; but the democratic parties together secured almost two-thirds of the vote.[8] Only 113 of the 300 members of the Constituent Assembly were Communists. Not even with the aid of a dozen or so fellow-travelers hidden in other parties could the KSČ hope to get its way by using normal legislative processes, let alone induce the Assembly to adopt a constitution that would be acceptable from the Marxist-Leninist point of view.

While the composition of the first two postwar legislatures differed substantially from that of prewar days, parliamentary procedures underwent no important change. Despite the presence of more than one hundred communist deputies and the explosiveness of the overall political situation of the first postwar years, prewar parliamentary traditions continued to predominate. Vigorous reaction against communist abuses made itself felt and heard ever more intensively on the Assembly's floor, even though there was little hope of translating it into effective action. Many a communist minister suffered a bitter verbal licking from the non-communist legislators. Except for the fact that no one ventured to aim any criticism at the Soviet Union, parliamentary debates were characterized by sharp exchanges much in the manner of prewar days.

Apart from the greatly changed party composition, the most conspicuous innovation of the 1945-1948 period was the adoption of the unicameral system. No other change secured such general agreement as the abandonment of bicameralism. Under the 1920 Constitution and political practice between the two World Wars, the Senate was indeed superfluous and became virtually a haven for retired politicians

---

[7] On the circumstances surrounding the 1946 elections see Josef Korbel, *The Communist Subversion of Czechoslovakia 1938-1948,* Princeton, 1959, pp. 150ff.

[8] See table in Diamond, *op.cit.,* p. 239.

and elder statesmen for whom a seat could no longer be found in the more powerful lower chamber. The democratic parties saw no need for its revival and the Communists did not wish to complicate matters for themselves by allowing an upper chamber that could check the lower. Since no full-fledged federal arrangement was contemplated for Czechoslovakia, a unicameral system was a foregone conclusion even before the end of the War.[9]

Finally, the minimum age requirement for the right to vote and for the right to be elected was reduced to eighteen and twenty-one respectively.[10] The initiative in this case was with the Communists who hoped to gain most by lowering the voting age.

Such was the situation in the legislative branch of the government when the Communists seized power in February 1948. Immediately, they arrested, purged, or put to flight the leading representatives of the non-communist parties and all those deputies whose willingness to submit to communist domination was in doubt. Many of the vacancies thus created were filled by pliable substitutes. Having thus converted the Asssembly into a body of yes men, they caused it to pass without a single dissent a new electoral law in April and a new Constitution in May 1948.

PARLIAMENTARY ELECTIONS UNDER THE DICTATORSHIP OF THE PROLETARIAT

Three parliamentary elections have been held in Czechoslovakia since the establishment of the dictatorship of the proletariat in 1948.

Having finished its job and outlived its usefulness, the Constituent Assembly vacated the field for a new legislature elected on May 30, 1948, under a new electoral law passed for that purpose by the Constituent Assembly on April 16, 1948.[11] Superficially, the new law, which retained the main features of the pre-communist electoral order, looked democratic enough. It followed much more the Western European than the Soviet pattern. In contrast to the Soviet system it retained the principle of proportional representation. The whole country was divided into twenty-eight large electoral districts and the three hundred legislative seats were apportioned among them on the basis of

---

[9] President Beneš personally pleaded for the abolition of the Senate and recommended an advisory economic council instead. *Demokracie Dnes a Zítra* (Democracy Today and Tomorrow), London, n.d., II, p. 244.
[10] Formerly, 21 years was the minimum age for voting while one had to be 30 years old to be eligible to the Chamber of Deputies and 45 to the Senate.
[11] Law No. 75/1948.

the ratio of registered voters. Candidates were to be nominated by electoral groups which comprised not only political parties but also groups of voters not previously organized. The conduct of the elections and the counting of ballots were to be supervised by two tiers of election committees appointed by the chairmen of the respective district people's committees and one central committee appointed by the Minister of the Interior. As in pre-communist days, all electoral groups were granted the right to share in this supervision through their representatives or at least through appointed watchers.

However, to guarantee against even the slightest danger of any organized opposition, the communist rulers inserted into the electoral law certain provisions not found in earlier legislation on the subject. In addition to the usual grounds for exclusion from the right to vote, such as conviction for certain crimes, a brand new one was introduced to include all those whom the Action Committees "had discarded from public and political life" for "having committed an offense against the people's democratic order or for having actively and knowingly attempted to cause economic disruption." The minimum of voters who had to sign a nominating petition in order to get their candidate on the ballot was fixed at one thousand instead of the previously required one hundred. The assumption was that while one hundred foolhardy desperadoes might possibly join hands, such a danger was virtually excluded if the requirement was so substantially raised. As Václav Kopecký put it with his notoriously brutal frankness, it was not probable that "one thousand suicides would be found."[12]

A similar purpose was pursued by the insertion of the permissive word "may" in reference to the use by the voter of a space where he could place the ballot in the envelope without being observed by the election officers. In view of emphatic communist assertions that voters ought to be proud of the way they cast their ballots, insistence on secrecy amounted virtually to a self-indictment of a hostile attitude toward the people's democracy. To make such insistence less likely, arrangements for secret voting in most polling stations were inadequate and one or another communist watcher was placed in a position from which he could observe what was going on in the booth. When the voter had cast the ballot, he had to discard the unused ticket in a wastepaper basket which was located within easy sight of almost everybody in the polling station. On top of all that, rumors were spread prior to election day that the ballot boxes were provided

[12] *Československý přehled*, II, 8 (1955), p. 7.

with special devices capable of laying one ballot on the other in the order in which they were dropped in the box, so that the way each voter had voted could thereafter be easily ascertained by comparing the order of the ballots with the list checking off the voters as they were cleared for balloting. Finally, in a great many localities Communists organized mass parades of voters marching to the polling stations with posters proclaiming such slogans as "We are proud to vote in public."[13]

Fearing that even all these safeguards might not be sufficient to get them all the votes they wanted, the communist leaders prevailed on the other parties of the regenerated National Front to agree to a united list of candidates for each of the twenty-eight electoral districts. What sort of agreement that was is clearly revealed by the ratio of communist and non-communist candidates given places on the united lists. Some 70 percent of them were KSČ members. About 10 percent were social democratic fellow-travelers and Communists-to-be, since the Social Democratic Party was already scheduled to be merged with the KSČ after the elections. The remaining 20 percent were assigned to the other parties of the National Front, but even there the communist-dominated Action Committees had the right to veto any undesirable candidate. Since no independent candidate managed to obtain the one thousand signatures required to validate his candidacy, the only choice offered the Czech and Slovak voters was to cast the official ballot, or risk the possible untoward consequences of inserting in the envelope a blank ticket.

Under such circumstances a sweeping victory was a foregone conclusion. Of the 7,419,253 voters who participated in the election 6,424,734 voted for the united lists; 774,032 cast blank tickets; 220,487 ballots were declared invalid. An additional 512,986 voters abstained from voting and 65,796 were excluded from voting. It may be safely assumed that, with few exceptions, those who failed to vote did so because they were against the united lists, and so were undoubtedly most of those who were excluded. Thus, in spite of the grave risk of doing so, over one and one-half million, i.e., almost 20 percent, out of 7,998,035 officially registered voters expressed their opposition to the regime in the first parliamentary election held under communist rule; and that does not include all those who were denied registration as voters.

All these are communist figures which could not be impartially

[13] See Josef Josten, *Oh, My Country,* London, 1949, pp. 237-238.

checked. Moreover, doubts were cast upon their accuracy by reports which leaked out from Czechoslovakia that a number of communist-controlled election committees juggled the results. However, even if accepted at their face value, these results bespeak a deep-seated opposition to the communist rule, considering the conditions in which the election was held.

By the terms of the constitutional law that created it, the newly elected National Assembly was supposed to function only "for a transitional period until the new Constitution became operative."[14] But this provision was subsequently rescinded by a contrary clause of the Ninth-of-May Constitution stating that the Assembly elected under the electoral law of April 1948 "shall be deemed a National Assembly elected in accordance with this Constitution" and that its six-year term "shall be deemed to run from the date of the election." Since the Assembly was elected on May 30, 1948, its term of office was to expire on May 29, 1954, and a new parliamentary election should have been held prior to that date. However, on May 26, 1954, a few days before the deadline, a constitutional amendment was passed changing the composition of the Assembly and extending the current Assembly's term of office until the end of the year so that elections could be adequately prepared under the new electoral law approved at the same time.[15]

Several reasons account for this postponement of parliamentary elections, which were eventually held in the last week of November 1954. After six years of incessant lip service paid to "direct people's government" through the people's committees the communist rulers held in May 1954 the first local government elections.[16] As these were also the first elections held in Czechoslovakia after Stalin's death, the rulers felt it even more necessary to concentrate on a single purpose rather than complicate affairs by holding local and parliamentary elections simultaneously. Their uncertainty about the electoral results in the era of relative post-Stalin relaxation also counseled against combining both elections or holding the politically more important parliamentary elections first. Although they knew that they would win, they were not so sure that the percentage cast for the National Front candidates would be as overwhelming as they wished it to be. But a mishap in local government elections could much more easily have

[14] Constitutional law No. 74 of April 16, 1948.
[15] Constitutional law No. 26 and law No. 27 of May 26, 1954.
[16] For a fuller discussion see Chapter xiii.

been blamed on local issues than could a failure to attain the coveted near-unanimity in the parliamentary balloting. Furthermore, holding local elections several months in advance of parliamentary elections could yield valuable clues as to whither the wind was blowing and thus enable the Party to take remedial measures, if necessary. Finally, the Party leaders were too busy with the preparation of the Tenth Party Congress convoked for June 1954 to undertake yet another exacting chore at the same time.

The rules that governed the second parliamentary elections differed substantially from the electoral system of 1948. The principle of proportional representation, used in all parliamentary elections since the establishment of an independent Czechoslovakia in 1918, was abandoned. The fixed number of three hundred representatives set by the Ninth-of-May Constitution was replaced by a flexible system of one representative for each 35,000 inhabitants. Accordingly, the whole country was divided into 368 electoral districts, each electing one representative by an absolute majority of valid votes, provided that at least one-half of the qualified voters cast their ballots. Candidates were to be proposed by "meetings of workers, peasants, and other working people in factories, offices, and rural communities as well as meetings of soldiers and members of other armed corps." But the right of disposal lay elsewhere. All these proposals had to go to the National Front which alone was authorized to nominate the candidates from among "the best workers, members of the Unified Agricultural cooperatives, small and middle peasants, and members of the toiling intelligentsia" and register them with electoral commissions. Since the National Front was fully controlled by the Communist Party, no candidate could appear on the ballot unless he was deemed acceptable to the KSČ. No longer was it possible, not even theoretically, for Kopecký's "one thousand suicides" to put their candidate in the running. To make doubly certain that nothing could go wrong, the supervisory machinery was also arranged in a manner that gave to the National Front complete control over the conduct of the elections and counting of ballots. Election commissions on all three levels, central, district, and precinct, were to be composed of representatives of working people's organizations nominated by the National Front. "Authorized representatives of working people's organizations and representatives of the press" were reserved the right to be present when the ballots were counted, but the law forgot to mention who should authorize them.

239

As is apparent from this outline of the 1954 Election Law, it was a virtual facsimile of the Soviet original; and so was the election held under it. A few days after the official proclamation of the forthcoming elections the so-called meetings of the working people began to propose candidates, guided by "unity and close adherence to the Communist Party and the government of the National Front."[17] Requests for the honor of having leading Party members as candidates piled up in central headquarters of the National Front. Within nine days from the announcement of the electoral districts the Presidium of the National Front could approve unanimously all 368 candidates.[18]

Although no one but official candidates of the National Front could be validly nominated, the Election Law contained a provision for a new election in case no candidate obtained an absolute majority and thus left the door open for the nomination of more than one candidate per district. However, like its Soviet counterpart, this clause remained a dead letter and only one candidate was nominated for each electoral district. Evidently, the Party leaders abhorred any kind of competitive election, even among candidates passed by the National Front and pledged to support the communist cause. Their reasons were revealed with rare frankness in an article in *Rudé právo* published at the time of the elections and entitled "Wherein Lies the Democratic Character of Our System":

"If there were more than one candidate in an electoral district, a struggle would be waged for the election of one of them and this would necessarily divide the working people. The effort to get one's candidate elected could be coupled with professional, regional, nationalistic, and other interests. All the old survivals and prejudices could be revived. All this would weaken the people's democratic order and would ultimately endanger the truly democratic character of our elections. That is why the workers consult each other in the selection of candidates . . . and eventually agree on the one candidate who will, in the opinion of the majority of workers, defend well their common and basic interests."[19]

With only one candidate in each district, with no write-in vote permitted, and with all electoral controls firmly in communist hands, the 368 candidates were as sure as elected the moment they were put on the ballot. Only a failure to secure an absolute majority of

---

[17] *Československý přehled,* II, 8 (1955), p. 10.
[18] *Rudé právo,* October 9, 1954.
[19] *ibid.,* November 12, 1954.

the votes or an abstention of more than one-half of the qualified voters could cause defeat, and neither alternative was conceivable. Nevertheless, the communist stage managers unleashed a gigantic election campaign that dwarfed the campaigning in the first parliamentary elections of 1948. All the media of propaganda were mobilized to press home with mounting intensity the duty of every citizen to participate in the election and vote for the candidate of the National Front. Packs of agitators directed by agitation centers were let loose and ordered "to visit every voter several times, to discuss the candidates with him, to explain again the importance of the elections."[20] Warnings were issued that those who would vote against the official candidate or fail to take part in the election would thereby aid and abet the enemies of the people and of the Republic. As *Rudé právo* said, "Every city and village, every factory, every family had to live through elections in the true sense of the word."[21]

On election day collective public voting was organized on a much larger scale than in 1948. Groups rounded up and led by the National Front propagandists marched to the polls in paramilitary fashion to cast their votes publicly for the official candidates. Cars and ambulances hauled those who could not walk. Bed patients who could not be moved were visited by flying election commissions carrying special ballot boxes. Facilities for secret voting were even shabbier than in 1948. Booths where a voter could adjust the ballot were set in such a way as to afford the least possible secrecy. Unlike the arrangement in 1948, envelopes were not provided and thus the favorite trick of depositing an empty envelope—the best possible chance of registering opposition to the regime without being detected—was effectively blocked.

These high-pressure tactics and punctilious stage management brought the desired results and the communist regime fared substantially better than in either the first parliamentary elections of 1948 or the elections for the people's committees held earlier in the year, when over 6 percent of the voters voted against the regime.[22] In this election, 8,711,718 votes were cast, representing 99.18 per cent of the electorate. Of these, 8,494,102, i.e., 97.89 percent voted for the candidates of the National Front, 182,928 (2.11 percent) voted against, and 34,688 (0.39 percent) ballots were held invalid.[23] Again,

[20] *ibid.*, November 18, 1954.
[21] *ibid.*
[22] See Chapter XIII.
[23] *Rudé právo,* December 1, 1954.

however, with no opposition able to check on the counting of the ballots, there is no way of saying how many antigovernment ballots were really cast or to what extent the results were padded to "prove" how solidly the "will of the people" was behind the Communists.

What has been said of the 1954 elections applies with equal weight to the elections of a new National Assembly that took place on June 12, 1960.[24] Once more, the same pseudodemocratic trappings were used to mask the same totalitarian substance. Again, one name only was allowed to appear on each ballot, and that name was chosen by the communist-controlled National Front. The secrecy of the voting was just as hypothetical as in the parliamentary elections of 1954. As reported by foreign correspondents who could observe the procedure, very few of the voters dared to use the privacy of the screened booths; in one electrical district only five of the 1,500 voters used the screen.[25] The sole difference from the previous occasion was that a new constitutional law fixed the size of the new Assembly at 300 rather than allowing one representative for each 35,000 inhabitants. The electoral results went accordingly: 9,085,432 voters representing 99.68 percent of the electorate went to the polls; of these, 9,059,838, representing 99.86 percent of votes validly cast, voted in favor of the official candidates, 12,775 voted against, 12,819 ballots were held invalid, and 29,581 voters abstained from voting.[26] So sure was the regime of the outcome of the election that the social and ethnic composition of the new Parliament was announced three weeks in advance of the election![27]

While communist figures can by no means be accepted as an accurate measure of how the voters actually voted, there can be little doubt that in the three parliamentary elections held thus far under the dictatorship of the proletariat attendance at the polls has been very high and that a substantial majority of the voters have cast their ballots in favor of the communist-sponsored candidates. How can that be reconciled with the assertions of so many students of communist politics and the claims registered elsewhere in the present book that an overwhelming majority of the Czechoslovak people are against the communist regime?

[24] Constitutional law No. 35 and law No. 37, both of April 9, 1960, enacted only minor changes in the electoral system.

[25] Paul Underwood's report "Czechs Ballot for Single Slate Amid Holiday's Entertainment," *New York Times,* June 13, 1960.

[26] *Rudé právo,* June 15, 1960.

[27] *Československý zpravodaj,* No. 298, June 7, 1960.

The explanation is simple and its main elements have been supplied on the preceding pages describing the absolute communist control over the whole electoral process from the nomination stage to the final counting of the ballots. A communist subject *can* step into the booth, scratch out the name of the one and only candidate listed on the ballot, and thereby cast a vote against the regime. However, in so doing, he will inevitably brand himself as a foe of communism and a note to that effect will be entered into his personal file. He will not be arrested and tried for this particular act of hostility but sooner or later he and his family are likely to suffer the adverse consequences of his action. He may be shifted to a less desirable job with smaller earnings or even transferred to another locality where a vexatious housing issue and other disagreeable problems of adjustment will await him. If he is an administrative employee he will be released for "productive work" in the mines or in heavy industry. His children may find it harder to gain admission to higher schooling. If a higher percentage of such black sheep appears in a given community, it can expect to become soon thereafter an object of special attention on the part of the Party, police, and other long arms of communist controls. That is, incidentally, why the local election managers, as some reports from Czechoslovak antiregime sources indicate, can seldom resist the temptation to interpret as many "adjusted" ballots as possible as having been actually cast for the regime. They may thus save their community from excessive intrusion of the regime's police and evade reprisals for their own "poor contacts with the masses."

Though people seek to avoid trouble, they would undoubtedly risk these untoward consequences of a negative vote—if they were convinced that it would help their cause. But most of them feel that it would not make any difference. They know that the communist rulers would not yield to the verdict of the ballot and that they would not hesitate to doctor election results whenever and wherever necessary. Why, then, expose oneself and one's whole family to possible reprisals for the sake of a vain gesture, a gesture that may not even be publicly recognized because of the suppression of true election results? It is this sense of utter futility that accounts more than anything else for the impressive majorities which the communist rulers secure in their elections.

Since both Party leaders and people understand that such elections are quite meaningless as indicators of the extent of support for the regime, why do the rulers go to the trouble and expense of holding elections at all? Why do they spend so much energy and permit millions of precious hours, which could be used in "productive work," to go to waste on campaigning and balloting for something that has already been decided? The main reason lies in the pretense that the will of the people is paramount in the communist system. Hence, the communist leaders never tire of deferring to the "will of the people" as the sole source of their authority and the guiding light of all their endeavors; and electoral success, i.e., striving after fullest attendance at the polls, and near-unanimity of electoral results, has become an indispensable part of the game.

THE PERSONNEL AND ITS STANDING

The manner in which candidates are nominated and elected determines the composition and the whole character of the National Assembly.

The Assembly's Political Complexion

Like its pre-communist namesake, the National Assembly is a multiparty body, five different parties being represented in its membership. However, all of them belong to the communist-controlled National Front. With no freedom to choose their own nominees, the four partners of the KSČ can only propose candidates whom they would like to have represent them; but it is up to the KSČ leaders, acting through the Presidium of the National Front, to grant or deny such wishes. As shown earlier, the number of seats assigned to the non-communist parties depends exclusively on the generosity of their communist superiors, and they have been anything but magnanimous toward their poor political relatives.[28] In the first legislature elected under communist rule in 1948 the non-communist parties were given sixty-one seats out of three hundred, i.e., approximately twenty percent, although these parties had won almost 49 percent of the popular vote in the last pre-communist elections of 1946.[29] In the National Assembly elected in 1954 they fared much worse and had to be satisfied with only forty-eight seats out of 368, which was less than 13 percent.[30] In the legislature elected in June 1960 their share was 37 out of 300, i.e., 12.3 percent of the total.[31]

[28] See preceding pages and Chapter vi.
[29] *Československý přehled*, iv, 3 (1957), pp. 12ff.
[30] Rattinger, *op.cit.*, p. 29.
[31] *Neue Zürcher Zeitung*, June 19, 1960, and *Volksbote* (Munich), June 25, 1960.

On the other hand, a new category of representatives "without political affiliation" appeared on the legislative scene and fifty-seven of them became members of the National Assembly after the 1954 elections and 44 in 1960.[32] They appear to be the Czechoslovak version of the notorious *bezpartyinye bolsheviki* of the Soviet legislatures. Like their Soviet counterparts they are Communists without Party membership cards and their presence in the National Assembly is designed to lend additional support to the communist claims of broad popular representation.

As a result of these measures all non-communists prominent in pre-communist political life have by now disappeared from the ranks of the legislators, except a dozen inveterate fellow-travelers needed as window dressing.[33] Quite the opposite is true of the KSČ. As of 1960 its parliamentary club could boast of having among its members not only all the newly risen stars, but also practically every living communist member of the prewar Czechoslovak Parliament, such as Široký, Dolanský, Kopecký, Harus, Krosnář, Hodinová, Zupka, Ďuriš, Valo, and Kohler.

Social Structure

The social composition of the National Assembly is apparent from Table II.

TABLE II
Occupational Background of National Assembly Members
Elected 1948-1960

Members' Occupations	YEAR OF ELECTION		
	1948	1954	1960
Workers	57	95	79
Farmers	44	70	45
Intelligentsia, Public and Party functionaries	192	182	166
Members of Armed Forces and Security	6	21	10
Clergymen	1		
	300	368	300

Sources: *Rudé právo*, December 16, 1954, *Prague News Letter*, January 8, 1955; Rattinger, *Nejvyšší státní orgány lidově demokratického Československa*. (The highest State Organs of the People's Democratic Czechoslovakia), Praha, 1957, p. 29, *Československý zpravodaj*, No. 298, June 7, 1960.

[32] *Československý přehled*, IV, 3 (1957), pp. 12ff.; *Neue Zürcher Zeitung*, June 19, 1960.
[33] Among those who were known to the general public in pre-communist days and were reelected to the National Assembly in 1960 are: A. Neumann, J. Plojhar, L. Jankovcová, Z. Fierlinger, F. Tymeš.

These figures would suggest that the number of legislators belonging to the "two friendly proletarian classes" of workers and peasants rose between 1948 and 1954, both absolutely and relatively, and that the members of the intelligentsia declined. While this runs counter to recent Soviet trends, it is well in line with similar Soviet developments in the first ten to fifteen years after the October Revolution when the percentage of workers and peasants elected to the Congress of Soviets generally increased and that of deputies from the rank of the intelligentsia fell off.[34] In marching thus in the earlier Soviet footsteps Czechoslovak rulers behaved in the best Marxist-Leninist tradition, for Czechoslovakia was supposed to be at a stage of development corresponding to that of Russia before the socialist construction was completed.

The communist claim of the increased workers' representation sounds genuine enough. The frantic endeavor of the KSČ leaders to pose as champions of workers' rights and the well-known Leninist emphasis on the "working proletariat" tend to make the Party chiefs place workers in the limelight where they can best be seen, and the legislature is a good device for such a purpose. Nor is there any contrary information that would cast doubt on the veracity of this particular claim. It is somewhat different with the communist claim regarding the number of farmers. In the same release in which the regime proudly announced the presence of seventy farmers in the 1954 legislature, it spoke of only "nineteen small and middle working farmers" and "twenty-four members of agricultural cooperatives" having been elected "together with directors of state farms, machine-tractor stations, agricultural scientists, etc."[35] This clearly indicates that not seventy but at the most only forty-three farmers were in fact sent to the National Assembly in 1954, while the balance was made up mostly of agricultural administrators who may never have been dirt farmers, except possibly as amateur gardeners. Nor is it by any means certain that all of the "twenty-four members of agricultural cooperatives" were farmers working actually in the fields. The chances are that some of them were collective farm managers or their assistants, often chosen from city Communists, sent to supervise collective farms after a snap course in agricultural affairs.

Other membership data released by the Assembly's Credentials

---

[34] See tables in Julian Towster, *Political Power in the USSR,* New York, 1948, pp. 317, 320, 327. For later elections see W. W. Kulski, *The Soviet Regime,* Syracuse, 1954, pp. 147, 755.

[35] *Prague News Letter,* 11, 1, January 8, 1955.

Commission show that there were 63 women among the 368 legislators elected in 1954 and 67 among the 300 legislators elected in
1960. As for the age factor, the most numerous age groups in the
1954 Assembly were those between 31 and 40 and between 41 and
50 with 136 and 111 legislators respectively, while 56 deputies were
younger than 31, and 65 were older than 50. According to their
nationality there were 253 Czechs, 98 Slovaks, 9 Hungarians, 3
Ukrainians, 3 Germans and 2 Poles. A comparison with respective
population figures shows that the Czechs and the Ukrainians were
overrepresented, the Slovaks and the Poles fared about even, and the
Germans and the Hungarians were underrepresented.[36] The same
basic trend is reflected in the ethnic composition of the National
Assembly elected in 1960 which consists of 205 Czechs, 83 Slovaks, 6
Hungarians, 3 Ukrainians, 2 Germans, and 1 Pole.[37]

The Legislators' Status

If an inhabitant of Mars or some other distant planet, unaware of
communist facts of life, read the Ninth-of-May Constitution, he could
not but reach the conclusion that the Czechoslovak legislators were
the most privileged group in the whole country. Indeed, the Ninth-of-
May Constitution retained all the extensive privileges and immunities
granted the members of the National Assembly by the democratic
Constitution in 1920. Not only were legislators exempt from prosecution for their voting and statements in the Assembly and its committees, but they could not be prosecuted "then or ever after" for any
other offenses or omissions unless an assent of the National Assembly
had first been obtained.[38] Nor could legislators be compelled to give
testimony "in respect to matters confided to them in their capacity
as members of the National Assembly," except when it was a question
of "inducement to a misuse of the mandate."

Besides granting them an almost absolute and life-long immunity
from prosecution except by permission of their own colleagues, the
Ninth-of-May Constitution protected the individual law-maker's freedom of action. According to his constitutional oath, each Assembly
member was supposed to be guided in the discharge of his functions
solely by "the best of his knowledge and conscience."

The guarantees of personal and political independence were sup-

[36] See Chapter II.

[37] *Československý zpravodaj*, No. 298, June 7, 1960.

[38] An exception was made in regard to the penal liability incurred by a representative as responsible editor of a journal.

plemented by provisions for the legislators' material security. As enacted in 1948, the Ninth-of-May Constitution entitled each legislator to a leave of absence from his regular employment, whether public or private, and a salary or compensation throughout the duration of his legislative mandate. The system was modified in 1954 when Czechoslovakia switched to the Soviet pattern under which law-makers continue to work in, and derive their livelihood from, the jobs they held prior to their election, and are compensated only for the extra expenses connected with their legislative work.[39] While this latest adaptation has undoubtedly deprived the legislative office of some of its erstwhile material advantages and comforts, it nevertheless continues to provide its incumbent with some extra income and other worthwhile amenities, such as a few weeks' respite from regular occupation coupled with two to four yearly excursions to the country's capital. Together with the honor and prestige that go with it, all these advantages make the legislative job a highly desirable position that is used to reward deserving citizens ranging from scientists, generals, and directors to *stakhanovite* cowgirls.[40]

That the guarantees of parliamentary freedoms and immunities provided for in the Ninth-of-May Constitution were not worth the paper on which they were printed hardly requires explanation. The futility of such guarantees stems from the very nature of the Leninist-Stalinist version of the dictatorship of the proletariat; and it could not be otherwise in an Assembly that owed its existence solely to the narrow oligarchy of topmost KSČ leaders. Hence, it comes as no surprise that there has not been a single case in which the National Assembly withheld assent to the prosecution of its members. Indeed, no one would have been more amazed than Slánský, Clementis, Šling, Husák, and other Assembly members, had they been released from the claws of communist justice by the Assembly's refusal to assent.

It is scarcely surprising, therefore, that the new Constitution of 1960 has turned thumbs down on the idea of legislator's responsibility to their conscience and has also substantially diminished the elaborate immunity provisions of the Ninth-of-May Constitution. Instead of

[39] Besides being reimbursed for the loss of his earnings while on leave in connection with the Assembly's sessions, a deputy gets 1,500 crowns (about 210 dollars) per month as compensation for his expenses, 100 crowns (about 14 dollars) per diem during legislative sessions and free transportation. See Decree of the Assembly's Presidium of July 13, 1960, No. 111.

[40] Fifty-seven of the legislators elected in 1954 were holders of various high decorations, state prizes, and "other great distinctions." *Prague News Letter,* 11, 1, January 8, 1955.

being guided by the best of his knowledge and conscience the legislators are now to "abide by the suggestions of their voters and to render to them regular accounts of their work." Insofar as parliamentary immunities are concerned, the 1960 Constitution disposes of the whole matter in one laconic sentence which makes the legislators' prosecution contingent upon the consent of the National Assembly. Protection, whatever it is worth, is evidently now granted only during the legislator's term of office.

But the deflated political status of the communist legislator is reflected most conspicuously in his duties. Policy-making is none of his business since that is an exclusive preserve of the highest Party leadership. His part in actual legislative work is a very minor one. There are very few sessions per year and his duty there is, in essence, to listen to speeches, applaud whenever and wherever applause is due, occasionally make short speeches of approval or raise a prearranged tame question, and cast his vote for whatever is proposed by his chiefs. Occasionally, he may get some extra work in phraseology when he is made committee *rapporteur* on a voluminous bill. As stated above, he has the duty to follow the instructions of his voters, which means in practice the directives of the Party chiefs who control them. "There is no such thing as an independence of the people's democratic representatives from the working masses that have elected them. On the contrary, the representative's dependence on the voters is absolute, lasts throughout the whole of his electoral term, and applies to all the work done by the representative in the performance of his mandate. This dependence corresponds to the constitutional right of the voters to control and to recall their representatives. Thus, politically as well as legally, the member of the National Assembly is a representative and a servant of the people."[41]

The representative's primary duty is thus to carry on a "systematic political work among the voters.[42] "The deputies of the National Assembly are not only legislators, but are simultaneously obligated to help carry out the laws in their electoral districts . . . ."[43] As prescribed by the 1960 Constitution and by the Standing Orders, the deputies have the duty to report to their voters on the activities of the National Assembly. In particular, they "must explain to the voters the meaning of the laws approved by the National Assembly and thus

[41] Rattinger, *op.cit.,* p. 52.
[42] *Rudé právo,* October 10, 1954.
[43] Rattinger, *op.cit.,* pp. 33, 53.

help the state and economic organs and citizens to observe the laws
. . . . In close cooperation with the people's committees and the organizations of the working people, they help carry out the laws and
the resolutions of *the Party* and the government, especially by recruiting the citizens of their electoral districts for the implementation of
the tasks of the socialist construction and by developing the creative
forces of the workers."[44]

Not the National Assembly, but his electoral district is thus the
Czechoslovak legislator's main arena. His front-line mission there was
aptly and authoritatively defined by the Assembly's Chairman, Zdeněk
Fierlinger:

"We must know how to make every citizen enthusiastic about the
great tasks of the socialist construction. We must strengthen even
more the close unity of the workers, peasants, and members of our
toiling intelligentsia [and] raise even higher the banner of our National
Front under the leadership of our glorious Communist Party . . . .
Our effort must be aimed at the increase of respect for our socialist
laws, at the strengthening of state discipline . . . at the liquidation
of the leftovers of old bourgeois morality and at the creation of a new
type of patriotic socialist man."[45]

Nor is it left to the legislator's own discretion and initiative how
he attends to these extralegislative chores, which must be usually performed after his regular daily work. Acting under specific instructions
from the National Front, the "people's" legislator must pay periodic
visits to factories, collective farms, offices, schools, and other establishments in his district.[46] He is directed to "encourage the workers
to socialist contests, stimulate the development of the innovators'
movement, and the fight against shortcomings . . . ."[47] At frequent
and regular intervals he must hold office hours in the center of his
district, usually in the premises of the district people's committee or
in a large industrial plan. He must make speeches and arrange for
conferences with his voters in order to "persuade the voters of the correctness of the Party's and government's decisions and gain them for
their implementation."[48]

In view of the exacting nature of many of these duties it is easy
to understand why the legislators seek to evade them or to dispose

---

[44] Article 43 of the Standing Orders. Italics added.
[45] *Rudé právo,* December 14, 1954.
[46] Rattinger, *op.cit.,* pp. 56-58.
[47] *ibid.*
[48] *ibid.*

of them as superficially as they can. To overcome these tendencies the legislators of each region are organized into regional associations which have the obligation to control the legislators' work in their electoral districts.[49] The meetings of these associations outline the work plans of individual legislators who in their turn have to report to their regional association regularly on all their activities. Needless to say, these regional associations are under the complete control of the KSČ. All the communist deputies elected from the region form a special Party group within each regional association, headed by a leader appointed by and responsible to the Party's regional committee. These Communist Party groups are directed to offer help and advice to the deputies of the other parties of the National Front as well as to non-party deputies. This supervision by the regional associations is further supplemented by controls exercised by the Party's district committees, especially by their secretaries who are in charge of both the communist and non-communist legislators from the electoral districts under their jurisdiction.[50]

Instead of a law-maker the National Assembly member has thus become the regime's propagandist. Instead of a representative of his voters and a custodian of their political rights, acting, in Burke's famous words, as "his unbiased opinion, his mature judgment, his enlightened conscience bids him," he has been converted into a cog in the iron wheel of government controls.

The Organization

The formal organization of the National Assembly reveals no striking departures from the pre-communist pattern save for the enhanced position of the presiding organs and officers. The Soviet influence has made itself felt in a few organizational aspects, but less so than in the electoral system and in the Assembly's operational pattern.

The chief presiding officer is the Chairman of the National Assembly. Under the Ninth-of-May Constitution he was elected annually by the Assembly. Since 1960 he is elected for the entire legislative session. The Chairman presides over the sessions of the National Assembly and its Presidium; signs, together with the President of the Republic and the Prime Minister, the laws passed by the Assembly and the decrees adopted by the Presidium; and reports to the As-

---

[49] Standing Orders, Article 44.
[50] Rattinger, *op.cit.,* p. 61.

sembly on the work done by its Presidium while the Assembly was not in session.

The Chairman is aided by several Vice-Chairmen elected in the same manner. Together with the Chairman they form a collective organ called the Inner Presidium. Although it was not set up by the Constitution but by the Assembly's Standing Orders, the Inner Presidium has become the directing organ of the Assembly. Besides handling various current affairs of administrative nature, it deals with certain matters which would be labeled as politically important if anything pertaining to the legislature's work in communist Czechoslovakia could be so labeled. It decides whether the motions made by individual legislators should or should not be placed on the Assembly's agenda; considers suggestions, resolutions, and petitions which it has decided not to place on the Assembly's agenda; assigns work to committees, regulates, and supervises their activities; and maps out the Assembly's sessions and order of business.

The Inner Presidium is aided by a Council of a Deputies that performs in Czechoslovakia the role played in the Soviet legislative system by the Council of Elders. Composed of the Inner Presidium and representatives of regional associations of the Assembly's members, it is supposed to coordinate and supervise the activities of the deputies.[51] It is also supposed to see that "the experience gained by the deputies in their regions and electoral districts be exploited in the proceedings of the National Assembly and its organs."[52] However, the Council of Deputies acts in a strictly advisory capacity.

The committee system comprises two types of committees: mandatory standing committees prescribed by law and *ad hoc* committees set up by the Assembly as the need arises.[53] With the approval of the Inner Presidium the committees may establish commissions and call upon experts and representatives of organizations of the working people to help them in their work.[54] Until 1960 there were seven standing committees to deal with the following matters: credentials, constitutional law, foreign affairs, budget and economy, agriculture, public welfare and health, and cultural affairs.[55] In July 1960 the

[51] Standing Orders, Articles 45 and 46; also, Juraj Hromada, *Prehľad československých štátnych orgánov* (An Outline of Czechoslovak State Organs), Bratislava, 1955, pp. 69-70; Rattinger, *op.cit.*, pp. 49-51.

[52] Rattinger, *op.cit.*, p. 50.

[53] Standing Orders. Also, Hromada, *op.cit.*, p. 70.

[54] Hromada, *op.cit.*, p. 70. A provision to that effect is also included in the 1960 Constitution.

[55] Rattinger, *op.cit.*, p. 48. Prior to 1954 there was also a committee on defense and state security.

number was increased to eight by dividing the budget and economy committee into two: one for the Plan and the budget, and one for industry.[56] Originally, the committee membership in the 1954 legislature ranged from eleven to twenty-five per committee. However, in April 1957 this was raised to thirty-five so that "a bigger number of deputies could actively participate in the work of the National Assembly."[57]

While the number of committees is considerably less than in the prewar Parliament, it is still double the number of committees used in either house of the Supreme Soviet of the USSR. Only three of the Assembly's committees correspond to similar committees of the Soviet legislature, those of credentials, foreign affairs, and budget. Whereas in the Soviet system there is only one committee for all legislative motions, the National Assembly has five different committees to consider bills and other items in the field of their authority. Thus the Czechoslovak system of legislative committees continues even under the dictatorship of the proletariat to bear some of the outward appearance of Western systems.

As can be seen from this brief outline, the management of the Assembly's affairs is in the hands of the Inner Presidium. Acting at all times under the supreme directives of the KSČ leaders, it operates as a little dictatorship whose rulings cannot be challenged by a contrary decision on the Assembly's floor any more than a platoon of privates can oppose the orders of their sergeant. Although formally elected by the Assembly, the Chairman and the five to six Vice-Chairmen who constitute the Inner Presidium are handpicked by the Party's Political Bureau from among its dependable henchmen. Both the provisions of the Standing Orders and actual practice reveal that the Inner Presidium reaches its decisions collectively and that its Chairman does not have any more authority than its other members. However, being simultaneously Chairman of the whole Assembly and of its Presidium, he is more in the limelight than his colleagues and, in the official government hierarchy, ceremonially ranks right behind the President of the Republic. That is probably why the Chairmanship of the National Assembly has been assigned ever since 1948 to former social democratic fellow-travelers, first to Dr. Oldřich John and since September 1953 to Zdeněk Fierlinger.

Throughout the Assembly's organizational framework the dominant positions are held by leading deputies of the KSČ. All Party

[56] *Rudé právo,* July 13, 1960.
[57] Rattinger, *op.cit.,* p. 48.

members elected to the National Assembly belong to a group of communist deputies headed by a bureau drawn from the Party members who sit on the Assembly's Presidium. Acting under the directives of the Party's Political Bureau, the leadership of the group sees that Party resolutions are carried out in all the organs of the Assembly and at all stages of its work. They also serve as "advisers and helpers of the nonparty deputies and members of the other political parties of the National Front . . . explaining to them the policy of the Party and of the National Front, and recruiting them for its active implementation."[58]

CONSTITUTIONAL POWERS

As defined in the Ninth-of-May Constitution, the powers of the National Assembly did not differ substantially from those enjoyed by a typical Western European parliament. The Assembly was "the supreme organ of legislative power." Bills could be introduced either by the Cabinet or by individual members and had to be passed by a simple majority. An earlier requirement that a private bill be submitted by at least twenty deputies was changed by the Standing Orders of 1954 so that any one member could introduce such a motion. The President of the Republic had the right to veto the Assembly's laws, but his veto could be overruled by an absolute majority of all the members, such a vote to be taken by roll call. The Assembly also adopted addresses and resolutions, made its own rules of procedure, verified the election of its members, and approved the state budget. It approved all political treaties, economic treaties of general character, and all other treaties that required legislation for their implementation. It also had the power to amend the Constitution and to declare war, both by a three-fifths majority of all its members.

As far as its relationship to the executive branch of the government was concerned, the Assembly not only elected the President of the Republic but could at all times force the Cabinet out of office by a vote of no confidence. It had the authority to summon members of the Cabinet to appear before the House and any of its committees and question them "in respect to matters within their jurisdiction." It could remove the President by impeachment procedure for high treason and any member of the Cabinet for violating, with intent or from gross negligence, the Constitution or other laws. On the other

[58] *ibid.*, p. 63.

hand, the Assembly was subject to dissolution by the President at any time except during the last six months of his term of office.

The Assembly was to be summoned by the President of the Republic for two regular sessions each year: a spring session in March and a fall session in October. The length of the sessions was not prescribed and the President could thus prorogue each and any session whenever he deemed it appropriate. However, a constitutional provision enabled the absolute majority of the Assembly to request an extraordinary session; and should the President fail to summon it, the Assembly's Presidium was authorized to do so.

The powers granted the National Assembly by the Ninth-of-May Constitution appear thus to have been a virtual transcription of the corresponding provisions of the 1920 Czechoslovak Constitution. Therefore, it is understandable that the position of the National Assembly in the system of communist transmission belts had to be revised to make it fit better into the new stage of the forthcoming completion of the "socialist construction." Like its Soviet counterpart, the Assembly has been elevated by the 1960 Constitution to the rank of "the highest organ of state power." It may no longer be dissolved and its laws may not be vetoed. It has newly acquired the right to elect the judges of the Supreme Court as well as the right to annul the ordinances and resolutions of the Cabinet. It may also invalidate the laws of the Slovak National Council and the regulations of regional people's committee if they do not conform to the Constitution or other laws. All the other organs of government, including even the President of the Republic, have been made responsible to the Assembly and the latter's powers of control over the executive and judicial branches of the government as well as over the local government organs have been spelled out in much greater detail.

Thus the 1960 Constitution has removed most of the Western elements from the definition of the Assembly's powers and refashioned its constitutional status after the Soviet model. But for its unicameral construction, the only matter of theoretical importance in which the National Assembly continues to differ from the Supreme Soviet of the USSR is the Assembly's lack of power to appoint the Cabinet and the Procurator General.

THE NATIONAL ASSEMBLY IN ACTION

While the National Assembly resembled, until the constitutional reform of 1960, Western European parliaments more than the Supreme Soviet of the USSR in the constitutional grant of power and the formal arrangement of the executive-legislative relationship, the opposite has been true of the way in which the Assembly has conducted its business. Since its very first session after the communist coup of 1948 the National Assembly has always behaved as the Party's transmission belt should.

As in the Soviet Union, unanimity and make-believe enthusiasm are probably the most characteristic features. Securing the prescribed quorums and majorities has been no problem. Under strict communist controls, playing hooky from parliamentary duties has become risky and underfulfillment of the legislative work norm would amount to a "betrayal of the people's trust." The near-perfect attendance has been more than matched by a perfect record of unanimous voting. Since February 1948 not one dissent has marred the Assembly's proceedings. Every bill and every treaty brought to the Assembly's floor have been approved unanimously. So have all the constitutional amendments, economic plans, state budgets and financial accounts, and each and every declaration or statement of policy laid before the Assembly, no matter what its topic or purpose. No amendment has ever been suggested from the Assembly floor, and all the bills and resolutions have been adopted in the version in which they have been introduced. Similar consensus characterized the three presidential elections held under the communist system. On all three occasions every legislator present voted for the one and only candidate for the highest executive office. That has also been true of the elections of the Assembly's own officers from the Chairman down to the last committee member.

This absolute harmony among several hundred politicians, supposedly belonging to different parties, reached on even the most complex political issues and sustained without a single exception over twelve eventful years, is too good to be true. Even the best pupils of the Party schools have found it hard to believe that such harmony was possible. Typical of the situation and illustrative of the unconvincing manner in which the regime has been trying to explain this phenomenon is the following statement of the Slovak Trade Union paper, *Práca:*

"We sometimes encounter the question: How is it possible that our National Assembly approves laws with complete unanimity? Is it really democratic? . . . Were not the parliamentary deliberations in the pre-Munich Republic more democratic when one talked for and against as much as one wanted, and when consideration of the laws was accomplished by a long and combative discussion? . . . Unanimity of voting in our National Assembly is not caused by our deputies being a group that . . . approves everything just as the government presents it. This unanimity stems most of all from the fact that the goals of the government and the goals of the National Assembly are identical: to express and defend the interests and the desires of the people."[59]

The introduction of bills has become a monopoly of the Cabinet, and the legislative initiative of individual members as provided by the Constitution and the Assembly's Standing Orders is virtually non-existent. The regime's explanation of this eclipse of individual motions has been as fictitious as its justification of the unanimity of voting. Individually-sponsored bills have become unnecessary, argues a communist textbook on government, "because the government carries out a policy that is in agreement with the political line of the deputies as representatives of the people."[60] The very few so-called private bills allowed to be introduced were actually government bills which the regime wanted to be initiated by individual legislators for tactical considerations and propaganda purposes. Typical of these maneuvers was the bill on the defense of peace which was introduced in December 1950 by a group of deputies as Czechoslovakia's contribution to the Soviet-sponsored peace campaign. Evidently, the communist leaders felt that their purpose would be better served by a seemingly spontaneous motion from the floor than by a government bill. Unlike prewar private bills, which were mostly gestures of defiance used especially by communist deputies and as such faced with almost certain defeat, the motion was not only passed promptly and unanimously, but was received with great applause and "enthusiastic ovations for the President of the Republic, Klement Gottwald, and the greatest fighter for world peace, Generalissimo J. V. Stalin."[61]

Similar spontaneous outbursts of enthusiasm, duly graduated in accordance with the occasion's importance, have been reserved for government bills and declarations.[62] Even such dry subjects as the annual budgets seem to have been able to elicit "stormy applause."[63] The debate on such occasions has invariably presented a spectacle of flattery toward the Kremlin and the native communist leaders, coupled

[59] *Práca,* October 23, 1954; *Československý přehled,* I, 9 (1954), p. 33.
[60] Hromada, *op.cit.,* p. 67.
[61] *Práce,* December 21, 1950.
[62] For examples see *Rudé právo,* July 12, 1951, November 1, 1951.
[63] *Lidové noviny,* March 23, 1951; *Rudé právo,* April 22-24, 1953.

with vicious abuse of the West. Those granted the privilege to speak praised their government's "wise and perspicacious political line" and vied with one another in giving thanks to their communist superiors while indulging in tirades against "imperialist war-mongers," "American monopolists," "capitalist interventionists," "reactionary *émigrés*," and other such enemies of the "camp of peace."[64]

The speed with which the Assembly has managed to dispose of its law-making and budget-making business has been truly miraculous. In a two-day session on December 20 and 21, 1950, it enacted seventeen laws, many of quite a complex character, and one bulky commercial treaty, besides attending to the usual administrative measures.[65] A new record was set in a two-day meeting on October 29 and 30, 1952. The legislators adopted thirteen laws, some of them quite weighty, approved one constitutional amendment and a number of government ordinances, and elected a new Presidium as well as members of all committees. Moreover, the Chairman still found enough time to commemorate the bolshevist seizure of power in Russia with a speech on the "historic importance of the Great October Socialist Revolution."[66] But even this speed record held for less than three months. On December 11, 1952, the Assembly considered and approved in one lump fourteen new laws in the field of taxation and financial administration and ratified two commercial treaties.[67]

Not even such shattering events as the deaths of Stalin and Gottwald in March 1953 could slow down the legislators' speed, shake their unanimity, or put a damper on their enthusiasm. It took them only three and one-half days in April 1953 to discuss and adopt the 1953 state budget, approve the final accounts of state finances for 1951, pass five new laws, ratify a number of government ordinances on the Five-Year-Plan, and fill the vacancies on committees.[68] Like efficiency has been apparent in the ensuing years. To cite just one typical example, less than ten days at the end of June and the beginning of July 1959 was enough for the Czechoslovak legislature to process, through all the committee and floor stages, twelve laws, most of them quite substantial, the state accounts for 1958, several international treaties, and a number of administrative matters.

---

[64] *Lidová demokracie,* March 21, 1951; *Rudé právo,* June 21, 1953, April 22-24, September 17 and December 4, 1953.
[65] *Rudé právo,* December 21 and 22, 1950.
[66] *Rudé právo,* October 30-31, 1952.
[67] *ibid.,* December 12 and 13, 1952.
[68] *ibid.,* April 22-25, 1953.

While the speed, the unanimity, and the synthetic enthusiasm with which the National Assembly performs its duties bear an unmistakable Moscow trade-mark, there is one notable aspect of legislative operations in which Czechoslovak law-making continues to differ from the Soviet pattern: namely, in the use of committees. Unlike the Supreme Soviet's Committee on Legislative Motions, which is so frequently by-passed in the Soviet legislative procedure, the legislative committees of the National Assembly have been used regularly for consideration of bills before they are sent to the floor for final reading. Only exceptionally has the committee stage been left out, as was the case with the law on currency reform of May 30, 1953, when the need for absolute secrecy precluded regular procedure.[69] The extent to which the committee system has been used is revealed by the official report on the work of the National Assembly elected in 1948. During its six-year term the Assembly's committees held 561 meetings of which 250 dealt with legislation, 230 were concerned with budgetary matters, and 81 with other business.[70]

This relatively frequent use of committees does not mean, however, that they can change anything of substance in the budgets, legislative drafts, or anything else assigned to them for consideration. Both the communist conception of the law-making organs as transmission belts for Party decisions and the evidence on the committee's actual operations suggest a rubber-stamp behavior and belie the communist assertion that "the work of the committees is very important because it is there that bills of law are thoroughly considered . . . before they are presented to the plenum for final decision."[71] Even if there were no other impediments, how thoroughly can the budgetary committee delve into such a huge and complex volume as the state budget when it is given only a few days to do so and the deadline for the presentation of its report to the Assembly is set by the presiding officers even before the committee gets a glimpse of the budget? How could the constitutional committee consider in three days (October 21-23, 1952) the merits of one constitutional amendment, five laws dealing with the whole judicial system and the pro-curator's office, and the revision of both civil and criminal procedure?[72] Obviously, the time allocated for committee consideration has in every instance been just long enough to go through the neces-

[69] *ibid.*, May 31, 1953. Also, Rattinger, *op.cit.*, p. 35.
[70] *Rudé právo*, October 28, 1954.
[71] Hromada, *op.cit.*, p. 70, Rattinger, *op.cit.*, p. 35.
[72] *Rudé právo*, October 24, 30, and 31, 1952.

sary formalities and allow the *rapporteur* to prepare the customary eulogy warmly recommending the bill for unanimous passage. This is also borne out by communist statistics. To consider 326 bills that were laid before the first National Assembly the committees met in only 250 sessions concerned with legislative work, i.e., less than one meeting per law![73]

In the field of legislative-executive relationship, crucial in democratic governmental systems, the elaborate provisions of the Ninth-of-May Constitution remained dead letters. The National Assembly had no use whatsoever for the constitutional devices of legislative censure of the Cabinet or presidential or ministerial impeachment. Nor could it have ever entertained any thought of forcing the President to call it for an extraordinary session. On the other hand, it proved unnecessary for the President to use his constitutional weapons of parliamentary dissolution or legislative veto. As explained by a Czechoslovak communist study, "Under the conditions of the people's democracy after the February victory of the working people, when the exercise of state power by the highest organs of the State expresses completely the interest and the will of the workers, this right of the President of the Republic was not used and it will hardly be necessary to use it in the future."[74]

The manner in which relations between the two branches of government have shaped up in actual practice is well illustrated by budgetary procedures, which are generally considered as the keystone of executive-legislative relationship in modern governmental systems. Commending the Assembly on its budgetary work, Jan Harus, a prominent member of the communist Old Guard and Minister of State Control, described the legislators' cooperation as follows: "The Chairman of the Assembly and the chairman of the budgetary committee ask individual deputies to see them and tell them to take part in the preparation of the budget in various ministries. The legislator goes there, no one asks him what party he represents, he is not looked upon with suspicion or mistrust, and the Minister himself provides him with information."[75]

Thus the pattern of executive-legislative contacts customary in democratic countries has been reversed in communist Czechoslovakia. It is not the committee that summons the ministers of their deputies

[73] *ibid.*, October 28, 1954.
[74] Rattinger, *op.cit.*, p. 37.
[75] *Rudé právo*, March 30, 1952.

to explain, defend their agencies' budgetary requirements, and plead with the committee not to cut them, but it is the legislators who have to go to the respective ministries and are informed, i.e., instructed how to report in the committee and on the floor. Cabinet members attend the final sessions of the committee in budgetary as well as other legislative matters affecting their departments. However, they are there, not because they might be called upon to answer embarrassing questions or because their help might be needed to defeat attacks by the opposition, but in order to receive due credit and applause, to check on the spot whether their directives are properly carried out, and, last but not least, to display communist zeal and uphold the semblance of democratic processes.

The legislative time table that has evolved in Czechoslovakia under communist rule is as follows:

As prescribed by the Constitution, the President of the Republic summons the National Assembly to two regular sessions per year. The spring session begins in February or March and usually lasts until May or June; the fall session begins in October and ends in December. Although the Assembly is thus formally in session for many months, in reality it meets only for some ten calendar days per annum. The main session is undoubtedly the one that is convened in the spring with the approval of the state budget as its main business. The Assembly is then in actual session for some two to five days. Thereafter it meets for a day or two in October and again for a brief session of one or two days for a pre-Christmas shift in December. On these latter instances it usually approves several laws, government ordinances on the Economic Plan, and (more recently) decrees of its Presidium. If parliamentary action is desired between the main session in March and the October session, as sometimes happens, one or two brief meetings may be held during the intervening months.

At the beginning of each legislative session the presiding officers meet first to determine, in accordance with the wishes of the KSČ leaders, the Assembly's agenda. They apportion work among the several committees and fix the dates of their meetings and the time limit by which they must have their reports ready. They then schedule the dates and approximate length of the Assembly's meetings and prescribe the order and the manner in which the Assembly shall dispose of its business. They also select the legislators who are to participate in the debate and decide the topic and length of their speeches. Thus nothing whatsoever is left to chance and the Assembly's impresarios, guided by the firm hand of the Party leadership, retain complete control over all phases of the session.

Finally, the political eclipse suffered by the legislative branch of the government under the communist system is clearly apparent from the statistics of the Assembly's legislative output. In 85 plenary sessions that the first communist National Assembly held since its first meeting on June 10, 1948, until its last meeting on October 27, 1954, it considered and passed 326 laws and approved 76 government ordinances on economic planning, 6 annual budgets, 8 final accounts of state finances and 33 international treaties. Altogether 488 reports and 472 "contributions to the discussion" were made on all these items. The nine committees of the Assembly met 561 times.[76]

Insofar as the making of the law is concerned, it was not a bad showing and the average annual legislative output of the first communist legislature roughly corresponded to that of the last Chamber of Deputies of prewar Czechoslovakia which had considered 151 bills from the beginning of its term on June 18, 1935, to its last meeting on December 16, 1938.[77] But this was owing to the fact that so many changes had to be made in the legal system during the initial years of the dictatorship of the proletariat. Almost two-thirds of the 326 laws were made between 1948 and 1950. When the situation returned to normal the production of laws slackened considerably, amounting to 22 laws in 1951, 37 in 1952, 16 in 1953, and 13 in 1954. This low rate of legislative activity continued during the term of the second communist Assembly elected in November 1954. From its constitution in December 1954 to its termination in June 1960 it adopted a sum total of 118 laws, i.e., about 21 per annum.[78]

The rubber-stamp nature of the communist legislature is revealed also by the correlation of plenary meetings and bills considered by them. While the last prewar Chamber of Deputies averaged approximately one bill per meeting (151 bills in 159 meetings), its communist successor was four times as efficient and could polish off almost four bills per meeting (326 bills in 85 meetings). Additional evidence pointing in the same direction is the silence of communist statistics on parliamentary interpellations. None are mentioned in Fier-

---

[76] *ibid.*, October 28, 1954.

[77] *Deset let parlamentní retrospektívy* (Ten Years of Parliament in Retrospect), Praha, 1948, p. 8.

[78] See *Sbírka zákonů* (Collection of the Laws) for the respective years. Two of the thirteen laws enacted in 1954 were adopted by the New Assembly elected in November 1954.

linger's review of the work of the first communist Assembly, although the legislators' right "to interpellate the Prime Minister and other members of the government" was specifically listed in the Ninth-of-May Constitution. By contrast, 2,081 interpellations were addressed to the Cabinet by the last Chamber of Deputies of prewar Czechoslovakia.[79]

THE ASSEMBLY'S PRESIDIUM

Whereas the Presidium of the National Assembly, which should not be confused with the Inner Presidium, holds a rather extraordinary position in the Czechoslovak legislative framework, it is preferable to consider it separately from the other legislative organs.

Under the Ninth-of-May Constitution the Presidium as a whole had little to do as long as the Assembly itself was in session. Despite its designation, the Presidium of the National Assembly did not actually preside over the Assembly as this function was left to the Assembly's Chairman and Vice-Chairman who constituted the Inner Presidium. The full Presidium of the National Assembly could consider matters which were not assigned to any committee and it had the authority to determine the order in which the Assembly's Vice-Chairmen deputized for the Chairman.[80] Thus, as an owl rests while it is daylight but comes to life as soon as darkness sets in, so the Presidium of the National Assembly shed its slumber and became an "inner assembly" only when the National Assembly was no longer in session.

The Ninth-of-May Constitution listed four instances in which the twenty-four members of the Presidium, elected annually by the Assembly, could step into the legislative picture: (1) when the National Assembly was prorogued or adjourned; (2) when its term expired; (3) when it was dissolved; (4) when its convention was made impossible by "exceptional circumstances."

If and when any one of these instances occurred, the Presidium was automatically authorized by the Ninth-of-May Constitution to "take up urgent measures, including such measures as would otherwise require a law," and to "deal with all matters lying within the scope of authority of the National Assembly." Excepted from this delegation of legislative authority at all times were the powers to elect the President of the Republic or the Vice-President and to pass con-

[79] *Deset let parlamentní retrospektivy*, p. 8.
[80] Law No. 61 of December 14, 1954.

stitutional amendments. Furthermore, unless the meeting of the Assembly was prevented by "exceptional circumstances," the Presidium was barred from the exercise of three additional powers: (1) to extend the term of military service; (2) to impose permanent burdens upon state finances; and (3) to declare war.

Yet another set of limitations applied to the Presidium's authority to legislate by decree. Such decrees in lieu of the laws had to be proposed by the Cabinet, passed by an absolute majority of all the members of the Presidium, and signed by the President of the Republic, the Chairman of the National Assembly, the Prime Minister, and not less than one-half of the Cabinet members. Moreover, both the President of the Republic and the Prime Minister had a right of absolute veto over such decrees. Finally, all decrees in lieu of the laws had to be laid before the National Assembly as soon as it met again. Unless ratified by it within two months, they ceased to be valid.

As is apparent from this outline of constitutional provisions regulating its powers and status, the Presidium of the National Assembly differed substantially from its Soviet namesake, the Presidium of the Supreme Soviet of the USSR. Unlike the latter, it did not act as the Head of State. Hence, it did not possess the prerogatives that the Soviet Presidium exercises in its capacity as the Head of the Soviet Union, such as the power to appoint Cabinet members and army commanders, grant pardons, award orders and medals, ratify treaties, and send and receive envoys. Nor did the Czechoslovak Presidium have the virtually unlimited authority, enjoyed by its Soviet counterpart, to legislate by decree and to conduct referendum.

All this reveals that the communist makers of the Ninth-of-May Constitution did not intend to pattern the Assembly's Presidium after the Soviet image but chose to retain, under a new name, the Permanent Parliamentary Committee of the bourgeois Constitution of 1920. This Committee, which was a specialty of the Czechoslovak parliamentary system, was designed for the purpose of disposing of urgent legislative business and keeping an eye on the executive branch of the government when the legislature was not in session. A comparison between the constitutional provisions of 1920 concerning the Permanent Parliamentary Committee of the First Republic and the provisions in the Ninth-of-May Constitution pertaining to the Presidium of the National Assembly shows that the latter were little more than a slightly altered version of the former.[81]

[81] Details in Eduard Táborský, *op.cit.*, pp. 73ff.

In one important aspect, however, the Ninth-of-May Constitution went far beyond the previous pattern and did follow the Soviet system. It conferred on the Presidium of the National Assembly authority to give a binding interpretation of laws and to decide whether a law was contrary to the Constitution or an ordinance contrary to a law. Through this far-reaching clause the Presidium of the National Assembly was elevated to the position of supreme guardian of the Constitution, a role performed in prewar Czechoslovakia by a special Constitutional Court. If the Constitution were the supreme law of the land that it is supposed to be, the Presidium of the National Assembly would have become a very powerful organ. Through the above-mentioned authorization it would have wielded a mighty check over both the executive and the judicial branches of the government. But the hard realities of communist dictatorship once again prevented constitutional theory from becoming anything but an empty shell, and reduced the Presidium to the level of political impotence characteristic of its technical mother, the Assembly.

Worse than that—for many years after the communist seizure of power it looked as though the Presidium was destined to be altogether a stillborn child. From the way the communist system operates, it was clear from the very outset that the Presidium would never be given an opportunity to declare laws unconstitutional or to challenge the Cabinet by invalidating its ordinances. Nor was it likely that it would have much chance of being asked to give a binding interpretation of a controversial law. But in view of Soviet practice one might have thought that the Presidium would be quite frequently called upon to substitute for the Assembly in passing decrees with statutory validity. Yet nothing of the sort happened and not one such decree was issued throughout the whole term of the first communist Assembly. It was not until 1955 that the Presidium began to issue such decrees. Fourteen of them were adopted in 1955, thirteen in 1956, but only one in 1957, five in 1958, and one in 1959.[82]

Why did the communist rulers make so little use of the Assembly's Presidium between 1948 and 1960? The main reason lies undoubtedly in their desire to keep the democratic façade as decorative and as attractive as possible. Because of the country's deeply entrenched democratic traditions, they feel that more trappings are needed in Czechoslovakia than in Russia to foster the delusion of constitutional legality and popular representation. Hence, it would be hardly politic to downgrade unnecessarily its main symbol, the National Assembly,

[82] See *Sbírka zákonů* for the respective years.

by extensive use of delegated legislation or by assigning the Presidium final authority over the meaning and validity of the Assembly's laws. Moreover, summoning 300 or even 368 legislators to Praha is much simpler and far less costly than convening four times as many members of the Supreme Soviet from all parts of the huge Soviet Union to Moscow.

This desire to bolster the symbolic value of the National Assembly, coupled with the recent emphasis on collective leadership, probably accounts for the adjustment made in the status of the Presidium of the National Assembly by the new Constitution of 1960. While the Presidium has retained its right to legislate by decree when the National Assembly is not in session, it has lost its authority to issue a binding interpretation of the laws, and its power to rule on the constitutionality of the laws and the legality of government ordinances has been transferred to the National Assembly. On the other hand, the new Constitution specifically confers on the Presidium the right and the duty to "direct the work of the National Assembly," a function hitherto carried out by the extraconstitutional Inner Presidium. Simultaneously, the Presidium's membership has been increased to thirty and it now includes also chairmen of all of the Assembly's committees. Furthermore, as in the Soviet Union, the Presidium is now elected for the entire legislative term of four years rather than annually. However, none of these adjustments is likely to have noteworthy effect on the Assembly's operational pattern, except that the inclusion of the committee chairmen in the Assembly's presiding organ may inject an even bigger dose of democratic centralism into the parliamentary proceedings.

The National Assembly—A Potemkin Village

Thus the National Assembly has ceased to be "the capitalist chatter house" and has been turned into a vehicle for communist propaganda. The libertarian verbiage of the electoral laws and the Constitution, the elaborate paraphernalia of parliamentary elections, the legislators' immunities and the pseudodemocratic aura surrounding the Assembly's proceedings have all been carefully planned to conjure the illusion of genuine democratic representation. As in a well-arranged theatrical performance, the communist stage managers see to it that all the spotlights are focused on that portion of the scene that the audience is supposed to notice and that beneficial darkness hides the rest. Delegations of miners, factory workers, people's militia, the Army, and other representatives of the working people are brought to attend the pageant as the Assembly's honored guests. Immune against any challenge of adverse criticism, the radio and newspapers give great publicity to the Assembly's sessions and carry the texts of the main speeches and substantial excerpts from parliamentary "debates," thus doing their best to spread the phantasmagoria of make-believe democracy country-wide.

However, despite their determined efforts to create a semblance of democratic law-making, the audience remains unconvinced. Like the reputed false-front villages of Prince Potemkin, the decorative façade of the Czechoslovak legislative structure can be taken for real only by a nonchalant passer-by from far away, satisfied with a cursory glance at the structure's outward appearance. It cannot conceal the hard realities of totalitarian dictatorship from those who have to live in the façade's dark shadow.

CHAPTER XII

SOCIALIST LEGALITY

"WHAT IS the state but a great robber band if it be lacking in justice?" When studying the communist system of justice, one cannot help thinking of this celebrated sentence of St. Augustine, written fifteen centuries before anyone had ever heard of Lenin and his "Revolutionary legality." Indeed, no story is sadder for anyone reared in the legal and judicial concepts of Western civilization than the progressive decay of these concepts in Czechoslovakia, a country that used to be justly proud of its rule of law and judicial integrity. It took the communist rulers of Czechoslovakia only a few years to tear down the elaborate palace of pre-communist justice and erect on its site a new structure dedicated to class warfare.

"Our people's courts stand in the first line of the struggle for socialism . . . educate citizens to respect socialist property . . . tighten the working and state discipline . . . ," wrote the Czechoslovak Minister of Justice, Štefan Rais, in February 1953.[1] His successor, Jan Bartuška, spoke in the same vein in May 1955: "Our people's democratic laws . . . are directed against those who disturb the foundations and the development of socialist construction of our fatherland and the rules of socialist life of our people . . . . Not only does our judiciary strictly and uncompromisingly punish all criminals, agents of imperialism, traitors and enemies of our people's democratic system, but it also provides for the education of these culprits and gives all those who have gone astray the opportunity of rejoining the building work after they have served their sentences . . . ."[2] Three years later, yet another Minister of Justice, Václav Škoda, urged the courts to make "better use of their functions of suppression and education" and to strengthen "the socialist consciousness of the citizens"; and he reminded them that, together with the organs of public prosecution—the Army and Security forces— they were responsible "for the liquidation of hostile elements."[3]

[1] *Rudé právo,* February 2, 1953.
[2] *ibid.,* May 11, 1955.
[3] *ibid.,* July 24, 1958.

These militant pronouncements, made by the highest administrators of socialist legality over a span of six years ranging from the peak of the Stalin era through the post-Stalin thaw to the refreezing of 1957-1958 unabashedly reveal the true nature of justice under communist rule.

THE PREWAR JUDICIARY[4]

Prior to the Second World War the Czechoslovak judicial system provided for four tiers of courts having general jurisdiction over both civil and criminal matters. The judges, all of whom had to have a law degree and pass a special judicial examination, were appointed for life by the President of the Republic or the Cabinet. They enjoyed as complete a security of tenure as judges anywhere in the world. They could be removed, transferred, or have their salaries reduced only upon conviction by a special senate of five judges of the Supreme Court or the Court of Appeals for gross malperformance of their duties.[5] Their independence was fully guaranteed. They were bound by law and had both the right and the obligation to deny validity to any government ordinance in conflict with an Act of Parliament. They had, however, no power to question the constitutionality of duly enacted laws. Judicial review of legislation was reserved exclusively for a special Constitutional Court, and could be exercised only on a very limited scale. With a few exceptions, all cases of original and appellate jurisdiction were tried before professional judges. Laymen took part in judicial proceeding only in special labor dispute courts, in courts dealing with commercial matters, in cases arising out of social insurance, and in certain types of offenses committed through the printed word. There was also a jury system that was used in criminal trials for felonies punishable with a minimum penalty of five years in the penitentiary.

Protection against unlawful acts of the administration was afforded, not by the ordinary courts, but by a special Administrative Court composed of experts in public law and administration appointed for life by the President of the Republic.[6] Acting under the same guarantee of independence enjoyed by the judges of the Su-

---

[4] A good review of the Czechoslovak judicial system of prewar days may be found under *"Soudy a soudnictví"* (The Courts and the Judicial System) in *Slovník veřejného práva československého* (Encyclopaedia of Czechoslovak Public Law), Vol. 4, Brno, 1938, pp. 429ff.

[5] The retirement age was 66 and was to have become 65 by 1940.

[6] For details see Eduard Táborský, *Czechoslovak Democracy at Work*, London, 1945, pp. 131ff.

preme Court, the judges of the Administrative Court became intrepid protectors of individual rights against interference on the part of any government agent—from the President of the Republic down to the village constable—thereby exercising a function similar to that performed by the French *Conseil d'État*.[7]

In fact, the resemblance to the French system of courts was marked throughout, except that there were neither *juges de paix* nor any lower administrative tribunals comparable to the French Prefectural Councils. There was an even closer similarity to the French system with respect to juridical preparation and appointment of judges, and the actual operation of the courts.[8] That was true also of the role of the Minister of Justice who had the authority to admit law school graduates to judicial apprenticeship, recommend judges for promotion, and supervise the entire judicial system. The Czechoslovak system of public prosecution and the organization of the legal profession were also patterned after the French model. All the members of the *parquet* were appointed by the Minister of Justice and were fully subordinate to him. This similarity of the prewar Czechoslovak and French judicial systems is hardly surprising if we bear in mind that Bohemia-Moravia, the nucleus of present day Czechoslovakia, while retaining certain older rules of her own in some fields, came quite early under the influence of Roman law and based her civil law system on the Code Napoléon.

In concluding this brief survey of the prewar system it may be said that the judiciary attended adequately to the functions that the courts of law are supposed to perform in a properly working democracy. Except for the rather slow work of the Administrative Court, it dispensed justice with reasonable speed and ample impartiality at a relatively low cost. It provided for full legal protection of the rights of the individual, not only against violations by private citizens and groups, but also against infringements by government authorities.

The 1945-1948 Intermezzo

In 1945 the judicial system was restored essentially to the form in which it had existed before the War. The only major postwar changes were the creation of special "people's courts" to handle certain crimes committed during the Nazi occupation and the failure

---

[7] According to the statistical data available for the period from 1931 to 1935, 28,947 cases had been handled by the Court, of which 7,803 were decided against the government. See *Ročenka,* 1937, p. 279.

[8] See below regarding legal education.

to reestablish the Constitutional Court.[9] Due to the chaotic conditions prevailing during the months following the liberation, the judiciary experienced some difficulties in reasserting itself and in attaining its high prewar standards. However, backed by the strong tradition of judicial independence and impartiality, as well as by the firm hands-off attitude against communist tactics taken by the democratic Minister of Justice, Prokop Drtina, the judicial branch of the government made quite a spectacular comeback.

The communist leaders had correctly anticipated that a full restoration of the prewar judiciary would only make the fulfillment of their plans more difficult. For that reason they assiduously claimed the Ministry of Justice for their Party during the strenuous negotiations between them and the leaders of democratic parties in Moscow in March 1945.[10] Their failure to get this post was one of the few setbacks they suffered in their early bid for power. And when the public prosecutors began to demand, and the courts to mete out, jail sentences against communist-commanded policemen for having exceeded their authority, and when, in addition, the Administrative Court even went so far as to throw out as illegal some of the confiscatory measures taken against private property by communist-directed local authorities, the Communists' ire erupted. They gave full expression to their feelings later when, in their retrospective criticism of the judicial system of pre-Communist days, they complained bitterly that "the reactionaries had taken advantage of legal opportunities within the state apparatus," and that "many judges were directly reactionary, while many others were nonpolitical, made decisions according to 'law' only," and thus "kept on thwarting the struggle against the bourgeoisie."[11]

The events of February 1948 rang the death knell of a free and impartial judiciary in Czechoslovakia. Klement Gottwald's choice of Alexei Čepička, the most fanatical representative of the younger communist generation, to succeed the judicious Drtina as Minister of Justice after the communist coup, was a symbol of the changes to come. The new chief of the socialist legality, who was also Secretary

---

[9] Another court which failed to be reinstated was the Electoral Court, a special tribunal with the authority to rule on electoral disputes. For details see Táborský, *op.cit.*, pp. 78ff.

[10] Concerning the Moscow negotiations in March 1945, see Eduard Táborský, "Beneš and Stalin—Moscow, 1943 and 1945," *Journal of Central European Affairs*, 13 (1953), pp. 181-182; also, Josef Josten, *Oh, My Country*, London, 1949.

[11] See *Lidové noviny*, October 15, 1950.

General of the Central Action Committee of the regenerated National Front, the main purging body, wasted no time. A colossal purge was immediately carried out in the Ministry of Justice and on all levels of the judiciary and public prosecution. When it was finished, the backbone of the pre-communist judicial system was broken and its whole character defaced. Almost overnight the independence of the judiciary was destroyed, and what had once been the staunch guardian of individual rights and freedom was turned into a sharp weapon of the class struggle.

All this was achieved without significant change in the structure of the judiciary and without formal amendment of the rules of procedure or the canons of substantive law. In fact, one finds in the field of the judiciary and the agencies related to it at the early stage of the dictatorship of the proletariat trends and developments similar to those that had occurred in the other two branches of the government. There was a speedy domination by the Communists, a sweeping purge of unreliables, and a complete imposition of communist will with little change in structure, machinery, and formal procedures. Institutional sovietization came later. It spread gradually, almost grudgingly, and usually under the stress of necessity created either by direct or indirect Soviet "suggestions" or by pressure on the part of overzealous homegrown Stalinists.

THE JUDICIARY IN THE NINTH-OF-MAY CONSTITUTION OF 1948

As has been the case with the legislative and executive branches of the government, the bulk of the Judiciary Article of the Ninth-of-May Constitution was little more than a slightly retouched version of the corresponding clauses of the bourgeois Constitution of 1920.

The essential constitutional principles governing the judicial system under the original version of the Ninth-of-May Constitution may be summarized as follows:

1. Separation of the judiciary from the administration on all levels of government.

2. Independence of the judges in the discharge of their office.

3. Adjudication of cases by benches composed of both professional and lay judges.

4. Appointment of professional judges by the executive branch of the government and their subjection to involuntary transfer, dismissal or retirement only in case of a general reorganization of the judiciary,

by virtue of a disciplinary finding, or upon reaching a prescribed age or length of service.

5. Appointment of lay judges by people's committees on the corresponding territorial level and their subjection to recall under conditions laid down in a special Act.

6. Duty of all judges to abide by the laws and government ordinances and to interpret both in the light of the constitution and the "principles of the people's democratic order"; the right to declare an Act of the legislature unconstitutional to be reserved exclusively to the Presidium of the National Assembly.[12]

7. Jurisdiction to be exercised by civil courts in matter of civil law, by criminal courts in matters of criminal law, and by an Administrative Court in administrative matters; the authority of military courts to be extended to civilians "only in time of war or of increased danger to the State, and only in respect to acts committed in such a time."

8. Liability of the State and the judge in respect to damages arising out of a violation of the law committed by the judge in the discharge of his office to be prescribed by law.

9. Organization of the courts, the qualifications of judges, methods of court procedure, and other arrangements relative to the exercise of judicial powers to be stipulated by acts of the legislature, thus withdrawing the regulation of such matters from the authority of the executive branch of the government.

10. No arrest to be lawful "except on a written and circumstantiated warrant granted by the judge," such a warrant to be "served at the time of arrest or, if this is not possible, within 48 hours thereafter."

When compared with the corresponding provisions of the 1920 Constitution, these principles were, for the most part, identical or represented only a slight rewording. A few items were added and a few of the prewar provisions omitted. The jury system was abandoned and the use of lay judges to sit with professional judges was made a general rule in both civil and criminal matters. The authority of the legislature to subject civilians to the jurisdiction of military tribunals was somewhat enlarged. These and a few other changes of lesser consequence could by no means in themselves have an important effect on the character and the operation of the judicial branch.

[12] On the Presidium see Chapter XI.

There were, however, one omission and two additions which cannot be dismissed so lightly. The omission concerned the Constitutional Court, the only Czechoslovak Court entitled to review the acts of the legislature.[13] For Communists, any type of judicial check on the legislative branch of the government has always been an anathema. Whenever and wherever an attempt was made to provide for judicial review, the Communists have been in determined opposition.[14] It is therefore not at all surprising that the Ninth-of-May Constitution did not provide for a Constitutional Court. Instead, the exclusive power to rule upon the constitutionality of the laws was vested in the Presidium of the National Assembly.

The two additions of importance reflected the communist concept of the judiciary as merely a subordinate organ of law enforcement instead of a coordinate branch of government with checks on the other two branches. The first addition ordered the judges to abide not only by the laws of the legislature, but also by government ordinances. That was a far-reaching departure from a well-established principle rigidly adhered to in Western democracies of both the presidential and the parliamentary variety.

The second notable communist addition served to instruct the judges as to the proper methods of legal interpretation by directing them to interpret statutes and ordinances "in the light of the Constitution and the principles of the people's democratic order." The purpose of this clause was self-evident and was fully borne out by its practical application considered below. No longer was the judge expected to follow traditional channels of legal interpretation. Instead, he was to apply the laws as required by the Party leaders, for the people's democratic order is what the communist rulers say it is, and its substance changes constantly as the march proceeds toward the completion of socialism and the ultimate utopia of pure communism.

Subsequent Sovietization of the Judicial System

Having achieved their main objective of transforming the courts into obedient executors of their orders through ruthless purge and a few constitutional changes, the communist rulers were content for a time to make only a few relatively unimportant changes in the judicial machinery. To expedite the business of liquidating the enemy classes,

---

[13] For details see Eduard Táborský, *Czechoslovak Democracy at Work,* pp. 74ff.
[14] This was the case in France, Italy, and Western Germany.

the so-called people's courts (which had gone out of existence in January 1947) were reestablished in April 1948, with their personnel thoroughly communized. In October 1948, a special State Court was created to deal with certain categories of crimes against the State and its external and internal security under a People's Democratic Republic Protection Act. And by January 1949, the four-tiered arrangement of prewar days had become a three-tiered system through the discontinuance of the provincial courts of appeal.[15] None of these changes could be considered as essential or as having anything to do with communist doctrine. Nor were any substantial changes made in the formal court procedure in the first two years of the communist rule. The results obtained, particularly in criminal matters, were quite different from what they had been in pre-communist days and drastic sentences against "spies, traitors, and saboteurs," as well as against the "village rich" began to be meted out in ever-increasing quantities. But the formal processes through which such judgments were reached continued, on the whole, to follow the pattern of earlier days.

Considering the Stalinist mania for imposing rigid uniformity on satellite governmental systems, it was obvious that such a situation could not last long since there remained far too many deviations from the Soviet model. Professional judges still continued to be appointed for life by the executive branch of the government rather than elected for a definite term of office as in the Soviet Union. There were no popularly-elected courts with broad, general jurisdiction corresponding to the Soviet people's courts.[16] Unlike the Supreme Court of the USSR, the Czechoslovak Supreme Court enjoyed no authority of general supervision over the other courts. There were two additional courts of final jurisdiction, both fully independent of, and on a footing of equality with, the Supreme Court: a Supreme Military Court and an Administrative Court. Also, the whole system of prosecution was completely out of step with that in the Soviet Union.

Conscious of the risk he would run if he failed to communize quickly enough in the field under his responsibility, the new Minister of Justice announced in March 1948 a Juridical Two-Year Plan designed to do away with bourgeois law and replace it with socialist

[15] In pre-communist Czechoslovakia the four levels of courts of ordinary jurisdiction were the district courts, regional courts, provincial courts of appeals, and the Supreme Court.

[16] The previously mentioned Czechoslovak people's courts were only extraordinary criminal courts with a limited purpose of providing speedy retribution for wartime activities of the Nazis and their collaborators.

law.[17] By the fall of 1950 the program was completed. The results, aided by what was termed "the broadest utilization of the experience of Soviet jurisprudence,"[18] were embodied in several voluminous codes covering, with few exceptions, the whole field of civil and criminal law, substantive and procedural.[19] A number of far-reaching innovations imitative of Soviet law were thus brought into the substantive law, but only a few changes of essential importance were made with respect to judicial procedure.

These procedural changes were motivated by the need to eliminate "old-fashioned bourgeois formalism."[20] For example, the court could no longer decide for the plaintiff on the sole ground that the defendant failed to file a reply to the suit. Again, new facts were allowed to be brought into the trial even on the appellate level. The main procedural change, however, and the one most detrimental to the position of the judiciary, was the transfer of the exercise of certain rights from the judge to the public prosecutor. Under prewar rules of criminal procedure, only a judge could order a suspected person to be held in custody for purposes of investigation for a limited time, and only judges could conduct such investigations or authorize searches and seizures of persons, dwellings, and mail. The new Criminal Procedure Act of 1950, borrowing from the Soviet system, gave all these powers to the prosecutor without even imposing a definite limit on the period for which he could hold a person incommunicado.[21]

As these changes were being prepared and enacted, the communist rulers kept on emphasizing the changed ideological foundation upon which the new people's democratic courts and their work were to be based. "The starting point for the solution of all legal questions," said Čepička, addressing the National Congress of Czechoslovak lawyers in September 1949, "is Marxism-Leninism which enables us to express in a precise and understandable way legal concep-

[17] *Právo lidu,* March 17, 1948. A good discussion of the Plan as it affected the Czechoslovak legal system may be found in Václav Beneš, "The New Legal System of Czechoslovakia," *Journal of Central European Affairs,* 12 (1952), pp. 215ff.

[18] *Zpráva o Československu,* I, 18 (1950), p. 5.

[19] Laws Nos. 86, 87, 88, and 89 of June 12, 1950.

[20] Explaining the intended reforms on December 17, 1948, *Lidové noviny* stated: "The purpose of this new judiciary will no longer be the preservation of certain meaningless formalities. The purpose will be above all to find material truth. The finality of a judicial decision will remain untouched, but it will no longer prevent the Court from admitting its mistakes and from remedying them."

[21] Other important powers granted the procurators by the new regulation will be considered below.

tions that bourgeois legal science sought to obscure."[22] In mentioning some of the purposes to be achieved by the new juridical order, the communist Minister of Justice primarily emphasized the need to strengthen the people's democracy and socialist legality, while relegating to third place the need of "legal security of the workers."

Čepička's successor as Minister of Justice, Štefan Rais, expressed similar views. In December 1950, he told the National Conference of court presidents and public prosecutors:

"In the struggle for the socialist rebuilding of the village, the prosecutors and the judges have the task to protect the agricultural cooperatives, to prosecute saboteurs, to hit hard at the village bourgeoisie. The trials in the village must become effective means to convince the broad masses as to who is the sworn enemy of their interests. The proceedings against the saboteurs found among the village rich and their associates have a great political importance . . . . The courts must be prepared and must take advantage of every opportunity to unmask the true face of the village rich . . . in reaching decisions they have to consider the class character of the accused and the threat his act represents for the community . . . . The basic task of the judiciary in connection with the building of socialism in the village is to pursue consistently the general line of the Communist Party of Czechoslovakia . . . ."[23]

Fifteen months later, addressing another national conference, the same Minister of Justice listed as the main functions of the judiciary such things as "helping to carry out the resolutions of the Party and the government concerning industrial and agricultural production, and intensifying the struggle against those who were stealing national property and violating socialist legality and working discipline."[24] He also advised the judges on how to tackle these all-important tasks: "There is no judicial case, be it criminal or civil, that would not require the judge to apply a political viewpoint in dealing with it. It is not enough that the judge knows the provisions and the sanction of the law. He must also know its essence and function, its political content, and its political purpose."[25]

These and many similar public explanations of the ideology underlying the function and operation of the judicial branch were not intended to pave the way for further structural reform. Having com-

[22] *Lidové noviny,* September 24, 1949.
[23] *Rudé právo,* December 6, 1950.
[24] *ibid.,* March 18, 1952.
[25] *Lidové noviny,* January 30, 1951.

pleted and put into operation their Juridical Two-Year Plan, the Czechoslovak communist leaders apparently believed that their reorganizing work in the judicial sphere had been substantially concluded. Rather, their main concern seemed to be to heighten the judges' and prosecutors' ideological level and hammer into their heads the new class concept of law enforcement. In January 1952, however, the *Sovietskoye Gosudarstvo i Pravo,* the principal Soviet review of political science and law, published an article strongly criticizing the Czechoslovak judicial system for not yet having done away with the subordination of the prosecutors to the Minister of Justice. Its author, V. S. Tadevosian, a Soviet jurist, expressed hope that the situation would soon be improved and that the prosecutor's office would be made into "a centralized and independent organ which would exercise supreme supervision over the exact implementation of laws."[26] Although it was concerned specifically with the prosecuting element of the judicial system, a criticism coming from such a source could be left unheeded only at grave risk for the responsible officials. The hint was not lost on Štefan Rais and his associates. Within a few months the Minister could report that appropriate laws had already been drafted. On October 30, 1952, the National Assembly approved with customary unanimity a constitutional amendment and three laws reorganizing the judiciary and the public prosecution and once again amending the rules of civil and criminal procedure.[27]

The most notable changes concerning the judiciary proper brought about by this further utilization of the "rich experience of the most mature, solely correct, and truthful science in the world, Soviet jurisprudence,"[28] can be summed up as follows:

1. The Administrative Court and the Supreme Military Court were abolished.

2. Three *collegia* were established within the Supreme Court, one for criminal matters, one for civil law matters, and one for military matters, the last of these taking over the function previously exercised by the Supreme Military Court.

3. The Supreme Court was vested with supreme supervisory and directive powers over all the other courts, including the right to issue

[26] English translation taken from *News,* 1, 8 (1952), p. 15.

[27] Constitutional law No. 64 and law Nos. 65, 66, 67, and 68, all of October 30, 1952.

[28] As stated by the Minister of Justice in an address to a conference of attorneys in June 1952. *Rudé právo,* June 12, 1952.

directives to the lower courts regarding the proper interpretation of laws and regulations.[29]

4. Similar powers of supervision were given to the regional courts over the district courts, which were renamed people's courts to match the Soviet courts of the same name.

5. The Supreme Court was authorized to withdraw a case "for important reasons" from one subordinate court and assign it to another. A similar authority was given to regional courts with regard to cases handled by the people's courts within their districts.

6. The oath which all judges take upon being sworn into office was modified to include a promise to decide cases "in accordance with the principles of socialist legality."

7. All judges, professional and lay, were to be elected.

8. The function of the courts was redefined in accordance with Marxist-Leninist doctrine. The Court Organization Act listed as the courts' first task the protection of "the social order and the state machinery of the Republic, its socialist construction, and socialist property," and only secondarily the protection of "the personal work and property rights and interests of the citizens which are safeguarded by law."

9. The Marxist-Leninist guidance of the courts, hitherto supplied by Party directives, was inserted directly into the law which spelled out the role of the courts to "educate the citizens in devotion and loyalty toward the Czechoslovak Republic, in strict and consistent observance of the laws and other legal regulations, in respecting socialist property, in labor discipline, in the fulfillment of the obligations imposed upon them by the defense of the State, and in the orderly observance of the rules of socialist common life."

The steady sharpening of socialist legality that had characterized the Stalinist era in Czechoslovakia came to a temporary halt during the post-Stalinist thaw, especially under the impact of the Twentieth Congress of the Soviet Communist Party of February 1956. At a self-critical session of the KSČ's Central Committee held in the last days of March 1956 the Party's First Secretary, Antonín Novotný, conceded at long last that the one-sidedness of Stalin's thesis led to a vulgarization of the class struggle which made "some workers in

---

[29] To enable the Supreme Court to perform better its supervisory function a Presidium of the Supreme Court was established in 1955. See a decree of the Presidium of the National Assembly, No. 21 of March 31, 1955.

Security and Justice incorrectly think that they were the main power in the class struggle" and resulted in "excesses, arbitrariness, and violations of socialist legality . . . ."[30] An even more repentent note was struck by Novotný's colleague, Viliam Široký, at the session of the Central Committee of the Slovak Communist Party in May 1956. In a major breast-beating speech the Czechoslovak Premier bewailed the serious violations of socialist justice that had occurred during the Stalin era. Besides blaming it, "in the interests of historic truth," on Rudolf Slánský, "the malignant influence of the cult of the individual," and "the incorrect ideological conception" of the sharpening of class struggle during the construction of socialism, he admitted that the judicial system was also at fault and should be corrected:

"The violation of socialist justice was also made possible by some abnormalities in our penal code, in its provisions for supervision by the prosecutor, and in the penal law. Up to now, our penal code in fact permitted a conception of justice according to which a confession by the accused was sufficient for the establishment of his guilt. Understandably, this abnormal and impermissible situation played into the hands of those who used incorrect methods. Instead of all attention being concentrated on the establishment of objective truth on the basis of thoroughly investigated evidence, the Security organs, prosecutors, and judicial organs saw their function in obtaining a confession from the citizen suspected or accused of criminal actions come what may. Furthermore, the fact that our penal code does not recognize the function of the examining judge has placed on the Security organs the entire focus of the work of preparing the trial, which thus to a great extent predetermined the results of the trial itself. The Central Committee of the Communist Party of Czechoslovakia has concerned itself with these serious shortcomings and has resolved to take measures to correct them with the greatest speed. The Communist Party of Czechoslovakia is firmly determined to build a court procedure that will guarantee the maximum enforcement of socialist justice."[31]

The matter was taken up by the National Conference of the KSČ held in June 1956. In his report to the Conference Novotný repeated his earlier criticism of the "shortcomings and serious errors" in the judicial system and announced that "the Party had already taken

[30] *Rudé právo,* April 10, 1956.
[31] *ibid.,* May 11, 1956. The part of Široký's speech dealing with socialist justice and judicial procedure was reprinted in English in *Prague News Letter,* 12, 11, May 26, 1956.

a number of important measures to correct the errors, and was submitting further proposals to correct the situation."[32] Unanimously approving these proposals, the Conference issued directives aimed at strengthening socialist legality through a revision of the laws concerning the system of prosecution and criminal procedure. Its resolution spoke promisingly of the protection of "political and personal rights of the citizens," "objectivity in criminal procedure," "the right of the accused to defense," and other such "guarantees" of fair trial. It insisted that "confession of the accused did not relieve the organs of the investigation and the court of the duty to use further means in order to establish the objective truth" and rejected "investigation procedures that did not secure . . . truthful proofs."[33]

Whatever hopes there may have been that the iron grip of socialist legality might be relaxed were blown away by the tempest that had meanwhile erupted in Poland and Hungary. Having before their very eyes a live example of what could happen if controls were softened, the communist rulers of Czechoslovakia quickly shed any ideas of "liberalizing" the socialist justice. As passed by the National Assembly on December 19, 1956, the four laws revising the criminal code and the judicial system were hardly worth the bustle and hustle with which they have been heralded.[34] To be sure, a few improvements were made. The penalty of twenty-five years' imprisonment may now be substituted for capital punishment, which was hitherto mandatory for certain crimes, and it also replaces imprisonment for life as the longest possible prison sentence. In order to give the courts "much broader possibilities for using educational sentences" the revised code allows suspended sentences for penalties not longer than two years (three in the case of juvenile delinquents) instead of the former limit of one year, and removes the lower limits of some penalties.[35] It also eliminates some of the vagueness that characterized the criminal law of the Stalin era. As the Party leaders promised, the new law on criminal procedure states that a confession by the accused does not free the organs involved in penal procedure from the duty of verifying such a confession in every possible way. It proceeds from the assumption that no person should be considered guilty until a valid sentence has been pronounced; and its prescribes that the accused has the right to consult with his lawyer without interference from the moment when

[32] *Rudé právo,* June 12, 1956.
[33] *Československý přehled,* IV, 10 (1957), p. 37.
[34] Laws Nos. 63, 64, 65, and 66, all from December 19, 1956.
[35] *Prague News Letter,* 13, 3, February 2, 1957.

formal charges have been made against him. A two-month time limit has been set for the period during which an investigated person can be held in custody, and an additional two-month extension is permitted in "justified cases."

But even these meager improvements in legal formulae were promptly offset by the renewed insistence on "revolutionary vigilance" and the increased demands for sterner repressive measures against "enemy agents and traitors" that followed in the wake of the Hungarian revolution.[36] Noting with profound gratification the neo-Stalinist trends in the Soviet Union, Czechoslovak communist leaders wasted no time in calling off their reluctant courtship with "liberalization." By the middle of 1957 the re-stalinization of socialist legality was in full swing. Addressing the Party's Central Committee, Politbureau member and Minister of the Interior, Rudolf Barák, scored "the erroneous interpretation of our laws" leading to "false conclusions that the observance of socialist legality implies a certain liberalistic attitude toward perpetrators of criminal acts." He reprimanded the courts, including even the Supreme Court, for being far too lenient in imposing penalties even for crimes "against the construction of socialist society" and against "socialist property."[37] Similarly, another top watchdog of socialist legality, Jan Bartuška, the Prosecutor General and former Minister of Justice, complained of "serious liberalistic tendencies in the judicial practice" that he blamed on "the idealistic view of judicial independence."[38] He particularly bemoaned the fact that even many Party members and officials "wished to see the main front of the struggle for the strengthening of socialist legality in revisions of trials and arrangements for clemency" and "forgot that class enemies and their allies wanted to exploit the Party's criticism of matters of socialist legality for their own benefit."

In the face of such resolute admonitions to hit harder at the "class enemy," the scanty ameliorations enacted by the laws of November 1956 dissolved like soap flakes in boiling water. Rather, the sovietization was carried yet another step further by the adoption, in July 1957, of two additional laws regulating the election and the status of the judges of people's and regional courts and their disciplinary responsibility.[39]

The law on the election of judges implemented, with a delay

[36] *Rudé právo,* January 26, 1957.
[37] *ibid.,* June 20, 1957.
[38] *ibid.*
[39] Laws Nos. 36 and 37 of July 4, 1957.

of almost five years, the directive of the constitutional law of 1952 that both professional and lay judges be elected. Under its provisions, the judges of the people's courts were to be elected by the district people's committees and those of the regional courts by the regional people's committees, in both instances for three-year terms of office. The number of judges to be elected for individual courts was to be fixed by the Minister of Justice, and the candidates were to be nominated by the councils of the respective people's committees from among Czechoslovak citizens twenty-three years of age or older who were "devoted to the people's democratic system." An additional requirement of "professional knowledge," presumably of the law, had to be met by candidates for professional judgeships. The presiding judges of both the people's and regional courts were to be appointed by the Minister of Justice from among the elected judges. In sharp contrast to the original version of the Ninth-of-May Constitution, which guaranteed professional judges life tenure, the new law introduced the Soviet-style system of judicial recall. The people's committee that elected the judge could recall him "for gross violation of his duties." However, before it could make such a decision, it had to obtain an opinion of the Minister of Justice and grant a hearing to the judge who was to be recalled. Furthermore, the law imposed on the judges the duty to present periodic reports on their work to the people's committees that had elected them.

The law on "disciplinary responsibilities" deals with disciplinary procedure and punishment of judges for violations of work discipline and behavior unbecoming a judge. It subjects the judges of the people's courts to the disciplinary senates of the regional courts and the judges of regional courts to the disciplinary senates of the Supreme Court.

With this "further step toward the deepening of socialist democratism," as *Rudé právo* hailed the new judicial arrangements, the degradation of the once exalted judicial profession reached a new low.[40] Ever since the communist seizure of power in 1948, judges have been reduced to obedient executors of the Party's will and their selection has rested in the hands of the KSČ. But at least professional judges, appointed as they were by the central government, enjoyed some independence vis-à-vis the administrative authorities of their districts and regions. That has now been changed and the subordination of the judges to the Ministry of Justice has

[40] *Rudé právo*, September 22, 1957.

been supplemented by their responsibility to the respective organs of the local government as well. Thus, in addition to control by higher Party chiefs, they are now subjected also to the control of local Party officials. "The fact that judges are elected, that they can be recalled, and that they are obliged to present reports on their work to the workers broadens still further the influence of the working class on our judiciary."[41] Provided that the euphemistic term "working class" is replaced by "Party," for which it really stands, this statement of the Czechoslovak Minister of Justice is an accurate appraisal of the net effect of the 1957 judicial "reform."

Finally, mention must be made of the institution of the so-called "comradely courts" which began to be established in Czechoslovakia in 1959. Copied after the like-named Soviet invention they follow the same purpose of meting out summary punishment, mainly for infractions of the socialist labor discipline. As *Rudé právo* put it, "These courts, elected by the whole collectives from among the employees, command the confidence of the entire body of the workers and will deal, in an ever-increasing manner and with the direct participation of workers, with minor offenses irreconcilable with the ethics of a socialist. In this way the trade unions or other social organizations will take over part of the functions performed thus far by the state.[42]

As a result of these successive rearrangements, the Czechoslovak judicial system became by 1957-1959 virtually a miniature reproduction of the Soviet original. In only two relatively minor aspects did it differ from the original: (1) judges of the people's courts continued to be elected by the organs of the district government, the district people's committees, rather than directly by the voters; (2) the judges of the Supreme Court were not chosen by the national legislature, but continued to be appointed by the President of the Republic.

THE JUDICIARY IN THE SOCIALIST CONSTITUTION OF 1960

These modifications of the Soviet pattern were corrected by the new Constitution of 1960 which vests in the National Assembly the right to appoint judges of the Supreme Court and provides for the

[41] *Práce,* October 2, 1957.
[42] *Rudé právo,* October 15, 1959. As of September 30, 1960, 776 such comradely courts existed in Czechoslovakia. *Rudé právo,* December 13, 1960.

election of judges of the district people's courts by the voters rather than by the people's committees. The new Constitution incorporates also the sovietization measures that have been introduced into Czechoslovakia's judicial system in preceding years. It confirms the Supreme Court in its role of chief supervisor of the judicial work of all the other courts. It reaffirms the judges' obligation to render regular accounts of their work to the voters and assemblies that have elected them and imposes on the Supreme Court the specific duty to report to the National Assembly on "the state of socialist legality." It embodies the institution of judicial recall and drops the time-honored provision of the Ninth-of-May Constitution that the judiciary is in all instances separated from the administration. Finally, it provides a formal constitutional basis for the Soviet-like "comradely courts" under a new label of "local people's courts," thus becoming the first satellite constitution to adopt this latest device of communist justice.

Thus, with the adoption of the new socialist Constitution of 1960, the sovietization of the Czechoslovak judiciary, initiated with the communist seizure of power in 1948, has been brought to completion.

PUBLIC PROSECUTION

In the Soviet Union the judiciary is closely integrated with the public prosecution. The courts and the prosecuting organs are dealt with in the same section of the Constitution under a joint heading. All experts on the Soviet judicial system agree that the office of the Procurator General of the USSR overshadows in importance and authority every court in the Soviet Union. Said Vyshinsky, who certainly ought to know, having served as Procurator General for so many years: "The Soviet Prosecuting Officer is the watchman of socialist legality, the leader of the policy of the Communist Party and of Soviet authority, and the champion of socialism."[43]

The Soviet arrangement stood in absolute contradiction to the very basis of the Czechoslovak prewar system of prosecution. However, being anxious to gain the good will of as many people as possible in the initial years of their rule, and hoping that they could achieve their objectives better by avoiding sudden drastic structural changes, native communist leaders shrank from remodeling the public prosecution along Soviet lines. To be sure, they made the prose-

[43] Andre Vyshinsky, *The Law of the Soviet State,* New York, 1948, p. 537.

cutors the central figures in the administration of criminal justice, but they did this by simply purging all prosecutors whom they considered unreliable and replacing them with full-fledged Communists. They dealt similarly with the personnel of the courts and thus placed both prosecuting officers and judges under the rule of rigid Party discipline. It was, therefore, no problem for them to make both cooperate along the desired lines and to induce both to comply with whatever wishes the Party expressed. This explains why the communist leaders felt no urgent need of any sweeping reorganization of the prosecuting branch.

A few formal alterations, however, were made. The Procurator General was granted somewhat broader powers, insofar as he was authorized to lodge "complaints to insure observance of the law" in both criminal and civil law suits against judicial decisions that he deemed not consonant with the law.[44] However, he was given no such authority with regard to the decisions of the Supreme Court. Moreover, he could lodge such complaints only if authorized to do so by the Minister of Justice, who continued to be the Procurator's chief. Nor did Čepička's Juridical Two-Year Plan bring any basic change in the Procurator's position. As indicated earlier, investigative powers and the right to authorize arrests and searches, hitherto belonging to the judge, were vested in the prosecutors, as was the supervision of prisons and penitentiaries. The Procurator's authority to join in civil proceedings was further enlarged. He could intervene in civil cases at any stage whenever he deemed it necessary in the interests of the State or of the working people. He could appeal against any judgment, and he could demand the resumption of proceedings in such matters that had already become *res judicata*. However, despite these extensive powers, going considerably beyond those granted to the prosecutors in pre-communist days, the Czechoslovak Procurator General and his aides were still far behind their Soviet counterparts in the extent of their authority and in their over-all position in the structure of government. No wonder that serious fault was found with the Czechoslovak prosecution when V. S. Tadevosian chose to review its organization in the people's democracies in his article in *Sovietskoye Gosudarstvo i Pravo* in

[44] Under the prewar Criminal Procedure Code the Procurator could lodge with the Supreme Court "complaints for the preservation of the law" against final judgments of criminal courts which he believed to be incompatible with the law. However, a person already acquitted under such a judgment could not be tried again for the same offense even though the judgment was pronounced illegal.

January 1952. Tadevosian's remarks touched off a hasty reform of the judiciary proper, and were bound to lead to a radical reorganization of the prosecuting branch which had become the direct object of Soviet criticism.

The result of that reorganization, undertaken simultaneously with the judicial reform of October 1952, was that the Czechoslovak system of prosecution became almost a duplicate of the Soviet model. A constitutional amendment adopted by the National Assembly on October 30, 1952, vested in the Procurator General the power to enforce strict observance of the laws and regulations not only by the courts, but by all the ministries, all agencies of central and local government, and all institutions, as well as all officials, and even private individuals.[45] An additional law passed on the same day spelled out the above general definition in more detailed terms, including among the Procurator's specific tasks such items as "watching over, carrying through, and strengthening socialist legality"; the "protection of the social order and the state machinery of the Republic, its socialist construction and socialist property, as well as the interests of the working population against enemies and other saboteurs"; the "protection of the fighting ability of the Armed Forces and their discipline and order"; the "strengthening of the authority of the commanders and contribution toward the safeguarding of the defense of the motherland"; and the "education of citizens in observance of the laws and other rules of socialist common life and in fulfillment of civic obligations."[46] Simultaneously, the Procurator General was released from his subordination to the Minister of Justice and was granted the authority to appoint, and exercise full disciplinary powers over, all the regional and district procurators, as well as, in agreement with the Minister of National Defense, over the military procurators. He also took over the functions of the Minister of Justice in matters of pardon and amnesty.

However, in one aspect the Soviet pattern was not followed. While the Soviet Procurator General is elected by the Supreme Soviet of the USSR for a fixed term of seven years, his Czechoslovak namesake continued even after the 1952 reform to be appointed by the President of the Republic upon the proposal of the Cabinet and remained responsible to the Cabinet. This striking noncompliance

[45] Constitutional law No. 64 of October 30, 1952.
[46] Law No. 65 of October 30, 1952. See also Juraj Hromada, *Prehľad československých štatných orgánov* (An Outline of Czechoslovak State Organs), Bratislava, 1955, pp. 91-92.

with the Soviet model, despite Tadevosian's suggestion that the procurator General ought to be "an independent organ of the National Assembly and its Presidium," cannot be explained solely in terms of the different executive arrangements of the two countries. It would certainly have been more in line with the communist concept of legislative supremacy to allow the legislature, rather than the President of the Republic, to choose the chief watchman of socialist legality. Moreover, as the Procurator General was also called upon to supervise the work of individual ministries, he should have been made accountable to the legislative branch rather than to the Cabinet. Evidently, the Czechoslovak rulers had no desire to establish an office that would be, at least technically, independent of the President and the Cabinet.

Nor was the status of the Procurator General affected in any substantial way by the new law on public prosecution issued within the framework of the much-advertised judicial reform of 1956.[47] As promised by the National Conference of the KSČ in June 1956, the new law authorized the Procurator General to appoint (and remove) special investigators to help in preliminary investigations of crimes, thereby enhancing the procurator's role in that respect at some expense to the police organs. It broadened the supervisory powers of the Procurator General over the prisons and penal institutions and made it his right and duty to insure that nobody be prosecuted, taken into custody or held incommunicado without reason, or in any other way be deprived of his legal rights.

Finally, the Czechoslovak Procuracy has been brought still closer to the Soviet model by the constitutional reform of 1960. Whereas the Ninth-of-May Constitution of 1948 ignored the Procuracy altogether, the 1960 Constitution elevates the Procurator General to a constitutional status equal to that of his Soviet colleague. Furthermore, like the latter, the Czechoslovak Procurator General is henceforth responsible to the National Assembly rather than to the President of the Republic and the Cabinet. However, in contrast to the Soviet practice, he continues to be appointed (and may also be dismissed) by the President of the Republic.[48]

Despite the sweeping powers conferred upon the Procurator General by the laws of October 1952 and December 1956, and their

---

[47] Law No. 65 of December 19, 1956.

[48] But the 1960 Constitution confers on the National Assembly the right to request the President of the Republic to dismiss the Procurator General.

confirmation by the 1960 Constitution, the office has not thus far developed into the kind of supreme guardian of socialist legality made possible by such a vast grant of authority. The Procurator's relatively modest activities in the administrative field have already been considered in Chapter x. A similar situation has prevailed in the judicial sphere. True, the status of the prosecuting branch exceeds considerably what it used to be in pre-communist days and public prosecutors have become leading figures in all stages of criminal procedure. But they have not yet attained the absolute predominance reserved for their counterparts in the Soviet judicial proceedings. The residuum of traditional pre-communist concepts of justice, deeply embedded in the minds of Czechoslovak lawyers under the protective Red overlay have probably more to do with this than anything else. That such "harmful, liberalistic tendencies" had penetrated even into the inner sanctum of the supreme watchdog of socialist legality was revealed by the Procurator himself.[49]

On the other hand, the Procurator General has by no means become a protector of the rights of loyal citizens against police excesses to the degree he is supposed to be. Although the 1956 Party Conference and the verbiage of the 1956 law on the Procuracy displayed some concern in that respect, the renewed emphasis on the repressive mission of the State Security organs nipped in the bud any attempts to translate these vague promises into reality. All the evidence at hand suggests that, except in extreme cases of harshness that evoke interest of prominent high-ranking Communists, the procurators cannot do much to shield victims of communist police.

The Legal Profession

These far-reaching changes made in both the judiciary and the prosecuting branch and the whole conception of justice and function of the law were paralleled by a drastic reorganization of the legal profession that converted the once-free profession into an agency of the omnipotent communist State. There were several telling reasons why the legal profession became an early object of communist attention.

In pre-communist days all the practising attorneys were organized in public corporations called Chambers of Advocates, which were established on a territorial basis and enjoyed a considerable

---

[49] *Rudé právo,* June 20, 1957.

amount of autonomy.[50] Though they had been patterned after the French *chambres des avoués,* their purpose and functioning were not dissimilar from those of the American system of State Bar Associations. A strong tradition developed, as it had in all democratic countries, that it was the attorney's duty to do everything possible for his client and to take advantage of any legal technicality and use any stratagem short of deceit in order to win the case. To be admitted to the Bar one had to be a graduate of a university law school, to have had at least five years of postgraduate practical training under the guidance of a practicing attorney, and to have passed successfully a rigorous State Bar Examination. Since it took long years of study and considerable money to be admitted to the Bar the legal profession was a preserve of the upper and middle class. A much higher percentage of lawyers than of any other occupational group was actively engaged in politics and only very few of them showed any inclination for communism.

Thus, lawyers did not fit into the communist system which has no room for any liberal profession, least of all for one so bourgeois-ridden and so bent on protecting, come what may, the individual's rights against public prosecution. Hence, the legal profession was a logical, high-priority target in the class struggle unleashed by the communist rulers when they seized power in 1948. As in every other institution, a thorough purge was first undertaken. Special communist-controlled Action Committees were created within the legal profession and these committees speedily barred hundreds of lawyers from the exercise of their profession and frightened the rest of them into subservience. What happened was well expressed in figures given by Mr. Stein, chairman of the Action Committee of the Praha Chamber of Advocates, in 1948. According to these data only 143 lawyers were members of the KSČ in Czech lands prior to February 1948, and only five attorneys belonged to the Party in the entire city of Praha prior to 1938. Yet, after February 1948, as many as 1,049 of the 1,940 attorneys still operating in Czech lands became Party members.[51] It is quite obvious that an overwhelming majority of these post-February converts joined the KSČ, not because of a sudden realization of communism's virtues, but rather because of a hope of postponing the inevitable.

[50] For detail concerning the prewar status of the legal profession in Czechoslovakia see *"Advokacie"* (The Practicing Attorneys), in *Slovník veřejného práva československého,* I, Brno, 1929, pp. 11ff.

[51] *Lidové noviny,* December 16, 1948.

Having thus broken the backbone of the legal profession as it had been conceived in prewar Czechoslovakia, the Communists temporarily refrained from organizational reforms. Nevertheless, the Minister of Justice announced as early as March 1948 that the whole legal profession would soon undergo a drastic reorganization which would involve such things as turning the practicing attorneys into public officers "rewarded from common state funds."[52] This radical reform was enacted by the National Assembly in December 1951, together with a similar reform affecting the institution of the notary public, which was another type of legal position previously open exclusively to law school graduates and primarily concerned with wills, sales, and other contracts.[53]

Under the new Legal Profession Act, "working collectives" of lawyers, called Legal Advisory Bureaus, were established wherever necessary and subordinated nationally to a Central Bureau. Each Advistory Bureau is headed by a director who is appointed (and subject to removal) by the Central Bureau. The director guides and organizes the work of the Bureau, promotes the "political and professional growth" of all its members, and is "personally responsible for the proper fulfillment of these tasks." There are varying numbers of lawyers, candidate-lawyers, and other personnel attached to each Advisory Bureau, the membership and the number of personnel being determined by the Central Bureau, which also has the authority to transfer employees from one bureau to another and has full disciplinary powers over them. The earlier emphasis on voluntary membership was abandoned and the Legal Profession Act explicitly prohibits private practice of law.

The conditions under which one can become a member and thus be entitled to practice law are more lenient in one sense, and more stringent in another, than before the War. They are more lenient so far as the professional qualification is concerned. The strict requirements of pre-communist days have been substantially relaxed. The new requirements are listed as "legal education," "two years of law practice," and "a professional examination." However, all and any of these may be "fully or partially waived" by the Minister of

[52] *Právo lidu,* March 17, 1948. See also *Lidové noviny,* August 6 and December 23, 1948.

[53] Laws Nos. 114 and 116 of December 20, 1951. The very first step toward the socialization of the legal profession was taken as early as 1949 through the establishment of "attorneys' associations." See Government ordinance No. 74 of February 21, 1949, implementing the law No. 322/1948.

Justice. While the requirements of legal proficiency became more lenient, the requirements of political reliability became more stringent. The candidate must now show conclusively that he is "loyal to the people's democratic regime." When appointed as lawyer, he must take an oath promising not only to observe laws and ordinances but also "to apply them, everywhere and in everything, in accord with the will of the people and the State, and in full harmony with the spirit of the people's democracy and its socialist goals." Thus, no one may be admitted to the Bar, or become a notary public, who has not been given a certificate of clean political health by the Communist Party.

The relationship between the lawyer and the client is also radically changed. No longer is the counsel bound by an absolute duty not to reveal what he learns from his client in performance of his legal functions. As the new law bids, whenever the Minister of Justice chooses, because of "important state interests," to relieve the lawyer of his duty to keep such matters in confidence, the lawyer may no longer invoke such a duty before the courts or any organ of the state administration. On the other hand, the citizen's right to choose his own counsel has been retained by the new arrangement— whatever value such a right may have under the given circumstances. In any case, individual cases are considered collectively by the Bureau's lawyers in regular weekly discussions presided over by the Bureau's director.[54]

The fees for various types of legal work are fixed by the Minister of Justice and are governed by a class scale. Very low fees are prescribed for legal assistance allegedly protecting workers' interests, such as appeals against dismissals from work or cases involving alimony. Moreover, those who cannot afford the fee may ask to be represented at a reduced rate or altogether free of charge. Conversely, rates are much steeper for legal work pertaining to private property. Fees are not paid by the client directly to the lawyer who works on his case but to the Bureau which rewards its members on a salary-plus-bonus basis.

Yet another notable feature emerges from this description, namely the great authority granted to the Minister of Justice over the entire legal profession. He is empowered to waive at his pleasure various requirements for the admission to the Bar, to fix mandatory rates of lawyers' compensation, and to force the counsel to reveal data which he had learned from his client. In addition to all this, he is clothed

[54] See *Prague News Letter*, 12, 7, March 31, 1956.

with complete supervisory powers. In the exercise of these powers he can annul or change any decision of the Central Bureau if such a step is required in the "public interest."

The sad fate that has befallen the legal profession is well documented by reports brought out by escapee lawyers, such as the following one on the situation in Praha in 1954:

"Notaries public and lawyers are concentrated today at Žižkov [a rather dreary section of the capital city] in a former apartment house for women in Kubelík street. They are packed two or three to a room. They are apathetic to the matters of their clients and display no interest in their problems. When they counsel someone well, i.e., on how he ought to proceed to obtain from the State what belongs to him, they have to answer for 'not protecting the interests of the State.' Often, the lawyer tells his client quite openly that he cannot do anything in such a state of lawlessness."[55]

THE NEW CONCEPTION OF THE
LAWYER'S FUNCTION

These changes are well in line with the new conception of a lawyer's function. As stated in the Legal Profession Act, the legal profession "provides legal aid to socialistic legal persons, other cooperative organizations, the organs of the state administration, and to the citizens; it protects their interests in harmony with the principle of material truth and with the interests of society and thereby contributes toward the strengthening of the socialist legality." What is actually meant was explained in considerable detail by the lawyers' supreme chief, the Minister of Justice:

"The lawyer must not blindly protect his client's interest, which is often selfish . . . . He must defend his client in accordance with the interests of society. Therefore, he must abandon all cunning, pretense, and twisting, and must instead help to seek truth and justice with decency and honesty. The lawyer must always have on his mind the higher interest of the whole community; he must protect and strengthen the socialist community and not to break it . . . . He must master the teaching of Marxism-Leninism; he must rely firmly on the most mature, solely correct, and truthful science in the world, the Soviet legal science; and he must thoroughly avail himself of the experience of the Soviet practice of the law . . . . Lawyers cannot, by using old forms of work based on bourgeois individualism, fulfill the important and responsible tasks given

[55] *Československý přehled*, I, 3 (1954), p. 28.

the legal profession by the new Act. They must acquire the socialist style of work."[56]

Under such an interpretation from the highest quarter, the sharp and well-defined lines that used to separate the threefold functions of the judge, the public prosecutor, and the defense are virtually erased and the traditional conception of the defense counsel is distorted beyond recognition. Lest he be misunderstood, the Minister of Justice accompanied his statement with several illustrations that provide ample evidence of the low point to which ideas of law and justice have sunk in communist Czechoslovakia. He gave the assembled lawyers the "deterrent example" of an attorney who had attempted to help an "enemy of the Republic" by claiming that the accused was a good-natured man who was unable to refuse when people asked him to do unlawful things. And the Minister angrily remarked that there still existed lawyers who secretly wrote letters of appeals for the village rich. When a lawyer dares not openly help the defendant prepare his appeal, it is hardly surprising that no defendant can find a counsel willing to take up a case that has a political tinge. Thus, the legal profession, fully communized and geared to the service of helping to enforce the socialist legality, has lost both its face and its soul. It can assert itself in its earlier traditional mission only in the sharply narrowed field of individual disputes and minor offenses, providing in both instances that no political issue and no socialist property are involved.

LEGAL EDUCATION

"Czechoslovak lawyers shared the fate of the Czechoslovak intelligentsia in their dependence on the ruling classes which they served, i.e., in their dependence on the bourgeoisie. Their whole education was subordinated to this interest and was channeled into a formalistic conservatism which the bourgeoisie considered as the most appropriate means toward maintaining its supremacy. Year after year young people were inculcated with a doctrine of individual rights and of the sanctity and inviolability of private ownership that was asserted to be the law of all laws. They were fed on philosophical distortions engineered in support of such goals, as well as on a dry, spiritless practice, playing with soulless, pedantic pettifogging, always directed against real life and the living man . . . ."[57]

[56] In a speech before the First National Conference of lawyers on June 11, 1952. *Rudé právo,* June 12, 1952.

[57] From an address of welcome to the conference of Czechoslovak lawyers in September 1949. *Lidové noviny,* September 23, 1949.

This retrospective criticism of the pre-communist preparation of lawyers, made by no less a person than the Chairman of the National Assembly, illustrates communist objections to the previous training of lawyers. That alone was an adequate reason to prompt the communist regime to revise drastically the former system of the "production of lawyers." But there was yet another reason that made it quite imperative. It was customary throughout Central Europe for graduates of law schools not only to fill all the judgeships and prosecuting positions and to monopolize the legal profession, but also to supply the bulk of the top administrative class of the civil service at all levels of government. Hence, considerably more was involved than would be the case in the Anglo-Saxon world where graduates of law schools do not permeate the administrative apparatus to that extent.

The first corrective measure to be taken was a thorough purge of the law school faculties. Most of the professors appointed in pre-communist days were removed, and the vacancies were filled with reliable Communists or subservient fellow-travelers, most of whom were not wholly unqualified, but who certainly fell below prewar standards. Simultaneously, a process of political screening was established with the purpose of barring undesirables from admission to the law schools. Though university studies were not too expensive in prewar days, they were, nevertheless, beyond the means of an average worker's family. As mentioned above, the consequence was that relatively few people of working origin could manage to enter law schools. This fact was eagerly seized upon by the Communists, and without delay they launched a campaign to correct the class composition of the student body in all schools above elementary level and in law schools in particular. Communist-dominated screening commissions were established with authority to admit or to reject applicants on the basis of both educational qualification and political reliability.

Hand-in-hand with persistent efforts to correct the class composition of the faculties and the student body, significant revision was undertaken in the law studies curricula in order to make them correspond to the new conception of the law and of its function and to transform the law schools into "the focuses of the new Marxist-Leninist legal science."[58] Public law is stressed, with particular emphasis on criminal law and procedure. Commercial law, having been done away with within the Juridical Two-Year Plan, disappeared altogether. Within the remaining field of civil law, which was de-emphasized considerably, the major items of study are the new institution

---

[58] *Lidové noviny,* June 28, 1949.

of socialist ownership, as well as the so-called economic agreements. So far as history of the law is concerned, the main attention is now centered on the recent past, instead of being devoted to all stages of its development from Roman law to modern times, as used to be the case. The purpose of this shift was explained by the Minister of Justice: "The main interest of the lawyer-historian must be concentrated upon the recent past, the consequences of which still assert themselves. The history of law reveals very clearly the antipopular and exploiting nature of the pre-Munich Republic where law and the legal profession readily aided the capitalists and their political representatives."[59]

New textbooks had to be quickly prepared to replace the "bourgeois" texts. An examination of a number of these hasty products of communist jurisprudence in Czechoslovakia indicates that they are, for the most part, inferior to the materials used in the law schools of the First Republic.[60] Not only are they replete with factual distortions, misrepresentations of "bourgeois" law, and unctuous references to Soviet legal science, but their over-all standard of scholarship is often below par even if the Marxist-Leninist viewpoint is granted. It is apparent that the Czechoslovak Communists have thus far failed to develop fully qualified academic personnel who could serve as adequate replacements for the purged professors.

The communist treatment of the law schools has caused a substantial deterioriation in the quality of law school graduates, compared with average graduates of prewar days; and as the former strict requirements of postgraduate legal practice were substantially reduced, the new graduates have even less chance to learn in practical work what they failed to gather while in law school. How low the standards have sunk since the coup is strikingly shown by the following illustra-

[59] From a speech at the meeting organized by the Law School of Charles University and the Juridical Institute of the Ministry of Justice on June 7, 1951.

[60] See, for instance, Pavel Levit, *Správní právo, část obecná* (Administrative Law, General Part), Praha, 1954, and *Správní právo, část zvláštní* (Administrative Law, Special Part), Praha, 1956; Juraj Hromada, *op.cit.;* Vladimír Klokočka, *Základy státního práva buržoasních zemí, obecná část* (The Fundamentals of the State Law of the Bourgeois Countries, General Part), Praha, 1957; Jaroslav Krofta, *Kapitoly z ústav lidově demokratických zemí* (Chapters from the Constitutions of the People's Democratic Countries), Praha, 1957; Jan Gronský, *Prehľad ústavného a politického vývoja ľudovodemokratíckych zemí* (An Outline of the State Law of the People's Democratic Countries), Praha, 1957; Radim Foustka, *Doplňková skripta z theorie státu a práva* (Supplementary Scripts on the Theory of the State and the Law), Praha, 1954; Radim Foustka, *Národnostní otázka* (The Nationality Question), Praha, 1952; Viktor Knapp, *Hlavní zásady československého socialistického občanského práva* (The Main Principles of the Czechoslovak Socialist Civil Law), Praha, 1958; Jan Bartuška, *Státní právo Československé republiky* (The State Law of the Czechoslovak Republic), Praha, 1952.

tion quoted by the Czechoslovak daily press as an outstanding example of the "new socialistic man" and his achievements: "He [Schubert, a former worker] managed to prepare himself for university studies in the one-year law course for state prosecutors. Comrade Schubert started his studies in February 1949. After having completed the course where he acquired a full knowledge of criminal law and deepened his knowledge of Marxism-Leninism, he became a prosecutor at the state prosecutor's office in Bratislava and soon thereafter an assistant professor of criminal law at the university."[61] Thus, what could at best have been achieved in prewar Czechoslovakia in nine years of senior high school and college studies was accomplished by the amazing comrade Schubert in a mere two and one-half years.

Despite all these glaring deficiencies, the preparation of lawyers can hardly be labeled as utterly inadequate for the task which they are now supposed to perform. With so little scope for varied interpretation of the laws; with the rigid guidance provided by the Communist Party, the communist Minister of Justice, communist Procurator General, and the communist-staffed Supreme Court; with the all-pervading concept of the socialist legality, and with so few private interests of any importance to be protected, the work of people's democratic lawyers, whether they serve as judges, prosecutors, or practicing attorneys, is of necessity immeasurably less complicated than is the case with their colleagues in the free society of the Western World.

THE ADMINISTRATIVE RETRIBUTION

Dicey's famous advocacy of "the amenability of everybody, high or low, to the ordinary law of the land, to the jurisdiction of ordinary tribunals" and his contempt for administrative courts no longer hold good, not even in his mother country. But the principle that penalties for breaking the law (except in minor matters) may be imposed only by independent courts is still considered as one of the fundamentals of democratic justice. That was true in prewar Czechoslovakia. Administrative authorities did have a very limited power to impose fines, disciplinary punishments, and minor jail penalties up to fourteen days for infractions of certain police, custom, and other regulations. But the ultimate decision even in these matters rested with fully independent courts.

The totalitarian regimes, on the other hand, spurn such notions

[61] *Pravda,* July 25, 1951.

as the rule of law. As illustrated in Fascist Italy, Nazi Germany, and Soviet Russia, it is typical for such systems of government to assign vast powers of criminal jurisdiction to administrative authorities and to allow them to impose penalties, even of forced labor, without any right to judicial review. Since such was the pattern adopted by the Soviet model, the Czechoslovak Communists could be expected to behave likewise.

The ground for administrative criminal justice was prepared by the Ninth-of-May Constitution which provided that "the jurisdiction in matters of criminal law shall be discharged by criminal courts except where general regulations prescribe that criminal cases shall be dealt with by administrative criminal proceedings." Acting under this broad constitutional authorization, the National Assembly passed in July 1950 an Administrative Criminal Code and an Administrative Criminal Procedure Act granting substantial penal powers to the people's committees.[62] The law authorized the people's committees to decree penalties for a long list of broadly defined offenses against the economic system and planning, agriculture, and forestry; against regulations relative to work, health, the supply system, public order, and cultural and community life. The types of punishable behavior are described so loosely that one can be punished for the commission or omission of almost anything. The favorite words used by the Code to define criminal activity subject to administrative prosecution, such as "he who impedes, disturbs or endangers" are elastic. They can be made to fit any circumstance and thus enable the administrative organs amply to fulfill the announced purpose of the law, namely to "educate toward the fulfillment of duties connected with the construction of socialism."

Details of procedure, which are very informal, are prescribed by government ordinances and regulations issued by the Ministry of the Interior, which supervises and directs the whole system. Decisions are made by penal commissions of three members consisting of the chairman of the people's committee and two members elected by the same committee. One appeal is permitted to the next highest people's committee, and the findings may be annulled by higher order "if they are in conflict with the interests of the working people." Under the original version of the Administrative Criminal Procedure Act, the penal commissions enjoyed broad powers in selecting the type of penalty, from

[62] Laws Nos. 88 and 89 of June 12, 1950, No. 102 of December 22, 1953 and No. 14 of March 6, 1957; government ordinance No. 65 of October 11, 1957.

plain admonition to confiscation of property and jail.[63] Ordinarily, the jail sentence was not to exceed six months. However, when the act committed revealed a hostile attitude toward the socialist construction, the maximum penalty could be raised as high as two years of hard labor. On the other hand, if the accused "conducted the proper life of a working man," punishment could be dispensed with unless required by the "interest of the working people."

This broad discretion in the matter of penalties was narrowed considerably in the post-Stalin era. A law adopted in December 1953 deprived the people's committees of the power to pass prison sentences and to declare confiscation of property, and limited their authority to the imposition of fines to a maximum of 3,000 crowns (approximately 420 dollars) and "correctional measures," consisting mainly of a downgrading of jobs and reductions in pay for a maximum duration of three months.[64] But it has left unimpaired the principle that a man could be punished by administrative authorities without any right of appeal to regular courts. Furthermore, a new method of penalizing by administrative fiat was enacted in 1958 when the Social Security Commissions of the district people's committees were authorized to lower or take away completely Social Security benefits of persons sentenced for certain crimes against the Republic, its economy, socialist property, peace and "analogous offenses according to the laws previously in force."[65] Yet another form of administrative retribution is provided by plant disciplinary commissions authorized to impose penalties for theft of socialist property.[66] Finally, the previously mentioned comradely courts also fall into the category of administrative criminal justice.

STATE ARBITRATION

A substantial number of cases that would be handled by court action in non-communist countries are removed from the court register in communist Czechoslovakia because they are subject to compulsory arbitration by government-appointed arbitrators. Patterned after the Soviet *Gosarbitrazh,* the Czechoslovak arbitration organs deal with disputes between nationalized enterprises resulting from their economic contracts, as well as similar conflicts arising between various organs

---

[63] However, the authority of the local people's committees was limited to minor infractions only. See government ordinance No. 65 of October 11, 1957.

[64] Law No. 102 of December 22, 1953.

[65] Law No. 40 of July 3, 1958.

[66] Law No. 24 of April 18, 1957.

of the state administration.[67] Disputes between enterprises subordinated to different ministries are settled by the State Arbitration Board attached to the Ministry of Justice. It has branch agencies in all the regions as well as a special State Arbitration Board for Slovakia. Controversies between bodies operating under the aegis of the same Ministry are handled by arbitration organs within the Ministry. Similarly, the Central Union of the Cooperatives establishes arbitration organs to cope with conflicts developing within the cooperative sector of the socialist economy.

Another type of arbitration procedure was provided in 1959 for labor disputes. Previously, controversies arising from the employee-management relationship were subjected to the ultimate jurisdiction of regular courts. But a new law adopted in July 1959 gave the authority to settle such cases to trade union works councils or special arbitration organs set up for this purpose in individual enterprises.[68] The philosophy behind this substitution of compulsory arbitration for regular court procedure was pointedly explained by the *rapporteur* on the bill: "A labor dispute is a matter for the whole collective of the respective working place and it is primarily up to this collective to contribute to the solution of controversies arising between the employees and the management" and thus to "create prerequisites for a quick and socially useful removal of labor disputes."[69]

THE "PEOPLE'S JUSTICE"—A WEAPON OF CLASS STRUGGLE

From what has been said in the preceding pages, the predominant character of the socialist legality as a sharp weapon of the class struggle stands out very clearly. In addition to innumerable official pronouncements to that effect (some of which have been quoted earlier) the class conception of the "people's justice" is amply revealed in everyday practice.

As elsewhere behind the Iron Curtain, the general trend of development has been away from civil law litigation and toward increasing adjudication in criminal matters. With the disappearance of private enterprise in industry and business and its swift eclipse in the field of agriculture, there is far less room for such civil law cases as usually

[67] Government ordinances No. 47 of May 12, 1953, No. 77 of September 11, 1953, No. 45 of September 21, 1954, and No. 28 of May 20, 1959. See also Hromada, *op.cit.,* p. 101.

[68] Law No. 38 of July 8, 1959.

[69] *Rudé právo,* July 9, 1959.

arise under a free enterprise system. At the same time, the continuous need to enforce rigid discipline and break every resistance necessarily multiplies the number of law violations and sharpens the application of criminal law. The class nature of the people's justice is best illustrated by the types of offenders and crimes tried and penalties imposed by the Czechoslovak courts under the dictatorship of the proletariat.[70]

Judging by published reports on court proceedings, the great majority of defendants brought before the communist courts have thus far been members of the former bourgeoisie. As claimed by the Minister of Justice in July 1958, "Former exploiters, members of the bourgeoisie and petty bourgeoisie comprise 70 percent of all sentenced persons."[71] Among them figure such "parasites" and "leeches and enemies of the new life" as former merchants, contractors and shopkeepers; physicians, lawyers, architects, and members of other formerly free professions; white-collar employees in previously private enterprises; priests and nuns; functionaries of former "bourgeois" organizations such as the Scouts, Sokol, and Legionnaires; workers who had been previously active in the Social Democratic Party and non-communist trade unions. But the most numerous single group among the victims of socialist justice have been the village rich, the *kulaks*. However, in recent years the sharp edge of the socialist legality has also been increasingly applied against industrial workers for various offenses against labor discipline, as well as against supervisory personnel of the socialist sector of the economy guilty of various crimes against the planning discipline and socialist property. And juvenile delinquents of all sorts have lately also been appearing before the communist magistrates in increasing numbers.

The two main categories of offenses that occupy the bulk of the courts' time are crimes against the people's democratic political institutions and those directed against the socialist economic order.

The first category consists of treason, espionage, and various acts aimed against the communist regime, such as "terrorizing peaceful citizens," "spreading subversive opinions," "advocating the return of capitalism," selling "anti-Soviet and other prohibited books," endeavors "to create mistrust toward the regime and the cooperative idea," and "teaching groups of boys to hate our regime." Also, the first category includes such malfeasance as collaborating "with the

[70] This is based on information gleaned from the daily press reports on trials over the years of the communist rule.
[71] *Rudé právo,* July 21, 1958.

treacherous *émigrés*," "interfering with the peaceful construction of our working people," "dishonoring the monuments of the Red Army," disseminating information broadcast by Free-Europe and Voice-of-America transmitters, and possession of mimeograph machines without permit.

The offenses against the country's economic order that fill the dockets of communist courts embrace a wide range of activities from capital felonies to minor infractions that would not qualify even as misdemeanors in a Western democratic system. They encompass an almost infinite variety of willful or negligent commissions and omissions detrimental to socialist economy, such as embezzlement of funds of national enterprises; stealing and pilfering state and cooperative property; concealment and unlawful disposal of merchandise; nonfulfillment of government deliveries, ploughing schedules and other prescribed agricultural quotas; dissemination of the "American beetle" and of foot-and-mouth disease; excessive absenteeism at work; stealing tools and materials from factories, produce from collective farms, hardware from government buildings, and silverware from publicly owned restaurants; and defrauding the government by unlawful payment of bonuses or unearned overtime compensation.

The class principle is also reflected in the imposed penalties. While personal guilt still continues to be the main consideration, penalties are increasingly assessed according to the object against which the offense has been perpetrated. Only a few months after the communist seizure of power, the case was stated clearly in an editorial in *Lidové noviny* which insisted that "stealing nationalized property was something essentially quite different from stealing property of a private entrepreneur."[72] The communist Civil Code is designed to give a preferred legal position to socialist legal persons and to socialist property.[73] According to the Criminal Code, the maximum penalty for larceny against socialist property is twice that prescribed for larceny against private property. An act otherwise criminal ceases to be considered criminal when it has been committed in order to "avert danger from the people's democratic Republic, its socialist construction, and the interest of the working class." Lesser penalties such as "corrective measures," may be imposed "only upon offenders from the ranks of the workers and in no case upon independent

[72] *Lidové noviny*, July 21, 1948.
[73] Gustav Přenosil, *Ochrana socialistického vlastnictví podle československého trestního práva* (The Protection of Socialist Ownership According to the Czechoslovak Criminal Law), Praha, 1957, pp. 9-10.

tradesmen, including those who were tradesmen in the past."[74] Guided by the directives of their communist chiefs "to consider the class character of the accused," the courts never fail to include the appropriate description of the defendants' social background in their judgments, and they award penalties accordingly.

As a result, truly Draconian penalties are imposed for acts that would be punished much more mildly or not at all in the democratic West. This was particularly true of the Stalin era when death sentences were pronounced, not only for treason, espionage and other major political offenses, but also for such relatively trivial matters as falsification of food ration cards and concealment of property from government authorities.[75] As one communist writer put it, the judge must act not like a "sentimental woman" but like a physician, who does not hesitate to make a surgical cut or to isolate a patient who could communicate the disease to others.[76] The post-Stalin thaw brought a certain mitigation that was primarily reflected by a major drop in capital punishments, but also in a generally more lenient attitude of the courts and less regard for the class principle. However, the renewed offensive of 1957 against the "liberalistic tendencies in judicial practice" and the strong reemphasis on the application of the "sharp edge" of the laws to the "class enemies" made the courts once again keenly class conscious and pushed the penalties upward, though the trigger-happy use of capital punishment characteristic of the Stalin era has not returned.

An especially notable stiffening of penalties has recently taken place in cases of stealing and pilfering national property, obviously as a concerted effort to curb their rampant growth. Hard labor sentences as high as five to fifteen years are known to have been imposed in some extreme cases. Even smaller pilfering may be punished by jail sentences although most of the lesser cases of first offenses are generally disposed of by fines.[77] As many as 5,047 persons were convicted on charges of stealing socialist property in the first half of 1958 alone.

Thus, as the regime's executor of socialist legality, the Czechoslovak judiciary has contributed its share toward the "completion of the socialist revolution."

[74] *Práce,* January 6, 1953.
[75] *Rudé právo,* July 13, 1951, April 30, 1952.
[76] *Lidové noviny,* August 12, 1948.
[77] See a list of such crimes for the latter part of 1957 and for 1958 in *Československý přehled,* v, 3 (1958), pp. 3ff.

CHAPTER XIII
THE LOCAL LEVERS

In no other country of twentieth-century Europe have matters of local government played more havoc with domestic peace and external security than in Czechoslovakia. Nor does modern history offer a more frustrating story than the process by which well-meant, though slow and hesitant, endeavor to meet claims for more local self-government was exploited for the opposite purpose, i.e., for crushing liberty and establishing a rigid totalitarian centralism.

The birth of the Republic itself in 1918 was bitterly opposed by most of its German minority, whose desire, however unrealistic, was to join the new Austrian state. The majority of the Sudeten Germans had scarcely begun to show a change of heart, and leaders of their major parties had hardly begun active cooperation with the Czechoslovak government by sending their representatives to sit in the Czechoslovak cabinet in 1926 and 1929, when Hitler came to power in Germany, and the Nazi acid quickly corroded the delicate fabric of Czech-German cooperation.

Having learned, in the holocaust of World War II and under the heel of Nazi occupation, how cleverly petty quarrels over more or less local self-government were subject to exploitation against them, the Czechs, Slovaks, and Ruthenians set out with high hopes to build up a new, almost federal pattern of decentralized government. They established, in 1944 and 1945, a system of elective people's committees vested with broad powers of self-government. Yet once again, as in the case of the Nazis in 1938 and 1939, what were to be institutions of greater freedom were gradually turned into the chief instruments of suppression, culminating in the communist coup of February 1948.

Thus, the story of Czechoslovak local government is not only an account of drastic changes in forms and institutions and in their practical working. It is also a story of the profound mutual mistrust of three major ethnic groups, Czechs, Slovaks, and Germans, a story of irreconcilable clashes fostered and exploited by foreign interests, a story of frustrated hopes, of two national, and millions of individual, tragedies. It is a story reminding one of the sad fate of Sisyphus and his marble block.

LOCAL GOVERNMENT FROM 1918 TO 1948[1]

Prior to the Second World War the local government of Czechoslovakia was organized on three territorial levels constituted by communes, districts, and provinces.[2]

The communal government consisted of an assembly of nine to sixty members elected on the basis of proportional representation for six-year terms; a council with a membership of one-third of the assembly, elected for six years from among the assembly's members; and a mayor with one or two deputies elected by the assembly from among its members and confirmed by the Provincial Office or, in the case of a city where the District Office was located, by the Ministry of the Interior.

The arrangements on district and provincial levels were almost identical. There were provincial and district assemblies with two-thirds of their members popularly elected on the basis of proportional representation and the remainder appointed by the central government, all for six-year terms. From their membership these assemblies elected smaller provincial and district committees, while their presiding officers—the provincial presidents and the district governors—were appointed by the central government.

The powers of these local government units were determined by a broad and vague formula under which each was authorized to manage its "administrative and economic needs" provided that such needs exceeded the scope of interests handled on the lower level and had not been taken care of by the central government or a higher level of local government. This formula permitted many activities on each

---

[1] There is comparatively little material in the English language dealing with the prewar Czechoslovak local government. A chapter is devoted to the subject in Eduard Táborský, *Czechoslovak Democracy at Work*, London, 1945. See also Eduard Táborský, "Czechoslovak Local Government," *Central European Observer* (London), January 12 and 26, 1945, and "Local Government in Czechoslovakia, 1918-1948," *The American Slavic and East European Review*, 10, 3 (1951), pp. 202-215. A brief, far too brief, outline of pre-Munich local government may be found in Malbone W. Graham's article "Constitutional and Political Structure," in R. J. Kerner's *Czechoslovakia*, Berkeley, 1940. Czech sources are plentiful. See, for instance, *"Samospráva"* (Self-government) in *Slovník veřejného práva* (Encyclopaedia of Public Law), Brno, 1938, Vol. IV, pp. 1ff., and *"Výbory národní"* (People's Committees), *ibid.*, Vol. V, Brno, 1947, pp. 350ff. Also, Eduard Táborský, *Naše nová ústava* (Our New Constitution), Praha, 1948, pp. 137ff., 276ff., 532ff.

[2] Originally, the highest level of local government was the region which was considerably smaller than the province.

level in the field of general welfare, but at the same time made it possible for the central government to curb at its pleasure virtually any local government operation. Having no rights guaranteed by the Constitution, and with the whole arrangement of local government left to the discretion of the national legislature, the local government units were virtually at the mercy of the central government, except that they could appeal to the Supreme Administrative Court against what they considered an unlawful encroachment upon their corporate activity by the executive branch of the central government.

Thus, prewar Czechoslovakia had a highly centralized system of government strongly reminiscent of the rigid centralism of the French Third Republic. The provincial presidents and district governors of Czechoslovakia were virtual duplicates of the French prefects and subprefects, appointed as they were by, and responsible to, the central government. As in France, they were the most important agents in the sphere of provincial and district government. With a staff of civil servants appointed by the provincial president in each province, they managed the bulk of general administration, presided over the rare meetings of the provincial and district assemblies, and drew up the programs of their sessions. They alone were entitled to carry out the resolutions passed by these assemblies, and even had the right and the duty to stay such resolutions and refer them to the central government for further decision if they deemed them contrary to law or beyond the powers of the respective assembly. On the communal level the local self-government was considerably broader. The communal assembly was wholly elective and free to choose its own executive officers who in turn appointed the administrative personnel of the commune.

There was, therefore, some basis for various criticisms leveled at the prewar Czechoslovak administrative system and its excessive centralism. However, most of these complaints were made not by the Czechs, but by the Sudeten Germans and some Slovak autonomist groups; moreover, the limited scope of self-government was not actually their primary target. As the Sudeten German leader, Konrad Henlein, subsequently admitted, he and his followers were wholly uninterested in any reforms of local government but rather in the "ripening" of Czechoslovakia for ultimate liquidation.[3] Father Hlinka's

[3] See his speech before the Administrative Academy of Vienna in March 1941 in which he said: "In the course of a few years the Sudeten Germans have succeeded in so deeply endangering the inner stability of Czechoslovakia and in so confusing her internal relations that she became ripe for liquidation." *Wiener Beobachter*, No. 64, March 5, 1941.

Slovak autonomists, on the other hand, were concerned only with seizing power in Slovakia, and nothing proves this better than their own behavior once they had achieved their purpose. Instead of providing for more local self-government for the Slovaks, they dissolved local councils, appointed governmental commissars to run local governments in their stead, and initiated a policy of rigid centralizing totalitarianism. For the proscribed "Praha centralism" they substituted a much stiffer "Bratislava centralism."

While those who had clamored most for more self-government, the Sudeten Germans and the Slovak autonomists, actually liquidated whatever self-government had existed before they took over, the man against whom they had been firing their biggest salvos, President Eduard Beneš, began from his London exile to lay the groundwork for sweeping local government reform. As early as 1941, he wrote in the enlarged Czech edition of his *Democracy Today and Tomorrow:*

"Free municipal self-rule, a well-equipped district and regional self-government, as well as a sufficient degree of decentralized administration and legislation in provincial and regional units—that is and always will be the prerequisite for a proper functioning of a regime which is truly democratic. This is true of all nations, be they small or big, as far as it corresponds to their geographic, economic, and cultural conditions. I have always advocated this, and I continue to advocate it today."[4]

Nor was it his personal belief alone that persuaded him to advance local government reform. Other weighty reasons were present, two of which in particular were impressive to Beneš. The first was the knowledge that the Slovaks would not be willing to accept the pre-Munich pattern but would insist on sweeping autonomy for Slovakia. The second reason, even more compelling, was that the exiled leaders of the Communist Party of Czechoslovakia had definitely declared themselves for a new system of elective people's committees to take over all local administration.

In a series of long talks which Dr. Beneš had with communist leader Klement Gottwald and his associates in Moscow in December 1943, Gottwald strongly insisted upon scrapping the previous system of local government and replacing it with elective local committees.[5]

---

[4] *Demokracie Dnes a Zítra* (Democracy Today and Tomorrow), London, n.d., pp. 247ff.; also, *Edward Beneš in His Own Words,* New York, 1944, p. 61, and Eduard Beneš, *Problèmes de la Tchécoslovaquie,* Praha, 1936, p. 18.

[5] Eduard Beneš, *Paměti* (Memoirs), Praha, 1947, p. 408, and Klement Gottwald, *Cesta k svobodě* (The Road to Freedom), London, 1944, pp. 18ff.

Dr. Beneš was well aware of the real reasons behind Gottwald's insistence. However, anxious as he was to deprive Communists of as much propaganda fuel as he could by removing real and alleged deficiencies which they could exploit for their own ends, he reluctantly gave his assent to the new scheme. In December 1944 he issued a constitutional decree providing for a system of people's committees to take over local government in Czechoslovakia after the War.[6] The decree amounted to a revolutionary break with the past. With one bold stroke the former parallelism of weak self-governing bodies and strong central government appointees was eliminated. The appointive provincial presidents and district governors who dominated the prewar scene of local government disappeared, and the powers of local government were placed squarely in the hands of what were purported to be elective representatives of the local population.

The new pattern was received with genuine enthusiasm by the broad masses of the Czech and Slovak peoples, fitting well into the hectic ecstasy of the first days of the liberation. But those who were familiar with the background of the decree, who knew the story of the use made by Communists of similar committees earlier in the fall of 1944 and since the beginning of 1945, whether in Rumania, Bulgaria, Hungary, Ruthenia, or in the short-lived Slovak uprising of the fall of 1944, were highly apprehensive. In the overcautious manner that was typical of him, President Beneš had expressed his own doubts at the very time he signed the decree on December 4, 1944, when he wrote to his Prime Minister: "The issue is left open as to how far in this or another field of public administration the people's committees shall directly replace the former organs and how far they shall administer matters through the latter's intermediary." And he added wishfully: "I believe that the question of the relationship between the present organs of public administration and the people's committees will be settled with a view not only to the fullest democratization of the whole domain of public administration but also to its expediency and without forgetting the need for expert qualification wherever necessary."[7]

Dr. Beneš's misgivings were fully vindicated by subsequent events that upset all his plans and placed before him accomplished facts. Using a combination of pressure, denunciation of political opponents, exploitation of the support generously given by the local commanders

---

[6] The decree was subsequently published in the Czechoslovak Collection of Laws in 1945.

[7] *Úřední věstník československý*, v, 6, 1945.

of the Red Army and the NKVD agents, and clever management of "direct democracy" in mass meetings and show-of-hands elections, the Communists secured majority and key positions in almost all the people's committees on every level.[8] As was admitted by communist spokesmen after they had seized power, the people's committees constituted in fact "the first, and one might say the most important, step in the process of breaking up the state apparatus . . . ."[9] Gottwald and his associates showed themselves to be worthy disciples of Lenin in following their teacher's slogan of "all power to the Soviets." The earlier suspicions of the Communists' real intentions regarding the role of the people's committees proved correct. Any hope that the committees would be only temporary organs until local government could be properly reorganized quickly vanished. The communist-influenced Košice Program of the Czechoslovak government of April 1945 left out any mention of the provisional aspect of the people's committee system. Thus Gottwald could confidently declare in a major speech in Brno in June 1945: "By the government program and according to the intentions of all of us, this new political organization of the Republic is to be permanent. The time when the districts and communes were ruled by bureaucrats shall not return . . . ."[10]

Nevertheless, as democratically minded citizens began to recover from the first shock of Soviet occupation, the picture brightened. Some of the evils of the first months of lawlessness and chaos were eliminated. Many an arbitrary "people's" functionary found his way behind the bars, where he rightly belonged. Many able local government officials of prewar days, dismissed in precipitate purges, were reinstated. The disproportionate communist overrepresentation was somewhat corrected. Thus, on the eve of the communist coup of 1948, local government was showing signs of improvement, although it still continued to be mostly communist-controlled and cluttered by incompetents.

No local government elections were held during the whole time between the liberation of Czechoslovakia and the communist coup. As early as May 1945 a government ordinance clearly stipulated

[8] For a discussion of methods used for that purpose, see Josef Josten, *Oh My Country*, London, 1949; Otto Friedman, *The Breakup of Czech Democracy*, London, 1950; Ivo Ducháček, "The Strategy of Communist Infiltration: Czechoslovakia, 1944-1948," *World Politics*, 2, 3 (1950).

[9] Juraj Hromada, *Prehľad československých štátnych orgánov* (An Outline of Czechoslovak State Organs), Bratislava, 1955, p. 32.

[10] Pavel Korbel, *Narodní výbory* (National Committees) (mimeographed), Free Europe Committee, New York, 1951, p. 3.

that the people's committees established in the territory liberated from the enemy would be replaced in the shortest possible time by new committees elected according to the principles of Czechoslovak electoral laws. But the "shortest time possible" never came. Instead, following the parliamentary elections of 1946, the membership of the people's committees was brought into proportion with the parties' relative strength by the simple device of assigning each party a number of committee seats corresponding to the ratio of the popular vote polled in the parliamentary elections in the local area concerned.[11]

Upon their seizure of power in February 1948, the Communists first undertook a thorough purge and ousted from the people's committees whomever they held to be inimical to the new regime. Since the people's committees were primarily a communist idea and most of them had been under communist control since 1945, no need for structural changes was felt after the February coup. After all, there was no political institution in Czechoslovakia by 1948 that resembled the Soviet model more closely than the people's committees. The only change which the Communists had advocated prior to 1948, and which they carried out soon after their seizure of power, was the abolition of the former provinces. These were split into a number of regions and a regional people's committee was created in each to take over the agenda of the disbanded provincial committees.[12] This was, however, only a minor matter which had nothing to do with communist doctrine.

LOCAL GOVERNMENT UNDER THE 1948 AND 1960 CONSTITUTIONS

Unlike its "bourgeois" predecessor which left matters of local government to be regulated by ordinary laws, the Ninth-of-May Constitution of 1948 devoted a special Article to the people's committees; and the official explanation of the Constitution referred to the provisions on the people's committees as "the core of the new Constitution."[13] However, the Constitution itself did not introduce

---

[11] Prior to that, in August 1945, the membership of the district and provincial committees was renewed in the following manner: the local committees, which were never elected, chose electors who then elected the new district and provincial committees.

[12] Law No. 280 of December 21, 1948.

[13] *Ústava devátého května* (The Ninth-of-May Constitution), Praha, 1948, p. 109.

any innovations but confirmed only what had been established in practice after 1945. It provided for three levels of people's committees—local, district, and regional—which were to discharge "public administration in all its branches within the territories for which they have been elected." Other administrative organs could be authorized to discharge public administration in the areas managed by the people's committees only in exceptional circumstances. Besides the usual functions assigned to local government organs in democratic countries, such as care for public safety, health, and welfare, the Constitution also required the people's committees to protect and strengthen the people's democratic order; to participate in tasks connected with the defense of the State; to help maintain and increase national property; to take part in the preparation and implementation of the Uniform Economic Plan and to plan and direct economic, social, and cultural developments within their respective territories, to take steps to insure a constant flow of agricultural and economic production; and to care for the supplies and feeding of the population.

In discharging their tasks the committees were directed to "lean on the direct participation and initiative of the people," and committee members were made "accountable to the people for their activities." At the same time, they had the duty not only to comply with "acts and ordinances," but also, "in the interest of uniform public administration and uniform state policy, to observe the directives and instructions of superior organs." To eliminate any doubt as to what this meant the Constitution specifically stated that "a people's committee on a lower level shall be subordinated to a people's committee on a higher level" and that all of them "shall be subordinated to the organs of governmental and executive power, in particular to the Ministry of the Interior." Moreover, a people's committee could be dissolved when it did not discharge its duties or when its activities "endangered the operation of public administration."

While the Ninth-of-May Constitution amply defined the people's committees' functions, it was somewhat vague regarding the manner in which they were to be elected. All it had to say on this important item was that the "details regarding the exercise of the right to elect the members of the people's committees and the holding of elections shall be prescribed by an Act."

On the whole, the provisions of the Ninth-of-May Constitution on the people's committees closely followed the Soviet pattern. While the committees were assigned many new duties, particularly in economic matters, they were simultaneously integrated into a tightly knit hierarchical pyramid in which each higher unit acted as an absolute boss over each lower unit, and with all subordinate to the central government. Although the Constitution promised that "the entire public administration shall be effectively decentralized," all the other provisions of the Local Government Article pointed in an opposite direction and clearly indicated that those who had drafted them, were guided by Marxist-Leninist "democratic centralism," rather than by any desire for decentralization, local autonomy, or local self-government.

The Ninth-of-May Constitution supplied only the basic framework for local government and left "the organizational principles of the people's committees and the principles governing their work and proceedings" to be prescribed by ordinary laws. No constitutional authorization was used more extensively by communist law-makers. Close to thirty laws and government ordinances regulating various aspects of the people's committees' activities were adopted between 1948 and 1960, including two constitutional amendments, but not counting a steady stream of sundry government resolutions and ministerial directives.[14] The gist of this regulatory output will be considered under appropriate headings below. As will be shown, its net result has been a gradual transfer of additional duties and responsibilities to the people's committees, coupled with the simultaneous retention of stiff controls and ever more vigilant tutorship from above.

Since the Article dealing with the people's committees was the most Soviet-like of all the clauses of the Ninth-of-May Constitution, no change of substance was necessary when the time came in 1960 to bring the Czechoslovak constitutional pattern more into line with the Soviet model. While local government provisions have been rephrased to sound more Leninist, the position of the people's committees in the framework of the communist transmission belts has remained the same.

[14] Constitutional laws Nos. 47 of May 18, 1950 and 12 of March 3, 1954; laws Nos. 280 of December 21, 1948, 76 of March 24, 1949, 142 and 143 of May 11, 1949, 83 of December 11, 1952, 13 of March 3, 1954, 10, 11 and 14 of March 6, 1957, and 65 of May 25, 1960; government ordinances Nos. 139 of June 7, 1949, 14 of February 28, 1950, 78 of October 9, 1951, 119, 120, 121, and 122 of December 11, 1951, 23 of May 7, 1954, 32 of July 16, 1954, 20 of March 22, 1955, 5 of January 16, 1957, 7 of February 22, 1957, 64 of November 30, 1957, 65 of October 11, 1957, 33 of June 27, 1958, and 71 of June 10, 1960.

THE ELECTORAL SYSTEM

Although the Ninth-of-May Constitution clearly stipulated that the people's committees were to be elected by the people and directed the legislature to work out the details of the electoral system, no local government elections were held until May 1954. Instead, in flagrant violation of its own Constitution, the communist regime decreed that members of the people's committees be appointed, assigned their functions, and, if necessary, removed by the supervising organs. The authority so to act was vested in the Minister of the Interior with regard to the regional and district committees and in the district committees with regard to the local committees.[15] All such appointments were made upon the recommendation of the committees of the communist-dominated National Front in the respective areas. Having previously denounced the First Republic for "strangling" local self-government by usurping the right to appoint one-third of the provincial and district committees' membership, the communist rulers of Czechoslovakia "corrected" that flaw by simply appointing all of them.

Since the communist leaders intended from the start to make the people's committees elective, why did they persist in appointing them from above for six full years after the adoption of the Ninth-of-May Constitution? Surely, it cannot be explained by any fear that local government elections might have weakened their hold over the country's administration. The same communist-style parliamentary election held on the national level a few months after their seizure of power in 1948 could have been arranged on the local level. Since February 1948 the communist-controlled Action Committees had been in a position to make certain that no candidate ran who would not be acceptable to the KSČ. Hence, the only plausible explanation of the delay lies in the committees' poor performance. As described below, their operations were marred by so many deficiencies that they were a permanent headache for their communist chiefs.[16] It seems, therefore, that the Communists kept postponing the promised elections until such time as the committees' work would improve and

[15] Laws Nos. 280 of December 21, 1948 and 142 of May 11, 1949; and government ordinances Nos. 139 of June 7, 1949, and 14 of February 28, 1950.

[16] Complaints to that effect are contained in virtually every speech that the communist leaders made on local government topics. See, for instance, *Rudé právo,* January 11, October 23, December 6, 1953, and March 3, 1954; *Zemědělské noviny,* September 13, 1953; *Život strany,* September 9, 1953.

the elections could be made an occasion for extolling the excellence of the new people's government over the bourgeois bureaucratic system of the past.

However, years went by and the people's committees showed no sign of improvement. Meanwhile, the death of Stalin and the beginning of the post-Stalin thaw encouraged critical voices within and without the Party and made people openly wonder why the long-promised local government elections had not been held. "The fact that the elections of the people's committees have not taken place has been criticized in the last session of the Central Committee [held in September 1953] as a serious drawback to our efforts to gain the confidence of every working man and to strengthen the people's democratic system," said Široký in his report to the Party's Central Committee in December 1953. "Therefore, it is correct to remove this serious shortcoming . . . ."[17] Thus, having for six years treated their promises of people's self-government as "piecrusts made to be broken," to use Lenin's expression, Gottwald's heirs caused the National Assembly in March 1954 to enact a hastily prepared electoral law and, two months later, staged the first local government elections ever held under the communist rule.

The election law was devised to accomplish the dual purpose of strengthening the Party's hold on all levels of local government while creating the illusion of broad popular representation. Since the 1954 law on local government elections, slightly amended in 1957 and 1960, is almost identical with the 1954 law on parliamentary elections (similarly amended in 1960) considered in Chapter xi, it is not necessary to deal with it in detail here.[18] Like the latter, it confers upon the communist-controlled National Front exclusive control over the final selection of all candidates from among nominees recommended by "meetings of workers, peasants, and other working people in factories, offices, and rural communities" and similar gatherings of "soldiers and members of other armed corps." It reserves to the National Front the monopoly of nominating members of all election commissions. Except for small communes whose population does not exceed 400 (600 since 1960), all local government areas are divided into precincts with each electing one member of the respective people's committee. As in the Parliamentary Elections Act, a candi-

---

[17] *Rudé právo,* December 6, 1953.
[18] Law No. 14 of March 3, 1954, slightly amended by law No. 11 of March 6, 1957, and No. 39 of April 9, 1960.

date must obtain an absolute majority of valid votes to be elected; otherwise a new election is held within two weeks between the two candidates with the largest vote. "Unworthy members" may be re-called upon a proposal of the National Front; and a by-election is held within sixty days to fill any vacancy occurring between the regular elections. The nature of the election law was appraised with disarming naïveté by the National Assembly Chairman, Zdeněk Fier-linger, who sought to explain its "democratic character" to the listeners of the Czechoslovak Radio: "There is no complex arith-metic, and the voters are not confused by electoral lists of diverse parties and factions as they used to be before the War."[19]

Since the people's committees on all levels had three-year terms of office (changed to four years in 1960), three local government elections were held between 1948 and 1960: the first in May 1954, the second in May 1957, and the third in June 1960. The electoral pattern, from the nomination of candidates and the election campaign down to the voting day and the counting of ballots, was in all three instances of the same totalitarian character as that of the 1954 and 1960 parliamentary elections discussed in Chapter XI. To that extent the five elections held in Czechoslovakia since 1954 were identical quintuplets. The voters of each precinct were given the choice of one out of one candidate allowed to appear on the ballot for each tier of the people's committees.[20] They were served with the customary warning that "there will not be a single honest citizen who would fail to use his honorable right to elect his representatives to the people's committees."[21] A nation-wide network of agitation centers was set up to cover every inch of territory.[22] Hospitals were visited by "flying election commissions." "Spontaneous decisions" of voters to go to the polls en masse and vote in public were a general occurrence.[23]

Although the KSČ's tactics were identical in the three local gov-ernment elections and an overwhelming communist victory in each was a foregone conclusion, the results differed markedly between the 1954 election on the one hand and the 1957 and 1960 elections on the other in the number of votes cast against the official candidates

---

[19] *Československý přehled*, I, 2 (1954), p. 32.
[20] For how it was done, see *Rudé právo*, April 8, 1954; *Nová svoboda*, April 11, 1954; *Mladá fronta*, April 13, 1954.
[21] *Rudé právo*, May 16, 1954.
[22] *ibid.*, May 20, 1954.
[23] *Práce*, May 14, 1954.

and, to a somewhat lesser degree, in the number of abstentions. In 1954, 6.4 percent of eligible voters dared to register opposition to the official candidates and 1.7 percent abstained. The corresponding figures were only 0.88 percent of negative votes and 0.74 abstentions in 1957 and 0.12-0.24 negative votes and 0.32-0.36 abstentions in 1960.[24] The explanation of this unusual contrast lies in the differing circumstances under which the elections were held.

In 1954 the atmosphere was one of hope. The post-Stalin New Course was still gathering momentum. The KSČ leaders had to forego brandishing the big stick too conspicuously. They had to make concessions and tolerate behavior that would have met with instantaneous reprisals prior to Stalin's death. Since fear was somewhat lifted, more people found courage to vote against the regime, and members of the election commissions did not consider it so important to adjust election results by a proregime interpretation of the negative ballots.

By 1957 the situation was changed. The relative condescension of the first post-Stalin years yielded to neo-Stalinist harshness, and once again the whip began to be cracked more resolutely. Most of those who had dared to defy the regime in 1954 found it wiser to refrain from sticking their necks out under worsened conditions, and the election commissioners were quick to realize their duty of a more appropriate interpretation of doubtful ballots. Oddly enough, some seventy candidates were reported defeated in 1957 and twelve in 1960 owing to a failure to secure an absolute majority of valid votes, while no such failures were announced in 1954.[25] However, with 216,302 candidates running in 1957 and 203,943 in 1960, the number of failures is so insignificant that reference to them tends to make the communist success seem even greater to those accepting communist claims at their face value.

On the occasion of the 1957 elections the government also released data on the occupational background of the 216,302 local government candidates: 33.8 percent were listed as workers; 14.3 percent as collective farmers; 16.7 percent as individual farmers; the remainder were "white-collar workers, professional people, housewives, etc."[26] Compared with corresponding figures for the social

[24] *Rudé právo,* May 20, 1954; *Prague News Letter,* 13, 11, May 25, 1957; *Rudé právo,* June 15, 1960. The 1960 figures were given according to the three levels of the people's committees, but not for the committee election as a whole.

[25] *Prague News Letter,* 13, 11, May 25, 1957; *Rudé právo,* June 15, 1960.

[26] *Prague News Letter,* 13, 11, May 25, 1957.

composition of the Czechoslovak legislature of 1954, where only 25 percent of its members were classified as being of working origin and 19 percent as farmers, the above figures show that the representation of the workers and peasants on local government levels was considerably higher than in the national legislature and that the opposite was true of the "toiling intelligentsia."[27] This is well in line with the over-all communist practice which is very generous to the "two friendly classes of workers and peasants" in granting them representation on lower echelons of the government, but less so when it comes to higher positions.

The Organization

In view of the communist obsession with democratic centralism as the guiding principle of the people's democratic administration, it is hardly surprising that the organizational pattern of local government is one of rigid uniformity and strict subordination.[28] The entire country is divided into regions whose number was cut from nineteen to ten in 1960 in order to fit administrative boundaries better into the emerging economic pattern.[29] Each region is subdivided into districts which were reduced in number even more drastically from 306 to 108. The base of the local government system consists of over 14,000 communes some of which are similarly scheduled to be merged wherever two or more of them form a natural economic unit. The capital city of Praha constitutes an independent city-region subdivided into boroughs, and several other major cities form independent city-districts.

The local government on all three territorial tiers is organized along identical lines. The primary organ on each level is the plenary assembly called the people's committee. Its membership ranges from 9 to 150 according to the territorial level and the population of the area.[30] Each people's committee elects, as its general executive organ, a council consisting of a chairman, his deputy or deputies, a secretary, and several other members. Originally, the people's committees on all

[27] For figures on parliamentary elections, see Chapter XI.

[28] Hromada, op.cit., p. 120; Pavel Levit, Správní právo, část obecná (Administrative Law, General Part), Praha, 1954, p. 24; also, Široký's explanation of the new laws on the people's committees in the National Assembly on March 2, 1954, Rudé právo, March 3, 1954.

[29] See the resolution of the Central Committee on the KSČ of January 14, 1960, Rudé právo, January 16, 1960; law No. 36 of April 9, 1960.

[30] For further organizational details, see laws Nos. 13 of March 3, 1954, 10 of March 6, 1957, and 65 of May 25, 1960; government ordinance No. 33 of June 27, 1958, No. 71 of June 10, 1960.

levels appointed individual council members as heads of various administrative departments. But the work of these department chiefs "from the people" was so disappointing that they were replaced in 1954 by professional administrators appointed by the respective people's committees on the proposal of their councils and subject in each instance to the approval of the head of the corresponding department of the next highest people's committee or by the corresponding minister. This arrangement was reversed once again in 1958 when the people's committees were directed to entrust council members with the headship of the most important departments and were given simultaneously the authority to appoint, upon the council's proposal, the chiefs of the remaining departments from among "politically and professionally qualified employees" without the need of higher approval.[31]

Actual administration on regional district, city, and borough levels is carried out by departments, each of which is assigned agenda along functional lines. On regional and district levels there are departments for matters of planning, finances, control, organization, agriculture, industry (local economy), trade, transportation, water economy and energy, education and culture, manpower, health, social welfare, and internal affairs. Additional departments may be created according to the needs of "economic and cultural construction." No departmentalization is mandatory for city and local levels, but communes with more than 10,000 population may set up administrative departments with higher approval. Similarly, communes under 10,000 population may establish an economic-administrative department after having secured permission to do so from the council of the district people's committee.

Finally, the people's committees on all levels are aided in their work by various commissions selected partly from committee members and partly from outsiders. Until 1960, these commissions had no part in direct administration, but acted only in an advisory and supervisory capacity, reporting their findings to the other organs of the respective people's committees. But the 1960 reform authorizes the commissions, hailed as "an embryo of future communist self-administration," to make also certain administrative decisions.[32] Both the administrative

[31] Government ordinance No. 33 of June 27, 1958; decree of the Assembly's Presidium No. 38 of July 10, 1958.

[32] See the resolution of the Party's Central Committee of April 1960, *Rudé právo*, April 11, 1960; also, law No. 65 of May 25, 1960, and government ordinance No. 71 of June 10, 1960.

departments and the commissions are in turn aided in their work, especially in the all-important "contacts with the masses," by citizens' committees, women's committees, and other groups of "activists."

POWERS AND DUTIES

"The people's committees, through their executive organs (the local organs of state administration), organize and direct economic, cultural, and social construction of their respective areas. In particular, they organize, direct, plan, and control local economy; take care of planned maintenance of public institutions serving the population; supervise maintenance and construction of housing; and are responsible for improvement of health service. They prepare and supervise the implementation of their budgets. They work for the incessant development and increase of agricultural production, food supplies, and the economic and cultural growth of their areas. They secure favorable conditions for fulfillment of the State Economic Plan. They take care of the health of the working people and the development of physical education and sports. They participate in the protection of peaceful constructive work against enemies from without and within and contribute to the strengthening of the Republic's defense. They protect socialist property."[33]

The people's committees must also "exploit the reserves of productive capabilities and sources of raw materials . . . as good economists procure by their own initiative the means for the fulfillment of their tasks from local resources . . . see to it that farmers fulfill their delivery quotas of agricultural products . . . educate citizens in a new attitude toward work and foster the development of socialist competition . . . attentively follow the work of all the organs of state administration and other organs of the state mechanism in their respective areas, evaluate the work of these organs, and facilitate its implementation."[34]

These statements, translated from two Czechoslovak communist textbooks on administrative law and government, illustrate both the breadth and the vague definition of the duties and functions that the people's committees are supposed to perform. The burden of these virtually all-embracing duties placed on the shoulders of the people's committees is very heavy indeed. This is especially true at the district

[33] Levit, *op.cit.*, p. 81.
[34] Hromada, *op.cit.*, p. 120.

level which is, in the words of a communist university lecturer in administrative law, "the focus of the operative work" and "the most important link of the administrative system."[35] A substantial increase in local government chores has resulted from the decentralization drive of 1956-1958 and another one in 1960 when a portion of the agenda, hitherto administered by ministries and other central agencies, was transferred downward, mostly on the executive organs of regional and district committees.[36] Similarly, much of the routine administration handled by the regional committees was shifted to district and city levels. As a result, the local committees' share of local government employees was scheduled to rise in 1960 from 11 to 25 percent, that of the district committees from 34 to 56 percent, whereas the regional committees' share was to decrease sharply from 54.5 to 19 percent.[37] The increased work load is also reflected in the stepped-up expenditures of the people's committees that have almost doubled between 1956 and 1959.[38]

While the scope of authority conferred upon the people's committees under the dictatorship of the proletariat looks very impressive, it must be realized that it has little in common with true local self-government in the democratic sense. In line with the principle of democratic centralism, each power granted to any local government organ must be used in strict compliance with the directives of higher authorities, which can also change or annul any decision of lower organs at their pleasure. However centralistic the administrative pattern may have been under the First Republic, it nevertheless distinguished between the functions performed by local government units such as subdivisions of the State and those in which they engaged as self-governing corporations. When acting in the latter capacity the local government organs were free to operate unhampered by higher directives and could even seek the protection of the Supreme Administrative Court against undue interference by the central government. Today no such distinction is made, and no judicial or other protection against higher orders is afforded. While there is indeed more government on the local level, there is infinitely less self-government than under the prewar bourgeois regime that

[35] Levit, *op.cit.*, p. 83. See also section 15 of government ordinance No. 33 of June 27, 1958, and section 15 of law No. 65 of May 25, 1960.
[36] Chapter XI.
[37] *Rudé právo*, April 14, 1960.
[38] These expenditures amounted to 16,697 million crowns in 1956, 28,590 in 1957, 31,269 in 1958, and 33,016 in 1959. *Ročenka*, 1960, p. 482.

the Communists never tired of denouncing as a strangler of local autonomy.

OPERATIONAL PATTERN

Since the people's committees were intended from their very inception to play the role of the USSR's soviets, the operative principles that were to guide them were adapted from the Soviet model faster and more completely than had been the case with any other people's democratic institution. "The Communist Party and the government desire and want the people's committees to be built into such organs of the dictatorship of the proletariat as are the soviets . . . ," said the communist Minister of the Interior in an address to a national conference of functionaries of the people's committees in January 1953.[39]

The very first operative principle that must be listed is, once again, the complete KSČ dominance on all levels of local government. "The Communist Party of Czechoslovakia is the leading and directing force of the people's democratic state administration."[40] Applying this precept to the local transmission belts, the 1958 government ordinance on the reorganization of the executive organs of local government instructs them in its very first article to "carry out in everyday work the line of the Communist Party of Czechoslovakia, the leading force of our society."[41]

To make sure that Party directives are followed, the key positions in local government are filled with dependable Communists whose supreme duty is to secure an unflinching obedience of all the organs of the people's committees. Not only the committee chairman and secretaries but also the department heads are recruited for the most part from the KSČ's ranks. Moreover, a recent resolution of the Party's Central Committee prescribes that all important matters handled by the people's committees must first be considered and cleared by the respective Party organs.[42] Thus, the practice that has governed the relationship between the Party and the government on the central level since the February coup of 1948 must now be rigidly enforced in the Party-government relationship on lower adminis-

[39] *Rudé právo,* January 31, 1953.
[40] Levit, *op.cit.,* p. 8.
[41] Government ordinance No. 33 of June 27, 1958. The leading role of the Party is also duly listed in law No. 65 of May 25, 1960—the new law on the people's committees.
[42] *Rudé právo,* June 19, 1958, and April 14, 1960.

trative echelons where it had not been applied quite so emphatically in the past.

Closely related to this iron law of Party supremacy is the principle of democratic centralism that permeates the whole local government system as thoroughly as it binds the Party's own organizational pyramid and the central transmission belts. Explaining the meaning of the local government reform of 1954, Široký could not have been more trenchant: "The bills consistently apply the principle of democratic centralism. The people's committees are directed by higher organs, i.e., by the people's committees on higher levels and by the government, and they are also responsible to them. Decisions of higher organs are unconditionally binding on lower organs."[43] Similar emphasis on rigid hierarchy and democratic centralism as the guiding operative principle of local government pervades the 1960 Constitution, as well as the resolution "on the broadening of the authority and responsibility of the people's committees and the increase of their role in the economic and cultural construction" adopted by the Party's Central Committee in April 1960.[44] As explained by *Rudé právo,* the Party's resolution insists on "a strict observance of the Leninist principle of democratic centralism which combines in a harmonious fashion the development of local initiative with the strengthening of central guidance. The brilliant application of this principle to our concrete conditions is yet another blow to those who would want to separate, and set in contradiction to one another, these two inseparable aspects of democratic centralism."[45]

While stressing democratic centralism, local government laws and their communist interpreters play up the principle of dual responsibility that makes the executive organs of the people's committees responsible both to the people's committee which has created them (horizontal responsibility) and to the corresponding executive organ on higher local government level and, in the last resort, to the ministry (vertical responsibility).[46] In theory, the principle of dual responsibility suggests that the executive organs of the people's committee serve two masters. But actual practice relegates such an impression to the realm of fiction. As borne out by overwhelming evidence based on reports from non-communist sources inside Czechoslovakia and depositions of escapees, the horizontal responsibility of

[43] *Rudé právo,* March 3, 1954.
[44] *ibid.,* April 14, 1960.
[45] *ibid.*
[46] Levit, *op.cit.,* pp. 32, 85.

the executive organs to their committees is hardly more than an empty form. True responsibility operates strictly upward. That this is so has once again been emphatically restated by the above-mentioned government ordinance of 1958 and the new 1960 law on the people's committees as well as by the 1960 Constitution. The 1958 ordinance and the 1960 law, in particular, bristle with references to the responsibility of the executive organs of lower committees to those of the higher committees and, in the last resort, to the Cabinet; the duty of committees' councils to control the executive organs of lower people's committees and to stay or to change their decisions; and the obligation of lower executive organs and their heads to abide by the instructions of the departments and department heads of the higher echelons of the state administration.[47]

Another feature of the operational pattern that has become more pronounced in recent years, despite verbal assurances to the contrary, is the rise of the bureaucratic element over the laymen. "Democrats of Masaryk's and Beneš's type did not trust the people's representatives," wrote Široký in his exposé of the 1954 local government reform. "They trusted only their bureaucrats, the district governors and notaries, who saw to it that the work of local assemblies did not exceed their emaciated authority."[48] However, while shedding crocodile tears over the local government's emaciation under the First Republic and praising the excellence of their own system, Široký and his colleagues did away with elective department heads and entrusted the actual conduct of local government affairs to a hierarchy of hand-picked professional administrators. Although the 1958-1960 rearrangement again permits council members to assume direct departmental responsibilities and abrogates the necessity of higher approval of the appointment of department heads, the Party's absolute control over all such appointments deprives this latest concession of most of its practical value.

As for the councils of the people's committees, they have been allowed to direct and control the work of their own departments and other organs of the respective people's committees. But in practice they have surrendered to the bureaucrats. As prescribed, the councils meet once every two weeks. Yet, judging by recurrent complaints in the communist press and by information obtained from escapees, the councils (often poorly attended) indulge mostly in generalities rather

[47] Government ordinance No. 33 of June 27, 1958.
[48] *Rudé právo,* March 3, 1954.

than concern themselves with the guidance and alert supervision of the executive departments.[49] Nor do they exert any real influence on the choice of the departments' employees. Although the councils are formally granted the authority to appoint department employees, they do so upon the proposal of the chief of the respective department whose word is actually decisive. Thus, the lay element can assert itself, subject to strict Party controls, only in the smallest communes that do not establish administrative departments and have no salaried employees.

Finally, it should be added that the monocratic principle operates in the local government administration almost as fully as on the central level. Administrative decision-making on all local government tiers is vested in the department head who is also personally responsible for the work of officials in his department. The collective principle applies only to the plenums of the people's committees and to their councils and commissions.

MAKING THE PEOPLE'S COMMITTEES WORK

When President Beneš, yielding to communist pressure, gave his assent to the creation of the people's committee system, he was fully aware of the serious consequences that such a radical change might have on administrative efficiency of local government, not to speak of its integrity and impartiality. He saw his doubts fully corroborated by facts as soon as the new system went into operation in 1945; and he lived just long enough to find his fears exceeded by harsh realities after the communist take-over in 1948.

In their turn, the communist rulers themselves were to discover soon enough that it is easier to destroy than to build. While all their government operations have been running into difficulties, it is in the area of local government that the situation has probably been worst. The people's committees represent the Achilles' heel of the huge communist administrative system. "The ministries and the chancellery of the President of the Republic are flooded by masses of letters from citizens complaining of the people's administration in various matters," reported government authorities in 1951.[50] The people's committees have thus become a target for a steady stream of complaints, and criticism appearing in the communist press alone in the course of the first twelve years of communist rule would fill a thick volume.

[49] *ibid.*, January 13, 1955.
[50] *Zpráva o Československu*, II, 11 (1951), p. 23.

Inefficiency and red tape have been perennial phenomena and have assumed an endless variety of forms. "Many bureaucratic pitfalls, particularly paper-pushing without knowledge of real life, hamper the work of the people's committees," confessed Široký in October 1953. "Bureaucratism manifests itself also in slow operation and in endless delays . . . . Nor is a sufficiently sharp struggle waged against the instances of indifference and negligence regarding the needs of the working men."[51] Such phenomena have indeed been of frequent occurrence. Citizens' applications have been lost or displaced; laws and ordinances violated; legitimate complaints unanswered. *Obezlichka* has been plaguing local government as much as the central administration. Some people's committees have "modernized" their methods of work in such a way that they no longer kept files and had no evidence as to how matters have been handled.[52] "I have gained one interesting experience from the manner in which the people's committees settle complaints," said Antonín Zápotocký. "When the complainant is not within his rights, he is answered immediately . . . . But when he is within his rights, the settlement takes months and even years . . . ."[53]

Irregularity of committee meetings, poor attendance, and other manifestations of sluggishness have also been a rule rather than an exception. "The plenary sessions of the district and local committees are not held regularly, in fact, they are seldom held at all," bewailed Fierlinger in a speech to the National Assembly in March 1952. "Politically, they do not live, and the same is true of the commissions of the people's committees."[54] "So many local committees do not meet and all their work falls on the chairman and the secretary," lamented *Zemědělské noviny* on September 18, 1953. "So behave also many members of the district and regional people's committees who attend the meetings irregularly, do not take part in the work of the standing commissions, and do not fulfill their duties . . . ." Such complaints have been a recurrent feature in the communist press, documenting thus a continued and widespread lack of interest in the work of the people's committees, not only on the part of the general public, but also on the part of the "people's representatives" themselves.[55]

[51] *Rudé právo,* October 23, 1953.
[52] *Pravda,* December 6, 1953; *Rudé právo,* September 17 and December 6, 1953, *Zemědělské noviny,* September 13, 1953; *Práce,* November 18, 1950.
[53] *Rudé právo,* February 1, 1953.
[54] *ibid.,* March 8, 1952.
[55] For samples, see *Rudé právo,* July 5, 1952, January 13, 1955; *Nová svoboda,* February 27, 1955; *Lidové noviny;* December 19, 1951; *Práce,* October 8, 1953.

Financial mismanagement has been another major communist headache. A convincing piece of evidence of the "lack of financial discipline" was supplied by the Minister of the Interior in 1951.[56] While one regional committee figured its annual need for fuel at 26,000 crowns, another one planned to spend 980,000 crowns for the same item. The budgetary requirements for lighting ranged from 100,000 to 430,000 crowns for regional committees that differed little in the number of employees and scope of operations. Cleaning materials cost one such regional committee 50,000 crowns per annum, but another one spent as much as 450,000 and looked no cleaner. Some committees concealed funds remaining unspent at the end of the fiscal year by placing them on special "black" accounts and pretending that the money had already been spent. One such committee in a relatively small city created fifty such black accounts totalling 2,975,000 crowns, i.e., almost 60,000 dollars at the then official rate of exchange. These funds were subsequently used for unnecessary purchases such as carpets, musical instruments, and radios.[57]

Two years later, a vivid illustration of similar prodigality from right under the noses of the communist leaders was reported by the trade union daily, *Práce*.[58] On December 11, 1952, the director of a technical high school in the capital city of Praha was notified by the education department of the central people's committee that he was permitted to exceed his school's budget by 313,000 crowns (6,260 dollars) and that the money must be used prior to December 23, 1952. "In twelve days," the paper continued with a rare touch of humor, "the school had to spend an amount that was one and one-half times its total budget for the whole year. The school turned into a lunatic asylum. The teaching staff scattered into the streets in frantic search of books, workshop tools, and similar items . . . . In bookstores the salesmen were gasping: 'You are the seventh such school. What has happened?' Finally, the school managed to get most of the things and to gaily spend the money . . . ."

Nor are these isolated cases. As documented by a wealth of similar complaints, wasteful use of public funds has been a fairly general characteristic of the "people's" administration. Accounts of revenues and expenditures have often been found defective: budgetary limitations have been circumvented; advance payments have remained un-

---

[56] *Rudé právo,* October 7, 1951.
[57] *ibid.*
[58] *Práce,* January 9, 1953.

accounted for; expense accounts for official travels of doubtful usefulness have been extensively relied upon to supplement employees' salaries; gross negligence has been displayed in the collection of revenues.[59] Instances of favoritism and dishonesty have also been in excess of anything experienced in prewar days. Both the information from non-communist sources and the revelations made by the communist press indicate that suspensions and removals of local government officials for corrupt practices and misuse of authority have been recurring in substantial numbers and with monotonous regularity.[60] Moreover, it is safe to assume that successful collusion has permitted most of these malpractices to go undetected.

A major source of communist dissatisfaction with the work of the people's committees has been what the KSČ leaders call "violations of state discipline."[61] This catchall term is applied to all sorts of behavior deemed contrary to communist interests. Foremost among such violations is an almost infinite variety of nonperformance or malperformance of assigned duties, due partly to mere negligence, but mostly to deliberation motivated by sullen disaffection with, and passive resistance to, the regime. Thus, "the people's committees in many cities and communes do not fulfill their tasks in the struggle for a further betterment of the life of the population and for higher productivity in the factories and the fields."[62] "Some of the workers of the people's committees, and even some people's committees as a whole, have succumbed to the temptation to resort to unilateral unlawful acts."[63] Others have displayed gross negligence in the "operative direction of harvesting" and other controlling activities over agricultural production, and failed to provide for "good supplies for the working people."[64] They have ignored socialist contests, disregarded the directives of the Communist Party and the National Front, and displayed "unhealthy manifestations of local patriotism."[65] They have even resorted to such acts of outright sabotage of government policies

[59] For other examples of the lack of financial discipline, see *Pravda,* January 5 and July 18, 1953; *Zemědělské noviny,* January 6, 1953.

[60] *Rudé právo,* January 11 and February 1, 1953; *Zpráva o Československu,* III, 2 (1952), p. 22, IV, 5 (1953), p. 9 and IB, 7-8 (1953), p. 11.

[61] Zápotocký's and Nosek's speeches to a national conference of the people's committee's, *Rudé právo,* January 31 and February 1, 1953.

[62] *ibid.,* July 11, 1953.

[63] *ibid.,* September 17, 1953.

[64] *Rudé právo,* July 22, July 24, August 1 and October 23, 1953; *Pravda,* July 15, 1953.

[65] *Rudé právo,* September 17, 1953, January 11, 1953; and *Zemědělské noviny,* September 13, 1953.

as illegal slaughtering, inciting peasants against joining the Unified Agricultural Cooperatives, or "advising cooperative farmers to take care of their own needs first and bother about government deliveries afterwards."[66]

Equally disappointing have been the accomplishments of the people's committees in their role as the main link of the Party with the masses, a role to which the communist leaders attach a particular importance. "The weakest spot in the work of the people's committees has been in their contact with the people," cautioned the Party's Secretary General, Rudolf Slánský, in his report to the Ninth Party Congress in May 1949. "Members of the people's committees seldom meet with citizens in their communities in order to report to them about their work and to hear their opinions."[67] To remedy this inadequacy the communist leaders brought to life in 1949 an institution of so-called "trustees of the people's administration," later renamed "activist of the people's committees." Patterned after the Soviet *aktivs* and composed of representatives of political parties, labor and youth unions, Czechoslovak-Soviet Friendship Union, women's committees, and other organizations, as well as individually drafted citizens, these groups are supposed to serve as two-way bridges connecting the people's committees, and through them the Party, with the masses. On the one hand, these groups are intended to activate the masses by making them work better, and by educating them for socialism and impressing upon them the necessity of more vigilance against the "enemies of the people," the *kulaks,* and other undesirable elements. On the other hand, they are to serve as "interpreters of the interests and needs of the people."[68]

All the evidence of their work shows, however, that most of the traffic over these bridges goes one way, namely from the government to the people. Each group of trustees-activists is assigned a certain area, street, or block of houses where it takes care of such thankless chores as collecting signatures for "peace petitions," organizing working brigades, helping to "mobilize manpower," prevailing upon married women to go to work, and dissuading parents from "discouraging their children from becoming miners."[69] The activists help take care of recreation facilities, parks, and nurseries, and are responsible for

[66] *Rudé právo,* December 19, 1952; *Zpráva o Československu,* III, 2 (1952), p. 22; *Rudé právo,* July 22, 1953.
[67] *Lidové noviny,* May 27, 1949.
[68] *Rudé právo,* January 24, 1950.
[69] *ibid.*

the general cleanliness of their area. They are to report people who infringe upon regulations. They are urged to be on the lookout for people who may be tuning in the Voice of America and other "enemy" broadcasts. And periodically they have to organize "talks with the public" in order to make people in their area understand and accept government policies.

The Party's determined efforts to improve the work of local government are bound in due time to correct many of the malpractices listed on the preceding pages, especially those caused by individual incompetence. To do so is imperative since the decentralization tendencies of recent years have added substantially to the administrative responsibilities of local government organs on all levels. Indeed, a slight improvement seems to have taken place in recent years. But it is more doubtful whether any notable improvement can occur in the people's committees' role as the main link with the masses, for this is not so much a question of the quality of local government as of how the people feel about the Party and its practice of Marxism-Leninism. As shown in Part IV of this study, twelve years of experience with communist rule have made matters worse rather than better in that respect for the Party and, by the same token, have further impaired the ability of the people's committees to "activate the masses" for the communist cause.

CHAPTER XIV

SLOVAKIA—AN ODD UNIT
OF PROVINCIAL GOVERNMENT

In the last years of the Second World War Czechoslovak Communists were among the most enthusiastic promoters of Slovak nationalism.[1] Temporarily shelving the time-honored Leninist principle of proletarian internationalism, they lent their fullest support to a political program which, had it been carried out, would have changed Czechoslovakia into a loose union of two states. Whenever the Slovak nationalist spokesmen wavered and were ready to yield to Dr. Beneš's persuasiveness and to settle for less than an extremist version of autonomy during the 1945 Moscow negotiations on the formation of a new Czechoslovak Cabinet, it was the quadrumvirate of Czechoslovak communist leaders headed by Klement Gottwald which prevailed upon the Slovaks to continue to press for the most radical demands.[2] The Communists attached such political importance to their Party's identification with the rights obtained for Slovakia that Gottwald, then only Deputy Premier, reserved for himself the task of proclaiming, upon the government's return to Czechoslovakia in April 1945, the "Magna Charta of the Slovak Nation" while allowing the fellow-traveling Premier, Zdeněk Fierlinger, to declare the rest of the government's program.[3]

This striking communist eagerness to secure a status of extreme

[1] Communist spokesman in exile, both in Moscow and in London, harped incessantly on the touchy theme of Czech-Slovak relations, deliberately encouraging the most radical among the Slovak autonomists. See various articles in the main Czechoslovak communist periodicals: *Československé listy,* published in Moscow, and *Mladé Československo,* published in London. Most authoritative among them were two articles by Václav Kopecký published in *Československé listy,* September 15, 1943, and February 1, 1944. See also, V. Široký's article in *Světový rozhled* (Paris), xv, 1, July 1939, reprinted in *Za svobodu,* 1956, pp. 44ff.; *Pravda* (Báňská Bystrica), October 8, 1944.

[2] I can bear testimony to this on the basis of first-hand knowledge of these negotiations which I obtained as Personal Aide to President Beneš at that time.

[3] See *Program prvé domácí vlády narodní fronty Čechů a Slováků* (The Program of the First Government of the National Front of Czechs and Slovaks on Native Soil), Košice, 1945, p. 41.

autonomy for Slovakia could hardly be taken at its face value. It ran too much afoul of the principle of democratic centralism that had guided the KSČ leaders in every phase and in every aspect of the country's reorganization. Indeed, when Czechoslovak Communists achieved a position of power and governmental responsibility following the end of the War, and, in particular when they seized complete control in February 1948, Gottwald's Magna Charta of the Slovak Nation was quickly deprived of its substance.

THE UPS AND DOWNS OF 1918-1948

The reasons why the political status of Slovakia was bound to become a hot issue following World War II are well known, not only to students of European politics, but also, mainly because of the dramatic events of 1938 and 1939, to laymen interested in world affairs in general. Therefore they will be discussed only very briefly.[4]

After centuries of separation from Czech lands, Slovakia became part of the Czechoslovak Republic in 1918, but at this time was granted no special status, though for a while a special Ministry for Slovak affairs was in existence.[5] An autonomist Slovak movement soon developed, however, fed mainly by the Slovaks' resentment over the poor-relative treatment that they met in some aspects of political and economic life at the hands of their more numerous Czech brethern. The Slovaks felt that they were discriminated against in the recruitment of the civil service because too many government officials, teachers, and other public employees operating in Slovakia were Czechs. They wanted more self-government and less dependence on central authorities. And they raised, as their main political goal, the creation of a special Slovak diet endowed with legislative powers in matters pertaining to Slovakia.

Following the Munich *Diktat* of 1938, which led to the territorial mutilation of Czechoslovakia and the resignation of President Beneš, Slovak autonomist forces, taking advantage of the weakened position of the central government, succeeded in obtaining a special status

---

[4] For an up-to-date story in English of developments relative to Slovakia and Czech-Slovak relations, see Harrison S. Thomson, *Czechoslovakia in European History,* Princeton, 1953, and Jozef Lettrich, *History of Modern Slovakia,* New York, 1955.

[5] The so-called "Pittsburgh Convention" of May 1918, which envisaged "her own administrative system, her own diet, and her own courts" for Slovakia, was only a *desideratum* expressed by Czech and Slovak organizations in the United States, composed predominantly of U.S. citizens of Czech and Slovak extraction. See Thomson, *op.cit.,* pp. 313-315.

for Slovakia in which she had a provincial legislature, a Prime Minister and a Cabinet with substantial executive authority, and a separate Slovak judiciary.[6] When Hitler ordered the complete liquidation of Czechoslovakia in March 1939, the Slovak provincial government headed by Tiso proclaimed, at Hitler's behest, an "independent" Slovak State which became, in fact, a Nazi protectorate.[7]

During the War an underground Slovak National Council was established which came into the open in August 1944. At that time, in agreement with Beneš's Czechoslovak government in exile in London, it organized an uprising in Central Slovakia behind the German lines. In its very first enactment the Council assigned to itself the exercise of the "entire legislative, governmental, and executive power in Slovakia" and subsequently provided for the creation of a Board of Commissioners as its administrative organ, appointed by, and responsible to, the Slovak National Council.[8] The Council itself was led by a Presidium of six men who also supervised the work of the Commissioners. All functions in these revolutionary Slovak government organs were evenly distributed among the Communist and the Democratic Parties, which were the only two parties permitted to exist.

The uprising was crushed by the Germans within two months and the Slovak National Council, with all its organs, had to disperse and go underground again. Previously, however, the Council managed to send a three-man delegation to London with a mission to prevail upon President Beneš and his government to accept the new arrangement. Though Beneš did not definitely commit himself at that time, he had to yield later to the joint pressure of the Slovak Democratic Party and the Czech and Slovak Communists. During the subsequent negotiations in Moscow in March 1945, he was

[6] This status was first agreed upon by several Slovak political parties on October 6, 1938 (the so-called "Žilina agreement") and was subsequently enacted by the Czechoslovak post-Munich rump parliament in the form of a constitutional amendment, No. 299 of November 22, 1938.

[7] Regarding the position of the Slovak State after March 1939, see Eduard Táborský, *The Czechoslovak Cause,* London, 1944, pp. 33ff.

[8] See ordinances Nos. 1, 3, and 37, *Sbírka nařízení Slovenské národní rady* (Collection of Ordinances of the Slovak National Council), 1944. For a good survey of political and constitutional developments in Slovakia from 1944 to 1947, see *"Zřízení Československé republiky po osvobození,"* *Slovník veřejného práva československého* (Encyclopaedia of Czechoslovak Public Law), III, Brno, 1948, pp. 802ff. A summary of the activities of the Slovak National Council during World War II may be found in Martin Kvetko, *K základom ústavného pomeru československého* (Concerning the Foundations of Constitutional Relations between the Czechs and the Slovaks), Bratislava, 1947, pp. 41ff.

forced to accept almost all of their radical demands. But even before the President could return to Czechoslovakia, the short-lived revolutionary pattern of 1944 was reestablished in Slovakia under the protective arm of the advancing Red Army.[9]

For a year thereafter the Slovak National Council through its Presidium and Board of Commissioners continued to govern Slovakia much as they pleased without bothering too much about the President of the Republic and the central government. A drastic change came, however, immediately after the first parliamentary elections in May 1946. Having polled only 30 percent of the votes in Slovakia, compared with 41 percent in the Czech provinces, the Communists realized that their support of the Slovak cause did not bring them the hoped-for dividends. Therefore, they abandoned their advocacy of Slovak autonomy and became, instead, instrumental in its radical curtailment.

Since the status of Slovakia had been determined primarily by political agreements between the Czechoslovak government and the Slovak National Council, the change was made in the same way. According to the new arrangement, the so-called Third Political Agreement of June 27, 1946, all enactments of the Slovak National Council had to be submitted to the Czechoslovak Cabinet.[10] If the latter disapproved of them on the ground that the enactments exceeded the jurisdiction of the Slovak National Council or were contrary to the government program, the Presidium of the Slovak National Council could place the matter before a Board of Arbitrators. As the Board, which consisted of the Chairman of the Constituent National Assembly, the Cabinet's Presidium, and the Chairman of the Slovak National Council, had a Czech majority and the Czech Communists, following their about-face of 1946, were definitely opposed to any far-reaching Slovak autonomy, it was a foregone conclusion that the Board would side with the central government in any such controversy. A radical restriction was imposed also upon the Slovak Board of Commissioners. In addition to being responsible to the Slovak National Council, the commissioners were made accountable to the Czechoslovak Cabinet, which was also given the power to approve their appointment and suspend their decisions.

[9] The Presidium of the Slovak National Council renewed its activities by February 1945 and the entire Slovak National Council in April 1945. See details in *Slovník veřejného práva československého, op.cit.*

[10] For a legal analysis, see *Slovník veřejného práva československého, op.cit.*, and Pavel Korbel's article in *Československý přehled,* III, 3 (1956), pp. 10ff.

Moreover, they were henceforth to be sworn in by the Czechoslovak Prime Minister.

CONSTITUTIONAL ARRANGEMENTS

The sharp curtailment of Slovak autonomy in 1946, made possible only through the communist reversal of policy with regard to Slovakia, clearly foreshadowed what was to come when the Communists seized complete power in February 1948.

The Ninth-of-May Constitution

The original version of the Ninth-of-May Constitution reaffirmed the existence of the Slovak National Council of one hundred popularly elected members as "the national organ of legislative power in Slovakia" and of the Slovak Board of Commissioners as "the national organ of governmental and executive power in Slovakia." And it used nine full pages of its Detailed Provisions to spell out the rights and obligations of these Slovak bodies and to determine their relation to the organs of the central government. But the provisions bristled with restrictive clauses which cut out the hard core of Slovak autonomy. This fact stands out very clearly if we compare the 1945 version of Slovak autonomy with that of 1948.

The original arrangement, the so-called First Praha Agreement of June 1945, vested in the Slovak National Council "legislative power on all questions, insofar as they are not reserved to the Czechoslovak legislative assembly." Similarly, all the executive power in Slovakia was vested in the Slovak National Council and its Board of Commissioners "insofar as it is not in the domain of the Czechoslovak [central] government." This presumption of authority in favor of the Slovak organs was completely reversed by the Ninth-of-May Constitution. The Slovak National Council was permitted to legislate in only ten fields of strictly limited political importance, specifically enumerated in the Constitution, such as cultural matters, elementary and secondary education, public health, funds and endowments, division of communes and districts, building codes and some highway maintenance, land development and conservation, handicraft and retail trade, statistics and research in the sphere of special Slovak interests, matters of guardianship and care of orphans. Moreover, these powers were assigned to the Slovak National Council "save for such matters as are or shall be uniformly regulated by Acts [of the national legislature]" or "save for matters within the scope of the Uniform Economic Plan," which embraced virtually everything of major importance.

The scope of Slovak authority in the executive field was reduced accordingly. With the exception of the above-mentioned ten narrow fields of activity, the Slovak commissioners could act only as executive organs of the central government and the central ministries. They had to "abide by the directives and instructions of the Cabinet" and individual commissioners had to follow the "directives and instructions of their respective ministers." Moreover, the members of the central Cabinet could, if they so chose, exercise their authority in Slovakia directly.

This drastic reduction of authority was accompanied by other provisions, even more illustrative of the communist disregard for past promises. The Czechoslovak Premier was given power to summon and adjourn the Slovak National Council and even to dissolve it. The Council's laws had to be signed, not only by its Chairman and by the Chairman of the Slovak Board of Commissioners, but also by the Czechoslovak Premier who had the right to refuse signature when he deemed the law incompatible with the Constitution or inconsistent with the Uniform Economic Plan of with the national budget. The final word in such a case rested with the Cabinet which thus enjoyed veto power over Slovak legislation.

While the Slovak National Council was authorized to give a binding interpretation of its laws, such an interpretation to be valid required the approval of the Czechoslovak Premier. The central Cabinet also shared in the right to initiate bills in the Slovak National Council, an arrangement that is most unusual in the relation of a central to a regional government. Equally centralistic was the provision that the method of election of the Slovak National Council was to be prescribed by an Act of the central legislature, rather than by the Slovak National Council itself.

The decline of the political status of Slovakia resulting from the original version of the Ninth-of-May Constitution is perhaps best illustrated by the change in the mode of appointment of the Slovak Board of Commissioners. In 1945 the commissioners were chosen solely by the Presidium of the Slovak National Council and were responsible to the Council. In June 1946 such appointments became subject to the approval of the Czechoslovak Cabinet and the practice was initiated of having the commissioners sworn in by the Premier.

In 1948 the appointive power devolved on the Cabinet, which also had the sole authority to determine which commissioner should direct a particular department.

Finally, the Ninth-of-May Constitution failed to provide for any guarantee that would protect the Slovak minority against the Czech majority. Such a guarantee has always been considered by the Slovak autonomists as a vital part of their political program and a condition *sine qua non* for their acceptance of any Czech-Slovak State. This is pointed up by the fact that they had always demanded that any new constitution must include a clause which would require the consent of the majority of Slovak members of the legislature to any constitutional amendment affecting the status of Slovakia. Their effort in that respect was crowned with success in April 1946 when the Constitutional Act establishing a Constituent Assembly provided that no constitutional law affecting the status of Slovakia might be adopted except with "the consent of the majority of the present members of the Constituent Assembly elected in Slovakia." However, no such clause was included in the Ninth-of-May Constitution which could be validly amended by a three-fifths majority of all the Assembly members, irrespective of whether they represented Slovakia or the Czech provinces. As more than three-fifths of Czechoslovak legislators come from the Czech provinces, anything could be done with the status of Slovakia, even if all the Slovak representatives opposed it.[11]

Constitutional Concessions of 1956

Although the communist leaders did their best to pass this silver-plated ware for sterling, the Slovaks knew that they had been cheated and communist assertions to the contrary embittered them even more. "Bourgeois nationalism" spread among them by leaps and bounds and, as shown in Chapter VI, penetrated even deeply into the ranks of the Slovak Communists. Meanwhile, Stalin died and the Twentieth Congress of the Soviet Communist Party, steering away from the harsh nationality policies of the late Soviet Dictator, prescribed a more liberal course. Following the new Soviet line, and perhaps hoping also that a more lenient pose might help to dull the sharp edge of the rampant Slovak nationalism, the KSČ leaders decided to "consider increasing the authority of the Slovak national

[11] Only 110 of the 368 members of the National Assembly elected in 1954 came from Slovakia (98 Slovaks, 9 Hungarians, and 3 Ukrainians). See Bedřich Rattinger, *Nejvyšší státní orgány lidově demokratického Československa* (The Highest State Organs of People's Democratic Czechoslovakia), Praha, 1957, p. 29.

organs."[12] The matter was put on the agenda of the National Conference of the KSČ that met in June 1956.[13] In obedience to the Conference's directives, the National Assembly, on July 31, 1956, removed through an appropriate constitutional amendment several unnecessarily vexatious restrictions on Slovak autonomy contained in the Ninth-of-May Constitution, but preserved all the essential central government controls.[14]

The Slovak National Council regained the authority to appoint and remove the Slovak Board of Commissioners, and this authority devolved on its Presidium when the Council was not in session. The Council's Presidium repossessed its pre-coup powers to summon and adjourn the Council's sessions, while the dissolution power was abandoned altogether. The Prime Minister, who had been granted these powers under the original version of the Ninth-of-May Constitution, was also stripped of his prerogative to sign the Council's laws. Finally, the Prime Minister lost his authority to swear in the Slovak Commissioners in favor of the Chairman of the Slovak National Council.

On the other hand, the delimitation of the legislative powers of the Slovak National Council remained essentially the same as before. While the 1956 amendment did not attempt to enumerate the various fields in which the Slovak National Council was allowed to legislate, it permitted such legislation only in matters which required "a special regulation in order to assure a full economic and cultural development of Slovakia," a rather enigmatic and obviously very elastic provision that could be made as broad or as narrow as the central government wished to make it. The central government retained the power to knock down any law of the Slovak National Council that contradicted the Constitution or was deemed to exceed the Council's vaguely defined legislative grant. The only modification in this respect was that the last-named right was transferred from the Cabinet to the Presidium of the National Assembly and that it could henceforth be used only to annul a Slovak law already adopted, and not to prevent its adoption. Nor was any meaningful change made in the status of the Slovak Board of Commissioners. Although the 1956 amendment did not mention their responsibility to the Cabinet, the commissioners continued, nevertheless, to be bound by the

---

[12] *Rudé právo*, April 10, 1956.
[13] *ibid.*, June 12-16, 1956.
[14] Constitutional law No. 33 of July 31, 1956.

directives issued by the Cabinet and the individual ministers; and the Cabinet retained the right to annul any decision or act of the Board of Commissioners or any of its members that did not conform to national laws or the Cabinet's directives.[15] Moreover, the manner in which the over-all administrative authority of the Board of Commissioners was defined in the 1956 amendment represented a deterioration of Slovak autonomy rather than an improvement. While the original version of the Ninth-of-May Constitution exempted from the Board's authority matters of national defense, foreign affairs, and foreign trade, the 1956 amendment embodied a vague formula referring to "matters administered by the [central] government directly throughout the whole state territory" and citing as examples matters of "foreign affairs, foreign trade, national defense, railways and air transportation." Moreover, it authorized the central government to designate the matters to be handled by the commissioners and to issue basic directives for their administration. Listed as such in the amendment were matters of education and culture, health, agriculture and forestry, local economy, food industry, purchases of agricultural products, and water economy, i.e., matters of only minor political consequence. About the only genuine concession to Slovak autonomism was the transfer of the power to appoint the Slovak commissioners from the central Cabinet to the Slovak National Council. However, since nominees for such offices may not in any case be appointed without approval by the Central Committee of the KSČ (not merely its Slovak branch), the increase in the authority of the Slovak National Council was more apparent than real.

The 1960 Constitution

Save for certain rephrasing and a few adaptations of secondary significance, the Constitution of 1960 leaves the constitutional and political status of Slovakia where it was after the amendment of the Ninth-of-May Constitution in 1956. Although the Slovak National Council is henceforth referred to as the "national organ of state power and administration" rather than merely a legislative organ, the definition of its authority encompasses the same fields and the Council continues to be relegated to the same subordinate position it held previously. That is especially true of the principal feature of the Slovak

---

[15] For details, see Pavel Korbel's article in *Československý přehled*, III, 7-8 (1956), pp. 12ff. Also, Jan Moural, *Slovenské narodní orgány* (The Slovak National Organs), Praha, 1958.

autonomy, the power of legislation. Under the new terms, the Slovak National Council may legislate solely when authorized to do so by the National Assembly or when a special arrangement is necessary to secure "an all-round economic and cultural development of Slovakia." Evidently, enactment of measures pertaining to politics proper remains outside the Council's scope of authority. Moreover, any of its laws may be annulled by the National Assembly if the latter deems them to "contradict the Constitution or any other [national] law," and no legal recourse is available against such a ruling. Nor can the Council's political stature be enhanced in any way by the provision authorizing it to present drafts of laws for consideration to the National Assembly, which is the only really new prerogative conferred upon the Slovak National Council.

Similarly, no change of substance has been made in the position of the Slovak commissioners, except that they are henceforth selected from among the members of the Presidium of the Slovak National Council and that they do not any longer constitute a joint Board of Commissioners, but operate rather as individual officers directed collectively by the Council's Presidium. Commissions staffed both by members and nonmembers of the Slovak National Council as the latter's executive and controlling organs have been established. While these new provisions undoubtedly weaken the position of the commissioners vis-à-vis the Slovak National Council and its Presidium, they do not affect their relationship to the central government. The Slovak commissioners must "attend to further tasks in the economic and cultural construction of Slovakia to the extent determined by the [central] government." Furthermore, judging by various official pronouncements made during the "nation-wide discussion" of the draft of the new Constitution, the obvious intention is to by-pass the commissioners more and more in favor of the three regional people's committees which constitute the highest local government tier in Slovakia and are under direct guidance and supervision of the central government.[16]

Thus both the 1956 amendment and the Constitution of 1960 have left the whole matter very much where it had been ever since the communist seizure of power in 1948. While adding a few frills to embellish its façade, the communist regime has done little to repair the basic flaws in the weak foundations of Slovakia's autonomy. Nor has it had any such intention. As frankly admitted in a recent

[16] See, for instance, the editorial in *Rudé právo,* April 14, 1960.

communist monograph discussing the status of Slovakia, that province's autonomy "does not interfere with the unity of the State and does not interfere with the unity of the working people; on the contrary, it raises [this unity] to a new and higher level of proletarian unity, proletarian democratic centralism."[17]

THE SLOVAK AUTONOMY IN PRACTICE

As Alexander Pope has said, "Words are like leaves; and where they most abound, much fruit of sense beneath is rarely found." Behind the leaves of the communist assurances few fruits indeed have matured; and even these have tasted more of centralism than of autonomy. This has been true almost as much of the post-Stalin crop as of the Stalinist harvest.

With the increasing practice of legislating through administrative fiats, little room has been left for the actual exercise of the narrowly defined Slovak legislative powers. A study of the available primary and secondary sources reveals that the legislative yield of the Slovak National Council for the first twelve years of its operations has been meager. Save for the first two years after the communist seizure of power, 1948 and 1949, when as many as fifteen legislative enactments were passed per annum, the Council's annual crop of laws has ranged from zero to four.[18] Also, with few exceptions, the Slovak laws have been confined to the regulation of matters devoid of political significance, such as the establishment of regional colleges, the creation of the Slovak Academy of Science, and the protection of the beauties of nature.[19] Thus, the rare meetings of the Council are convened primarily for the purpose of hearing and approving the reports of the commissioners, and the Council's chief mission is to serve as a convenient platform for pronouncements of the Party leaders relative to Slovakia. Apart from this, the bulk of the Council's agenda consists of an annual "discussion" and formal approval of the Slovak part of the national budget and the development plan of Slovak economy, both of them within the detailed framework prepared by the central government.

Since the Slovak National Council is subject to the same absolute

---

[17] Eduard Kučera, *K některým otázkám autonomie a postavení Slovenska v rámci Československé republiky* (Concerning Some Questions of the Autonomy and Position of Slovakia within the Framework of the Czechoslovak Republic), Praha, 1954, p. 22.
[18] See Pavel Korbel's article in *Československý přehled*, III, 4 (1956), p. 30.
[19] Moural, *op.cit.*, p. 27.

control by the KSČ leadership as the National Assembly, its entire operational pattern is a small-scale fascimile of the national model. Therefore, what has been said about the operative principles with regard to the National Assembly applies also to the Slovak National Council.[20] Similarly, the rules governing the election of the Council were and are an exact duplicate of the Election Acts governing the elections for the National Assembly.[21] Under the 1954 arrangement the whole of Slovakia was divided into single-member electoral districts on the basis of a ratio of one deputy to 3,000 inhabitants. In 1960 the number of members of the Slovak National Council was fixed at 87 and their term of office at four years to match the four-year terms prescribed for the National Assembly and the people's committees.[22] The provisions for the eligibility and nomination of candidates and all the other electoral procedures, as well as the recall of deputies, are a literal transcription of the corresponding clauses regulating parliamentary elections. Since the Slovak elections were held jointly with the parliamentary elections of November 1954 and June 1960, and were thus subjected to the same totalitarian formula described in Chapter XI, the results of both were virtually identical. According to the official release 99.14 percent of the registered voters participated in the elections of 1954; 97.27 percent of the voters cast their ballots for the official candidates, while 2.73 percent voted against them and 0.5 percent of the ballots were invalid. In 1960 the attendance at the polls was 99.59 percent of which 99.79 percent voted for the official candidates.[23]

The highest organ of the Slovak administration, the Board of Commissioners (meanwhile abolished by the 1960 Constitution), was more active than the Slovak National Council, although its bondage to the central government was just as complete. It met fairly frequently, usually once a month or oftener. However, the bulk of its agenda consisted of trivial administrative matters. A study of official press communiqués reporting on the Board's activities reveals that it concerned itself with such matters as securing performance of agricultural work, assigning youths to jobs in accordance with the needs

[20] See Chapter XI.
[21] See Slovak law No. 7 of June 4, 1954, *Sbírka zákonů Slovenské narodní rady* (Collection of Laws of the Slovak National Council); also, *Pravda,* June 5, 1954; constitutional law No. 35 of April 9, 1960; and law of the Slovak National Council No. 38 of April 11, 1960.
[22] Constitutional law No. 35 of April 9, 1960.
[23] *Pravda,* June 15, 1960.

of economic planning, measures to improve tourism, publication of new textbooks for Slovak schools, and improving telephone service. However worthy and necessary such agenda may be, politically it is petty business.

Yet another trend detrimental to Slovak self-government began to emerge soon after the adoption of the Ninth-of-May Constitution. Originally, the Slovak commissioners were to administer the implementation of all laws in the territory of Slovakia, i.e., not only the enactments passed by the Slovak National Council, but also the statutes adopted by the national legislature. The Czechoslovak ministers were thus debarred from operating in Slovakia, except indirectly through the intermediary of corresponding Slovak commissioners. In June 1946 this principle was weakened and the Third Political Agreement provided that "a minister shall also be entitled to exercise his jurisdiction in Slovakia directly through the organs of his own department"; but the minister could not exercise this authority in Slovakia without the knowledge of the respective commissioner. The original version of the Ninth-of-May Constitution adhered substantially to the same arrangement in so far as it stipulated that "the Board of Commissioners (individual commissioners) shall *in principle* discharge all governmental and executive power in Slovakia . . . save for matters of foreign affairs, national defense, and foreign trade."[24] It provided also for twelve departments through which the Slovak commissioners were to carry out the executive power in Slovakia, both in their own right and on behalf of the central ministers.

This constitutional pattern required that, whenever a change occurred in the scope of authority of central ministries or a new central agency was established, the Slovak administrative machinery be rearranged accordingly. Such procedure was followed on several occasions in 1948 and 1949. But in 1950 the practice was modified. When a new Ministry of State Security was created on the Soviet model in May 1950, no corresponding Commissioner's Office was set up in Slovakia.[25] The same failure to establish Slovak departments as counterparts of newly founded ministries was repeated in a number of cases, although there were other instances in which corresponding Slovak departments were created.[26] Thus, the constitutional principle

---

[24] Italics added.

[25] Government ordinance No. 48 of May 23, 1950.

[26] When seven new ministries were created in September 1951 (State Control, Foundries and Ores, Fuel and Power, Chemical Industry, Heavy Engineering, Light Engineering, Forest and Timber Industry), only one of them, Forest and Timber

that the central ministries concerned with domestic affairs (except defense) should operate in Slovakia through the instrumentality of Slovak commissioners ceased to be honored.

This widespread practice of direct central government operations in Slovakia was somewhat restricted, and the authority of the Slovak commissioners correspondingly increased, in connection with the decentralization drive of 1956-1958. For instance, a Slovak Commissioner of State Control was appointed in January 1957 to take over the area hitherto administered by the Slovak branch of the Ministry of State Control. Also, the Board of Commissioners seems to have been granted the powers to direct and supervise the work of the people's committees located in the Slovak territory, which, oddly enough, it did not have under the previous arrangement.[27] But the 1960 reform designed to broaden the scope of local government activities has reversed the trend once again to the detriment of the Slovak Commissioners. "There is no reason whatsoever for the regional people's committees to have less authority in Slovakia than they have in the Czech regions," explained *Pravda*, denouncing a contrary attitude as "Slovak national stupidity." "The developments in Slovakia demand the same degree of decentralization."[28] Indeed, the 1960 Constitution expressly assigns the power to direct and control the work of the people's committees to the Czechoslovak Cabinet while it leaves the Slovak organs conspicuously out of the entire local government picture.

Finally, in any evaluation of the actual practice of Slovak autonomy under communist rule one must never lose sight of the all-pervasive character and the absolutist habits of communist totalitarianism. As prescribed by the Statutes of the KSČ, the Party representatives sitting in the Slovak National Council and all its organs must be approved by the Central Committee of the Communist Party of Czechoslovakia. This is equally true of the tiny group of non-communists granted membership in the Slovak National Council,

---

Industry, was given a counterpart in a corresponding Slovak department. See government ordinances Nos. 74 and 75 of September 7 and 11, 1951. Nor were Slovak departments created to parallel further additions to the roster of ministries in May and July 1952. See government ordinances No. 18 of May 27, 1952, and No. 33 of July 29, 1952. In the ministerial reorganization that took place in January 1953 some of the new ministries were given corresponding Slovak departments while others were not. See government ordinances Nos. 6 and 7 of January 31, 1953.

[27] For an admission to that effect, see *Prague News Letter*, 12, 16, August 18, 1956.

[28] *Pravda*, April 19, 1960.

for the National Front, which alone is entitled to nominate them, is fully controlled by the KSČ leaders. So long as this is the case, and so long as the KSČ's Politbureau can keep its Slovak lieutenants in the present strait jacket of rigid Party discipline, there can be no genuine Slovak autonomy even if the Constitution granted the Slovaks a legislative, executive, and judicial carte blanche.

Slovakia—the Ever-disgruntled Stepdaughter

This is also the reason why the slight concessions of 1956-1958 were bound to leave the Slovaks unimpressed and could in no way detract from Slovak bitterness toward the treatment to which they had been exposed ever since the KSČ leaders abandoned their calculative support of Slovak autonomism in 1946. Ample evidence of continued Slovak resentment is provided by recurrent warnings, criticisms, and exhortations delivered by Party leaders and the communist press, as well as by reports from underground sources.

The touchy problem of Czech-Slovak relations and the "poison of bourgeois nationalism" have figured high on the agenda of all the Slovak Party congresses and Central Committee meetings held since 1948. "We are still frequently faced with dangerous expressions of bourgeois nationalism in the shape of populist separatism deliberately implanted and maintained in Slovakia by the church hierarchy," complained Široký at the Congress of the Slovak Party in April 1955.[29] One year later, *Pravda* used the solemn occasion of the May First festivities to deplore the "lack of confidence and the suspicion of fear" between the Czechs and the Slovaks and lay blame on "the neglect of Leninist principles."[30] By 1958 the situation had not improved. According to bitter complaints made by the Slovak Party's First Secretary, Karol Bacílek, at the session of the Central Committee in January 1958, "bourgeois nationalistic tendencies" have penetrated "various fields of our cultural, political and scientific life; sports; the state apparatus; economic organs; and so on." They have infiltrated "the films, press, and radio" and "have recently appeared even in some commissioners' offices" and the Party itself.[31] Similarly, the specter of Slovak nationalism cast its long shadow over the Twelfth Congress of the Slovak Communist Party held in April 1958. In a gesture of appeasement, Václav Kopecký, speaking on behalf of

[29] *News*, 4, 6 (1955), p. 52.
[30] *Pravda*, May 1, 1956.
[31] *ibid.*, January 10 and 11, 1958.

the KSČ's Czech hierarchy, unleashed a sharp retrospective attack on "Czechoslovakism," the concept that the Czechs and the Slovaks were one nation, and took great pains to expound his Party's consistent opposition to "Czechoslovakism as an imperialist conception of national oppression of the Slovaks."[32] Seeking to exorcise the same evil spirit of Slovak nationalism through a different approach, Pavol David, a ranking member of the highest command of the Slovak Party, indulged in lavish praise of "the brotherly help of the Czech working class and the Czech public" in the "magnificent work" of Slovakia's industrialization and asserted that "the Slovak people had always cherished the warmest feelings of real and sincere brotherhood toward the Czech people."[33]

While such declarations might have flattered the Slovaks in 1945, they fell on deaf ears in 1958. Nor could the communist leaders derive much comfort from the "improvement" in the Slovak class structure resulting from the communist industrialization and collectivization drive. The transformation of the predominantly agrarian Slovakia of prewar days into a province where industrial output accounted for 70 percent of the province's production by 1956 and over 80 percent of all arable land was collectivized by the end of 1959, did substantially increase the number of the industrial proletariat who, together with the collective farmers, are supposed to be the backbone of the communist system.[34] But the communist hopes that these "two friendly classes of workers and [collective] peasants" would rise in resolute defense of proletarian internationalism against the dire threat of "bourgeois nationalism" have failed to materialize. Typical of the situation is the following excerpt from an article in *Pravda* published in March 1958:

"Local patriotism in the Košice plant of the East Slovak Machine Works is one of the sources of conflict that divide the workers into two competing groups: workers from Košice and those from elsewhere. What is most harmful is the narrow, parochial outlook that prevents people from seeing that their factory could not exist without the help of the other, particularly Czech, enterprises . . . . Some of the leading personalities have evinced a wrong and negative attitude toward the Czechs. This wrong attitude has led them into the arms

[32] Pavel Berka's article in *Československý přehled*, v, 5 (1958), p. 27.
[33] *ibid.*, p. 26.
[34] See Bacílek's report at the Slovak Party Congress of April 1957, *Prague News Letter*, 13, 10, May 11, 1957; *Československý přehled*, iii, 3 (1956), pp. 15ff.; *Ročenka*, 1960, p. 261.

of the bourgeois nationalists. They have acquired anti-Party opinions."[35]

That this is no isolated instance, but a general phenomenon, is documented not only by the continuous concentration of fire on Slovak bourgeois nationalism registered elsewhere on these pages, but also by nonofficial reports from Slovakia reaching the outside world. Aside from confirming the obvious fact that the communist fight against Slovak nationalism has made no headway among the Slovak peasantry, these reports indicate that the communist industrialization drive had backfired in an unexpected manner. By building up Slovakia's economic potential and bringing new industries to the province's backwoods areas, the regime has unwittingly prodded the Slovaks' pride and self-confidence, and thus helped to underpin the same Slovak nationalism it has been trying so hard to blot out.[36] Having acquired the know-how and the ability to run the system themselves, the Slovaks—Communists and non-communists alike—resent being ordered around by their elder Czech brethern.

[35] *Pravda,* March 30, 1958. English translation in *East Europe,* 7, 6 (1958), p. 37.

[36] *Československý přehled,* v, 2 (1958), pp. 14ff.; also, J. Šafránek, *op.cit.*

PART THREE

"OUTPRODUCING CAPITALISM"

CHAPTER XV

THE INDUSTRIAL CHALLENGE

THE CLAIM of economic superiority of the communist over the capitalist system has always been a major ingredient of the Marxist-Leninist lure. This is all the more so today when, speaking on behalf of the whole socialist camp, Khrushchëv has proclaimed economic competition to be the main tool with which he plans to "bury" capitalism by overtaking economically the most advanced of the capitalist countries, the United States, and by providing the subjects of communism with "the highest living standards in the world."

Khrushchëv's slogans have found a resounding echo among the KSČ leaders who have been ever since their seizure of power in 1948 at least as boastful of Czechoslovak economic achievements as the Soviet rulers have been of theirs. Capitalizing on the fact that Czechoslovakia was by far the most industrialized of all the countries that succumbed to communism, the new rulers have consistently striven to prove the excellence of the communist cause primarily in terms of economic successes. "The main battlefield where the completion of the socialist construction in our fatherland will be decided is the national economy," declared Novotný in his report to the Eleventh Party Congress in June 1958.[1] And, as did his predecessors, he staked claim to an impressive array of economic gains, past, present, and future, made possible by the communist victory. Joining enthusiastically in Khrushchëv's latest slogan of defeating capitalism by outproducing it, the Czechoslovak Communists even came out into the open with a cocky assertion that "of all the countries of the socialist camp Czechoslovakia is closest to the fulfillment of the basic economic task of catching and overtaking the most advanced capitalist countries in per capita production."[2]

How real are the communist claims of tremendous economic advances attained in the first twelve years of their rule? How true is, in the case of Czechoslovakia, the communist assertion that a social-

[1] *Rudé právo*, June 19, 1958.
[2] *Zahraniční obchod*, March 1957.

ized, centrally directed economy works so much better and brings so much more benefit to the common man than the free enterprise system with its guiding rationale of private profit? Has the KSČ implemented its promises to abolish the exploitation of man by man and provide for a more equitable distribution of material wealth? And, above all, to what extent, if at all, have the regime's economic achievements (whatever they are) offset the adverse effects of the rigid regimentation inherent in the Marxist-Leninist operational pattern? Or, to approach the matter from a somewhat different direction, to what extent, if at all, have communism's subjects in Czechoslovakia become reconciled to the curtailment of their civil rights and political freedoms by virtue of whatever economic advantages might have accrued to them under the dictatorship of the proletariat?

In considering these matters it is proposed to begin with industry, turn in the next Chapter to agriculture, and conclude with an inquiry into the issue of material well-being and the human cost entailed by the totalitarian character of the economy.

Prewar Background

Without attempting to detract from whatever credit may be due to the communist regime, it is only fair to point out that the communist task has been made much easier by the high level of industrialization attained in the precommunist era. Hence, a short review of economic developments in pre-communist Czechoslovakia can serve a useful purpose by providing a basis of comparison and contrast.

Prior to World War II Czechoslovakia had a free enterprise system based on private ownership of the means of production and affording as much opportunity for private initiative as existed anywhere in the world. The government owned and operated railroads, postal and telegraph services, radio transmissions, and a tobacco monopoly. Apart from these few fields, considered to be a traditional sphere of public ownership in most of Europe, the Czechoslovak government owned and operated a small number of sundry enterprises, such as a few sawmills, breweries, sugar refineries, stone quarries, one steel plant, and one aircraft factory.[3] Thus, measured by customary European standards, the government's share in direct business activities in prewar Czechoslovakia was negligible. A few statistics may be quoted in order to enable the reader to obtain a general

---

[3] In all, there were about sixty such state-operated enterprises in the field of industrial production. See *Ročenka,* Praha, 1937, p. 275.

picture of the Czechoslovak economy prior to World War II. Unless otherwise stated, they are the 1930 data as this was the last decennial census taken in prewar Czechoslovakia.[4]

There were a total of 720,007 industrial and commercial establishments employing 3,076,982 persons. Of these establishments, 350,427 were engaged in industrial production proper and their total employment amounted to 1,994,594 persons. Engaged in construction were 27,588 units with 297,303 employees. In trade, banking, and insurance, there were 299,927 units with 657,405 employees, and in transportation (exclusive of the railways and postal services which were government-operated) there were 16,077 units with 33,573 people. As many as 91 percent of these establishments employed from one to five persons each and only 5.9 percent used the services of six to nineteen persons and 2.2 percent, twenty or more. Of the 14,729,536 inhabitants of Czechoslovakia in 1930, 5,101,614, i.e., 34.64 percent, derived their livelihood from agriculture, forestry, and fisheries; 5,146,937, i.e., 34.94 percent, from industrial production and construction; 1,094,063, i.e., 7.43 percent, from trade and banking; 814,468; i.e., 5.53 percent, from transportation; and the remaining 17 percent from other occupations, such as the public services, Armed Forces, and liberal professions.

The Czechoslovak national income of 1929 was estimated at 66.1 billion crowns which was equivalent to some two billion dollars at the official rate of exchange at the time. The main branches of industrial production were coal mining, steel and iron, textiles, machinery, and armaments. A few output figures for 1937, the last full year of pre-Munich Czechoslovakia, may serve to illustrate the character and the capacity of the Czechoslovak industry of prewar days. The output of hard coal amounted then to almost 17 million tons, that of brown coal exceeded 18 million and of hard coal coke 3¼ million tons.[5] Over 2¼ million tons of crude steel, almost 1¾ million tons each of rolled steel and pig iron were produced. Some typical figures in the field of consumer goods included 55 million pairs of shoes, over 377 million meters of cotton, and over 33 million meters of woolen textiles, 208 thousand tons of paper, 604 thousand tons of refined sugar, over 12 thousand automobiles and 14 thousand motorcycles, over 8¼ million hectoliters of beer and close to 12 billion cigarettes.

[4] Unless otherwise stated, the figures for prewar Czechoslovakia are from *Ročenka,* 1937.

[5] *Statistická příručka Československé republiky* (Statistical Handbook of the Czechoslovak Republic), London, n.d., p. 49.

As can be gathered from this rudimentary selection of statistical data, prewar Czechoslovakia had a reasonably well-balanced economy with only about one-third of her population depending for their livelihood on agriculture, which was considerably less than in any other country of Central-Eastern Europe. Her industry consisted mainly of small and medium-sized workshops and factories which might have used a good deal more mechanization than was provided. He would be mistaken, however, who would conclude that there was only a negligible number of large-scale enterprises. The low average of only a little better than six employees per establishment was caused mainly by the specific nature of certain branches of manufacturing unsuitable for mass assembly-line production, such as artistic china and glassware, and by a high number of independent craftsmen operating their workshops with little or no outside help, rather than by the absence of mass producing plants. Indeed, prewar Czechoslovakia could boast of huge industrial establishments employing tens of thousands of personnel and using the most modern machinery, such as the world-famous Škoda Works of Pilsen, the Zbrojovka armament and engineering corporation of Brno (the home of Bren guns), Baťa's shoe production plant at Zlín (Europe's largest), and many others.

Before leaving the prewar era, a word must also be said about Czechoslovakia's foreign trade. Having inherited over 70 percent of the industrial capacity of the Austro-Hungarian Empire in 1918 but only about 25 percent of its population, Czechoslovakia became strongly dependent on foreign trade. At its peak in 1928, the volume of the Czechoslovak foreign trade reached almost forty and one-half billion crowns, which was almost two-thirds of her whole national income. In the second best year, 1929, exports alone were equal to 30 percent of Czechoslovakia's national income, amounting to twenty and one-half billion crowns.[6] Although the depression of the thirties made a deep cut in her foreign trade, Czechoslovakia continued to rank among the first six or seven nations of Europe in the absolute volume of exports. The structure of her foreign trade reflected strikingly the nature of Czechoslovakia's economy. The first place among her imports was held consistently by raw materials and half-finished products, which usually constituted more than half of all imports. On the other hand, Czechoslovak exports consisted predominantly of manufactured articles, which generally accounted for about three-fourths of all the exports. Thus Czechoslovakia's well-being depended greatly

[6] *Statistický zpravodaj,* x, Nos. 7-8 (1947), p. 262.

352

upon her ability to sell abroad a substantial part of the fruits of her skilled labor, and any disruption or curtailment of international trade was bound to cause serious trouble. Indeed, it tended to hurt her more than most other industrial countries as a considerable part of her exports consisted of nonessential merchandise, such as china, glassware, and jewelry.

MIXING SOCIALIZATION WITH FREE ENTERPRISE—1945-1948

The memories of the Great Depression and of the havoc it had played with the Czechoslovak free-enterprise economy were still very much alive when World War II came to its end and Czechoslovakia began to rebuild her economy. Most Czechoslovaks believed that the former liberal economic system must be so adapted as to prevent recurrence of economic crises. The prevailing opinion among the workers and even a considerable number of the intelligentsia was that planning and socialization of key sectors of national economy would do the job. It was felt, also, that the colossal tasks of postwar reconstruction with its need of tremendous investments could by no means be met by a prewar type of free enterprise, but had to be handled directly by the government. Moreover, most of the major industrial plants had been taken over by the Germans following the Nazi occupation of Czechoslovakia. Even if there had been any desire to return such enterprises into the hands of the original owners or their legitimate heirs, it would have been quite a complex procedure. "In solving all these new and incredibly complex property, legal, and social problems and relationships there may not perhaps be any other way than that the liberated State take over the administration of such property and seek then the methods of a new general arrangement according to specific conditions in each particular country," wrote Beneš before the end of World War II.[7]

Thus the reasons which operated in favor of nationalization in Czechoslovakia were not dissimilar to those which prompted nationalization in France and Britain. But there was, in the case of Czechoslovakia, one additional factor of major importance which was absent from Western Europe: the geographical proximity of the Soviet Union and the presence of the Red Army throughout the crucial year of

[7] *Demokracie dnes a zítra* (Democracy Today and Tomorrow), London, n.d., II, p. 200.

1945 when foundations were being laid for the new political and economic system. Explaining the circumstances under which nationalization was undertaken, Beneš stated rather euphemistically: "The final reason is of a geographical nature; we are Slavs and neighbors of the Soviet Union which is mainly a Slavonic State. It is only natural that its socialistic system should have an influence upon us."[8]

This gave a tremendous advantage to the Communists and a corresponding disadvantage to their opponents for whom a resolute advocacy of free enterprise invariably meant being attacked as reactionaries and "abettors of fascism." Nevertheless, at that early stage of their political endeavors, the KSČ leaders were rather cautious in their approach to the matter of nationalization. Considering the avowed goals of Marxism-Leninism and the results obtained on its basis in the Soviet Union, the KSČ attitude in the years preceding the February coup of 1948 must indeed be designated as quite moderate. Writing in April 1944, Rudolf Slánský, then member of the Big Four of the KSČ leadership in exile, made it clear that major industrial plants taken over by the Nazis would not be returned to their original owners. But at the same time he declared that smaller enterprises up to 500,000 prewar crowns' worth (i.e., some 17,000 dollars) would be "immediately returned to former owners" while the remainder would be "placed under temporary public administration until the properly elected National Assembly could decide about their ultimate fate."[9]

Nor was the Košice Program of April 1945 outspoken about the economic system to be established in liberated Czechoslovakia. It confirmed the principle that property held by citizens of enemy states and by Czechoslovak citizens who "actively aided" the enemy would be placed under national administration and that property taken by the occupants from "workers, employees, shopkeepers, farmers, and members of liberal professions" would be returned to the former owners or their heirs. Though the above wording obviously did not apply to factory owners, nevertheless the Košice Program promised to "support the private initiative of entrepreneurs, artisans, and other producers" as well as "private and cooperative trade." On the other hand, the Program left the gate wide open for socialization by listing as one

---

[8] From an article in the *Manchester Guardian,* reprinted as an introduction to the Czechoslovak government publication *Nationalization in Czechoslovakia,* Praha, 1946, pp. 8-9.

[9] *Cesta k svobodě* (The Road to Freedom), London, 1944, i, pp. 86-87.

of the government's objectives "placing the whole banking and credit system, the key industrial enterprises, the insurance business, natural resources, and sources of energy under general state direction and into the service of the reconstruction of national economy and revival of production and trade." Though the word socialization or nationalization was not used, it was nevertheless understood by all parties to the Košice Program and by President Beneš that the above-mentioned sectors of economy would be transferred into direct state ownership and operation. Opinions differed only as to how far socialization should go, the Communists and most of the Social Democrats pressing for more, the other parties attempting to save as much private enterprise as they could, and President Beneš advising caution and moderation. With regard to the power relationship among these three political factors in 1945, it is hardly surprising that the Communists achieved virtually all that they wanted. This was easy for them because their policy at that time was to nationalize, with a promise of full compensation, only major industrial and financial establishments while leaving the small and medium-size enterprises alone.

As enacted by four presidential decrees of October 24, 1945, nationalization was applied to different fields of production in varying degrees.[10] Mining, sources of energy, iron and steel, armament production, the pharmaceutical industry, the cellulose and gramophone industry, and certain types of chemical and glass production were completely nationalized irrespective of size or capacity. Exception was made only in case of enterprises run by, or belonging to, cooperative societies. In other fields of industrial production only such plants were nationalized as exceeded a certain minimum size, determined in most branches of production by the number of employees and by technical capacity in others. The minima of employees which made an enterprise subject to nationalization ranged from 150 in enterprises producing porcelain and ceramics to 500 in case of cotton-weaving mills and establishments of metallurgical industry and electrical engineering. Banking and insurance business was nationalized in its entirety. The only sectors of nonagricultural production left out from the scope of nationalization were building and printing, though even in them the government took into possession a number of units.

As a result of these arrangements the extent of nationalization

[10] Nos. 100-103 of 1945. For an English translation see *Nationalization in Czechoslovakia.*

differed substantially from one industry to another, reaching 100 percent in such sectors as mining and power generation, 84 percent in metal industries, 51 percent in textiles, and 20-24 percent in the food industry. While a mere 17.4 percent of individual plants had been nationalized in 1946, in terms of persons employed they represented 57.7 percent and, by January 1948, 63.9 percent.[11]

Along with nationalization, another major innovation brought into the Czechoslovak economy in the 1945-1948 intermezzo was economic planning. On this point, there was no disagreement among the parties, for it was realized by all of them that the urgent need of economic reconstruction and rehabilitation could hardly be met without a careful economic plan setting the main goals and assigning scarce raw materials, hard-to-get equipment, and manpower according to a definite schedule of priorities. On October 28, 1946, Czechoslovak Independence Day, President Beneš signed into law the first Czechoslovak Economic Plan aiming at raising the over-all industrial output 10 percent above 1937 by the end of 1948 and emphasizing especially the heavy and basic industries where the scheduled increase was to average a full 50 percent above the 1937 level.[12]

Thus two of the main points of the communist economic program, i.e., the socialization of business, banking and industry, and all-embracing economic planning with emphasis on capital goods production and investment, were substantially achieved even prior to the communist coup of February 1948. As stated above, they were not exclusively communistic because all parties and all people in responsible positions in postwar Czechoslovakia as well as the average man-in-the street accepted economic planning and some amount of nationalization as desirable or at least necessary. But due to the overwhelming political influence which they had gained in 1945, the Communists were able to secure powerful strongholds throughout the nationalized industries and establish thus an excellent basis for further operations as well as for the future obliteration of what was still left of free enterprise. It was no coincidence that the communist clamor for further nationalization of all enterprises with more than fifty employees, coupled with a parallel accusation that the "reactionary" leaders of

[11] Nicolas Spulber, *The Economics of Communist Eastern Europe*, New York, 1957, p. 50; Josef Goldman, *Czechoslovakia, Test Case of Nationalization*, Praha, 1947; *Plánované hospodářství v Československu* (Planned Economy in Czechoslovakia), Praha, 1947.

[12] For an English translation of the Czechoslovak Two-Year Plan see *The First Czechoslovak Economic Plan*, Praha, 1947.

other parties wanted to return the nationalized enterprises into "capitalist hands," became the main rallying battle cry ushering the February putsch of 1948.[13]

FURTHER NATIONALIZATION AFTER
THE FEBRUARY COUP

Their complete victory in February 1948 enabled the KSČ leaders to carry out their will on the economic front, as everywhere else, without being hampered by opposition. Responding promptly to the victorious "will of the people," Gottwald's lieutenants took over, during and immediately following the February coup, private enterprises with more than fifty employees (and even many with less than that) and placed them under "national administration." Only subsequently, in April and May 1948, was this revolutionary take-over validated retroactively by the Ninth-of-May Constitution and nine new Nationalization Acts banning private enterprise altogether from a great many additional industries and limiting it to small plants employing not more than fifty employees in the remaining less important fields of manufacturing.[14]

As a result of these early post-coup arrangements private ownership in industry and business was drastically reduced. As late as February 1948, 20.4 percent of industrial production, measured in terms of the number of employees, was in private hands while the ultimate fate of an additional 12.8 percent, which had been confiscated from the Sudeten Germans, remained still undecided.[15] After the second wave of nationalization resulting from the February coup, the private sector was cut to a mere 5.1 percent.[16] In wholesale and foreign trade the change was even more drastic. As much as 75 percent of such trade was managed by privately owned firms and only 25 percent by state and by cooperative societies prior to 1948. After the coup, wholesale and foreign trade was socialized in its entirety.

Although sharply curtailed, private ownership and operation of the means of production continued nevertheless to be permitted even after the communist seizure of power. Nor was that an oversight on the part of the KSČ leadership. Addressing the Constituent Assembly

[13] See Ludvík Frejka, *26.únor 1948 v československém hospodářství* (February 26, 1948, in the Czechoslovak Economy), Praha, 1948.

[14] Laws Nos. 118-126 of 1948, all of them made effective retroactively from January 1, 1948. For the economic provisions of the Ninth-of-May Constitution see Chapter VIII.

[15] *Statistický zpravodaj*, XII, Nos. 5-6 (1949).

[16] *ibid.*

prior to its final vote on the above-mentioned Nationalization Acts of April 1948, Antonín Zápotocký emphatically promised protection of the remaining private enterprises and reprimanded publicly those overzealous comrades who pleaded for its total abolition:

"The question arises as to how far we intend to nationalize. And I do not hesitate to declare: We do not want to nationalize either the medium enterprises or small trade. We could have done so after February [1948], we could have broken our promise and overstepped the limit which we imposed upon ourselves. We have not done so and we will not do so . . . . I do not hesitate to state from this rostrum that we do not agree with the endeavors of those individuals who would like to nationalize everything . . . . That is why we do not hesitate to embody the protection of small enterprises into our Constitution. We make promises in order to keep them, and not in order to break them when there seems to be a propitious occasion to do so."[17] Furthermore, the Ninth-of-May Constitution, adopted shortly thereafter, specifically guaranteed "private ownership of small and medium enterprises of up to fifty employees" and thus formally sanctioned private employment of hired labor even under the dictatorship of the proletariat.

However, these solemn promises notwithstanding, private enterprise became an object of ever-mounting repression. After a slight temporary reprieve following the death of Stalin, the recrudescence of neo-Stalinism in the wake of the Hungarian uprising lent a new impetus to a relentless drive against the remnants of "petty-bourgeois capitalism." Although represented, as of 1956, by a mere handful of 30,000 persons engaged mostly in metal-working, wood-working, textiles, and clothing,[18] these private entrepreneurs have been continually attacked by communist spokesmen in recent years for allegedly defrauding government, violating tax and currency regulations, and taking undue advantage of certain "weaknesses" of the socialist economy.[19] Many of them have been hauled before the people's courts and sentenced to stiff penalties in well-publicized trials evidently designed to "unmask" these "hidden enemies" of socialism and create a suitable atmosphere for their ultimate economic liquidation. Simultaneously, the regime's spokesmen have been lashing out at those man-

[17] *Svobodné noviny,* April 29, 1948.
[18] *Postavení Československa ve světovém hospodářství* (Czechoslovakia's Position in the World Economy), Praha, 1957, p. 16. Hereafter cited as *Postavení.*
[19] For instance, *Rudé právo,* April 4 and 29, 1958; *Lidová demokracie,* May 4, 1958; *East Europe,* 8, 2 (1959), pp. 21ff.

agers of state enterprises who still continued to place orders with such private entrepreneurs.[20] In issuing its directives for the completion of the socialist construction, the resolution of the Eleventh Party Congress of June 1958 called specifically and unequivocally for the removal of the remaining private entrepreneurs.[21]

Thus, while formally committed by their oath of office to abide by the solemn constitutional guarantee of "private ownership of small and medium enterprises up to fifty employees," the communist rulers of Czechoslovakia have never relented in their efforts for their undoing. The number of private retail stores, which have for many years been the main residue of nonagricultural private enterprise under the communist rule, sank from 5,442 in 1951 to 204 by the end of 1959 and their volume of business from 20.1 percent of the over-all retail trade in 1949 to 0.03 percent.[22] The number of self-employed persons in the entire nonagricultural private sector of the national economy is listed as a mere 9,000 by the end of 1959.[23]

That individual enterprise in communist Czechoslovakia came to these sorry ends is, of course, a logical consequence of the basic Marxist-Leninist attitude toward private ownership and operation of the means of production, an attitude in which the KSČ leaders concurred. Nor has it been any departure from the prevalent satellite pattern of tolerating a modicum of private enterprise at the initial stage of the socialist construction. The Moscow-approved precepts of the Marxist-Leninist strategy prescribe a degree of gradualism in this respect; and private enterprise was and still is formally allowed by the East European satellite constitutions, including the new Czechoslovak Constitution of 1960.[24] What makes the Czechoslovak case somewhat different, however, has been the sharp contrast between the relative initial leniency and the recent excessive harshness. Of all the constitutions in the Soviet orbit Czechoslovakia's Ninth-of-May Constitution offered the most elaborate protection of private enterprise. As illustrated by Zápotocký's above-mentioned pronouncement of April 1948, the KSČ leaders went to greater lengths than their colleagues elsewhere behind the Iron Curtain in professing their respect for private ownership of small-scale production. Yet, they were more

---

[20] *Rudé právo,* August 15, 1957, and February 5, 1958.

[21] *ibid.,* June 23, 1958.

[22] *Ročenka,* 1959, p. 333 and *Ročenka,* 1960, pp. 326 and 346.

[23] *ibid.,* 1960, p. 91.

[24] See Article 9 of the Czechoslovak Constitution of 1960, Chapter II of the Bulgarian Constitution, Article 19 of the East German Constitution, and Chapter II of the Hungarian Constitution.

reluctant than their satellite counterparts in making concessions to private enterprise during the post-Stalin thaw; and since 1957 they have ranked among its foremost repressors. What is the explanation?

Most of their initial leniency of 1948 was undoubtedly motivated by tactical considerations. Having seized power with a claim that the KSČ was not only the advocate of the workers' rights, but also the best protector of small and medium entrepreneurs, the Party leaders felt the desirability of continuing the pretense while consolidating their power. But Gottwald's and Zápotocký's instinctive pragmatism, hidden under the thick layer of dogmatism, has also been a contributory factor.[25] While the two topmost architects of the February coup were firm believers in socialized economy, they were aware of the pitfalls and problems involved in its operation. Hence, mindful of the experience which the Bolsheviks had with their first postrevolutionary nationalization, they did not want to complicate matters for themselves at the initial stage of the dictatorship of the proletariat by a sweeping nationalization of small enterprises. On the contrary, their behavior at the time and all the evidence at hand indicate that Gottwald and Zápotocký were in no hurry in that respect and that they reckoned originally with a fairly long coexistence of nationalized industry with a narrowly delimited private sector in small-scale manufacturing.

But subsequent developments caused the Party leaders to switch to ever-sharpening restrictions. To satisfy the Gargantuan appetite for more and more manpower and materials caused by the excessive industrialization forced upon Czechoslovakia by Moscow in the early fifties, it was natural for Gottwald and his associates to dip, first and foremost, into the leftovers of private enterprise. The hard-pressed entrepreneurs fought back by securing the needed raw materials and labor through various semilegal or illegal devices, such as paying higher "black wages" than the nationalized enterprises, bribing government controllers, and colluding with trade union officials and managers of state enterprises. This in turn induced the regime to an even more violent persecution of these "vicious saboteurs of the national economy." How much and how quickly the situation changed since the days of Zápotocký's lofty assurances of 1948 is well illustrated by the following statement of the Party's ideological magazine, *Nová Mysl,* in October 1952:

"Comrade Lenin shows that small-scale production gives birth to

[25] For a discussion of their mentality see Chapter v.

capitalism and the bourgeoisie . . . . This tendency is countered by the policy of our people's democratic State which fulfills the main functions of the dictatorship of the proletariat. Taxing policy, state purchases, class-conscious imposition of quota deliveries, regulation of the market, price-fixing policy—all that is directed against the capitalistic element, aimed at reducing and eliminating them."[26]

Having broken the promises given to small tradesmen prior to 1948 and so emphatically repeated even after the communist coup, the KSČ leaders had good reason to fear the political consequences of the "petty-capitalistic" revival which made itself apparent in the satellite orbit after Stalin's death. Furthermore, the workers' enthusiasm for socialization, in which they had seen, prior to the communist seizure, a panacea for most ills and a sure key to prosperity, petered out by 1953 and the small private entrepreneurs began to be looked upon by many a worker as victims worthy of sympathy rather than petty-bourgeois villains to be hated. Also, despite all the restrictions to which they were exposed, private entrepreneurs gave better and faster service than the top-heavy, overbureaucratized national enterprises, belying thus the communist claim of the superiority of the socialist economy. As conceded by the communist press itself, "In some cases the private entrepreneur was cheaper, quicker, and simpler to work with."[27] Granting concessions to private enterprise under such circumstances looked like playing with fire among combustibles to the overcautious KSČ leaders, especially when their fears were so amply vindicated by the 1956 explosions in Poland and Hungary.

ECONOMIC PLANS: TARGETS AND RESULTS

In the nationalization of industrial establishments the original targets have certainly been exceeded and the liquidation of the "capitalist sector" attained much earlier than initially anticipated. But what about production itself? What have been the salient trends of Czechoslovak industrial developments in the era of the dictatorship of the proletariat? What major targets have been set and what have been the actual results?

The basic Czechoslovak pattern has been much like those of the other East European satellites. A postwar period of economic reconstruction with top priority given to heavy industry was followed by an overambitious First Five-Year Plan (1949-1953) characterized by

[26] *Nová mysl,* October 4, 1952, p. 660.
[27] *Rudé právo,* August 15, 1957.

TABLE III

Percentile Production Increases under the Economic Plans

| | TWO-YEAR PLAN (1947-1948) (percent over 1937) | | FIRST FIVE-YEAR PLAN (1949-1953) (percent over 1948) | | | 1955-1956 INTERMEZZO (1954) (percent over 1953) | | (1955) (percent over 1954) | | SECOND FIVE-YEAR PLAN (1956-1960) | | | THIRD FIVE-YEAR PLAN (1961-1965) | |
	Plan	Actual	Original Plan	1951 Super-Plan	Actual	Plan	Actual	Plan	Actual	Original Plan (percent over 1955)	1958 Revision	1959 Actual (percent over 1948)	(percent over 1957) Original Plan	(percent over 1960)
Industry as a whole	10	8	57	98	93a	5.8	4.4	9	10.6	50	54.4	233	90-95	56
Producer goods	50		66	133	119	6	4.2	9	9	57	61	284		70
Consumer goods	50	-10	50	73	68b	5.3	4.7	9	12	40	44	181		34
Agriculture	0	-25.2	37	53	17c	12.1	-2.5	12.6	11.5	30	27	31	40	22-23
Electricity			52		65					68	72	213	115	61
Hard coal					15					26			40	19
Brown coal			35		46					49		100	57	31
Iron ore					79					46				
Pig iron			49		69					60	59			63
Crude steel					67					46	51		77-87	57
Rolled steel					73					47	55			62
Cement					40					56	61		89	75
Engineering goods			93		223						77	477	130	83
Chemical goods			62	64d	138						61	370	150	97
Labor productivity in industry	10	4	32	59e	73	8.8	2	8	8	44	35	149	75	43
Reduction in production costs									0.3	12.4	12.4		per annum 2.5-3	12.4

a According to previous claims, 102; b according to previous claims, 80; c according to previous claims, 14; d heavy industry; e light industry.

Sources: Ročenka, 1960, official Plan announcements; Rudé právo, June 19, 1960.

a lopsided emphasis on capital goods production and by an even sharper upward revision of the initial targets in 1950-1951. The impossibility of sustaining the murderous pace, coupled with the post-Stalin necessity of granting at least some of the long overdue concessions to the neglected consumer, led to the New Course intermezzo of 1954-1955 during which the over-all pace of industrialization was slowed down and an attempt was made to correct somewhat the gross imbalance between the consumer and capital goods sectors. But the Second Five-Year Plan, begun in 1956, reverted to the extremely preferential treatment of heavy industry typical of the First Five-Year Plan, although the over-all rate of industrial growth has been held well below the back-breaking pace of the 1950-1953 era. And more of the same scheduling will be enforced by the Third Five-Year Plan for the 1961-1965 period.

In the original layout of the present volume this general characterization of Czechoslovak economic developments under the communist rule was followed by a more detailed review of the four successive stages through which the Czechoslovak economy traveled between 1948 and 1960. However, the necessity of conserving space counseled concentration on an analysis and evaluation of results rather than back-tracking the tortuous road trodden by Czechoslovak economic planners. Such a course seems all the more advisable as the concern of this book is not with economic developments per se but with their political implications. Moreover, excellent accounts in English of the various stages of the Czechoslovak economic developments under communism may be found in the publications of the United Nations Economic Commission for Europe, such as its *Economic Surveys of Europe* and *Economic Bulletins of Europe*.[28] Hence, in lieu of a detailed chronology of economic developments, a table of percentile indices (Table III) concerning the major aspects of industrial development is offered below. It is hoped that, together with the table of absolute production figures (Table V) appended to this chapter, it will provide at least some insight into the basic trends over the years.

INDUSTRIAL BALANCE SHEET

What is, then, the industrial balance sheet of Czechoslovak communism after twelve years of the dictatorship of the proletariat? Naturally, in a study of politics industrial attainment cannot be meas-

---

[28] *Economic Survey of Europe Since the War*, Geneva, 1955, and ensuing *Surveys* for each year beginning with 1955; also, Spulber, *op.cit.*

ured solely or even mainly by strictly economic yardsticks, but must be considered first and foremost in terms of their contribution to man's over-all well-being and happiness, material as well as spiritual. No matter how spectacular production achievements may be from a strictly economic viewpoint, if they are attained by excessive harshness and regimentation, resentment rather than contentment is the result, especially if the promised material improvements lag behind expectation. Thus even unquestionable excellence in economic performance may sometimes produce adverse results in politics.

In the present chapter communist industrial developments from 1948 to 1960 will be balanced in terms of economic achievements. However, as Western students of communist economics find far too frequently, accurate measurement of the economic attainments of the Soviet orbit countries in the manner in which such results can be gauged in the democratic West is well-nigh impossible. Although the extreme economic secretiveness of the Stalin era was abandoned soon after the Dictator's death and statistical data have since then become much more abundant, there is still no fool-proof way of verifying communist claims. And the fact that the communist morality condones deceit if it contributes to communist victory counsels caution in accepting communist figures at their face value.

Communist Czechoslovakia has been no exception to the rule. The scanty production data released in the Stalin era, mostly in the form of percentile indices, were made virtually worthless for purposes of comparison by constant methodological shifts. At first, the output was computed according to various industrial sectors and the products transferred for further processing to other sectors were counted as the part of gross output as many times. Thereafter, statistical data began to be gathered according to the several economic ministries under which related enterprises were grouped. Since these groupings did not correspond to the former "sectors" and, furthermore, were changed as new economic ministries were added and the old ones split and merged again, the basis for meaningful comparison was all but lost. Moreover, the changing value of the crown—the yardstick used for computing the gross output—added still further to the statistical confusion; and so did the deeply embedded communist habit of withholding disagreeable data and the almost irresistible temptation on the part of factory managements to camouflage deficiencies by inflating results through various statistical sleights-of-hand. The bankruptcy of the Czechoslovak statistics of the Stalin era was confirmed by the communist statisticians themselves. Caught in the web of their own sins, they confessed in November 1952: "The fact is that today we have no reliable data on the over-all production of our industry for the past years and that we shall have to reconstruct with much effort and a great deal of guessing the development of production and labor productivity in our industry during the First Five-Year Plan."[29]

Having learned the hard way how detrimental the absence of dependable statistics had been for their economic planning, the KSČ leaders readily complied with the post-Stalin emphasis on the improvement of statistical work. As a result, ample data are available today on all but a few facets of the Czechoslovak industrial production; and they include also a wealth of absolute output figures which cannot be juggled with over a span of many years quite as easily as percentile indices of industrial growth. It is improbable that the upward bias, which is inherent in the very nature of the Marxist-Leninist economic reporting system, could have been wholly eliminated. Nor would it be prudent to believe that Czechoslovak Communists have discarded altogether the practice of manipulating statistical data if and when such course is warranted by considerations of communist strategy and needs of communist propaganda. But in spite of these reservations, most of the economic data released by the Czechoslovak State Office of Statistics in recent years do yield a much better insight into the country's economy than did the deceptive statistical gobbledygook of the Stalin era.

Seen in the light of official figures, checked for dependability by whatever other pertinent information could be secured from non-communist sources, the balance sheet of Czechoslovak industrial production at the close of the Second Five-Year Plan presents a mixed pattern ranging all the way from spectacular successes to dismal failures.

Credit Items

1. Foremost on the positive ledger of the economic balance sheet ranks the impressive increase in the volume of industrial production. According to official claims, the over-all industrial output rose an even 200 percent above 1948 by 1958 and stood 233 percent above 1948 by the end of 1959.[30] The lion's share belonged to capital goods

---

[29] *Politická ekonomie,* No. 1, 1953. Cited after Ota Karásek's article in *Československý přehled,* I, 2 (1954), p. 9.
[30] *Ročenka,* 1960, p. 137.

production which jumped a full 284 percent between 1948 and 1959. Czechoslovak communism's economic pet child, engineering, led the field with a whopping 477 percent rise from 1948 to 1959, followed in order by chemical production (384 percent), construction materials (366), rubber industry (312), extraction of black metal ores (234), electricity (213), and fuels (179).[31] As shown in the table appended to this chapter, the absolute production figures in the key sectors of heavy industry are similarly impressive.

Spectacular as these results are, Czechoslovakia's rate of industrial growth has been slower than that of any other of Moscow's European satellites except East Germany. This is due, of course, to the fact that the countries in question were far less industrialized than Czechoslovakia prior to their engulfment within the Soviet orbit. Hence, because of the low base against which it is measured, the same or lower output represents in their case a faster rate of growth. On the other hand, in the over-all rate of industrial growth for the period 1937-1957 Czechoslovakia ranked above most of the industrial countries of the non-communist world. However, should 1948, the year preceding the first Czechoslovak communist long-term plan, be taken for the base, the Czechoslovak industrial growth of 2.7 times the 1948 volume by 1957 was greatly exceeded by that of Japan, which quadrupled her 1948 output by 1957, and West Germany, which almost quadrupled hers, and was more than equalled by small neighboring Austria and by Greece. A similar comparison for the period 1954-1959 reveals that Czechoslovakia's industrial growth by 69 percent over 1953 by the end of 1959 was equalled by France and Italy while Western Germany with a 68 percent growth was a mere 1 percent behind.[32]

Nor could Czechoslovakia as yet take the much-coveted lead either in per capita output or the rate of growth in any of the sectors of heavy production given top priority, such as electricity, coal, steel or iron. As of 1958, her per capita output of electricity lagged well behind such capitalist countries as Austria, Britain, Finland, France, West Germany, Norway, Sweden, Switzerland, Luxemburg, Australia, Canada, and the United States, relegating thus Czechoslovakia to a

[31] *ibid.*

[32] The data for this and the following comparisons were taken from various statistical publications of the United Nations, especially the *Economic Surveys of Europe, United Nations Yearbooks of Statistics* and *Monthly Bulletins of Statistics.* The Czechoslovak rate of industrial growth for 1954-1959 was calculated from the Czechoslovak official indices of 193 percent for 1953, 300 for 1958 (1948-100) and a 10.9 percent claim of increase in 1959 over 1958.

none-too-glorious eleventh place in Europe. Even in the rate of growth for the 1937-1958 period Czechoslovakia had to yield to Australia and the United States, not to speak of such industrially less-developed countries as Ireland, Spain, and Portugal. In the per capita output of hard coal, Czechoslovakia figured on sixth place in Europe in 1958 but was behind Belgium, Britain, West Germany, South Africa, Australia, and the United States, and trailed South Africa and Australia in the 1937-1958 rate of growth. Similarly, she took fifth place in per capita production of crude steel and continued to be topped by Belgium, Luxemburg, Britain, West Germany, and the United States while in the rate of growth Czechoslovakia was preceded by a long list of capitalist countries, such as Austria, Italy, the Netherlands, Finland, Norway, Denmark, Spain, Canada, and Australia. Finally, in the per capita output of pig iron Czechoslovakia placed fifth in Europe in 1958 and was behind Austria, Belgium, Luxemburg, West Germany, and the United States, whereas in the rate of growth since 1937 she had to yield to Austria, Italy, Norway, Finland, the Netherlands, Sweden, Japan, South Africa, Canada, and Australia.

These figures, taken from the various statistical compendia of the United Nations, are not recited here with an intention of belittling the results attained by communist Czechoslovakia in the main sectors of heavy production. Considered solely in terms of quantitative levels and without regard to quality, production costs, and other factors, the Czechoslovak record is very good indeed, even though Czechoslovakia still remains behind the "most advanced capitalist countries" that she strives to "outproduce." But these few comparisons with the simultaneous economic achievements in the non-communist world are designed to underline the fact, often obscured by the bombast of communist self-praise, that there are free countries capable of successfully competing with the best the communist world has to offer even in such economic sectors as enjoy top priorities behind the Iron Curtain; and that the free countries can do so without totalitarian regimentation and without imposing artificial ceilings on consumer goods production and services.

2. The reorientation of Czechoslovak production away from light industry and toward heavy industry, in particular engineering and chemical production, must be considered as another credit item on the communist industrial balance. In prewar Czechoslovakia, industrial production was weighted too much on the side of branches which

were highly vulnerable to economic depressions. Textiles, fancy glass and china ware, footwear, and gloves, which were all major items of prewar Czechoslovak exports, definitely fall into such a category. Since Czechoslovakia lost some three million inhabitants after World War II, it was all the more sensible to effect a better balance in the country's economy by concentrating more on capital goods production. Indeed, the desirability of such a reorientation was agreed upon by all the Czechoslovak parties prior to the communist seizure of power. Unfortunately, after they had assumed absolute control of the country's economy, the Communists pushed, mainly at Moscow's behest, the emphasis on heavy industry far beyond a reasonable limit; and their exaggeration in this respect must be considered as a debit item.

3. A particularly striking communist contribution to the betterment of Czechoslovak industry lies in their elimination of small-scale production and their concentration of all industrial production in larger units. By 1958 the 350,427 units engaged in industrial production proper in prewar Czechoslovakia had been reduced to a mere 1,689 of which 771 employed over 500 workers each.[33] Thus the average number of employees per enterprise has reached 1,245 as compared to 5.7 as registered by the last prewar census of 1930. A similar development has taken place in the construction industry and retail business. By 1958, the 27,588 construction firms with 297,303 employees of the prewar days have been replaced by 463 enterprises with 449,000 employees and the 263,347 retail stores and catering establishments employing a total of 557,498 persons have been simultaneously reduced to 110,522 with 409,000 employees (including the factory canteens). While the inhuman coercive class-struggle methods used to attain these results must be condemned on moral grounds, from the strictly economic point of view the replacement of small-scale manufacturing by large-scale production, more suitable for modern mass-production techniques, must be considered as a definite improvement.

4. Finally, the Czechoslovak communist planners should be commended for their endeavors to speed up the industrialization of Slovakia and thus spread the benefits of industrial growth more evenly throughout the entire country. True enough, the foundations for this development were laid prior to the communist seizure of power. The Two-Year Reconstruction Plan of 1946 included a spe-

[33] *Ročenka,* 1959, p. 137.

cific directive "to speed up the process of raising Slovakia's economic level to that of the Czech provinces."[34] But the communist regime gave the drive an additional momentum. By 1950 the percentage of the Slovak population dependent on industry rose from 14.6 percent in 1930 to 18.4 percent while the corresponding figure in the Czech provinces remained virtually stationary (33.2 percent in 1930 as against 33.3 in 1950).[35] A similar trend took place in construction and transportation. That the trend has continued into subsequent years is documented by the fact that employment in Slovak industrial production has risen by almost 70 percent between 1948 and 1959, whereas the corresponding increase for the country as a whole has been 44 percent.[36] Even more significant in this respect is the 347 percent rise in Slovak industrial production between 1948 and 1959 as compared to 233 percent for the country as a whole.[37]

Debit Items

Against the several more or less pronounced successes listed above there has been a number of failures or other untoward developments which must be put on the negative side of the communist balance sheet.

1. The lopsided emphasis on producer goods was bound to have an adverse effect in the consumer goods field. In terms of official over-all indices everything seems all right since the output of consumer goods by 1959 is claimed to have risen as much as 181 percent above 1948. Since the production of consumer goods was still some 10 per-cent or more below the prewar level by the end of the Two-Year Plan in 1948, the above-mentioned 181 percent represents at the most a rise of only about 163 percent above prewar figures. But even with this downward correction such a volume of output should suffice for a population which still remains below the prewar figure. Yet, the consumers' incessant complaints of all sorts of shortages and deficiencies belie the rosy façade of the consumer goods indices.[38]

The standard official explanation of this contradiction is that not even the greatly stepped-up output can keep pace with the rapidly

---

[34] Section i of the Plan.
[35] *Ročenka,* 1958, p. 52.
[36] Industrial employment in Slovakia rose from 212,000 in 1948 to 375,000 in 1959. *Ročenka,* 1960, p. 31. The corresponding increase for the whole of Czecho-slovakia was from 1,543,000 to 2,230,000. *ibid.,* p. 21.
[37] *ibid.,* pp. 29, 20.
[38] See Chapter xvii.

rising consumers' demand resulting from the communist policy of continually increasing wages and lowering prices. Although this explanation is partly true, to the extent to which it is true it actually amounts to an unwitting self-indictment. It is an implicit admission of an intentional disregard for the wishes and needs of the broad masses of people, which may be met only from what is left over after the voracious appetite of capital industries had been satiated. But there are other factors that help to explain why high production indices did not bring more satisfaction to the general consumer. Such absolute output figures of consumer items as have been published and can be compared with corresponding prewar levels reveal that the production of the everyday necessities of life has not generally kept pace with the rate of growth claimed for consumer goods as a whole. Thus, for instance, the output of such basic needs as textiles, clothing, and shoes rose by a mere 3 to 15 percent in the entire twenty-one year span of 1937 through 1957.[39] Although the situation improved in 1958-1959, the main production increases continue to be registered in certain branches of metal consumer goods, such as automobiles, radio and television sets, refrigerators, washing machines, and watches. However welcome and desirable the stepped-up production of such articles may be, it cannot offset the fact that twelve years of communist planning have failed to provide the citizens of Czechoslovakia with consumer goods that would be anywhere near, in quantity, assortment, quality, and price, merchandise available in the retail stores of non-communist countries of Western, Northern, and even Central Europe.[40]

2. Another major weakness of Czechoslovak industry under the communist rule lies in the poor quality of the products. Year after year, while claiming fulfillment and overfulfillment of the Economic Plan, communist spokesmen have bewailed the defective quality of many products and taken plant managers to task for turning out excessive quantities of rejects amounting in some instances to as much as 35 to 40 percent of the individual plants' total output. The losses caused by the production of rejects exceeded one billion crowns in 1953.[41] Five years later, in 1958, they still amounted to 873 million crowns (125 million dollars).[42] By communist admission, 6,000 of the 26,000 tons of coal extracted daily in 1957 in the main

[39] See table in the appendix to this chapter.
[40] See Chapter XVII.
[41] *Rudé právo*, April 16, 1954.
[42] *Život strany*, No. 16, August 1959, p. 999.

Czechoslovak mining region of Ostrava-Karvinná consisted of rock.[43] And in 1959 *Rudé právo* had to report as follows on a spot check of textiles offered for sale in retail stores: "We have found that 65 percent of the checked merchandise was deficient and should not have appeared on the market."[44]

Persistent consumers' complaints appearing in the columns of daily papers tell the same story. Offered for sale have been items such as knives which ceased cutting after having been used a few times; clothes that shrank beyond use after the first washing; locks that refused stubbornly to unlock; pencils that could not be sharpened as they always broke in the process; bicycles that lasted only one ride; razor blades that did not raze; agricultural and other machines that required costly repairs after a few days of operation; electric boilers that leaked from the very first day they were installed. One sample of such complaints may perhaps be quoted verbatim to serve as a striking illustration of what the Czechoslovak consumer has had to put up with:

"Comrade janitor has just bought nine classroom thermometers. He bought them in the National Enterprise *Chemodroga* . . . . Before distributing the thermometers among individual classrooms we hung them in one room; and we found that one thermometer showed 17 degrees Celsius, one 18, two 19 each, two 20 each, one climbed to 24, while one did not register at all because the tube was broken. Nor does their outward appearance point to good workmanship. A sheet of paper with the scale is crudely attached to a rough board by an ordinary nail. The glass tube is not placed vertically and hangs loosely so that there is danger that it will break any minute."[45]

While recurrent consumers' complaints and the regime's ever so frequent admonitions do not warrant even an approximate estimate of the economic losses due to the turnout of defective products, they leave no doubt as to the persistence of what the Minister of Finance once called "the plague of production."[46] Why this has been so lies in the very nature of the communist economic system. Pressed ever harder by steadily "strengthened" work norms, the workers display an understandable tendency to obtain the desired production volume at the expense of quality. Wherever and whenever feasible, local

[43] *Rudé právo,* August 11, 1958.
[44] *ibid.,* August 18, 1959.
[45] *Svět práce,* June 5, 1952.
[46] *Rudé právo,* April 22, 1953.

supervisors and factory managers close their eyes to such practices since they, in turn, are interested in meeting and exceeding the prescribed targets in order to stay out of trouble and earn welcome bonuses. In the sectors earmarked for special attention, such as production for export, stiff controls manage usually to secure adequate standards. But the more neglected sectors of production, especially merchandise for home consumption, suffer.

3. Besides contributing to the output of defective products, the reckless drive takes a terrific toll of the machinery and equipment. Racing against time to meet and exceed planned goals, managers and their personnel find it nearly impossible to take proper care of their tools. Often they have to run them day after day with maintenance reduced well below the safe minimum. When repairs become inevitable, hasty stop-gap repair is sometimes all that they can afford. That is particularly so toward the close of the year when many plants have to catch up with earlier production delays so that they might report the Plan's fulfillment by the year's end. Typical of the dilemma is the following complaint of a steel furnace operator: "This furnace has been working more than 10 years without repair. It deserves a general overhaul. We cannot stop it now, yet one day it will have to be stopped. But who will then produce those thousands of tons of steel before such a repair is finished?"[47]

Such abuse of machinery tends to shorten its average span of life by many years. Hence, much of the investment allocations which could have otherwise been used for the expansion of industrial capacity must be spent on mere substitution for machinery worn out prematurely by such gross neglect of adequate maintenance.[48] In the Stalin era this wasteful use of investment money was further aggravated by the notorious "gigantomania" which led the Czechoslovak Communists to invest their overstrained resources in new overambitious projects which had subsequently to be scaled down or abandoned. The most glaring example thereof has been HUKO which was begun with tremendous fanfare in 1951 as the supposedly best and biggest steel and iron plant in the whole of Europe. By 1953 the construction was abandoned, and only recently has work on it been resumed.

4. A recurrent headache for Czechoslovak planners has been the

---

[47] *Nová svoboda,* October 14, 1951. Cited after *Československý přehled,* I, 3 (1954), p. 9.

[48] Ota Karásek's article in *Československý přehled,* I, 3 (1954), pp. 4ff.

"fuel and raw materials basis" which has persistently lagged behind developments in other production sectors. The main villain has been hard coal. While impressive results could be claimed in most of the other fields of capital production, the annual output of 25 million tons, supposed to be reached as early as 1953, was attained only by 1958, i.e., five years behind the schedule. This has been especially painful for the communist rulers since coal mining, from which Czechoslovakia derives the bulk of the power turning the wheels of her industries, has been from the very beginning the center of their attention in terms of manpower recruitment, high wages, output bonuses, and other preferential treatment.[49]

5. Although the continued dearth of meaningful data makes a dependable estimate impossible, it is my belief that the results attained in labor productivity deserve listing as a debit rather than a credit item on the Czechoslovak industrial balance. The official story is one of outstanding success. According to communist statistics labor productivity in industry was more than doubled between 1948 and 1959, having risen by 149 percent in that period. Since it was claimed to be already 4 percent above the prewar level in 1948, the increase in labor productivity between 1937 and 1959 would thus amount to some 154 percent.[50] But a closer analysis of these impressive indices removes much of their outward glamor.

To begin with, it must be pointed out that the statisticians of communist Czechoslovakia have adopted the Soviet practice of computing labor productivity in man-years rather than man-hours as is customary in the non-communist world. They simply divide the estimated gross value of the annual industrial output by the average annual number of industrial workers. Hence, the longer the workday and the work week and the more "donations" of additional work hours and Sunday or holiday shifts, the higher rises the index of labor productivity, although the actual results per hour may be the same or even lower. Such a method by-passes altogether the true test of industrial efficiency, namely how much a worker can produce per hour of actual work. Furthermore, it necessarily transmits to the indices of labor productivity the upward bias caused by the well-known communist tendency of exaggerating the estimates of gross value of output. Nor is it clear what Czechoslovak statisticians do

[49] For a detailed analysis of the earlier stages of the "battle for the coal" see *News,* 3, 3 (1954), pp. 3ff.

[50] Spulber estimates the industrial output per man to have been actually three percent below 1937 in 1948. *op.cit.,* p. 387.

with the untold millions of work hours "volunteered" annually by the innumerable brigades of pupils, students, office employees, and other white-collar workers. If the value thus contributed is simply added to the dividend of the gross output without increasing proportionately the corresponding divisor of the annual average of regularly employed workers, the resulting index of labor productivity is further increased irrespective of any change in output per man-hour.

Consequently, the official Czechoslovak indices of labor productivity are of little help in answering two basic questions: (a) How much more does a Czechoslovak worker produce today *per work hour* than he did before the War? (b) How does Czechoslovak output per man-hour compare with that of the industrial countries of the non-communist world? Fortunately, at least a partial answer has been supplied by Czechoslovak communist spokesmen themselves. A recent government publication on the position of Czechoslovakia in world economy conceded that the coal output per miner per shift still lagged behind the prewar level.[51] And this has once again been confirmed in October 1959 when *Rudé právo* complained that prewar levels of productivity in coal mining would not be reached before 1962-1963![52] Similarly, while praising recent Czechoslovak advances in the volume of textile production, the above-mentioned communist publication admitted that Czechoslovakia was still "lagging behind in technical level."[53] According to my own computations, labor productivity seemed to be in 1957 below the prewar level also in steel and iron production while, by contrast, output per man-hour in U.S. steel production has been rising by about 2.6 percent annually between 1947 and 1957.[54] These are, of course, only exceptional cases and an evaluation of all the pertinent elements leaves no doubt that in most of the other fields of production not only the output per man-year but also the output per man-hour has by now risen well above the prewar level.

That this should be so is no special merit of the communist system but only a logical result of technological developments over the years. But how does Czechoslovak labor productivity stand in

[51] *Postavení*, p. 31.

[52] *Rudé právo*, October 2 and 5, 1959, *Československý zpravodaj*, No. 264, October 22, 1959.

[53] *Postavení*, p. 48.

[54] When the actual output of crude and rolled steel and pig iron of 1937 and 1957 are divided by the number of workers employed in the respective industries in the two years, the respective output figures per man are 110 for 1937 as against 109 for 1957.

comparison with that of non-communist countries of a comparable stage of industrial development? The reply to this is provided by the above-quoted official publication on Czechoslovakia's position in world economy: "The productivity of labor [in terms of man-years] grows substantially faster in Czechoslovakia than in all the other capitalist countries, the United States not excluded. But the level of *labor productivity proper* [in terms of man-hours] in Czechoslovakia remains substantially below the levels of the advanced [capitalist] countries."[55]

Thus, after twelve years of persistent promotion of industrial efficiency through a tightening of the "socialist labor discipline," an unending stream of "socialist contests," and huge sums spent on technological streamlining, as of 1960 communist Czechoslovakia continued to lag behind the advanced industrial countries of the non-communist world in genuine labor productivity as expressed in terms of output per man-hour.

6. In part, the problem of labor productivity has been aggravated by unnecessary job-hopping and an excessive absenteeism at work. "Absenteeism and job-hopping are the curse of our production," complained Zápotocký in an address before a trade union conference in 1952.[56] And the same tune with only minor variations has been played over and over again like a broken record throughout the ensuing years. Job-hopping reached its peak in 1953 when, according to official statistics, almost one-half of the industrial labor force changed jobs (459 of every thousand).[57] The adverse effect which such a disproportionate turnover had on production and productivity is self-evident. Although the situation has improved since that time, due mainly to the strengthening of various "antifluctuation" measures, job-hopping continues to pose a serious problem, especially in those production sectors where a shortage of labor is more pronounced. Thus even at its lowest point, reached in 1959 the workers' turnover amounted to 224 per thousand.[58]

---

[55] *Postavení*, p. 50. Italics added. *Prague News Letter* conceded in 1960 (Vol. 16, No. 4, February 20, 1960) that only 970 tons of pig iron were produced per worker in Czechoslovakia in 1958 whereas the corresponding figures were 1,108 in Britain in 1959 and 1,372 in France. *The Czechoslovak Statistical Yearbook of 1960* is the first in the series to mention labor productivity of industrial workers per man-hour. But it lists only the increase since 1953 and claims that it had risen 49.9 percent above 1953 by the end of 1959 (see *Ročenka*, 1960, p. 153).

[56] *Práce*, June 12, 1952.

[57] *Ročenka*, 1960, p. 154. The figure includes all those who left their jobs for any reason except death.

[58] *ibid.*

Even more damaging has been the widespread absenteeism from work. The omnipresence and persistence of this practice of evading work is amply revealed by communist announcements and statistics. Thus, almost three million work shifts were lost through unexcused absences in 1952 and an average of 200,000 workers were absent daily from work because of sickness and accidents.[59] By 1956 the daily rate of absenteeism rose to 245,000.[60] The stubbornness with which the plague of absenteeism withstands all the communist countermeasures is documented by the official statistics on the number of workdays missed per worker from 1953 to 1957. While 28.9 out of 294.4 workdays were missed in 1953, 28.3 out of 292.6 were not honored in 1957.[61] Only in 1958 did the situation improve slightly and the number of missed workdays sank to 24, which was also the rate of absenteeism in 1959.[62] As for absenteeism on account of sickness and accidents, the rate has been rising slowly but steadily from 18.9 per worker per annum in 1953 to 20.7 in 1957, but declined to 16.4 in 1958.[63] That such a high level of absenteeism, exceeding by far anything experienced in prewar days, harmed industrial production by causing delays and interruptions is a foregone conclusion. But it also contributed eventually to increased production costs. As most of those who stayed away from work did so on account of sickness, real or successfully simulated, they drew fairly high sickness benefits which had ultimately to be paid from the nationalized production.

7. The inability to achieve any meaningful reduction in production costs is another major item that rightly belongs among the debit items of the communist industrial balance. These costs have sky-rocketed since prewar days far beyond the levels caused by the over-all inflationary pressures of the postwar era. "The most serious deficiency has been nonfulfillment of the planned productivity of labor and planned reduction in production costs," bewailed *Práce* in 1955. "Rather than leading all the trade union members to overcome all the difficulties of production, the functionaries think of ways to prove that the prescribed goals of the state plan are unrealistic."[64]

The situation was worst during the First Five-Year Plan when the necessity to meet the steep production targets led to a reckless dis-

---

[59] *Rudé právo,* January 23, 1953.
[60] *Práce,* December 14, 1956.
[61] *Ročenka,* 1960, p. 153.
[62] *ibid.,* and *Hospodářské noviny,* April 1, 1960.
[63] *Ročenka,* 1960, p. 153.
[64] *Práce,* March 26, 1955.

regard for the costs of production. Thus, for instance, in the course of the First Five-Year Plan production costs in hard-coal mining rose admittedly by 39.4 percent.[65] While the much-pampered coal industry was probably the worst offender, wastefulness was a general hallmark of Czechoslovakia's economy under the first long-term plan. In recent years the stepped-up emphasis on more economical production seems to have brought some improvement, as Table IV would indicate.

TABLE IV
Reduction in Industrial Production Costs
(percentage below preceding year)

1955	1956	1957	1960	1961-1965 (Plan)
5	0.3	2.5	2.2	2.63 (per annum)

Source: *Economic Survey of Europe in 1957*, Chap. I, p. 111; *Rudé právo*, November 17, 1960, and February 8, 1961.

To what extent these claims represent a genuine reduction of costs cannot be reliably determined. But recurrent communist lamentations about the continued high costs of production and bits of information gleaned from various other sources suggest that the above figures are more artificial than real. This is further indicated by the rather small gap between the 1949-1957 rates of growth of industrial production and the total wage bill, 170 and 146 percent respectively, especially if the notorious upward bias built into communist production indices is taken into consideration.[66] Matters would be even worse were it not for the many millions of unpaid hours of "brigade" and other work which the citizens of Czechoslovakia are made to contribute annually to the socialist construction.[67]

The reasons behind the communist failure to reduce industrial production costs to reasonable levels are several. As shown on preceding pages, the disagreeable consequences of a failure to fulfill planned targets are often avoided by hasty work detrimental to quality, by excessive and uneconomical use of manpower, abuse of machinery, and waste of fuels and raw materials—all of which necessarily increase the costs of production. So does the eagerness of factory managers to avoid delays by securing the much-needed materials, hard-to-get spare parts, and tool replacements through various under-

[65] *News*, 3, 3 (1954), p. 6.
[66] The wage factor was calculated by multiplying the average wage in industry by the number of employees for 1948 and 1957 respectively.
[67] See Chapter XVII.

hand methods involving even graft, which must then be hidden in production-cost calculations. Occasionally, the regime itself pushes the costs up when it seeks to step up the output in certain important areas, such as mining, by granting economically unwarranted wage increases and bonuses.

8. This trend toward uneconomical procedures has been further enhanced by the bureaucratization which constitutes an ever-present threat to any government-operated economy, but finds an especially fertile ground in a totalitarian system. The imperative need for an elaborate machinery of multiple checks and controls throughout the top-heavy industrial apparatus tends to create an altogether excessive number of nonproductive administrative and supervisory functions. So does the well-nigh irresistible urge to provide enough soft jobs for deserving Party members, a vice which is especially hard to combat where genuine freedom of public criticism is seriously curtailed. The inevitable result has been what the Party's theoretical journal, *Tvorba,* calls rather euphemistically "an unfavorable development" in the ratio of workers-at-the-bench to employees in other categories.[68] While there were 4-5 workers for each nonworker employee in 1948, the ratio became 3-4 and the prewar ratio of one technical or administrative employee for each 4 workers in engineering sank to 2.9 in 1956.[69] As revealed by the *Czechoslovak Statistical Yearbook* for 1958 the ratio of workers to employees of nonworker categories in the industry as a whole stood at less than 3:1 by 1957. And that does not include the personnel of the overgrown state apparatus who, in the last analysis, live off the production of national enterprises although they do not draw their salaries directly from the wage funds of the individual factories. Some improvement has recently taken place in this respect through the reorganization and simplification measures adopted in 1957-1959 whereby certain smaller units were merged and more authority delegated from the economic ministries to plant managements and local government units.[70] Nonetheless, as revealed in the above-quoted article in *Tvorba,* the basic problem has not thereby been solved.

The overbureaucratization of Czechoslovak industry, as well as managements' and workers' indifference to the ultimate disposition of merchandise they produce, contributes to the rise in production

---

[68] *Tvorba,* February 13, 1958.
[69] *ibid.*
[70] See Chapter x.

costs also by encouraging various costly malpractices connected with labor discipline. This is particularly reflected in persistent cheating in work norms. The understandable desire of workers, managers, and foremen responsible for their work is to keep work norms as low as possible so that they can be easily exceeded. Thus a whole array of more or less ingenious devices is continually contrived to frustrate the regime's untiring efforts to strengthen the norms. "It is a frequent phenomenon," complains an official communist study of the planned economy, "that the plan is fulfilled only by 80 to 90 percent while the work norms are exceeded by 150 to 200 percent."[71] How this is done is well illustrated by a typical case reported by a communist correspondent who asked the foreman at a construction site why his workers were pushing carts loaded with dug-out dirt upward and the empty carts downward, although the opposite was feasible: "The answer was grotesque: When workers push the load upward, they earn more according to the norms. So we have arranged it this way."[72]

The adverse effects of such collusive feather-bedding, which assumes an infinite variety of forms throughout the whole nationalized industry, are further worsened by pilfering and other acts of defrauding the socialist economy. As shown elsewhere in this volume, economic crimes of this kind overcrowd the dockets of the people's courts.[73] Economic losses resulting from such widespread stealing are bound to push production costs upward, especially if they are added to the economic waste caused by the negligence which seems to flourish in Czechoslovakia's economy.

Thus, viewed strictly in economic terms, the over-all balance of Czechoslovak industry after twelve years of the dictatorship of the proletariat reveals both successes and failures. The successes are represented mainly by the high output levels of the capital goods sector and its greatly expanded productive capacity resulting from high investments and concentration on large-scale production. The failures lie primarily in the high production costs, a questionable rate of growth in man-hour output, and quality deficiencies in many, though not all, sectors. A comparison with corresponding develop-

[71] Jiří Řezníček, *Organisace plánování v ČSR* (The Organization of Planning in the Czechoslovakia Republic), Praha, 1956, p. 45; also, *Rudé právo*, June 3, 1956, and *Práce*, August 17, 1956. For work norms as weapons of regimentation, see Chapter XVII.

[72] *Rudé právo*, March 23, 1955.

[73] Chapter XII.

TABLE V
Output of Selected Industrial Goods, 1937-1965

Type of Goods	Unit	1937	1948	1953	1958	1959	1960 Plan	1960 Actual	1965 Plan
PRODUCER GOODS									
Hard coal	million tons	16.7	17.7	20.3	25.8	26.5 }	93.8	29.8	31.4
Brown coal	" "	18.4	22.6	32.8	54.3	51.1 }		55.5	70.2
Hard coal coke[a]	" "	3.3	4.3	6.5	7.4	7.9	8.2		11.6
Iron ore	" "	1.8	1.4	2.3	2.8	3.0		3.1	4.4
Pig iron	" "	1.7	1.6	2.8	3.8	4.2		4.7	7.7
Crude steel	" "	2.3	2.6	4.4	5.5	6.1	6.8	6.8	10.6
Rolled steel[b]	" "	1.6	1.8	2.7	3.8	4.0	4.6	4.5	7.3
Cement	" "	1.3	1.7	2.3	4.1	4.7	4.7	5.0	8.7
Electricity	billion kw-hr	4.1	7.5	12.4	19.6	21.9	24.2	24.4	39
Nitrogenous fertilizers	thousand tons t/N	24.5	29.4	35.4	108.0	133.0	141.0	140.0	320.0
Phosphorous fertilizers	thousand tons t/P_2O_5	58.5	54.3	66.8	117.4	135.0	157.0	147.0	285.0
Sulphuric acid	thousand tons	165.0	215.0	311.0	463.0	513.0		553	
Paper	" "	246.0	260.0	310.0	404.0	429.0	433.0	443.0	595.0
Trucks	thousands	2.0	7.2	11.4	9.6	11.5	15.8	16	19
Tractors	"	0.2	9.1	6.5	24.6	29.2	28.3	32	43.1
Railway wagons (freight)	"	1.4	5.4	6.1	5.4	4.7			
Bricks	billions	1.13	0.92	1.21	2.2	2.4	2.4	2.5	3
CONSUMER GOODS									
Fabrics	million meters								
Woolen	" "	33	42	40	43	45	453	45	52.0
Cotton	" "	365	264	331	403	424		445	492
Linen and half linen	" "	38.7	34	51	62	64		67	
Silk	" "	35	26	43	56	61		65	80.8
Footwear	million pairs								
Leather	" "	55 }	28	23	34	39 }		44 }	
Rubber	" "		26	26	34	36 }	76.1	38 }	101
Other	" "			8	12	12 }			
Suits and dresses	millions		7.9	24	24	26		31	35
Socks and stockings	"			66	76	75			
Knitted underwear	"		17	28	34	36		40 }	
Knitted outerwear	"			24	36	41		}	101
Automobiles	thousands	12.6	18	7.3	43.4	51	56	56	113
Motorcycles	"	14	68	46	146	151		160	
Bicycles	"	208	231	259	316	295			
Cameras	"		23.4	65	147	142			
Electric washers	"		2.1	40	313	296			
Sewing machines	"			67	109	135		217.5	236
Vacuum cleaners	"			30	189	176			
Radios	"	144	268	182	303	280		243	330
Television sets	"			12	134	197		283	410
Refrigerators	"			8	80	104	130	132	265
Cigarettes	billions	12	13	16.2	17.7	17.6			
Meat (except horse meat)	thousand tons	353	163	335	415	413	458	440	583
Canned meat	" "			12	13	14		13	

(table continues)

TABLE V
Output of Selected Industrial Goods, 1937-1965 (*concluded*)

Type of Goods	Unit		1937	1948	1953	1958	1959	1960 Plan	1960 Actual	1965 Plan
			CONSUMER GOODS							
Meat products	"	"			139	173	183		191	
Poultry	"	"			6	14	18		22	
Refined sugar	"	"	630	517	657	856	723	897	881	1,222
Butter (factory production)	"	"	14.3	22.9	35.3	58.1	55.4	70	58	81
Cheese (factory production)	"	"	8.4	12.9	18	38.6	43		41	
Vegetables	"	"			71					
Wheat flour	"	"	621ᶜ	589	922	935	1,018		1,094	
Bread	"	"			1,021	940	960			
Chocolate and chocolate products	"	"			17	19	18			
Margarine	"	"		62.8	66	55	52			
Soap	"	"			44	43	44			
Milk	thousand tons			23		58	55			
Beer	million hl.		8.3	8.2	11	12.6	13.6			

ᵃ With 6 percent moisture until 1956, with actual content of water since 1957; ᵇ without pipes;
ᶜ 1936.
Sources: *Czechoslovak Yearbooks of Statistics* and official announcements on the Plan fulfillment.

ments in the industrial countries of non-communist Europe yields a similarly mixed pattern. Czechoslovakia has certainly done as well, or better, in some industrial aspects, but not so well in others. However, this comparison with non-communist countries which are at a similar stage of industrial development shows quite unmistakably that high levels of industrial output, even in capital goods, can be attained without the penalty of a drastic regimentation of men's lives such as has accompanied the forced industrialization pace of communist Czechoslovakia.

CHAPTER XVI
THE AGRICULTURAL DEMISE

AGRICULTURE has been the soft underbelly of the communist economy, and the individual peasant one of its leading villains. Both Marx and Lenin considered the peasant to be too backward to grasp the meaning of their doctrine. Neither had room for the individual farmer in the social fabric of the communist utopia. As Lenin frankly admitted, whatever concessions he made to the peasantry were only temporary expedients dictated by tactical postulates of the revolution. As soon as his successor Joseph Stalin felt strong enough in the saddle, he rode roughshod over the peasantry and forced them into *kolkhozes.* And in his last ideological pronouncement, *The Economic Problems of Socialism in the USSR,* the Soviet Dictator openly proclaimed his intention of liquidating eventually even the collective farmers by transforming them into full-fledged agricultural workers.[1]

Although the post-Stalin New Course with its gestures of leniency addressed particularly to agriculture granted the peasants a welcome respite, the emergence of Nikita Khrushchëv as the number-one Communist of the Soviet Union augured nothing good in that respect. It was Khrushchëv who, in the early fifties, had advocated merging collective farms into *agrogorods,* agricultural cities, thus transforming collective farmers into hired laborers and depriving them of their last remnant of personal landholding, their small individual household plots. That the new Soviet ruler has by no means abandoned the idea has been reaffirmed in his official report to the Twenty-first Congress of the Soviet Communist Party in January 1959. Among the changes to be effected in the course of the transition from socialism to communism he listed an eventual fusion of the "collective, cooperative, and state forms of ownership" into "a single communist ownership," thereby solving "the deep problem of overcoming the difference between the town and the country."[2] Since Khrushchëv's ideological precepts are considered by the communist rulers of Czecho-

---

[1] English text in Leo Gruliow, *Current Soviet Policies,* New York, 1953, pp. 18ff.

[2] *Pravda* (Moscow), January 28, 1959.

slovakia just as binding as Stalin's had been, the eventual liquidation of the Czechoslovak peasantry as a class is an integral part of the long-term political plans of the KSČ.[3] The ominous reference to the "overcoming of substantial differences between physical and mental work and between the town and the country" in the new Czechoslovak Constitution of 1960 points unerringly in the same direction.

It is this gloomy background of the forthcoming doom that lends all the elements of live tragedy to the uneven struggle which has been going on between the Czechoslovak peasantry and its communist superiors ever since 1948, and indeed even since 1945. Or, rather than calling it a struggle, a more fitting word would be a chase, a chase in which the communist regime represents the well-armed stalking hunter and the peasantry the hunted deer.

Prewar Background

It is customary for communist propagandists to shed tears over the fate of the Eastern European peasantry under "capitalist" rule. The blackest colors are used to paint a crude picture of rich landowners ruthlessly exploiting poor peasants, depriving them of their measly livelihood by auctioning off their small-holdings for nonpayment of debts at a fraction of their real value. These and other wicked deeds are perpetrated with the obliging cooperation of the heartless *gendarmerie* and other media of enforcement at the disposal of the bourgeois-capitalist landlords. While it would go beyond the scope of the present study to inquire into the validity of such assertions with regard to other countries of Eastern Europe, they must be emphatically rejected insofar as they refer to Czechoslovakia. Everything had not been rosy in Czechoslovak agriculture between the two World Wars; the peasant's life was one of hard work and lacked many amenities; there was certainly room for improvement in many respects. Nonetheless, the agricultural attainments of prewar Czechoslovakia and the standard of her peasants ranked high above those of the rest of Eastern Europe and corresponded, on the whole, to a

[3] In his speech before the Eleventh Party Congress Novotný rejected "the opinions of some comrades" suggesting "mergers of collective farms and creation of great villages" as unnecessary. While this may reflect the Party's attitude now and for the nearest future, it can hardly be doubted that the Czechoslovak collective farms will be "elevated" to the "higher form of socialized property" when the situation therefor will be considered ripe. His 1958 assurances notwithstanding, Novotný in November 1959 proposed further merging of' collective farms into bigger units. *Rudé právo,* November 13, 1959.

good European average. A quick glance at a few pertinent data will bear this out.

The Czechoslovak agricultural output per capita was 15 percent higher and the output per hectare 29 percent higher than the European average and even higher than the average of other countries of Eastern Europe.[4] In net agricultural production per person dependent on agriculture (including forestry and fishing) Czechoslovakia, with an index of 96, approximated the European average (100) while, again, all the other East European countries that have subsequently fallen to communism lagged far behind, with figures ranging from 76 for Hungary to 50 for Poland and a mere 38 for Albania.[5] A similar pattern prevailed in yields per hectare of the principal crops of the area, such as wheat, rye, barley, oats, sugar beets, and potatoes. In each and every one of them Czechoslovakia was well ahead of all the other Eastern European countries, and even ahead of France, although trailing somewhat neighboring Germany, mainly because of lower yields in the less developed easternmost parts of the country.[6] Consequently, while all the other Eastern European nations with 51 to 80 percent of their population dependent on agriculture were debited with an agricultural overpopulation ranging from 22.4 to 77.7 percent, Czechoslovakia with only 33-34 percent of her population deriving livelihood from agriculture registered only an estimated 4.7 percent excess in this respect.

These few selected figures suffice to show that, unlike the rest of the present Soviet satellites, Czechoslovakia could by no means be considered agriculturally backward when measured by prewar European averages. Moreover, Czechoslovak agricultural lag in productivity behind the more highly developed farming of Western Europe was caused to a considerable extent by a measure which was psychologically and politically necessary and socially justified: namely, the splitting up of large land properties and their distribution among the landless peasants and small-holders. Subjecting to expropriation, with some exceptions, all estates exceeding 150 hectares (375 acres) of agricultural land or 250 hectares (625 acres) of any land, and distributing most of the arable land thus acquired among almost 650,000 new owners, the Czechoslovak land reform of 1919-1920

---

[4] N. E. Moore, *Economic Demography of Eastern and Southern Europe,* Geneva, 1945, p. 35. Figures are for the 1931-1935 average.

[5] *ibid.,* p. 51.

[6] Averages for 1932-1936. See *Annuaire International de Statistique Agricole,* Rome, 1937.

went a long way toward satisfying "the hunger for land" of the landless and quasi-landless peasants and gave virtually every one of them the opportunity to obtain at least the minimum of land necessary for his family's subsistence. As a result, Czechoslovakia became predominantly a country of small-sized family farms of up to 10 hectares (86.6 percent of all farms), although larger farms of over 50 hectares (0.9 percent of all farms) comprised over 19 percent of all agricultural land and over 13 percent of all arable land as of 1930.[7]

However, the breaking up of so many large estates necessarily retarded the modernization and mechanization of a substantial part of Czechoslovak agricultural production. Although this did not prevent the country from keeping well ahead of the general agricultural backwardness of Eastern Europe, it certainly impaired its agricultural efficiency in comparison with the better developed agriculture of Western and Northern Europe. On the other hand, the land reform helped to ward off the danger of social radicalism among the poorer strata of the rural population and contributed thus to the social and political stability of the reborn country. The political gains were well worth the price paid in retarded productivity. The peasant felt that the government cared about him and his problems. The communist propagandists, who began to descend upon the villages in the early twenties in an endeavor to secure the support of the small and medium peasants in the well-known Leninist pattern, met with failure. To be sure, all rural poverty was not done away with through the land reform. There continued to exist, particularly in the mountainous areas of Slovakia and Ruthenia, poor rural families subsisting largely on a daily diet of potatoes. There were in almost every rural community a few people whose own holdings alone could not provide them a sufficient livelihood and who, therefore, had to supplement their income by helping their more prosperous neighbors, and this for very meager rewards, mostly in kind. But even among this very small minority—only 7.6 percent of agricultural holdings were two hectares or less—there was relatively little mood for communism.

Thus the average Czechoslovak peasant of prewar days was a rather conservative creature, wary of innovations and suspicious of "isms." He was a rugged individualist endowed with a strong posses-

[7] *Ročenka*, 1937, p. 53. For further details about the 1919-1920 land reform see Robert J. Kerner, *et al.*, Czechoslovakia, Berkeley, 1940, pp. 219ff., and A. Rozehnal, *Land Reforms in Czechoslovakia*, a mimeographed paper published by the Free Europe Committee, New York, 1953.

sive mentality and an attachment to private ownership. While he was not opposed to joining cooperatives for specific, strictly delimited purposes, such as credit and warehouse cooperatives, he had little liking for producers' cooperatives.[8] He lived in a small but usually well-kept stucco house. Across his backyard he had a wooden barn and sheds for tools and domestic animals. Nearby he had his compost and manure, often uncomfortably close to his water well. His daily diet was plain, based as it was mostly on potatoes, homemade rye bread, milk, butter, eggs, several kinds of pastries, home-grown vegetables and fruits, and occasional poultry, fish, or game. Meat was not eaten regularly in most peasant families, but after the customary annual slaughtering of the pig there was a real feast of homemade sausages, smoked ham, and other pork delicacies which the Czechoslovak peasants were expert in turning out on such occasions. Their wardrobe, too, was relatively simple. Besides sturdy clothing for work, patched and repatched to make it last as long as possible, they had good quality, though not too well-tailored, "Sunday clothes" kept in impeccable condition for long years and worn only on Sunday or other special occasions.

Yet, behind this plain appearance, which was at times mistaken by superficial observers for inadequacy of means or even poverty, one could often discover men of property. Not infrequently, these shabby looking peasants had substantial bank accounts or sizable amounts of cash hidden at the bottom of their hand-painted wooden chests, for the average Czechoslovak peasant was an extremely thrifty person. Rather than spend his money on fancy foods or clothing, he preferred to save it and use it later to buy additional land or more cows, to provide his daughter with a better dowry so that she might get a wealthier husband, or to compensate the younger sons for his leaving the farm to the eldest. His main ambition was to make his farm more profitable, to enlarge and improve it. That was also, he knew, the best way to enhance his standing in the community and his prestige among his fellow-farmers.

Politically, the Czechoslovak peasants and their interests were represented by several parties. In the western half of the country their main spokesman was the Republican Party of the Farmers and Smallholders, usually referred to as the Czechoslovak Agrarian Party. After

[8] Of the total number of over 12,000 agricultural cooperatives that existed in Czechoslovakia in 1938, virtually none pursued joint cultivation of the land. For further information see Ladislav Feierabend, *Agricultural Cooperatives in Czechoslovakia,* New York, 1952.

the drastic weakening of the Social Democratic Party following the communist secession of 1920-1921, the Czechoslovak Agrarian Party came out of each and every election as the country's strongest party. It held consistently the Ministry of Agriculture and, except for a few instances, also the Premiership. Although the Agrarian Party was frequently criticized by its opponents for supporting the interests of the bigger landowners rather than those of the smaller peasants, such criticisms, valid or not, did not seem to weaken in any notable way its electoral appeal among the farmers, rich or poor. Hence, it can be said that the average prewar Czechoslovak peasant considered his interests to be reasonably well attended to by the Agrarian Party. In case he was not satisfied he had, furthermore, a suitable alternative in the Czechoslovak Catholic People's Party. Although this Party sought and found support also among the Catholic population in urban areas, it had to depend quite considerably on rural votes. The Slovak peasants gave their solid backing to the Slovak People's Party and they, too, were reasonably well satisfied with the way in which this Party took care of their interests. Similarly, the German- and Hungarian-speaking peasants of prewar Czechoslovakia had their own agrarian parties to represent them.

Thus, contrary to what the present KSČ leaders want to make them believe, the peasants of prewar Czechoslovakia enjoyed ample political representation and felt, on the whole, well pleased with the manner in which their interests were taken care of. Conditions in Czechoslovakia differed in that respect from those in some of the other countries of Eastern Europe where parties representing the peasants were gradually excluded from power and reduced to impotence with the emergence of dictatorial regimes in those areas. In Czechoslovakia there was actually what might be called an overrepresentation of agrarian interests, not dissimilar in its political impact (though not in form) to that known in United States politics. When depression hit in the thirties the Czechoslovak government sought to help the farmers by enacting a Czechoslovak AAA program of acreage limitation and government purchases of grain at fixed prices. Moreover, Czechoslovak tariff policy was largely governed by the farmers' interests, although oftentimes such an attitude hurt Czechoslovak industry.

This brief review of the conditions of Czechoslovak agriculture and the status of the peasantry before World War II makes it sufficiently clear why the Czechoslovak peasant longed for communism as little as for a bear's embrace.

The 1945-1948 Intermezzo

The KSČ leaders were well aware of the dearth of sympathy for communism among the Czechoslovak peasants. They knew that it was beyond their capabilities to make Czechoslovakia's farmers accept willingly any form of collectivization, no matter how much sugar-coating would sweeten it. Yet, according to Leninist teaching and the Kremlin's directives, they were supposed to gain the cooperation of the small and medium peasants at the preparatory stage of the revolution planned by the Kremlin's staffers for the first postwar years. Hence, they resorted to a weapon ever ready in the communist arsenal for that purpose: pretense and deception. While the communist-sponsored Košice Program in April 1945 spoke of "a state direction" of banking, key industrial enterprises, the insurance business, natural resources, and sources of energy, it refrained with meticulous care from suggesting a similar possibility for any sector of agriculture. Quite to the contrary, it declared categorically that the land confiscated from the Sudeten Germans and native collaborators with the Nazis would be distributed among small and medium farmers and agricultural laborers, and that the price they would be expected to pay for it would not exceed the equivalent of an average yield of one or two annual crops. Only in one oblique reference did the Košice Program mention cooperatives, and this for the sole purpose of using the confiscated buildings and inventory.[9]

The stand taken by Gottwald and his associates in 1945 was well in line with the over-all communist strategy at that time. All over the world, save in the Soviet Union proper, native communist leaders donned the robes of benevolent "agrarian reformers" and posed not only as staunch advocates of the peasants' private ownership of the land, but also as generous Santa Clauses distributing land right and left wherever there occurred the opportunity of doing so. "The land belongs to those who till it." In innumerable variations this and similar slogans were spread in every country earmarked for communist conquest by all the communications media at the Communists' disposal. And to add to the persuasiveness of their assertions, communist leaders went on record with crystal-clear pronouncements stating that no *kolkhozes* were intended, planned or desired by them, that conditions in Russia were different and what had worked all right in the

[9] See *Program prvé domácí vlády Čechů a Slováků* (The Program of the First Government of Czechs and Slovaks on Native Soil), Košice, 1945.

Soviet Union would not work outside Russia. Communist newspapers and magazines of 1945-1946 are replete with such assurances.

That these communist abjurations of any thought of collectivizing Czechoslovak agricultures were only temporary stratagems was subsequently shown not only by communist deeds when they seized power, but also by their own admissions. Said the leading KSČ agricultural expert, J. Koťátko, addressing the meeting of the association of Czechoslovak journalists in March 1949: "In Czechoslovakia land reform preceded a change-over to social forms of [agricultural] production because otherwise the support of the peasants would not have been gained for the working class during the February events [of 1948]."[10]

Indeed, the Czechoslovak communist leaders returned to Czechoslovakia from Moscow in 1945 well prepared to make the best of their disguise as agrarian reformers. In the very first Czechoslovak Cabinet to govern again on Czechoslovak soil they secured for the Party the Ministries of Interior and Agriculture which were to play a key part in their early agricultural policies based primarily on the distribution of land confiscated from the expelled Germans and the native "traitors." Both these ministries, headed by two rigidly disciplined Old Guard Communists, V. Nosek and J. Ďuriš, and staffed by dependable Party members in all key positions, were in fact converted into agencies of the Central Secretariat of the KSČ, carrying to the letter the Party's directives. And so were the local people's committees and farmers' commissions which were to help these ministries in matters of land confiscation and allocation.

The results of this communist stranglehold over agriculture were soon apparent. With almost one and one-quarter million hectares of cultivable land confiscated, there was abundant acreage to be distributed; however, fertility and other factors affecting the value of the land earmarked for distribution varied greatly. And applicants quickly found out that the one document necessary for securing a better allotment was a membership card in the Communist Party—a requirement true also, to a great extent, for allocations of fertilizers or for priorities in purchases of tools and other agricultural supplies, all of which were almost impossible to obtain without official authorization. The peasants' dependence on the good graces of the KSČ was further enhanced by the catastrophic drought of 1947. To compensate peasants for the huge losses sustained through the drought the Communists called for

[10] Quoted from Dana A. Schmidt, *Anatomy of a Satellite,* Boston, 1952, p. 406.

a so-called "millionaire tax." Under the demagogical slogan "Let the millionaires pay for the drouth" they proposed a one-time capital levy on all properties valued at or above one million crowns (50,000 dollars at the then official rate of exchange). Simultaneously, they launched with great ado a campaign for a further splitting up of land properties exceeding 50 hectares.[11]

In making such a proposal at a time when the drought pushed agricultural production into a quandary, the KSČ leaders knew perfectly well that nothing but more economic harm could come from the adoption of this third land reform. Moreover, abundant land for distribution was still available from the land property confiscated in 1945, and much of it still lay fallow because there were not enough people to settle it. The economic unsoundness of their proposals did not bother them, however, for their motive was to improve the communist chances by creating more mutual envy, fear, and uncertainty, and thus to undo whatever stabilization had been brought about in 1946. At the same time, by breaking up the remaining larger private estates among small-holders who could not afford modern agricultural machinery, the communist leaders were in fact laying a foundation for the collectivization which they planned to consummate later.

Both these communist strategems, the millionaire tax and the third land reform, were resolutely opposed by the democratic parties. On the first count, the democratic parties won and the millionaire tax failed to materialize. But on the second point, which was politically far more important, they sustained defeat. By the slimmest possible margin of one vote, achieved thanks to the ill-advised support of the communist attitude by the Social Democrats, the Communists pushed their bill through the parliamentary agricultural committee and got it enacted in July 1947. Since the carrying out of the new Act was entrusted to the communist-dominated Ministry of Agriculture, yet another potent weapon was added to the communist arsenal of political and economic intimidation which they used to their utmost advantage in paving the way for their victory in February 1948.

AGRICULTURAL POLICIES UNDER THE DICTATORSHIP OF THE PROLETARIAT

For those conversant with Marxism-Leninism and its practice in the Soviet Union there was no doubt as to what the February coup meant for Czechoslovak agriculture. The Czechoslovak peasant knew

[11] See Hubert Ripka, *Le coup de Prague,* Paris, 1949.

next to nothing about communist theories and very little about their application in the USSR. But the many bitter pills which the communist chiefs had made him swallow since 1945 left no room for any illusions. While a great many factory workers, misled as they were by lofty communist promises, hailed the February Revolution as the beginning of a better era, the peasantry received the news with sullen despondency. The officially decreed jubilation over "the people's victory" contrasted strangely with the glum silence of the Czech and Slovak peasantry, and the shrill hilarity of the communist agitators found no echo throughout the countryside.

No immediate change came, however, in the wake of the February coup. On the contrary, in the first months after the coup the KSČ leaders were doing their best to assure the peasants that any idea of collectivizing agriculture was utterly alien to them, at least with regard to properties of less than 50 hectares. "We want the new Constitution specifically to provide that private ownership of land is constitutionally guaranteed to those who work on it," said Gottwald, addressing the congress of peasants' commissions on February 28, 1948. "That will once and for all stop the idle chatter that someone wants to establish *kolkhozes* in our villages."[12] In another speech, delivered on the following day, he was even more outspoken: "We want no one to spread the lie that we shall make *kolkhozes* here. Remember that he who comes to your village with such rumors, is a saboteur . . . ."[13] In pursuance of these categorical assertions the Ninth-of-May Constitution declared that "the economic system of the Czechoslovak Republic rests . . . on the ownership of the land in accordance with the principle, the land belongs to those who till it." While limiting to 50 hectares the maximum area of land "which may be held in private ownership by individual or joint owners or by a family working together," the Constitution expressly guaranteed "the private ownership of land, up to the limit of 50 hectares, to farmers who till the land in person."

However, the respite granted the peasantry in 1948 proved to be only a calm before the storm, mainly for two reasons: First, the regime had to concentrate primarily on establishing and consolidating its control over the administration, the Armed Forces, and industry. Second, it was vitally concerned with obtaining the best possible yields

---

[12] Klement Gottwald, *Kupředu, zpátky ni krok* (Forward, Not One Step Back), Praha, 1948, p. 49.
[13] *ibid.*, p. 57.

from the 1948 harvest in order to remedy the failures of the dry year of 1947. Hence, it was desirable to disturb the peasants as little as possible. As soon as the crops were safely in and the communist leaders felt firmly in the saddle, the truce was off. At the session of the Party's Central Committee in November 1948 the steam roller which was ultimately to flatten the peasantry as a class and to effect a hundred percent collectivization of agriculture was set into motion. Advancing at an uneven pace, at first very slowly, often pausing and zigzagging, it gained speed in 1951 and 1952. Soon after Stalin's death it came to a temporary halt and even backed a little, in response to the tactical needs of the post-Stalinist New Course. But it resumed its forward rolling again in 1955 and has since then been pushed with ever-growing vigor toward the desired goal of total collectivization.

The "gaining of the village for socialism" has implied two main and mutually complementary elements: (1) the destruction of the *kulak,* and (2) the gradual collectivization and reorganization of agriculture along the Soviet pattern.

The Destruction of the Kulak

Together with the factory owner the *kulak,* the "village rich," has been in the forefront of the communist gallery of rogues. Wherever the Communists had seized power, they promptly unleashed an all-out offensive against the better-off peasants. Learn "to come to an agreement with the middle peasant," Lenin bade his comrades in November 1918, "while not for a moment renouncing the struggle against the *kulak* and at the same time firmly relying solely on the poor peasant."[14] In deference to this Leninist precept the KSČ leaders began their anti-*kulak* campaign even prior to the February coup. When they embarked on their drive for a further limitation of landholding to a maximum of 50 hectares in 1947, they supported it by brutal attacks upon the "village capitalists" whom they accused of sabotaging the Two-Year Plan, black-marketeering in foodstuffs, and failing to meet their delivery quotas.[15]

After the communist seizure of power the anti-*kulak* campaign was intensified and soon became the major plank in the ferocious class struggle designed to liquidate the enemies of communism and make

[14] V. I. Lenin, *Selected Works,* English Edition, London, 1943, viii, p. 150; quoted also in *History of the Communist Party of the Bolsheviks, Short Course,* 1939 edition, pp. 233-234.

[15] See, for instance, *Černá kniha kapitalistického hospodaření před únorem* (The Black Book of Capitalist Economy prior to February), Praha, 1948.

Czechoslovakia into a Marxist-Leninist "classless" state. "Saboteurs of national economy," "faithful companions and helpers of American imperialists and incendiaries," "repugnant leeches," "implacable enemies of socialism," "bloodthirsty vampires," "exploiters and hatchers of treacherous intrigues"—these are just a few specimens of abuse heaped upon the unfortunate village rich by the communist spokesmen through all the media at their disposal. Not even the New Course touch of leniency toward the peasants in 1953 and 1954 brought any real respite to the *kulaks*. "A *kulak* sits like a louse in your fur coat," Antonín Novotný, in a 1954 harvest-time speech, summarized the Party's attitude.[16] And in the summer of 1955 an editorial in *Rudé právo,* appropriately entitled "To Detect, Restrain, and Suppress *Kulaks,*" ordered Party members "to look thoroughly for *kulaks* in every village, unmask them as exploiters and expose them as enemies of the working people."[17] As a result of this stepped-up anti-*kulak* drive, befitting the recrudescence of neo-Stalinism after the brief post-Stalin thaw, Novotný could inform the Eleventh Party Congress in June 1958 that the amount of arable land still left in *kulak* hands sank from 14.1 percent to 1.6 percent in the previous six years; and he could confidently predict that a "consistent continuation of this policy [of restricting and suppressing the *kulaks*] will lead in a foreseeable time to the liquidation of the *kulaks* as a class."[18]

While the *kulak* came in handy as a fitting scapegoat for communist bungling in agriculture, and anti-*kulakism* served the regime's divide-and-conquer strategy in the countryside, the primary reason behind this exterminatory process lay elsewhere. As mentioned previously, a typical Czechoslovak peasant, whether he owned 50 hectares or much less than that, took good care of his property, put in a lot of hard work, and was generally successful in his ventures. If allowed to remain outside the collective farms, he would be a dangerous living example of peasant independence. Moreover, as he himself tilled the land which he owned, worked as hard as, and dressed in the same manner as, the poorer peasants, the odious label of "capitalist" could not be pinned on him as easily as on factory owners. On the other hand, if forced into the collective farm, the *kulaks,* being the ablest and most experienced farmers, would have in many instances gained prestige and the confidence of their fellow-members. Remaining at

[16] *News,* 3, 4 (1954), p. 54.
[17] *Rudé právo,* August 4, 1955.
[18] *ibid.,* June 19, 1958.

heart bitter enemies of communism and collectivization, they would have been able to work against communism even more efficiently from within the *kolkhozes* than from without. "A *kulak* within the JZD [Unified Agricultural Cooperative] is an even greater enemy than the *kulak* without the JZD," announced the Party's theoretical journal, *Nová mysl,* in 1954.[19] Hence, the *kulak* could be permitted neither to stay in business on his own nor to become a member of the collective farm, but had to be totally annihilated.

This ideological and practical need of the speediest possible liquidation of the *kulaks* gave birth to the dilemma: Who was and who was not a *kulak?* How could a *kulak* be distinguished from *středňák,* the middle peasant, a moderately well-off farmer? Such a differentiation was of basic importance in the early years of the dictatorship of the proletariat. As Marxism-Leninism prescribes, the *kulaks* are to be liquidated at the initial stage of the socialist construction, whereas the middle peasants are to be gained for cooperation and persuaded to join the collective farms. "To confuse *sredniaks* with *kulaks,*" ruled the Bolshevik Party Congress in 1919, "to apply to them in any extent the measures which are directed against *kulakism,* means to violate in the most flagrant fashion not only all the decrees of the Soviet government and its entire policy, but all the basic principles of communism . . . ."[20]

Aware of the fate awaiting a Party member who would "violate in most flagrant fashion" the basic principles of communism, and confronted with the problem which the Russian comrades had faced thirty years earlier, the Czechoslovak Communists were hard put to devise a dependable definition which would prevent confusing the *středňáks* with the *kulaks.* Pestered repeatedly by their rank and file with requests for proper directives on how to separate the wolves from the lambs, the Czechoslovak Party leaders again and again had to indulge in semantic acrobatics. As early as May 14, 1950, *Rudé právo* sought to answer the frequent inquiries of its readers on who ought to be considered as village rich:

"Acreage alone is not decisive. You will tell the village rich by noting that he exploits the agricultural workers who depend on him. He need not own 30 or 50 hectares. He may be a miller upon whom the village depends, or the innkeeper who lends money, or the village

---

[19] *Nová mysl,* No. 12, 1954; *Rudé právo,* June 8, 1954.

[20] *Vsesoiuznaia Kommunisticheskaia Partia (b) v rezoliutsiakh i resheniakh s'ezdov, konferentsii i plenumov Ts. K. 1898-1935* (The All-Union Communist Party (B) in Resolutions and Decisions of the Congresses, Conferences, and Plenums of the C.C. 1898-1935), Moscow, 1936, i, pp. 314-315.

usurer who buys various produce and sells them at high profit, and the like. It is not a matter of the number of hectares. The determinative mark of a village rich is that he exploits the country folk, one way or another."[21]

Nor could the *kulak* redeem himself by giving away his land. "A *kulak* is and remains a *kulak* even today when he has no hired hands and works mainly by himself on his farm," explained *Rudé právo*. "What is decisive is not his present situation but his whole life."[22] No matter how social-mindedly he may have behaved, the *kulak* thus continued to be "a lamb in wolf's skin."[23]

A number of devices were adopted for the purpose of gradually "limiting and suppressing the *kulaks*."

The first and probably the basic means for this purpose was *třídní rozpis,* which can perhaps best be translated as exactions of compulsory deliveries according to class origin. As defined by an editorial in *Rudé právo, třídní rozpis* meant that "deliveries of agricultural products are to be apportioned according to the size of property and according to potentialities of production, with the proviso that far greater obligations will be imposed upon the village rich than upon the small and middle peasants." Thus, it "will become a most effective weapon in the hands of the alliance of the working class and the working peasantry in their struggle against rural capitalists and exploiters."[24]

This discriminatory device, adopted for the first time after the harvest of 1948, was made to bear upon the hapless *kulak* more heavily with every coming harvest. Said the communist Minister of Domestic Trade, giving directives to a national conference of the district people's committees in April 1951: "Such obligations must be imposed on the village rich as will force them unconditionally to deliver [to the State] everything they produced except seeds and feeds which they need and their own grain rations . . . . We must thus make sure that the village rich may not speculate, may not mar by their intrigues the evolution of the village toward socialism, nor interfere with food-purveying."[25]

Compulsory delivery quotas were set up accordingly. The two most socialized types of cooperative farms (types III and IV) were assigned

[21] See also *Rudé právo,* June 8, 1954.
[22] *ibid.*
[23] See also *Lidové noviny,* March 22, 1951, *Práce,* February 27, 1951, *Zemědělské noviny,* July 18, 1952.
[24] *Rudé právo,* January 15, 1949.
[25] *Práce,* April 27, 1951.

the lowest quotas while members of the less socialized types (I and II, subsequently discontinued) and such independent farmers as managed to escape being brandmarked as *kulaks* were charged more heavily.[26] For those classified as *kulaks* the quotas were raised an additional 10 percent in 1952.[27] Although this *kulak* "sur-delivery" was rescinded with the inception of the New Course (as an incentive to increase food-growing), the sharp anti-*kulak* discrimination in the apportionment of delivery quotas remained. Since deliveries above the prescribed quotas were purchased at a much higher price, this discriminatory policy meant a substantial loss of income for the *kulaks*. The system of dual prices was finally abolished in 1959, but by then the *kulaks* were already eliminated.[28]

This ruthless class criterion was applied also in the regulation about *who may grow what and in what quantities*. *Kulaks* were simply prohibited from growing the crops which were more lucrative and were allowed to engage only in such fields of agricultural production as were less profitable. At the same time, their ability to meet the stepped-up compulsory deliveries was systematically undermined by the growing difficulty they experienced in obtaining tools and other means for adequate and timely performance of their "planned" agricultural chores. Though they were supposed to be assigned enough fertilizers to enable them to meet their delivery quotas, this principle was frequently violated in practice. Moreover, the *kulaks* were forced to sell to the government (and at a fraction of its real value) their main agricultural machinery. What the regime wanted to achieve thereby was revealed in an article in the communist weekly *Tvorba*:

"The [government] purchase of agricultural machinery was a heavy blow for the village rich . . . . By losing his tractor, his threshing machine, the village rich lost his economic supremacy over the small peasant. The situation has changed. Today, he cannot plough, mow, or thresh for himself first, as he used to do, and then only for others in the order in which they paid him respect. On the contrary, he must now go to the state machine-tractor station, to the local people's committee, or to the chairman of the Unified Agricultural Cooperative, and ask them not to forget him . . . ."[29]

Unable any longer to hire outside help, the *kulak* became thus

[26] *Zpráva o Československu*, II, 5 (1951), p. 101.
[27] Government ordinance No. 57 of November 4, 1952, and *Zemědělské noviny*, November 16, 1952.
[28] *Zemědělské noviny*, June 20, 1959.
[29] *Tvorba*, September 6, 1950.

fully dependent on the machine-tractor stations which would accommodate him only after they had served all the others. Frequently, he would get no service at all as the tractors and machines would break down before they were through with preferential work on collective farms. Moreover, the *kulak* had to pay about double the rates charged to collective farms.

The *kulak's* misery was further heightened by discrimination in the imposition of the agricultural tax which was designed to hit private farmers, especially those with somewhat larger acreage, much harder than collective farmers. In 1950, for instance, a peasant holding five hectares paid six to seven times less than a peasant with twenty hectares. In 1952 peasants owning not more than twenty hectares were freed from the agricultural tax provided they met their delivery quotas. But those with more than twenty hectares had to pay 100 percent surtax if they failed to meet their deliveries.[30] Also, while collective farms were granted tax reductions of varying degrees, the district people's committees were authorized to increase the *kulak's* taxable income by 30 percent for the purpose of tax computation. The true purpose of these discriminatory taxation practices was openly proclaimed by the regime's spokesmen: "The chief principles of the law on agricultural taxation are as follows: to encourage the entrance of small and middle farmers into collective farms . . . to tax rich farmers and *kulaks* in such a way that their economic position in the village will be gradually and systematically weakened; to adjust the taxes of the wavering middle farmers in such a way that the taxes do not serve as a barrier to their voluntary entrance into collective farms."[31]

Finally, the *kulaks* were excluded from various important advantages which were made available to collective farmers, such as state medical care and use of the regime's recreational facilities. They were made to pay much higher premiums for old age insurance. Nor were they granted the tax and debt moratoria which were conceded to collective farmers in 1955.[32] A particularly brutal anti-*kulak* measure was the exclusion of the village rich from the allocation of ration cards for clothing in 1948 and 1949 and for sugar and soap in 1952 on the ground that they could supposedly afford to pay the much higher prices charged in the open market.

[30] *Zásobovací zpravodaj*, No. 48, December 1, 1952, *Zpráva o Československu*, III, 1 (1952), p. 123.
[31] *East Europe*, 7, 1 (1958), p. 31.
[32] Government ordinance No. 36 of July 6, 1955.

Exposed to such treatment, the *kulak* became the pariah of the countryside. Frozen, together with his family, into a permanent status as the chief class enemy in the rural areas, he existed only on the sufferance of communist authorities, seeing his fellow-*kulaks* succumb one after the other and waiting helplessly for his own turn to be liquidated. By 1960 the process of *"kulako-cide"* was virtually completed.

Agricultural Collectivization and Reorganization

As in Soviet Russia, rural collectivization in communist Czechoslovakia has been pressed home through the three classical Leninist-Stalinist institutional devices: the collective farm, the state farm, and the machine-tractor station.

THE COLLECTIVE FARMS (JZD). The collective farm became the main vehicle of agricultural socialization owing not only to imitation of the Soviet model, but also to the desire of the KSČ leaders to take the fullest possible advantage of the comparative popularity of the cooperative idea in prewar Czechoslovakia. Had it been possible to make the peasants believe that the Unified Agricultural Cooperatives which the Party leaders wished them to join were merely an improved version of the cooperative movement of prewar days, rural collectivization might indeed have been smoother, at least in its first stages. It was this postulate of tactics, together with an understandable desire not to rock the agricultural boat before the completion of the 1948 harvest, that accounts for the very cautious communist approach to the agrarian question at the initial stage of the dictatorship of the proletariat.

In the first few months after the communist coup any mention of rural collectivization was strictly taboo. Next, communist spokesmen started talking in a roundabout way about the difficulties which the scattered small-holdings represented for efficient agricultural production and which might be remedied by "higher forms" of agricultural organization. By October 1948 they began to mention "agricultural producers' cooperatives" as the best form of agricultural production.[33] Finally, on February 23, 1949, the National Assembly adopted the Unified Agricultural Cooperatives Act, thereby setting up a legal framework for a course of action which, when carried to

[33] See, for instance, a speech by Deputy Volavka before the Agricultural Committee of the National Assembly on October 13, 1948. *Lidové noviny,* October 14, 1948.

its conclusion, was to make the individual farmer in Czechoslovakia a memory of the past.[34] To make the unpalatable pill taste sweeter, the phraseology of the Act was relatively mild and its ultimate purpose was carefully hidden below a thick veneer of seemingly innocuous verbiage: "In order to insure the salutary development of agricultural cooperatives and to eradicate the fragmentation of operations inherited from the past, unified cooperatives shall be founded on a voluntary basis which shall unite existing associations and produce significant benefits for the class of working farmers." The law's objectives were couched in relatively suave language as "consolidation of the scattered strips," "mechanization of agricultural work," "participation in drawing up and assuring the fulfillment of agricultural production quotas," "participation in the actual purchase of produce . . . its care and storage," "improvement of the efficiency of labor and productivity in agriculture," "promotion of the cultural and social level in rural communities" and "alleviation of female work on the farm." Also, a choice of four different types of cooperatives was offered and, to make the bait look more attractive, formal title to the land was left vested in the original owners.

Furthermore, in 1949 the emphasis was rather on patience, practical example, and persuasion. "The basic method of our policy and of our work in the village is the method of persuasion by examples and of active participation of the broad masses of the small and middle peasants," said Gottwald speaking to the Ninth Party Congress of the KSČ in May 1949. And addressing the same Congress one day later, even such a doctrinaire Communist as Slánský urged Party members to proceed cautiously, not to hurry, but first to find out how the peasants felt about the matter, to unfold a campaign of personal door-to-door persuasion, to use women to approach peasant wives. He also warned against "chasing after quantity" and advised the Party's agricultural workers "rather to establish the first cooperatives in a modest number of villages where conditions therefor were best."[35]

However, persuading a typical Czechoslovak peasant to join voluntarily the Unified Agricultural Cooperatives (JZD) proved to be impossible. Through several years of bitter experience with the communist directors of Czechoslovak agriculture prior to 1948, the Czechoslovak peasants learned to mistrust communist assurances and acquired a capacity for reading between the communist lines. Although

[34] For a fuller discussion of the Act see Ladislav Feierabend, op.cit., pp. 64ff.
[35] Rudé právo, May 26, 1949.

lip service continued to be paid to the "patient-and-friendly-persuasion" concept and occasional reprimands were addressed by the Party leaders to those "shamefully violating the principle of voluntary membership in the cooperative farms" and "resorting to methods of administrative and economic pressure,"[36] ever-stiffening coercive measures had to be applied to keep the collectivization wagon rolling. In substance, methods used to make the individual peasants hand over their land and stock to the collective farms were similar to those employed against the *kulaks* and need not therefore be recounted here. The main difference was that peasants who escaped being labeled as *kulaks* could, and indeed had to, join a collective farm, adding their property thereto, whereas the *kulak*-labeled peasant could not and, if previously admitted, had to be expelled.

The process of collectivization in a typical village would begin with the establishment of a preparatory committee of some five to ten members chosen from among the poorer peasants whose holdings were so small that they had little to lose and something to gain from sharing land with others. Wherever they were unavailable, suitable tools were usually recruited from among the so-called "metal-farmers," i.e., factory workers living in the village and possessing small plots of land on which they used to do a little farming, or rather gardening, on week ends. Next, pairs of Party agitators would be dispatched to pay repeated visits to individual farmers to induce them to join the nascent cooperative. They were aided by periodic trips of groups of factory workers from nearby cities organized by the communist-controlled trade unions for the purpose of "convincing the peasants of the advantages of common farming, helping them organize their work, forming working groups, setting up work norms and a proper accounting system."[37] Individual factories would assume patronage over various collective farms, patterned after the similar Soviet institution of *shefstvo*. The main function of such patrons was to help the JZD members "to persuade the other small and middle peasants of the advantages which they could gain through joining the JZD."[38] Under the slogan "Every village teacher an enthusiastic agitator for a socialist village," the teachers in rural areas were mobilized for the collectivization drive and directed to "show the perspective of bright life in the cooperative" and to "crush the whispering propaganda

[36] Široký's speech in the National Assembly, December 13, 1954.
[37] A resolution of the Central Council of Trade Unions of June 19, 1952.
[38] *Práce,* April 20, 1952, and February 7, 1951.

spread by the village rich."[39] Their pupils in the rural schools were made to participate in well-publicized contests under the slogan, "Which school will do more toward establishing the JZD."[40] The children were also directed to compose letters addressed to their peasant parents, urging them to join the agricultural cooperatives.

Simultaneously, a mammoth nation-wide campaign of public village meetings was unfolded for the recruitment of JZD members.[41] Every eligible peasant was individually invited to attend. Those who failed to attend or to display a "positive attitude" at such gatherings were exposed to the communist-manipulated "wrath of their fellow-neighbors" of which the following is a typical sample: After one such meeting in a small village in eastern Slovakia the names of fifteen peasants who failed to comply with such communist invitations were publicly posted with the threatening inscription: "The above persons are notorious *kulaks* and enemies of our state. They are waiting for help from the West, but they are waiting in vain. They will never be allowed to exploit our people. The small and middle peasants will never let them join our ranks." Moreover, the houses of several of them were daubed in red with the words: "*Kulaks, you are through!*"[42]

Since this combination of propaganda and threats persuaded but a small number of peasants of the superior virtues of collective farming, the inevitable result was an increasing dosage of covert and overt compulsion. That is where the distinction between *kulaks* and non-*kulaks* dwindled to microscopic proportions. Higher compulsory deliveries, stepped up year after year to and beyond the breaking point; prohibitions on growing more profitable crops; discriminatory treatment in purchases of equipment and fertilizers, in matters of taxation, health care, and social welfare—all these favorite anti-*kulak* weapons began to be applied after 1950 with increasing vehemence to all peasants unwilling to give up independent farming.

An abrupt, though only temporary, reversal came in 1953. Under the impact of anti-Stalinist developments in neighboring Hungary, where farmers were granted, upon the Kremlin's own advice, the right to withdraw from collective farms, the KSČ leaders felt it advisable to call for a pause in the frantic collectivization drive characteristic of the Stalin era. However, sensing the dangers inherent in the post-Stalin

[39] *Rudé právo*, February 5, 1955.
[40] *Lidové noviny*, November 4, 1950.
[41] *Rudé právo*, December 1, 1951; *Tvorba*, December 20, 1951.
[42] *Zpráva o Československu*, III, 9 (1952), pp. 103-104.

relaxation, Czechoslovak agricultural policy-makers were far less yielding than their Hungarian comrades. Although they halted coercive collectivization measures in 1953 and even refrained from forcible reprisals against peasants who chose to return to individual farming, they never wavered in their insistence on collectivization as the only acceptable solution of the agricultural question. Using the occasion of the festive opening of the Klíčava Dam on August 1, 1953, Zápotocký tackled the ticklish issue in no uncertain terms:

"Establishing cooperatives administratively, by decrees and perhaps through coercion, will not do. Such cooperatives will barely vegetate. People there will not work properly, they will not like it, and such cooperatives will be of no use. That is why we shall have to reexamine the matter of agricultural cooperatives, we shall have to fortify them and help them. To those who think that they will help themselves by leaving the cooperatives we can say quite openly: 'You will not help yourselves. In a few years you will have to build anew the cooperatives which you may have run away from today. We shall not hinder you, but take note of the fact that we must raise agricultural output . . . .' "[43]

The Party's Central Committee, summoned especially for an urgent consideration of agricultural problems in June 1955, sounded the clarion for a renewed collectivization drive. Having condemned "the stagnation in the numerical growth of cooperatives" and "the opportunist theories of an autonomic and spontaneous progress in the establishment of cooperatives," it ordered all Party and state organs to show the peasants the road of socialism more boldly and more forcefully.[44] Thus, after two years of relative leniency, the kid gloves were replaced once again with bare knuckles and persuasion resumed the true meaning given it by communist semantics. A better awareness of the importance of raising agricultural output, characteristic of the post-Stalin era, brought a little more subtlety into coercive techniques. Such was, for instance, the permission granted private farmers in 1957 to purchase small gasoline, diesel, and electric motors, which in its turn served as a convenient justification for raising their compulsory deliveries by an average 20 percent in 1958.[45] But this did not divert the regime one iota from its announced goal of "completing in essence the transition to cooperative production" by 1960 and of doing

---

[43] *Rudé právo*, August 2, 1953. See also *Práce*, August 18, 1953.
[44] *News*, 4, 8 (1955), p. 51.
[45] *Zemědělské noviny*, January 24, 1957.

away with private farming altogether by 1961.[46] The inexorable march toward the total liquidation of individual farming, interrupted only at the height of the post-Stalin New Course, is strikingly illustrated by Table VI.

TABLE VI
Collective and Individual Farming, 1948-1960

	1948	1953	1954	1955	1956	1957	1958	1959	1960
Cooperative farms types III and IV	28	6,679	6,502	6,795	8,016	11,090	12,140	12,560	10,816[e]
Members (thousands)		381		329	395	656	852	970	994
Persons working in the private sector[a] of agriculture (thousands)		1,159	1,169	1,320	1,318	1,183	816	542	
Agricultural land (million hectares)									
coops III and IV[b]		2.17	1.9	1.95	2.24	3.46	4.3	4.79	4.9
private sector[a]		3.88	3.94	4.08	4.14	3.74	2.46	1.72	
Arable land (million hectares)									
coops III and IV[b]		1.64	1.46	1.48	1.7	2.62	3.21	3.57	
private sector[a]		2.72	2.78	2.88	2.88	2.57	1.6	0.98	
Cattle (million head)									
coops III and IV[b]		1.06	1.12	0.95	0.96	1.15	1.83	2.53	
private sector[a]		2.94	2.52	2.64	2.67	2.48	1.73	1.07	
Pigs (million head)									
coops III and IV[b]		1.33	1.34	1.4	1.55	1.75	2.47	3.13	
private sector[a]		2.5	1.87	2.35	2.63	2.5	1.84	1.05	
Sheep (million head)									
coops III and IV[b]		0.28	0.32	0.31	0.32	0.36	0.39	0.41	
private sector[a]		0.41	0.4	0.41	0.39	0.33	0.24	0.17	
Percentile share of the entire socialist sector[c]									
Agricultural land	10.9[d]	44.7	41.9	42.6	47.8	65.4	77.5	84.4	87.4
Arable land	8.0	45.1	42.1	43.2	49.0	67.9	80.6		

[a] The private sector comprises individual farmers and coops types I and II; [b] coops III and IV also include household plots of collective farmers; [c] coops III and IV, state farms, etc.; [d] in 1949; [e] the reduction is due to the merging of collective farms into bigger units.

Source: *Ročenka*, 1960, and other official announcements of the Czechoslovak Office of Statistics.

Considering the stepped-up pace at which land has been gobbled up by the "socialist sector" and the remnant of private farmers fed into the collectivization grinder in the last few years, especially since

[46] Novotný's speeches to the Eleventh Party Congress *Rudé právo*, June 19, 1958, and to the Fourth Congress of collective farmers in March 1959, *Zemědělské noviny*, March 20-23, 1959.

the suppression of the Hungarian uprising in the fall of 1956, there is little doubt that rural socialization will be completed on schedule.

State Farms

Having chosen the collective farm to be the key device of rural socialization, the KSČ leaders have by no means neglected the alternative Leninist approach to the agricultural question, namely via the government-owned state farm. In so doing they have been prompted by considerations both of ideology and of pressing practical necessity.

Of all the avenues of agricultural socialization the state farm, the *sovkhoz,* comes closest to an ideal Marxist-Leninist image. As a fully government-managed enterprise, the state farm becomes, in its final form, an agricultural factory and peasants are converted into factory workers working a specified number of hours per day and paid essentially the same as industrial workers. An all-embracing system of such state farms would eliminate the "antithesis between town and country" the removal of which has been considered as one of the prerequisites of the transition from socialism to communism by the chief interpreters of Marxism-Leninism from Lenin to Khrushchëv. It would thus attain the coveted communist goal of liquidating the peasantry as a class and of creating a "classless society." At the same time, the maximum mechanization made possible by the large size of the state farms and their specialization in one or only a few lines of agricultural production would supposedly bring nearer to its solution yet another prerequisite of pure communism: the overcoming of the contrast between mental and manual labor. Indeed, both Stalin and Khrushchëv made it amply clear that even the collective farms must be "elevated" to a "higher form" of full public socialist property before the final stage of communism can supervene. Hence, the agricultural policy-makers of communist Czechoslovakia acted in the best Marxist-Leninist tradition when they did not allow the state-farm concept to go to seed at a time when the cooperative approach was the slogan of the day.

The practical reason for establishing state farms lay in the over-abundance of agricultural land. The seizure of land owned by the expelled Sudeten Germans and the Czech and Slovak landowners accused rightly or wrongly of collaboration with the Nazis left the government with so much land that it became impossible to find enough people to settle it. Additional expropriations undertaken after the communist seizure of power and the continued confiscations of *kulak* properties made the problem even worse. Some of this land was assigned to adjacent agricultural cooperatives. But much of it was located in areas where no cooperatives existed at the time or where they were in no position to take proper care of additional tracts of land. Under such circumstances the logical way out was the creation of state farms to fill the gap.

As a result of these ideological reasons and practical necessities, state farms registered a sevenfold increase in holdings of arable land between 1948 and 1950, expanding in area from 67,000 hectares to 466,00 hectares. Although their initial production achievements were so poor that Zápotocký himself felt it necessary to warn in 1952 that "for the time being the collective farms are not to learn from the state farms,"[47] the state-farm sector resumed its slow but steady growth after the very slight New Course retrenchment of 1953-1955, as the Table VII indicates.

TABLE VII
State Farms, 1948-1960

	1948	1953	1955	1956	1957	1958	1959	1960
Number of farms				2,895	3,038	3,062	3,154	
Employees (in thousands)				185	177	183	193	
Arable land (in thousand hectares)	67	482	594	660	694	735	782	
Arable land (in percent)		10	12	13	14	14	15	
Agricultural land (in thousand hectares)				900	942	985	1,047	1,104
Agricultural land (in percent)			11	12	13	14	16	
Cattle (in thousand head)			355	384	395	450	513	
Pigs " " "			724	718	621	639	737	
Sheep " " "				222	206	191	170	
Poultry " " "				541	520	680	949	
Share in gross agricultural production (in percent)[a]		12.2	13	12.2	12.7	13.7	14.8	

[a] State farms plus other agricultural enterprises operated by the government.
Source: *Ročenka*, 1959, especially p. 261; 1960, especially page 254, and other official announcements of the Czechoslovak Office of Statistics.

While state farms thus embrace only a relatively small portion of Czechoslovak agriculture, recent Soviet ideological pronouncements on the prerequisites for the transition from socialism to communism and the gradual rise in the share of the *sovkhozes* in Soviet agricultural production in recent years seem to assure the Czechoslovak state farms of an increasingly important position in the communist agricultural system.

[47] *Rudé právo,* September 28, 1952.

The Machine-tractor Stations (STS)

While the Czechoslovak state farms can look with hopeful anticipation toward the days ahead, this is not true of the country's machine-tractor stations. Khrushchëv's recent decision to disband the Soviet MTS system spelled a quick end for its Czechoslovak counterpart, at least insofar as its original role is concerned.

Although a few state-owned machine stations existed in Czechoslovakia prior to the communist coup—twenty-three of them to be exact—the foundation for their development into a full-fledged nation-wide system along Soviet lines was laid in January 1949 with the creation of a Central Office for the Mechanization of Agriculture. To enable the new office to attend to its task of taking care of the bulk of the machine work for both the individual and collective farms, it was authorized to requisition the machinery owned by private farmers and subsequently also that possessed by the collective farms. Thus the government acquired a monoply over agricultural machinery and private farmers as well as agricultural cooperatives became dependent upon the communist State for virtually all agricultural work that could not be carried out by hand tools and horse- or oxen-drawn vehicles.

The actual field work was assigned to a vast network of machine-tractor stations, each of them consisting of a number of tractor brigades and auxiliary personnel. At the peak of its expansion the network comprised 2,770 tractor brigade centers subordinated to 260 machine-tractor stations. The system employed 59,305 persons and its machinery included 35,473 tractors in terms of 15 Hp units, 17,477 binding machines, 10,107 threshing machines, 13,511 mowing machines, 20,264 sowing machines, 10,567 weeding machines, 36,335 ploughs, and 3,752 grain combines. It performed machine work of various kinds on 13,173,000 hectares of agricultural land of which 92.2 percent was done for the Unified Agricultural Cooperatives.[48]

The types of work which the STS were called upon to execute—ploughing, sowing, harvesting, and threshing—afforded them an excellent opportunity for the performance of their other major function, that of supervising their clientele and becoming, as the Party's Central Committee put it, "the apostle of collective cultivation of the soil and of the new forms of agricultural production." In carrying out his machine work on the cooperative or individual farm, each STS em-

[48] *Ročenka,* 1959, p. 268.

ployee was under specific instructions to watch all the time for instances of cheating, economic sabotage, and land concealment, and to report violators of the socialist discipline to his communist superiors. Every tractor driver ploughing the fields or harvesting the crops, every agronomist or veterinarian coming to offer his services, every accountant eager to help out in the JZD bookkeeping problems, were so many scouts poking their inquisitive noses into the farmers' affairs. The STS employees thus became thousands of tentacles enabling the communist regime to reach down into every farm and supplementing the other Party and government controls.

This being so, it can be easily understood why the KSČ leaders were anything but enthusiastic about Khrushchëv's sudden decision to do away with the MTS in the Soviet Union. Hurriedly, they launched in January and February of 1958 a press campaign designed to explain why the new Soviet policy was not suitable for Czechoslovakia where cooperative farms were smaller and the machine-tractor stations "have not by far fulfilled as yet their historical mission."[49] As late as June 1958 Novotný assured the Eleventh Party Congress that "the machine-tractor stations will continue to be an important factor in the development of the Unified Agricultural Cooperatives and will constitute a base where the principal means of mechanization will be concentrated."[50] However, by the end of 1958 a change of mind occurred. Since 1959 the STS have begun to sell their machinery to the collective farms and the process was substantially completed by the end of 1960.[51]

What has caused the Czechoslovak agricultural policy-makers to reconsider? While the question cannot be answered with certainty, it seems that the main reason for the regime's second thoughts lies in a combined effect of the Soviet example, the deep over-all resentment against the STS among the farmers, and the imperative need of breaking at long last the Gordian knot of the lingering agricultural malaise. Ever since their establishment the STS have been a thorn in the side of the Czechoslovak farmer, individual or collective. Desiring to exceed their work norms and secure the coveted bonuses, STS workers developed a tendency to make work easier for themselves through various short-cuts (such as, for instance, shallower ploughing than contracted), which harmed the farmers' interests through re-

---

[49] *Mladá fronta,* February 4, 1958.
[50] *Rudé právo,* June 19, 1959.
[51] *Pravda,* January 3, 1959, and *Prague News Letter,* 16, 3, February 6, 1960.

duced harvest yields. This was one of the main reasons why the government introduced in 1954 a system of paying the STS in kind rather than cash and made the size of the payments dependent on the actual yields per hectare.[52] Moreover, not even the communist members of the collective farms had any liking for the prying activities of their fellow-comrades from the STS. Hence, when Khrushchëv's decision to abolish the Soviet MTS bestowed an imprint of Marxist-Leninist legitimacy upon the arguments for a similar course in Czechoslovakia, the many foes of the STS could come into the open with so resolute an attack on that hated institution that the regime thought it wiser to yield. While counterattacking the "zealots" who wished to dissolve the STS right away and stressing the important role which the machine-tractor stations had yet to play in the final stage of rural collectivization, the KSČ leaders came reluctantly to a decision allowing a transfer of machinery from the STS to the collective farms.[53]

While the STS were relieved of the main function for which they had originally been established, they have not been abolished. Rather, their role has been changed and adapted to the new agricultural pattern. Though they no longer plough the fields and harvest the crops, they nevertheless continue to serve socialized Czechoslovak agriculture in several ways:

1. They attend to various land improvement projects, such as irrigation, drainage, digging of ensilage pits, and insecticide and fungicide spraying and dusting.

2. They act as machinery maintenance and repair stations for cooperatives, state farms, and the state forest service.

3. They perform technical inspection service by keeping track of the use and condition of machinery owned by the cooperative farms and instructing their members on its proper operation and maintenance.

4. They help to train mechanics for the agricultural cooperatives.[54]

Thus the STS have not surrendered all their controls over the collective farms. Moreover, the rearrangement of their role was cleverly taken advantage of by the regime for the purpose of planting additional controllers directly in the JZD's midst. The KSČ leaders made sure that the transfer of machinery from the STS to the

[52] *Prague News Letter,* 11, 17, September 3, 1955.
[53] *Rudé právo,* January 20, 1959; *Zemědělské noviny,* February 1, 1959.
[54] *Prague News Letter,* 16, 3, February 6, 1960.

JZD was accompanied by a corresponding transfer of "politically and professionally mature" employees of the STS to the JZD.[55]

AGRICULTURAL PLANNING: TARGETS AND RESULTS

"In the growth of agricultural production we are not catching up with the capitalist countries but are rather falling behind. While Czechoslovak agricultural production in the years 1955-1957 was 3 to 5 percent lower than before the War, in the countries of Western Europe it was on the average 25 percent higher."[56] This frank admission which appeared in *Nová mysl,* and which is typical of innumerable other communist lamentations about the sorry state of Czechoslovak agriculture, contrasts sharply with the glowing praise which the KSČ spokesmen bestow liberally on the country's achievements on the industrial front. By the same token they bear witness to the fact that in Czechoslovakia, as in the Soviet Union, agriculture has been the weakest part of communism's economic system. That this should be so is the cumulative result of a number of factors, most of which have a common denominator in the lopsided communist emphasis on industrialization and the parallel Cinderella treatment reserved for agriculture.

The extent to which agriculture has been downgraded in relation to industrial production under the dictatorship of the proletariat stands out very clearly in the following table (Table VIII) comparing planned targets and actual results in two sectors of the economy.

Except for the New Course intermezzo of 1954 and 1955, when the cogent circumstances of the post-Stalin thaw compelled the KSČ leaders to make extraordinary NEP-like concessions, communist planners set the goals of agricultural production far below those fixed for industrial growth. Nonetheless, considering the postwar population decrease of well over two million, the planned production targets should have been adequate—had they been reached. But they never were and this failure was by no small margin. As shown in Table VIII below, instead of attaining its prewar level in 1948 as scheduled by the Two-Year Reconstruction Plan of 1947-1948, agricultural production remained more than 25 percent behind it. The 53 percent increase envisaged by the First Five-Year Plan fizzled out into a negligible 17 percent. Even more catastrophic were the results of 1954 when the call for a 12 percent increase was answered by a

[55] *Život strany,* No. 15 (1959), p. 919.
[56] *Československý zpravodaj,* No. 260, September 30, 1959.

decrease of almost 3 percent. Thus it was only in 1955 that agricultural production came anywhere near the prescribed annual target. However, with the inception of the Second Five-Year Plan in 1956, agriculture has promptly reverted to its habitual pattern of underfulfillment of its planned targets by alarming proportions, as indicated by Table IX.

TABLE VIII

Indices of Planned and Actual Results in Agriculture and Industry
(percent above pre-plan year)

| | AGRICULTURE | | INDUSTRY | |
	Planned	*Actual*	*Planned*	*Actual*
Two-Year Plan	0	−25.2	10	8
(1947-1948)				
First Five-Year Plan	37[a] 53[b]	17	57[a] 98[b]	93
(1949-1953)				
New Course Intermezzo				
1954	12.1	−2.5	5.8	4.4
1955	12.6	11.5[e]	9	10.6
Second Five-Year Plan	30[d] 27[e] 16.5[f]		50[d] 54.4[e]	
(1956-1960)				
Third Five-Year Plan	22-23		56	
(1961-1965)				

[a] Original version; [b] 1951 superplan; [e] originally 9.5 percent was claimed; [d] original plan; [e] 1958 revision; [f] 1959 revision.

Source: *Ročenka*, and other official announcements on the plans and their fulfillment.

TABLE IX

Indices of Planned and Actual Agricultural Output
1956-1960
(percentage over preceding year)

	1956	*1957*	*1958*	*1959*	*1960*
Planned	8.3	6.8	11.9	12.3	6
Actual	2.0	−1.0	3.4	−1.4	7

Source: Official announcements on plans and plan fulfillments.

As a result of this persistent nonfulfillment of the planned goals the prewar level of agricultural production which was supposed to have been reached as early as the end of 1948 was still unattained in 1959, thus putting Czechoslovak agriculture under communist rule eleven years behind schedule! This dismal story told by percentile indices is corroborated and amplified by absolute production figures as well. As is apparent from the table of output in major fields of agricultural production (Table XV) appended to this chapter, the average annual yields of recent years barely hover around those attained back in 1934-1938, i.e., twenty or more years ago. Nor can the communist regime derive much comfort from a per-hectare comparison (Table X), of current levels of agricultural production with prewar levels:

TABLE X
Prewar and Postwar Yields

	1929-1933 Average	1934-1938 Average	1954-1957 Average	1958-1960 Average	1960 Plan	1965 Plan
AGRICULTURAL LAND (quintals per hectare)						
Wheat	17.6	17.1	19.5	21.4	22	27.0
Rye	17.8	16.0	18.2	19.9	20.5	25.0
Barley	18.6	17.0	19.8	21.5	21.8	26.5
Oats	17.6	16.2	17.9	18.8	17.0	
Corn		21.4	24.2	28.5		
Potatoes	129.8	135.0	137.9	103.4	153	180.0
Sugar beets	261.7	286.0	262.8	283.8	293.9	327
				1958-1959 Average		
		(per 100 hectares)				
Milk (liters)		611.0	501.0	500.5	541.0	746
Eggs (thousands)		24.2	28.4[a]	28.8	35.4	41.7
Cattle (head)		55.4	56.6	58.0		
Cows		30.7	28.7	28.4		
Sheep (head)		5.9	13.4	10.5		
ARABLE LAND (per 100 hectares)						
Pigs		56.1	102.3	106.7		
Poultry		708.2[b]	461.2	515.0		
Hens		270.3[b]	403.8	456.8		
Milk (thousand liters per cow per year)		1.87[c]	1.66[d]	1.76	1.9	2.35

[a] In 1957; [b] summer level of 1935-1936; [c] in 1937; [d] 1954-1958.
Sources: *Ročenka* and other official announcements.

Only in pigs and in sheep have there been substantial increases over prewar levels. In all other fields of vegetable and animal production, increases in per-hectare yields have been either extremely modest or none at all. But the very small margin of most of these increases, averaging only 4.2 percent for the over-all gross agricultural production per hectare between 1936 and 1959,[57] amounts actually to a major failure. After all, modern advances in technology attained in the last twenty years should have paved the way for a much steeper rise in the yields per hectare than are the meager increments registered in communist Czechoslovakia. Small-scale farming has been mostly

[57] *Ročenka*, 1960, p. 211.

replaced by large-scale or at least medium-scale production. The 500,000 hectares that have remained uncultivated in the postwar era, and are not, therefore, taken into account in the per-hectare computations, comprise much marginal farmland of poor fertility. Similarly, much of the worst agricultural land was separated from Czechoslovakia through the loss of Ruthenia to the Soviet Union in 1945. Moreover, as shown by Table XI, the use of fertilizers and tractors has increased tremendously since prewar days and since the communist seizure of power in 1948:

TABLE XI
Use of Fertilizers and Tractors

	Unit	1937-1938	1948-1949	1958-1959
Fertilizers (per hectare of arable land)				
Nitrogenous	kg/N	4.7	7	25.2
Phosphorous	kg/P$_2$O$_5$	9.5	11.2	25.6
Potassic	kg/K$_2$O	5.3	8	49.4
			1948	1958
Tractors (in 15 hp units per 1,000 hectares of agricultural land)			3.2	7.2

Source: *Statistické zprávy*, No. 7, 1959, p. 22; *Ročenka*, 1959, p. 22.

All these factors should have raised the average yields per hectare in each and every instance far above those of prewar days.

The Agricultural Balance Sheet

With these meager results the over-all balance sheet of Czechoslovak agriculture after twelve years of the dictatorship of the proletariat looks bleak indeed. In sharp contrast to industry with its mixed pattern of successes and failures, Czechoslovak agricultural accounts at the threshold of the Third Five-Year Plan are almost exclusively in the red.

Credit Items

About the only entry that can with some justification be made on the positive side of the balance pertains to the gradual integration of agricultural production into bigger units. As shown earlier in this chapter, less than 1 percent of prewar Czechoslovak farms were over fifty hectares; and over 80 percent of the agricultural land was split among 1,632,569 farmers. On the other hand, the typical collective farm in Communist Czechoslovakia averaged some 300 hectares of arable land by 1958–1959, and as revealed by Novotný in November 1959, this average is to be further increased "so as to take advantage of large-scale production and intensified methods of management."[58] Such a concentration of land formerly scattered in lots of a few hectares each among many independent peasants greatly facilities mechanization and the use of modern labor-saving devices and processes.

This high level of integration has in its turn allowed a cut in agricultural manpower from 2,222,000 in 1948 to 1,775,000 in 1958 and to 1,455,024 by February 1, 1960, as compared with over two and one-half million in 1930.[59] It must be added, however, that the last-mentioned figure includes one million "helping family members." As all of the latter could by no means be considered as "permanent agricultural workers" in the present communist meaning of the word, the prewar and postwar sets of figures are not fully comparable.

For the same reason (as well as those mentioned in the preceding chapter with regard to labor productivity in industry) it is impossible to accept at its face value the communist claim that by 1959 the gross agricultural output per "permanent worker in agriculture" has risen 105 percent above 1936.[60] That labor productivity in agriculture must have risen considerably above the prewar level is a foregone conclusion. The tens of thousands of tractors and other agricultural machinery delivered to Czechoslovak agriculture and the greatly stepped-up use of commercial fertilizers were bound to be reflected in an increased output per man. But the actual increase is most probably well below the official figure which evidently credits the permanent workers with the additional untold millions of hours' worth of work performed annually, especially at harvest time, by the hundreds of thousands of "volunteers" sent from cities in notorious brigades as well as compulsory agricultural work carried out by school children, students, and the Army.

Debit Items

The keynote of the overwhelmingly negative balance sheet of Czechoslovak agriculture is the almost unbelievable fact that in the

[58] Rudé právo, November 13, 1959. By the end of 1960, 3,477 collective farms were merged into larger units averaging 654 hectares of agricultural land each. Rudé právo, February 8, 1961.

[59] Ročenka, 1959, p. 92, and 1937, p. 19, Statistické zprávy, No. 6, 1960, p. 157.

[60] Ročenka, 1960, p. 211.

twelve years of its rule the communist regime did not manage to raise the output levels of Czechoslovak agriculture to where they had been a quarter of a century ago! A similarly dark picture is revealed when communist agricultural attainments are measured in terms of yields per hectare. In spite of all the advantages of larger scale production, increased mechanization, and a spectacular rise in the use of chemical fertilizers, the gross vegetable production per hectare has stood year after year below prewar levels, reaching them only once, in 1955, and still trailing behind them by almost 6 percent in 1959.[61] Although the gross animal production per hectare finally rose above prewar level by 1955 and exceeded it by 18 percent in 1959, this rather modest increase is due mostly to successful pig raising which, though commendable, does not compare in economic importance with cattle raising, which has been standing virtually still all the time.

The degree of stagnation of Czechoslovak agriculture under the dictatorship of the proletariat is perhaps revealed most strikingly when its results are measured against those registered by non-communists countries endowed by nature with approximately similar conditions for vegetable and animal production, such as Western Germany, Austria, Belgium, or France. Whether it be the question of total output or yields per hectare, such a comparison (Table XII) shows that communist Czechoslovakia has lost ground in virtually every major sector of vegetable production.

As can be seen from the Table XII, Western Germany and Belgium, which were already ahead of Czechoslovakia in prewar days in per-hectare yields, have further increased their lead, while Austria and France have come from behind to overtake her. A comparison with other advanced capitalist countries presents the same general pattern.

In the animal sector of agricultural production, heavily emphasized by the communist planners, the comparative picture, as seen in Table XIII, is somewhat more favorable.

However, the comparison looks good for Czechoslovakia only in pig and sheep raising. In the key section of animal production, cattle, all but one of the above-listed non-communist countries have done better than Czechoslovakia, while the remaining one, Austria, has done about the same. Similarly unimpressive look the Czechoslovak attainments in various other aspects of animal production whether measured per hectare or per capita (Table XIV).

[61] *ibid.*

TABLE XII

Prewar and Postwar Crops in Five Countries

	CZECHOSLOVAKIA		AUSTRIA		WEST GERMANY		FRANCE		BELGIUM	
	1934-38	1955-57	1934-38	1955-57	1934-38	1955-57	1934-38	1955-57	1934-38	1955-57
Wheat	1,513[a]	1,513	417	564	2,505	3,570	8,143	9,023	472	702
	(17.1)[b]	(20.8)	(16.7)	(22.5)	(22.1)	(30.2)	(15.6)	(22.3)	(26.9)	(35.0)
Rye	1,577	989	539	417	3,081	3,682	769	461	424	203
	(16.0)	(19.2)	(14.7)	(19.6)	(18.5)	(25.0)	(11.6)	(12.4)	(23.9)	(29.4)
Barley	1,109	1,354	287	374	1,699	2,298	1,074	4,252	91	288
	(17.0)	(20.5)	(17.6)	(22.5)	(21.0)	(27.5)	(14.5)	(23.5)	(26.3)	(33.5)
Oats	1,212	969	438	359	2,843	2,386	4,572	3,653	655	473
	(16.2)	(18.2)	(15.2)	(19.3)	(20.2)	(25.3)	(13.9)	(18.1)	(26.8)	(37.2)
Corn	225	412	170	149	51	56	541	1,417		
	(21.4)	(24.2)	(25.5)	(28.2)	(30.0)	(28.8)	(15.8)	(25.6)		
Potatoes	9,635	8,765	2,845	3,423	19,603	25,303	17,158	16,057	3,169	2,087
	(135)	(140)	(137)	(190)	(166)	(225)	(713)	(756)	(201)	(253)

[a] Total output in thousands of tons;   [b] (output per hectare in quintals).

Source: *Statistical Yearbooks* and *Bulletins* of the United Nations and the respective countries.

TABLE XIII

Prewar and Postwar Numbers of Livestock in Five Countries

(in thousands of head)

	CZECHOSLOVAKIA		AUSTRIA		WEST GERMANY		FRANCE		BELGIUM	
	1938-39	1957-58	1939	1957-58	1938	1957-58	1938	1957-58	1939	1957-58
Cattle	4,706	4,091	2,620	2,297	12,187	11,948	15,622	17,924	1,600	2,596
Pigs	3,538	5,435	2,830	2,917	12,280	15,418	7,127	8,131	856	1,423
Sheep	543	889	818	207	2,097	1,127	9,875	8,573	187	174

Source: *Statistical Yearbooks* and *Bulletins* of the United Nations and of the respective countries.

As a result of the sluggish behavior of her agriculture, communist Czechoslovakia has been compelled to import huge quantities of agricultural products of all sorts. While in 1937 foodstuffs constituted 11 percent of the country's imports and 8.2 percent of its exports, leaving thus a net import of less than 4 percent, the average share of foodstuffs in Czechoslovak imports for the years 1949-1958 jumped to 27.3 percent and that of exports stayed at 9 percent, creating thereby a net import surplus of 18.3 percent.[62] Thus a country that

TABLE XIV
Recent Output Levels in Animal Production

	CZECHOSLOVAKIA 1956	AUSTRIA 1955	WEST GERMANY 1955	FRANCE 1956	BELGIUM 1955
PER 100 HECTARES (in quintals of dead weight except where stated otherwise)					
Beef	22.7	27.2	56.8	39.7	104.5
Pork	45.1	41.9	94.4	31.9	117.1
Lamb	0.3	1.5	1.7	3.4	1.1
Milk	510.7	619.6	1,193.1	580.4	2,031.2
Eggs (in thousands)	143.7	134.2	116.6	305.3	270.6
PER CAPITA (in kilograms)					
Beef	12.7	15.9	15.9	30.6	20.5
Pork	25.3	24.5	26.4	24.5	23.0
Lamb	0.2	0.9	0.5	2.6	0.2
Milk	280.0	363.0	340.0	852.0	400.0
Eggs	143.7	134.2	116.6	305.3	270.6

Source: *Statistical Yearbooks* and *Bulletins* of the United Nations, FAO, and of the respective countries.

was almost self-sufficient in foodstuffs when it had fourteen and one-half million inhabitants cannot now feed a population smaller by more than one million without heavy foreign purchases of all sorts. It had to import in 1954 twenty-five times as much wheat and forty-five times as much butter as in 1937, and "every other kilogram of meat either directly as meat or in the form of fodder";[63] and during 1954-1957 one-third of its consumption of cereals and over one-fifth of its needs in fodder and butter had to be secured by purchases abroad.[64] The persistence with which the problem of excessive agricultural imports continues to plague the regime has been corrob-

[62] Prewar figures from the *Statistical Digest of the Czechoslovak Republic*, Praha, 1948, p. 97; postwar figures from *Ročenka*, 1958, p. 280.
[63] *Práce*, November 26, 1954, and Prague radio, March 9, 1955, as monitored by the Free Europe Committee, *News*, 4, 5 (1955), p. 11.
[64] *Rudé právo*, November 27, 1958.

orated by agricultural indices published by the official press organ of Czechoslovak agriculture, *Zemědělské noviny,* which revealed that in 1958 Czechoslovak meat imports were higher than in 1937 by 250 percent, fodder by 272 percent and wheat by a fantastic 1,850 percent.[65] Since it has been an avowed communist purpose to make the country essentially self-sufficient in the main food resources, the failure to do so, and by such a wide margin, must definitely be considered as a debit item on the communist balance.

This failure throws also an altogether different light on the matter of the 500,000 hectares of arable land that remain uncultivated despite continuous communist efforts to the contrary. While arable land, including utility gardens, amounted to 5,712,156 hectares in prewar Czechoslovakia (without Ruthenia), it sank to an all-time low of 5,000,700 in 1954, and still stood only at 5,143,000 in 1960.[66] As mentioned before, part of this uncultivated land is poor and its exclusion from cultivation makes good economic sense. But a considerable part of it is fertile enough and should have been ploughed under, especially in view of the continued inability to meet planned targets of agricultural output. If enough manpower or machines were not available for a more intensive cultivation, such land should have been converted to meadows or to pastures to provide additional grazing and hay. That this has not been done is revealed by the fact that the present acreage claimed for meadows and pastures is also well below prewar levels.[67]

However, not all of these "fallow lands" have been really left fallow. An unspecified portion of them have been cultivated, and often very efficiently so, without the knowledge of the authorities. The massive land transfers which accompanied the several waves of confiscation and expropriation since 1945 brought much chaos into matters or rural landholding. This created good opportunities for land concealment through failure to report possession of some of the land to the proper authorities. Since compulsory deliveries have been determined mainly according to the size of the registered landholding, such unregistered land has become a lucrative device for lowering one's compulsory deliveries and for selling the saved items at higher

[65] *Zemědělské noviny,* September 3, 1959.

[66] Prewar figures based on data from *Ročenka,* 1937, postwar figures on *Ročenka,* 1958 and 1960.

[67] In 1936 there were 1,122,944 hectares of meadows and 894,503 hectares of pastures, not counting Ruthenia; in 1960 the corresponding figures were 1,091,000 and 833,000.

free-market prices. The widespread prevalence of such practices was documented by a report of the Ministry of Agriculture of January 1952 which revealed that a full 13.4 percent of all arable land was not accounted for.[68] Not only individual farmers and collective farms, but also state farms took part in such land concealment.[69] Naturally, as soon as the regime became aware of these stratagems, it took resolute measures to combat them. In view of stiffening Party and government controls over agriculture it cannot be doubted that most of this concealed land has by now been uncovered.

The main reason why huge tracts of arable land have remained fallow in spite of lagging agricultural output lies in the muddling communist policy regarding agricultural manpower. The basic communist endeavor to reduce the number of workers in agriculture was certainly a needed course of action. However, hard pressed to satisfy the industry's voracious appetite for more and more labor under the First Five-Year Plan, the regime depleted the agricultural manpower far beyond the initially planned 4 percent reduction. By 1952 the number of persons engaged in agriculture had dropped from 2,239,000 in 1948 to 1,850,000, i.e., by some 18 percent.[70] As progress in agriculture mechanization simultaneously fell behind schedule, the inevitable result was a collapse in the agricultural sector of the First Five-Year Plan. With the relative reemphasis of agriculture in the New Course, the policy of depleting agricultural manpower came to a halt. "It certainly is not a healthy phenomenon that the number of workers engaged in agriculture was lowered by several hundreds of thousands in the last years," proclaimed Zápotocký in January 1954. "The decrease of [agricultural] manpower does not correspond to the progress of mechanization and causes many deficiencies." [71] Acting upon these second thoughts, the regime reversed its previous manpower policy and decreed that 320,000 new workers be recruited for Czechoslovak agriculture between 1954 and 1957.[72] However, despite offers of bonuses and other inducements to those willing to leave cities for farms, the campaign was anything but successful. In 1955 the number of persons engaged in agriculture rose slightly from its 1952 low of 1,850,000 to 1,933,000. But it began to fall

[68] *Lidová demokracie,* January 31, 1952.

[69] *Statistický obzor,* No. 9, 1954.

[70] *Ročenka,* 1960, p. 90. *Nová svoboda,* January 4, 1955, listed as high a decrease as twenty-one percent between 1949 and 1953.

[71] *Zemědělské noviny,* January 4, 1954.

[72] *Rudé právo,* May 23, 1954, December 18, 1954; *Prague News Letter,* 11, 2, January 22, 1955.

again in 1956 and by 1959 it slipped to the above-mentioned 1,623,000.

Equally unsuccessful have been the regime's recent efforts to improve the age structure of agricultural manpower. To inject more young blood into the aging ranks of the farmers it was directed that 205,000 of the 320,000 persons to be recruited for agriculture between 1954 and 1957 were to be young people leaving schools. Yet the fact that the average age of farmers was listed as 44.8 years and over 46 percent of them as being over fifty in 1960 shows that the rejuvenation campaign has thus far failed.[73] That today's younger generation does not feel inclined toward farming is a socio-economic phenomenon which is not limited to the communist world. But there is a powerful additional reason why the youth of Czechoslovakia should abhor any idea of becoming farmers. In view of the persistent communist glorification and heroization of the industrial worker and the parallel downgrading of the peasant it is small wonder that the occupation of farming has so little attraction.

Since advanced age impairs working efficiency, especially in occupations requiring physical effort, the high median age of the Czechoslovak farming population has undoubtedly contributed to the general deterioration in the quality of agricultural manpower, which is yet another conspicuous item to be listed on the debit side of the communist agricultural balance. But the main blame for the qualitative deterioration must be ascribed to the earlier-mentioned communist policy of suppressing the *kulaks* who were actually the best and most experienced farmers. Since they are barred from membership in the collective farms, Czechoslovak agriculture has thereby denied itself the services of thousands upon thousands of the best qualified men. At the same time, the management of a great many collective farms has fallen into the hands of persons who may be dependable Communists but whose knowledge about farming is often only what they have learned in hastily organized short courses. Moreover, in view of the low repute of farming as an occupation, it has been difficult to meet the ever-growing need for various categories of specialists and technically trained personnel necessary to operate modern mechanized agriculture. Persons with such qualification are most reluctant to give up city and factory positions for assignment on farms; and the better qualified among the agricultural laborers strive for more desirable urban jobs.

[73] *Lidová demokracie,* April 19, 1958; and *Ročenka,* 1960, p. 249.

However, of the many dilemmas that plague the communist directors of Czechoslovak agriculture, the worst is the peasantry's sullen opposition to communism in general and to communist agricultural policies in particular. Being a rugged individualist endowed with a strong possessive instinct, the typical Czechoslovak peasant hates collectivization in any form. Furthermore, he considers the communist regime to be a gangster who has robbed him of his property, livestock, and tools, and on top of that forces him to toil as an underpaid laborer on the very land he once owned. Hence, he feels no inclination to help a system which he so thoroughly detests and uses every opportunity to steal since, in so doing, he only takes back a little part of what should rightly be his. Guided by this philosophy, the majority of the Czechoslovak peasants, herded in the collective and state farms, work as little as the communist controls permit, cheat the regime as much as they can get away with, and concentrate on the cultivation of their small household plots as much as possible.[74] A collection of the recurrent communist complaints about the neglect and subterfuge with which the Czechoslovak peasantry retaliates daily against the regime would constitute a thick volume; and another one could be composed from reports brought out by escapee farmers. But a few samples, taken at random from the communist press, must suffice to illustrate the problems rising from this relentless battle between the peasantry and the regime.

While cows owned collectively refuse persistently to meet the prescribed targets of milk output, cows owned by collective farmers individually and fed on their household plots, often on fodder "borrowed" from collective farm supplies, seem to be much more responsive. To cite just one recent example, an agricultural cooperative with 108 cows has been delivering daily a mere 131 liters of milk, whereas cows belonging privately to the members of the same cooperative have been averaging 8 liters per cow.[75] In another instance, the problem of increasing milk deliveries was conveniently solved by "forgetting" a little water in each milk can after washing, thereby providing an additional 20 liters a day.[76] Yet another collective farm, which fulfilled its prescribed quota of potato deliveries by 27 percent only, could nevertheless distribute among its members 2 to 3 kilograms of potatoes per each labor unit so that "they might

[74] *Rudé právo,* November 9, 1951, June 15, 1953; *Zemědělské noviny,* January 8, 1955; *Dikobraz,* June 9, 1955 and March 29, 1956; *Rudé právo,* July 10, 1959.
[75] *Československý zpravodaj,* No. 221, November 20, 1958.
[76] *ibid.,* No. 271, December 4, 1959.

feed more pigs on their plots and have a bigger income from their personal holdings."[77] Another favorite means to the same end seems to be to collude with potato diggers so that they leave a part of the potato crop in the ground during the "official" harvest—and dig them out clandestinely for private use later. In a district in Northern Bohemia the potato situation in 1958 thus reached a point where fewer potatoes were harvested than had been planted![78] Similarly, sugarbeets are sometimes withheld surreptitiously to be used as feed rather than handed over for sugar production.[79] Not only feeds but also fertilizers and even livestock seem to have a persistent tendency to vanish from state and collective farms and find their way into private possession. For instance, on a state farm in Bohemia a sudden check by the controlling organs found twenty-three employees to be in unlawful possession of 499 chickens, 30 ducks, 145 geese, 23 sheep, 34 goats, and 20 pigs.[80] A convenient method of effecting such "transfers" has been to cut in on the deal all those concerned with certifying animal deaths and thus get the desired animal offspring recorded officially as having perished. Together with genuine deaths caused by natural causes and neglect, these artificial reductions account for the high mortality of collective livestock.

Similar neglect, evasion, and downright cheating has characterized the work of the machine-tractor stations. With monotonous regularity they have been taken to task year after year for gross negligence in maintenance, resulting in much of their machinery being incapacitated when it was needed most.[81] Stealing and illegal trading of hard-to-get spare parts has been commonplace; and before even a minor part could be obtained through official channels the time for ploughing or harvesting was often gone.[82] This goes a long way toward explaining why the impressive statistical figures of huge deliveries of tractors and other agricultural machinery have not been reflected in similarly impressive output results. Also, the all-important purpose of checking on collective farms through the STS has frequently been defeated by mutually advantageous collusion between tractorists and collective farmers, such as having the tractor brigade plough, illegally and on the

---

[77] *Rudé právo,* January 6, 1958.
[78] *Zemědělské noviny,* January 27, 1959; *Československý zpravodaj,* No. 233, February 18, 1959.
[79] *Rudé právo,* November 19, 1959.
[80] *Zemědělské noviny,* October 3, 1952; *Rudé právo,* December 24, 1952; *Zemědělské noviny,* May 13, 1953.
[81] *Rudé právo,* January 13, 1953.
[82] *ibid.,* October 14, 1953.

government's time, the farmers' private plots or concealed land in exchange for special rewards, and covering up the deal by falsifying data on the documents of work performance.[83]

Aware of these practices, the KSČ leaders have combated them relentlessly through the notorious combination of the whip and the carrot, but as yet with meager results. Undoubtedly, after the completion of agricultural collectivization scheduled for 1961, the regime will be able to apply its controls more effectively and thus reduce

TABLE XV
Prewar and Postwar Output of Agricultural Goods

Commodity	Units	1926-1930	1934-1938	1948	1953	1958	1959	1960	1965 Plan
Wheat	million tons	1.32	1.51ᵃ	1.43	1.56	1.35	1.65	1.5	
Rye	" "	1.67	1.58	1.14	0.95	0.94	0.97	0.88	
Barley	" "	1.29	1.12	0.9	1.25	1.12	1.47	1.74	
Oats	" "	1.40	1.21	1.0	0.87	0.87	0.94	1.04	
Potatoes	" "	8.78	9.64	6.07	9.7	6.59	6.59	5.25	
Sugar beets	" "	6.66	4.7	4.29	5.59	6.95	4.9	8.40	
Corn	" "	0.24	0.23	0.3ᵇ	0.4	0.48	0.50	0.59	
Fruit and nuts	" "		0.48	0.64	0.72	0.77	0.47		
Meat (live weight)	" "			0.44	0.70	0.89	0.90		1.3
Beef	" "			0.20	0.30	0.31	0.32	0.34	
Pork	" "			0.27	0.36	0.54	0.55	0.55	
Raisins	million quintals			0.66	0.35	0.93	0.49		
Hops	thousand tons	11.3	7.0	4.99	5.63	6.51	5.95		
Tobacco	" "	8.0	13.1	9.01	11.8	7.85	7.08		
Cattle	million head			4.71	3.66	4.08	4.18	4.3	4.8
Cows	" "			1.87	1.87	2.15	2.08	2.07	2.3
Pigs	" "			3.54	3.42	4.17	5.28	5.69	5.7
Sheep	" "			0.54	0.46	1.02	0.82	0.73	0.6
Poultry	" "			16.39	21.09	25.36	27.57		
Milk	million hl.			25.0	31.5	36.5	36.6		54.0
Eggs	millions			1.1	2.0	2.1	2.1	2.6	3.0

ᵃ 1.98 in 1933; ᵇ estimate.

Sources: *Czechoslovak Statistical Yearbooks* and other announcements of the Czechoslovak Office of Statistics.

the peasants' peculative practices. With the aid of agricultural schools and its courses on agrotechnics and zootechnics the regime will in due time overcome the glaring lack of agricultural know-how among many of those made to volunteer for agricultural work to replace the aging farmers of pre-communist days. However, as long as the KSČ leaders remain guided by the present Marxist-Leninist agricultural precepts, they are likely to be confronted with peasants' resist-

[83] *Pravda,* May 12, 1953.

ance, which is the primary source of the regime's agricultural troubles. Hiding wisely behind a protective cloak of anonymity, a Czechoslovak peasant hit the nail on the head when he wrote in a recent letter to the editor of a regional communist paper in Czechoslovakia:

"After the First World War we were looted to the very bones—and how long did it take before we recovered? No one had to prod our farmers and remind them of the agrotechnical timetables, yet everyone knew when to sow and when to harvest. And how did they manage under the Occupation [during World War II]? Though the Germans took what they wanted, there still was enough left over. Now we have been talking for eleven years about large-scale production, and agricultural products continue to be so expensive. Many mistakes were made. There have been many methods, but none has brought any miracle. *The miracle could occur only when love for the land returns and the children of the farmers and agricultural workers tread in the footsteps of their old parents—as it used to be.*"[84]

[84] *Cesta míru,* September 19, 1959, *Československý zpravodaj,* No. 268, November, 16, 1959. Italics added.

CHAPTER XVII

THE HUMAN COST

IN THE PRECEDING two chapters an attempt has been made to evaluate Czechoslovak industrial and agricultural developments under the dictatorship of the proletariat strictly in terms of economic achievement. The present chapter will consider them in terms of their contribution, or lack of it, to the over-all well-being of the Czechoslovak man-in-the-street.

The consideration of communism's economic attainments within such a frame of reference is crucial for their correct over-all evaluation. With all its emphasis on economic determinism the teaching of Marx and Lenin regards economic arrangements only as a means to an end. The elimination of private ownership of the means of production, the all-embracing economic planning, the reckless industrialization drive, and the lopsided emphasis on capital goods production—all this is allegedly done for the sake of abolishing the exploitation of man by man, promoting a more equitable distribution of goods and services, and providing for higher levels of social welfare than those obtainable under a capitalist system. It is supposed to generate an overabundance of material values that is considered to be one of the chief prerequisites for the establishment of the communist millenium when man's needs rather than his work should serve as the criterion of his reward. By releasing wage-earners from dependence on the "profit-greedy capitalist bread-givers" the communist economic system claims not only to improve man's material well-being but to substitute "genuine" freedom that only communism can offer for the meaningless "formal" freedom provided under the capitalist rule. "Only socialism is destined to create for the first time in history dignified humane conditions for all and provide freedom for all; and this is possible solely because of the unprecedented development of production and only to the extent in which such a development will continue."[1]

How does the balance sheet of Czechoslovak economy under the dictatorship of the proletariat look in these respects?

[1] *Práce,* July 31, 1958.

LIVING STANDARDS

First to be considered, for several reasons, are living standards. As proclaimed by the law enacting the very first of Czechoslovakia's long-term economic plans, the main purpose of economic planning is a "substantial increase in the living standards of all working masses of the town and the country."[2] Although the First Five-Year Plan failed miserably in this particular respect, the post-Stalin era brought a notable improvement and the standard of living in present-day Czechoslovakia is considerably higher than in her sister-satellites. Some Western observers of the Czechoslovak scene even suggest that this higher level of material well-being played an important part in keeping Czechoslovakia quiet while unrest and outright rebellion were sweeping the neighboring people's democracies of Poland and Hungary in 1955-1956. More recently, the KSČ leaders have been using the issue of improved living conditions to score for communism in the Khrushchëv-sponsored international competition of ideas between capitalism and communism. Capitalizing on the fact that Czechoslovakia had always had a higher standard of living than her less fortunate Eastern European neighbors, they have striven hard to portray communist Czechoslovakia as a show window of socialism. "At the end of the Third Five-Year Plan [in 1965]," boasted *Pravda* in January 1960, "Czechoslovakia will be far ahead of the United States, Great Britain, the German Federal Republic, and France, and she will be a model for these states, not to speak of other capitalist countries, insofar as the standards of living are concerned."[3]

In order to decide what, if any, credit is due to the communist regime of Czechoslovakia in this respect, the results which it has attained in the field of the citizens' material well-being must be measured with a fourfold yardstick: (1) Have living standards under the rule of communism risen above pre-communist levels? (2) If the answer is in the affirmative, have they risen by a greater margin than would have resulted from normal technological, economic, and social progress irrespective of political system? (3) Is the material well-being distributed more equitably in present-day Czechoslovakia than prior to the communist seizure of power? (4) If the answer is in the affirmative, to what extent is it due to communist efforts rather than the general world-wide postwar trend toward the welfare state?

[2] Law No. 241 of October 27, 1948.
[3] *Pravda* (Bratislava), January 3, 1960.

Evidently, such a measurement calls for a comparison of present Czechoslovak living standards, not only with those of pre-communist days, but also with corresponding developments in those non-communist countries whose prewar pattern of material well-being approximated that of Czechoslovakia.

Real Wages

The most telling barometer of material well-being is real income, i.e., the expression of nominal earnings in terms of their actual purchasing power. Hence, a comparison of the average real income of the Czechoslovak wage earner under the communist regime with that of prewar days on the one hand, and with that in non-communist countries on a comparable level of economic development on the other, should go a long way toward answering the first two of the above-stated four questions.

Comparing real wages and salaries in communist Czechoslovakia with those earned before the War, the communist regime claims massive increases ranging from 30 percent upward. According to a 1957 government publication on Czechoslovakia's position in the world economy, real wages of workers and employees in 1956 were 30.8 percent higher than in 1937 so that "the working people of Czechoslovakia could buy and obtain for their wages in 1956 . . . almost one-third more merchandise of everyday need and services than in 1937."[4] The *Prague News Letter,* communist Czechoslovakia's propaganda mouthpiece in the Anglo-Saxon world, puts the rise of real wages by 1957 at "more than 36 percent" above the 1937 level and *Statistické Zprávy* estimates the increase to have reached 56 percent by 1960.[5] If these and similar claims could be accepted at their face value, then the communist record in this respect would have to be highly commended. While such an increase in real earnings in the course of more than two decades would not be unusual, it would certainly be commendable. But a closer examination sets the matter in an altogether different perspective.

To begin with, the communist comparison distorts the reality by a partisan selection of only such prewar data as suit the regime's purpose of depicting life in prewar Czechoslovakia in blackest colors so as to make the present look so much whiter. Thus, for instance, the

[4] *Postavení,* p. 123.
[5] *Prague News Letter,* 14, 8, April 26, 1958, and *Statistické zprávy,* No. 8, 1960, p. 21.

above-mentioned issue of the *Prague News Letter* compares the average 1957 earnings of 4.6 million wage earners, comprising all persons working in the socialist sector of the national economy except the members of collective farms and apprentices, with only 3.2 out of some 4 million persons engaged in gainful occupations outside agriculture before the War. In order to lower prewar average earnings, the communist propagandists deliberately disregarded almost one million gainfully employed persons earning higher incomes in prewar days while including, on the other hand, such better-paid individuals in their calculations of the average wages and salaries in 1957.[6] Moreover, prewar Czechoslovak statistics of workers' wages were based on data used for accident and old age insurance which did not accurately reflect actual earnings because of the widespread practice of many enterprises of reporting lower wages than were actually paid in order to save on insurance premiums. Nor were overtime pay and Christmas and other bonuses, customarily paid workers by many prewar enterprises, included in the computation of prewar wages, whereas premiums and bonuses were counted in arriving at current average earnings.[7] Only in this way could the communist propagandists come up with a figure of 742 crowns as the average monthly pay per employed person in 1937 and an average of 476 crowns per worker in the same year. In reality, monthly pay of the manual worker in 1937 came to 826 crowns while the average monthly earnings of salaried personnel ranged from 1,366 to 1,192 crowns between 1929 and 1936.[8]

A similar distortion characterizes the communist computation of living costs. Since the index of real wages is simply the ratio between the indices of nominal wages and the cost of living, its accuracy is gravely impaired whenever items composing the statistical consumer basket are not readily obtainable at prices used in the computation of the cost-of-living index. Yet this is precisely what has been happening in communist Czechoslovakia, and on a quite substantial scale. As

---

[6] For prewar data see *Ročenka,* 1937, p. 19.

[7] That these factors made wages appear lower than they actually were was conceded even by a communist writer in 1957. See Jan Křen, *Československo v období dočasné a relativní stabilisace kapitalismu* (Czechoslovakia in the Period of a Temporary and Relative Stabilization of Capitalism), Praha, 1957, p. 252.

[8] See J. A. Trutnovský, *Worker's Standard of Living in Czechoslovakia, 1949-1951,* a mimeographed study of the Free Europe Committee, New York, 1952; *Ročenka,* 1937, p. 223. *The Yearbook of the International Labor Office,* Geneva, 1951, p. 301, lists the weekly earnings of a Czechoslovak worker in 1937 as 192.47 crowns and his family income as 286.06 crowns.

documented both by non-communist sources and by the communist press, the Czechoslovak market for consumer goods has been plagued continually by a sort of Gresham law in reverse, substituting costlier merchandise for cheaper assortments. Whenever the government lowers the prices, the lower-priced merchandise begins invariably to vanish from retail counters, and consumers have no choice but to buy more expensive substitutes. "In connection with the price reduction [of March 1959]," wrote *Rudé právo,* "it is necessary once again to condemn phenomena which have been criticized by our working people in the [recent] nation-wide discussion, such as the attempts of some of our production plants and trade establishments to eliminate the cheapest classes of merchandise and to replace them with the so-called better and naturally also more expensive products."[9] Thus, as the paper conceded, "the consumer is compelled against his will to buy costlier articles." That the difference is by no means negligible is revealed by specific complaints which occasionally make their way into the daily press.[10] Not even the display of wanted items in the shop's window guarantees their availability to the customer. Under the pretext that it would "spoil the display" salesmen often refuse to sell articles put on display.[11] Yet another favorite stratagem, used particularly in food stores, is to let customers have the merchandise, such as lemons, if they agree to purchase at the same time another article that the store wishes to dispose of, such as apples.[12]

As a result of these malpractices, which are of general occurrence despite the regime's effort to curb them, the communist cost-of-living index reflects reality about as accurately as would its American equivalent if it were based predominantly on "specials" or "white sale" prices designed to lure customers to the store or to get rid of "cats and dogs." Therefore, the communist claim that the 1959 indices of the cost of living for worker and employee households and agricultural households stood only at 17.8 and 28.8 percent, respectively, above the 1937 levels must be considered as grossly misrepresentative.[13]

[9] *Rudé právo,* April 5, 1959.

[10] For instance, a man's shirt supposed to sell for 39 crowns could not be had for less than 50; the cheapest nylon stockings priced at 23 crowns were unavailable and the customer had to buy a "better" assortment for 42 crowns; children's leather shoes cost a mother 100 crowns instead of 50 listed as the official price; etc. *Rudé právo,* December 13, 1959; *Pravda,* December 29, 1959; *Práce,* January 5, 1959.

[11] *Československý zpravodaj,* No. 264, October 22, 1959, and No. 279, January 26, 1960.

[12] *ibid.,* No. 227, January 6, 1959.

[13] *Ročenka,* 1960, pp. 389, 391.

This misrepresentation of reality is further enhanced by the deterioration in the quality of many of the items going into the statistical consumer basket. Incessant customer complaints citing innumerable and often shocking examples of poor quality unheard-of in prewar days leave no doubt that merchandise retailed in communist Czechoslovakia is often markedly inferior in quality to similar wares in prewar days.[14] What this means for the actual cost of living is obvious: If, for instance, a given suit or dress costs twice as much today as before the War but wears out twice as fast, its price has in fact quadrupled. Since many of the articles covered in the present cost-of-living index do not compare in quality with their prewar counterparts, the customer's purchasing power is in reality lower than the communist index would suggest, though it is impossible to estimate by how much.

Finally, in evaluating the communist claims of real-wage increases, it must be borne in mind that they had to be paid for by more work. While the average work week in Czechoslovak manufacturing was 44.98 hours in 1939, it jumped to 48.87 hours after the communist seizure of power in 1948.[15] In 1957 it was formally reduced to 46 hours, but there is strong evidence indicating that the extra work which is habitually needed to meet the Plan's exacting goals continues to keep the work week generally above the prescribed maximum. As of 1958 the actual work hours in Czechoslovak manufacturing were listed as 8.1 hours per work day.[16] Also, until the 1959-1960 wage reform, over 70 percent of workers' earnings were derived from piece work and various bonuses for overfulfillment of the plan as against only some 13-16 percent earned in straight time wages.[17] Moreover, as corroborated by a flood of recent complaints, many Czechoslovak wage earners seem to have been hurt by the overhaul of the entire wage and work norm system undertaken in 1959-1960. Introduced with the avowed purpose of "increasing and consolidating

[14] See examples in Chapter xv.

[15] *The Yearbook of the International Labor Office 1949-1950,* Geneva, 1951.

[16] *Statistical Yearbook of the United Nations,* 1959, p. 60. The Czechoslovak work week includes Saturdays as a regular workday with somewhat shorter work hours. How illusory the 1957 work-week reduction really was has been revealed by *Hospodářské noviny* which stated on August 26, 1960, that the average shift of the construction workers was 8.1 hours in 1957, 8.2 hours in 1958, 8.4 hours in 1959, and 8.5 hours in the first half of 1960.

[17] *Ročenka,* 1959, p. 160. Also, Valerian Rizga and Michal Hronský, *Odměňováni práce ve výrobě* (Remuneration for Work in Production), Praha, 1959, p. 34. After the 1959 reform of the work norms, the proportion of work hours covered by piece rates sank to 54 percent.

the material incentive of the workers so as to insure an uninterrupted rise in output and productivity,"[18] the new system evidently has brought an over-all strengthening of work norms which resulted in reduced earnings for those who would not or could not live up to the tougher work schedules.[19]

Viewed in the light of the above-mentioned factors the communist regime's record in the real-wage area is far less impressive than the first cursory look at the released statistical data would suggest. While the absence of dependable over-all data precludes an accurate measurement, there is nevertheless enough material on which to base at least an approximate evaluation of the communist record in this respect.

The first obstacle to be overcome is the fact that prewar Czechoslovak wage statistics give data only for certain categories of workers and employees and, being based mostly on basic wages as reported for social insurance purposes, do not reflect actual earnings in their entirety. Hence, it is impossible to determine accurately one of the key figures for a dependable computation of the real-wage index: namely, what was *in toto* the average nominal income of a gainfully employed Czechoslovakian before the War. Nevertheless, a rough estimate can be made on the following basis: With the exclusion of agriculture all the gainfully employed persons in prewar Czechoslovakia were divided statistically into four broad categories:[20]

Independent operators	585,541
Office personnel	469,435
Custodial personnel	479,291
Manual workers and apprentices	2,604,374

Income data published in prewar statistical yearbooks cover only the office personnel in private employment (over 300,000) and workers covered by workmen's compensation insurance (some 1,700,000). The average annual earning for the first-named group, both men and women, as reported for old age insurance was 16,400 crowns in 1929

---

[18] See the open letter of the Party's Central Committee, *Rudé právo,* November 20, 1958.

[19] *Práce,* May 28 and December 8, 1959; *Rudé právo,* September 22, 1959, January 3 and February 18, 1960; items 244/60 and 673/60 from the files of the Free Europe Committee, New York.

[20] *Ročenka,* 1937, p. 19. In addition to agriculture, which must be left out because the corresponding communist statistics omit not only private farmers but also members of the JZD from their calculations, the only groups excluded are persons living off subsidies and pensions and inmates of institutions.

and 15,800 in 1931, which would correspond to a mean monthly income of 1,341 crowns. The average monthly earning of the second-named group, as registered for workmen's compensation insurance, amounted to 710 crowns.[21] As similar income averages are not available for other categories, independent operators and civil servants will be added to office personnel and custodial personnel to manual workers. This can be done as a rough rule of thumb on the assumption that the average monthly income of civil servants was close to, and that of independent operators undoubtedly exceeded, the average salary of office personnel in private employment while the average monthly wages of custodial personnel approximated those of manual workers. Thus two broad categories of gainfully employed persons obtain: that of independent operators and office employees comprising 1,054,886 persons with the estimated average monthly income of 1,341 crowns and that of manual workers and custodial personnel, comprising 3,083,665 persons, with an estimated average monthly wage of 710 crowns. The ratio of the two categories being roughly 1:3, monthly earnings computed for both together would average 868 crowns. This is a conservative estimate and the actual average earnings in prewar Czechoslovakia were probably higher than that. Nonetheless, though deliberately downgraded, this computation sharply reduces the communist claim of a 68.2 percent rise of nominal earnings between 1937 and 1956 to a much more modest 44 percent increase between 1937 and 1957. Even if one would accept at its face value the communist index of the cost of living registering a simultaneous 20.8 percent increase over 1937, the result would be an increase in real wage of 19.2 over the prewar level rather than "over 36 percent" as claimed by the communist propagandists. However, since the real cost of living is considerably higher than asserted by the official communist index, the real-wage index must be cut down correspondingly.

That is indicated also by Table XVI below which compares the purchasing power of the Czechoslovak workers' earnings for 1937 and 1957. The main problem encountered in the preparation of the table has been the absence of any data on the workers' average hourly earnings. While the communist catalogues of work list hourly rates for various categories and classes of workers, no over-all figures are available on what the Czechoslovak worker actually averages for one

[21] *ibid.*, pp. 221 and 223. Monthly earnings were ascertained by dividing the total of reported wages by the number of insured individuals for 1929 and 1931.

hour's work. Hence an approximate estimate of 6.76 crowns per hour was arrived at by dividing the mean annual earning per worker by the estimated sum total of hours for which he received wages in the same year.[22] That the estimate is close to reality is corroborated by the partial data of selected hourly earnings supplied by the Czecho-slovak government in response to the inquiry of the International Labor Office in 1958.[23] Actual average hourly earnings of unskilled laborers in various sectors of industrial production range from 5.24 crowns in textile production to 6.08 in machine industry and 6.35 in construction, whereas the corresponding hourly earnings of skilled workers seem to fall mostly within the 6-8.50 brackets for all but the privileged branches of mining, steel, and heavy machinery. On the other hand weekly earnings cause no problem as they can be computed from the given monthly earnings. As for the prewar period, the only data on hourly earnings found in the *Czechoslovak Yearbooks of Statistics* refer to the average hourly rate for thirty-two different types of industry and trade in the capital city of Praha, which is listed as 4.34 crowns for 1936 and 4.32 for 1938.[24] The corresponding weekly rate is listed as 207.91 for 1938. Despite its obvious limitations, a comparison based on these approximate sets of figures can nevertheless serve at least as another useful clue for the evaluation of the communist claims in the real-wage field.

As the Table XVI reveals, as of 1957 the Czechoslovak worker under communism was still worse off than his fellow-worker in prewar Czechoslovakia when shopping around for his everyday necessities. Except for bread, potatoes, milk, sirloin beef, beer, and cigarettes, he had to work longer to be able to buy the same quantity of food than before the War. He suffered likewise when he needed clothing, footwear, or home furnishings. While he did not have to put in as many hours of work as in prewar days to pay for his utilities and heating, this could improve his position only very slightly as the bulk of his income is spent on food, clothing, and durable goods. The modest price reductions enacted in 1959 and 1960 and the wage increase by about 4 percent registered between 1957 and 1959 have certainly

---

[22] For this purpose, the 286.1 days for which the average industrial worker was paid wages in 1957 (264.3 on which he actually worked, 17.6 of paid leave, 2.5 of fulfillment of other duties, and 1.7 of free time formally granted) were multiplied by 8 in line with the ILO statistics giving 8.1 as an average workday in Czechoslovak manufacturing in 1957.

[23] See *Statistical Supplement* to the *International Labour Review*, LXXX, 1 (1959), p. 22.

[24] *Ročenka,* 1937, pp. 226-227, and *Yearbook of Labor Statistics,* 1939, p. 110.

TABLE XVI
Purchasing Power of Hourly and Weekly Earnings of Czechoslovak Workers,
1937 and 1957

Hours of Work[1] Needed to Buy in		Unit	Article	Quantity of Same Articles that Could Be Purchased with One Week's Pay in[2]	
1937	1957			1937	1957
0.52	0.39	1 kg.	Rye bread	92.44	110.0
0.65	0.66	"	White flour	74.29	81.71
0.71	1.07	"	Rice	68.19	39.72
3.95	3.58	"	Beef sirloin	12.23	11.91
3.09	4.18	"	Pork loin chops	15.64	10.24
3.66	3.73	"	Sausages	13.12	11.44
2.53	2.79	"	Margarine	19.08	15.88
3.84	6.28	"	Butter	12.6	6.81
0.12	0.09	"	Potatoes	416.0	461.0
1.48	1.64	"	Sugar	32.75	26.0
8.37	31.34	"	Coffee	5.77	1.36
1.16	1.28	"	Soap (laundry)	41.6	33.25
0.11	0.15	1 piece	Eggs	416.0	286.0
0.35	0.30	1 liter	Milk	138.66	143.0
0.60	0.36	"	Beer	80.0	119.17
1.4	1.2	1 pack	Cigarettes	29.7	35.7
4.84	2.39	100 kg.	Household coal (brown)	10.0	17.93
6.28	1.19	10 kw-hrs	Electricity	7.70	35.75
34.88	7.46	100 cu.m.	Cooking gas	1.39	5.72
1.05	2.36	1 meter[a]	Cotton shirt cloth	46.22	18.10
1.02	2.11	1 meter[b]	Cotton dress cloth	47.27	20.14
27.91	59.57	1 meter[c]	Wool suit cloth	1.73	0.72
63.95	72.74	1 piece	Man's suit, half wool	0.75	0.59
116.27	161.19	"	Man's suit, all wool	0.42	0.24
39.07	50.30	"	Man's overcoat, wool	1.24	0.85
36.28	41.04	"	Lady's dress, all wool	1.33	1.04
71.16	86.56	"	Lady's overcoat	0.68	0.49
21.39	24.18	"	Boy's suit (9 years)	2.26	1.77
6.51	6.94	"	Man's cotton shirt	7.43	6.17
0.93	0.81	1 pair	Man's cotton socks	52.0	53.15
18.37	26.27	"	Man's leather shoes	2.63	1.63
15.12	23.28	"	Lady's leather shoes	3.20	1.84
2.79	3.05	"	Man's leather soles	17.33	14.06
534.88	544.77	1 suite	Bedroom furniture	0.09	0.08
300.0	369.0	"	Kitchen furniture	0.16	0.12
138.37	80.59	1 piece	Man's bicycle	0.35	0.53
1,160.5	1,313.4	1 piece	Motorcycle (Jawa)	0.04	0.03

[1] Hourly wage for 1937: 4.3 crowns; for 1957, 6.7 crowns.
[2] Weekly wage for 1937: 208 crowns, and for 1957, 286 crowns.
[a] 80 cm. wide; [b] 70 cm. wide; [c] 140 cm. wide.
Source: For 1937 and 1957 prices, *Ročenka*, 1959, pp. 383-384, and 1958, pp. 324-325.

helped to stretch the purchasing power of the earnings above that of 1957.[25] However, since the decreed 1959 and 1960 price cuts apply only to very few food items, it does not appear that the over-all purchasing power of the hourly earnings could have as yet been raised above that of 1937. Nor should it be forgotten that the above table applies only to manual workers who enjoy a privileged position in the distribution of material well-being in communist Czechoslovakia. If a similar comparison could be made for other categories of gainfully employed persons, the communist system would fare much worse.

And how do the real wages in communist Czechoslovakia compare with those prevalent in her non-communist neighborhood? That there is little to boast about is suggested by the profound communist silence in this respect. While extolling everything possible in Czechoslovak economy and indulging in numerous other comparisons with non-communist countries, the official publication on *The Position of Czechoslovakia in World Economy* evades painstakingly any comparison of real wages, using as an excuse "the methodological difference" of non-communist indices.[26] Nevertheless, it unwittingly reveals the real reason for its reticence by claiming that "the average earning of the ordinary worker is . . . distorted considerably" by the high salaries of some of the more privileged employees in the capitalist countries and that capitalist calculations are "embellished for purposes of exploitation."

That something other than the methodological difference in the making of indices accounts for the obvious Czechoslovak reluctance to compare real earnings in Czechoslovakia with those of non-communist countries is shown by the Tables XVII and XVIII below.[27] Table XVII considers the over-all level of earnings in terms of hours which an average worker in manufacturing has to work to be able to buy a stated quantity of various consumer goods of everyday use.[28] Table XVIII is based on data on hourly earnings in individual occupations which were sent to the International Labor Office in response to the above-mentioned inquiry in October 1958. Since occu-

---

[25] For price reductions see *Ročenka*, 1959, pp. 383-384; *Prague News Letter*, 15, 6, March 21, 1959, and 16, 9, April 30, 1960. For wage increase in 1958 see *Ročenka*, 1959, p. 18; for that in 1959, *Rudé právo*, February 9, 1960.

[26] *Postavení*, p. 123.

[27] Austria, Belgium, France, and Western Germany were selected as the non-communist countries of comparable economic development and the United States was included for the benefit of the U.S. reader.

[28] For the computation of the average hourly earnings of the Czechoslovak workers see n. 22 above.

pations on which information was supplied do not always coincide, only twelve such occupations could be chosen for which comparative data are available. The purchasing power has been expressed in terms of the number of hours which a person employed in each of the twelve occupations must work in order to be able to buy a specified package of food.[29]

TABLE XVII

Purchasing Power of Hourly Earnings of Workers in Manufacturing, 1957

| Unit | Merchandise | HOURS OF WORK NEEDED TO BUY IN | | | | |
		Czecho-slovakia[a]	West Germany	Belgium[b]	United States	France[c]
1 kg.	White bread	0.54	0.48	0.27	0.21	0.28
"	Wheat flour	0.66	0.37	0.55	0.18	
"	Rice	1.07	0.48	0.63	0.20	
"	Boneless sirloin beef	4.03	2.42	4.52	1.11	3.5
"	Loin pork chops	4.18	2.75	3.36	0.96	
"	Boneless cooked ham	8.98	3.85	4.36	0.65	4.0
"	Margarine	3.73	0.98	0.89	0.32	1.0
"	Butter	6.28	3.40	3.51	0.80	3.25
"	Potatoes	0.09	0.10	0.08	0.05	
"	Sugar	1.55	0.57	0.52	0.12	0.41
"	Roasted coffee	25.37	9.57	4.63	1.04	4.0
"	Apples	0.90	0.80	0.47	0.11	
100 kg.	Household coal	2.63	3.6	7.69	1.5	4.5
1 liter	Pasteurized milk	0.31	0.20	0.27	0.13	0.20
"	Beer	0.42	0.65	0.22		
1	Egg	0.22	0.12	0.10	0.03	0.07
100 gr.	Laundry soap	0.13	0.9	0.04	0.02	
20	Cigarettes	0.48	0.80	0.30	0.12	0.39
10 kw-hrs	Electricity	1.2	1.1	1.26	0.3	1.1
100 cu.m.	Cooking gas	7.46	15.5	13.32	2.3	

[a] Figures differ on a few items because of the difference in prices and quality; [b] in 1958; [c] workers in the Paris region.

Sources: Data on prices and wages in 1957 taken from *Yearbook of Labor Statistics*, 1958; data for Belgian prices from *Statistical Supplement, International Labour Review*, LXXX, 1, July 1959; data on Belgian wages from Belgian Embassy, Washington, D.C.; wages for Czechoslovakia computed from monthly earnings in the manner statedho-note 22. For purposes of computation, wages have been rounded as follows: Czec in slovakia, 6.7 instead of 6.76; West Germany, 2.1 instead of 2.13; Belgium, 28 instead of 27.91; U.S., 2.07 as listed. Wherever different prices were listed, the highest has been used. Data on France taken from "Le débat du niveau de vie," *Entreprise*, No. 195, May 30, 1959, pp. 53-55.

As Tables XVI, XVII, and XVIII reveal, with few exceptions, the Czechoslovak worker can buy with his earnings less than his counterpart in the non-communist neighborhood, not to speak of the United States. Indeed, reality is even worse than indicated because, in contrast to the other countries except West Germany, the data per-

[29] France could not be included but for a few items because of the lack of comparable data.

TABLE XVIII

Purchasing Power of Hourly Earnings of Manual Workers in Twelve
Occupations in 1958[1]

Occupation	Czechoslovakia	Austria	Belgium[a]	France	West Germany
Coal hewer	37.94	56.54	26.76	37.52	32.12
Coal loader (underground)	51.49	62.20	31.71	37.52	50.00
Baker (ovenman)	68.90	67.06	46.52		42.40
Weaver	107.50	103.84[a]	45.63		44.17
Unskilled laborer in textile	112.02	113.71[a]	57.59		56.99
Cabinet-maker	79.11	83.49[a]	41.61		44.91
Upholsterer	91.43	83.49[a]	41.61		50.48
Unskilled laborer (in steel)	90.03	78.73	58.65	40.38[b]	46.08
Machinery fitter (assembler)	71.93	65.48	52.21	38.62[b]	40.62
Bricklayer	78.79	73.61	39.56		39.85
Unskilled laborer (in construction)	92.52	79.74	46.60		48.40
Electrical fitter (outside lines)	69.55	62.20	42.96		40.00

[1] Purchasing power is expressed in the number of hours of work required to buy a food package containing: 10 kg. white bread, 10 kg. wheat flour, 3 kg. rice, 1 kg. boneless sirloin beef, 1 kg. boneless pork loin chops, 1 kg. boneless cooked ham, 1 kg. margarine, 1 kg. butter, 10 liters pasteurized milk, 5 dozen eggs, 10 kg. potatoes, 5 kg. cabbage, 5 kg. apples, 5 kg. sugar, ½ kg. coffee, 3 liters beer, and 100 cigarettes.

[a] Minimum rate; [b] exclusive of overtime.

Source: Computed from data taken from the *Statistical Supplement, International Labour Review*, LXXX, 1, July 1959.

taining to Czechoslovakia in Table XVII refer to workers in the entire industry rather than manufacturing alone. The inclusion of workers of extracting industries who represent by far the highest paid category creates an upward bias.[30] So does the exclusion of 58,000 employees listed as "other" in Czechoslovak statistics who were earning 1,000 crowns per month in 1957 as compared to 1,292 for those labeled "workers."[31] Such auxiliary labor in other countries is lumped into one category with the workers. Nor should it be forgotten that the comparison would look much worse for Czechoslovakia if it included nonmanual employees whose salaries, save for a narrow managerial and technical élite, are far below those of the above-mentioned non-communist countries.

The disadvantage in which the Czechoslovak citizen finds himself under the dictatorship of the proletariat in relation to citizens of non-

[30] For instance, the average hourly earning of an underground coal hewer stood at 15.47 crowns in 1958, i.e., almost three times the hourly earning of an unskilled laborer in textiles.

[31] *Ročenka*, 1958, p. 124.

communist countries when shopping around in his retail stores is somewhat lessened when it comes to paying rent. Though the absence of fully comparable data does not permit an accurate computation, the figures in Tables XVI, XVII, and XVIII pertaining to utilities and household fuels show that, with the exception of electricity, the said items cost less in Czechoslovakia than in the European countries used for comparison. These are also the only goods of everyday use that are today cheaper in Czechoslovakia even in terms of nominal prices than they used to be before the War; and the same is true of rents.[32] Rent constituted in 1958 only 1.6 percent of the expenses of the Czechoslovak worker family and 2 percent of those of nonmanual employee, which is well below the corresponding percentages for accommodation in non-communist countries.[33] However, as shown below, the dwelling quarters that the average Czechoslovakian gets in return are pitifully inadequate even by the rather crowded Western European standards.

Another advantage which the Czechoslovak worker and employee enjoys over his counterparts in the Free World is the higher security of his earnings. Although they are lower than those of his fellow-workers in the economically advanced countries of the non-communist world, they are more secure against the pitfalls of unemployment. Moreover, the relative dearth of manpower which characterizes the present stage of the socialist construction in Czechoslovakia provides better opportunities for gainful employment of married women. Thus the worker's wife contributed 13.5 percent and the employee's wife 18.8 percent to the average family income in 1958.[34]

While the available statistical data allow a meaningful, though only approximate, real-income comparison with the levels in prewar Czechoslovakia and in the non-communist countries with regard to industrial workers and, to a lesser extent, other nonagricultural employees, no such comparison can be made in the field of agriculture. It is possible, of course, to compare nominal wages of agricultural

---

[32] The average rent for a kitchen-and-bedroom apartment in Praha in 1937 was 1,350 crowns per annum in older houses under government rent control and 3,300 in newer houses not subject to rent control; the average for the two was 2,650 crowns. Corresponding figures for a kitchen-and-two-bedroom apartment were 2,462 and 5,292 crowns. *Annuaire Statistique de la République Tchécoslovaque*, Praha, 1938, p. 159. Today rent ranges from 900 to 1,200 crowns per annum and a kitchen-and-two-bedroom apartment with central heating in Praha rents for 2,200 crowns, according to Czechoslovak official sources.

[33] *Ročenka*, 1959, p. 381.

[34] *Ročenka*, 1958, p. 323.

laborers; and such a comparison reflects favorably upon communist Czechoslovakia in relation both to prewar levels and to wages paid agricultural workers in non-communist countries of Central and Western Europe.[35] But the overwhelming majority of persons engaged in agriculture in prewar Czechoslovakia were self-employed independent peasants; and that is true also of non-communist Europe of today. The nearest equivalent in present-day Czechoslovakia are, together with the small and steadily dwindling leftover of individual peasantry, collective farmers; and these two categories together outnumber the state farm and machine-tractor station employees, the only group of agricultural laborers of today, almost by 9 to 1.[36]

Although replete with other data on agriculture, the official *Czechoslovak Yearbooks of Statistics* are altogether silent about the average earnings of either individual or collective farmers. However, a Czechoslovak economics magazine stated in 1958 that the money income of the individual peasant averaged 4,409 crowns per annum in 1956 and the agricultural products which he kept were worth 6,859 crowns. Simultaneously, the money income of a collective farmer in the same year was said to be 6,730 crowns and his income in kind was estimated at an additional 5,274 crowns.[37] Thus the collective farmer earned about one-quarter less than an average industrial worker in 1956 and the much-abused individual peasant was still farther behind.[38] In terms of real income the farmer's disadvantage was even more pronounced as the cost-of-living index for agricultural households stood then at 33.3 percent above 1937 whereas that for "workers and employees" was listed as having risen only by 23.2 percent.[39] While these data confirm, not at all surprisingly, the regime's discrimination against farmers, they offer no figures upon which to base a dependable comparison of the real income of the present Czechoslovak farmers with that of their counterpart in prewar days, or their equivalent in the countries of non-communist Europe. But all the circum-

---

[35] Data on daily earning of agricultural workers in prewar Czechoslovakia in *Ročenka,* 1937, pp. 220, 221, 226; for current earnings in non-communist countries see the *United Nations Statistical Yearbook,* 1958; *Statistical Supplement* to the *International Labour Review,* LXXX, 5, November 1959, p. 433.

[36] In 1959 954,000 persons worked in agricultural cooperatives and 542,000 operated private farms as against 214,000 employees of state farms and machine-tractor stations.

[37] *Politická Ekonomie,* No. 2, 1958, cited after *Československý zpravodaj,* No. 214, October 2, 1958.

[38] The industrial worker's average monthly earning amounted then to 1,285 crowns.

[39] *Ročenka,* 1958, pp. 328 and 326 respectively.

stantial evidence that could be gathered seems to suggest that, save for agricultural laborers, such a comparison could hardly be in communist Czechoslovakia's favor.

Thus, when all things are considered, the conclusion seems warranted that, after twelve years of communist rule, the average Czechoslovak citizen's real earnings are probably still below prewar levels. Undoubtedly, the real wages of certain categories of industrial workers have gone up. The same is true of the real earnings of some groups of workers who used to be grossly underpaid before the War, such as the above-mentioned agricultural laborers. Similarly, the virtual disappearance of domestic servants, poorly paid in prewar days, has helped to raise the over-all average. But these gains seem to have been offset by the elimination of the independent businessmen and free professions and by the substantial downgrading that has occurred under the communist rule in the real earnings of salaried personnel.

Social Welfare Benefits

Although the real earnings of the family's breadwinner or breadwinners is by far the most important determinant of material well-being, it is not the only one. The various social benefits conferred in steadily increasing doses upon the citizens of the modern welfare state must also be considered when measuring the populace's living standards.

As her communist rulers never tire of emphasizing, present-day Czechoslovakia ranks high among the nations of the world in this respect. Her virtually all-embracing system of Social Security from cradle to grave provides the majority of her citizens with all the social benefits the welfare-state philosophy has devised: maternity leaves of eighteen weeks with 75-90 percent of net wages, depending on the length of uninterrupted employment in the same enterprise; contributions for the purchase of the layette; free medical and dental care; state-supported recreation; invalidity and sickness pay equal to 50-90 percent of net wages up to a maximum of 100 crowns per day; monthly children allowances ranging from 70 crowns for the first child up to as much as 260 crowns for the seventh and decreasing with higher wage brackets; tuition-free schools and an impressive number of college scholarships; old-age pensions at the age of 55-60 after 20-25 years of employment in amounts ranging from 50 to 60 percent of average annual earnings in the last five or ten years, with 1-2 percent increments for each additional year of work up to 85-90 percent of net earnings;[40] survivor benefits for widows up to 70 percent of the breadwinner's would-be pension, contingent upon the widow's age, length of marriage, and children cared for; and funeral benefits up to 1,000 crowns. Of the social benefits granted by the most highly developed welfare states of the non-communist world, only unemployment compensation is not supplied by communist Czechoslovakia since unemployment is not supposed to occur under communist rule.[41] Furthermore, except for the collective farmers and self-employed persons, no employee contributions toward any part of the Czechoslovak social insurance program are required.[42]

All this sounds quite impressive; and the various benefits granted under the Czechoslovak health and social insurance program, most of all the free medical care and the family allowances, help indeed the man-in-the-street to meet the steep cost of living, especially if he has a large family. But a closer analysis of such statistical data as are available on the operation of the program indicates that the program's contribution toward the rise of the average standard of living is comparatively modest. Thus in 1958 the family allowance raised the income of the worker's family by 5.7 percent, that of an employee's family by 5.1 percent, and that of a collective farmer's family by a mere 0.5 percent.[43] If all the benefits paid by the government in 1958 under its entire health and social insurance program, save the old-age and survivors pensions, are added up and divided by the number of gainfully employed persons, the results shows that nominal earnings were thereby increased by no more than some 8 percent.[44] Most probably the actual increase was less than that since the statistics on paid out social benefits include also the employees of the

[40] The maximum is set at 1,600-2,200, depending on the category of employment.

[41] See the Czechoslovak Social Security laws Nos. 99 of April 15, 1948, 54 and 55 of November 30, 1956, 41 of July 3, 1958, 16-18 of March 26, 1959; and government ordinances Nos. 56 and 57 of December 18, 1956, and No. 19 of March 26, 1959. For a discussion in English, see "Social Insurance Programs in Eastern Europe," *East Europe*, 8, 8 (August 1959), pp. 3ff.

[42] However, all gainfully employed persons contribute indirectly because a portion of the progressively graduated income taxes which they have to pay is applied to the coverage of social security; all enterprises contribute an amount equal to 10 percent of their respective gross wage bills.

[43] *Ročenka*, 1959, p. 381.

[44] The total of 6,572 million crowns listed as spent on the program was divided by 6.105 million stated as employed in national economy in 1957, thus giving 1,076 crowns per annum. Average annual earnings were estimated as having been somewhere in the neighborhood of 14,250 crowns. This was arrived at by adding 12,000 crowns as the approximate annual earning of farmers (one-fourth of the 6.1 million) to three times the annual earning of the 4.53 million of others and dividing the result by four.

Armed Forces and the police whereas such employees are not included among the 6.1 million persons engaged in the national economy.[45]

Similarly, the rather liberal legal provisions about old-age and survivors pensions lose much of their glamor when a simple division of the totals paid out on old-age pensions by the number of recipients reveals an average monthly pension of 462 crowns in 1958 and a similar computation yields as little as 322 crowns as the average monthly allowance of widows and orphans.[46] Moreover, these figures reflect already the "far-reaching improvements in the health and social insurance payments" that became effective in 1957.[47] Finally, the actual purchasing power accruing from the social benefits is further lowered by the fact that the cost of food, clothing, and footwear toward the purchase of which the bulk of these benefits is evidently applied rose three to four times more than the over-all cost-of-living index.[48]

In view of all these limiting factors the improvement in the social welfare system under the dictatorship of the proletariat in comparison to the pre-communist era has been far less spectacular than claimed by the communist propagandists. Being already well advanced in matters of social welfare, prewar Czechoslovakia had a well-developed system of social insurance supported by employee and employer contributions on a matching basis. It provided virtually all wage earners with benefits covering sickness, invalidity, maternity, old-age, and death. Its health insurance part offered a thorough and good quality coverage for all cases of sickness as well as dental care. Its old-age provisions arranged for pensions that averaged 872 crowns per month in 1935, but suffered from a gross disparity in pensions paid to salaried personnel and manual workers.[49] On the

---

[45] *Ročenka*, 1958, p. 88.

[46] *ibid.*, 1959, p. 88. In 1958 6.7 billion crowns were paid out to 1,207,641 recipients of old age and invalidity pensions, including 110,647 pensions for wives; 491,760 widows and 64,105 orphans were paid 2.14 billion crowns. The official announcements of the Plan fulfillment for 1959 and 1960 claimed that the average old age and invalidity pension of employees was 584 crowns in 1958, 610 in 1959, and 645 in 1960 (*Rudé právo*, February 9, 1960, and February 8, 1961). But these computations leave out the 219,000 old-time pensioners whose pensions are much lower.

[47] *Postavení*, p. 145. It was considerably worse prior to that; the average pension in 1955 was only 278 crowns per month.

[48] As of 1958 food prices stood at 61.1 percent above the prewar level and the corresponding price increases for footwear and textiles were 72.5 and 84 percent respectively. The over-all cost-of-living index for the same year is listed as 20.6 percent above 1937. *Ročenka*, 1959, p. 385.

[49] *Ročenka*, 1937, pp. 230-231. The figure of 872 crowns was reached by dividing the sum total of benefits by the number of recipients. The manual worker's pension then averaged only 146 crowns.

other hand, children allowances were paid only to state employees and a few other groups. But the two last-mentioned deficiencies were remedied after the War prior to the communist seizure of power. Thus the communist regime deserves credit for relatively few improvements over those offerings prior to 1948, and these improvements have been often sullied by a ruthless application of the discriminatory class criterion to the whole social welfare system.[50]

Nor does comparison with non-communist countries bear out communist assertions about the unexcelled superiority of the communist Social Security system. It is quite true that the average Social Security benefits paid in communist Czechoslovakia rank among the highest in the world when measured in proportion to wages; in that sense they are for the most part higher than those available in the four non-communist countries used for purposes of comparison in this chapter.[51] However, as Table XIX reveals, it is equally true that the

TABLE XIX

Comparative Food Prices in Four Countries, 1957
(computed in dollars at the 1957 official exchange rates)

Article	Unit	Czechoslovakia	West Germany	Belgium	France
Beef sirloin	1 kg.	3.75	1.21	2.53	2.59
Cooked ham	"	8.88	1.93	2.46	3.09
Butter	"	5.83	1.69	1.97	2.26
White bread	"	0.50	0.24	0.15	0.16
Potatoes	"	0.08	0.07	0.05	0.07
Sugar	"	1.45	0.22	0.29	0.26
Coffee	"	23.66	4.78	2.59	2.86
Milk	1 liter	0.28	0.10	0.15	0.13
Eggs	1 piece	0.20	0.06	0.06	0.08

Source: *Yearbook of Labor Statistics*, Geneva, 1958.

disproportionately high cost of food in communist Czechoslovakia makes the advantage more apparent than real.

Thus, to cite a few examples, the Belgian monthly allowance of 9 dollars for the first child buys considerably more food than the corresponding Czechoslovak allowance of 9.70 dollars. Similarly, the 30 dollars that constituted the French allowance for three children in the Paris area in 1957 exceeded in terms of purchasing power the 43 dollars paid to a corresponding Czechoslovak family with three children at that time. Nor could it be said that the Czechoslovak pen-

[50] See below.
[51] For figures on social expenditures and numbers of beneficiaries see the *Yearbooks of Labor Statistics*, 1958, pp. 499ff., and 1959, pp. 481ff. and the Statistical Yearbooks of the respective countries; also, *Social Security in France*, Paris, 1957, and Helmut Arntz, *Facts about Germany*, Wiesbaden, 1959.

sioner could eat better on his average pension of 62 dollars in 1957 than his German counterpart on his basic 32 dollars, irrespective of the fact that many of the German pensioners undoubtedly drew additional benefits from other sources.[52]

Services

A role of ever-rising prominence in the living standards of modern society is played by services. To be assured of prompt, dependable and reasonably priced repairs and maintenance care for the many appliances without which everyday life would be unthinkable today is just as important for the modern consumer's welfare as his ability to buy them in his neighborhood store. The spectacular rise in the volume of such services in Western industrial civilization in the last decades bears ample witness thereto. But it is precisely in this respect that the communist regime of Czechoslovakia has been grossly neglectful of its subjects' needs. Even *Prague News Letter* had to confess in 1958, after ten years of the dictatorship of the proletariat, that "the long wait for repairs and services—shoe repair, plumbing, electrical appliances, cleaning, laundry, etc.—and the poor quality of these services when they are performed, has long been a blot on the otherwise rapidly improving consumer goods picture."[53]

Indeed, a long list of recurrent consumer complaints in the daily press shows the services to the Czechoslovak consumer to be woefully inadequate even by the most modest Western standards. Many of the services considered as a matter of course in the non-communist West simply do not exist at all in communist Czechoslovakia or, at best, have only recently become available in a few major cities. Interminable delays mar the usefulness of such services as are maintained. It takes months before an ordinary kitchen appliance is repaired, a dress is dry-cleaned, or shoes are resoled; it may be many months until the plumber or the electrician deigns to answer the call of the desperate housewife.[54] As *Prague News Letter* nostalgically

---

[52] Figures for France taken from *Social Security in France,* figures for Germany from *Facts about Germany,* figures for Belgium obtained from the Belgian Embassy in the United States.

[53] *Prague News Letter,* 14, 14, July 5, 1958.

[54] Thus it took the communal services of the city of Nymburk over one-half year to clean work clothes of factory employees; a similar service in another city needed five months to clean a uniform; a typewriter for a district health agency had to be sent to another city for repair, but was still being repaired after three months despite eighteen reminders (*Československý zpravodaj,* No. 221, November 20, 1958; *Práce,* August 16, 1959; *Rudé právo,* May 24, 1960); *Nová svoboda,* August 16, 23, and 30, 1960. *Československý zpravodaj,* No. 321, December 6, 1960.

remarked, grossly understating the dilemma, "The happy days when a few telephone calls will keep the household running smoothly are still a long way off . . . ."[55] Occasionally, a few of the services which used to be commonplace before the War have been restored and hailed as a wonderful socialist achievement. Such was, for instance, the case when home delivery of milk was introduced in some districts of Northern Bohemia in 1958;[56] or when Praha's *House of Shoes* allowed its customers once again "to sit down comfortably in modern chairs" and have shoes tried on by a salesgirl.[57] The distribution of goods and the retail services continue to be so poor that fifteen years after the War's end and twelve years after the establishment of communist rule long lines of waiting customers are a frequent phenomenon. Poor quality of repairs and of other services has also been a cause of perennial complaints, not only on the part of individual customers but also of such public enterprises as had the misfortune to need the services of their nationalized sister-enterprises engaged in maintenance work. So has been the matter of repair costs which are often out of proportion to the benefit offered, mainly because of the widespread practice of overcharging customers, a practice encouraged by the dearth of such services and the absence of competition.[58] Moreover, courtesy in dealing with customers is conspicuous by its absence. Judging by the overwhelming evidence from communist and non-communist sources, the treatment meted out by the personnel of most of the nationalized stores and services in communist Czechoslovakia is such that a businessman applying it to his clientele in America would soon be out of business.

There is no question that the blame for this demise of services to the customer must be laid squarely on the shoulders of the communist regime. Of all the sectors of nonagricultural activities, repairing and maintenance services are probably the least suitable for collectivized methods of work. Yet, except for a brief respite after the death of Stalin, the KSČ rulers kept right on forcing them into the Procrustean socialized pattern, mainly in the form of unwieldy municipal enterprises deeply buried in rigid bureaucratism, devoid of personality, and plagued by nepotism. Moreover, the regime's disparaging attitude toward the individual craftsmen, artisans, and repairmen, considered as a petty-bourgeois leftover of the capitalist past,

[55] *Prague News Letter,* 12, 22, November 10, 1956.
[56] *Československý zpravodaj,* No. 225, December 17, 1958.
[57] *Mladá fronta,* October 18, 1958.
[58] *Práce,* August 16, 1959.

has been quite successful in discouraging the young generation from seeking careers in such fields of activity. The consequence has been such that, for instance, in the most populous of Czechoslovakia's regions, that of Praha, only ten boys and two girls chose the glazier's trade and only seventeen boys were shoemaker apprentices in 1959.[59]

Shortchanging of the captive clientele that has nowhere else to turn has infiltrated also the government's social services, especially the medical service, hospital treatment, and the spa and vacation assignments. One of the reasons adduced for the prohibition of private practice of medicine and dentistry in 1958 was the "frequent superficiality" of treatment of patients at health centers by physicians anxious to devote as much time as they could to more lucrative private practice.[60] Whatever the real cause, the fact that medical and hospital care for the average patient in communist Czechoslovakia does not measure up to the standards of the advanced countries of the non-communist world seems to be well substantiated by the consensus of opinion among escapees from Czechoslovakia as well as by occasional criticism in the communist press.[61] Unless the patient belongs to the communist elite or has a relative or a personal friend in the proper place, he receives a sort of assembly-line treatment somewhat like that in an overcrowded American charity clinic. If it is an emergency case or an easily diagnosed ailment requiring simple therapy the treatment is adequate, though of a utility nature. But when the case is complicated, especially if it is of chronic character, the physicians at the health center have neither the time nor the patience for the elaborate treatment such an illness may require.

[59] *ibid.*, October 30, 1959.
[60] *Rudé právo,* August 22, 1958.
[61] A particularly shocking example of poor hospital care was cited by *Mladá fronta* on August 9, 1958, in a report on the sorry state of affairs in a district hospital in Northern Bohemia. Dust from the unpaved road leading to the hospital penetrated everywhere. Twice a day it was supplemented by stinking smoke caused by the burning of used bandages on the hospital grounds. Food was prepared in a small "dungeon-like" kitchen with old-fashioned equipment located in the basement; and the kitchen personnel had to change in the pantry and use rest rooms together with the patients on the second floor. Ashes, rotten vegetables, and cans were also heaped on hospital grounds and this "romantic corner" was crossed by a "bubbling creek" receiving all the waste from the hospital which lacked proper canalization. The reporter found the chief physician and his assistant carrying a maternity patient up a steep staircase. While this was certainly an extreme case of hospital neglect, it is amazing that even a single case of this kind could exist as late as 1958 in a country boasting of the excellence of her nationalized medical and hospital care.

Housing

Deficient as the Czechoslovak customer services are, their inadequacy is exceeded by the pitiful state of the country's residential housing. Undoubtedly, if a public opinion poll could be taken in present-day Czechoslovakia to find out which is the citizens' main economic grievance, the public's accusing finger would point first and foremost to the housing situation.

TABLE XX
Newly Built Dwellings per Thousand of Population, 1949-1958

	1949	1950	1951	1952	1953	1954	1955	1956	1957	1958
Czechoslovakia	2.4	3.1	2.5	3.1	3.0	2.9	3.9	4.8	4.8	4.0
Austria	4.2	6.7	5.0		5.5	5.8	6.0	6.0	4.9	
Belgium	4.2	5.2	4.1	3.8	4.5	5.1	5.0	4.9	5.5	5.2
Denmark	5.9	4.8	5.0	4.4	4.9	5.3	5.4	4.4	5.8	4.6
Finland	7.3	6.5	7.0	7.7	7.1	7.7	7.8	7.1	7.5	6.9
France	1.3	1.7	1.8	2.0	2.7	3.8	4.9	5.4	6.2	6.5
Greece	2.9	6.4	5.7	7.7	6.5	5.6	7.0	7.7	6.3	6.7
Italy	1.0	1.6	2.0	2.5	3.2	3.7	4.5	4.8	5.6	5.7
Netherlands	4.9	5.4	6.3	5.5	6.0	6.6	5.8	6.4	8.1	8.1
Norway	5.7	6.9	6.3	9.8	10.4	10.4	9.4	7.9	7.5	7.5
Sweden	6.1	6.4	5.8	6.4	7.3	8.2	7.9	7.9	8.8	8.5
Switzerland	4.3	5.3	6.3	5.7	6.0	7.3	7.9	7.8	7.6	5.0
United Kingdom	4.4	4.3	4.2	5.0	6.5	7.0	6.4	6.1	6.0	5.5
Western Germany	4.5	7.5	8.5	9.1	10.5	10.9	10.7	11.2	10.5	9.4

Source: *Annual Bulletin of Housing and Building Statistics for Europe*, Geneva, 1959, pp. 14-15.

The reckless industrialization pace of the Stalin era and capital production's insatiable appetite for investments, construction labor, and materials relegated the population's housing needs to a very low level of priorities. Although matters took a turn for the better after the death of Stalin, the annual programs of dwelling construction have been fixed far too low to improve the situation; moreover, they have chronically suffered from underfulfillment of the planned goals. Table XX gives a striking illustration of how poorly communist Czechoslovakia has taken care of the people's needs in this respect in comparison with the countries of non-communist Europe, irrespective of whether they sustained substantial losses as a result of World War II:

Instead of narrowing the gap, communist Czechoslovakia has thus been falling still further behind the countries of non-communist Europe. In view of these poor results it is hardly surprising that the

446

number of apartments per 1,000 inhabitants advanced at a snail's pace from 288 in 1953 to 293 in 1959[62] while the ratio of persons to one dwelling unit actually worsened from 3.05 in 1946 to 3.28 by 1955.[63] As a result, Czechoslovakia is today far behind even such countries as have suffered tremendous loss of dwellings in the course of the military operations of the Second World War, such as Belgium, the Netherlands, Britain, and Western Germany. Simultaneously, the living area per newly built apartment has decreased from 53.2 square meters in 1948 to 39.3 in 1955, and to an all time low of 35.9 in 1959.[64] Thus the average apartment built today measures a mere 400 square feet. This reflects adversely on the communist regime in Czechoslovakia because, besides suffering comparatively little property damage as a result of the War, the country retained empty residential property left behind by over three million expelled Sudeten Germans. Nor do the above figures tell the whole dismal story as they reflect neither the poor quality of the housing and the excessive building costs nor the widespread favoritism and corruption pervading the apartment allocation system.

The low quality of residential housing is documented by innumerable complaints of tenants and recurrent censures of the home-building industry by the Party's spokesmen. One would be tempted to dismiss some of these lamentations as mere anti-communist propaganda were they not printed in black and white in the communist press itself. How else could one believe that, after having joyfully moved into new houses that had just been completed, the nonplussed tenants found that doors would not close because of uneven floors; railing of balconies had a tendency to topple over; asphalt was dripping from the ceilings; basement floors were under water; window frames had to be held in place by wire; central heating units, unable to stand the pressure, cracked when put into operation for the first time; window blinds fell out at the first attempt to pull them down; stucco was falling from the walls; badly leaking faucets almost caused flooding of the apartments.[65] Although these are probably some of the more extreme cases of sloppy construction work, the very fact that the regime allows them to be aired in the daily press suggests that

[62] *Postavení,* and *Prague News Letter,* 15, 10, May 16, 1959.

[63] *Plánované hospodářství,* December 1, 1958, cited after *East Europe,* I, 7 (1959), p. 23.

[64] *Ročenka,* 1959, p. 123, and 1960, p. 117.

[65] *Nová svoboda,* November 5, 1959; *Rudé právo,* December 28, 1959, and March 3, 1960; *Československý zpravodaj,* No. 277, January 12, 1960.

they are by no means infrequent. Also, if the builders in communist Czechoslovakia dare to hand over as ready for occupancy houses fraught with such shocking flaws, one can well imagine how many other defects there must be that the tenants do not even mention. Nor is it difficult to visualize how fast such poorly built houses are likely to deteriorate, especially when, as documented by overwhelming evidence, proper maintenance care of apartment houses is virtually nonexistent.[66] Evaluating the record of residential housing, the Party's journal *Život strany* summed up its opinion as follows: "The comrades from the construction work and related fields should be ashamed of themselves."[67]

Even with this low quality, construction costs seem to be extremely high. According to the *Czechoslovak Statistical Yearbook,* the average delivery price per apartment with an actual living area of 385 square feet was 100,760 crowns ($13,966) in 1956.[68] The average building costs for an apartment with kitchen plus two bedrooms in a cooperative housing project in a rather commonplace suburb of Praha was quoted in 1959 to be in the neighborhood of 72,000 crowns (10,000 dollars), which would be almost equal to an average employee's earnings for five full years.[69] Hence, it can be easily understood why the regime's persistent appeals that people build houses "cooperatively" at their own expense fall mostly on deaf ears.[70] Since a full one-third of the 1.2 million new dwelling units planned to be completed by 1970 is supposed to be built in this cooperative fashion with the participating individuals footing the bill, the whole construction plan itself seems to be built on rather shaky foundations.

To offset the high construction costs the socialized building industry tends to economize, not only by using inferior materials and encouraging hasty work, but also by leaving out various desirable interior features such as built-in closets and other conveniences which are standard in modern home-building in the West.[71] Thus most of the newly built houses are in fact obsolete by Western standards even before they are given their final coat of paint.

[66] For instance, *Práce,* October 28, 1959; *Rudé právo,* December 28, 1959; March 3 and May 24, 1960.

[67] *Život strany,* No. 16, August 1959, p. 1004.

[68] *Ročenka,* 1958, p. 109.

[69] *Práce,* May 30, 1959.

[70] *Rudé právo,* September 6, 1959.

[71] See complaint about it in *Plánované hospodářství,* December 1, 1958. As conceded by *Ročenka,* 1960, p. 118, only 53.1 percent of apartments built in 1958 and 58.2 percent of those built in 1959 featured gas, central heating, and hot water.

Social Justice with Built-in Class Bias

The consideration of a nation's material well-being in terms of mathematical averages supplies valuable data on the over-all mean standard of living and permits useful comparisons with the welfare levels of other times and other nations. But it says next to nothing about the equity in the distribution of well-being which is, of course, a most important element of social justice. Whether it be big or whether it be small, how is the welfare loaf sliced and how equitably is it allocated among the major social groups? In particular, how does Czechoslovakia under the rule of communism compare in this respect with Czechoslovakia of pre-communist days?

Naturally, the answer depends very much on one's concept of social justice. Evaluating the communist performance from a viewpoint which could be described as fairly sympathetic toward the welfare state idea, I find both positive and negative factors.

Foremost among the positive factors in the communist distribution of material well-being is undoubtedly the elimination of the grossly underpaid agrarian proletariat which numbered over one-half million and was the main blot on the otherwise good social record of prewar Czechoslovakia. It is true that this group mostly disappeared even prior to the communist coup of 1948 when the landless peasants who did not switch to factory work after the War were assigned adequate acreage from land taken from the Sudeten Germans. However, credit therefore should not be denied the KSČ leaders who, guided by the Leninist strategy of attracting the poor peasants, were certainly most instrumental in bringing this about.[72]

Another development which belongs on the positive side of the communist balance in the field of socio-economic justice is the equalization of the financial burden of large families by children allowances graduated in inverse ratio to the income of the main family breadwinner and increasing with each successive child. With wage tax reductions granted in relation to the number of dependents and with free medical care extended since 1959 even to children of parents who are not themselves eligible, the present system is greatly superior to the prewar arrangements and ranks certainly among the most generous in the world.

Finally, credit should be given to the communist regime, though

[72] Another low social group that benefited economically from the advent of communism along somewhat similar lines were the domestic servants.

not without substantial reservations, for having upgraded the economic status of manual workers in relation to salaried employees, civil servants and managerial personnel. In prewar Czechoslovakia the average manual worker was at a great disadvantage in comparison to white-collar personnel. This was reflected not only in the worker's wages but even more so in his fringe benefits, particularly in old-age pensions which were shockingly disproportionate in comparison with those reserved for public employees and salaried personnel in private employment. However, prompted by their concept of merciless class struggle, the Communists went so far beyond what would have been a fair correction of previous iniquities that the desiderata of social justice have been more harmed than helped in the process.

Permeating the economic sphere of the communist system as much as, and possibly even more than, its other sectors, this ruthless class criterion is primarily responsible for the several negative aspects that gravely impair the communist distribution of material well-being.

Worst from the standpoint of social justice is class discrimination in matters of social welfare. Thus the free health service is denied independent tradesmen and farmers, *kulaks,* and capitalists. Until 1959 even children were penalized for the wrong class profile of their parents so that some one and one-half million persons were discriminated against in matters of health protection. Nor are the above-mentioned categories entitled to family allowances for their children. Even the persons who are otherwise eligible for them have them cut by about two-thirds if they possess a private plot of land in excess of one-half hectare. Class origin is also a determining factor in selections for spas, sanatoria, and recreation resorts. The control of all such facilities and admission to them is in the hands of the communist-controlled trade union organs which are under specific directives to apply a rigid class viewpoint in disbursing these benefits and to use them mainly as "rewards to the best workers and victors of socialist contests."[73]

But probably the most heartless of the communist class-struggle devices is the regime's manipulation of the old-age and survivors benefits. Nowhere does the communist vindictiveness look more naked than in the treatment reserved for old people labeled with the bourgeois stigma. While raising at long last pensions of those retiring after January 1, 1957, the regime granted increases only to one-half of those pensioned prior to that date, using class origin and socialist merit as

[73] *Práce,* March 20, 1959, and November 22, 1958.

the main yardstick.[74] In ruling whether or not to increase pensions of persons previously retired the Social Security Commissions of the district people's committees were directed to take into consideration "the pensioner's merits in the past and in the period of the socialist construction" and "thus to reward the work of those pensioners taking active part in our public life."[75] The commissions were also given the authority to lower pensions of those who used previously to employ hired labor or had been "prominent representatives of the former political and economic system" and to reduce even the benefits of survivors of such persons![76] Similarly, they were authorized to reduce or altogether cancel pensions of persons convicted of certain political and economic offenses against the people's democratic order.[77] Thus there are in present-day Czechoslovakia, boasting of superior social justice, poor wretches receiving old-age "pensions" as low as 190 crowns per month, which is just about enough to pay rent and utilities for a shabby room and to buy a loaf of bread and a quart of milk a day.[78]

Yet another form of discrimination is aimed at self-employed persons and, despite all the communist talk of the two "friendly classes of workers and peasants," the collective farmers. Not only must persons belonging to these categories pay fairly steep Social Security premiums, but their pensions are so low that they are almost all below the 400 crown minimum guaranteed now to workers and employees, though the latter do not pay any premium at all. For premiums amounting to 10 percent of their income the self-employed persons are eligible for maximum monthly retirement benefits ranging from 210 to 300 crowns, depending on the years of insurance and the average annual basis of assessment.[79] The collective farmers qualify for a monthly old-age pension of 230 crowns costing them 14 crowns per month. They may contract for a higher pension up to 440 crowns but then they have to pay a much steeper premium equal to as much as 88 crowns per month for the 440 crowns pension.[80] Furthermore, the collective farmer forfeits his Social Security rights if he leaves, or is

[74] According to *Finance a úvěr,* Nos. 2-3, 1957, there were 2,025,000 persons receiving old age and invalidity benefits of various types in 1956. Of these only 1,012,000 were chosen to receive increases. *East Europe,* 8, 8 (1959), p. 10.

[75] *Práce,* March 8, 1959; also *Život strany,* No. 6, March 1959, pp. 328ff.

[76] Law No. 41 of July 3, 1958.

[77] *ibid.*

[78] *Československý zpravodaj,* No. 208, August 19, 1958.

[79] Government ordinance No. 56 of December 18, 1956.

[80] *ibid.*

expelled from, the collective farm or if he fails to work off the pre-scribed minimum of labor units without an acceptable excuse.[81]

Finally, it should be pointed out that differentiation unwarranted by considerations of social justice vitiates even the main body of the pension system as it applies to workers and other employees of the socialist economy. They are divided into three categories supposedly determined by the "social importance and difficulty of work done."[82] The first category that commands the highest benefits is reserved for miners working underground and aviators. The second one, comprising miners working on the surface and workers employed in heavy or dangerous occupations, such as steel and chemical industry, is less generous. The third category which is by far the largest in numbers and least liberal in benefits, includes all the rest, i.e., all but some 8 percent of persons covered by the Social Security provisions. While it may be justified to pay higher wages to and even allow an earlier retirement of miners and workers in other health-affecting or unusually hazardous lines of work, it is hardly fair to discriminate against employees in other occupations when it comes to old-age pensions and survivors benefits. Surely it cannot be said that a retired textile worker or retail store employee and their families eat less, dress less, and have lesser needs than their fellow-workers engaged in mining or chemical industry.[83]

Discriminatory measures taken in the field of social security and welfare have been paralleled by similar arrangements in the entire wage system. In line with their philosophy of extolling manual

[81] Vladimír Chalupný, ed., *Příručka pro nově založená družstva* (A Handbook for Newly Established Cooperatives), Praha, 1958, pp. 173-174.

[82] Laws Nos. 55 of November 30, 1956, and 17 of March 26, 1959; *Prague News Letter,* 12, 21, October 27, 1956, and 15, 9, May 2, 1959.

[83] How great the disparity may be is shown by the following calculation of old-age pensions of several typical employee groups based on the assumption that the hypothetical beneficiaries would retire after 25 years of work and their monthly average earnings for the last five or ten years before retirement were equal to their average wages of 1957:

	monthly pension	
occupation	*in crowns*	*in dollars*
underground miner	1,260	174
clerk in manufacturing	555	77
employee in retail trade and catering	520	72
engineer in manufacturing	835	116
average employee in the socialist sector of the economy (not counting collective farmers)	625	87

workers as the main creators of economic values, the communist rulers have turned the pre-communist pay scales upside down. Worst hit have been administrative and managerial personnel so that their average monthly pay is below that of the manual worker. Engineers and technicians have fared better, but the difference between their earnings and those of manual laborers has been sharply reduced as against prewar days. Thus the average 1959 monthly earnings of a worker were 1,348 crowns in industry and 1,449 in construction, whereas administrative personnel averaged 1,193 and 1,219, and engineering-technical employees 1,808 and 1,842.[84] While a certain reduction of the prewar disparity between the wages of manual workers and the salaries of managerial and technical personnel was undoubtedly justified, the opposite is true of the extreme to which the rulers of communist Czechoslovakia have resorted. It is hardly justifiable on moral, social, or economic grounds to pay an engineer, who had to study long years to obtain his diploma, only some 30 percent more than a manual worker with no more schooling (beyond compulsory school attendance) than after-work apprentice school.

The discriminatory effect of the class viewpoint is supplemented, further, by the well-known communist bias in favor of heavy industry and capital construction over the other sectors of economy. While the average 1959 monthly earnings per employee amounted to 1,496 crowns in construction and to 1,379 in industry as a whole, the corresponding figures were 1,089 in agriculture, 1,066 in retail trade and catering, and 1,223 in the "nonproductive" branches.[85] This bias affects not only salaried personnel but manual workers themselves. Thus the hourly earnings of an underground coal hewer averaged 15.47 crowns in 1958 and those of a steel melter 12.42, whereas upholsterers were getting only 6.42, furniture polishers 6.20, spinners 5.67, and weavers 5.46.[86] Although it may be argued that the disagreeable and more hazardous work of underground miners and steel melters should command higher pay than that of weavers and upholsterers, the disparity is too wide to be acceptable on ethical grounds.

Last but not least, the equitable distribution of material well-being in communist Czechoslovakia is interfered with by widespread nepotism and favoritism which necessarily flourishes wherever check on the government by the opposition and freedom of public inquiry and

[84] *Ročenka,* 1960, pp. 21 and 23.

[85] *ibid.,* p. 92.

[86] *Statistical Supplement* to the *International Labour Review,* LXXX, 1, July 1959, p. 22.

criticism are curtailed. One's standing in the communist hierarchy or connection with persons in proper places seems to be very helpful, and sometimes even decisive, in securing a better deal. That is so when special treatment is needed beyond the everyday routine medical care of the health centers or when trade-union controlled recreation is allocated among the "best workers" most of whom often turn up to be trade union functionaries and their friends.[87] That is so when it is a question of squeezing out a better apartment from the housing authority of the city people's committee cluttered with thousands of applications or when the Social Security Commissions use the authority conferred upon them to raise or lower old-age benefits according to the pensioner's "socialist merit." And that is so again not only when job vacancies are filled but also when employees are assigned to the respective classes of the prescribed wage schedule that largely determine their earnings.[88]

ECONOMIC REGIMENTATION

In the preceding pages the economic system of communist Czechoslovakia has been analysed and evaluated in terms of its contribution (or lack of it) to man's material well-being. But man does not live by bread alone and the workingman's aspiration is not only to secure a bigger slice of the loaf but also to be able to so under conditions of fairness and decency. Even in the frame of reference of communist theory and propaganda the "abolition of exploitation of man by man" implies not only a redistribution of material wealth along Marxist-Leninist concepts but also an equitable adjustment of nonmaterial values pertaining to man's economic and professional status.

Yet it is in these nonmaterial aspects of its economic system that communism has brought the bitterest disappointment both to those who had placed their faith in its tenets and to those who had thought that the anticipated curtailments of political freedoms would at least be balanced by the wage earners' enhanced status in the economic

---

[87] *Odborář,* No. 25, 1958, cited after *East Europe,* i, 8 (1959), p. 8; *Rudé právo,* November 13, 1957.

[88] Recent information from Czechoslovakia reveals that such favoritism flourishes even in the most pampered profession of coal mining. According to the report, the favorite Party members among miners were assigned easier work in shafts where coal deposits were one to two yards high whereas non-communists had to dig in shafts with coal deposits of less than one-half yard. This resulted in much higher earnings for the communist miners. *Československý zpravodaj,* No. 206, August 4, 1958. For a recent glaring example of favoritism in housing see *Rudé právo,* August 10, 1960.

sphere. Having been promised that they will be their own masters in factories in which they worked, the workers have been subjected instead to a "socialist labor discipline" far harsher than had been the impositions of the "capitalist leeches." Having been similarly assured of the unconditional right of self-management reserved for them in the cooperative farms, the peasants "persuaded" to join them have been made painfully aware of the real meaning given such terms in communist semantics. Freed from its dependence on the "capitalist exploiters" the entire working population of communist Czechoslovakia, with nowhere else to turn for its livelihood, has been pushed into a much more thorough dependence on the almighty communist State that has usurped the monopoly of regulating all aspects of economic life. Thus total economic and professional regimentation supplements and greatly strengthens regimentation in the fields of politics, culture, and social life, as recounted elsewhere in the present volume.

It would take a great many pages and extend this book to altogether unwieldy proportions to tell the full story of the economic and professional regimentation brought about upon all strata of the Czechoslovak population by the dictatorship of the proletariat. Hence, it must suffice to point out only some of the most essential things and hope that they will illustrate adequately enough the heavy human cost which the average Czechoslovakian has to pay for his captive participation in the communist campaign of "outproducing capitalism." Those familiar with the Soviet scene will readily see that, as in so many other respects, the KSČ leaders have followed closely in the footsteps of their Soviet mentors.

The Ubiquitous Norm

The basic device of the stick-and-carrot strategy with which the rulers of communist Czechoslovakia seek to win the production battle is "the norm." The work norm prescribes what minimum result each worker or peasant has to attain in what time. The "norm of the consumption of materials" determines the quantity of raw materials which he may use. The "fuel norm" does the same for the consumption of fuels and the "norm of electrical energy" for the use of electricity while the "norm of capacity" directs the worker as to how much work should be squeezed out of the machines in a given time. Since these norms are of crucial importance both for production costs and output levels, on the one hand, and the level of employees' earnings on the other, their determination has been a perennial bone of contention be-

tween the employees and the regime. Motivated by a desire to work
less and earn more, a "bourgeois" attitude which holds firm in face
of all communist indoctrination to the contrary, employees try hard
to keep the norms as "soft" as possible.[89] But the interest of the regime
and its economic planners runs in exactly opposite direction. Striving
hard to increase the productivity of labor upon which hinges the fate
of their ambitious economic planning, the KSČ leaders must insist on
a continuous "uncovering of concealed labor reserves" and "strengthening" of norms. "To impart to our [economic] plans a truly mobiliz-
ing character," says an official manual on the organization of planning
in Czechoslovakia, "they must be based on progressive norms that
mobilize the working masses for the increase of production and pull
up those workers who are lagging behind to the level of those who are
the best. The plans must not be based on norms representing mathematical averages which only brake further advancement."[90]

Of all the stratagems used for this purpose the favorite one is to
induce the ablest among the workers themselves to exceed substantially
the respective work norms by offering special bonuses and other rewards for so doing. In this manner a positive proof is provided that
such norms are indeed soft and a strong argument is gained for the
strengthening which follows in due time. To sweeten the bitter pill,
the stiffening of the work norms is usually coupled with a simultaneous increase in wage rates. However, since the actual amount of
work required to meet and exceed the new work norms is usually
raised more than the corresponding rate of pay, more often than not
the employees lose more than they gain in such a bargain. As shown
by the experience of the first twelve years of the dictatorship of the
proletariat, the outcome of this tug-of-war over the work norms and
wage rates between the regime and the workers has depended on how
effectively the regime could at any given time apply the power of the
stick. In the first years of the post-Stalin thaw, when the regime felt
it necessary to refrain from harsh coercive measures, especially against
industrial workers, wages rose faster than work norms, causing dismay
and alarm among the KSČ leaders openly committed to the precept
that "labor productivity must grow faster than wages."[91] But when

[89] For the methods used for this purpose see, for instance, Jiří Řezníček, *Organisace plánování v ČSR* (The Organization of Planning in the Czechoslovak
Republic), Praha, 1956, p. 45.

[90] *ibid.*, p. 12. Also, Razga-Hronský, *op.cit.*; F. Kutt's article in *Plánované
hospodářství*, No. 8, September 30, 1955; *Československý přehled*, II, 11 (1955),
p. 25.

[91] *Rudé právo*, May 8, 1956.

the subsequent recrudescence of neo-Stalinism in the Soviet orbit enabled the regime to act more forcefully, a wholesale strengthening of the work norms was undertaken in 1959 and 1960 with the result that many workers have suffered a decrease in their earnings while others have to work harder in order to earn as much as they earned before the "wage reform," and much harder still to secure pay increases.[92]

The Socialist Pledges and Contests

Another favorite device used on a massive scale to whip up the production effort is the so-called socialist pledge and socialist contest. Year after year, individual workers as well as various groups of employees working together as a unit are prevailed upon to sign formal pledges whereby they assume obligations to exceed their planned output by a specific percentage, bring projects to completion in less time than prescribed, save more on materials and fuel than stipulated by the respective norms, and so forth. These pledges are further supplemented by socialist contests in which individuals and work units are made to compete with other individuals and groups engaged in the same type of work within the same enterprise as well as in corresponding establishments throughout the entire country. After some initial experimentation in the first years of the communist rule a government resolution of January 1953 placed socialist contests "on a firm organizational basis" and developed them into an all-embracing nation-wide system covering all branches of production.[93]

Although the signing of socialist pledges and participation in socialist contests is voluntary, pressures of a varying degree are nevertheless made to bear on the workers to induce them to volunteer. Since the various honors conferred upon the winning individuals or teams, such as honorable mentions, certificates of achievement or even titles of

[92] This is borne out both by information obtained from non-communist sources as by reports published in communist press: *Práce* revealed on December 8, 1959, that two-thirds of the factories in a province in Northern Bohemia failed to strengthen their norms and, as a consequence, will earn less. (See also items 673/60 and 4721/1959 from Free Europe Committee's files.) According to a communist survey of 1960 some 12 to 20 percent of workers suffered a wage reduction while wages of 20 to 25 percent remained unchanged and the rest secured unspecified wage increases (*Rudé právo*, January 3 and 23 and February 18, 1960). But the survey is silent about the stepped-up amount of work which must be done to secure wage improvement or even to retain previous earnings under the new system. As revealed by the State Planning Commission, the overfulfillment of work norms in factories operating under the new system fell from 173 to 111 percent. (*East Europe*, 9, 9, 1960, p. 22).

[93] Government resolution of January 27, 1953, *Úřední list ČSR*, 15, January 31, 1953, p. 151; also, *Rudé právo*, January 28, 1953.

"Hero of Socialist Labor" provide little incentive, they have been supplemented by more tangible rewards in the form of pecuniary remuneration from the enterprise funds, paid vacations, priorities in the assignment of apartments, or purchases of hard-to-get merchandise.[94] But the most effective means of making people take part in contests, which most of them heartily dislike, is the realization of possible adverse consequences that they might suffer if they stood aside. "Socialist contests are a school of socialist patriotism, a struggle for a new man and for his attitude to socialist ownership."[95] They are "the most efficient tool of the struggle for the fulfillment of our plans."[96] Hence, a stubborn refusal to participate amounts virtually to an open display of lack of interest in socialist achievements. A corresponding black mark is duly entered into the personal files of the culprits who may then find themselves by-passed in promotion or assignment to better jobs, and even be shifted to work falling under lower wage rates. Initially, it was possible sometimes to get by with such vague undertakings as "taking proper care of the technical process of the production," "studying technical literature," "keeping the workshop tidy," or "learning Russian." But such easy escape routes have since been barred by more effective controls over the socialist pledges by the trade union works councils which keep close watch over the progress made by contestants in the respective plants.

The Work Brigades

A particularly obnoxious design of man's exploitation in communist Czechoslovakia are the so-called work brigades. Initially, they were used mainly as an additional supply of manpower at the time and in the places of special need, such as helping farmers at the peak of the harvest or digging coal to reduce the recurrent winter fuel shortages. But the steadily growing drain on labor contributed toward transforming the brigades into a permanent institution. In addition to short-term brigades sent out for a few days or a few weeks, the government offices, business enterprises, and other establishments not engaged in heavy industry were directed in 1952 to supply the mines, steel plants, and construction work with a prescribed number of brigade-men on a more or less permanent basis and to send replacements for those whose

[94] For details see A. Rozehnal's article in *Československý přehled*, II, 3 (1955), pp. 5ff.
[95] *Práce*, February 3, 1953.
[96] Řezníček, *op.cit.*, p. 48.

brigade contracts would end.[97] A further refinement took place in later years when the customary stop-gap brigades, used mainly in agricultural work, have been supplemented by brigades organized under a variety of so-called actions. The most burdensome of them for the average citizen is probably Action Z, a nation-wide, year-round enterprise in which all adults and often even youngsters over fourteen have to volunteer for unpaid work, mainly of construction and maintenance type, for the purpose of amelioriating their respective communities. Added to these year-round actions and the regularly recurrent harvesting brigades must be innumerable special brigades organized to commemorate various communist red-letter days, and thus to "strike back at capitalist imperialism," through donations of work whether the occasion be the anniversary of the Great October Socialist Revolution, the launching of the Soviet Lunik or "honoring the peaceful visit of Comrade Khrushchëv to the United States."[98]

Thus, after they are through with the long hours of regular work governed by ever-stiffening piece-work norms, the citizens of communist Czechoslovakia have to deliver millions after millions of additional hours of work, mostly unpaid. The magnitude of the values which the regime obtains in this manner without paying for it is revealed by a recent official estimate that the average work donated in 1960 on melioration projects alone will be worth approximately two million crowns (278,000 dollars) per day.[99] According to another communist claim the Czechoslovak citizens participating in melioration Action Z worked off a sum total of 670 million work hours in five years and their voluntary contribution was valued at 8.5 billion crowns (1.2 billion dollars).[100] If such work donations were truly voluntary, as they are supposed to be, the whole arrangement would be a highly commendable display of selflessness and civic mindedness. But overwhelming evidence shows that much the same high-pressure techniques are used for making people volunteer for the brigades as for inducing them to participate in the socialist contests. Typical of

[97] A government regulation of June 24, 1952. With the subsequent transfer of many office workers to "productive" work in the post-Stalin era these long-term brigade assignments were abandoned.

[98] Communist radio and press are replete with reports of various types of such brigade work. See, for instance, *Rudé právo*, June 25, 1952, October 23, 1959, September 10, 1952, January 21, 1960; *Zemědělské noviny*, October 7, 1952; *Práce*, August 28, 1959; *Československý zpravodaj*, No. 262, October 14, 1959.

[99] *Československý zpravodaj*, No. 284, March 1, 1960.

[100] *Rudé právo*, March 16, 1960. For reports on other such contributions see *Práce*, August 28, 1959, and *Rudé právo*, October 20, 1959.

the way in which this is done has been the following directive printed in *Práce,* on how to secure participation of Praha residents in brigade work in 1960: "Couples of agitators from the National Front will visit all the families in the precinct [and] will talk with citizens about when and where they want to fulfill their obligations in the action 'For a More Beautiful Praha' . . . ."[101] Evidently, citizens are given some choice as to when and where to donate their work, but none as to whether they want to donate it in the first place.

Curtailments in Employment Freedoms

A somewhat similar situation prevails in regular gainful employment. For a Czechoslovakian of today there is no such thing as simply pulling out of work for a while if and when it pleases him, not even if he had sufficient financial means therefor. Unless duly retired, an able-bodied adult man and an unmarried woman without a regular full-time job are considered as social parasites facing a possible criminal or administrative prosecution on that charge. Substantial psychological and social pressure to take up gainful employment is also exerted on married women, although the sheer economic necessity to raise the family income above a mere subsistence level is the main explanation why women constitute today over 42 percent of the Czechoslovak labor force.[102]

The citizen's choice of career and occupation has also been hemmed in by many restrictions. Theoretically, the subjects of communist Czechoslovakia may select whatever "socially useful" work they wish to pursue. But in practice this freedom is sharply curtailed by the necessity to feed available manpower to various branches of the economy according to the priorities prescribed by the Economic Plan. In fact, it can hardly be otherwise if the right to gainful employment is to be guaranteed to all. Hence, a Czechoslovak youth enjoys an ample freedom of choice—provided he wishes to work in mining, construction, steel and iron works, or such other sectors in whose expansion the government has a particular interest at the time when he is making his choice. However, unless he happens to have influential friends, his freedom of choice virtually dwindles to zero should he take a fancy to become a bank clerk or a retail salesman, or to embrace some other "unproductive" line of work, especially if the small allowable quota for such occupations has already been filled.

[101] *Práce,* January 19, 1960; see *Rudé právo,* August 10, 1960.
[102] *Ročenka,* 1960, p. 90.

Although the stiff State Labor Reserves system comprising compulsory work assignment for the graduates of the Labor Reserve Schools was abandoned after the death of Stalin, manpower continues to be channeled into the economic sectors where it is most needed through a combination of semicoercion, material enticement, and psychological high-pressure.[103]

Once a man is fitted to a job in a production field considered important for the country's economic advancement, the regime is interested in keeping him there as long as he is needed. On the other hand, the worker's natural interest is to look for a better position wherever he may find it, especially at times when jobs are plentiful. Since this has been the situation on the labor market of communist Czechoslovakia, particularly in the key sectors of industrial production, the inevitable result has been the workers' tendency toward excessive drifting from one job to another and the regime's parallel efforts to put an end to it. The techniques used in this "battle against fluctuation" have followed the customary carrot-and-stick pattern.

The highest point of regimentation was reached at the height of Stalinism when a government ordinance of July 1952 chained the worker to his job by decreeing that no worker may be hired unless he has first obtained a proper release from his previous employment, which was possible only with the consent of the management and approval by the labor department of the respective people's district committee.[104] Although this revival of serfdom could never be fully implemented and was subsequently abandoned, the regime nevertheless continues to penalize unauthorized job-hopping by discriminatory measures, mainly in the field of social welfare. The length of uninterrupted employment in the same enterprise is a major factor in computing the amount of an employee's sickness and maternity benefits as well as the length of his annual vacation.[105] Wage rates are fixed

[103] State Labor Reserves Act No. 110 of December 19, 1951, and government ordinance No. 128 of December 27, 1951. A Government ordinance No. 20 of May 6, 1952, extended such compulsory assignments also to graduates of universities and professional schools. See also government ordinance No. 43 of August 19, 1952, No. 56 of June 23, 1953, No. 24 of April 17, 1959, and law No. 70 of October 17, 1958.

[104] Government ordinance No. 38 of July 29, 1952.

[105] The maximum sickness and maternity benefits of 90 percent of the net daily wages are granted only to employees who have served without interruption in the same enterprise for ten or five years, respectively. Similarly, the basic annual vacation of two calendar weeks can be extended to three weeks after five years and to the allowable maximum of one month after fifteen years of uninterrupted employment in the same enterprise.

much higher in key industries so as to encourage workers to stay. "Loyalty bonuses" and other advantages are offered and preferential treatment in matters of housing, selective recreation, and higher rewards from the "workers' fund" is reserved for workers in such production fields.

"Antifluctuation" measures have also been applied with increasing vigor to collective farmers, especially in the recent years of stronger emphasis on agricultural production. Although members of the JZD are theoretically free to end their cooperative membership, the way it operates in actual practice is well illustrated by the following case of a collective farmer who was trying to use his right: "He has twice applied to be released from the cooperative membership. Thus far his request has not been complied with, and rightly so. He owned twelve hectares of fields and joined the JZD when he realized that he was no longer capable of taking care of his farm by himself. Now he would like to leave the land to the JZD and find another occupation."[106] Even when a member is granted permission to leave the collective farm, he is not entitled to get his land back but must accept substitute property. Also, he forfeits irrevocably the 20 percent of livestock and equipment which he had to contribute to the JZD's "indivisible fund" as well as his household plot and all his social insurance rights. Under a new 1959 law on the Unified Agricultural Cooperatives he must even return to the JZD a part of the income which he had earned in the last three years prior to his separation from the cooperative.[107]

The regimentation resulting from antifluctuation devices is further stiffened by the measures with which the regime seeks to combat absenteeism from work. Besides being penalized by curtailment of annual vacation, bonuses, and other rewards, unexcused absence from work makes the delinquent party vulnerable to charges of unsocialistic attitude toward work which, if recurrent, may eventually lead to prosecution for hampering or delaying the fulfillment of the Economic Plan. Similarly, the JZD management has the right to apply various disciplinary measures to collective farmers who fail to work off the prescribed number of labor units, including even unexcused absence from meetings or the cooperative's work school.[108]

However, since the bulk of absences results from sickness, real or alleged, the regime's main attention has been focused on reducing the

---

[106] *Zemědělské noviny*, December 30, 1959; see also *Československý zpravodaj*, No. 294, May 9, 1960.

[107] Law No. 49 of July 9, 1959.

[108] Krumbholc, *op.cit.*, especially article 19 of the Model Statutes.

incidence of simulated illness. Physicians have been warned repeatedly against "buying cheap popularity" by declaring workers unfit for work because of sickness. To discourage such "irresponsible benevolence" a large number of doctors and other employees of the health service have been tried and given stiff penalties for issuing sickness certificates to healthy workers.[109] The national insurance commissions set up to supervise health care on factory level are under strict instructions to pay "comradely visits" to sick fellow-workers and to expose those suffering from "potato rheumatism," "gardening fever," and other such "seasonal illnesses."[110] While the frequent abuses, prompted especially by the relatively generous sickness benefits, justify the necessity of thorough controls, they tend to enhance the regimentation from above which characterizes labor-management relations under the dictatorship of the proletariat.

THE ROLE OF THE TRADE UNIONS

In gauging the communist economic system in terms of human cost a mention must be made of the sad fate that Czechoslovak communism has had in store for the trade unions. For nothing belies the communist promises of better economic freedoms more glaringly than the manner in which the communist regime has perverted trade unionism's traditional role. From resolute fighters for workers' rights with a primary target of higher wages and shorter work week, the trade unions have become pliable tools of communist-controlled management in helping to enforce the socialist labor discipline and to make the workers work harder.

This conversion of an organization supposed to represent the employees' interests into a company union in the worst sense of the word is fully documented by the statutes and resolutions defining the functions of the trade union organs. As restated in the resolution of the Fourth Trade Union Congress, and given the force of law by a legislative enactment, the main task of the works councils, which serve as the basic organs of the Czechoslovak trade union movement in factories and other production units, is to mobilize workers for the successful fulfillment of socialist construction and to serve as "a school of communism" in the factories.[111] They are directed to "lead the

---

[109] In one such trial held in October 1959 thirty-six physicians and health service employees were sentenced for issuing certificates to jail terms up to 18 years (*Rudé právo*, October 20, 1959).

[110] *Práce*, August 8, 1959.

[111] Law No. 37 of July 8, 1959.

workers toward a socialist attitude toward the work"; "organize socialist contests and evaluate their results"; "organize in cooperation with the management a massive development of the improvers' and inventors' movement"; "help in introducing new working methods"; "consider measures for strengthening labor discipline and raising the protection of the socialist property"; "take care of the improvement in the socialist attitude and professional qualification of the workers"; help in "raising productivity and the quality of labor."

That the primary role of the trade unions in communist Czechoslovakia lies in fostering production by "winning the widest possible active participation in the socialist construction" and developing "a correct socialist attitude toward work" has been further confirmed by recurrent Party directives and innumerable pronouncements by the KSČ leaders.[112] On the other hand, trade union officials have been repeatedly urged to show firmness in opposing the workers' tendency to cause wages to grow faster than labor productivity; to prevent work stoppages and nip in the bud any attempts at solving work disputes by resorting to strikes; and to wage a ruthless struggle against the holdovers of "social democratic" and "anarcho-syndicalist" beliefs that the trade unions' mission is to defend the workers' interests against "their socialist State."

This emphasis on the trade unions' task as production promoters does not mean that their officials should not be concerned with the improvement of working conditions or with the protection of the employees against possible abuses on the part of their factory superiors. Indeed, the trade union organs are granted by law a number of rights in this respect, some of which go even beyond those enjoyed by the strongest labor unions of the free world. Thus the management may not hire, fire, and transfer workers from one job to another without the approval of the works council. It must obtain the works council's consent for changes in work regulations, working hours, overtime arrangements, setting of work norms and premium systems, or allocation of apartments in the factory's apartment houses.[113] Also, the works council codetermines with the management how to use moneys from the factory enterprise fund and participates in the drawing up of the enterprise's production plans. However, all these rights must be interpreted and exercised in strict conformity with "the interests of the

---

[112] *Prague New Letter,* 12, 20, October 13, 1956, and 15, 15, July 25, 1959; *News,* 5, 11 (1956), p. 51.
[113] Law No. 37 of July 8, 1959.

society" and the requirements of production, which are paramount. If compliance with the workers' interests promotes, or at least does not obstruct, the fulfillment and overfulfillment of the prescribed production goals, it is perfectly all right for the trade union organs to attend to their traditional mission as protectors of the workers. But if the two do not coincide, as happens far too often, the communist State and its Economic Plan must be served first, no matter how much the workers' rights may be trodden underfoot in the process.

To strengthen their hand in the promotion of socialist labor discipline the trade unions have since 1952 taken over the operation and control of health care and sickness benefits as well as the distribution of family and maternity allowances.[114] Although this imitation of the Soviet system was hailed officially as a major democratization of the social insurance system, replacing supposedly a "bureaucratic apparatus with almost no contact with the workers," the real purpose was clearly revealed by *Práce:* "The trade unions have been given an important instrument. Its correct use will enable the trade union organizations to deepen their care for the workers by improving health and working conditions, by increasing the struggle against invalidism and absenteeism, and by educating workers toward a new attitude toward work and socialist ownership."[115] That seems also to have been the main reason behind yet another important function conferred upon the works committees in 1959, namely the power to decide disputes between individual workers and management. By withdrawing the authority to adjudicate conflicts arising from the employee-employer relationship from the jurisdiction of regular courts and subjecting them to compulsory trade union arbitration, the workers' individual interests have been even more effectively subordinated to the interests of the "whole collective of the respective working place."[116]

Clothed with such vast powers the trade unions of communist Czechoslovakia enjoy today a position that is legally superior to anything available to their counterparts in the democratic world. One needs little imagination to visualize the overwhelming power labor unions operating in a typical Western democratic country would have in labor-management relations if they were endowed with similar prerogatives. Yet, paradoxically, the very magnitude of these powers makes it all the more imperative that the Party leadership keep the

[114] Laws No. 102 and 103 of December 19, 1951.
[115] *Práce,* July 2, 1953.
[116] Law No. 37 of July 8, 1959; also, *Rudé právo,* July 9, 1959.

trade union movement under the most stringent controls lest it become a Frankenstein that might destroy its creator and master. Since the methods used for this all-important purpose are essentially the same as those employed in exacting obedience from the Party's other transmission belts and its own rank and file, it would be a duplication to recount them here.

CONCLUSION

What, then, are the answers to the several questions raised at the start of this inquiry into the human cost of Czechoslovak economic attainments under the dictatorship of the proletariat?

1. The over-all living standards of the average Czechoslovak citizen are higher today than they were in 1947, the last pre-communist year, but it is doubtful whether they are higher than in 1937, the last year before the Munich mutilation of Czechoslovakia. Since a substantial rise in living standards over the prewar years has been simultaneously registered in non-communist countries of a comparative economic structure as Czechoslovakia, the conclusion seems to be warranted that communist economic policies have thus far delayed rather than accelerated the country's progress toward higher living standards.

2. Material well-being is distributed today somewhat more evenly than before the War in the sense that there are today fewer people who are extremely poor and even fewer who could be described as even moderately wealthy. However, from the viewpoint of social justice, the removal of prewar iniquities has been more than offset by the creation of new ones, mainly as a result of the vindictive communist class struggle. Moreover, improvement in the economic and social status and Social Security benefits of industrial workers and the agrarian proletariat of prewar days had been well on the way in Czechoslovakia even prior to the communist seizure of power. Both social and economic developments in pre-1948 Czechoslovakia and the general trend toward the welfare state that has swept across the non-communist part of postwar Europe lend strong support to the assumption that Czechoslovakia would have worked out for herself a more equitable welfare system had she not succumbed to communist rule.

3. Exploitation of man by man, which the communist regime of Czechoslovakia proclaims in the 1960 Constitution to have already been abolished, has become worse. Piece-work and other capitalist practices of making men work faster and harder, practices that the

Communists used to decry so bitterly in prewar days, have become a commendable method of forcing higher production. They have been perfected and have spread beyond anything experienced prior to the communist seizure of power. By withholding an excessively high portion of the national income from consumption the communist regime usurps in fact a larger "surplus value" of labor than the "profit-greedy capitalist" has ever done.

4. Except for "freedom from unemployment," the promised economic freedoms have failed to materialize and the citizens' total economic dependence on the communist state has become a major factor in the over-all regimentation of life in communist Czechoslovakia. The conversion of trade unions into mere transmission belts for the regime's directives has deprived employees of the most potent weapon with which to fight for their economic interests.

Thus, whatever the economic achievements of communist Czechoslovakia may be, the human cost paid for them has been extremely high; and it has been prohibitively high if measured in terms of happiness which is, after all, man's main purpose in earthly life.

PART FOUR

THE MAKING OF THE NEW COMMUNISTIC MAN

CHAPTER XVIII

ERECTING AN IRON CURTAIN AGAINST WESTERN INFLUENCES

THE FATE of communism hinges in the last resort on whether a new species of "communistic man" can be produced who would believe that communism can give more happiness, more of the good things of life, than Western democracy has to offer. Unless the communist rulers win this crucial battle for men's minds, unless they succeed in supplementing their expropriation of the means of production by a collectivization of men's souls, they are headed irrevocably for an eventual defeat, no matter how many records they may yet break in their output of coal, steel, or other production exploits. Because of their awareness of the vital role that the conquest of the mind plays in the "construction of socialism" and in the attainment of the ulti-mate Leninist goals, not to speak of their own self-preservation, the communist leaders have imposed rigid thought control and have launched a colossal campaign of indoctrination in each country they control.

Czechoslovakia has been no exception. "We shall change human nature in accordance with our needs," announced the foremost com-munist intellectual, Zdeněk Nejedlý. "We shall not be satisfied with the innate gifts of man." And indeed, as soon as they had broken the resistance of ailing President Beneš in February 1948, the communist rulers of Czechoslovakia embarked upon a gigantic program of collec-tive brainwashing designed to develop a new conformistic progeny of Czechs and Slovaks who would turn away from their country's Western European traditions and trade the heritage of their fathers and forefathers for the gospel of Leninist-Stalinist totalitarianism.

SETTING THE STAGE

The KSČ leaders could get their indoctrination machine rolling at full speed with a minimum of delay because they had been warm-ing it up ever since the German invasion of Russia in 1941 when the "imperialist" war became the "Great Patriotic War." In line with the Soviet "brotherhood-in-arms" attitude of the 1941-1945 era, Gottwald and his associates hid their true designs under a garb of selfless patriotism and moderate social reform, as though they had no other thought than to destroy the Nazis and bring freedom back to their tormented Czech and Slovak fatherland. They offered their cooperation to President Beneš's government in exile; and their resistance movement inside Nazi-held Czechoslovakia began to collaborate with the non-communist anti-Nazi underground. They became ardent promoters of national unity among all the Czechoslovak "patriotic and democratic" forces. They raised high the banner of all-Slav brotherhood and of ferocious anti-Germanism, and thereby exploited national bitterness toward the Germans and sentimental sympathy with the Russians. At the same time, however, they jealously guarded their own tightly-knit Party organization to prevent its merger with other groups. And they missed no opportunity to remind "the masses" of the Anglo-French responsibility for Munich and to assure them that a new Munich would never happen again now that Czechoslovakia's national security was guaranteed by the "big Slav brother."[1] As shown in Chapter I, they had suave words and lavish promises of a better deal for all major segments of the population, save only a small group of the biggest factory and land owners.

These themes were continually beamed at the receptive minds of the Czechs and Slovaks who regularly listened to Radio Moscow in the latter years of the War. Some of these promises were even embodied in 1945 in the Košice Program of the Czechoslovak government. And promises continued to be fed to the people by communist-directed broadcasts and by the rich flow of communist literature in the years from 1945 to 1948. Although the bitter experience with the Red Army in 1945 cured many Czechs of their pro-Russianism, the comparative suavity of the native communist propaganda lulled many of them into believing that the kind of communism offered by Gottwald and his aides was more acceptable than the Russian variety. Thus, even prior to the communist seizure of power, a sizable segment of the Czechoslovak population was conditioned for the major indoctrination drive that was to follow.

During this early stage of communist strategy, known as "the over-

---

[1] See, for instance, various articles in *Československé listy* and *Mladé Československo,* the periodicals published by the KSČ during World War II in Moscow and London, respectively; also, *Za svobodu, passim.*

growth of the national revolution into a socialist revolution," communist indoctrination efforts were greatly facilitated by the virtually complete communist control over the country's media of information and communication. In the communist-dominated interparty negotiations (in Moscow in March 1945) about the formation of a new Czechoslovak government the KSČ leaders had secured for themselves the two key positions of thought control, the Ministries of Information and Education. At the head of these ministries they placed two of the most fanatical Communists, Václav Kopecký and Zdeněk Nejedlý. As Minister of Information, Kopecký became the supreme controller of the country's state-operated broadcasting network, film industry, government publishing, and news distribution. His powers to allocate newsprint and paper to publishers enabled him to determine the volume of newspaper circulation and the size of book editions. His Party colleague, Zdeněk Nejedlý, obtained in his capacity as Minister of Education the supreme command of the country's schools and faculties, and thereby gained a large degree of control over the indoctrination of the malleable minds of the youth. Both Ministers made the best of their opportunities. They staffed all the important organs in the ministries and agencies subordinate to them with dependable Party members and pliable fellow-travelers; and they did their best to convert their departments into branch offices of the KSČ's propaganda and agitation center. The only major setback the Communists suffered in their early bid for the control of men's minds was their loss of the Ministry of Education to their staunchest opponent, the Czechoslovak Socialist Party, after the parliamentary elections of 1946. Hence, the KSČ leaders and their indoctrination experts were well prepared for the gigantic collectivization of men's minds on which they have since been engaged.

The first communist concern after their victory was to seal off Czechoslovakia from the non-communist world by a sky-high Iron Curtain. This incarceration of a whole nation in an isolation ward was designed to serve essentially the same purpose in the process of collectivizing the mind of a whole nation that solitary confinement serves in the process of individual brainwashing. Not only did the Communists attempt to cut the nation off from sources that might contradict communist propaganda, but they also sought to generate feelings of abandonment, despondency, and hopelessness and thereby to weaken the mental resistance of the victim. A variety of devices were and are used to achieve this all-important goal.

THE BARBED-WIRE FRONTIER

Nothing symbolizes better the communist attitude than the elaborate barbed-wire barrier erected along the Czechoslovak border facing the non-communist world. With its machine-gun towers, searchlights, alert-signaling devices, and Frontier Guard patrols equipped with packs of bloodhounds, it belies the official communist calls for fraternization and free competition of ideas.

Although the barbed wire does not prohibit authorized transit across the state boundaries, the once lively traffic between Czechoslovakia and the Western world came to a virtual standstill after the communist seizure of power. The possession of a passport valid for travel abroad, such as prewar Czechoslovakia took for granted, became a rare privilege under the dictatorship of the proletariat. At the peak of the Stalin era permits to go abroad were issued solely to carefully screened persons traveling on official business or in the interest of the State. Except for the personnel of Czechoslovak missions abroad, such permits were rarely extended to whole families, thereby diminishing any temptation to remain abroad.

The post-Stalin thaw brought a slight relaxation. According to official reports, 54,000 people went abroad in 1956, most of them on collective tours organized by Čedok, the Czechoslovak counterpart of the Soviet Intourist.[2] In 1957 over 75,000, in 1958 close to 90,000, in 1959 over 115,000, and in 1960, 160,000 availed themselves of a similar opportunity.[3] Although this is a notable improvement over the Stalinist years, it is still less than one-tenth of the more than one million Czechoslovaks who traveled abroad year after year prior to World War II.[4] Also, whereas the prewar tourists could go wherever they pleased, the majority of the present people's democratic vacationers are directed to the countries in the Soviet orbit; very few of them are permitted to venture into the hostile territory of the capitalist world. Not even such an exceptional occasion as the Brussels World Fair of 1958, which would have ordinarily attracted tens of thousands of travel-hungry Czechs and Slovaks, caused the Communists to relax their restrictions. As a result a mere 4,000

[2] *Prague News Letter,* 12, 22, November 10, 1956; *Statistický obzor,* April 1958; *Ročenka,* 1958, p. 318.
[3] *Prague News Letter,* 13, 18, September 14, 1957; *Rudé právo,* February 10, 1959; *Statistický obzor,* April 1958; *Ročenka,* 1959, p. 371, and 1960, p. 371. *Rudé právo,* February 8, 1961.
[4] A total of 1,255,502 Czechoslovaks went abroad in 1935, exclusive of the local border traffic. *Ročenka,* 1937, p. 37.

Czechoslovaks were allowed to witness in person the success of the prize-winning Czechoslovak pavilion; and the total number of Czechoslovak tourists who could visit non-communist countries was only 6,032 in 1958 and 4,431 in 1959.[5] Furthermore, those who are granted the opportunity of traveling to the West undergo a thorough screening. Only those are allowed to go whose ideological level is deemed to be high enough to withstand the bourgeois temptations to which they would be exposed. While abroad they are under as much surveillance as can be managed. Those traveling in groups organized by Čedok are almost constantly under the watchful eyes of their Čedok guides; and such groups are the only way an ordinary Czechoslovak tourist can get out of the country in the westerly direction.[6] Those who are members of delegations, such as athletes and artistic troupes, are looked after by communist guides who seldom let their flocks out of sight. Any suspicious contacts render a person ineligible for further travel abroad and may result in reprisals back home. For instance, several members of the Bratislava soccer team were given five-year prison sentences for having supplied "intelligence information" while on soccer trips in Austria in 1955 and 1956.[7]

Hardest hit by these restrictions have been those who would benefit most by foreign travel—the students. Typical of the negative communist attitude is the experience of the director of one of the Free World's Foundations who went to Praha for the specific purpose of exploring the possibilities of providing facilities for Czechoslovak students to study abroad. He was received with stiff correctness by high officials of the Charles University of Praha who were anything but enthusiastic when their guest expressed the desire to talk with the students. Since he was insistent, they agreed to let him talk to a student delegation. Next day, some fifteen students were marched into the Rector's office in the presence of the Minister of Education and several other administrators. The Foundation Director went straight to the point: "Who of you would like to study one year at Cambridge or Harvard?" The students seemed startled, looked at each other, but said not a word. "Well?" the Director prodded them; still no student dared to speak out. Finally, the Minister of Education broke the op-

[5] *Rudé právo,* August 12, 1958, and February 10, 1959; *Statistický obzor,* April 1958; *Ročenka,* 1959, p. 371, and 1960, p. 371.

[6] Of 90,000 Czechoslovak tourists who went abroad in 1958 according to *Rudé právo,* February 10, 1959, 88,642 went through the intermediary of *Čedok. Ročenka,* 1959, p. 371.

[7] *Rudé právo,* December 29, 1957.

pressive silence and bade the students answer. "Well," said one of them at last, "I would like first to study at the University of Moscow and then I'd go to Harvard."

Traffic in the opposite direction, from the Free World into Czechoslovakia, has followed the same general pattern. At the height of Stalinism it was limited almost entirely to foreigners coming on official business, such as accredited diplomats, newspaper correspondents, businessmen, and various official or semiofficial delegations. Some sympathizers from the West, such as the Red Dean of Canterbury, were let in for propaganda reasons. When Khrushchëv launched the fraternization campaign in 1954-1955, his Czechoslovak lieutenants fell into the new line with more than customary obedience. They remembered that foreign visitors used to bring a substantial amount of useful foreign currency before the War. Hurriedly, they ordered some of the internationally known spas of prewar fame refurbished. "The hotels which were mistakenly closed down will be put into operation again," wrote *Lidová demokracie* on August 31, 1955. "In addition to the curative provisions of the spas for workers in need of medical treatment, arrangements will be made for recreation so that people will be able to visit the spas at private expense for pleasure. Not only for business reasons but for *other reasons as well* our spas will serve foreigners from any part of the world."[8] Hotel employees were reported to have begun studying foreign languages.[9] Visa procedure was simplified and the tourist exchange rate was raised in the foreigners' favor by a lucrative 200 percent bonus.[10]

Despite the increase in tourist travel to Czechoslovakia which has resulted from the reversal of the previous prohibitive attitude, the inflow of guests continues to be pitifully small when measured by prewar yardsticks. Less than 35,000 foreign tourists visited the country in 1956. In 1957 the number rose to 82,000, in 1958 the figure was 80,000, in 1959 133,000, and in 1960, 176,000.[11] Thus, in spite of the post-Stalin increase in tourism, the influx of foreign visitors into Czechoslovakia remains a mere trickle in comparison to the well over one and one-half million foreigners who used to visit Czechoslovakia

[8] Italics added. See also *News*, 5, 1 (1956), pp. 5ff., and *East Europe*, 8, 7 (1959), pp. 7-8.

[9] *Svobodné slovo*, March 25, 1955.

[10] *Prague News Letter*, 12, 17, September 1, 1956.

[11] Data on 1956-1960 tourism taken from *Statistický obzor*, April, 1958, *Ročenka*, 1958, p. 318, and *Ročenka*, 1960, p. 371; also, *Prague News Letter*, 12, 22, November 10, 1956, and *Rudé právo*, February 8, 1961.

annually prior to World War II.[12] Furthermore, a substantial majority of the postwar visitors have come from countries within the
Soviet orbit rather than from the non-communist world. Thus, only
24,922 of the 80,332 foreign tourists who visited Czechoslovakia in
1958 came from the West, while corresponding figures for the preceding years were 28,528 in 1957, 11,822 in 1956, and 2,749 in
1955.[13]

While the desire to earn more foreign currency and the need to
follow the current Moscow line have been the two main reasons for
the partial lifting of the Iron Curtain with regard to visitors from
the West, they are not the only reasons. A collateral consideration has
been the hope of gaining at least a few points on the propaganda
scoreboard. As the Czechoslovak press reported, "Our primary aim
is to show foreigners what our working people are capable of and
what we have achieved in a short time in our socialist system. We
have many well-wishers abroad who will talk, upon returning home,
about the progress in our country and will appreciate our socialist
hospitality."[14] To foster this purpose communist organizers have been
doing everything possible to keep visitors away from the seamy side
of life and from contacts with the "remnants of the class enemy"
within the country. Although individual travel is not prohibited, most
foreign guests are encouraged to come in organized groups with their
itinerary carefully mapped and guided by Čedok. If they want to
benefit by the tourist bonus in currency exchange, visitors must buy
hotel vouchers for the scheduled length of their visit and are directed
for the most part to hotels reserved for foreigners. While there is
no official ban on private accommodation of foreigners, crowded
housing conditions make a stay with native friends or relatives seldom
practicable.

In spite of the regime's efforts to make visiting foreigners see only
the "right" things and the "right" people, many of them do nonetheless manage to have contact with non-communists who are eager to
talk to someone from the free part of the world. This was particularly

[12] According to *Ročenka,* 1937, p. 37, 1,698,029 citizens of foreign countries
entered Czechoslovakia in 1935, exclusive of the local border traffic.

[13] *Hospodářské noviny,* March 3, 1959, and *East Europe,* 8, 7 (1959), p. 7.
Of the non-communist countries Austria sent the largest number of tourists both in
1957 and 1958 (7,812 and 8,410, respectively), followed by the United States in
1958 (4,341). *Ročenka,* 1959, p. 371. In 1959, 10,598 tourists came from Austria; 5, 514 from the United States; and 4,697 from France. (*Ročenka,* 1960, p.
371.)

[14] *News,* 5, 1 (1955), p. 6.

true at the height of the post-Stalin thaw. During this period many visitors to Czechoslovakia reported that people were no longer afraid to talk to them and even openly broached their discontent with the communist system.[15] Those who wished to avoid direct contacts found various other ways to let visitors know of their feelings. An example from one of many incidents is the experience of two Canadians who drove to Czechoslovakia for the *Spartakiad* in 1955. During their trip the car was parked overnight in the streets; and invariably, the next morning they would find antiregime messages scrawled on slips of paper placed on the roof of their automobile.[16] Nor could the renewal of communist vigilance that followed the Soviet suppression of the Hungarian uprising plug this hole in the Iron Curtain. Czechoslovakia's non-communists continue to enjoy the slight breath of fresh air brought by visitors from the Free World, though they must do so more cautiously than during the 1954-1956 respite.

A special problem in this respect is posed by foreign citizens of Czechoslovak descent. These people, who have relatives in the old country, and an understandable longing to revisit the places of their childhood memories, constitute the main tourist potential from Western countries, especially from America with its large number of Czech and Slovak immigrants. Of all the Western tourists, they are the ones relied upon to contribute most heavily to Czechoslovakia's foreign currency funds and have thus been the main target of the post-Stalin tourist wooing. Yet the very fact that they have kin within the country and speak or at least understand Czech or Slovak makes it extremely difficult for the government to control their movements and prevent their interference, whether intentional or unwitting, with the processes of indoctrination. While visiting with their kinfolk even the most taciturn American guests are usually forced into talking marathons by the insatiable curiosity of their relatives. Under the prodding of endless questions they talk themselves hoarse telling and retelling the story of free America. The unfolding of the drama of the speaker's fortunes in America is all the more impressive for being told as their real-life stories related in ordinary words and without political intent. The net result is that the kinfolk who do not like the regime are strengthened in their disaffection; the doubts or uncertainties about America that some of them may have had under the impact of the regime's ceaseless anti-American propaganda are dispelled; and

[15] See, for instance, *Československý přehled*, III, 10 (1956), pp. 28-29.
[16] *ibid.*, II, 10 (1955), p. 27.

the apodictic beliefs of the few who may have succumbed to communist tales about the "rottenness of American capitalism" are countered and often shaken.

Communist propagandists have been almost as luckless with their claims that each year more of the visiting countrymen "will become convinced through their own eyes of the advantages of the socialist system that brings a perspective of joy and peace."[17] They have, of course, no difficulty in now and then getting a fellow-traveler to write a laudatory article in one of the few pro-communist periodicals that still appear in dwindling editions in the Free World. They also score a partial success with a small proportion of the foreign visitors who do not quite realize that a guest living in the best hotels on money exchanged with a 100-200 percent bonus, who is able to leave whenever he pleases, is in quite another position from that of a subject locked up for life in the drab everyday existence of the communist super-State. They also manage to impress a few old-timers who emigrated from the country prior to World War I when it was still part of the Austro-Hungarian Empire and find the country quite modernized after their long absence. These old-timers are not fully alive to the fact that most of the improvements occurred prior to the communist seizure of power. But the majority of the visitors return with a keen realization of the lack of genuine freedom and the low over-all standards of living prevalent in the old country. These impressions are clearly apparent in the travelogues which returned travelers have written in various Czech-language magazines in the United States.[18]

KEEPING OUT BOURGEOIS THOUGHT

Another major interference with the communist processes of indoctrination has been the transmission from abroad of western thought via the printed word and the air waves. This form of "bourgeois infiltration" has been a more serious menace than personal contacts. Direct personal experience, such as foreign travel, leaves the deepest and longest-lasting impression. But even if such travels were unimpeded by official restrictions, they would still be limited to only a few occasions in a man's lifetime and to the relatively small proportion of the population which has the financial means for travel abroad. On the other hand, periodicals, books, movies, and the radio

---

[17] *Práce,* August 10, 1958.
[18] Such articles have been appearing regularly in many periodicals, such as *Denní hlasatel* (Chicago), *Newyorské listy* (New York), *Naše hlasy* (Toronto).

are ordinarily within the reach of everyone and are available the year round. Cutting off these avenues of penetration by alien ideologies has therefore become a vital part of the communist battle for the mind.

Foreign Periodicals

First among the casualties of the communist campaign were foreign newspapers and periodicals. The better-educated Czechs and Slovaks were avid readers of foreign magazines. Their popular cafés and numerous public reading rooms, even in smaller provincial cities, were well supplied before the War with all sorts of periodicals. These ran the gamut of the main European languages and every shade of political opinion, from the conservative *London Times* and the Roman Catholic *Osservatore Romano* to the French communist *L'Humanité* and Soviet *Izvestia*. Many of them were for sale in newspaper kiosks. Since the communist seizure of power there was an end to this variety. Apart from their home-produced press, the ubiquitous Soviet *Pravda,* and over one thousand other Russian magazines regularly imported from the USSR, the Czechoslovak readers have at their disposal today only a handful of Western European communist papers, such as *L'Humanité, The Daily Worker,* East Germany's *Neues Deutschland* and Austria's *Wiener Volkstimme*. But even their supply is very short. The situation is amply illustrated by the following report from a Czechoslovak escapee:

"The former Café Šroubek on St. Venceslaus Square in Praha [the best-known of Praha's fashionable prewar cafés] is now called *Evropa* and has one great and rare attraction: placed on a special table there are foreign newspapers. To be sure, they are communist, official organs of the respective communist parties, but all the same it is something from the outside. Western communist papers are bound to contain some information since they must react in some way to their free surroundings. Even the East Berlin papers are a more valuable source of information than native publications. Thus *L'Humanité, The London Daily Worker, Volkstimme,* and *Neues Deutschland,* the only ones that are available, go from hand to hand and often the patron must sit in the café for one or two hours before he can get to them. In particular, when one reads *The Daily Worker,* several people are sure to come and notify the reader that they are next in line to have it. If the reader takes too long the head waiter comes and suggests that he should hurry a little so that other interested customers may have their chance."[19]

For a while residents of three or four major cities could read foreign magazines in reading rooms operated by the United States and British Information Services, the British Council, and the French Institute. Although only a negligible fraction of the population could avail itself of these facilities, not even this minute keyhole into the free press was allowed to stand. By 1950 the Czechoslovak government had closed the reading rooms on the ground they had been "unmasked as centers of espionage, sabotage, and enemy propaganda against the Republic."[20]

For obvious reasons scientific and technical journals have fared better than newspapers and periodicals concerned with politics, philosophy, history, economics, and related fields. The former are still available in the libraries of universities and various scientific institutes; but often even these utterly nonpolitical periodicals are available only through special permits. In spite of some improvement in the post-Stalin era these powerful obstructions to the flow of ideas continue. The resolution sent to the government by Czechoslovak students at the height of the post-Stalinist thaw in 1956 put a complaint to that effect high on the list of the students' grievances and asked especially for the importation of foreign periodicals dealing with philosophy, political science, and *belles lettres*.[21]

Western Books

Similar Iron Curtain practices have been used regarding foreign books. Upon seizing power in 1948, the KSČ leaders promptly barred publication of translations from Western literature deemed prejudicial from the communist viewpoint. In 1947, the last pre-communist year, there were 350 translations from Anglo-American literature against 99 from the Russian. By 1949 the situation was completely reversed: only 91 Anglo-American translations were published, against 312 from the Russian.[22] Furthermore, the only translations from Western languages allowed to be published throughout the Stalin era were works of "truly progressive authors fighting consciously for peace and

[19] *Československý přehled*, II, 8 (1955), p. 29.
[20] *Lidové noviny*, July 13, 1951.
[21] *Československý přehled*, III, 6 (1956), p. 9.
[22] Jindřich Filipec, *"Radostná bilance vydavatelské činnosti"* (The Joyful Balance of the Publication Work), *Slovanský přehled*, No. 1, 1950.

democracy against the forces of imperialism."[23] Among these authors were Howard Fast, Pablo Neruda, Andersen-Nexö, M. Sayers, A. E. Kahn, and G. Selders. Also, permission was granted to publish certain standard classics, such as Shakespeare, Dante, and Homer. The latter were usually prefaced with introductions pointing out the "progressive" nature of their writings and tending to portray them as precursors of "socialist realism." Finally, readily approved for publication were works by Western authors that depicted the seamy side of life in capitalist countries. This group included such writers as Dickens, Balzac, London, and Dreiser. It was hoped that such books might aid communist indoctrination by leaving a suitably distorted impression in the mind of a reader unaware of present conditions in the Western world. A thorough purge along similar lines was undertaken in library and bookstore inventories.[24]

These stiff restrictions on foreign literature were somewhat liberalized after Stalin's death. Faced with literary ferment instigated and fed by the rebellious attitudes of Soviet, Polish, and Hungarian writers, communist censors sought to appease their critics by swinging the censorship ax less vehemently and by allowing publication of works which would have never been granted admittance prior to the Dictator's death. Thus the monotonous literary diet of the Czechoslovak readers was made more palatable by the inclusion of such dainties as Hemingway, Steinbeck, Faulkner, Sandburg, Wilde, Verlaine, Baudelaire, de Musset, Strindberg, Thomas Mann, Kafka, Sagan, Miller, Rimbaud, Galsworthy, G. Hauptmann, and Chamisso. Nor have the youngsters been altogether forgotten. While they have been given no respite from their everyday Marxist-Leninist ideological pudding, they could henceforth share in the adventures of Mark Twain's *Tom Sawyer* and *Huckleberry Finn* and the exciting exploits of Jules Verne's heroes; and they have been allowed to read such a "reactionary" as Kipling. The latter's *Jungle Books* were actually referred to by the Czechoslovak teachers' newspaper as "a great poem in prose."[25] After the Soviet pattern a new magazine, *Světová literatura* (World Literature) was started in 1956 with the avowed aim of "helping to fill the gap in our knowledge of . . . contemporary [world] literature."[26] Literary critics began to bewail the "immeasurable harm" caused by the "isolation from Western literature." "We

[23] *ibid.*
[24] For more about the fate of libraries see Chapter xx.
[25] *Učitelské noviny,* February 7, 1957.
[26] *Rudé právo,* April 20, 1956.

were like astronomers who saw only half the moon," wrote *Literární noviny,* the official organ of the Czechoslovak Writers' Union, "and the less perfect our methods were, the bolder our conclusions became in regard to the whole moon and its second half. Indeed, we were more like astrologers than astronomers."[27] Even such an archconformist as Jiří Hájek, present editor-in-chief of *Plamen,* monthly publication of the Czechoslovak Writers' Union, dared to turn thumbs down on "the entirely untrue concept that in capitalist countries— with the exception of writers who had adopted the communist position in politics—literature was universally and automatically rotting."[28]

However, the orthodox counteroffensive unleashed against rebellious writers and artists in the Soviet orbit in the wake of the Hungarian uprising has threatened once again to smash these fragile literary openings to the West. "The completion of the cultural revolution," announced by Novotný and approved by the Eleventh Congress of the KSČ in 1958 as one of the five main points of the Party's program for the forthcoming years, can hardly be reconciled with tolerant views of modern Western literature. In Novotný's own words, it is the main task of the cultural revolution at its present stage "to overcome the influence of bourgeois ideology."[29] Hence, Party censors are not likely to overlook the infiltration of such alien ideologies from the West via *belles lettres.*

Films, Theater, and Music

The sad experience which the KSČ leaders have had with Western books has been duplicated with films, the theater, and music.

Prior to World War II the Czechoslovak cinema field was dominated by films imported from the West, primarily from the United States; the Soviet film was a rarity. Similarly, the live theaters were almost entirely Western orientated. Apart from native works, their repertoires were replete with Western products. The East was represented almost exclusively by pre-communist Russian classics, such as Gogol and Chekhov, and dramatized novels of Tolstoy and Dostoievsky.

The situation changed when the Communists assumed control over the nationalized film industry and the theater with the appointment of Václav Kopecký as Minister of Information in 1945. From

[27] *Literární noviny,* September 29, 1956.
[28] *ibid.,* January 26, 1957.
[29] *Rudé právo,* June 19, 1958.

the start, the new Czar of Czechoslovak culture did his best to promote Soviet films and plays. At the same time, he put obstacle after obstacle in the way of Western products seeking admittance. Yet, no matter how hard he tried, Kopecký was unable to completely eliminate the public's elemental craving for Free World films and plays. During the first years of his czardom he had to permit imports of a substantial number of them. Even after the communist coup of 1948 movie houses throughout Czechoslovakia continued for a while to feature American, British, French, and other foreign movies; and the theater-going public ignored the sour muttering of communist critics who objected to the lack of "message" and "educational mission" in Western works. As a matter of fact, such censures had just the opposite effect and served to advertise the very performances they wished to harm. While theaters showing Soviet and "people's democratic" plays performed to near-empty houses, those featuring films and plays imported from the West were packed to capacity. People were willing to travel long distances and queue for hours or pay black market prices for tickets to see such unpretentious and shopworn prewar comedies as those featuring Laurel and Hardy.

Such flagrant disregard of well-meant communist advice could not be endured for long. In March 1950 the Central Committee of the KSČ met to consider the matter and to issue new directives which resulted in a strict ban on all Western movies, except for a few films whose "progressive" character was deemed conducive to the new "socialist morality."[30] The few foreign films approved were a number of Italian and French films which unfavorably depicted certain aspects of capitalist life. Similar strictures were imposed on the live theater. "The Czechoslovak dramaturgy has succeeded in crushing the remnants of bourgeois ideologists and in removing plays with bourgeois themes," boasted a prominent fellow-traveling theater director in 1952. "The repertoire of our theaters has gradually been filled with Soviet plays and with comedies on contemporary [socialist] themes."[31] Except for the classics, such as Shakespeare, Molière, or Shaw, only plays by "progressive" foreign playwrights, such as Howard Fast's *Thirty Pieces of Silver*, were offered. Occasionally, classical plays were rearranged to make them more "educational." Such liberty was taken, for instance, with a performance of Shakespeare's *Romeo and Juliet* in 1951. As a Czech paper put it, "The new concept of the play cor-

[30] *ibid.*, April 19 and 28, 1950.
[31] *Literární noviny*, July 19, 1952.

rectly stressed that a pure and strong love must end tragically wherever the love union is conditioned by social and power relationships" and that the two lovers had to die because their families belonged to the exploiting class which did not appreciate the feelings of youth longing for a world of peace and love.[32]

As in the field of *belles lettres,* the post-Stalin era brought a certain alleviation. The theater-goer's heavy ideological fare has been somewhat lightened by the inclusion of entertaining imports without a message. However, this reluctant concession to Czechoslovak movie fans came under fire almost as soon as it was granted. "The Praha movie theaters are all too often supplied with films that impede our struggle and are harmful to the education of the youth," complained the Youth Union paper, *Mladá fronta,* on February 4, 1955. Apart from their concern with the "educational mission" of Western movies and dramas, the communist rulers resented the eager response evoked by them among the public. As was the case before the issuance of the March 1950 restrictive edict, Western showings attracted full houses, whereas the communist propagandists had a hard time producing attendance for the best Soviet productions. Hence, it came as no surprise that the advent of neo-Stalinism in 1957-1958 led to stiffer ideological criteria for admission of film imports. Of the 140 full-length films imported in 1958 only five came from the United States as compared to forty-nine from the Soviet Union and of the 151 films imported in 1959, 61 were from the USSR while none came from the United States.[33] The live theaters seem to have withstood the onslaught of neo-Stalinism somewhat better and have continued to offer at least a few works of modern Western authors, such as Giraudoux, Remarque, and Priestley.[34]

In sharp contrast to the rigid bar against Western periodicals, books, films, and plays, the influx of foreign music has been subjected to relatively slight restrictions. To be sure, Soviet standards of evaluation with their rejection of "formalism" have as a matter of course been applied to the native musical output since 1948 and Soviet music and performers have invaded the country on a grand scale. Nonetheless, serious music from the West has continued to be accepted, primarily in the form of the old classics and famous nineteenth-century composers with some mixture of the more modern ones. Music cannot easily

[32] *Lidové noviny,* February 13, 1951.
[33] *Ročenka,* 1959, p. 466, and 1960, p. 467.
[34] *Lidová demokracie,* August 31, 1958.

be divided into the favorite communist categories of "progressive" and "reactionary," nor can it be exploited as a vehicle of propaganda to the extent possible with the written or spoken word. For these reasons communist rules can afford to make concessions to the centuries-old traditions that unite Czech music with that of Central and Western Europe.

But while liberal in their treatment of serious Western music, communist censors are dead set against its lighter genres. After the Soviet example, they lash out periodically at jazz, rock'n'roll, and other kinds of Western dance music.[35] Although they claim that they reject such "decadent" music for aesthetic reasons, their real motivation is political. They know that the Western dance and songs are tremendously popular among the youth. For the youth instinctively seek in them an expression of their suppressed individuality and at least temporarily find escape from the everyday regimentation to which they are exposed under the dictatorship of the proletariat. The rulers know that the youngsters who fall in love with this kind of music are well aware of the fact that it comes from the West, especially from America, and that this somehow brings the West closer to them and operates to the detriment of communist indoctrination. That is also why the Praha regime has recently adopted a somewhat different policy. Unable to destroy the popularity of jazz music among the youth, the communist watchdogs of the "people's recreation" seek now to control it and even to benefit from it by arranging for special jazz orchestras, clubs, and dancing lessons. Thus, through an ironic twist of fate, what was intended originally as an utterly apolitical entertainment has been projected into politics behind the Iron Curtain.

Fighting the Spoken Word

Most successful at piercing the Iron Curtain is the spoken word. Needing neither a visa nor the approval of the communist censors, Czech and Slovak transmissions by Radio Free Europe, Voice of America, the BBC, and other broadcasts of the Free World can cross at will the barbed-wire frontier, elude the communist guards, and carry their message from the West straight into the people's homes. With more than three million radio receivers in the country, most of them with two or three wave-bands, and with their close geographical proximity to the West, radio reception of these transmissions is not

[35] *Mladá fronta,* December 10, 1955; *Směna,* October 6, 1957; *Práce,* November 29, 1959.

difficult. Virtually, every Czechoslovak family is capable of tuning in foreign radio stations. Both the habit of doing so and the skill necessary to avoid detection had been acquired during the War when the Czechs listened en masse to foreign stations and depended on them for reliable information. Hence, when the darkness of totalitarianism again descended on their country, people reverted to their wartime habit of dialing the available Czech and Slovak broadcasts from the West. These have become the people's main link with the Free World and the major source of interference with communist processes of indoctrination.

The communist rules of Czechoslovakia have been trying hard to plug this dangerous leak in the Iron Curtain. At first they adopted a pose of indifference and sought to disparage the impact of foreign transmissions by behaving as if they were wholly unperturbed by whatever the "imperialist enemy" might say. But soon this pretense had to be abandoned, especially when the American *Crusade for Freedom* put into operation in 1951 the powerful Free Europe transmitter with its complete morning-to-night program beamed directly to Czechoslovakia. Radio Free Europe became at once the number-one target of communist propagandists. To counter its effect, the Praha regime since 1951 has been engaged in the large-scale jamming of foreign broadcasts in the native language. Reversing its earlier policy of official silence the regime has begun to take issue with such broadcasts, to contradict them, to ridicule and denounce them. It has loudly and repeatedly protested to the governments responsible for such "gross interference" with internal Czechoslovak affairs; and it has been trying hard, with Soviet aid, to prevail upon Western Germany to expel Radio Free Europe from its vantage point in Munich and to ban all activities of *Crusade for Freedom* on the neighboring German soil.

Since Radio Free Europe frequently transmits talks by, and reports on activities of, prominent Czechoslovak anti-communist exiles, communist propagandists have also unleashed a vicious campaign against the "treacherous *émigrés*" who "sold themselves" as "lackeys of Western Imperialism" and thus "betrayed their own fatherland."[36] They have ordered all Party members and activists to watch for people listening to foreign broadcasts. House wardens and street trustees have been directed to eavesdrop on apartment dwellers and report their

[36] For a few examples, see *Rudé právo*, August 17 and 22, 1951; Eduard Táborský, "Czechoslovakia in the Khrushchëv-Bulganin Era," *The American Slavic and East European Review*, XVI, 1 (1957), pp. 55ff.

findings to the authorities. Lest a parallel be drawn with the Nazi era, the Praha regime has not made individual listening to "enemy broadcasts" a criminal offense. However, this does not apply to "spreading malicious rumors" based on such broadcasts or inviting others to such auditions. Stiff penalties have occasionally been imposed for such illicit behavior, amounting in some instances even to jail sentences of several years and confiscation of property.[37] In meting out punishment for other "anti-State" activities, the courts frequently refer to the defendant's habit of listening to "enemy propaganda" and consider it an aggravating circumstances.[38] After all, as *Lidové noviny* expressed it in 1951, "The vicious voice incites to murder. Whoever listens to it places himself between the two camps and gets near to the camp of the warmongers."[39]

More recently, the communist rulers have begun attacking the thorny problem through another promising avenue of approach modeled after the well-tested Soviet pattern—the long-distance "wired-radio," which carries radio programs by special telephone wire over local radio diffusion exchanges to the homes of the listeners. Initiated in 1954, the wired radio system has been slowly but steadily extended throughout the country.[40] In 1959, 19,062 out of the 80,872 broadcasting hours were devoted to transmissions via the wired network, and there were 427,000 holders of wired radio licenses by the close of 1960.[41] Its propagators point to several important advantages of the wired radio over the wireless sets: It is much cheaper to buy and to operate; reception is much better since there are no atmospheric and other disturbances; no tuning or modulation is necessary so that "even inexperienced people are able to obtain perfect reception"; should the need arise, citizens can be supplied with information which cannot be intercepted by "hostile monitoring services."[42] But the main reason was mentioned by the Minister of Communications himself who stated

---

[37] A three and one-half-year jail term and loss of property was imposed by a Czechoslovak people's court on a man who spread Czechoslovak transmissions of Western capitalist nations; a district court sentenced another man to six years' imprisonment for "plotting against the Republic by listening to Western broadcasts and spreading slanderous and inciting reports of Western broadcasts." *Československý přehled,* II, 5 (1955), p. 14, and *Zpráva o Československu,* II, 8 (1951), p. 37.

[38] *Rudé právo,* October 28, 1952.

[39] *Lidové noviny,* July 15, 1951.

[40] *Rudé právo,* January 7, 1955.

[41] *Ročenka,* 1960, p. 471, and *Rudé právo,* February 8, 1961.

[42] *News,* 2, 8 (1953), p. 62.

quite openly that the wired radio system would be one of the chief means of preventing transmissions by imperialist countries from "interfering with a large number of stations in Central Europe . . . ."[43]

Cutting Off Other Western Links

With the thoroughness so typical of them when it comes to fighting Western influences, the KSČ leaders struck at all the other contacts between their subjects and the Free World. Various non-communist groups with international connections outside the Iron Curtain had to close shop one after the other. Such was the fate of the YMCA and YWCA, the Rotary, the Boy Scouts, the Free Masons, and other similar organizations. The Scout movement, in particular, incurred the wrath of the regime when its leaders refused to participate in the communist-sponsored World Peace Appeal. It was denounced officially as "a Fifth Column pledged to support capitalism."[44]

Communications by mail have also been the subject of communist attention. Although the privacy of mail is solemnly guaranteed and no formal mail censorship has been established, there is overwhelming evidence that international mail is tampered with. As reported by underground connections within the postal service as well as by defectors among postal employees, all mail destined for abroad passes through a special post office in Praha where it is checked by the State Security organs. As for the mail coming from abroad, postal authorities are supplied with lists of persons whose correspondence the police specifically want to check. All mail addressed to these persons must be sent first to the Security organs; only after this check can it be delivered to the addressees.[45]

In their persistent de-westernization drive the communist zealots have even moved into areas which most people would consider quite irrelevant. Periodic campaigns have been organized against striped socks, gay ties, narrow trousers, shoes with thick soles, and certain types of feminine and masculine coiffures—all on the ground that these styles betray pernicious alien influences. Not even such utterly apolitical documents as restaurant menus have escaped the attention of communist purists. Thus, such Western-sounding designations as "rumpsteak Jackson," "Chateaubriand" or ordinary "ham-and-eggs" were

[43] *Svobodné slovo,* May 7, 1954.
[44] Prague Radio on October 23, 1952, as monitored by the Radio Free Europe staff, *News,* v, 11 (1952), p. 55.
[45] *Československý přehled,* i, 4 (1954), pp. 19-20.

rejected as "relics of feudalistic times when culinary delicacies were stylishly called after statesmen, artists, and their mistresses."[46]

Severing Sentimental Ties with the West

A very important role in the making of the communist man is assigned to the severance of sentimental ties with the West. To discredit the capitalist West in the eyes of their subjects is, in the communist view, a necessary prerequisite to victory in the battle for men's minds. This is especially true of Czechoslovakia because her birth in 1918 was attended exclusively by Western midwives and her independence was first proclaimed from Independence Hall in Philadelphia. Throughout the twenty years of its independent life the "godchild of America" remained deeply grateful to those who had helped it to rise from its three-hundred-year-long alien domination. Although the painful Munich experience had badly damaged Czech sympathies for Britain and France, the wartime support Britain extended for the Czechoslovak cause and the genuine repentence of a renascent France went a long way toward cicatrizing the wound. On the other hand, Soviet postwar behavior cured most Czechs of their superficial wartime pro-Russianism. Hence, the communist rulers of Czechoslovakia wasted no time in mounting an extensive hate-the-West and hate-America campaign.

Expropriating Czechoslovakia's Birthright

A crucial part of this campaign has been the persistent effort to deny the West any merits for its contribution to the birth of Czechoslovakia in 1918 and thus to obviate the need for any feelings of gratitude in the "wrong" direction. As soon as they seized power, the Communists virtually abolished the Twenty-Eighth of October, Czechoslovak Independence Day, as a national holiday. They baptized it instead as the Day of Nationalization in commemoration of the first decrees nationalizing the country's economy that had been signed by the President of the Republic in October 1945. Since then their propaganda machine has been working overtime to make people believe that the West was actually an enemy of Czechoslovak independence and that the 1918 liberation resulted mainly from "the inspiration by the Great October Revolution of 1917." To clothe this fantastic assertion with a seemingly scientific garb, a conference of historians was convened in Praha in November 1949. Its "findings" in support of the communist thesis

[46] *Lidová demokracie,* December 18, 1953.

were published in Czech and in Russian as a symposium under the self-explanatory title *The Great October Socialist Revolution and Our National Liberation.*[47]

The role of principal villain in the communist version of the Czechoslovak liberation was allotted to Woodrow Wilson. "Bourgeois historiography has falsified recent historical facts as if Wilson were almost the creator of our independence," reported *Tvorba* in 1950. "In reality, however, Wilson was an enemy of the independence of the Czechs and Slovaks, and he negotiated with out *émigrés* only in order to save some forces from the rotten Austria and to continue with the help of these forces in his endeavor to suppress the Great October Revolution."[48] The vilification of the American President reached a peak in 1953 with the publication of J. S. Hájek's book, the *Wilsonian Legend in the History of the Czechoslovak Republic.*[49] This book supplied the Communists with additional themes. Wilson was described as "collaborator of the American billionaires, racist, initiator of the intervention against the Soviet Republic, and master of hypocrisy." The "Wilsonian legend" was denounced as belonging among "the crudest, most mendacious, and most humiliating attempts at falsifying our national history."[50] Wilson's statues, honoring the American President for his support of the Czechoslovak cause, were removed. Praha's Wilson's Station was renamed, as were the many streets and squares bearing his name.

But no matter how hard they have tried, communist propagandists have not been able to make people forget either the correct date of their country's birth or the truth about its Western sponsors. This being the case, the communist rulers ordered a partial diversion—a tactic often used when frontal attacks bog down. Having refused year after year to recognize the Twenty-Eighth of October as Czechoslovakia's Independence Day, they suddenly reversed their stand in October 1958 and sponsored an ostentatious commemoration of the fortieth anniversary of the Republic's birth. But this concession aside, they have not retreated one inch from their denial of any Western contribution to the country's liberation in 1918. When he addressed

[47] *Velká říjnová socialistická revoluce a naše národní svoboda* (The Great October Socialist Revolution and Our National Freedom), Brno, 1950. See also *Rudé právo,* October 28, 1950.

[48] *Tvorba,* February 28, 1950.

[49] *Wilsonská legenda v dějinách ČSR,* Praha, 1953.

[50] *Svobodné slovo,* May 14, 1953; see also *Literární noviny,* March 28, 1953, *Práce,* May 14, 1953.

the solemn assembly held for the anniversary commemoration in Smetana Hall in Praha under the aegis of the Party's Central Committee, Kopecký attacked "the reactionary falsifiers of the historical truth" who "try to make believe that the realization of the national independence in October 1918 was the work of the liberating Western Powers: France, England, and the United States . . . ."[51]

Harping on the Munich Betrayal

But the most potent anti-Western charge that the Czechoslovak Communists have incessantly pressed home has been the Munich *Diktat*. Year after year they have consistently reminded the Czechs that the French and the British turned their backs on Czechoslovakia in the hour of her direst peril while the Soviets were eager and willing to help. Books and monographs have been published which analyze in pseudoscholarly fashion the attitudes of the Great Powers and which conclude with the customary clichés that paint the West in deep black and Russia in snow white.[52] Speeches, commentaries, magazine and newspaper articles, and innumerable cartoons devoted to this perennial topic would fill many volumes. Films and live theater have been utilized for this purpose. Communist disregard for historical truth even went so far that Winston Churchill, "the veteran of all warmongers," was called "the father of the Munich Pact"![53]

While it has not been difficult to build a rather strong case against France and Britain, especially by resort to typical Marxist-Leninist interpretations, it has been much harder to pin the blame on the United States. But nothing seems to be impossible for communist propagandists when it comes to denigration of communism's number-one enemy. In 1950, for instance, John Foster Dulles was added to the roster of the "Munich men."[54] Having linked America to Britain in some of the earlier anti-Munich diatribes, the regime came out in 1953 with a definitive study of American responsibility for the Munich tragedy in a book by M. Gus, *American Imperialists—Instigators of*

---

[51] *Rudé právo,* October 29, 1958.

[52] See, for instance, Rudolf Beckman, *K diplomatickému pozadí Mnichova; kapitoly o britské mnichovské politice* (The Diplomatic Background of Munich; Chapters on British Munich Policy), Praha, 1954; Václav Král, *O Masarykově a Benešově kontrarevoluční protisovětské politice* (On Masaryk's and Beneš's Counter-Revolutionary and Anti-Soviet Policy), Praha, 1953; M. Gus, *Američtí imperialisti—inšpirátori mnichovskej politiky* (American Imperialists—Instigators of the Munich Policy), Bratislava, 1953.

[53] Praha Radio, September 29, 1950, as monitored by Radio Free Europe, *Zpráva o Československu,* I, 10 (1950), p. 13.

[54] *ibid.*

the Munich Policy. The book's tenor and purpose were stated in a review in *Lidová demokracie:* "The book clearly convicts the United States of America of participation in the Munich policy, which it plotted from the background, while hiding behind German Fascism which had been cultivated and armed by American monopolies."[55] Thus, the country which historically took no part in the Munich settlement is made to appear as the main villain manipulating the outcome from behind the scenes.

The "Infamous Role of American Occupants"

Even cruder are the communist assertions with regard to American intentions and behavior vis-à-vis Czechoslovakia at the close of World War II. The most vicious of them is probably the claim that the American Command deliberately halted America's advance into Czechoslovakia to give the Nazis time to wipe out the "people's revolution" and to help the "reactionaries" to seize power. Typical of these statements is the following excerpt from *Tvorba:*

"Toward the end of the War, the Command of the American Army which, with the remnants of the Nazi soldiery, was fully occupied with anti-Soviet intrigues, had neither interest in, nor intention of, liberating our people from Hitlerite occupation. According to its agreement with the Command of the Hitlerite armies, it wished to give to the Nazi executioner Schoerner every opportunity for the toughest possible resistance to the Soviet Army advancing in the face of hard struggle. It gave Schoerner time to suppress, through scorched-earth tactics, the revolutionary wave that was passing through our lands with every step of the Soviet Army. It enabled K. H. Frank [The Reich's Protector in Bohemia-Moravia], according to the promise given to the Americans, to murder the imprisoned Communists and to break the resistance of the Czech people. These designs are clearly revealed by the fact that the American Command issued an order to halt the advance in April 1945 . . . . The American Command had precise understanding about these moves with the Supreme Command of the Hitlerite bands . . . ."[56]

These assertions have been repeated again and again on various occasions, especially at the time of the anniversaries of the Praha anti-Nazi uprising of May 1945. Yet it is an established historical fact,

[55] *Lidová demokracie,* March 22, 1953.
[56] *Tvorba,* September 6, 1951; K. Bartošek and K. Pichlík in *Tvorba,* May 3, 1950; *Lidové noviny,* May 4, 1951; K. Bartošek, *Američané v západních Čechách v roce 1945* (The Americans in Western Bohemia in 1945), Praha, 1953.

well-known to the communist rules themselves, that it was the Soviet Supreme Command which barred any further American advance, including American help to relieve Praha, by its stubborn insistence on the original Eisenhower-Antonov arrangement on the division of operational zones between the Western and Soviet armies.

Similar evil intentions have been imputed to the Americans and the British in connection with their bombing of military targets within Czechoslovakia. As the communist version goes, Anglo-American air operations were not prompted by any desire to fight the Nazis but by a "joint endeavor of Hitlerite Fascists and Anglo-American imperialists to destroy the Czech and Slovak cities and factories."[57] Their real purpose allegedly was to cripple Czechoslovakia economically, delay her postwar recovery and thus weaken her as a competitor of the West in world markets. In the "reckless pursuit of their selfish capitalist aims the British and the Americans burned homes, destroyed churches, and were responsible for needlessly killing a great many Czech patriots." Nor have these accusations been toned down in the post-Stalin era. Thus, in May 1958, a full thirteen years after the events, Radio Plzeň reminded its audience once again that the "air heroism of the American aviators" resulted in the death of hundreds of men, women, and children. "The Nazis have murdered and leveled Lidice and Ležáky to the ground. Aren't those who come to us from the West in the name of 'liberation and humanity' just like them? It is not accidental similarity; it is an innate kinship of the swastika and the dollar."[58]

Even worse have been the horror stories spread about the behavior of American soldiers in the small portion of western Czechoslovakia they liberated in 1945. According to *Tvorba,* "the American soldiers introduced a system of arbitrary shooting, beating, raping, and humiliating honest Czech people . . . forced upon our people their beastly culture, pornography, and prostitution." The prostitutes which the American officers were said to have brought with them were not enough and so they picked better looking local women and forced them to participate in their orgies. "If they resisted, the Americans took them by force to their quarters and raped them." They also "kidnapped in a gangster-like fashion and abducted many Czechoslovak industrial specialists to Germany."[59] Hence, the Czechoslovak

---

[57] *Tvorba,* May 3, 1950, and February 1, 1952.
[58] *Československý přehled,* v, 4 (1958), p. 33.
[59] *Tvorba,* February 1, 1952.

people ought to be grateful that the Red Army saved them, as Gottwald put it, from "falling under the yoke of those who have become the heirs of Hitler's striving after world rule" and from becoming "the instruments of the criminal war and the exploiting policy of foreign imperialists."[60]

The "Imperialist" and "Decadent" West

These distortions of recent history are matched by the warped image of the present-day West which the Czechoslovak rulers seek to induce in the minds of their captive audience. In drawing their caricature of Western capitalism communist propagandists do not shrink from resorting to pure fiction. However, wherever possible, they prefer to proceed from generally acknowledged facts which they then twist, stretch, magnify, and generalize into the desired pattern. Their favorite device is to raid the columns of the free press for the capitalists' admissions of their own shortcomings. These are padded liberally, brighter colors are deleted, and the result is offered as commonly recurrent features of capitalist life. America is the chief object of criticism, closely followed by West Germany. A collection of the abuse thus heaped upon the West in the Czechoslovak communist press and radio would run into hundreds and hundreds of pages. Only a few samplings are registered below to illustrate the main themes and overall tenor.

"Bloody Ike, as the new President of the USA is called by the nations of the world, is a foremost propagator of the so-called 'American way of life' which consists, apart from a chase after maximum profits, of war, fascism, and sterilization." This tirade, which appeared in the leading Czechoslovak pictorial magazine in 1953, is characteristic of the savage treatment of America by Czechoslovak propaganda throughout the Stalin era.[61] Imitating their Soviet colleagues, Czechoslovak propagandists echoed and reechoed in a variety of ways Moscow themes on the alleged American dissemination of a crop-destroying potato bug, the "American beetle," the use of disease-spreading germs in the Korean war, and other such crimes of American imperialism.[62] Both Presidents Truman and Eisenhower have been repeatedly attacked as heirs of Hitler and of his designs for world domination.[63]

[60] Gottwald's speech on the fifth anniversary of the liberation of Praha by the Red Army, *Rudé právo,* May 8, 1950. See also *Rudé právo,* May 4, 1950.

[61] *Svět v obrazech,* March 7, 1953.

[62] *Rudé právo,* June 13, 24, 28, 1951 and June 18, 22, 25, 1952, and March 19 and September 16, 1952.

[63] Jean Beaumier, *Od Hitlera k Trumanovi* (From Hitler to Truman), Praha, 1951.

"The scientific work of General Eisenhower at Columbia University lay in further development of the ideas of Hitler, Goebbels, and Rosenberg," asserted *Rudé právo* in 1951. Upon his election to the Presidency, the KSČ's main daily announced that "there is no substantial difference between the old and the new President with regard to the main policy of aggressive American imperialism," since "both are directed by the same chiefs, monopolistic Wall Street magnates."[64] After all, Eisenhower had actively collaborated in "Truman's policy of unleashing the Korean war . . . forming war blocs, and arming German and Japanese revenge-seekers . . . ."[65]

The main purpose of this constant harping on the alleged pro-Nazi and fascist leanings of American leaders has been to plant the belief that America has thrown her unreserved support behind the West German "Fascists and militarists whose ultimate aim is, once again, to grab the Sudeten areas of Czechoslovakia and to destroy the country's independence." For the KSČ leaders know that, if they could make their subjects believe that this might be true, they would deal a knock-out blow to the stubborn Czechoslovak pro-Americanism. Hence, they portray Konrad Adenaur and his West German associates as aggressive neo-Nazis whose evil designs enjoy the full support of their American "masters."[66] No stone has been left unturned in the search for evidence on "the imperialist conspiracy of the dollar with the swastika." Activities of expelled Sudeten Germans in Western Germany are followed to the last microscopic detail and anything which fits in with the communist line is promptly utilized.[67] The 1950 defection of the former member of the De-nazification Office of the U.S. military government in Germany, George Wheeler, who asked for an asylum in Czechoslovakia, was exploited to the hilt to "prove" how America had all the time been protecting the Nazi and pro-Nazi elements in Germany behind a false façade of de-nazification, and how the U.S. "representatives of international cartels and trusts," together with representatives of the British capital, helped the pro-Nazi German industrialists to remilitarize the country.[68] As documented in the case of Associated Press correspondent W. N. Oatis, trumped-up charges were

[64] *Rudé právo,* September 8, 1951.
[65] *ibid.,* November 9, 1952.
[66] *ibid.,* September 8, 1953; also, Radio Praha on September 20, 1953, as monitored by Radio Free Europe, *Zpráva o Československu,* iv, 9 (1953), p. 12.
[67] For a recent example, see *What They Want,* Praha, 1959, a government booklet, in English, denouncing the activities of the expelled Sudeten Germans.
[68] *Rudé právo,* April 8 and 9, 1950.

brought against "spies and saboteurs" and other "foreign agents"; and their trials were so arranged as to yield a maximum of anti-Western propaganda.[69] Cartoonists vied with one another in the creation of gangster-like caricatures of Eisenhower, Dulles, Adenaur, and other Western leaders.

Another recurrent topic of communist propaganda has been that of gruesome atrocities allegedly perpetrated by American troops and "terrorist agents." The Korean War, in particular, was utilized for this defamatory campaign. Thus a Czech paper had this to say in 1951:

"In Seoul the American bandits scalped 12 Korean patriots. In the Kocha district of Kongi province the Americans arrested 135 members of democratic parties along with their families, bound them, laid them on the road, and crushed them by tanks. Twenty-eight patriots were burned alive by the Americans in the province of Hakman. In the Bongeni village the Americans bound twenty people who were relatives of the members of the workers' party and slew them with axes. The Americans cut off the nose and ears of the peasant Li Yn Dzun from the village of Unenni, picked out his eyes, and stripped off his skin. Because six children in the Kocha district sang patriotic songs, the occupation troops killed them after having first cut their lips and torn out their tongues with pliers."[70]

Similar hair-raising stories were used to describe the American treatment of the Korean and Chinese prisoners of war. According to the communist press, torture chambers, nicknamed "death-on-credit," were set up in the American prison camps where the prisoners were "tortured by electric current and red-hot irons" and hanged by the neck with a steel collar.[71] When a prisoner of war screamed, the American "murderers" pulled him behind an iron plate, opened his mouth by force, poured in gasoline, and ignited the gas.[72] The prisoners were constantly beaten so that their "skin and flesh were torn and blood kept running."[73] There was also a "steam prison" in the camp. "It was a huge case with hot steam. They throw a man into it and when his body is boiled, they throw it to the dogs."[74]

---

[69] *Rudé právo*, March 16, 1952, July 4 and 5, 1951. For a thorough analysis of the Oatis case, see Dana A. Schmidt, *Anatomy of a Satellite*, New York, 1952, pp. 30ff.; also, *Rudé právo*, August 25, 26, 28, 1951.

[70] *Stráž severu*, August 26, 1951, *Zpráva o Československu*, II, 8 (1951), pp. 31-32.

[71] *Rudé právo*, November 20, 1952.

[72] *Květy*, June 29, 1952, *Zpráva o Československu*, III, 6 (1952), p. 35.

[73] *ibid.*

[74] *ibid.*

While the preceding samplings are of above-average viciousness, they are by no means only isolated instances. Many more quotations of a similar nature could be cited. Although most of the communist diatribes against American imperialism are not so luridly detailed, their essence and purpose are the same.

Along with imperialism, the whole Western way of life has been under constant communist attack. Again, the United States has been the primary target. As portrayed by the communist press, America is a class-rent plutocracy with ruthless profit-chasing as its supreme law; an oppressive system where riches and freedom belong to a few pot-bellied capitalists, while the masses of the people live in fear and poverty, and are deprived of the most elementary human rights; a decadent, dehumanized, and thrill-seeking society of drab uniformity with no sense for cultural values; a body politic passing through an advanced stage of economic, political, and moral decay. Evidences of the real face of the "glorified American way of life" have been tirelessly collected from all parts of the American scene, squeezed through the Marxist-Leninist strainer, seasoned with peppery ideological comments, and served in rich abundance to the public.[75]

In strict accordance with Marxist-Leninist clichés, the real political power in the United States is in the hands of the Wall Street bankers. It is customary for Czechoslovak cartoonists to portray the U.S. President and his chief aides as puppets manipulated from behind the stage by grimacing Wall Street characters who sit on money bags with ostentatious dollar signs on them. Naturally, such a government of Big Money serves only the interests of a narrow clique of "fascist millionaires and their lackeys" and disregards the legitimate needs of the people whom it keeps in subjection by "Americanized methods of Himmler's Gestapo," "criminal persecution of progressive citizens," and even "judicial murders."[76] And to keep their power U.S. rulers make a farce of elections through mass arrests so that "the American elections proceed in an atmosphere of advancing fascistization in an atmosphere to terror against progressive forces and stultification of the American voters."[77]

So it is, in the communist view, with all American political and

[75] B. Vronský, *Americký způsob života* (The American Way of Life), Praha, 1950; Miroslav Galuška and Adolf Hoffmeister, *Tři měsíce v Novém Yorku* (Three Months in New York), Praha, 1951; D. Kartun, *U.S.A. 1953. Pravda o Eisenhowerově Americe* (U.S.A. 1953. The Truth about Eisenhower's America), Praha, 1953.

[76] *Rudé právo,* April 1, 1950; *Práce,* March 6, 1951.

[77] *Rudé právo,* November 2, 1950.

civil rights. The exploitation of America's racial problem has been a recurrent feature of Czechoslovak propaganda.[78] But the "American racists" (among whom the Czech press even included William Faulkner) are also said to have no better regard for the members of their own race.[79] "The best, purest, and most truthful in this country are persecuted, murdered, or jailed," wrote *Rudé právo,* quoting from a letter sent by Howard Fast to a committee of the "Defenders of Peace."[80] "Honest citizens," such as the Rosenberg couple, become "victims of the dark police and judicial machinations of the American reactionaries."[81] "Defenders of peace" are "criminally persecuted."[82] "People are sent to prison for their thoughts" and books "are burned" because "the ideals which had once given birth to American democracy, freedom of expression and free literature, are today perilous for their despicable heirs."[83] The American press is dominated by "Fascists," such as the "cannibal" W. R. Hearst, who finally "choked to death on his own poisonous saliva."[84] Hence, as one of the communist scribes expressed it, "the huge Statue of Liberty turning its mendacious, hypocritical face toward Europe cannot hide behind its back an America of lynching and racial discrimination, an America of the Ku Klux Klan, and of furious fanatics on atomic and bacteriological war . . . [Nor can the Statue of Liberty hide] the most repugnant symbol of barbarism—the heavy chains in which one of the greatest writers of America [Howard Fast] was taken to the federal prison in Washington.[85]

Equally dim is the view which Czechoslovak propagandists take of the capitalist economy and living standards. Whether they actually believe it or not, they still swear publicly by Marx's and Lenin's predictions of the permanent crisis and the impending collapse of the capitalist economy. They concede that it may be concealed and

[78] Paul Robeson, *Boj černochů za svobodu a mír* (The Struggle of the Negroes for Freedom and Peace), Praha, 1951; G. S. Vojtovič, *Černá Amerika* (The Black America), Praha, 1950; Jaroslav Bouček, ed., *O Americe zpívám* (I Am Singing about America), Praha, 1951; also, *Lidové noviny,* May 12, 1951; *Práce,* November 2, 1950, and March 6, 1951.

[79] *Lidové noviny,* July 6, 1951.

[80] *Rudé právo,* June 21, 1950.

[81] *Mladá fronta,* March 18, 1951.

[82] *Lidová demokracie,* December 25, 1952.

[83] Praha Radio on January 16, 1952, as monitored by Radio Free Europe, *Zpráva o Československu,* III, 1 (1952), p. 41, commenting on Howard Fast's book on Thomas Paine.

[84] *Květy,* January 27, 1952.

[85] *Rudé právo,* June 17, 1950. Subsequently, Howard Fast fell out of communist grace because of his critical attitude toward the Soviet intervention in Hungary.

even temporarily delayed as a result of military spending. But they assure their captive audience that this artificial postponement cannot avert the ultimate crash of capitalism, and will only make it all the more thorough. Naturally enough, as the most accomplished specimen of capitalist economy, the United States has been the center of communist attention in this respect. Since the Czechs and Slovaks have always had a very high opinion of the American standard of living, the communist rulers of Czechoslovakia have felt it important to convince them of the opposite. They seek to show that the reputed high standard of living is enjoyed by only a small minority of wealthy exploiters, that the bulk of the American people live at best in a precarious hand-to-mouth existence fraught with all manner of privations and uncertainties. Nor can the exploited workers hope to better their sad fate through their labor unions whose leaders have betrayed them and thrown in with their exploiters. Thus, Walter Reuther is described by the communist propagandists as, of all things, "a darling of the American automobile magnates with whom he has always collaborated" and as belonging "to the worst enemies of the working class."[86] The over-all image which they seek to plant in the people's minds was well drawn by *Rudé právo:* "While the well-being of the broadest masses rises day by day in our country, the militarization program of Wall Street brings with it hunger and the impoverishment of the working people in the United States."[87]

The most commonly used technique for this purpose is the publication of "eyewitness reports." These focus the readers' attention on sharp contrasts of luxury and poverty in American life and utterly ignore the class of Americans living comfortably between these two extremes. Typical of these distorted insinuations drawn from unwarranted generalizations is the following excerpt from *Rudé právo's* New York correspondent under the heading "Such is America":

"The U.S. press, financed by Wall Street, reports economic prosperity. Contrary to facts, it attempts to claim that there is a decent standard of living for the masses. To prove this, the *New York Times* recently published a report on the pre-Christmas market. In order to give the most favorable picture, there was a description of stores on Fifth Avenue, New York's most fashionable street. I went to have a look at these extravagant stores. They were indeed overflowing with

[86] *ibid.,* December 6, 1952. The vilification of Reuther and other U.S. labor leaders was renewed in 1959 after their clash with Khrushchëv during the latter's visit to the U.S. See *Rudé právo,* September 26, 1959, *Práce,* September 27, 1959.

[87] *Rudé právo,* July 17, 1951.

merchandise, and jammed with customers. However, walking further down Fifth Avenue, I came to stores in the Bowery, a section bordering on the fashionable part of New York. There, the shops look quite different from those on Fifth Avenue described by the *New York Times*. The customers there are not the people who amass fat dividends, but common citizens, suffering severely from the constantly rising prices. And what are they buying? I have seen stores where you can buy, for instance, one single shoe lace, second-hand. I saw a fellow carrying a sign saying that he was willing to sell whatever he had on in order to get a few cents for a meal. I saw shelters for the unemployed, where people have to sleep sitting up, in order to save space. The American press boasts of the splendid stores on the ground floors of skyscrapers in the heart of Manhattan, claiming that this is America. In fact, however, this center, resplendent with neon lights, is in the middle of an endless sea of poor little houses and miserable shops where people buy fruit not by the pound, but piece by piece and bread by the slice . . . ."[88]

Another favorite source of these "proofs" about the alleged hollowness of American boasts has been that of the few *émigrés* who have returned home. Invariably, they have been prevailed upon to hold press conferences, make public declarations, or even write articles and deliver talks expressing their bitter disillusionment with life under capitalism. "Citizen Jandík has returned home after fifty-three years in Cleveland where he was driven to misery and starvation," wrote *Práce* about one such case in 1955. The paper quoted him as saying, among other things, that "81 percent of infants in the U.S. are born without hospitalization and under unsanitary conditions" and that "thousands of other Czechs and Slovaks [from America] would like to return home, but not many of them are fortunate enough to remain healthy so that they can save for the trip in their old age."[89] Another ex-emigrant spoke of "millions of unemployed young people and thousands of students walking the streets, looking for leftovers in garbage cans, happy to find work shining shoes or washing dishes in restaurants."[90]

Finally, to put the finishing touches to this blackened picture of "capitalism," Czechoslovak Communists have reached into culture,

[88] *Rudé právo*, December 28, 1952. English text in *News*, 4, 8 (1955), pp. 9-10. For other samples in the same vein see *Směna*, November 28, 1954; *Rudé právo*, July 9, 1954; *News, l.c.*

[89] *Práce*, January 18, 1955.

[90] *Směna*, October 17, 1954; *News*, 4, 8 (1955), p. 11.

sports, and the country's mores. They peer into the darkest corners they can find and present their findings, duly magnified and distorted, as typical phenomena of "the decadent bourgeois civilization" and then contrast them with the "shining achievements of the proletarian culture":

"In the present struggle for peace, which is also a struggle of two cultures, the decadent bourgeois culture of the West has long been in the camp of the enemies of mankind, in the camp of imperialism and war. Marching under the banner of objectivism, formalism, and cosmopolitanism, this venal legion of the propagandists of hatred, nausea, putrefaction, and darkness, of lies and imperialistic war, fights to save the profit of those who pay them. These writers have long since ceased to be Englishmen, Frenchmen, Italians. They are people without a country, without nationality, they are people cringing at the feet of American imperialism . . . . The era when the bourgeoisie had its art, its literature, when it was still capable of creating values, ended a long time ago."[91]

No facet of Western civilization has escaped the censure of communist mentors; and American has been the primary target. "Fascistization of the schools" and education of the youth "in the spirit of *Hilterjugend*"; "contempt for smaller nations"; "artificial development of war hysteria"; debasement of science and art; a standardized and dehumanized vulgarity in the form of the "dollar culture," which sees the highest accomplishments of civilization in "perfect pantbraces, chewing gum, and gay ties"; the book market flooded with cheap comic books, pornography, and crime stories; the pernicious influence of horror shows on television and in movie houses; the "unsurpassed brutality" of American sports, of which "most characteristic features" are "roughness, bloodshed, and death."[92] These are among the main ingredients of the American way of life as uncovered by communist critics to show the public that "the reality of American life is the sum total of the worst things that mankind has ever experienced . . . ."[93] Whatever might contradict this wholesale indictment has been consistently suppressed. Even innocent details are singled out and twisted. One writer's complimentary remark that some American

[91] *Lidové noviny,* July 6, 1951.
[92] *Rudé právo,* February 22, 1952; *Směna,* October 17, 1954; *News,* 4, 8 (1955), p. 18; *Rudé právo,* May 7, 1953; *Lidové noviny,* October 15, 1951; *Svět v obrazech,* February 24, 1951; *Československý sport,* September 1, 1953; *News,* 4, 8 (1955), p. 17.
[93] *Literární noviny,* November 21, 1953.

museums have rooms in which to smoke and eat exposed the author to a devastating attack in *Tvorba*. These "advertising stunts," the magazine wrote bitingly, made the author forget that "American museums do not at all document the truthful history of the class struggles of the American working masses and do not unmask the historical role of American imperialism."[94]

The post-Stalin thaw brought a few lighter colors into the uniformly black picture of the West depicted during the Stalin era. A slight touch of objectivity occasionally found its way at least into reports on Western literature and art. However, the neo-Stalinist recrudescence following the suppression of the Hungarian revolt seems to have nipped in the bud these promising beginnings. The tone is somewhat less vitriolic, especially in nonpolitical matters; and some of the uncouth crudeness typical of the anti-Western tirades of the Stalinist days has been abandoned in favor of somewhat more subtle techniques. But the character assassination of the West in general, and of the United States in particular, goes on; and, as in the Stalin era, distortion of facts and unwarranted generalizations are the favorite methods.

Depression, inflation, unemployment, sharp contrasts of rags with riches, and other "evidences of capitalist decay" continue to be among the most popular themes.[95] "Dirty, stinking streets on the North, South, East, and West" of Broadway are still used by correspondents of the Czechoslovak press reporting on the American scene to press home the idea that the fashionable neon-lit façade of Broadway and Fifth Avenue are a colossal hoax intended to hide the poverty of underprivileged masses.[96] Economic data are manipulated to make it appear that "the celebrated high living standards" in the United States can be enjoyed only by a small minority of Americans. "Approximately only one out of twenty families has the material conditions for the way of life which American propaganda passes on as typical for the entire population of the U.S.," claimed *Nová mysl* in 1956. It arrived at this sweeping conclusion by taking an annual income of 5,465 dollars as the subsistence minimum for an American worker with three dependents in 1955 and by pointing out that almost

[94] *Tvorba*, September 13, 1952.

[95] *Rudé právo*, September 26, 1956; *Květy*, January 10, 1957; *Nová mysl*, August, 1956; *Dikobraz*, February 21, 1957; etc.

[96] See, for instance, Joseph Marrow's "Letter from New York," in *Květy*, January 10, 1957, *East Europe*, 6, 6 (1957), p. 20. For other samples of anti-American propagande in the post-Stalin era see *Československý zpravodaj*, No. 295, May 17, 1960.

70 percent of American families had an income under 5,000 dollars in 1954.[97]

The previous wholesale defamation of Western art and literature has also been somewhat toned down. Some of the formerly denounced authors and artists have been "amnestied," among them even that advocate of the "permanent slavery of the negroes," William Faulkner. It has become possible to give credit publicly to Western troupes occasionally performing in Czechoslovakia. However, the disparagement of Western culture as a whole has by no means ceased and it is still customary to blame all sorts of violations of "public order and socialist morality" on the "pernicious influences of bourgeois morality."[98]

While the tone (if not the substance) of communist defamation of the West has become somewhat less abusive in the field of culture since the death of Stalin, that has not been the case in the sphere of politics. The tactical considerations of the "smiling-spree" era around the Big Four Geneva Conference forced the Czechoslovak propagandists for a while to watch their tongues and pens more carefully. But as soon as the smiling spree subsided, attacks on "Western imperialism" erupted again in full strength and their virulence quickly reached near-Stalinist levels. The hunt for "spies and saboteurs" has been greatly stepped up. Special emphasis has been laid on their connections with, and work for, "U.S. military intelligence," "the center of American espionage services in Munich," the NATO "espionage center in Frankfurt," and other such agencies of "Western imperialism."[99] Nor may any change for the better be hoped for in the foreseeable future. This was confirmed by the militant speech delivered by Novotný at the Eleventh Congress of the KSČ and adopted unanimously at the directive for the Party's work in the forthcoming years:

"Recent experience confirms the correctness of the Leninist attitude toward the present imperialism, held consistently by our Party . . . . How could the economic substance of the capitalist system have changed when it could not prevent the growth of an army of more than five million unemployed in its richest country—the United States? How could its political substance have changed when fascistization is

[97] *Nová mysl,* August 1956, *East Europe, l.c.*

[98] For recent samples see *Lidová demokracie,* October 22, 1957, *Československý zpravodaj,* No. 283, February 24, 1960; *Literární noviny,* June 4, 1960.

[99] *Rudé právo,* June 1, October 26, 1957, February 14, 1958; *Pravda,* February 22, 1958; *Rudé právo,* January 25 and 29, 1958.

504

its main way out of its class contradictions? . . . No, the 'mission' of capitalism in the world has not changed in the least. The main export articles of the U.S.A. today are atomic weapons and rockets, and the primary objective of the persistent efforts of the American militarists is the transformation of countries that have until recently been neutral and peace-loving into military bases against socialist countries.

"The role of American imperialism as the center of world reactionaries, the sworn enemy of all progressive and peace-loving nations has appeared very clearly in the latest period. The narrowing of the sphere of imperialism has prompted American monopolies to try all the more ferociously to strengthen their positions of hegemony in the capitalist world, to build hastily various aggressive blocs under their command and to take over the role of the main carrier of contemporary colonialism to the detriment of the other imperialist partners. We see the dirty hands of American monopolies wherever plots are hatched against the freedom and independence of nations . . . ."[100]

Although made in June 1958, Novotný's speech ranks side by side with the pronouncements of the Stalin era; the late Soviet Dictator would have wholeheartedly approved both its spirit and contents. Thus, the attitude of Czechoslovak communist rulers toward the West can best be summarized by the well-known French saying:

Plus ça change, plus c'est la même chose.

[100] *Rudé právo,* June 19, 1958.

CHAPTER XIX
THE EDUCATIONAL WEAPON

THE LOWERING of an Iron Curtain against Western influences is only half of the communist battle for the human mind. The other half consists of a monumental endeavor to purge the people's brains of adverse native influences and to substitute new sets and criteria of values. While mercilessly cutting off contacts with the outside world, the KSČ leaders and their ideologists have been doing their utmost to convince their subjects of the superiority of communism and to win acceptance of Marxist-Leninist precepts. Along with the growth of a socialist economy the "completion of the socialist revolution in the field of ideology and culture," has been given top priority by the Eleventh Party Congress. "Without it," emphasized Novotný in his report to the Congress, "the construction of a socialist society is unthinkable."[1]

Schools rank foremost among the communist media of indoctrination. "In solving this task [of overcoming the influence of bourgeois ideology and broadening the impact of communist ideas] the Party places school education first."[2] Keenly aware of the necessity of shaping the mind when it is most malleable, communist leaders have converted the country's classrooms from the kindergarten to the university into workshops for the making of the new "communistic man." "We must educate our new intelligentsia in our courses and schools in the spirit of the most progressive world outlook, in the spirit of dialectical and historical materialism, in the spirit of Marxism-Leninism," declared Gottwald in issuing directives to the Ninth Party Congress in 1949.[3] And in unfolding his strategy for the "completion of the cultural revolution" at the Eleventh Party Congress in 1958, Gottwald's successor, Novotný, emphatically restated the Party's resolve to anchor youth education "fully on the foundations of Marxism-Leninism and to lead it decisively in the communist spirit."[4]

Throughout the nine years separating the two Party congresses no

[1] *Rudé právo*, June 19, 1958.
[2] *ibid.;* also, *Život strany*, No. 2 (January 59), pp. 77ff.
[3] *Rudé právo*, May 26, 1949.
[4] *ibid.*, June 19, 1958.

occasion has been missed to stress over and over again the paramount ideological mission of the people's schools. Although mentioned in a somewhat subdued form in the laws regulating the school system it has been emphasized repeatedly and much more forcefully by Party spokesmen and by the resolutions and the decrees of the Ministry of Education.[5] It has become a recurrent *leitmotif* of innumerable "ideological conferences," teachers' workshops, "methodological consultations," sessions of "pedagogical councils," "associations of parents and friends of the school," and similar groups and assemblies designed to serve as transmission belts for Party directives in the field of education. As culled from the flowery rhetoric of high communist spokesmen on these various occasions, "communist morality" and the "Marxist conception of life," which the Czechoslovak schools are to instill into the new socialist generation under the dictatorship of the proletariat, comprise the following: "boundless love for the Soviet Union, the protector of our freedom, independence and socialist development" and, prior to Stalin's death, "limitless love for the Great Stalin who leads all the working people of the world toward the victory of communism"; "love for the working class and the Communist Party, the foremost fighter for a joyful and happy tomorrow," and, until his death, "love for President Gottwald who has worked all his life for a happy future for children"; "firm determination to fight for peace and stand solidly in the front against imperialism"; "warm feeling of alliance with the other people's democracies" and "solidarity with the workers and the working people of all countries"; "socialist patriotism and proletarian internationalism," "socialist relation to work and collective ownership," and "socialist discipline"; "placing the interests of society above those of the family"; "mastery of the Russian language—the language of brotherhood among the nations"; "love for the new collective life in the village" and rejection of "all the remnants of bourgeois thinking and behavior," especially "religious survivals and superstitions."[6] The shining example which the Czecho-

[5] Law No. 31 of April 24, 1953; the resolution of the Presidium of the Central Committee of the KSČ of May 28, 1951; a decree of the Ministry of Education of August 16, 1951, *Ministry of Education Gazette*, VII, p. 298, excerpts in Josef Keprta, *Organisace a správa československého školství* (The Organization and Administration of the Czechoslovak School System), Praha, 1956, pp. 58-59; the resolution of the Party's Central Committee of June 1955, *Rudé právo*, June 19, 1955; the resolution of the Eleventh Party Congress, *Rudé právo*, June 23, 1958.

[6] See, for instance, *Rudé právo*, August 18, 1952, March 25 and 27, and August 4, 1955, January 10, 1956; *Učitelské noviny*, January 5, 1955; Jaroslav Kopáč and Bohumil Uher, *Úloha učitele v dnešní škole* (The Teacher's Role in Today's School), Praha, 1956, pp. 50, 130.

slovak youth is encouraged by its educators to follow is that of "the little hero Pavlik Morozov," the Soviet boy who was so loyal to communism that he denounced his own *kulak* family and "did not hesitate to sacrifice his life for his fatherland, socialism, and Stalin."[7]

THE SCHOOL'S NEW PROFILE

The new mission of the schools necessitated a drastic adaptation of curricula, a thorough rewriting of textbooks, and radical surgery on the whole teaching profession. On the other hand, it required only minor changes in the organizational structure, except for the completion of state monopoly over education through the abolition of private schools and the traditional academic autonomy enjoyed by Czechoslovak universities. Any excessive experimentation with the organizational pattern was likely to hamper rather than help the communist purpose of converting the schools into the main vehicles of indoctrination. Nonetheless, since the communist seizure of power, the Czechoslovak school system has been in a constant flux which has not only gravely impaired over-all educational standards, but has made even harder the task of creating the new communistic man, an objective hardly attainable under any circumstances.

The first reorganization of the school system, adopted in April 1948, less than two months after the communist coup, was moderate and sensible.[8] It provided for a five-year elementary school and two successive levels of secondary schooling of four years each. All children were to attend elementary and lower level secondary schools, i.e., nine years in all. Thereafter, boys and girls who left school were to spend one day per week for three to four years in basic vocational schools. Those selected to continue in full-time studies beyond the nine compulsory years had a threefold choice: (1) lower vocational schools lasting two to three years and providing for essential training in specific professions; (2) four-year higher vocational schools offering, as the law put it, "advanced specialized training and at the same time advanced general education to such an extent as to enable pupils to proceed to study at schools of university rank"; (3) four-year *gymnasia* designed to "provide advanced general education on a basis of scientific perception . . . extend the knowledge of the pupils in natural science, cultural, technical, and social subjects [and] thereby

---

[7] *Zpráva o Československu*, II, 9 (1952), p. 61.

[8] Law No. 95 of April 21, 1948. English translation in *School Reform in Czechoslovakia*, Praha, 1948, pp. 11ff.

develop their personality in all directions and prepare them for university study." Preschool age children over three years were to be cared for by a nation-wide network of kindergartens which could be made compulsory for children above the age of five.

Besides the prohibition of all private schools and an extension of compulsory school attendance from eight to nine years, only one other organizational change of any consequence was enacted by the 1948 school reform. This provided for the establishment of a unified lower level of secondary education by merging the four lower grades of the *gymnasia,* the Czechoslovak equivalent of French *lycées* or English grammar schools, with junior high schools providing three to four years of lower secondary education for those who did not plan to go to college. But this was by no means an exclusively communist idea. Many Czechoslovak educators had favored such a merger in the past, and a unified school system for the whole span of compulsory education had been recommended by a congress of Czech teachers as early as 1921. In fact, strange as it may sound, Nejedlý, who fathered the 1948 reform, brought the structural framework of Czechoslovak schools somewhat closer to the American public school system than it had been in the pre-communist era when children earmarked for later college studies, like their schoolmates in Western Europe, attended separate schools from the age of eleven. The same is true for the greater emphasis on vocational training and practical work in the new secondary schools.

Since the Soviet Union has also organized the lower level of its secondary education on a uniform basis, and works vocational training into its school curricula, it could be argued that the 1948 changes in the Czechoslovak school system reflected to some extent the Soviet experience. However, except for a cursory reference to the devotion to socialism and the "community of Slav peoples," and the introduction of Russian as the main compulsory foreign language, neither the wording of Nejedlý's school reform law nor its over-all spirit revealed any Soviet influences. Listed among the main educational aims of the new schools were things with which Free World educators would have no quarrel: "national traditions" and "ideals of humanity"; "independent thinking," "purposive action" and "creative work and harmonious cooperation"; encouragement of "the desire for self-education and progress" and of an "active participation in the life of the school and in the constructive tasks of the Republic"; "a sense of social community," "the community of the family," and the "community of humanity."[9] Moreover, the elementary and lower secondary schools were made "liable to care for the religious instruction of children in accordance with their religious faith, save for cases where parents (legal guardians) countermand such instruction." Although the supreme supervision over religious education was reserved for the Ministry of Education, the issuance of syllabi on religious teaching and the actual religious instruction were left in the hands of churchmen. Nor was there, significantly, even the slightest reference to the Soviet system in the speech with which Nejedlý introduced his school reform bill in the National Assembly.[10] Instead, he spoke of "awakening our youth to love of our beautiful country, our glorious past, and our mature and capable people." While bewailing the absence of a proper legal basis for the Czechoslovak school system of the past, he lavishly praised the teachers for having "done all they could," and gave ample credit to several prominent Czechoslovak educators of the bourgeois era without uttering one single word about the idol of Soviet pedagogy, Makarenko.

What caused such a die-hard Communist as Nejedlý to behave in this manner, and what persuaded his communist colleagues to support a scheme that virtually ignored the Soviet experience? In part, they were guided by tactical considerations. In the first months after the February coup the communist leaders were willing to make concessions to "bourgeois survivals" for the sake of a smoother consolidation of their power. Furthermore, they still sought to support their claim to legitimacy by retaining the ailing President Beneš as nominal Head of State, and knew that he would not sign a law that did too much violence to his convictions. But the main reason for the rather moderate approach of 1948 lay undoubtedly in Nejedlý's belief in the intrinsic value of his plan, a belief that seems to have been shared by most of his associates who knew something about education. They strove earnestly to preserve the good quality of the Czechoslovak schools while also making them the principal medium of communist indoctrination. In so doing, they acted on the wishful assumption that they could use their own "specifically Czechoslovak" method of "constructing socialism" in their own country.

However, this assumption withered in the scorching heat of Stalinist totalitarianism. Their dependence on the Kremlin forced the KSČ leaders to defer more and more to the "rich Soviet experience"

[9] *School Reform in Czechoslovakia,* pp. 11-12.
[10] *ibid.,* pp. 9-10.

and to apply it in the field of education just as much as they had to follow it in other spheres of activity. Moreover, the overwhelming needs of additional manpower dictated by the stepped-up goals of the First Five-Year Plan made it imperative to put the youngsters on the production line as quickly as possible. Thus "the needs of the general economic plan and the perspectives of Soviet education" became, by official admission, "the two chief considerations that led the Czechoslovak government to reorganize the basis of the educational system" in 1953.[11] After five years of life the glorified Nejedlý Act was thrown to the winds with the uncharitable remark that it "was not able to prepare young people for the arduous tasks of socialist construction in the way the Soviet system could."[12] It was replaced in April 1953 by a new Education Act[13] prepared, as proudly announced by the chief of the education section of the Party Secretariat, "with the direct help of Soviet experts."[14]

The repeated references to Soviet aid were hardly necessary because the Kremlin's guidance was clearly visible in the law itself, and the resulting educational blueprint was nothing more than a slightly retouched copy of the Soviet system. The five-year elementary schools and the four-year lower secondary schools were merged into uniform eight-year "secondary schools" providing "basic general education and preparing pupils for their vocations, for technical school or for higher general education." The four-year *gymnasia* were abolished and "eleven-year secondary schools" were established after the fashion of the Soviet ten-year schools. The first eight grades of these eleven-year schools corresponded to the above-mentioned eight-year "secondary schools." The remaining three grades (9-11) were designed to prepare students, admitted on a selective basis, "primarily for university studies." The eighth-grade pupils not preparing for college could seek admission to selective technical schools, corresponding to the Soviet *technicums*, which were designed to provide "vocational training for the individual branches of the national economy, state administration, and cultural life." The pupils who reached fourteen years of age and gained admittance neither to the ninth grade of the eleven-year

[11] *Act Relating to the School System and the Training of Teachers in Czechoslovakia*, Praha, 1953, p. 10. Hereafter cited as *Act*; Keprta, *op.cit.*, p. 55; *Práce*, April 28, 1953.
[12] *Act*, pp. 8-9.
[13] Law No. 31 of April 24, 1953.
[14] Bohumil Mucha, addressing a conference of educators in December 1952, Pavel Korbel's article in *Československý přehled*, III, 2 (1956), p. 13.

secondary schools nor the technical schools (and that was an over-whelming majority of children) had to go to work. Those who "attained the necessary standard of general education" were, until 1959, given additional vocational training, together with a little general education, in the State Labor Reserve schools that were patterned after similar Soviet *uchilishcha*.[15] The remainder of the fourteen-year olds were given on-the-job training in apprentice schools resembling the Soviet FZO (factory-plant instruction) system.

The 1953 Education Act also made a brief reference to nursery schools. As did the Nejedlý Act of 1948, it visualized such schools for children above the age of three, but stipulated that they shall be established "chiefly for children of employed parents." Moreover, in striking contrast to the School Act of 1948 that envisaged mandatory attendance of children above the age of five, the new law expressly stated that "attendance at nursery schools shall not be compulsory."

Although compulsory education was thus reduced from nine to eight years, and higher secondary education from four to three (in order "to supply places of work with young people at an earlier age than hitherto")[16] the public was assured that the quality of education would actually be raised rather than lowered. "We want the school to give us much more, despite the reduction in the length of attend-ance," explained *Rudé právo*. "The Soviet school has shown us that this is possible."[17] And without even bothering to wait for practical results, a government booklet published shortly after the adoption of the new Education Act confidently announced that "the problem was satisfactorily solved because it became evident that the period of general education could not only be shortened, but at the same time the pupils could be given a deeper, more thorough and comprehensive knowledge than the schools had hitherto provided."[18]

This miracle of imparting more knowledge in less time was to be achieved by drastic surgery designed to cut from the school curricula whatever the communist regime considered as "unnecessary for the life of the socialistic man."[19] "Everything in fact depends on the actual content of teaching," declared the above-mentioned government booklet.[20] Mindful of the directives of the Nineteenth Congress of the

[15] These schools were run separately from the general school system under special laws. Law No. 110 of December 19, 1951.

[16] *Act*, p. 8.

[17] An editorial in *Rudé právo*, April 26, 1953.

[18] *Act*, p. 9.

[19] *Rudé právo*, April 26, 1953.

[20] *Act*, p. 9.

Soviet Communist Party that stressed further polytechnization of primary and secondary education, the KSČ sponsors of the 1953 school reform ordered that the disproportion between general and technical education be removed by reducing the instruction in humanities in favor of technical subjects and practical vocational training.[21] In line with this strong emphasis on polytechnical education, the 1953 Act dropped from its definition of the purpose of education the 1948 references to the "ideals of humanity," "national traditions" or "independent thinking" and simply listed as the mission of the new schools the duty to educate "new socialist citizens—workers, farmers, and the intelligentsia—to be well developed and perfectly prepared for the socialist society." Similarly, the earlier concession of religious instruction was left out, and since 1953 religion could be taught only on the parents' special request, and this solely in elementary schools and in after-school hours.[22]

Although the 1953 Education Act was hailed officially as a pedagogical masterpiece wonderfully suited for the "cultivation of an all-round, mature personality" and "the education of a new generation of proud and courageous builders of socialist society,"[23] its private reception by the country's educators, including many Party members, was negative. At the time of its adoption, only a few weeks after Stalin's death, when Stalinism still reigned supreme, the opponents of the Act cautiously refrained from publicly voicing criticism of what was supposed to "enable Czechoslovak education to follow consistently the Soviet example."[24] But as soon as the post-Stalin thaw began to take effect in Czechoslovakia, critics of the new school system became more and more outspoken. Gradually, a lively exchange of views developed on the pages of pedagogical journals and spilled over into general magazines and the daily press.[25] Teachers, parents, Party spokesmen, and even students and pupils took part in the "great debate," which was characterized primarily by complaints about overburdening the pupils; substantial loss of class work because of too many working brigades, various socialist contests and other extracurricular chores; high ratio of failures; waste of teachers' time by innumerable out-of-class duties; defective qualification requirements

---

[21] This will be considered more fully below.

[22] *Keprta, op.cit.*, p. 57.

[23] *Act*, p. 13.

[24] *ibid.*

[25] A very good selection illustrative of this exchange may be found in A. Rozehnal's articles in *Československý přehled,* III, 9 and 11 (1956), pp. 27ff. and 32ff., respectively.

and excessive turnover of teachers; and constant tampering with curricula and textbooks.

The criticism reached its climax in 1956. Encouraged by the demolition of the Stalin myth at the Twentieth Congress of the Soviet Communist Party, the most daring among the critics shifted from oblique maneuvering to a frontal attack on the very core of the reform. The attack was spearheaded by university students who in May 1956 demanded the abolition of the 1953 school reform in resolutions sent to the government and who wanted, as alleged by Kopecký's counter-attack in *Rudé právo,* "to push our school system back not only to the era prior to the [1953] reform, prior to February [1948], but even back to its state during the First Republic."[26] Similar negative attitudes were voiced by various other groups and individuals, including even Party members in good standing.[27] The quality of secondary education was scored repeatedly as providing a wholly inadequate preparation for university studies. Demands were made that compulsory school attendance be prolonged, the former *gymnasia* restored, and obligatory study of Latin and classical civilization reintroduced into the secondary school curricula.[28]

Thus the battle line of 1956 cut straight across the Party itself, dividing it into two embittered camps: the Stalinist leadership and its henchmen defending tooth and nail the 1953 school reform, and the revisionist group attempting to use the post-Stalin relaxation to restore those qualities for which Czechoslovak education had been highly valued in the past. As had been the case in all other areas where the Stalinist and revisionist forces collided in the post-Stalin era, the neo-Stalinism that enveloped the Soviet orbit after the suppression of the Hungarian uprising helped the KSČ's Stalinist wing to reassert its authority. Nevertheless, the great debate was not wholly in vain. Realizing that widespread dissatisfaction with the 1953 school system existed not only among the population at large but also within the Party's own rank and file, the KSČ leaders felt constrained to make certain concessions. Addressing the Eleventh Party Congress in June 1958, Novotný promised that "in the next two to three years the basic

[26] *Rudé právo,* May 29, 1956.

[27] See Pavel Korbel's article in *Československý přehled,* III, 12 (1956), pp. 33ff.

[28] *Lidová demokracie,* March 23, 1956, reporting on a discussion held by the cabinet for Greek, Roman, and Latin studies of the Czechoslovak Academy of Science, which adopted a unanimous resolution asking for compulsory instruction of Latin. Also, critical articles by the former Deputy Minister of Education, Ondrej Pavlík, in *Kulturný život,* June 30, and October 20, 1956.

compulsory education will be prolonged to nine years as our public has requested" and that the eleven-year schools will be correspondingly extended by one year.[29] Also, a new education plan was formulated which introduced some amount of differentiation on the higher level of general secondary education. Obligatory instruction was restored in descriptive geometry for students preparing for technical colleges and in Latin for those preparing for other university studies.

However, while yielding ground to its critics with regard to the length of school attendance and a few other points, the KSČ leaders did not budge from their determination to "strengthen the link between school and life." The manner in which Novotný described this "new conception of education" to the Eleventh Party Congress in 1958 speaks for itself:

"It is no longer possible to be reconciled with the fact that our secondary school does not prepare pupils for practical occupations, and that it does not educate them adequately toward love for physical work. It must therefore become the chief task and mission of our schools to prepare universally educated men who have grasped the fundamentals of science and technology and are at the same time capable of skilled work and ready to participate conscientiously in the construction of the communist society. To create such a truly socialist school system involves linking teaching even more closely with the production practice of the pupils so that they acquire not only good working habits but also, in the upper grades of the secondary school, a basic qualification for workers' occupations. Bringing the school system substantially closer to production will lead to an improvement in general education and create conditions for a further enhancement of the school's influence on political education in the spirit of socialism."[30]

This pronouncement reveals Novotný once again as an accomplished disciple of the Kremlin. What he had to tell the assembled Party delegates sounded like an echo of Khrushchëv's "Theses on the Strengthening of the Link between School and Life and on Further Development of the System of Public Education in the Country" which were first outlined by the Soviet leader in April 1958 and were subsequently adopted by the Central Committee of the Communist Party of the Soviet Union.[31] Stamped with such a mark of Marxist-

---

[29] *Rudé právo,* June 19, 1958.
[30] *ibid.,* June 19, 1958; see the resolution in *Rudé právo,* June 23, 1958.
[31] *Pravda* (Moscow), November 16, 1958, and September 21, 1958.

Leninist authenticity, the educational directives of the Eleventh Congress of the KSČ were promptly put to work. Four major steps were taken to implement Novotný's "new conception of education":

First, manual work, dubbed "The Fundamentals of Production," was added to school curricula beginning with the sixth grade so that pupils would become versed in, and acquire from early youth, "a proper relationship to productive work."[32] Not less than ten hours weekly or 30 percent of all class hours are reserved for polytechnical education.[33] It includes a minimum of one day of manual work per week to be performed partly in school workshops, but for the most part in nearby factories and collective farms. Manual work during the school year is to be supplemented by "work practice" during summer vacations.

Second, experiments were begun in a few selected schools with a new "improved curriculum" designed to give pupils "a more thorough preparation for life."[34] The new plan, which includes eight hours of factory or collective farm work per week, was to be put into effect in the whole school system beginning in 1962. However, prompted by the Soviet example and by the need of additional manpower, the KSČ leaders in September 1959 decreed that compulsory production work for all pupils fifteen years of age or older must begin in the 1959-1960 school year.[35] The students of the last two or three years of secondary school must thus spend a minimum of six hours per week "at the factory bench or in the cowshed or vegetable patch" while an additional four hours are given to lectures related to their work.[36] Through this further polytechnization, all high school graduates are expected to secure an apprentice certificate in one or another basic branch of production in addition to their high school diploma. As revealed by the official teachers' journal, in the 1959-1960 school year 47 percent of the students were scheduled to work in machine production, 26 percent in agriculture, 8 percent in construction, 5 percent in chemical industry and 14 percent in other industries.[37]

Third, an improvement has been made in the schooling of young-

[32] *Rudé právo,* November 20, 1958; also, a monitored broadcast of the Praha Radio, *Československý přehled,* v, 6 (1958), p. 33.

[33] *Prague News Letter,* 16, 10, May 14, 1960.

[34] Law No. 89 of December 12, 1958. Also, *Prague News Letter,* 14, 19, September 27, 1958.

[35] *Československý zpravodaj,* No. 267, October 14, 1959.

[36] *Prague News Letter,* 16, 10, May 14, 1960.

[37] *Učitelské noviny,* August 8, 1959.

sters who go to work following the completion of prescribed compulsory school attendance. A law adopted in December 1958 abolished
the hitherto existing system of Labor Reserve Schools and other types
of apprentice training, and substituted for them a network of specialized schools attached to the larger industrial plants.[38] Their pupils are
trained as apprentices in practical work in the plant to which the
school is attached and given classroom instruction in history, geography, science, and languages. Smaller plants, where the creation of
separate schools would be uneconomical, send their apprentices for
theoretical instruction to apprentice schools run by the local or district people's committees for this specific purpose. Two-thirds of this
schooling, which lasts two to three years, consists of practical work
in the plant and one-third of theoretical study. Since the first of these
specialized schools were established only in the 1959-1960 school year,
it is as yet impossible to evaluate them. If the law is properly implemented, the new system will undoubtedly offer more than the apprentice schools which it will eventually replace. But even if the
optimum is attained, it is obvious that these schools cannot compare
with the full-time education offered by the three highest grades of the
twelve-year school or the three to four years of the technical schools.

Fourth, a new type of secondary education after work was further
developed and reorganized in 1959 under the name of "secondary
schools for the working people."[39] They are established by, and attached to, district people's committees and some of the larger factories.
Resembling somewhat the American evening high schools, they offer a
regular three-year program of courses for employed people leading to
a high school diploma. Since the overwhelming majority of all the
graduates from the nine-year compulsory schools are expected to complete their secondary education in such after-work schools, Novotný's
promise of "full secondary education for the great majority of the
youth by 1970," made to the Eleventh Party Congress, appears in a
different and far less glamorous light.[40]

Finally, a new School Act, adopted on December 15, 1960 (No.
186) to formalize the several steps taken toward the implementation
of the educational directives of the Eleventh Party Congress, provided for yet another category of schools which has recently become

[38] Law No. 89 of December 12, 1958. Also, *Prague News Letter*, 14, 23,
November 22, 1958, and *Rudé právo*, October 11, 1960.
[39] A resolution of the Central Committee of the KSČ on linking the school
closely with life. *Život strany*, No. 9 (1959), pp. 520ff.
[40] *Rudé právo*, June 19, 1958, and August 3, 1960.

fashionable within the communist orbit: the residential school as "an educational institution of a higher type which secures all the necessary conditions for an all-round education of youth for the communist society."

THE DESTRUCTION OF UNIVERSITY AUTONOMY

The profound changes made in elementary and secondary education have been paralleled by an equally radical transformation in institutions of higher learning. As with its lower echelons, the "highest link of the people's democratic school system" had to be given a new profile closely fashioned after the Soviet model. Hence, Czechoslovak colleges and universities have been subjected to a process of sovietization that has found its way into every corner and facet of higher learning. Apart from the general considerations determining communist educational policies, the KSČ leaders had an additional reason for being strict with the country's institutions of higher learning. It was the student bodies of Praha's universities and colleges that had marched into the streets to protect actively against the communist coup of February 1948. Since university students comprised the only group to stage such an open mass demonstration at that time, communist leaders were confirmed in the belief that the universities were the hotbed of reactionary elements. From that time they marked them as a particular target of attention.

The mission of the universities has been redefined along Marxist-Leninist lines. "It is the task of the institutions of higher learning," states the University Act of 1950, "to educate professionally and politically highly qualified workers, loyal to the people's democratic Republic and devoted to the idea of socialism . . . ."[41] But most decisive for the university's role under the dictatorship of the proletariat is the communist concept of science, for even the communist State recognizes that science and its advancement is the primary function of institutions of higher learning.

One of the most authoritative pronouncements seeking to define the new progressive science for the benefit of Czechoslovak educators and scientists was contained in a speech delivered by the KSČ's chief spokesman on matters of science and higher education, Ladislav Štoll, then President of the Praha School of Politics and presently Director of the Institute of Social Sciences at the Central Committee of the Communist Party of Czechoslovakia and Chairman of the Committee

[41] Law No. 58 of May 18, 1950.

of Socialist Culture. Addressing a mammoth Ideological Conference, convened in February 1952 to instruct more than 2,000 top Czecho-slovak educators and scientists about the proper place and function of science in the people's democratic system, Štoll had this to say:

"It is obvious that there is no objective science as distinguished from partisan science. There is only one science which is objective and partisan at the same time, a science in which objectivity and partisan-ship are necessarily interconnected. Long ago, Lenin showed that one of the worst failures of the old-type education lay in its disruption of the unity of idea and action, of theory and practice. Only the meta-physicists do not see this unity, only the vulgarizers can believe that there are two truths: a partisan and an objective truth, a proletarian and a bourgeois truth . . . . A strictly scientific, objectively theoreti-cal activity must necessarily include an element of partisanship, a practical, subjective alignment with the new healthy forces of life against death. Without such an element scientific activity becomes devoid of ideas: it becomes sceptical and lifeless, and it turns into a passive erudition, a routine, and instrument of livelihood and profit . . . . Never before has a doctrine, a scientific theory, re-ceived such confirmation and historic verification as Marxism and Leninism. Marxism-Leninism is just as much a product of men's ob-jective love for the truth and irrepressible theoretical curiosity as have been the other great and ingenious discoveries, such as Men-deleyev's periodic law. Marx's critique of political economy, Lenin's discovery of the law of the uneven development of capitalism, Stalin's discoveries of the laws of development in the epoch of socialism, his definition of nationality, or his theory of the evolution of language are just as much a product of the tremendous strength of truthful sci-entific abstraction and are just as objectively truthful as, for instance, the mathematical theorem of Pythagoras . . . . Science must shake off the weight and the shackles of its disastrous heritage of ideological superstitions and prejudices; it must overcome yesterday's emptiness of ideas, crude empiricism, the indifference of bourgeois objectivism, the subjectivist, reactionary sediment of false abstractions which gave science the alien imprint of class selfishness. It must adopt the stand-point of dialectical materialism, which is not just one philosophical view, but the only truthful world outlook."[42]

Other speakers at the Conference, among them Václav Kopecký and František Trávníček, the Rector of Brno University, spoke along

[42] *Rudé právo,* February 29, 1952.

the same lines.[43] Similar attitudes have been expressed on many other occasions.[44] Reduced to plain terms, this fuzzy formula means that scientists, professors, and students have to tow the Party line and discard all views that are at variance with whatever is the official interpretation of Marxism-Leninism at any given time. To make certain that all university activities proceed within the prescribed bounds, the centuries-old tradition of academic freedom and university autonomy could no longer be tolerated. Having first seized control of all colleges and universities through extralegal Action Committees following the 1948 coup, the communist regime issued in May 1950 a new University Act that placed the whole system of higher education on a new highly centralized basis.[45]

As in pre-communist days, each university is headed by a rector, the Czechoslovak version of the American college president. Whereas he was formerly elected annually by his fellow-professors, the rector is now appointed by the President of the Republic on the motion of the Cabinet and does not necessarily have to be a professor. The rector directs and administers the university, is responsible for its pedagogical, ideological, and scientific (artistic) activities, its personnel and administration.[46] He is assisted in this work by the Rector's Office, headed by a quaestor appointed by the Minister of Education. On basic pedagogical and scientific matters the rector is advised by the University Council, over which he presides. This Council is composed of two prorectors appointed by the Minister of Education to serve as the rector's deputies, the deans and prodeans of the individual schools of the university, departmental chairmen, representatives of the faculty, and outside experts who are appointed (and removed) by the rector. Additional "experts" as well as representatives of student organizations and university employees may be invited by the rector to attend individual sessions of the Council in an advisory capacity. If the rector is

[43] *ibid.,* February 28, 29, and March 2, 1952.

[44] See, for instance, speeches on the occasion of the creation of the Czechoslovak Academy of Science in November 1952. *Rudé právo,* November 16, 18, and 19, 1952; also, A. Klečka in *Rudé právo,* August 21, 1954, Viktor Knapp in *Mladá fronta,* August 24, 1954; František Trávníček in *Mladá fronta,* August 20, 1954; and Jaroslav Procházka in *Rudé právo,* December 14, 1957.

[45] Law No. 58 of May 18, 1950, amended by law No. 46 of September 24, 1956; also, Pavel Levit, *Správní právo, část zvláštní* (Administrative Law, Special Part), Praha, 1956, pp. 309ff.; Keprta, *op.cit.,* pp. 87ff.; the decrees of the Ministry of Education of May 4, 1957, No. 28/1957, and of September 1, 1950, No. 130.

[46] Decree of the Ministry of Education of May 4, 1957, No. 28/1957.

in disagreement with the Council's decision, he may refer the matter to the Minister of Education.

This pattern is paralleled by the organization of individual schools or colleges of the university. The deans, who were elected by their fellow-professors in pre-communist days, are now appointed by the Minister of Education who may delegate this authority to the rector. The dean is assisted by the Dean's Office headed by a secretary appointed by the rector, the prodeans who serve as the dean's deputies, and by a College Council composed of the dean, his two prodeans, department chairmen, representatives of the teachers, and outside experts appointed by the rector. Additional "experts" as well as representatives of the student organizations and college employees may be invited by the dean to attend individual sessions of the College Council in an advisory capacity. The outline of the Dean's and the College Council's functions and their mutual relationship resembles closely that of the rector and the University Council. Cases of disagreement between the dean and the Council are settled by the rector. Once a year the Dean reports to the general assembly of the faculty, staff, and student body of the college on the work of the college and considers proposals that may be raised on such an occasion.

Each school or college is further divided into departments named *katedry* (cathedras) after their Soviet counterpart which served as their model. Originally, departments were created and their heads appointed by the Minister of Education; but this authority devolved on the rector in 1956. Finally, the departments may be and usually are subdivided into cabinets set up by the rector for individual subjects taught within the department. Their heads are appointed by the dean upon the recommendation of the departmental chairman.

As is apparent from this description, the new organizational pattern of the Czechoslovak system of higher education is fully governed by the two Leninist-Stalinist principles of democratic centralism and *edinonachalie,* one-man management. Every level of the university system is run by administrators appointed from above and responsible to their superiors, rather than by academic senates of professors as was the case prior to the communist seizure of power. The University and College Councils are only consultative organs, as is the State Committee on Universities which is supposed to advise the Minister of Education on matters of university studies, organization, personnel, and management. Thus, strict monocratism permeates the system from top to bottom, governing even the contents of the lectures, choice of text-books, and similar matters that used to be an exclusive prerogative of individual teachers in pre-communist days. In spite of the slight de-centralization of 1956-1957 the dominant figure of this hierarchy of higher learning is the Minister of Education who "administers in prin-ciple all the colleges and universities and directs them uniformly in matters of ideology, science, and pedagogy."[47] He issues the organiza-tion statutes for all colleges and universities and regulates all their activities within the framework of the University Act. He recommends appointments for rector; appoints (and recalls) prorectors, deans, and prodeans; determines how the University and College Councils are to be composed and names the members of the State Committee on Uni-versities; appoints all the faculty members below the rank of full pro-fessor and recommends suitable persons for presidential appointments as full professors. Since security of tenure has been abandoned, he can transfer and remove any faculty member, provided that his action does not meet with the disapproval of Party leaders. In particular, it is for him to decide whether a professor or lecturer continues to ful-fill the conditions under which he may retain his position. He de-termines the length of studies, admission procedures, codes of be-havior, and examination plans for every discipline; approves text-books and acts as the supreme guardian of the ideological purity of all college work. Finally, he exercises, with the help of a State Commis-sion for Scientific Degrees, supreme control over the awards of all scientific degrees. Without the Commission's approval no doctorate can be validly conferred by any Czechoslovak institution of higher learning and the Minister of Education is granted authority to cancel awards of scientific degrees in "important cases."[48]

Similarly, drastic changes have been made in the inner pattern of university studies. Voluntary class attendance, a centuries-old Euro-pean tradition shared by the Czechoslovak universities, has been abandoned in favor of compulsory attendance. Simultaneously, the prescribed class load has been steeply raised to as much as 36 to 52 hours per week throughout the entire length of undergraduate studies, lasting usually five years. Since this proved to be virtually beyond the limit of the students' endurance, the communist regime yielded, at least to some extent, to student demands made at the height of the post-Stalin thaw. A resolution of the Party's Central Committee of

[47] Law No. 46 of September 24, 1956.
[48] Government ordinance No. 60 of June 23, 1953.

April 1956 ordered a reduction of the work-load to a maximum of 32 weekly hours of compulsory lower division courses and 30 or 28, respectively, in upper division technical and nontechnical curricula.[49] Even so, there is hardly any room left for elective courses and the students must therefore adhere strictly to the detailed study plan prescribed for each discipline and each specialty by the Ministry of Education.

Another major departure from the pre-communist pattern has been the introduction of periodic quizzes designed to keep the students constantly at work in place of the former reliance upon a few comprehensive examinations taken by the student when he felt ready for them. Nor are students given freedom in their after-class hours. They are divided into study circles, consisting usually of some twenty students pursuing the same curriculum and supervised by a dependable communist tutor. These study groups have a dual purpose of rehearsing materials covered in the lectures and encouraging and checking upon the desired ideological growth of the students.[50] The groups are also urged to enter into socialist contests with one another much in the same manner as various brigades of factory workers are pitted against one another in competitions for higher production goals.

Furthermore, under the slogan of "unity between theoretical studies and production practice" a heavy supplementary load of practical production work was imposed on the overburdened college students in 1959. According to this new arrangement they have to work in factories, collective farms, and other production plants to the extent of four full months per annum.[51] Citing a typical example of what this polytechnization of college studies meant in practice, *Mladá fronta* reported on May 3, 1960, that the weekly work load of the students consisted of thirty hours of unpaid work in production and an additional sixteen hours of classroom teaching.

THE ADJUSTMENT OF CURRICULA

The changes in the organizational pattern of the Czechoslovak school system have provided the broad contours of its new profile; but it was the drastic revision of the curricula and the radical shift in the whole treatment and interpretation of the study programs that

[49] See *East Europe*, 7, 10 (1958), p. 19.
[50] *Mladá fronta*, October 9, 1953; *Československý zpravodaj*, No. 277, January 12, 1960.
[51] *Večerní Praha*, May 18, 1959, and October 29, 1959; *Svobodné slovo*, February 19, 1960; *Mladá fronta*, December 3, 1960.

contributed the new profile's most decisive traits. No school level and no subject escaped the knife of the communist surgeons.

Indoctrination in communist Czechoslovakia begins literally on the kindergarten level. "We cannot afford to leave the children at the mercy of anybody," said Nejedlý, explaining his cherished scheme of compulsory kindergarten to the National Assembly in March 1951.[52] As it has been impossible to provide the needed physical facilities and personnel for such a purpose, Nejedlý's dream has thus far failed to materialize. Nevertheless, the number of kindergartens rose well above the prewar figure of 1,812 such schools and reached 6,309 with 262,146 children in the 1958-1959 school year.[53] Their ideological mission has also been steadily developed. A good insight into their working methods is offered by the following excerpt from a report given by an escaped kindergarten teacher:

"The six-hour long daily program consists of games and basic instruction. Politico-emotional elements are as much a substantial part of the games as of the rest of instruction. Children are often made to attend collectively political activities, such as the May Day parades . . . . They are used frequently as 'live decorations' for allegorical floats where they have to sit for hours and wave the flags . . . . The teachers are given periodical directives as to what and how to teach children in 'political education.' It is done mainly through little poems, songs, and nursery rhymes about Stalin, Gottwald, and the Party."[54]

This and other similar reports also cite samples of teaching aids. One specimen of this poetry prescribed for children from four to six tells how the Germans robbed Czechoslovakia while she stood all alone. They would have tortured her to death had it not been for the "Big Brother of Slav birth" who came from the East to save her. Now it is all changed; we shall never perish because "Stalin shook hands with Gottwald." Another story designed for children five to six years old tells the children about the sun. Where it rises in the morning, there is the East where Czechoslovakia's good friends, the Russians, live. Where the sun goes down, that is the West. There, behind a big sea, is America where a few rich people have everything and workers and peasants live in misery.[55] In this subtle manner even children below school age are fed increasing doses of this ideology. They are

---

[52] *Lidové noviny,* March 15, 1951.
[53] *Ročenka,* 1959, pp. 392, 395.
[54] *Zpráva o Československu,* IV, 1 (1953), p. 27.
[55] Edward Taborsky, *Conformity Under Communism,* New York, 1958, p. 11.

taught what the Communists call "collectivist habits according to the principles of socialist morality" by means of toys, games, songs, and even fairy tales in which the old-fashioned princes are replaced by the "heroes of socialist labor" and the dainty fairies by muscular *stakhanovite* girls in blue overalls.

By far the most important stage of youth indoctrination is, however, in elementary and secondary education. While only a minority of children can as yet be exposed to the impact of the kindergarten, all of them receive eight to nine years of full-time elementary and lower secondary education supplemented by supervised and virtually compulsory extracurricular activities that take an additional slice of the pupils' free time. The selective upper grades of the secondary schools in their turn provide further indoctrination for the better-qualified portion of the youngsters from among whom the future leaders are to come. Thus elementary-secondary schools constitute the pivot of the communist effort to make the new communistic man. To make them live up to their function as an all-embracing medium of collective brainwashing, their subject offerings have been reorganized accordingly.[56]

Teaching of religion, for which two hours of instruction weekly had been reserved throughout the first nine school years by the Nejedlý Act of 1948, was left out of the regular curricula of all schools after 1953. Russian is taught as the main foreign language beginning with the fourth grade; and its weekly load was raised in 1953.[57] While three to four hours per week of another foreign language was prescribed for the four highest grades of secondary schools under the 1948 Education Act, the 1953 reform reduced this to two hours weekly to be offered only during the last three grades. Latin, which had been retained for *gymnasia* after 1948, was dropped altogether as a compulsory subject in 1953, although it has remained optional for the three highest grades of the general secondary schools.[58] In order to do away with the disproportions between the technical disciplines and the humanities, more hours are reserved since 1953 for mathematics, physics, chemistry, and technical subjects. And, as mentioned above, in line with the poly-

[56] For the curricula for the years 1948-1953, see *School Reform in Czechoslovakia*, pp. 43, 44, 47; for those after 1953 see Keprta, *op.cit.*, p. 69.

[57] Under the 1948 Education Act there were two weekly hours in the fourth and fifth grades and three weekly hours in the sixth to thirteenth grades. The 1953 Act raised these weekly loads by one hour.

[58] Under the pressure of the great debate on education in 1956 the Minister of Education announced that some classes would have Latin beginning with the ninth grade. *Československý přehled*, III, 12 (1956), pp. 35-36.

technization fashion dominant in the Soviet orbit, more and more manual work has been mixed into the study plans. Thus, school curricula have been freed from "the survivals and inadequacies of the bourgeois school," from materials "wholly unnecessary for the life of the socialistic man" and filled with knowledge deemed more useful for "the builders of socialism."[59]

Significant though they are, the changes resulting from the omission and addition of individual subjects are dwarfed by the drastic surgery applied to their content and interpretation. "The political nature of the schools [and] the socialist character of education in our schools cannot lie only in one subject, but must penetrate all subjects," said a prominent Party theoretician, G. Bareš, addressing a national conference of teachers in July 1950.[60] In pursuance of such high Party directives, pressed home repeatedly at periodic teachers' and school administrators' conferences and workshops on all levels, embodied in binding regulations of the Ministry of Education, and enforced by hordes of controllers, the "Marxist-Leninist world outlook" has been made the basis of all subjects.[61]

The chief means of indoctrination is instruction in the native language and literature, in Russian, history, and geography. The prescribed syllabi, readers, and all other aids used in these classes, as well as home assignments, are heavy with materials calculated to mold the youngsters' minds into the desired pattern and to make them "hate the exploiters of the workers and the plotters of a new war." The pupils read and hear of "the most beautiful examples of labor heroism in our plants and collective fields," the "glorious Soviet Union, our liberator, best friend, and protector," and the "Western imperialist aggressors." The wonderful world of socialism where people live in freedom, justice, and happiness is contrasted in word and pictures with life under capitalism, characterized by the lust for profit, and fear of unemployment, where riches are for the few and misery for the many. The bright socialist present and the even more brilliant communist tomorrow is compared with the dreary past in which police fired into crowds of hungry workers striking for more bread to feed their suffering children. Youngsters are taught that Beneš sold Czechoslovakia to the German Fascists and conspired with Western imperialists to keep the country in the camp of capitalism and war; but that the Com-

---

[59] Editorial in *Rudé právo*, April 26, 1953.

[60] *Rudé právo*, July 7 and 8, 1950.

[61] See, for instance, extensive directives on the school textbooks issued by the Presidium of the Central Committee of the KSČ on May 28, 1951, *Lidové noviny*, June 17, 1951.

munist Party, with generous Soviet help, stopped these vicious intrigues and secured a happy socialist future for the peoples of Czechoslovakia. They are shown, through a clever selection of antireligious materials going back to the Spanish inquisition and medieval burning of heretics, that the Church had for long centuries been the staunchest ally of reactionaries and oppressors and that religion has always been used to deceive the common man. They are assigned to read such stories as *Fireman of Train 71* (dramatizing Lenin's escape to Finland in 1917), *Pioneer Pavlik Morozov,* and *How Workers Lived in Olden Days.* An all-out effort is made to strengthen the pupils' "socialist morality" by highly idealized sketches of the life and work of such "revolutionary fighters" as Lenin and Gottwald, such "heroes of socialist labor and science" as Stakhanov and Michurin, and to precondition them for the right choice of a future occupation by richly embroidered and romanticized tales of the work of miners, tractor drivers, blast-furnace attendants, and other such meritorious builders of socialism.[62]

While the courses in Czech and Russian language and literature and in social sciences take a decisive lead in the battle for the making of the new communistic progeny, other subjects are by no means allowed to "rot in bourgeois objectivism." The natural sciences are assigned the specific task of conditioning the children for atheism. Courses in other languages, such as English or French, have been found suitable for a further elaboration of the distorted picture of the respective countries presented in history and geography classes.[63] Not

[62] See, for instance: Decrees of the Ministry of Education of July 27, 1951, August 10 and August 16, 1951, *Ministry of Education Gazette,* 1951; Decree of the Ministry of Education of August 29, 1950, on the study plans and syllabi for the elementary and secondary schools, *Ministry of Education Gazette 1950; Obrázky z dějin* (Pictures from History), a History Textbook for the Fourth Grade: J. Bělič, ed., *Český jazyk pro III. postupný ročník* (The Czech Language for the Third Progressive Grade), a Czech language textbook; *Učební plány a osnovy pro odborné školy s docházkou kratší než čtyřletou* (Teaching Plans and Syllabi for Technical Schools of Less than Four Years), Praha, 1949; Julius Alberty, *Úvod do vyučování dějepisu* (An Introduction to the Teaching of History), Bratislava, 1959; František Musil, ed., *Národní škola* (The National School), Praha, 1956; the textbook resolution of the Party's Presidium of May 28, 1951, *Lidové noviny,* June 17, 1951; the resolution of the Party's Central Committee on increasing the standards of general education of June 1955, *Rudé právo,* June 19, 1955; also, *Československý přehled,* II, 5 (1955), pp. 7ff., and V, 4 and 6 (1958), pp. 32 and 7-8, respectively; *Rudé právo,* October 16, 1951; *Mladá fronta,* August 16, 1951; *Lidové noviny,* March 17, 1950; *Zpráva o Československu,* II, 2 and 7 (1951), pp. 53-54 and 47-48, respectively.

[63] The French textbook for the high schools is replete with Marxist-Leninist clichés: *Cvičebnice francouzského jazyka pro 3. a 4. třídu gymnasií a vyšších hospodářských škol* (The Textbook of French Languages for the Third and Fourth Grade of *Gymnasia* and of Higher Economic Schools), Praha, 1950.

527

even such an inherently apolitical discipline as mathematics is spared: arithmetical word problems are subtly phrased to inject the prescribed ideological slant into the most exact of the sciences.

The magnitude of the distortions illustrated by these samplings from various textbooks and other school materials, from Party and Ministry of Education directives and from information gathered from escaped teachers and students, are corroborated by official instructions regarding the themes and methods for final examinations. Their prescribed purpose is to ascertain not only the pupils' educational level, but also to indicate how prepared they are "morally and politically for further study or occupation."[64] The manner in which this is done is illustrated by the following examples of themes prescribed by the Ministry of Education for final examinations held at the end of the compulsory lower level of secondary education:

"How Workers Lived in the Pre-Munich Republic"; "The Fulfillment of the Five-Year Plan and the Struggle for World Peace in Our Literature"; "Life and Struggle of the Working Class under Capitalism"; "Which Czechoslovak Poets and Novelists Teach Us to Understand and Love Lenin and Stalin?"; "The Heroes of Soviet Literature Who Are Models for Our Life"; "Without the October Revolution There Would Not Be a Free Czechoslovakia"; "Lenin's Legacy: To Learn."

Accompanying instructions direct the examiners to check on whether the pupil is "aware that without the experience and brotherly aid of the Soviet Union we would not have our independence; what his attitude is toward out great model and friend, the USSR . . . why the capitalists won in Czechoslovakia in 1920 . . . how the Red Army liberated us . . . how the people defeated in February 1948 the attack of the reactionaries . . . how Michurin's biology helps the Unified Agricultural Cooperatives . . . ."[65] Similar instructions apply to maturity examinations with which the pupils complete the upper level of secondary education.[66]

The results of the final examinations are evaluated by special commissions that are directed to consider equally the student's knowledge and his "political maturity and ideological dependability." To insure

[64] A circular of the Ministry of Education of January 18, 1954, *Ministry of Education Gazette*, 1954.

[65] *Ministry of Education Gazette*, May 10, 1951, *Zpráva o Československu*, II, 9 (1951), pp. 53-55.

[66] Ministry of Education decree of January 1, 1952, and of January 18, 1954, *Ministry of Education Gazette*, 1952 and 1954.

this inspection, representatives of the people's committees, invariably dependable Communists, sit on the examining commissions and participate on an equal footing with educators in determining students' grades. Their right to do so has been publicly reaffirmed in 1958 by the official teachers' journal in an answer to a group of teachers from a Praha borough, inquiring whether political representatives of the people's committees should codetermine the students' grades even though they may not be familiar with the subjects of the examination. The journal replied in the affirmative and explained that a denial of the right to participate on an equal footing in the grading of the pupils would defeat the very purpose of the "workers' share in the education of the youth . . . ."[67]

The ideological axe has fallen with a similar weight on the study plans and syllabi of the colleges and universities. "For the first time in our history our universities are given complete, precise, and unified study plans and syllabi," proudly proclaimed a Deputy Minister of Education when the new college study plans were approved by the State Committee for Universities over which he presided.[68] As a result, all curricula have been revised from the point of view of the Marxist-Leninist *Weltanschauung* and whatever did not square with it has simply been cut out or duly amended. As in secondary education, the grossest mutilation has taken place in the social sciences and in law; but hardly any field escaped unscathed. Biology departments and agricultural colleges have had to "enrich themselves" post-haste with Michurin-Lysenko theories. Departments of languages and literature, as well as schools of fine arts, must swear by socialist realism. Bourgeois sociology has been thrown out while the study of Soviet literature, law, and history was steeply upgraded. Russian has become a compulsory subject to enable the students to "draw from the rich sources of Soviet science in the original . . . ."[69] Western languages have been downgraded, although the situation in this respect improved somewhat in 1956-1957 when, on the insistence of the professors, requirements of some of the Western European languages have been reintroduced for some fields.[70] No matter what his major may be, the student must take basic courses in Marxism-Leninism; the 1956 stu-

---

[67] *Učitelské noviny,* November 30, 1958.
[68] *Rudé právo,* June 29, 1951.
[69] *Pravda,* October 3, 1951.
[70] It is interesting to note that the German language was reintroduced in the colleges of chemistry, agriculture, forestry, and architecture in Praha in 1953-1954. See *Aufbau und Frieden,* November 13, 1953.

dent demands that this requirement be dropped or at least reduced were scornfully rejected. Studies in the humanities have been consistently pushed back in favor of technical subjects. Atomizing of curricula for the sake of ever narrower specialization was the fashion of the day until 1958 when the trend was slightly reversed and the number of areas of specialization reduced from 200 to 154 to make future specialists more versatile.[71]

The implementation of the new "precise and unified study plans and syllabi" necessitated a new type of college textbook. While little mutilation was needed in exact sciences, the opposite is true of the social sciences, law, and the humanities. There truth, half-truth, distortion, and even outright lies are all presented to the students, together with quotations from the classics of Marxism-Leninism and contemptuous abuse of "bourgeois science." That is the general impression gained from a perusal of college textbooks used currently in social science and law studies at Czechoslovak universities. To make certain that all textbooks meet the prescribed standards, particularly those of communist ideology, they must be approved by the Ministry of Education. Manuscripts are prepared by the "collectives" of teachers of the respective departments under the leadership of the departmental head. They are then sent through the rector's office to the Ministry of Education where they are studied by "commissions of experts," considered by the Textbook Commission, and finally approved by the Minister of Education.[72] Usually, only one such textbook is used for a given subject. When more than one textbook is used, the second book is frequently a Soviet product. As for collateral readings and the use of library materials, it seems that the choice is left to individual departments. However, books, periodicals, and other study and research materials objectionable from the Marxist-Leninist viewpoint have been classified as *libri prohibiti* and may not be borrowed except by special permission.[73]

Finally, mention must be made of the departments of Marxism-Leninism that have been set up for the express purpose of supplementing the college curricula with ample doses of the proper "scientific world outlook." As explained by a communist lecturer, it is "the task of the departments of Marxism-Leninism to help our scientific workers to master Marxist-Leninist science of the laws of the development of

[71] *Lidová demokracie,* February 18, 1958.
[72] *Mladá fronta,* April 14, 1953; *Rudé právo,* June 4, 1953.
[73] *Československý přehled,* ii, 6 (1956), p. 9. See also Chapter xviii.

society, to help them to become real patriots, publicly active in politics, interested in the destinies of their country, and in the struggle of the peace-loving camp against the instigators of war . . . just as Soviet scientists are . . . ."[74] The departments of Marxism-Leninism offer courses in Marxism-Leninism and the history of the Communist parties of the Soviet Union and Czechoslovakia that constitute a mandatory part of all college curricula. By 1956 sixty-two such departments were in operation in Czechoslovak colleges and universities, employing 750 instructors selected from among hard-core Party theoreticians.[75] To assure these key media of college indoctrination a steady influx of dependable instructors, an Institute for Advanced Training for Instructors of Marxism-Leninism has been established at the Charles University in Praha with branches at the universities of Brno and Bratislava.[76]

IMPROVING THE CLASS PROFILE

Hand in hand with the preoccupation with the ideological aspect of education goes a deep concern about the correct social structure of the student body in the higher selective schools, both on the upper secondary and college levels. It has been shown in Chapter II how sensitive the KSČ leaders are about the proper class composition of the Party and how hard they strive to "improve its proletarian character." They are similarly concerned with the future "toiling intelligentsia." This is indeed one of the most striking examples of how some of the rosiest Marxist-Leninist postulates are twisted in actual communist practice. While thundering against privileges by birth, and while claiming to have provided equality of opportunities for all citizens, the communist regime has in fact established an aristocracy in reverse, based on birthright almost as much as was the medieval nobility. Membership in it, however, is attained by birth at the lower end of the social ladder. The children of manual workers and small and middle peasants, argued a Deputy Minister of Education in 1952, "already carry in their origin the prerequisites for their development and growth into a new class-conscious intelligentsia."[77] On the other hand, those who have had the misfortune of being born in middle-class or upper-class families or whose fathers happen to be designated

---

[74] *Lidové noviny,* December 29, 1951; also, *Pravda,* October 3, 1951.
[75] *Rudé právo,* February 7, 1956.
[76] A decree of the Ministry of Education of August 8, 1957.
[77] *Rudé právo,* May 27, 1952.

as *kulaks* are marked with a stigma which makes them only second-class citizens who are to be denied their constitutional right to equal access to education.

Children of bourgeois origin "must choose manual labor so that they may at last do the work that their class always gladly left to the proletarians . . . they must become miners and foundry workers . . . . There, underground, let them dig coal. There, in the glowing light of the furnaces and the red-hot iron, a brand new world will open for them, a world of active work. There will be their new high schools and universities. There we will hammer and educate them into builders of socialism."[78] Although not always stated in such a dramatic fashion, this basic attitude has been pressed home relentlessly year after year by the communist press, by KSČ spokesmen issuing Party directives to assemblies of teachers and school administrators, and in the admission rules issued by the Ministry of Education.[79] Having been toned down somewhat during the post-Stalinist thaw, the decisive influence of class origin in the access to education has been sharply re-asserted in 1958-1960 in connection with the "completion of the cultural revolution" ordained by the Eleventh Party Congress. The Party press stepped up once again its attacks on teachers who recommended pupils on the basis of their aptitude and without considering their class origin. "Again, cases have occurred this year," bewailed *Rudé právo* in August 1958, "that people have been recommended for further study without due consideration for their political profile and opinion and for their social origin. For instance, as if it did not matter, the Electrotechnical School has recommended the son of a wealthy farmer who owned over ninety hectares of land . . . . In the Plzeň rural district they approved the son of a miller who employed several hired hands . . . ."[80] Therefore, stiff directives were issued by the Ministry of Education in 1959 ordering all those concerned with admission procedures to consider, first and foremost, the applicants' class origin and political attitudes, as well as their entire family background, past and present.[81]

Various measures have been adopted with a view toward eliminat-

[78] A. Jungwirthová, a communist woman-legislator, in *Lidové noviny*, April 27, 1951.

[79] *Rudé právo*, May 27, 1952; *Lidová demokracie*, March 3, 1954; directives of the Ministry of Education of February 12, 1954, *Ministry of Education Gazette*, 1954; *Rudé právo*, January 14, 1956; *Učitelské noviny*, March 22, and June 26, 1956; *Rudé právo*, February 13, 1957; *Lidová demokracie*, October 23, 1951.

[80] *Rudé právo*, August 20, 1958; also, *Mladá fronta*, August 5, 1958.

[81] *Československý zpravodaj*, No. 286, March 15, 1960.

ing "incomprehensible leniencies" toward the bourgeois elements and toward securing an adequate supply of college students with impeccable class profiles.

As initial measures for this purpose the communist regime set up special preparatory courses for factory workers and small peasants who had an excellent work record and demonstrated their loyalty toward the people's democratic order by active participation in political life.[82] Originally, these were one-year courses; but their length was extended to two years in 1953 because one year proved to be far too short for even the most rudimentary preparation for college admission. As conceded by *Rudé právo,* it "laid big claim on the students' health" and caused many "older gifted students" to drop out because "they needed a slower tempo at the beginning."[83]

Scholarships have become another weapon of the class struggle in the field of education. "Today the scholarship is a class instrument helping to improve the social composition of the student body," stated one of the leading communist school administrators when in September 1950 he admonished a "working conference" of 2,000 Slovak teachers to "mobilize their strength for a more resolute implementation of the Party's educational policies."[84] The importance of the role played by scholarships in this respect is underlined by the fact that almost a third of Czechoslovak college students are recipients of scholarships.[85] In 1958 new types of factory, collective farm, and regional scholarships were introduced carrying a generous stipend of 600 crowns (83 dollars), in addition to allowances for dependents.[86] They are awarded upon the recommendation of the factory works councils and the people's committees on condition that the recipients will return to work in the respective factory or geographical region for five years after having finished their studies. Furthermore, the recipients of state scholarships since 1958 have been selected by the district and local people's committees rather than by the universities as had hitherto

---

[82] *Rudé právo,* December 5, 1951, November 2, 1952; *Práce,* January 6, 1951; *Lidové noviny,* January 4, 1951.

[83] *Rudé právo,* November 2, 1952.

[84] *Lidové noviny,* October 1, 1950.

[85] Of the 77,777 students attending the Czechoslovak colleges and universities in 1957-1958, 25,548 were recipients of scholarships; the corresponding figure for 1958-1959 was 19,855 out of 74,896 (*Ročenka,* 1959, pp. 418, 427). Figures include both regular students and students studying in extension, by correspondence, and other extraordinary types of studies. Regular full-time registration was 52,368 students in 1957-1958 and 52,462 in 1958-1959. The stipend ranges from 70 to 420 crowns (some 10 to 58 dollars per month).

[86] *Rudé právo,* May 16, 1958; *Prague News Letter,* 15, 4, February 21, 1959.

been the case.[87] This latest innovation is likely to sharpen still more the class edge of the "educational weapon." While applying the prescribed class criteria, college organs had an understandable self-interest in preventing their schools from being overrun by the inept and were, therefore, bent upon granting as many scholarships as possible to qualified applicants, even though they may not have fully met the stiff requirement of being proletarian thoroughbreds. Being not so directly and immediately affected, the people's committees, dominated by the district Party secretaries, are likely to be concerned more with the applicants' class profile than with their aptitude for college studies. Moreover, the new arrangement provides a broader field of operations for personal favoritism and local bossism in the selection of scholarship recipients.

But none of the various facets of class discrimination in the field of education violates the elemental principles of justice more than the double standard in the evaluation of examinations. Impartial grading, regardless of social status, should be a fundamental right of every student in any political and social system. But due to the high ratio of failures among pupils of working class origin, the communist directors of Czechoslovak education have been consistently trying to induce teachers to slant their evaluation according to the examinees' social status. "Abilities must not be judged mechanically," cautioned a Deputy Minister of Education in 1952 in an article which appeared in *Rudé právo* on the very eve of final examinations. "It is necessary to distinguish the causes of weaker achievements of some of the pupils . . . . I have in mind especially children of the workers and other working people where both parents are employed, work as functionaries, etc."[88] Similarly, in 1954 *Učitelské noviny* urged teachers to "remove the inequality between children of workers and collective farmers whose parents cannot as yet adequately help their children in their studies, and the children of the intelligentsia."[89] Two years later, the Minister of Education took up this delicate matter in an address before a national teachers' conference. He directed the school principals together with the teachers to analyse "the causes of failure of every pupil" and "in so doing, to take a social viewpoint of the pupil's achievement and failures and thoughtfully improve the situation."[90]

[87] *Rudé právo*, May 16, 1958.
[88] *ibid.*, May 27, 1952.
[89] *Učitelské noviny*, October 6, 1954.
[90] *Československý přehled*, III, 12 (1956), p. 36.

What was meant by this "social viewpoint" and "thoughful improvement of the situation" has been clarified by information supplied by escaped teachers and students. The examinees of the desired class origin are given easier questions of a more general nature, while those with a bourgeois background are subjected to a thorough and detailed quizzing.[91] The latters' answers are appraised with extreme rigor, while the replies of the candidates possessed of an appropriate class profile are given substantially more than the benefit of the doubt. Thus downgraded, the examination achievements of bourgeois pupils and students are pressed down still further by adverse grades in political maturity, which constitutes the truly decisive half of the finals on any school level.

Furthermore, the class criterion was given still more leeway through the abolition of entrance examinations for upper secondary schools, colleges, and universities in 1957. Instead, conferences are held with applicants by admission authorities "to determine the extent of their interest in, and capacity for, further study and the level of their preparation in the chosen field.[92] Similarly, additional room for class bias is provided by a new arrangement whereby suitable applicants both for the upper secondary schools and the institutions of higher learning are selected by the communist-controlled people's committees, which are assisted in the cities by the so-called street committees.[93]

Finally, as decreed by the Eleventh Party Congress, plans have been worked out to "improve the method of admission to colleges by way of preferential selection of applicants who have already gained production practice and thus a richer life experience."[94] This sounds very much like Khrushchëv's 1958 theses on education and, judging by past experience, there seems little doubt that the Czechoslovak Communists will eventually work out the new admission plans fully along Soviet lines. Of the 11,903 students admitted to Czechoslovak colleges and universities in 1959, 1,900 came from "work places and schools for the working people" and an additional 2,000 from industrial schools.[95] Thus the student body for Czechoslovak colleges and universities, and most probably also for the upper secondary schools, may in due time be drawn predominantly from youngsters who have first worked some years in factories and collective farms. The class

[91] See, for instance, Zpráva o Československu, II, 9 (1951), p. 58.
[92] Prague News Letter, 13, 6, March 16, 1957.
[93] Rudé právo, February 13, 1957; Mladá fronta, August 13, 1958.
[94] Rudé právo, June 23, 1958: Resolution of the Eleventh Party Congress.
[95] Lidová demokracie, October 15, 1959.

criterion in the candidates' choice will then undoubtedly become ever more pronounced.

THE NEW PROFILE OF THE TEACHERS

The crucial role in the communist endeavor to convert the schools into assembly lines turning out adequate numbers of properly indoctrinated communistic men is assigned to the teachers. An authoritative communist work on *The Role of the Teacher in Today's School* explains their mission without equivocation:

"The success of education through instruction lies almost exclusively in the hands of the teacher because the richness of the materials taught and the frequent opportunity for influencing the emotions [of the pupils] gives the teacher possibilities which no other educational factor, including even the family, can possess. That is why the educational work of the teacher has such importance. If his work has the correct ideological and political foundations and is organized systematically, it can fully prevail over the reactionary influences of the family and any other nonscholastic factor . . . . The teacher's work in educating the growing generation has a militant character: the teachers, to whom belongs the main role in education in the spirit of socialism and communism, must lead the fight not only for the creation of a new, higher socialist morality of the young generation, but also against the survivals which manifest themselves in the minds of the children and the youth through the influence of adults. That is why the Ninth Congress of the Communist Party of Czechoslovakia directed us to fight for the soul of the youth against those who would like to lead it away from the road to socialism. In his report to the Congress, Klement Gottwald imposed upon us the duty: educate people loyal to the cause of the people and the nation, educate in the spirit of Marxism-Leninism."[96] Hence, ever since their conquest of power, the communist leaders have striven to transform teachers on all levels and in every discipline into pliable instruments for the making of communistic men.

The very first step taken in that direction was a purge of undesirable elements. Following the February coup of 1948 a number of prominent college professors, especially in the field of social science and law, who were known for their staunch democratic convictions, were removed from their positions. Similar measures were taken on the secondary and elementary levels. However, lest the continuity of school-

[96] Kopáč, *op.cit.*, pp. 129-130.

ing be interrupted, actual dismissal was applied only in extreme cases and where replacements were available from among dependable Communists. Below the college level the purge resulted primarily in the substitution of trusted Party members for doubtful personnel in the ranks of school inspectors, principals, and other positions in the school administration and teacher supervision, with reassignment of the persons so removed to lesser ranks. After the initial wave of purges subsided, removals and transfers for political reasons have become less conspicuous, although, as reported by various escaped teachers, they have continued. Only occasionally did the purge among the faculties acquire a more sweeping character, and this solely on the college level. One such purge occurred in Slovakia in 1955 when more than sixty professors and lecturers of Slovak colleges were dismissed or shifted to lesser positions for bourgeois-nationalistic tendencies.[97] About the same time a number of instructors in the departments of Marxism-Leninism in Czech universities were removed after having been criticized for laxness in combating the influence of bourgeois ideologies among their students.[98] In 1957 the Party made a less dramatic but, in the long run, more ominous move. As announced by the Minister of Education, all colleges and universities were to draw up plans for a gradual replacement of teachers lacking "the potential for proper educational and political activities."[99] A convenient provision for such a purpose was included in the 1956 amendment to the University Act which authorized the Minister of Education to separate from college faculties persons who no longer fulfilled the "conditions for their continuation as professors or lecturers."

Since the communist regime had to retain the major portion of the predominantly non-communist faculties, it had to embark upon the battle for children's minds in the Czechoslovak classrooms by using teachers who were anything but convinced of communism's virtues. Hence, it has become imperative to convert to, and confirm in, the communist creed those teachers who could be so converted, and to bend to the regime's will those who would not. No effort has been spared and no stone left unturned in the pursuit of these key objectives. Year after year conferences of teachers and school administrators have been held on national, regional, and district levels to impress upon the participants their new role and their ideological and political

---

[97] *Československý přehled,* II, 10 (1955), p. 27.

[98] *ibid.,* II, 12 (1955), p. 30, and *Information,* a mimeographed magazine of the Council of Free Czechoslovakia in Great Britain, No. 2 (1956), p. 5.

[99] *Tvorba,* December 26, 1957.

duties. A vast network of summer courses and workshops has been set up combining indoctrination in the Marxist-Leninist ideology with pedagogical instruction.[100] Extension courses have been offered along similar lines, consisting of home studies periodically checked by extension instructors in special consultation centers and supplemented by summer pro-seminars, practical exercises, and "production experience."[101]

Teachers have been urged year after year to study systematically the classics of scientific socialism, to deepen their knowledge of the foundations of Marxism-Leninism, and to become thoroughly acquainted with all Party documents on education.[102] They have been directed to read the main works of Soviet pedagogy, especially Makarenko and Kairov, all of which have been translated into Czech and placed in all libraries. They have been urged to shed the "survivals of the old school," "the leftovers of pedagogical reformism," and "the disastrous heritage of the formalistic conception of the teacher's work."[103] They have been reminded again and again of the necessity to gain a thorough knowledge of Russian which will enable them to obtain "first-hand information of the problems of Soviet pedagogy," and will also serve as "proof of a sincere relationship to the Soviet Union and its people."[104] These exhortations may not be disregarded with impunity. Should they go unheeded, the negligent teacher is likely to fail the prescribed periodical tests for promotion. Furthermore, an adverse notation will be entered in his personnel report which may one day cause him to be transferred from teaching to less desirable work. The danger is more real at the present time than ever before since the previous shortage of teachers has been largely overcome. On the other hand, if the teacher takes good care of his professional qualification as well as his "ideological and political growth," and if his "materialistic world outlook bears results in his classwork," he may reap honorary and material rewards. The Medal of Jan Amos Komenský, the famous Czech seventeenth-century educator known as Comenius, may be conferred upon him. He may be cited on the eve of

[100] *Rudé právo*, May 13 and August 19, 1953; also, *Lidové noviny*, August 17, 1951, and July 10, 1951; *Zpráva o Československu*, III, 1 (1952), p. 53.

[101] *L'ud*, March 26, 1953.

[102] *Učitelské noviny*, September 8, 1954; *Rudé právo*, June 26, 1954; *Kopáč, op.cit.*, passim.

[103] *Kopáč, op.cit.*, pp. 52-53.

[104] *ibid.*, p. 62.

the annual Teacher's Day as an exemplary or meritorious teacher and granted pedagogical awards in the form of an additional monthly bonus.[105]

In each school the improvement of the teachers' "ideological, political, pedagogical, and professional qualifications" is primarily the responsibility of the school principal. Besides supervising the teachers in their everyday work he presides over monthly meetings of pedagogical councils composed of all the teachers, leaders of the youth groups, and the leader of the pioneer school organization. The council has the duty to consider all pertinent matters of education and instruction, "especially the official directives of the Party, the government, and the school authorities" and raise the pedagogical as well as ideological and political level of the teachers.[106] This is also the main purpose of methodological groups, commissions on individual subjects, set up wherever the same subject is taught by at least three teachers, and regular consultations of home-room teachers.

Finally, teachers are aided in their educational mission by Associations of Parents and Friends of the School, pupils' committees and classroom mayors, as well as by the leaders of the Pioneer organization and the Czechoslovak Youth Union.[107]

As prescribed by the 1953 Education Act, it is the task of the Parents and Friends of the School Associations "to secure the cooperation of the school and the family and to assist the school in its educational purpose." Since family influence has been the main focus of interference with the communist indoctrination of their children, it is the primary role of the Parents' and Friends' Associations to persuade the parents to desist by making them realize how harmful their action could be for their children's future. Here is where the "friends of the school" enter into the picture. Recruited from dependable Communists, mostly workers residing or employed in the respective schools districts, these friends of the school are supposed to better the class composition and the ideological attitudes of the Parents Associations and see that Party directives are observed. This is particularly important in the upper secondary schools where, despite persistent communist efforts, the ratio of pupils of bourgeois origin still remains high and where, as a consequence, the class structure of the parent-

---

[105] Government ordinance No. 73 of July 21, 1953; also, Kopáč, *op.cit.*, p. 152; *Prague News Letter*, 11, 6, March 19, 1955.

[106] Keprta, *op.cit.*, p. 129.

[107] *ibid.*, pp. 131-135.

teacher group would be far from desirable without an addition of such friends of the school.[108]

Pupils' committees are established in all secondary schools to assist the principal and the teachers in "the organization of the socialist education of the youth."[109] Furthermore, mayors are to "help the home-room teachers to create a healthy public opinion in the classrooms and develop a responsible attitude toward duties among the pupils."[110] That is also the prescribed function of the Pioneer organization and the school groups of the Czechoslovak Youth Union. Copied after similar Soviet institutions these organizations are established in all Czechoslovak schools to serve as auxiliary organs of the school principals and the teachers and, in particular, to extend care for the pupils' ideological growth well into the out-of-class hours.

While doing everything possible to reeducate the teachers retained from pre-communist days, the KSČ leaders pin their main hopes on the new teachers turned out in increasing numbers by the reorganized and thoroughly communized pedagogical schools. More care is taken to secure a steady influx of students of working class origin to teacher training institutions than to any other field of education, and their class structure is considerably "better" than in other schools on corresponding levels. While 41.3 percent of the pupils admitted in 1956 to the ninth grade of general secondary schools in Czech regions and 52.3 percent in Slovakia were children of workers and collective farmers, the corresponding percentages for the pedagogical schools were 58.8 in the Czech regions and 74.4 in Slovakia. At the same time there were 43.8 percent of students of worker and small peasant origin in Czechoslovak colleges and universities.[111]

The study programs of the pedagogical schools have been thoroughly reorganized to meet the new role of education and equip the new teachers with all that is needed in the classroom battle for children's minds. The following excerpts from the Ministry of Education directives regarding the topics to be considered in the pedagogy classes illustrate this shift in emphasis:

"The class character of education in a class society . . . the objective and tasks of socialist education . . . the classics of Marxism-

---

[108] Only 36.5 percent of students in upper secondary schools of general education came from worker families and only 8 percent from the families of working peasants in the 1958-1959 school year. *Ročenka*, 1959, p. 421. Corresponding figures for 1959-1960 were 37.7 and 6.8, respectively. *Ročenka*, 1960, p. 426.

[109] Keprta, *op.cit.*, p. 133.

[110] *ibid.*, p. 134.

[111] *Učitelské noviny*, September 6, 1956.

Leninism on education . . . the development of the Soviet school and pedagogy after 1917. Compulsory reading: Makarenko, *We Begin to Live* . . . .

"The creation of the foundations of the dialectical-materialist world outlook in the process of education. Education for socialist patriotism . . . a socialist attitude toward work . . . . "[112]

Even the field of musical education has been drawn fully into the service of indoctrination and the future music teachers are to be well acquainted with such topics as "the struggle for socialist realism in music . . . . Spiritual and court music in connection with the struggle of the feudal rulers for the maintenance of their power . . . the orientation in contemporary music as a struggle for socialist realism against musical formalism and cosmopolitanism . . . the struggle for a new music in the people's democratic countries and the tasks of the socialist school . . . . "[113]

CONTROLS

The whole educational establishment is permeated, as is every other sphere of activity in the communist state, by a thorough system of interlocking checks and controls governed by the notorious principles of democratic centralism and one-man management. The supreme controller is the Minister of Education. As a plenipotentiary of the Party leadership in the most crucial sector of the battle for men's minds he wields an almost absolute authority over every important facet of the country's education. While the actual operation of all schools below the college level, including the power to appoint and dismiss teachers and to create new schools, is in the hands of the school departments of the people's committees, these are bound in every phase of work by a maze of detailed directives and regulations that leave them little discretion.

The principal instrument of the Minister of Education in the exercise of his control is a nation-wide network of regional and district school inspectors who, as their instructions specify, "are responsible for the work of the principals, teachers, and other school workers entrusted to their supervision from the political, professional, pedagogical, and administrative viewpoint."[114] The school principals in their

[112] Regulations of the Ministry of Education of July 27, 1951. *Ministry of Education Gazette 1951; Zpráva o Československu,* III, 4 (1952), pp. 53-54; Alberty, *op.cit.;* and Musil; *op.cit.*

[113] *Zpráva o Československu,* III, 4 (1952), pp. 53-54.

[114] Keprta, *op.cit.,* p. 136.

turn are personally responsible for the work of all the teachers attached to their schools. On the basis of the study plans issued by the Ministry of Education the principals must prepare detailed annual programs for their respective schools and split them into quarterly work plans. From these the teachers draw their own individual day-to-day schedules of instruction which, after having been approved by the principal, are posted so that everyone can see what is to be covered in each class hour, including commemorations of major communist events. In this way the principals "may control the teacher's work with relative ease."[115] Another useful device of control over the teachers, as well as the pupils' classwork, are the "pupil's books" in which are kept a regular record of the pupil's work, his failures and success, and his "socialist commitments."

Together with these official or formal controls are multiple informal controls involving school administrators, teachers, and pupils, as well as outsiders. The key role in this respect is assigned to the KSČ's primary units in the schools. "The primary Party unit in the school is the first and the most active aide of the school principal in the fulfillment of his responsible work," wrote *Tvorba* in 1950.[116] The Party organizations in the school, stressed *Rudé právo* five years later, "answer not only for the work of all the school workers, but also directly for the education of all the students. They must strive incessantly to increase the ideological, political, and professional qualification of all the teachers, Communists and non-communists alike."[117] In pursuance of these crucial objectives the communist teachers check on their non-communist colleagues to help them "fulfill their tasks in an exemplary fashion." By using the prescribed devices of criticism and self-criticism they must see that the education of youth is carried out in the Marxist-Leninist spirit. They must report shortcomings to the proper authorities. Although they may not replace the principal, they have the right and the duty to criticize him whenever necessary and to make recommendations for improvement in school work. They are instructed to gather information from selected communist students in the Pioneer and Youth Union organizations who bring them "a view from below" regarding the teacher's work. As reported from many different sources and implicitly confirmed from communist quarters as well, these informers from among the communist pupils

---

[115] Kopáč, *op.cit.,* p. 114.
[116] *Tvorba,* December 6, 1950.
[117] *Rudé právo,* January 26, 1955. See also *Život strany,* No. 9 (1959), p. 527.

are a constant menace both to their classmates and to the teachers, particularly in the upper secondary schools.[118] They engage in conversations with other pupils, especially those of bourgeois origin, during school intervals. They keep close watch over the teachers' lectures and behavior as well as the pupils' reactions. Sometimes they remain in classrooms, locked during the noon interval, for the purpose of searching through other pupils' satchels and papers. Information obtained through such spying activities is handed over to the secretaries of the Party units in the schools and finds its way eventually into the cadre reports of the pupils and teachers.

Finally, these intramural Party controls are supplemented by frequent informal checks from the outside. "Friends of the school" participate through the Associations of the Parents and Friends of the School, in meetings of pedagogical councils, and through other contacts with the schools. Party units and work councils of various socialist enterprises visit classrooms and pupils' and teachers' gatherings, organize discussions with the pupils, and invite them to their plants. An additional avenue of outside check has also been opened by the recent inclusion of actual work in factories and collective farms as a substantial part of the school curricula.

Results and Problems

How successful has the communist regime been in its use of the "educational weapon"? To what degree has it attained the objectives of its educational policies? What problems remain unsolved? The results obtained in the pursuit of the regime's most important objective, that of creating a new generation of "communistic men," will be considered within the framework of the over-all evaluation of the communist experiment in the concluding chapter. Therefore, only such educational matters will be considered here that are not predominantly ideological in nature; and this only insofar as they have not already been sufficiently covered on the preceding pages.

The most outstanding communist achievement in the field of education is undoubtedly the fact that the door to higher education has been thrown wide open for the children of manual workers and the poorer strata of the peasantry. By organizing special preparatory courses and other short cuts in lieu of full secondary education for such chil-

[118] See, for instance, *Zpráva o Československu,* II, 16 (1951), p. 49, II, 1 (1951), p. 45, and II, 9 (1951), p. 55; *Československý přehled,* I, 1 (1954), pp. 28ff.; *Lidová demokracie,* October 23, 1951; *Tvorba,* December 6, 1950.

dren, and by offering scholarships and hostels for those whose parents cannot defray the cost of education, provided that they are deemed dependable and possess the right class profile, the communist leaders have brought college education within easy reach of the broad masses. The result has been a substantial increase in college attendance as compared with prewar days. According to Czechoslovak statistics the regular full-time student body in Czechoslovak institutions of higher learning reached 56,935 in 1959-1960 against 23,937 (exclusive of colleges with German language) in 1934-1935.[119] Communist Czechoslovakia has thus, with her 389 full-time students per 100,000 of population in 1956-1957, a higher student-population ratio than any country of free Europe, although she is still far behind the 1,752 per 100,000 in the United States in 1956.[120]

The rise in the student body has been paralleled by an increase in the number of institutions. By 1954 the number of universities and independent colleges reached forty; it stood at fifty in 1959-1960 compared with thirteen in 1935.[121] However, only a relatively small part of this large increase is due to the establishment of new universities; most of the increase is the result of the favorite communist practice to set up specialized institutions outside the regular university system, such as separate pedagogical colleges and individual colleges for various branches of industry, mining, construction, and agriculture.

Furthermore, there has been an unprecedented development in university extension teaching, an area completely neglected in prewar Czechoslovakia. A variety of "extraordinary forms" of study has been introduced after the Soviet model enabling qualified persons of working class and peasant origin to obtain college diplomas while being gainfully employed in "productive work." Those residing in university cities and near them may enroll in evening courses. Those who live elsewhere may take courses by correspondence, supplemented by radio classes, periodic short-term extension classes, and consultations. Maintenance scholarship and leave from work is usually granted for final examinations. Most of these "extraordinary forms" of college studies provide further training in technical fields for those already engaged in technical work in industry. Some courses, however, are offered in nontechnical disciplines, such as the Russian language,

---

[119] The postwar figures are from *Ročenka,* 1960, p. 420, the prewar figures from *Ročenka,* 1937, p. 238. (With the addition of students enrolled in German language colleges the student body amounted to 31,640 in 1934-1935.)

[120] *Postavení,* 1957, p. 154.

[121] *Ročenka,* 1960, p. 420.

pedagogy, psychology, library science, and journalism.[122] As many as 23,983 students took college courses by extension in the 1956-1957 school year, 20,903 in 1958-1959, and 20,773 in 1959-1960.[123]

Without attempting to minimize the positive aspects of these broadened educational facilities, it must be emphasized, however, that the rise in quantity has been accompanied by a definite decrease in quality. The shortcomings of the new educational system and their causes were amply revealed in the "great debate" of 1955-1956 when innumerable complaints were raised about these matters by parents, pupils, teachers, and school administrators.[124] The exacting study plans prescribed by the Ministry of Education in the attempt to attain in eleven years what was previously done in thirteen, has led to an excessive overloading of the pupils. Moreover, mandatory participation in various working brigades and in other extracurricular activities cuts deep into school programs and reduces the time left for the burdensome home work. The hastily rewritten textbooks are voluminous, overburdened with details, and often pedagogically defective. As explained in a striking example by one of the many critics, children of the seventh grade had to work 50 to 60 hours per week and in a single year had to study 1,834 pages set in small print.[125] Another critic complained that "the package of knowledge," in the form of textbooks and other school materials, which his eighth-grade daughter had to carry daily to and from school weighed 17 to 20 pounds.[126]

The logical consequence of this has been a colossal number of failures. Twenty percent of Czechoslovak children completed their compulsory education in 1956 without ever reaching the eighth-grade.[127] According to another authoritative source only 60 percent of Slovak youngsters finishing their compulsory school attendance in 1956 managed to do so from the eighth grade; and as many as 24,657 out of the 84,207 Slovak children who had begun their school attendance in the school year 1949-1950 got not further than the fifth grade.[128]

[122] Information in various magazines and newspapers, such as: *Práce,* September 20, 1952; *Rudé právo,* November 12, 1952; *Prague News Letter,* 11, 4, February 19, 1955; *Rudé právo,* January 9, June 5, July 11, September 1 and October 23, 1953; *L'ud,* March 26, 1953; *Pravda,* May 26, 1954.

[123] *Ročenka,* 1960, p. 420.

[124] *Učitelské noviny,* November 24, 1954, December 15, 1954, May 12, 1955, and June 2, 1955; *Rudé právo,* June 20, 1955.

[125] *Učitelské noviny,* February 12, 1955: a complaint of a pediatrician warning about the effects of such a system on children's health.

[126] *Literární noviny,* July 7, 1956.

[127] *ibid.,* August 11, 1956.

[128] *Kulturný život,* October 20, 1956.

Since an additional 25 percent failed to advance to the eighth grade, the author of the article, the former Deputy Minister of Education, came to the conclusion that the 43 percent of the eighth-graders who entered the upper secondary schools actually represented only 29 percent of all fourteen-year-olds. His estimate was corroborated by *Mladá fronta* which revealed on June 27, 1959, that "almost one-third of the boys and girls failed to go as far as the eighth grade."

What perturbed KSČ leaders most was the fact that the overwhelming majority of the casualties were children of working class parents. Such results should have been anticipated. Children of the middle-class intelligentsia average a higher IQ than those of manual workers. After all, it may be reasonably assumed that their parents' or grandparents' higher aptitude had a good deal to do with the fact that they had risen above the manual workers' status in the first place. Furthermore, pupils from such families can get aid with their homework that less-educated parents cannot provide. However, a Party built on the assumption of the superiority of the working class over the "bourgeoisie" cannot be expected to accept such an interpretation. Rather, it laid the blame on the "bourgeois attitude of some teachers toward the working people."[129] To remedy this situation, as shown above, strong pressure has been applied to the teachers to use a "social viewpoint" in grading the pupils' achievements. To ease the burden of the less-qualified pupils, the Party's Central Committee in June 1955 adopted a resolution that criticized the excessive load imposed on the pupils and directed the Ministry of Education to remedy the situation by 1960.[130] As explained subsequently by Novotný, it is not the purpose of the schools "to give the youth just any amount of knowledge . . . but above all, as Lenin had taught, to select from the volume of human knowledge only that which is needed for a true communist education."[131] In line with this educational philosophy the new school curricula have steered more and more away from what the Minister of Education condemned as "a predominantly intellectual character" and shifted toward ever more "polytechnization." Also, under a new arrangement adopted in 1959 and breaking sharply with the previous practice, the pupils of nine-year schools are to be promoted to higher grades even if they fail, pro-

---

[129] *Lidové noviny,* October 1, 1950.
[130] *Rudé právo,* June 19, 1955.
[131] Address to a national teachers' conference in Praha in August 1955, *Československý přehled,* III, 9 (1956), p. 35.

vided they failed in not more than two subjects.[132] Nor is it likely that the planned prolongation of secondary school attendance by one year will bring any substantial improvement of educational standards, for the eight hours or so of practical production work per week scheduled for the last three grades under the new plan will account for most of the time thus gained insofar as theoretical subjects are concerned.

The deterioriation in the quality of secondary education, the abandonment of college entrance examinations, and the admission to college studies of workers without full-fledged high school preparation has in its turn lowered the standards of Czechoslovak universities. The student resolutions of 1956 squarely labeled the system of higher education as inadequate and demanded substantial improvements.[133] High school graduates have reached the universities "with an immature attitude toward studying and without firmly established habits of independent work that is so important in college," bewailed a Party organization chairman at Brno University in 1957.[134] A series of articles on higher education published in *Mladá fronta* in October and November 1957 also complained of the low standards of college courses and said that the ratio of failures continued to be extremely high. As revealed in 1955 as many as 40 percent of the students dropped out before they reached the junior level.[135] And *Rudé právo* complained on September 16, 1960, that 30 percent of daytime and as many as 50 percent evening and extension college students fail to complete their studies. Among the reasons, the paper listed poor high school preparation, students' irresponsible attitude, low working discipline, and "a poor ability to do independent thinking." Evidently, these casualties include an especially high proportion of freshmen and sophomores of working class origin. That is probably one of the main reasons why, despite all the communist efforts, the percentage of students from the ranks of workers and "working peasants" remains unsatisfactory, amounting only to 44.3 in 1959-1960.[136]

The communist endeavor to secure teachers with a "new profile" has also had an adverse effect on the quality of the faculties. To facilitate the recruitment of persons with the desired social back-

---

[132] *Rudé právo*, June 27, 1959.
[133] *Československý přehled*, III, 6 (1956), p. 136.
[134] *Rudé právo*, December 30, 1957.
[135] *Práce*, November 5, 1955.
[136] *Ročenka*, 1960, p. 426.

ground and to speed up the output of this new species of dependable teachers, the initial plan of giving all teachers a full college education was abandoned. Under the 1953 Education Act teachers for the first to fifth grades are trained in special four-year pedagogical schools which they enter after having completed their eight years of compulsory education. To qualify for teaching in the sixth to the eighth grades an additional two years in a higher school of pedagogy are prescribed. Thus only those who wish to teach the ninth to eleventh grades or corresponding levels in technical and pedagogical schools must secure a diploma from a pedagogical college corresponding to the American bachelor of education degree. Moreover, even these reduced requirements are sometimes waived. As conceded by the Minister of Education, 34 percent of all the teachers of the sixth-to-eighth grades lacked the prescribed qualifications in 1956.[137]

A similar lowering of faculty standards occurred on the college level. Again, the social sciences and the law schools have suffered much more than the physical and technical sciences. To what extremes the emphasis on class origin can lead is illustrated by the previously mentioned case of Ladislav Schubert, a worker without previous high school education, who secured a degree of Doctor of Law and Political Science and became assistant professor in criminal law at the Law School of the Slovak University in Bratislava, all within less than two years.[138] Although this is a unique case, the fact remains that the communist regime has encountered major difficulties in keeping university positions staffed by well-qualified teachers in disciplines concerned with politics or economics. After all, the straitjacket of rigid ideological conformity can hardly encourage top-notch scholarship, especially in social science fields. The problem has been further complicated by the cumulative effect of a substantial increase in college enrollment and the introduction of compulsory attendance at lectures, both of which require many more college teachers than had been the case before the War. To cope with this situation a system of postgraduate fellowships, called "aspirantships," was established to give "talented college graduates devoted to the working class and outstanding practical workers an opportunity for further professional and political growth" and to prepare them for careers as college

---

[137] *Československý přehled,* III, 12 (1956), p. 36. Since 1959 a three-year study at a pedagogical institute is required for teachers of the first to fifth grades and one additional year for teachers of the sixth to ninth grades. *Mladá fronta,* December 10, 1960.
[138] See Chapter XII.

teachers.[139] However, the trouble was that such aspirants were appointed in due time as regular college teachers almost automatically without any adequate check being made of their qualifications. Since even persons with neither college nor high school education could be admitted to the aspirantship according to ministerial directives, it is easy to understand why the quality of many of these instructors must have been below par. To improve the selection of suitable candidates requirements were tightened in 1956. Would-be lecturers now have to defend a dissertation, college positions are filled on the basis of nation-wide competitions, and college teachers have to prove their continued scientific and pedagogical qualifications at regular intervals. Undoubtedly, that will in due time enhance the over-all professional standards of Czechoslovak college teachers in a technical sense. However, insofar as the social sciences are concerned, it can hardly encourage them to venture beyond the narrow boundaries prescribed by rigid insistence on the Marxist-Leninist world outlook.

Yet another adverse result of communist liberality in university admission policies has been a surplus of college graduates for whom no places could be found in the national economy that would correspond to their college preparation. This is a rather puzzling phenomenon. The admission of students to Czechoslovak universities is planned to correspond with the requirements of national economy. Definite quotas are fixed for each particular branch of the studies, and when that planned quota is reached, eligible applicants are channeled into other fields where vacancies still exist. Furthermore, persistent complaints were heard in the past about a shortage of college graduates, especially in the technical fields, and of an insufficient number of entering freshmen. "As of the beginning of the coming academic year [1953-1954]," lamented the Minister of Education, "the graduates of our *gymnasia* will not cover even half of the requirements of our colleges for their first academic year. We shall have difficulties in this respect until 1956."[140] The Ministry of Education literally begged for applicants, encouraging even those who had previously flunked their entrance examinations to try again, and organizing for them special preparatory courses.[141] But by 1957-1958 the over-all "overproduction"

---

[139] *Prague News Letter,* 12, 20, October 13, 1956; Keprta, *op.cit.,* p. 94. By the end of 1959 there were 602 full-time aspirants and 2,635 part-time aspirants. *Ročenka,* 1960, p. 427.

[140] A speech on the 1953 Education Act before the National Assembly. *Rudé právo,* April 25, 1953.

[141] For instance, *Rudé právo,* September 13, 1953.

of college graduates became so pronounced that it led to a sharp reduction in the number of admissions to the institutions of higher learning from 14,000 in 1957 to 11,500 in 1958.[142] Evidently, a miscalculation occurred in the Czechoslovak manpower planning. The drastic curtailment of the college admission quotas has in its turn led to an "overproduction" of high school graduates, thus creating a problem of what to do with a substantial number of youngsters who were not prepared and felt little inclination for practical "productive work." It has been estimated by communist sources that of an annual crop of some 30,000 such high school graduates only from 11,000 to 14,000 could be admitted to further college studies.[143] To dispose of this "disproportion" the bulk of surplus students had been given short courses in technical training, while the more promising ones have since 1956-1957 been sent to hastily established two-year schools to be trained as "middle technicians."[144]

Thus, in addition to the difficulties surrounding its crucial ideological mission, the Czechoslovak school system continues to confront the communist regime with a number of unsolved or only partially solved problems.

[142] *East Europe,* 7, 10 (1958), p. 16.
[143] *Prague News Letter,* 14, 19, September 27, 1958.
[144] *ibid.*

CHAPTER XX

THE INDOCTRINATION OF THE ADULT MIND

THE HEAVY concentration of communist indoctrination efforts on the youth does not mean that the adult population has been allowed to "rot in bourgeois prejudice." While allocating to the schools topmost priority in the making of the new communistic man, the KSČ leaders have done their utmost in the adult sector of the battle for the mind. Since the special measures applied to the Party's own rank and file have already been discussed,[1] what is left to consider are the techniques employed for the general public.

RADIO AND TELEVISION

The most ubiquitous medium for general indoctrination of the Czechoslovak masses is the radio. Radio listening has always been more widespread in Czechoslovakia than in other countries of Eastern Europe; and there has been a steady and substantial rise in the ownership of radio receivers in the postwar years. By the end of 1952, sets numbering 2,717,000 were reported in Czechoslovakia which contrasted with 887,000 in Hungary and with 1,747,148 in the more populous Poland by the end of 1951.[2] With one radio set for each 4 persons in 1959 Czechoslovakia ranked among the most radio-minded nations of Europe.[3] Also, as mentioned in Chapter xviii, the wired radio network has been steadily expanded; the public address systems have been installed after the Soviet fashion in squares, streets, and other public places. Moreover, since radio is the cheapest and most readily available means of entertainment, the habit of regular daily radio listening has become firmly established. Granted daily access into virtually every household in the country, the Czechoslovak broadcasting system thus offers facilities unsurpassed in breadth by any other vehicle of adult indoctrination.

[1] See Chapter iv.
[2] *Rudé právo*, December 17, 1952.
[3] *Ročenka*, 1960, p. 379. According to *Rudé právo*, August 3, 1960, there were 3,105,000 holders of wireless radio licenses and 398,000 holders of wired radio licenses as of June 30, 1960.

Aware of the tremendous propaganda potentialities the KSČ leaders quickly took advantage of their political dominance to secure for the Party an almost absolute control over the air waves. Having first placed (in 1945) a pliable fellow-traveling Social Democrat, V. Patzak, at the head of the state-operated Czechoslovak Radio Broadcasting, they soon replaced him with a full-fledged and fanatical Communist, B. Laštovička, and filled all the key positions in radio programming with dependable Party members. Thus even prior to the communist seizure of the government in 1948 the Czechoslovak broadcasting system was virtually a subdivision of the Party's *agitprop* rather than the non partisan, semi-independent government agency which it was designed to be. While its communist directors carefully refrained from pushing matters to an extreme during the 1945-1947 period of "the overgrowth of the national revolution into a socialist revolution," they did their best to keep the air waves free from anything that could damage the communist cause.[4] At the time of the coup of February 1948, the remaining non-communist radio employees were promptly removed and Party control over the whole broadcasting system was completed.

Freed from any further need to defer to the feelings of their National Front partners, communist leaders converted the radio into a potent weapon in their battle for the mind. Its function was stated with sharp clarity in one of *Rudé právo's* editorials on *"The Tasks of Our Broadcasting"*:

"In the capitalist countries broadcasting is in the hands of the exploiters and enemies of the people; it serves only the financial and industrial magnates and the aggressive plans of the imperialists. The program of the broadcasting stations, dominated by a handful of capitalistic beasts of prey, is aimed at leading the ordinary citizen away from thinking about serious matters, at making people apathetic, deceiving them by a web of lies and thereby disarming them morally so that the instigators of war may more easily pursue their dark objectives . . . . [On the other hand] broadcasting in the Soviet Union and other countries of the camp of peace serves the people. It is an instrument of political education of the masses and aids in their

---

[4] This also happened to me. After the War a number of people wrote to me expressing a desire to hear once again a series of talks on the new Czechoslovak Constitution which I had delivered over the BBC's Czech transmission from London toward the close of the War. Therefore, I offered the Director of the Czechoslovak Radio, B. Laštovička, to deliver the series over the Praha Radio. However, Laštovička declined on the ground that the talks were "controversial."

general cultural growth. Here broadcasting brings the words of truth . . . . In these countries broadcasting is an important propagator of Marxism-Leninism, the progressive production experience and socialist culture . . . . Czechoslovak broadcasting has before it a brilliant example, that of Soviet broadcasting . . . ."[5]

In pursuance of this and similar Party directives radio programs were heavily loaded with items of indoctrination. Although still predominant, the time allotted to musical programs was cut down and the time thus saved allocated to news and commentaries, lectures, reviews of the Soviet and communist press, including a daily reading of *Rudé právo* editorials, the "University of the Air," answers to listeners' questions, lengthy reports on the main events of the "socialist construction" on national and regional levels, commemorations of various communist red-letter days, Russian language courses, and similarly nonentertaining topics. As revealed by a breakdown of a typical 1953 broadcasting week of the two main Czechoslovak radio networks, *Československo* (Czechoslovakia) and *Praha,* musical transmissions accounted for 9,205 minutes of the broadcasting time compared with 7,215 devoted to nonmusical programs.[6]

However, in their efforts to make the maximum use of radio for indoctrination purposes, the KSČ leaders overshot their target. For fear of being found lacking in the ideological zeal and fighting qualities becoming a Bolshevik, the regime's propagandists often laid on the message so thickly and so crudely that they unwittingly repelled instead of attracting. The public's dissatisfaction with this monotonous fare was becoming more and more apparent and listeners' letters of complaints, mostly anonymous, kept coming in. Also, the necessity was keenly felt to do something more positive about the challenge of Radio Free Europe than simply jamming its programs. To meet the situation, notable changes were made in radio programs in late 1953 and early 1954. Musical transmissions were somewhat expanded at the expense of the nonmusical portion of the program, and serious music was made to yield some ground to lighter genres. Sports reportage, the most popular of all the radio features, and dramatic production were allowed additional time. A determined effort was made to enliven radio programs with more humor. More attention began to be paid to the wishes of listeners and the time allotted to

---

[5] *Rudé právo,* July 8, 1952. The indoctrination tasks of Czechoslovak broadcasting were restated in a resolution on broadcasting adopted by the Party's Central Committee in June 1960. See *Život strany,* No. 12, June 1960, pp. 740ff.

[6] *Československý přehled,* I, 7 (1954), p. 22.

straight ideology was reduced.[7] But this lightening of the listeners' diet was by no means intended to detract from the radio's political mission. On the contrary, its primary purpose was to make it into a better medium of indoctrination and, as stated by its supreme political chief, Václav Kopecký, "to enable it to fight even more efficiently against the enemy radio propaganda."[8] It is the Party's hope that by making radio listening more entertaining, and using the ideological message less conspicuously and somewhat more sparingly, it will be possible to indoctrinate more subtly and thus more successfully.

This more recent trend of peddling ideology in smaller doses and in a more appealing wrapping has been even more conspicuous in television. Introduced in Czechoslovakia only in 1953, television viewing has spread by leaps and bounds. By June 1958 the number of sets passed the one-quarter million mark and by the close of 1960 it reached 795,000.[9] Ten transmitters served the country in 1960.[10] From 845 hours in 1955, the television transmissions rose to 5,426 in 1959.[11] In striking contrast to radio broadcasting, political indoctrination made comparatively little headway in television programs in the first years of the Czechoslovak video's growth. Evidently, as long as video was limited to a small audience representing only a negligible fraction of the population, its relative unimportance as a medium of indoctrination hardly warranted the effort to establish its ideological function. But the recent spectacular rise in Czechoslovak televiewing made the Party realize the "great possibilities, as yet unexploited, which exist in television for the political education of the people."[12] Since 1957-1958 more and more politics has been gradually worked into the television programs; and Novotný's mention of the "stormy development in our television" in connection with the "completion of the cultural revolution" in his speech to the Eleventh Party Congress left no doubt about the way in which television was headed.[13] As restated most emphatically in a lengthy resolution on the state and the new tasks of Czechoslovak television adopted by the Party's

[7] ibid., pp. 19ff. In 1959 the distribution of the 80,872 broadcasting hours was as follows: music, 22,370; political, 8,532; regional, 13,131; dramas and literary works, 2,914; children's broadcasts, 2,210; broadcasts abroad, 31,715. Ročenka, 1960, p. 471.

[8] Rudé právo, December 13, 1953.

[9] Novotný's speech at the Eleventh Party Congress, Rudé právo, June 19, 1958, and Rudé právo, February 8, 1961.

[10] On television in Eastern Europe, see also East Europe, 7, 4 (1958), pp. 22ff.

[11] Ročenka, 1959, p. 467, and 1960, p. 471.

[12] Rudé právo, June 7, 1957.

[13] ibid., June 19, 1958.

Central Committee in June 1960, television must "educate working people in the ideas of communism, in the spirit of proletarian internationalism and socialist patriotism, in the new social morality and in progressive aesthetic taste . . . disseminate the teaching of Marxism-Leninism and the knowledge of materialistic science; organize the masses of the working people for the fulfillment of the tasks of the socialist construction . . . carry effective atheist propaganda . . . overcome the survivals and influences of bourgeois ideologies . . . ."[14]

THE NEWSPAPERS

Next to radio and television the newspapers are made to serve as the main vehicles of day-to-day political indoctrination of the masses. In the words of its supreme communist chief, Václav Kopecký, the press is "one of the decisive agents of national, state and moral education of the people and an effective helper in our building effort. A prerequisite for the attainment of this objective was, above all, the removal of all the remnants of the decadent, antipopular bourgeois journalism and the transformation of our press after the great Soviet model into a collective organizer of the working masses, into the fighting instrument of the endeavor of all progressive people in the world for the maintenance and building of a lasting peace. Its further task is to equip both of our nations [Czech and Slovak] ideologically, with the ideas of scientific socialism, to educate men with a new socialist attitude toward work, and to educate them in the spirit of the proletarian internationalism."[15]

To insure the implementation of this important ideological mission the whole system of the Czechoslovak press and the journalistic profession have been patterned in all essential aspects after the Soviet model. As in the case of the air waves, the foundations of communist controls over the periodical press were laid immediately after the War. Claiming that the press ought to be the property of the nation and not a source of personal profit, the KSČ leaders in 1945 forced upon their reluctant democratic partners the principle that the right to publish newspapers and other periodicals should be reserved solely for recognized political parties and public organizations. This could be done very easily since all but two of the major newspapers of prewar Czechoslovakia had been published by political parties and there

[14] *Život strany,* No. 12, June 1960, pp. 735ff.; see also *ibid.,* No. 23, December 1959, p. 1448; and *Rudé právo,* June 15, 1960.
[15] An address before the Cultural Committee of the National Assembly, *Lidové noviny,* March 21, 1950.

had been no individual local papers. Therefore, the exclusion of individuals and private corporations from the newspaper business was not considered by the general public as being such a major encroachment upon the freedom of the press as it would have been in a country familiar with newspaper ownership and operation by private publishers and with a maze of independent local papers. However, the restriction on private publishing led inevitably to an enhancement of the status of the communist-held Ministry of Information which was in charge of newspaper licensing and eleven other press affairs. The Ministry's power over publishing was further increased by its authority to ration and allocate newsprint which was in very short supply after the War.[16] Finally, by a law adopted at communist insistence in 1947, the exercise of the journalistic profession was made conditional upon membership in the Union of Czech or Slovak Journalists.[17] Since these unions were strictly communist-controlled and subject to supervision by the communist Minister of Information, the new law also tended to strengthen the Party's hold over the journalistic profession. Thus, all that the KSČ leaders had to do when they seized complete power in 1948 was to replace undesirable elements in the Journalists' unions, the ČTK (Czechoslovak News Agency), and the editorial boards of non-communist periodicals with Communists and dependable fellow-travelers.

The establishment of the dictatorship of the proletariat spelled the end of journalism as a liberal profession. Although journalists continue to be employees of the parties and other public organizations publishing the newspapers for which they write, they are under as tight governmental control as if they were on the government's payroll. Their professional organization, the Union of Czechoslovak Journalists, became yet another transmission belt in the KSČ machinery manipulated by the Ministry of Education and Culture, a successor to the Ministry of Information, which acts on behalf of the Party leaders. Prior to 1958 the Union was not even given the right to adopt its statutes, for they were issued for it by the then existing Ministry of Information and Enlightenment.[18] A law passed in July

---

[16] On these matters see K. F. Zieris, *The New Organization of the Czechoslovak Press,* Praha, 1947; also, *Newspapers and Newspapermen in Czechoslovakia,* Praha, 1947.

[17] An English translation of the law in J. Hrabánek, *The Legal Position of Journalists in Czechoslovakia,* Praha, 1947, pp. 23ff.

[18] Law No. 184 of December 20, 1950, and the ordinance of the Ministry of Information and Enlightenment, No. 21/1951.

1958 declared the Union to be "a voluntary organization," and as such it is now allowed to draft its own statutes.[19] But this change is a mere formality. Under the law on "voluntary organizations and assemblies" adopted at the peak of the Stalin era in 1951, the statutes of all such organizations are subject to government approval and the state "sees to it that they develop in harmony with the Constitution and the principles of the people's democratic system."[20]

The journalists' role was redefined so that their main function now is to indoctrinate people in the spirit of Marxism-Leninism and to help implement the Party's policies. As stressed once again in the letter sent by the Party's Central Committee to the Second Congress of Czechoslovak Journalists in June 1957, they must display "militant partisanship and ideological purity," wage a "systematic struggle against opinions hostile and injurious to the cause of socialism," and be guided by "implacability in the face of any manifestation of hostile ideology and revisionism."[21]

This important mission in the battle for the mind can be carried out satisfactorily only by men who are themselves staunch believers in the cause of communism. Hence, "political maturity" is an indispensable prerequisite for admission into the journalistic profession. A severe process of selection was established and only holders of impeccable cadre reports can gain membership in the Union of Czechoslovak Journalists which alone entitles a newspaperman to practice his profession. As in the procedure with regard to Party membership, the person seeking admission into the Union first becomes a candidate for membership. Only after having proved his worth during the probationary period and having successfully passed a qualifying examination, may the candidate be admitted to full membership. To take care of the journalists' further political growth special courses are held in Roztěž Castle, which was assigned to the Journalists' Union for this purpose.[22] They consist of a series of lectures, discussions, and individual study of such subjects as the history of the Soviet and Czechoslovak Communist parties, socialist and capitalist economics, foreign policy, political science, public law, and the aesthetics of socialism.[23] The participants are divided into small discussion and study circles. Each of them includes at least one dependable Com-

[19] Law No. 44 of July 3, 1958.
[20] Law No. 68 of July 12, 1951.
[21] *East Europe*, 6, 7 (1957), p. 48.
[22] *Zpráva o Československu*, III, 12 (1952), pp. 69-70.
[23] *ibid.*

munist who checks and reports on the participants' political attitudes and loyalties. No final examinations are held in these courses, which usually last three months, but the leaders of the school supply the Journalists' Union with reports evaluating individual participants which are placed in their respective personal files.

The editorial staffs of all newspapers and other periodicals are subject to strict supervision in every aspect of their work. Every paper has an editor-in-chief who directs, and is personally responsible for, the activities of his editorial staff. In particular, he is responsible for seeing that his staff abides by the directives distributed by the government's press organs. Government guidance is provided by the Ministry of Education and Culture and by the Division for Press, Recording, Publishing, and Book Distribution of the Government Presidium. Press releases and directives are teletyped every day from these headquarters to the regional bureaus of the ČTK, which in turn distribute them to the papers in their respective regions. These directives contain news, speeches, commentaries, and other materials to be printed. They dictate the manner in which every item of importance is to be handled, including the location, emphasis, and sometimes even the type of headlines. Government controls are supplemented by Party controls applied directly to the KSČ's own press and indirectly to the non-Party periodicals. On the central level controls are exercised by the Agitation and Propaganda section of the Party's Central Committee and on the regional level by corresponding departments of the regional Party secretariats.

Through this elaborate system of multiple press checks, the KSČ leaders have succeeded in effectively nullifying the constitutional guarantees of freedom of the press without any need to resort to formal censorship. Only during the few months of 1956 between the Twentieth Congress of the Soviet Party and the suppression of the Hungarian uprising did the Party's iron grip over the country's press seem to show signs of weakening. At that time a refreshing touch of nonconformism appeared here and there on the pages of the noncommunist press, particularly in connection with the calls for more creative freedom heard at the Second Congress of the Czechoslovak Writers.[24] According to eyewitness reports, editorial meetings were held at that time to consider what changes should be made in Czechoslovakia as a consequence of the Twentieth Soviet Party Congress; and

[24] See below.

they resulted in an overwhelming condemnation of Stalinist practices and in demands for more freedom.[25] But the worst chaos, though only of a short duration, occurred during the first days of the Polish and Hungarian revolts in October 1956. The speed of the developments caught the organs of the press controls completely off guard and their directives lost their habitual self-assurance. However, the neo-Stalinist counter offensive of 1957-1958 soon recovered most of the ground lost during the post-Stalin thaw.

Naturally, the rigid Party and government controls are reflected in the content of the newspapers. Whether they be published by the Communist Party, its non-communist National Front partners, the Youth Union, the Trade Union movement, or any other of the mass organizations, the Czechoslovak newspapers are all dull peas from the same pod. Day after day they dwell upon virtually identical Party-prescribed themes and topics channeled to them through the official Czechoslovak Press Agency. They include pronouncements of native and Soviet Party leaders; proceedings and resolution of various meetings and conferences; reports on the Plan fulfillments, socialist contests, and other economic achievements; patriotic propaganda articles from the production and collectivization front; centrally edited international news comparing progress in the "camp of the peace" with the "imperialist camp"; information on various happenings in the "construction of socialism." Year after year they commemorate such communist exploits as the Great October Socialist Revolution, the Liberation of Czechoslovakia by the Red Army, May Day, and other annual features such as Czechoslovak-Soviet Friendship Month, Press or Teachers' Day. They report somewhat briefly on cultural events and sports. On the other hand, crime and gossip items are meticulously ignored by the papers, although occasionally brief censuring reports are published on crimes against the State and socialist property or on such vices as alcoholism and hooliganism if such reports are deemed to serve as a deterrent or a means of indoctrination. Advertising is tolerated on a sharply reduced scale in some of the non-Party papers. Needless to add, independent columns customary in America do not exist at all.

Similar uniformity prevails in journalistic style, which has quickly acquired certain characteristics distinctive from those of the free press. Communist newspaper writing bristles with militant terms, such as "battle," "struggle," "discipline" or "mobilization." Journalists rarely

---

[25] *Československý přehled*, 4, 7-8 (1957), pp. 20ff.

use the techniques of matter-of-fact, straight reporting, but prefer to moralize, admonish, harangue, and pontificate. They have developed a vocabulary of odious adjectives used repetitiously whenever reference is made to the men and affairs of the capitalist world and a parallel vocabulary of adorning epithets for the description of the Soviet and other communist leaders and achievements.

Apart from the few outbursts of journalistic nonconformism in the post-Stalin era, the only relief Czechoslovak readers get from the dreary monotony of their press comes occasionally from the pages of non-Party newspapers and magazines, especially their cultural and sport sections. In its effort to reach every stratum of the population, the communist regime has retained a certain number of non-Party papers and, closely following the Soviet pattern, has even caused some new ones to be founded. In addition to the several press organs of the non-communist parties mentioned in Chapter VII, the major mass organizations are permitted to publish their own papers. Thus there are Czechoslovak counterparts of the Soviet *Trud* (*Práce*), *Komsomolskaya Pravda* (*Mladá fronta*) *Literaturnaya Gazeta* (*Literární noviny*), etc. There is also quite a number of "nonpolitical" weeklies and monthlies, including the humor magazine *Dikobraz,* a Czechoslovak equivalent of Moscow's *Krokodil,* and even periodicals in minority languages, such as *Aufbau und Frieden* for the Germans, *Glos ludu* for the Poles, *Druzhno vpered* for the Ukrainians, and *Uj Szo* for the Hungarians. Finally, there are regional papers designed to "reflect in their pages the richness of regional life."[26] While attending to their task of persuading their readers of the virtues of communism and the "rottenness" of capitalism, these poor relatives of the Party press have little choice but to paraphrase the themes prescribed by the regime's directives. But having done so, they are allowed more latitude than the orthodox Party press on strictly nonpolitical topics. Such concessions are granted primarily on the assumption that their readers, who are supposedly politically less mature than the readers of Party periodicals, can more easily be indoctrinated if the ideological fare is lightened by a few tastier tidbits.

To strengthen and simplify their press controls, the KSČ leaders reduced the number of individual periodicals, particularly the daily papers. By 1958 there were only seventeen dailies in the whole of Czechoslovakia in contrast to fifty-five published in the Czech provinces alone in 1940; and the number of regional newspapers was sim-

---

[26] *Rudé právo,* February 21, 1953.

ilarly curtailed.[27] On the other hand, there was a tremendous increase in various factory and village papers which were rare in prewar Czechoslovakia. By 1955 there were 1,380 factory papers and 270 village papers. But the number of factory papers fell sharply to 486 in 1956. With the inclusion of factory and village papers there were 1,447 periodicals in Czechoslovakia in 1959 of which 17 were dailies, 487 weeklies, 393 bi-monthlies, and 397 monthlies.[28] Furthermore, the printed magazines are supplemented by untold numbers of "wall newspapers" (equivalent to the Soviet *stengazety*) which are posted virtually in every factory, collective farm, school, and other establishments throughout the country.

While the number of daily papers was reduced, every effort has been made to increase their volume of circulation. Thousands of Party members and activists have been engaged in recurrent circulation campaigns climaxing on the annual Press Days. The main endeavor has been centered on stepping up subscriptions for the Party periodicals. Hard pressed from above, the salesmen of the Party press resort to various high-pressure tactics to obtain the desirable results. As a consequence, the circulation of the KSČ periodicals has risen many times above the prewar levels and that of non-Party papers has sharply dropped. About one-half of the present daily circulation of some two million claimed for the daily papers falls to the two principal Communist Party dailies, the Czech *Rudé právo* and the Slovak *Pravda,* while close to one-fifth is credited to the trade union dailies, the Czech *Práce* and its Slovak equivalent *Práca.* The balance is made up by the dailies of the other mass organizations and the three dailies published by the non-communist parties.[29]

Thus, what had been billed as an attempt to prevent the press from being abused by "uncontrollable groups or anonymous agents who made newspaper enterprise a profitable business"[30] has in fact been used to kill freedom of the press and convert newspapers into a daily instrument of communist indoctrination.

[27] The first figure is from *Ročenka,* 1959, p. 470, the second figure from *Newspapermen and Newspapers in Czechoslovakia,* p. 32.

[28] All figures from *Ročenka,* 1960, p. 472. However, in September 1959 *Život strany,* No. 18, p. 1122, claimed that there were factory papers in over 600 factories. In 1960 the number of dailies was increased from 17 to 18 through the establishment of a new daily for the industrial region of Plzeň. *Rudé právo* of February 8, 1961, mentions 21 dailies in 1960 with an annual circulation of 968 million copies and 1,032 other periodicals with an annual circulation of 437 million copies.

[29] *East Europe,* 9, 2 (1960), p. 39.

[30] Zieris, *op.cit.,* p. 6.

BOOKS

While using the newspapers as their central vehicle of indoctrination via the printed word, the KSČ leaders did not by any means overlook the great potentialities of nonperiodical literature as a carrier of the Party's ideological message. "The new literary and artistic production is an important agent of the ideological and cultural rebirth in our country and it is destined to play a great role in the socialist education of the broad masses," explained Kopecký when setting binding directives for the new socialist culture at the Ninth Congress of the KSČ in May 1949.[31] Hence, soon after they had seized power in February 1948, the communist leaders slapped stiff controls over the whole field of literature and art. The entire publishing industry and book distribution network became a monopoly of the State. All libraries were put under government control. Writers and other creative artists were herded into monolithic professional unions patterned after Soviet models and fully communist controlled. Apart from stopping the entry of undesirable books from the West,[32] the communist policy in the field of literature and art has been preoccupied with two basic problems: (1) to eliminate those creations of the bourgeois past which interfered with communist indoctrination efforts; (2) to secure an adequate supply of new books with the proper ideological message.

Taking Over the Book Business and the Libraries

To facilitate its task of converting books into "the arms of progress and peace" and to "free literature from bourgeois morality," the regime in 1949 took over the assets of all the publishing houses and reorganized them after the Soviet pattern. The 515 publishing firms of pre-communist days were merged into thirty-one, each of them assigned to a public organization specializing in the publication of certain types of books. Supreme control over all publishing was entrusted to the Ministry of Information (replaced now by the Ministry of Education and Culture), and a central Publishing Council was set up to advise the Ministry on the selection of manuscripts to be published.

Similarly, the distribution of books ceased to be an enterprise for profit. All private bookstores were liquidated and a socialist distribution network was created. It consists partly of book stores of various

---

[31] *Lidové noviny,* May 29, 1949; also, Baštovanský's speech to the Ninth Congress of the Slovak Communist Party, *Lidové noviny,* May 27, 1950.
[32] See Chapter XVIII.

collectivist enterprises, but primarily of those run by *The People's Book,* a central government agency that directs and supervises the entire book market. Finally, to close the controlling circle, a new Library Act of 1950, replaced in 1959 by a new law, welded all the libraries in the country into a unified library system and subjected them to supreme ministerial authority.[33]

Thus a rigid system of book censorship and thorough control over all book publishing, marketing, and distribution was established. As admitted with brutal frankness by Kopecký, the system is designed to act as a "guardian of ideological purity"; to "revise thoroughly our whole book market" and purge it of "bad literature"; to liquidate "the leftovers of bourgeois and petty-bourgeois ideology" and "ideologically confused intellectualism"; and to prevent publication and circulation of books "with a negative attitude to the victorious truth of our working class."[34]

Eliminating Obnoxious Books of the Bourgeois Past

The first logical step in the battle against "the leftovers of bourgeois ideology" in the realm of literature was to remove from the reach of the reading public objectionable books which had been published and placed in circulation in the pre-communist era. "Taking over the cultural heritage of the past," Kopecký informed the Ninth Party Congress in May 1949, "we are reappraising the fruits of Czech and Slovak literature and carrying out a revision of the literary works created in the bourgeois epoch. We see to it that only [such] works of our national literature are propagated among the people as can . . . contribute to the spiritual rebirth of the nation and help us in our socialist efforts."[35]

Reports gathered from many sources indicate that this reappraisal amounted in fact to a colossal purge involving many millions of volumes.[36] Detailed lists of books considered objectionable from the communist point of view were sent to bookstores and libraries with orders that they not be sold or lent. Squads of censors descended on hundreds of private libraries located in many of Czechoslovakia's castles, convents, and other individual collections and went through them with an

[33] Law No. 53 of July 9, 1959.
[34] *Lidové noviny,* March 21, 1950.
[35] *Lidové noviny,* May 29, 1949.
[36] *Zpráva o Československu,* ɪ, 1 (1950), p. 7; ɪɪ, 6 (1951), p. 57; ɪɪ, 8 (1951), p. 43, ɪɪ, 10 (1951), p. 69; *News,* 1, 1 (1952), p. 26; *Lidové noviny,* August 5, 1951; *Svět práce,* March 13, 1952; *Československý přehled,* ɪɪ, 10 (1955), pp. 24ff.

ideological fine-tooth comb. Volumes passed by the censor were distributed to public libraries and those which were condemned were either disposed of as scrap paper, or stored in special places, or sold abroad. Typical of the communist attitude at the peak of the Stalin era is the following passage which appeared in a Czechoslovak magazine:

"We need paper. We all know that old paper is a valuable raw material for new paper. Nevertheless, even people who understand this harbor heaps of useless old paper in their houses. Such paper lies around and even shines out from bookshelves in form of books. With the exception of a few classics there is very little indeed that is worth preserving of the past bourgeois era. What can all those decadent novels tell today's realistic reader? . . . This kind of literature has already vanished from our bookstores. It is time that it disappears from individual libraries as well. A library reflects a person's cultural level. Throw out of your library the trash you should be ashamed of! You will see that this check will be interesting. By what you discard you will learn to what extent you have managed to free yourself from the dead weight of the past and how your taste has changed. Your library will be smaller, but it will gain in quality. Moreover, you will deliver an armload of scrap paper that will help the development of our new progressive literature."[37]

It seems that huge masses of books did indeed end their journey in scrap paper dumps. According to reliable information obtained from Czechoslovakia in 1955, one-half of the fourteen million books from the liquidated private collections were consigned to scrap paper, some three million were transferred to public libraries, and the remaining four million were stored pending further decision about their ultimate fate.[38] Nor were the sentences of death by grinding or banishment to secluded storerooms or special shelves reserved solely for books of political or philosophical nature. These sentences were also meted out to huge quantities of novels, poetry, and drama, particularly those labeled "decadent" and those which might have contradicted the communist black legend about life under T. G. Masaryk's First Republic.

New Publication Programs

The same ideological yardstick has been applied since 1948 to publication programs. "The criterion [of all artistic production] is its relation to the ruling working people, its relation to the workers, and

[37] *Svět práce,* March 13, 1952.
[38] *Československý přehled,* II, 10 (1955), p. 25.

its relation to socialism," decreed Kopecký in his address to the Ninth Party Congress in 1949, heralding "the advent of a true golden age for all forms of culture and especially for literature."[39] As a result, the Czechoslovak publication programs under the dictatorship of the proletariat have concentrated primarily on books, booklets, and pamphlets of two kinds: (1) textbooks, manuals, and other practical how-to-do-it materials designed to provide guidance and instruction for socialist construction and contribute toward a better fulfillment of the Economic Plan; (2) Marxist-Leninist and Party literature to supply accurate ideological directives to Party workers and activists and to propagate knowledge of Marxism-Leninism among the masses.

Year after year the Czechoslovak printing presses have been turning out mammoth editions of the works of Lenin, Stalin, and Gottwald as well as untold millions of propagandistic pamphlets and brochures. The following few figures culled from communist sources suffice to illustrate the nature and the magnitude of the KSČ's indoctrination effort through the nonperiodical press:

Lenin's works, almost three million copies between 1950-1954; Stalin's works, over four million; Marx's *Das Kapital,* 100,000; *Short Course of the History of the Soviet Communist Party,* 652,000; Gottwald's collected works, almost two million; Gottwald's report to the Party's Central Committee in February 1951, 1,345,000; Slánský's report on the Unified Agricultural Cooperatives, 928,250; Dolanský's report on Economic Planning, 928,150; classics of Marxism-Leninism and works explaining their teaching, 1,403,000 between 1950 and 1953; translated Soviet nonfiction, over sixteen million copies in 1951 alone.[40] Of the 4,890 titles published in 1959 only 1,242 were works of fiction, including children's books.[41] This same 3:1 ratio in favor of nonfiction prevailed also in the preceding years, whereas it had approximated 2:1 before the War.[42]

In the reduced realm of *belles lettres* the publication programs consist mostly of three categories of books: (1) writings by Soviet authors and by "progressive" writers of other nations; (2) carefully selected works of native and foreign classics; (3) works of the few Czechoslovak men of letters who had belonged to the Party prior to World War II and the products of living native writers meeting the

[39] *Lidové noviny,* May 29, 1949.
[40] *Rudé právo,* April 1, 1951, March 28 and April 8, 1952; *Práce,* April 20, 1951; *Rudé právo,* March 27, 1954.
[41] *Ročenka,* 1960, p. 473.
[42] *ibid.,* p. 473; *Ročenka,* 1937, p. 250.

prescribed standards of "socialist realism." The most spectacular contrast as against the prewar era is offered by the tremendous increase, both in the number of titles and sizes of the editions, of translated Soviet fiction. As shown in Chapter xviii, such translations were relatively few prior to the War and the volume of their editions very modest. But in 1951 almost five million copies of translated Soviet fiction were published and editions of individual Soviet novels ran into hundreds of thousands. Thus Gorky's *Mother,* which was published before the War in an edition of 3,000 copies, reached 212,000 by April 1952; Azhayev's *Far From Moscow* skyrocketed to an unbelievable 346,000, and Babayevsky's *The Knight of the Golden Star* to 110,000.[43] According to a report by the director of the Main Administration of Publishing of the Ministry of Culture, 5,069 of the 19,635 titles published in the years 1950-1953 were translations of Soviet authors.[44] Similar gigantic proportions were reached by novels written by some of the native communist authors of prewar fame, such as Olbracht's *Anna, The Proletarian* (316,000), Majerová's *The Siren* (284,000), and, of course, Zápotocký's *New Fighters Shall Rise* (200,000).[45]

Of the native non-communist classics, Alois Jirásek, Czechoslovakia's Sir Walter Scott, was selected for an especially intensive process of glorification and popularization; and a somewhat similar treatment was reserved in Slovakia for the famed Slovak poet Hviezdoslav.[46] Begun in 1949, Jirásek's buildup culminated on the occasion of his hundredth birthday in August 1951 when Party leaders and communist magazines vied with each other in extolling Jirásek as "the greatest Czech writer" and a fine representative of "the ideology of militant democratism" who had never succumbed "to the cosmopolitan fashion."[47] His novel of the Hussite era, *Against All,* was published in a fantastic 253,000 copies, and his other works also appeared in huge editions. Theaters offered dramatized versions of his novels. Statues were erected in his honor and a special museum was established to collect materials related to "the life and work of the great teacher of the nation's history."[48] Jirásek's birthplace at Hronov was converted virtually into a national shrine.

[43] *Rudé právo,* April 8, 1952, and April 27, 1954.
[44] *Rudé právo,* March 27, 1954.
[45] *ibid.*
[46] Kopecký's speech to the Ninth Party Congress, *Lidové noviny,* May 29, 1949.
[47] *Lidové noviny,* December 14, 1952; F. Nečásek's and Pachta's articles in *Tvorba,* August 23, 1951; Čepička's article in *Rudé právo,* August 23, 1951; *Rudé právo,* August 24, 1951.
[48] *Lidové noviny,* August 4, 1951.

The strangest thing in all this is that the man whom the communist rulers attempt to present almost as an antibourgeois tribune of the class struggle was actually a resolute anti-communist who served after World War I for a short while as senator for a right-wing party in the Czechoslovak Parliament. Fortunately for the communist propagandists, Jirásek's political views do not appear in his historical novels. Furthermore, once the Communists decided to exploit the glorious Hussite era of Czech history for their own ends, it was natural enough to draft posthumously the noted writer whose novels about Hussite exploits endeared him to so many Czechs, proud of their ancestors' glories. Also, the communist rulers seem to cherish a hope that the cult of Jirásek might help them in their anti-Masaryk campaign. That is clearly evident from their persistent endeavors to contrast the "anti-bourgeois" and "revolutionary" Jirásek with Masaryk's "reformism" designed "to save capitalist society and paralyze the fighting capacity of the popular masses."[49]

While the ultraconservative Jirásek was thus built into a literary idol and a certain number of literary figures of the nineteenth century were selected to follow him into the communist Olympus, others of equal or better literary repute were marked, to use George Orwell's famed dictum, to be "lifted out from the stream of history." Among them were a good many who had unmistakable leftist inclinations and were infinitely less bourgeois than Jirásek. The most striking—and very typical of the behavior of the regime's literary censors—is the case of Karel Čapek, the most outstanding Czechoslovak writer of the twentieth century (died in 1939) who had been generally thought of as the best Czechoslovak candidate for the Nobel prize in literature. Despite his impeccable anti-Fascist record, he was among those chosen for oblivion after the Communists seized power in 1948. In part, this was due to the fact that Čapek had made his anti-communist stand publicly known through a booklet *Why I Am Not a Communist.* Also, the regime's censors perhaps felt that the sharply antitotalitarian tenor of some of Čapek's best-known dramas might make the public draw undesirable parallels with the present. But most probably the main reason for the negative communist attitude toward Čapek was his spiritual and personal closeness to T. G. Masaryk. It would have been indeed hardly logical from the communist standpoint to attack Masaryk's memory and at the same time to accept and esteem one of his foremost spiritual associates.

[49] Nečásek's and Pachta's articles in *Tvorba,* August 23, 1951; also, *Lidové noviny,* December 14, 1951.

However, when all seemed to be proceeding smoothly according to plan, the State Literary Publishing House in Moscow published a selection of Čapek's works prefaced by a flattering evaluation of the Czech writer's talent from the pen of a Soviet literary critic, S. V. Nikolsky. The dilemma thereby caused to the KSČ's literary mentors is revealed by the following announcement of the event in *Práce:* "Nikolsky's study brings a clear insight into the numerous embarrassments of our literary criticism concerning Karel Čapek. It expounds the progressive orientation of Čapek's work and dwells, in particular, upon Čapek as one of the most talented Czech writers of the twentieth century and ends by stressing that the Soviet reader knows and loves him."[50] Evidently, once Moscow had spoken, the KSČ leaders could hardly go on behaving as if the greatest Czechoslovak literary figure of the twentieth century had not existed. Therefore, they allowed the publication of a few of Čapek's works, but not without omitting certain portions which they found obnoxious for them. As pointed out in the May 1956 student resolutions protesting such "undignified changes in literary works," this kind of literary surgery was administered to Čapek's famed drama *The War of the Newts.*[51]

During the post-Stalin thaw the rigid controls over the publication programs were notably relaxed. Emboldened by the sudden turn toward freer publishing in the Soviet Union, Poland, and Hungary, and bored to death by the dreary cultural diet of Stalin days, both the Czechoslovak readers and authors began to press for more variety, more entertainment and less propaganda. "Publication programs should be revised with regard to the demand for good literature (Čapek, Seifert)," demanded the student resolutions of May 1956. "Publication of propaganda materials of doubtful value should be curtailed. Paper will thus be saved."[52] Yielding to such persistent proddings from below, the Czechoslovak publishing houses began to accept manuscripts which they would not have dared to touch at the peak of the Stalin era. Party censors, shaken by the unexpected course of events and lacking guidance from Moscow, lapsed temporarily into passivity. As a result, a refreshing change took place. As shown in Chapter XVIII, the Czechoslovak book market was enlivened by a number of works by Western authors other than the customary "progressive" species. Many more books by native pre-communist

[50] *Práce,* October 10, 1952.
[51] *Československý přehled,* III, 6 (1956), p. 9.
[52] *ibid.*

authors were published than during the Stalin era. But even more spectacular was the appearance in print of manuscripts by living authors composed with utter disregard of the prescribed formulae of "socialist realism," such as, to cite just a few outstanding samples, A. Lustig's *The Night of Hope* and *The Diamonds of the Night,* J. Škvorecký's *The Cowards,* M. Macourek's collection of verses *One Would Not Believe One's Eyes,* as well as works by Seifert and Hrubín, the two main literary rebels of the 1956 Congress of the Czechoslovak Writers.[53]

However, the ever-mounting attacks by the KSČ spokesmen on such damnable departures from "socialist realism" and on "the loss of revolutionary perspective" suggest that the post-Stalin literary leniency has come to an end.[54] The "completion of the cultural revolution in the near future," announced by Novotný at the Eleventh Party Congress in 1958, can hardly be attained without the reimposition of a rigid bar against ideologically obnoxious books. The substitution in 1959 of orthodox neo-Stalinists for more liberal-minded elements in the leadership of the Union of Czechoslovak Writers and in their publishing house also spells more regimentation for the Czechoslovak Parnassus.[55] So does the creation in 1960 of a new Socialist Culture Committee, headed by one of the most doctrinaire of Czechoslovakia's communist intellectuals, Ladislav Štoll, to serve as yet another watchdog over the ideological purity of cultural activities.

The regime's effort to mobilize books for the battle for men's minds is indicated also by the volume of publication programs which has risen high above prewar levels. While thirty-two million nonperiodical publications were published in Czechoslovakia in 1937, their number reached 103.5 millions in 1951, of which almost 90 million were books, for a population which was then one-fifth below the prewar level.[56] Although the high publishing rate attained in 1950-1951 leveled off noticeably in the ensuing years, it has remained nevertheless well above prewar averages, amounting to 50.2 million books in 1958,[57] 44.4 million in 1959, and 48 million in 1960.

This increased volume contrasts sharply, though not at all surprisingly, with the notable decrease in the variety of publication pro-

[53] For information on the publications programs of the post-Stalin era see *Československý přehled,* I, 1 (1954), pp. 25ff.; *Rudé právo,* September 17, 1954; *Československý zpravodaj,* No. 231, February 5, 1959.

[54] *Rudé právo,* February 28, 1959; *Pravda,* January 29, 1959.

[55] *Rudé právo,* March 6, 1959.

[56] *ibid.,* March 28, 1952; *Ročenka,* 1959, p. 463.

[57] *Ročenka,* 1960, p. 473, and *Rudé právo,* February 8, 1961.

grams. Whereas 17,531 titles were published in the years 1950-1953 and 17,831 in 1955-1958, the corresponding prewar figures for a similar period of four years, 1932-1935, was 35,359.[58] Even more striking is the contrast in the ratio of translations to original works. Of the 35,359 works published between 1932 and 1935 only 2,989 were translations.[59] On the other hand, translations of Soviet authors alone accounted for 5,069 out of a substantially smaller number of titles published in the years 1950-1953.[60]

Libraries

Although there are no statistical data showing how much of this colossal book production could actually be sold to individuals, information from many sources, official as well as unofficial, indicates that only a small portion can usually be disposed of through individual sales. That is true both of the huge editions of Marxist-Leninist literature and of the "socialist-realistic" fiction. Despite the persistent promotion campaigns much of such literature has repeatedly remained unsold.[61] The only books whose supply has invariably been exceeded by the demand are novels of Western literature other than the so-called "progressive," works of those native pre-communist authors barred from publication during the Stalin era and such products by living authors as break out from the stifling embrace of socialist realism.

Hence, the bulk of the literature with the correct ideological message is channeled into the vast network of public libraries which have thus become a major vehicle of communist indoctrination. While the present 15,000 people's libraries still run about 2,000 short of the number of communal libraries in prewar Czechoslovakia, the numbers of borrowers and borrowed books (Table XXI) greatly exceed the corresponding figures of prewar days.

Furthermore, there are over 12,000 factory libraries and almost 1,200 libraries attached to colleges, universities, and scientific institutes.[62] The regime began also to experiment on a small scale with "bibliobuses," the Czechoslovak equivalent of American bookmobiles. Some of them were used, according to reports in the Czechoslovak press, to bring communist culture even to the vagrant gypsies whom

[58] *ibid.*, p. 471; *Ročenka*, 1937, p. 250.
[59] *Ročenka*, 1937, p. 250.
[60] *Rudé právo*, March 27, 1954.
[61] *Zpráva o Československu*, ii, 12 (1951), p. 55, and iii, 4 (1952), p. 61.
[62] *Ročenka*, 1960, pp. 468, 470.

they supplied with books printed in extra large letters depicting "the flourishing life in the USSR" and the "ravages" of the Americans in Korea.[63] Since a new law adopted in 1958 orders that all vagrants be permanently settled, these special arrangements for the indoctrination of the gypsies will presumably no longer be necessary.[64]

TABLE XXI

Public Libraries in Czechoslovakia, 1935 and 1959

	Number of Libraries	Volumes (in thousands)	Books lent (in millions)	Borrowers (in millions)
1935	17,089	8,529	18.7	0.97
1958	15,005	20,743	36.9	1.74

Source: For 1935: *Statistická příručka Československé republiky*, London, n.d.; for 1959: *Ročenka*, 1960, p. 454.

The fact that a book is borrowed does not mean, of course, that it is actually read. As borne out by information gathered from many escapees, people frequently check out Marxist-Leninist literature from public libraries merely for the sake of establishing a verifiable record of having borrowed it. Instead of reading such books they just look through them cursorily and copy a few quotations which they could refer to should it become necessary to prove that they had read the books. Well aware of such practices, the regime has tried hard to counteract them. With regard to KSČ members and candidates subject to prescribed Party schooling, class discussion and final examinations serve to some extent as a convenient medium of checking on whether the prescribed books have actually been read. As for the general reader, adequate controls are much more difficult. The main method consists of reading and discussion circles set up mostly within the various organized groups to which most citizens have to belong, such as the trade unions, Youth Union and Pioneer groups, factory clubs, and collective farms. Discussions of this kind pursue people even into sanatoria and holiday resorts where they constitute a regular part of the "recreational" activities.

THE WRITERS' NEW ROLE

In order to convert books into the kind of ideological weapons which the KSČ leaders want them to be, it is absolutely essential to

[64] Law No. 74 of October 17, 1958.
[63] *Mladá fronta*, March 19, 1951.

secure the active cooperation of living Czechoslovak writers. While the classics of Marxism-Leninism and translations from Soviet literature are deemed indispensable, the main contribution to the making of the new communistic man must necessarily come from contemporary native fiction. As living witnesses of the "exciting new Czechoslovak reality," native contemporary writers alone are in a position to create works that can "generate enthusiasm and mobilize our people for a work full of *élan;* draw the themes from the ebullient building effort of the workers and from the living and never-drying sources of the Marxist-Leninist teaching; adhere proudly and honorably to the ideals of progress and socialism, and openly proclaim their fighting class-consciousness, and Party-mindedness."[65] They alone can portray "in all their vitality, richness, beauty, and humanity the splendid heroes of the socialist era"; can express "the greatness and beauty of the era"; and can "light the great flame of concrete faith, a flame of a stubborn and passionate dreaming . . . and permeate with it our whole vision of the future . . . ."[66]

What the Party expects of Czechoslovak writers has been spelled out for them over and over again by the Party chiefs with elaborate details strictly along the Soviet lines.[67] They are directed to sing the glory of communism and to contrast it with the evils of the bourgeois past. They are to write about "the oppression of our people in the past and their work for a piece of bread, and a more joyful tomorrow; the heroic epopee of the anti-fascist struggle and the national uprising; the great battle for the construction of socialism, the building of a new, full, gay life in the cities and villages; the powerful effort for the socialist transformation and full exploitation of nature and its tremendous forces; the struggle for peace."[68] They are to look for their themes primarily in the mines, factories, building sites, collective farms, and machine-tractor stations. They are to draw in rich and exciting colors artistic images of the new communistic men in action and to show convincingly how the inspiration of Marxism-Leninism trans-

[65] Baštovanský's speech at the Ninth Congress of the Slovak Communist Party, *Lidové noviny,* May 27, 1950.

[66] A speech by J. Drda, Chairman of the Czechoslovak Writer's Union, at the Ninth Party Congress, *Lidové noviny,* May 31, 1949.

[67] See, for instance, Kopecký's speech at the Ninth Party Congress, *Lidové noviny,* May 29, 1949, and another speech at the Cultural Committee of the National Assembly, *Lidové noviny,* March 21, 1950; Baštovanský's speech at the Ninth Congress of the Slovak Communist Party, *Lidové noviny,* May 27, 1950; Novotný's speech at the Eleventh Party Congress, *Rudé právo,* June 19, 1958.

[68] *Lidové noviny,* May 27, 1950.

forms them into better beings and helps them to overcome all obstacles. Only such men are to be the positive heroes in the works dealing with contemporary people's democratic life; and they are to be found preferably among the persons with a correct class profile. For "the central hero of their new works cannot be anyone else but the working people, building with enthusiasm and sacrifice their socialist fatherland."[69] On the other hand, the leading villains are to be recruited from the ranks of the *kulaks,* former capitalists, and other such reactionary elements. Whenever a Party member figures among the negative characters he must be portrayed as one of the few black sheep who failed to grasp the true meaning of communism and thus laid himself open to pernicious bourgeois influences. Moreover, the contradictions must be solved by a happy ending in which the cause of socialism triumphs over the "dark forces of the reaction."

The production methods which Czechoslovak writers are to use in order to become "honest workers of the literary art" have also been amply defined by various pronouncements of the Party leaders. They are to discard "enemy ideologies and elements," such as formalism and "ultraformalism," decadence, symbolism, cosmopolitanism, clericalism, naturalism and "ultranaturalism," futurism, "poetism," ideological neutralism, subjectivism, and any theories of "art for art's sake." Instead, guided by the "shining example of the mighty and brilliant Soviet literature," they must abide by the principles of socialist realism as formulated "in the resolutions of the Central Committee of the Soviet Communist Party and the Soviet discussions of the questions of artistic creation."[70] "A writer must at all times be armed with the Marxist-Leninist theory and his works must contribute to its application in everyday practice."[71] So that they may be able to "create realistically in the spirit of socialism," the writers are sent to factories and villages to "look there for their new heroes, the heroes of labor."[72] Also, like their journalist colleagues, authors are subjected to special indoctrination courses held regularly at Dobříš Castle near Praha. They listen to lectures on communist ideology by leading Party theoreticians; and established communist writers enlighten them on

[69] Drda's speech, *Lidové noviny,* May 31, 1949.

[70] Kopecký's speech, *Lidové noviny,* May 29, 1949; Drda's speech, *ibid.,* May 31, 1949.

[71] F. Kubka on the task of the writers on the Praha Radio on March 19, 1951, as monitored by Free Europe Committee, *Zpráva o Československu,* II, 3 (1951), pp. 53-54.

[72] Kopecký's speech, *Lidové noviny,* May 29, 1949; also, *Pravda,* January 29, 1959.

the proper way of socialist writing and help them by criticizing their works.[73]

To secure the writers' compliance with the Party's political and literary directives the KSČ leaders fall back essentially on the same basic stick-and-carrot techniques which they have been using to get desired results in other sectors of socialist construction. Those authors who comply get their books published, often in huge editions, and reap a rich harvest of literary honors, prizes, and fat royalties. Those who insist on their creative freedom, find it almost impossible to get their manuscripts published; and if they insist too much, they may as a last resort be expelled from the Writers' Union and see themselves transferred to other production work. The communist leaders began to apply these techniques to writers even prior to their seizure of power in 1948. Taking advantage of his ministerial powers of over-all control over culture, Kopecký did his best to reward communist and fellow-traveling writers and to make things complicated for others. Not only was he quite magnanimous in helping his favorites with the publication of their literary products, but he also appointed a good many of them to various well-paid positions in the Ministry of Information.

After the 1948 coup a thorough purge was undertaken in the Writers' Syndicate, which was replaced in March 1949 by a new Union of Czechoslovak Writers patterned after the Soviet model. Of all the Czechoslovak writers only 280 were admitted to the new Union and an additional 100 younger authors were accepted as candidates.[74] Although the Writers' Union is theoretically an autonomous organization entitled to elect its own leaders and to attend to its business without outside interference, in reality it is yet another of the KSČ's transmission belts and operates as the Party's watchdog over the writers' behavior. The Union's congresses, conferences, plenary sessions, and other meetings held from time to time are made to serve as convenient platforms for communist pronouncements on the literary canons which are to guide the writers of the socialist epoch. There high communist spokesmen deliver the Party's directives which keynote the meetings, set the tenor and the limits of the discussion, and predetermine its results. Invariably, the final resolutions thank the Party leaders for their wise guidance and contain the writers' promise of zealous compliance. Whenever new organs are to be elected, a slate

---

[73] *Lidové noviny,* July 27, 1951, and September 3, 1950.
[74] Dana Adams Schmidt, *Anatomy of a Satellite,* Boston, 1952, p. 279.

of candidates acceptable to the KSČ leadership is prepared in advance and its approval secured without much difficulty.[75]

The pressure was at its worst during the Stalinist era. The slightest departure from the rigid Zhdanov line, which Kopecký proclaimed as absolutely binding for Czechoslovak literature, meant literary banishment.[76] Authors and literary critics who sought refuge in silence or avoidance of contemporary topics were attacked with increasing vehemence. Some, such as Slovak writer L. Novomeský, were expelled from the Writers' Union and thus stripped dishonorably of the writer's status for having "knowingly propagated unpatriotic, cosmopolitan tendencies" and "oriented literature toward the rotten shoots of the capitalist culture in order to put it into the service of our class enemy."[77] Others, such as the poet K. Biebl and the old-time communist literary critic K. Teige, could not stand the persecution and committed suicide.[78]

The post-Stalin thaw brought a substantial relaxation. The literary ferment which erupted in Russia, Poland, and Hungary after Stalin's death invaded the Czechoslovak Parnassus. Noting the conciliatory mood with which the Kremlin tackled the thorny problem of the writers' demands for more creative freedom in the initial years of the post-Stalin era, the KSČ leaders adopted a somewhat similar course. Even such an inveterate Stalinist as Kopecký thought it advisable to retreat a little. Speaking before the Party's Central Committee in December 1953 he bewailed the lack of humor in contemporary satire, lashed out against those "dry fellows" who "scooped out ideology by the bucketful" and "presented cultural and social life under socialism as if its slogans were poverty, self-denial, asceticism, boredom, grayness."[79]

The liberalizing trends reached their climax at the Second Congress of the Union of Czechoslovak Writers in April 1956. Encouraged by the iconoclastic events of the Twentieth Soviet Party Congress and the mounting rebelliousness of their Polish and Hungarian colleagues,

---

[75] On the proceedings of the writers' congresses and other meetings see, for instance, *Československý přehled*, III, 5 (1956), pp. 8ff.; *Rudé právo*, April 24 and 30, 1956; *Lidové noviny*, October 24, 1950; *Literární noviny*, May 23, 1953, and April 29-May 5, 1956.

[76] *Lidové noviny*, May 29, 1949.

[77] *Rudé právo*, March 15, 1951.

[78] M. Grygar, "Teigism, a Trotskyite Agency in Our Literature," *Tvorba*, October 18, 1951; *Lidové noviny* November 14 and 20, 1951. For a review of the developments on the literary front see P. Korbel, "Writers in Czechoslovakia under Communism," *Thought Patterns*, Vol. 6, pp. 91ff.

[79] *Rudé právo*, December 13, 1953.

the rank and file of the Union turned the tables on the communist stage managers. Thus the halls of the Czechoslovak parliament, where the Writers' Congress was being held, became, if only for a few hectic days, the scene of a spontaneous outburst of stinging criticism of the Party's repression. Writer after writer rose to condemn the malpractices and humiliations of the Stalinist era; to confess how they had to distort reality in order to get their works published. They told how "a man who did not even know Czech [Paul Reiman, a Sudeten German Communist] reigned over Czech literature after 1948 and determined the fate both of Czech writers and Czech books." They compared the tragic fate of recent Czech poetry to the agony of Mallarmé's swan who could not free its wings from the ice. They demanded justice for their colleagues who had been driven into isolation and sent to jail.[80] However, the KSČ leaders had no intention of yielding to these overwhelming demands for creative freedom any more than was absolutely necessary. With an utter disregard for the facts, the Central Committee's letter, read personally by Antonín Zápotocký, assured the assembled writers that "the Party has never prescribed and never will prescribe to the writers regarding their literary work."[81] But when the writers took him at his word, Zápotocký rose to denounce the two most prominent advocates of creative freedom, the poets Hrubín and Seifert, as demagogues.[82] Also, the Party's henchmen among the writers managed to push through the congress a sycophantic reply to the Central Committee's letter, greeting the Party as "the inspirator and organizer of a great revolutionary change" providing for a "happy future" and thanking the KSČ for its "correct and wise suggestions."[83] Similarly, the Party succeeded in getting all but two of its favorite candidates elected to the new Central Committee of the Writers' Union, although it had to compromise and include in the new committee several of the regime's critics, among them Hrubín and Seifert.[84]

The writers' revolt of 1956 made the Party chiefs realize more than anything else the grave risks implicit in the liberalizing tendencies of the post-Stalin era. Coming on top of other difficulties engendered by the leniencies of the New Course, it convinced the KSČ leaders that nothing could be gained by concessions and that unswerving

[80] Jarmila Uhlířová's article in *Československý přehled*, II, 5 (1956), pp. 8ff., and Korbel, *op.cit.*, pp. 112-113.
[81] *Rudé právo*, April 24, 1956.
[82] *Literární noviny*, April 29, 1956.
[83] *Rudé právo*, April 30, 1956.
[84] *Lidová demokracie*, April 30, 1956.

ideological firmness was the best course for them. Hardly had the Writers' Congress adjourned when the Party leaders unfolded a determined counteroffensive against the "pernicious" influences among Czechoslovak writers.[85] Their "unprincipled liberalism" and "attacks against our people's democratic system" were sharply condemned by Novotný at the National Conference of the KSČ in June 1956, while Kopecký appealed simultaneously to those writers who had demonstrated "devotion to our regime and our Party" to see to it that the Writers' Union and its paper, *Literární noviny,* go to a "correct destination."[86]

From then on the Party has been slowly but relentlessly tightening its reins over the writers. Helped by the revival of neo-Stalinism throughout the Soviet orbit after the suppression of the Hungarian uprising, the KSČ chiefs missed no opportunity to narrow and cut down the concessions granted during the post-Stalin thaw. Ever since the summer of 1956 the Czechoslovak press has been replete with sharp attacks on writers "succumbing to pessimistic voices from abroad" and to "nihilistic" tendencies. The writers have been criticized for shunning the socialist realism, "retreating from the revolutionary concepts of art," and indulging in "lamentations and melancholia over the hopelessness of life." They have been taken to task for their "lack of true Marxist-Leninist spirit," for displaying "escapist" tendencies of avoiding contemporary topics, for resorting to a "conspiracy of silence," and "relying on the grandeur of uncertainties" and "bourgeois abstractionism."[87] They have been admonished repeatedly to abide strictly by socialist realism and warned that the Party "will not tolerate artistic creative freedom to be misused for the dissemination of views which we reject . . . ."[88] Nor has the regime been satisfied with exhortations alone. Once again the unsavory Stalinist practice of public self-flagellation was revived. At the plenary session of the Writers' Union in June 1957 the poet František Hrubín was made to recant his fighting speech which had touched off the writers' revolt at their congress in April 1956.[89] In a less conspicuous way, a number

[85] See, for instance, J. Pilař's article in *Literární noviny,* May 5, 1956, and J. Hájek's article, *ibid.,* May 12, 1956.

[86] *Rudé právo,* June 12, 1956, and *Svobodné slovo,* June 15, 1956.

[87] See *Mladá fronta,* December 28, 1956, and January 10, 1958; *Kulturní život,* October 20, 1956; *Rudé právo,* July 23, 1957, January 26, March 7 and May 25, 1958; *Pravda,* April 27, 1957, and January 29, 1959.

[88] Kopecký's speech at the Slovak Communist Party Congress in 1958, *Pravda,* May 18, 1958.

[89] *Rudé právo,* June 29, 1957.

of other authors were made to eat crow and the editors of several literary magazines had to bow publicly to the Party's criticism.

Finally, unable to subdue the writers by the method of "persuasion" alone, the Party leaders switched from recriminations and exhortations to direct action. A hastily convened national conference of the Writers' Union in March 1959 removed from the Union's leadership most of the writers who had led the struggle for liberalization at the Writers' Congress of 1956.[90] They were replaced by die-hard Stalinists, among them the notorious advocate of rigid orthodoxy in science and culture, Ladislav Štoll, and Jiří Taufer, whom the writers detested so much that he had failed in his bid for reelection to the Union's leadership in 1956.[91] And in the middle of 1959 the Party closed down the two most courageous of Czechoslovakia's literary magazines, *Nový život* and *Květen*.[92]

That is where the tug-of-war between the regime and the writers stands today. The Party leaders and their lieutenants in the Writers' Union flex their muscles to the utmost to undo "the harm" done by the post-Stalin thaw. Especially, as revealed so conspicuously by Štoll's keynote speech at the 1959 Writers' conference, they try very hard to blot out the dangerous slogan "The Writers—The Conscience of the Nation" raised at the rebellious writers' Congress of 1956. But so far they have been only partially successful. The Czechoslovak writers as a whole seem to be anything but "meritorious workers on the construction of socialism" in the manner in which the Party leaders would want them to be.

FILMS

The great popularity of motion pictures as the leading source of general entertainment made the film industry logically a prime target of the communist search for suitable indoctrination media. Kopecký spoke as a faithful disciple of Lenin and Stalin when he explained his ideas on the subject to the Cultural Committee of the National Assembly in 1950:

"As the cultural and educational medium serving the broadest

[90] *Rudé právo*, March 6, 1959. Removed thus were among others: J. Seifert, V. Kaplický, F. Rachlík, D. Tatarka, and K. Lazarova. Hrubín evidently managed to save his skin by his timely repentence of 1957.

[91] Others thus added were: Z. Pluhař, author of a novel denigrating the democratic exiles; K. Bendová, a Stalinist literary critic; also J. Glazarová, M. Krno, J. Lenko, and I. Skála.

[92] For a detailed discussion of the reasons see *East Europe*, 8, 9 (1959), pp. 26ff.

masses our film industry is first and foremost destined to fulfill the great educational mission assigned to it by our people's democratic Republic. This requires that our creative film workers provide our people with worthy motion pictures which would convince by their truthfulness and would be an incentive for our construction effort and a source of enthusiasm for joyful socialist work."[93]

To secure a correct implementation of the film industry's new mission the Ninth-of-May Constitution reserved for the State the exclusive right to "produce, distribute, publicly exhibit as well as to import and export motion pictures."[94] The whole field of cinematography from the preparation of the scripts to the showing of the finished product in the local theater was thus placed under the all-inclusive controls of the Ministry of Culture. Not even amateur films may be shown without state approval. Actual film production is concentrated in a national enterprise, the Czechoslovak State Film, which operates all the studios and directs the "creative collectives" put in charge of shooting individual motion pictures. A Film Council composed of dependable Communists assists the Minister of Culture in his supervision of film production from the artistic and ideological point of view while a Film Commission, attached to the Writers' Union, helps in the selection of the scripts.[95]

The basic directives for the film industry were laid down by a resolution of the KSČ Central Committee of 1950 on the "high ideological and artistic level of the Czechoslovak film."[96] It called for films that would fill people "with optimism and faith" and follow the "great example" of the Soviet motion pictures. It turned thumbs down on films of nonpolitical nature made for the sake of mere entertainment and prescribed that the overwhelming majority of motion pictures must deal with contemporary problems of the construction of socialism. While allowing film comedies, the KSČ leaders ruled that, to be acceptable, they must "ridicule the remnants of the bourgeois views" and "emphasize the positive humorous and optimistic features

[93] *Lidové noviny,* March 21, 1950.

[94] The production of the motion pictures was nationalized in 1945, but the distribution of films was taken over by the state only after the communist seizure of power in 1948.

[95] The first chairman of the Film Council was Jiří Hendrych, one of the most zealous Party *apparatchiks* who was later promoted to full membership of the Party's Presidium. *Rudé právo,* April 20, 1950.

[96] *Rudé právo,* April 19, 1950. See also the directives contained in the keynote speech of the Minister of Education and Culture at the Czechoslovak Film Festival in February 1959 (*Mladá fronta,* February 24, 1959).

of the present." "Socialist realism" was installed as the sole permissible method of work. "Creative film workers" were directed to abandon "all the remaining tendencies toward films of nonideological and non-political nature, the leftovers of formalism, addiction to routine, and attempts to escape contemporary reality."[97] Instead, they must help "to strengthen steadily, through their film production, the power of the working class, the building of socialism . . . and a new morality, new ethics and aesthetics."[98]

Special attention is given by the communist censors to the choice of suitable themes and topics. As stressed by Kopecký, "The great educational mission of our film industry requires it to concern itself with new themes from real life; to show the heroism of our people in the construction of socialism, express the immense variety of the contemporary era and the great perspective which the transformation of our economy, industry, agriculture and our Five-Year Plan offers all honest working people. Our film industry must pay special attention to the problems of the struggle of the world front of peace led by the USSR, to the problems of the socialist transformation of our village, the relation of the new man to his work as it is manifested in the shock-workers' movement and in the socialist competition. In must show the growing heroes of labor and help to reeducate our people into men of a new socialistic type."[99]

In deference to these stiff directives the Czechoslovak film industry has been engaged predominantly in the production of motion pictures glorifying the "joyful life" under communism, disparaging life under capitalism in general and in pre-communist Czechoslovakia in particular, and belaboring historical topics so as to fit them into the Procrustean bed of communist interpretation. Here are a few representative samples taken at random from the repertoire of the Czechoslovak picture theaters of various years:

Warning: describes the struggle for the Stalin Works, a huge synthetic gasoline plant in Northern Bohemia, against traitors and foreign agents;

They Emerge from the Darkness: depicts the evil deeds of the *kulaks;*

New Fighters Shall Rise: a filmed version of Zápotocký's novel about the beginning of socialism in Bohemia;

[97] *Lidové noviny,* March 21, 1950.
[98] Kopecký, addressing a meeting of "creative film workers" summoned in April 1950 to discuss the Party's film directives. *Rudé právo,* April 28, 1950.
[99] *Lidové noviny,* March 21, 1950.

Kidnapping: deals with "gangsters kidnapping [Czech] citizens and taking them by air to Germany";

Grinder Karhan's Shift: designed to encourage the shockworkers' movement;

The Churchwarden and the Hen: a story of a farmer's wife persuaded to join the collective farm despite the saboteur efforts of a churchwarden;

The Wooden Village: depicts development in a Slovak village leading to victory over the *kulaks;*

Katka: shows how a naive country girl is reeducated through factory work to become a socialist worker;

The Rocks and the People: based on the motto, "To work in the socialist manner and to live in the socialist manner."

With the importance attached to motion pictures as media of indoctrination and the communist endeavor to keep out bourgeois movies from the West, one would have thought that the output of native films would increase by leaps and bounds after the communist seizure of power. The Barrandov film studios of prewar Czechoslovakia were the largest east of Germany and they were further enlarged by the Germans during the war. However, such anticipation has not thus far materialized. Repeatedly the Czechoslovak film production fell short of the Plan, and insofar as full-length feature films were concerned, for a time it kept decreasing rather than increasing. From 29 full-length films produced in 1949 it fell to 15 in 1954, then rose again to 29 in 1958, 35 in 1959, and 36 in 1960.[100] This is a meager result, especially in view of the initial plans of an annual output of over 50 full-length feature films. Communist admissions and information gathered from non-communist sources indicate that the main causes of the lag lay in the slow pace of film-shooting, official red tape, made even worse by numerous reorganizations in the complex approbatory machinery, and the dearth of scripts that would combine good artistic merit with the necessary ideological slant.[101] Occasionally, delay was caused also by the need to delete "falsifications of historical data smuggled into the scenario"

[100] Unless otherwise stated, these and other figures on Czechoslovak cinematography are taken from *Ročenka,* 1959, pp. 462, 465. Figure for 1960 taken from *Rudé právo,* February 8, 1961.

[101] Kopecký's complaint in 1950 of "deficiencies in creative work," *Lidové noviny,* March 21, 1950; *Československý přehled,* IV, 12 (1957), p. 11; *Svobodné slovo,* July 12, 1953, complaining that the Czech film comedy does not as yet fulfill the responsible task assigned to it in our new society: to amuse the spectator and help him at the same time in the struggle against everything that stagnates and brakes progress; *Literární noviny,* January 17, 1953; *Lidová demokracie,* January 29, 1953.

by persons meanwhile unmasked as "traitors."[102] The situation has been substantially better in the output of short films of which 821 were produced in 1960. Since the supply of full-length native films cannot cope with the demand, it has to be supplemented by imports of foreign motion pictures, especially those from the Soviet Union and other countries of the socialist camp. However, the indoctrination value of such imports can hardly ever equal that of native films, no matter how low the effectiveness of the latter may be.

While the film output has been anything but impressive, there has been a steady and substantial increase in the number of movie theaters. By 1959, 3,531 movie houses were in operation in Czechoslovakia, which was 1,693 more than in 1937.[103] They offered 1,088,090 performances in 1959.

Even more spectacular has been the increase in picture theater attendance. While 84.5 million people attended film showings in 1937, the corresponding claim for 1958 was 183.8 million, 174 million in 1959, and 176 million in 1960. However, mere attendance figures, no matter how impressive, cannot by themselves serve as an accurate indicator of the extent and intensity of the public's exposure to indoctrination via the screen, let alone its effectiveness. Unable as yet to meet the needs of the growing movie theater network from the laggard native film production and from imports from the socialist camp, communist film distributors must permit at least a limited entry of motion pictures from without the socialist camp.[104] Naturally, every effort is made to select only progressive films that fit, or at least do not contradict, the communist line. Nonetheless, the indoctrination value of these films, if any, is more often than not outweighed by the manifold echoes of the Free World which permeate them, even though they may depict the darker sides of life. But these are precisely the pictures which have people scrambling for tickets and buying them under the table at black market prices. On the other hand, most of the communist-made movies have been suffering chronically from poor attendance because people, bored to death with repetitive overdoses of the omnipresent dogma, do not want to have more of the same in the movies.

These attitudes of the movie-going public affect rather adversely the usefulness of the screen as a medium of indoctrination. To over-

---

[102] This delayed, for instance, the completion of the motion picture *Sokolovo,* dealing with the Czechoslovak Brigade on the Russian front during World War II. *Literární noviny,* January 17, 1953.

[103] *Ročenka,* 1960, p. 463.

[104] See Chapter xviii.

come this drawback the Party encourages collective viewing by various organized groups. Tickets for performances of motion pictures considered especially important from the ideological point of view are distributed to labor unions, youth organizations, party units, and similar groups which have to sell them to their members. In this manner some check is also possible on whether or not those who have bought the tickets actually attend the show. Furthermore, communist-slanted newsreel or documentary short films invariably precede the main feature. Since the Czechoslovak picture theaters use the system of reserved seats for each performance the patrons are thereby forced to swallow the ideological hors d'oeuvre before they can touch the main dish even when they choose a picture imported from outside the Iron Curtain.

THE THEATER

Although the live theater cannot compete with motion pictures in terms of attendance, it is by no means unimportant as a medium of indoctrination. Traditionally, the Czechs have always been great theater lovers, yielding to no other nation in that respect. Hence, the use of the theater for ideological purposes, once the Communists gained full control of the country, was a foregone conclusion. "It is the mission of Czechoslovak theaters to contribute to the enhancement of the cultural level and the development of the artistic creativity of the people and to the socialist education of the citizens," decrees the Czechoslovak Theater Law.[105] "We will strain every nerve to encourage new creative work filled with communist ideas and revolutionary struggles," promised, on behalf of the "theater workers," the director of the National Theater, the most famous of the Czechoslovak stages, on the festive occasion of the theater's seventy-fifth anniversary in November 1958; and Novotný used the occasion to warn against the dire consequences which would ensue should the theater "close its doors to the struggle for communism."[106]

To provide against any such calamity the Theater Law contains a peremptory prescription that "the state directs all the theaters whether they are theaters employing professional artists or amateur performances, and inclusive even of puppet shows." Naturally, only major theaters are operated directly by the central government, acting through the Ministry of Education and Culture. All the other state theaters are run by the regional, city, and local people's committees.

[105] Law No. 55 of October 31, 1957.
[106] *Rudé právo*, November 19, 1958.

"Non-state" theaters may be established and operated only by "social-ist legal persons" upon the approval by the regional people's committee which "determines the conditions and the manner of operation." They are supervised by the people's committee of the district in which they are located. Not even amateur shows may be staged without the ap-proval of the district people's committee; and permission to do so may be granted only to recognized organizations, such as schools, Houses of Culture, and collective farms. The primary responsibility for the artistic and ideological level of each theater lies on the shoulders of the theater director, hand-picked by the respective Party organs and aided by a Party-controlled council elected by the theater employees.

In preparing their annual repertoires the theater directors must follow the directives issued by the Ministry of Education and Culture. As in the case of motion pictures, the prescribed formula calls primar-ily for plays with an appropriate ideological message. Apart from the customary Soviet and other "progressive" foreign plays, high priority is assigned to contemporary native dramas dealing with suitable themes from socialist construction and abiding by the rules of socialist realism. However, as revealed by recurrent complaints, it is precisely in the last-mentioned category that the communist repertoire-makers run into most trouble. Repeatedly, KSČ spokesmen press playwrights to write plays portraying the glories of the socialist epoch and comedies ridicul-ing the remnants of bourgeois morality. Year after year socialist pledges are undertaken, promising early delivery of plays extolling the virtues of socialism and unmasking the evil schemes of the class enemy. Even definitive state contracts for delivery of such plays are signed on behalf of the State with individual authors.[107] But the results have thus far fallen short of communist expectations, for most of these made-to-order products are so dull and so crudely tendentious that they often defeat the very purpose for which they have been ordered.[108]

As in the case of motion picture houses, the network of live theaters has been expanded. By 1959 there were seventy-eight permanent theaters—twenty-six more than in 1937—and they staged 27,655 performances.[109] Similarly, theater attendance rose to 12.56 million by 1958, to 12.8 million in 1959, and almost 13 million in 1960 as against 5 million in 1937. However, as borne out by communist complaints,

---

[107] *ibid.*, November 1, 1951.

[108] *Pravda*, August 1, 1953; *Rudé právo*, October 18 and 25, 1953; *Svobodné slovo*, October 4, 1953.

[109] Unless otherwise stated, these and following figures on live theaters are taken from *Ročenka*, 1960, p. 463.

the dilemma which the regime encounters in the motion picture field is duplicated in the arena of the live theater. Plays with pro-communist bias are mostly performed before near-empty auditoriums or before "planned" audiences. On the other hand, pre-communist classics and such nonideological modern plays as manage to slip by the censors draw full houses.[110] A theater critic complained bitterly in March 1959 that only 12 percent of Praha's theater-goers went to see original socialist plays whereas the remaining 88 percent preferred showings of dramas which "might have been played even in the bourgeois republic."[111] Hence it seems that only a small minority of the theater-going public is really exposed to indoctrination via the live theater in spite of the regime's persistent efforts to the contrary.

While speaking of the theater it is appropriate to add that not even such a traditionally apolitical entertainment as the circus has been omitted from the all-embracing purview of the communist battle for the mind. Having nationalized the film industry and the live and puppet theater, the government took over all the circuses and reorganized them into a national enterprise under the slogan: "To build the Czechoslovak circus art to such an ideological and artistic level that it may help the cause of socialism."[112] A special law on circuses was issued in 1957 with the avowed purpose of "raising their ideological and artistic level and providing for the artistic and ideological growth of the circus artists."[113]

OTHER MEDIA OF INDOCTRINATION

Since it is inherent in the concept of totalitarianism, especially its communist variety, to use each and every institution for the propagation of its infallible credo, many more instrumentalities could be considered that attend to this all-pervasive task, at least as their secondary mission. This would include the trade unions whose statutes impose on them the duty to raise the ideological level of the workers; the Army enlightenment officers who take care of the correct ideological orientation of the soldiers; and so forth. However, such a discussion would exceed the scope of this chapter which is concerned solely with the indoctrination of the public in general rather than any specific groups. Hence, only three other media of general indoctrination remain to be mentioned in addition to those already listed: the Houses of Culture,

[110] *Zpráva o Československu,* IV, 1 (1953), p. 24; *Rudé právo,* March 24, 1959.
[111] *Rudé právo,* March 20, 1959.
[112] *Práce,* September 14, 1950.
[113] Law No. 82 of December 19, 1957.

the Union of Czechoslovak-Soviet Friendship, and the Society for the Dissemination of Political and Scientific Knowledge.

Patterned after the like-named Soviet institutions, the Houses of Culture are designed to serve as "the unified social-cultural centers of the community."[114] They are established by the respective people's committees in the districts and cities with the approval of the regional people's committee and the Ministry of Education and Culture. According to a communist textbook on administration, the main task of the Houses of Culture is "to provide above all methodical aid to the cultural establishments of their respective areas."[115] In particular, as stated by a new law of 1959, they are to help in improving "the political level and professional qualification of voluntary cultural workers."[116] They form various circles for reading, singing, reciting, amateur acting, and discussion groups for purposes of further political education. They set up cultural brigades, led by Party-chosen cultural activists, which compete with each other in various ideologically motivated activities and carry socialist culture into the rural areas. They coordinate and supervise the activities of numerous cultural clubs established in factories, collective farms, and small villages.

However, all the available information at hand suggests that the Houses of Culture and the factory and village clubs of culture have not yet been developed in Czechoslovakia to the extent found in Soviet Russia or some of the other East European satellites. As revealed during the processing of the new law on cultural work in the National Assembly in July 1959, collective farms, in particular, have been procrastinating in establishing clubs of culture. A 1957 Czechoslovak publication, replete with figures on communist achievements in a wide variety of fields inclusive of culture, was altogether silent about the number of Houses of Culture, although it listed the numbers of theaters, motion picture houses, libraries, museums, and other cultural establishments. The only statistical reference it contained concerning this matter was the statement that one of every 213 citizens was a member of some circle of the clubs of culture in 1956.[117] This means that less than 60,000 of the thirteen and one-quarter million Czechs and Slovaks were members of such clubs in 1956, a very poor ratio indeed. According to the *Czechoslovak Yearbook of Statistics* of 1960 there

[114] *Pravda*, March 2, 1954.
[115] See Pavel Levit, *Správní právo, část zvláštní* (Administrative Law, Special Part), Praha, 1956, p. 326.
[116] Law No. 52 of July 9, 1959.
[117] *Postavení*, 1957.

were 298 Houses of Culture in the entire country in 1959. In addition
to them there were 3,383 "chambers of enlightenment," i.e., assembly
rooms provided with propaganda materials and designed for periodic
indoctrination meetings, 5,889 cultural circles, 761 trade union factory
clubs and 6,424 "red corners."[118]

In contrast to the rather late and comparatively slow development
of the Houses and Clubs of Culture was the quick growth of the massive Union of Czechoslovak-Soviet Friendship which reached 2,200,000
in 1952 and made the Union the second biggest mass organization,
surpassed only by the United Trade Union movement.[119] As its name
indicates, the Union is designed to contribute to the victory of communism by extolling the virtues of the Soviet system and thus fostering
the desire to follow the Soviet way. As emphasized by the KSČ spokesmen, "the Union must . . . explain to the broadest masses of our
people the leading and decisive role of the USSR in the struggle for
peace . . . . Through its activities the Union can help beat off effectively reactionary anti-Soviet propaganda. Further, it is the task of the
Union to acquaint the working people with Soviet experiences, propagate to the utmost the inexhaustible wealth of Soviet science, technology, and culture among the workers, especially in factories and villages
. . . . Simultaneously, the Union must help to unfold the fight against
cosmopolitanism and servile bowing to the capitalist West . . . ."[120]

In pursuance of this mission the Union and its huge network of
branch offices throughout the country engage in an array of activities.
They organize lectures, conferences, and discussions on various Soviet
topics; exhibitions of Soviet art and achievements. They sponsor
visits of Soviet writers and scientists, performances by Soviet artists
and showings of Soviet films. They propagate Soviet gramophone
records, books and magazines of which 1,057 were imported in 1958
for 300,000 subscribers.[121] They establish and take care of "Soviet
corners" in factory and other libraries and club rooms and keep them
well supplied with current Russian books and periodicals. They initiate
various quiz programs with questions on Soviet affairs and reward
the winners with "valuable books."[122] Their activities culminate in the
Month of Czechoslovak-Soviet Friendship held annually in November,

[118] *Ročenka*, 1960, p. 468.
[119] *Rudé právo*, July 13, 1952. The membership stood at 2,150,000 by the end
of 1959. *Rudé právo*, December 19, 1959.
[120] *ibid.*, July 13, 1952.
[121] *Rudé právo*, October 19, 1958.
[122] *Lidové noviny*, November 3, 1951.

the month of the "Great October Socialist Revolution." But the main undertaking of the Union is undoubtedly the huge network of Russian language courses. Year after year it organizes between 10,000 to 19,000 study circles attended by 130,000 to 300,000 people in all parts of Czechoslovakia.[123] It also sponsors supplementary Russian courses on the radio. In 1953 it even prevailed on the streetcar conductors to hang out each week posters with two *Azbuka* letters so that the passengers could learn the Russian alphabet while traveling to and from work.[124]

While the Union of Czechoslovak-Soviet Friendship is a mass organization in the fullest sense of the word and strives after maximum membership, the Society for the Dissemination of Political and Scientific Knowledge is rather an elitist group. Like its Soviet name-sake, it is composed mainly of scientists, technical intelligentsia, writers, artists, cultural workers, and an admixture of selected "inno-vators" and shockworkers from among the factory and collective farm laborers. Unlike most other communist instruments which seek to serve ideological pills with sugar coating, the Society administers them straight and does not attempt to conceal its strictly Marxist-Leninist ware. The Society's role and major purposes were well explained in Kopecký's keynote speech to its constituent assembly in June 1952:

" . . . in developing our educational and enlightenment activities among the masses we have thus far lacked an institution which would secure a broad and systematic cooperation of the workers in our public life and the workers in our science . . . . It is a great and important task of the Society . . . to contribute to the propagation and popular-ization of the scientific understanding of socialism through a systematic educational work . . . . There are many people who do not yet fully understand what a tremendous social revolution has taken place in our country; they do not realize that . . . the expropriation of the means of production . . . is a factor which cannot be reversed and which takes effect under the impact of social forces . . . . If our people will understand socialism in this scientific fashion as a higher develop-mental stage of the social order, they will gain clarity also concerning

[123] *Rudé právo,* May 12, 1951, May 25 and July 7, 1952, December 8, 1953, January 21, 1954, and August 26, 1960. According to the last-mentioned magazine a total of 2,448,207 persons attended the 166,394 courses organized in the eleven years ending with the 1959-1960 school year. However, the number fell to 10,840 courses, attended by 134,471 persons in 1959-1960 and to 10,600 courses at-tended by "over 133,000 citizens" in 1960-1961. See *Rudé právo,* August 26, 1960, and *Svobodné slovo,* December 23, 1960.

[124] *Práce,* August 22, 1953.

other questions . . . the question of freedom, democracy, state, legal order, morality, culture, etc. They will gain clarity concerning the leading role of our native Party, the Communist Party of Czechoslovakia . . . . It is a matter of disarming completely the reactionaries and offering thorough information on developments on the international scale; making those who vacillate, who are confused and prejudiced, realize that it is a crime and high treason to rely on the military plans of American imperialists, that it makes no sense to oppose the forces of progress and that it is sensible to accept the new forms of life, to join in the construction of our Republic as a socialist Republic . . . ."[125]

Guided by these high Party directives the Society wages a merciless battle against such pernicious isms as cosmopolitanism, nationalism, the "leftovers of the Masaryk and Beneš ideology," and all the other "remnants of obsolete thinking."[126] But its most crucial task is, in Kopecký's words, "the struggle against religious obscurantism, superstition, and against the reactionary concepts of the churches . . . ."[127] To enable the Society to carry out more effectively these important functions its creators organized it into a number of sections each of which is assigned a certain field of operations. Following a "central thematical plan" prepared by the Society's Presidium and Central Committee, these sections work out suitable lectures and send out lecturers to deliver them and to lead discussions with various groups. The Society holds national and regional ideological conferences on political, philosophical, economic, and other topics; organizes exhibitions and showings of documentary films "unmasking the reactionary role of the church" and "exposing other pernicious influences of the bourgeois past"; cooperates with radio, film, and other people's democratic institutions and mass organizations with a view toward popularizing Marxism-Leninism; publishes various pamphlets, books, and magazines designed to raise the public's ideological level.

RESULTS AND PROBLEMS

Reserving once again the evaluation of the crucial issue of the making of the new communistic man for consideration in the concluding chapter, what have thus far been the other results of the communist battle for the adult mind?

[125] *Rudé právo,* June 22, 1952.
[126] *Literární noviny,* June 28, 1952.
[127] *ibid.,* and *News,* 1, 8 (1952), p. 37.

To begin with, the system of controls over, and the degree of regimentation of, all the media of adult indoctrination follow closely those of the USSR; and so does the over-all pattern of development. When regimentation was at its peak in the Soviet Union, so was it in Czechoslovakia. The mollifying effects and after-effects of the post-Stalin thaw were much the same in Czechoslovakia as in Russia. And when Khrushchëv and his associates began to shorten the leash again, the KSČ leaders did likewise.

The Soviet trends are also reflected in the degree to which the controls are applied to the various indoctrination media. They are most complete in broadcasting and in libraries. Being administered directly by the State under the supreme and constant direction of the Ministry of Education and Culture, these two institutions remained under strict control even during the post-Stalin relaxation. This is true also of the Society for the Dissemination of Political and Scientific Knowledge which belongs among the most orthodox and most doctrinaire of the Party's transmission belts.

Next in line in the thoroughness of communist control are the newspapers. But for a few flashes of nonconformism at the height of the post-Stalin thaw, the Czechoslovak daily press has ever since the communist coup of 1948 kept within the prescribed bounds of Party directives, even though it did so with an obvious lack of enthusiasm. The situation is well characterized by a critic who dared to speak out in 1957: "It looks as if journalists—personalities with judgment and opinions of their own—have already died out in our midst, as if there were no more voices speaking for the people . . . . It seems that there exists only a formless mass of employees of newspapers who are unable to rise above and beyond the bulletins of the Czechoslovak Press Bureau."[128] Although this prostration of the journalistic profession could be attained and can be maintained solely through the Party's absolute powers of coercion and repression, the communist enslavement of the Fourth Estate was undoubtedly facilitated by some of the less desirable pre-communist traditions of Czechoslovak journalism. Since virtually all Czechoslovak daily papers used to be party-owned and no institution of independent columnists ever developed, newspaper editors have always acted mostly as stylists clothing other people's thoughts into attractive phraseological garb. An independent editor-crusader like some American newspaper colum-

[128] An article by Štefan Drug in *Kulturný život,* February 2, 1957.

nists and courageous local editors was rare in Czechoslovakia even prior to the communist seizure of power.

Although the motion picture industry is as fully government-controlled as the radio, it has nevertheless withstood the onslaught of ideological regimentation somewhat better. Having had no previous experience in the field of film production, the Party controllers have evidently found it more difficult to impose their will there than in the operation of the air waves. As a consequence, Western influence and the traditional concept of the motion picture as a means of entertainment rather than a medium of indoctrination have lingered on despite persistent communist efforts to weed them out. The Czechoslovak film industry had to be warned repeatedly against such gross ideological *faux pas* as a "superficial and narrow portrayal of the role of the KSČ," "inaccurate portraiture of the types of the middle peasants and of the village rich" or plain "escaping from reality."[129] As revealed once again in February 1959 by the Minister of Education and Culture in his address to the national congress of the Czechoslovak film producers "there still remain many . . . who proclaim that the [film] art should only be a testimony of the period . . . a passive and objective picture of our life . . . " and thus flout the prescribed formula of "Party-mindedness."[130]

Similar difficulties confront the regime in the live theater area which continues, according to communist complaints, to be plagued by unhealthy individualism and leftovers of bourgeois attitudes. In spite of stiff communist controls the theaters still somehow manage to show socially neutral plays without an appropriate ideological message.[131] One way of doing this is to include in the repertoire a disproportionate number of classical plays. Another method, scored recently by a Czech communist broadcast as "a clever move designed to circumvent the crux of socialist problems," is the "exaggerated staging of progressive plays by authors writing within a capitalist society."[132]

But the most persistent dilemma which the KSČ leadership has to cope with is the continued rebelliousness among writers and artists. Not even during the worst repressive years of the Stalin era did the

[129] *Lidové noviny*, January 4, 1951; *Literární noviny*, October 11, 1952, and January 17, 1953; *Mladá fronta*, February 22, 1959.

[130] *Mladá fronta*, February 24, 1959.

[131] *Pravda*, August 1, 1953; *East Europe*, 8, 4 (1959), p. 50; *Československý zpravodaj*, No. 239, April 2, 1959.

[132] Radio Praha, February 13, 1959, as monitored by Free Europe. *East Europe*, 8, 4 (1959), p. 50.

regime succeed in disciplining writers and artists in any manner comparable to the subjection of their journalistic colleagues.[133] As with other groups, there were and are among them individuals prepared to trade their artistic integrity for the glitter of publicity and material advantages reserved for such authors, painters, and sculptors as are willing to bow to Party wishes. However, with a few exceptions, only second-rate writers and artists seem thus far to have succumbed to the temptation. The most talented among them continue to resist the Party's carrot-or-stick tactics as best they can. While the cultural repression was at its worst between 1949 and 1952 they resorted primarily to various devices of passive resistance, such as choosing safer historical or foreign topics rather than contemporary native subjects, seeking refuge in intimate lyrical poetry and other ideologically neutral creations, or in a conspiracy of silence. When the rigid Zhdanov line gave way under the impact of the liberalization trends of 1953-1956, they promptly shed their escapism and came out with a veritable torrent of works written, painted, and sculptured in flagrant disregard of every precept of the socialist realism.[134] Nor has the radical stiffening of Party controls in 1958-1960 met thus far with much success in subduing the writers' and artists' oppositional mood. Evidently, of all the groups with which the regime has to battle in its indoctrination efforts, the writers and artists are the hardest to regiment.

Another major impediment of the communist endeavors to create a new species of communistic man is the boredom which seems to be an inseparable bedfellow of all the indoctrination media. Peddling ideology is seldom a hilarious venture, but judging from incessant complaints even on the part of communist spokesmen, there is evidently more tedium in the communist processes of collective brainwashing than can be condoned even by such humorless fellows as the KSČ leaders. Realizing the serious handicap implicit in the dullness of the indoctrination diet fed to their subjects, the communist leaders have striven to make it more palatable. In particular, while persisting in their emphasis on the ideological message, they have repeatedly urged writers, playwrights, librettists, and film-makers to abandon

---

[133] For complaints about the writer's resistance during the Stalin era see Kopecký's speech to the Ninth Party Congress, *Lidové noviny*, May 27, 1949; *Tvorba*, April 19, 1950 and January 18, 1951; *Rudé právo*, June 28, 1950; *Lidové noviny*, October 22, 1950.

[134] For the continued rebellion of Czechoslovak artists see *Československý zpravodaj*, No. 286, March 15, 1960, No. 304, July 19, 1960; *East Europe*, 9, 5 (1960), pp. 6ff.

schematism, bring into their works more vitality and, above all, inject into them more joy and more humor.[135] But all such efforts have borne only meager results, and it is not difficult to see why. While asking for more wit and humor, Party spokesmen have never relented in their condemnation of humor for humor's sake and never tired stressing that "the arrows of satire must hit the real enemies," but must stop at the Party's own door.[136] "On no account can satire be permitted to ridicule the activities of the Party," warned Kopecký. "Not a shadow of blame or ridicule must touch our glorious native Party which deserves to be esteemed and loved to the utmost."[137] Under such narrow limitations it is hardly surprising that, for instance, no prize could be awarded to any one of the 280 works which had been entered for a 1954 comedy contest.[138] As long as it is safe, in the words of an editor of *Dikobraz,* to direct barbs at the doorkeeper but extremely risky to joke about a Cabinet minister, the constructive humor is bound to suffer from anemia; and boredom will vitiate the effectiveness of communist indoctrination through the media meant for entertainment.

This is very apparent from the reaction of the general public which expresses its displeasure with the insipid ideological diet by avoiding it wherever and whenever it can. Judging by recurrent communist complaints, no sector of the battle for the mind has escaped the adverse effects of these negative attitudes which amount at times to a truly massive passive resistance. The most telling illustration thereof is offered by the general public's selectivity as to what books to buy and to read and what showings of plays and films to attend. The stubborn refusal of the Czechoslovak man-in-the-street to see motion pictures and plays with the correct ideological message and his sweeping preference for nontendentious screen and live theater entertainment have already been mentioned. A similar situation prevails in book buying and reading. Despite continuous promotions and sales campaigns, substantial quantities of communist literature remain habitually unsold. On the other hand, whenever a book by a non-communist author is published, the whole edition is sold out in a matter of days,

---

[135] Kopecký's speech at the Party's Central Committee in December 1953, *Rudé právo,* December 13, 1953; *Rudé právo,* December 6, 1953; Novotný's speech at the KSČ Congress, *Rudé právo,* June 12, 1954; *Literární noviny,* March 20, 1954.

[136] *Kulturný život,* July 17, 1954; *Československý přehled,* v, 3 (1958), pp. 20ff.

[137] *Rudé právo,* June 14, 1954.

[138] *L'ud,* November 2, 1954.

as has been the case with Hemingway, Steinbeck, Sagan, Brain, Čapek, and others.[139] This "literary snobism," as the regime calls it, is widespread and makes people buy such books, allowed to be published mostly in small editions, at black-market prices. It also makes them pay fantastic prices for some pre-communist books which are now on the index, such as the works of Thomas Masaryk and Eduard Beneš. Furthermore, recent information from Czechoslovakia shows that, to defeat the efforts of communist censors, younger intellectuals have recently been embarking more and more upon the device of study and reading circles of their own.[140] Meeting in inconspicuous small groups in private homes, they gather and pool whatever banned literature they can lay their hands on. Each of the participants selects certain themes on which he concentrates and shares his findings with other members of the circle.

Nor are the "wrong" reading habits limited to the intelligentsia; they are deeply embedded among the working people as well, though in a less sophisticated form. Very illustrative evidence to that effect was supplied, for instance, by a zealous Slovak Communist who checked incognito what the working people read while traveling to work on a train to Bratislava, the capital of Slovakia, and published his "shocking" findings in a Slovak literary magazine.[141] To his bitter disappointment he found no one on the crowded train reading any Soviet authors, Gottwald's works, or any worthy product of socialist realism. Instead, walking from one compartment to another, he saw young workers of both sexes reading proscribed paper-back thrillers and love stories from pre-communist days, some of them even cut out and carefully preserved from old newspapers, such as *Montana Mounts a Horse, The Pious Gunman, Half-Time: One to Nothing, Murder by the Alphabet, Magda's Fate, The White Lady of Levoča,* or *Two Loves of Franz Joseph.*

Evidently, twelve years after the communist seizure of power, widespread "escapism" and passive resistance still continue to hamper KSČ propagandists in their indoctrination of the adult mind.

[139] *Práce,* January 6, 1959; *Svět práce,* April 2, 1960.
[140] *Československý zpravodaj,* No. 215, October 9, 1958.
[141] Josef Váh in *Kulturný život,* No. 29, 1954, *Československý přehled,* i, 9 (1954), pp. 18-19.

CHAPTER XXI

CONCLUSION AND PROSPECTS

WHAT THEN, are the main trends and characteristics of Czechoslovak communism at the completion of its first twelve years of rule? What conjectures, if any, may be ventured about its further prospects?

One of the most conspicuous trends, and one of Czechoslovak communism's chief headaches, has been a steady deterioration in the relationship between the Party's leadership and its rank and file. The Party entered the era of the dictatorship of the proletariat in February 1948 in a festive mood of triumphant unity. Although some of its members had their private doubts about some aspects of the 1948 *putsch,* most of the Party membership stood wholeheartedly behind their leaders and were genuinely excited about a new era where the wicked capitalists would no longer be able to sabotage comrade Gottwald's promising plans for a better future. Even the opportunistic "mayflowers," who had swelled the Party's ranks in and after May 1945 for purely selfish reasons, rallied round the Party leaders in eager expectation of the spoils.

However, as ordinary Party members came to realize more and more that, far from bringing the implementation of the rosy promises of yester-years, the Party's acquisition of the monopoly of power actually made matters worse in many respects, the initial intoxication gave way to growing disillusionment. The humiliating spectacle of the KSČ chiefs cringing before Moscow and willing to sacrifice Czechoslovak interests to those of the Kremlin badly shattered members' confidence in their Party superiors. So did the purges of high-ranking Communists, such as Slánský and Clementis, once acclaimed as the best sons of the Party and suddenly found guilty of the worst crimes against the communist cause. Nor could the situation be improved in any way by the few post-Stalin concessions which were far too obviously intended by the KSČ leaders as a temporary lengthening of the political leash until it could be shortened again.

Thus the one-time strong bonds of Party unity, born from the common struggle for the establishment of the coveted dictatorship of the proletariat and based to a high degree on the voluntary subordination of the members, were in the course of the twelve years under review replaced with a deep-seated alienation between the leaders and the led. Outwardly, unity remains, and seems to a superficial onlooker to have been even enhanced. But its very substance has radically changed as the elements that hold the Party together now are fear and opportunism rather than voluntary and genuine acceptance.

That is also why inner-Party democracy, which had found expression in the Party's proceedings in prewar days, virtually vanished after 1948. Although a full-fledged one-man rule never developed within the KSČ, not even at the peak of Klement Gottwald's era, the leadership of the Party has been ever since the coup in the hands of a narrow, self-perpetuating oligarchy of a small group of chiefs sitting in the Party's Political Bureau.

The chasm between the leaders and the rank and file of the Party is paralleled and further aggravated by the gulf that has developed between the Party and the broad masses, particularly the workers. This is especially significant because Czechoslovakia had by far the highest ratio of industrial workers of all the countries behind the Iron Curtain. Most of them had backed the Communist Party, impressed as they were by its glorification of the working class and by its sweeping promises of a workers' millenium in the era of communism. Thus the KSČ took over in February of 1948 not only as the biggest communist party of the satellite orbit, but also as a party enjoying a massive support of the majority of industrial workers who thought that they could lose nothing and gain a good deal from the communist power monopoly.

However, twelve years of experience with communism in practice have proved their hopeful expectations to have been mostly wishful thinking. As a result, growing disaffection vis-à-vis the Party has spread among the great majority of the Czechoslovak workers. Except for the open rebellion in Plzeň and riots in several other areas in 1953, prompted by the drastic currency reform of that year, the workers' disaffection has not acquired in Czechoslovakia the explosive character which triggered the Polish and Hungarian revolts of 1956. Rather, it manifests itself in passive resistance, occasional sitdown strikes, widespread absenteeism from work and functions, and, most of all, recurrent demands for the fulfillment of the Party's many abortive promises, demands that the Party leaders scornfully reject as social democratism and anarcho-syndicalism. Nor can it be said that the opposition of the working class is as thorough and unequivocal as that of the peasantry or the former middle and upper classes. For the workers' disappointment tends to be partially offset by certain positive improvements, such as the elevation of the workers' social status, the premiums given to working-class origin in various ways, and the fact that the living standards of the workers has withstood the strictures of the communist system better than those of the other classes.

Nonetheless, the workers' disenchantment is very real and constitutes a grave long-term, although so far only latent, danger to the Party which would perish if it lost connection with the masses of the toilers, as stressed again and again by communist leaders from Lenin to Khrushchëv. While in February 1948 the Party could count on a more or less active support of a majority of the working class, and this was its main political trump next to Soviet backing, the same is no longer true today.

A similar loss of faith in the Party and the virtues of Marxism-Leninism has occurred among the intellectuals. Taken as a whole, only a small portion of Czechoslovakia's intellectuals succumbed to the lure of communism. Among those who did, most conspicuous and most numerous were writers and artists of previous leftist inclinations, including some of the most reputed Czechoslovak men of letters. They were impressed by communist assurances of a new wonderful era of true creative freedom and spiritual and cultural regeneration once capitalism with its alleged sordid profit motive as a decisive criterion of cultural values had been done away with. However, the higher their hopes, the more shattering their disillusionment when they became aware, soon after the communist coup, of the abysmal contrast between the pre-1948 lofty promises and the post-1948 harsh realities. As František Halas, a communist poet and one of the most prominent figures of the Czechoslovak Parnassus, said in the essay written shortly before his death in 1949, "Instead of a varied and exacting culture came something unbelievably poor, monotonous, and low . . . ." That is why, of all the groups opposing the communist regime, the writers have been the most outspoken, the most persistent, and the most determined in their criticism and heretical behavior in spite of continuous communist admonitions, warnings, and reprisals.

Yet another major failure of Czechoslovak communism in the first twelve years of its rule has been its signal lack of attraction for the youth. As shown in the present volume, the Party has constantly run into difficulties in its recruitment of young people. By the Party's own admission, the communist-sponsored Czechoslovak Youth Union has been in a state of stagnation. Although an unswerving loyalty to the cause of communism has been a prerequisite for admission to any institution of higher learning ever since the establishment of the dictatorship of the proletariat, the entire student body of Czechoslovak universities, with negligible exceptions, revealed in the forceful and unequivocal resolutions of 1956 how negative the attitude of the cream of the Czechoslovak youth, from which the new generation of leaders is supposed to be developed, is toward things communistic. Private study circles of young intelligentsia which have been spreading throughout the country in recent years for the purpose of merging and sharing whatever private information can be obtained on the scientific, literary, political, and cultural trends in the Free World, point in the same direction. Although much less sophisticated, negative attitudes toward the regime and indifference to Marxist-Leninist ideology are evident also among the working youth, not to speak of young peasants. As reported in unison by Western visitors to Czechoslovakia and corroborated by Czechoslovak non-communist sources as well as complaints of communist leaders, the majority of the Czechoslovak youth are seized by a truly insatiable hunger for almost everything coming from the West, especially America. It is one of the strangest phenomena of the Czechoslovak situation that the one country which is supposed to be hated most, America, continues instead to be the object of general admiration.

Thus it seems that the colossal indoctrination efforts unfolded in Czechoslovak schools and supported by other media of communist propaganda have so far transformed only a small minority of Czechoslovak youth into true believers in communism. Unavoidably, the communist school is fairly successful in withholding from children objective data on life in pre-communist Czechoslovakia and in the capitalist world in general. Despite cautious parental endeavors to the contrary, schools manage to plant in children's malleable minds a picture distorted to fit communist needs. But as children attain the age of reason and are increasingly confronted with everyday practice, doubts begin to creep in. The natural curiosity of the young mind sets to work and, sooner or later, the school-injected illusions are worn out by recurrent friction with the contrasting facts of life under a totalitarian system. To be sure, some of these new communistic men, turned out by today's Czechoslovak schools, never shed the impact of their childhood's indoctrination, especially, if they attain positions satisfying their personal ambitions. Others free themselves only of a part of their addiction to the doctrine and often hover in a strange state of ideological weightlessness, no longer sure of where the truth ends and falsehood begins.

But all available evidence suggests that an overwhelming majority of Czechoslovakia's young men and women above the age of sixteen are definitely non-communist. Although they may know progressively less and less about pre-communist Czechoslovakia and their knowledge of the Free World may be sketchy and inaccurate, they are well aware of what they are denied under the communist regime. Above all, they resent the absence of what they instinctively covet most: freedom— freedom to express themselves, to display their suppressed individuality; freedom to read whatever they wish, or not to read; freedom to enjoy themselves the way they like and to use their scarce leisure as they please without the communist mentors breathing down their necks; genuine freedom to choose their occupations; freedom not to join, and not to attend the meetings of, the Youth Union and other voluntary-compulsory groupings without being classified, berated, and penalized as reactionaries. It is precisely this elemental longing of the youth for freedom and self-expression that constitutes the most potent barrier to the communist efforts to create a new species of robot-like communistic men.

While the four major problems considered so far in this chapter have plagued the KSČ as much as the other communist parties of the Soviet orbit, and in some instances possibly even more, the opposite is true of revisionism. For reasons explained in Chapter VI there have been considerably fewer genuine revisionists in Czechoslovakia than in Poland or Hungary, and most probably, in proportion to Party membership, less than anywhere else behind the Iron Curtain. Most of those whom the KSČ leaders brand as revisionists do not desire merely to revise certain outdated tenets of Marxism-Leninism and thus restore its vigor, but want to replace it with something very close to democratic socialism of a Western European type. Czechoslovak revisionists, however, are sorely lacking in the caliber of leadership, courage, and missionary zeal which lent such an impetus to the revisionist cause in Poland and Hungary. They pay lip service to Marx and Lenin and assert that they wish to streamline their theories only because they feel that to behave thus is a lesser risk than to offer direct opposition. Hence, revisionism as a separate ideological challenge to orthodox Marxism-Leninism from within the doctrine's confines poses less of a danger for the KSČ leaders than is indicated by their incessant antirevisionist tirades.

Thus Czechoslovak communism has lost substantial ground on precisely the most crucial sector of its operations, the battle for the mind. After twelve years of continuous cradle-to-grave indoctrination there are today in Czechoslovakia considerably fewer believers in Marxism-Leninism than when Klement Gottwald led his Party to victory in February 1948. In view of the gigantic communist effort spent on making new communistic men, outside observers find this sometimes hard to believe and tend to mistake outward conformism for genuine acceptance. But on no other aspect of the Czechoslovak situation is there a greater consensus among those who are familiar with true conditions inside communist Czechoslovakia. Naturally, this does not mean that under the present regime there are not things which find favor with some segments of the population and in a few instances, such as social welfare, with the people as a whole. It does mean that a substantial majority of the Czechoslovak people of all walks of life would, if given freedom to choose, overwhelmingly reject the Marxist-Leninist system in favor of Western democracy combined with a substantial amount of social welfare and industrial socialization.

The fading ideological appeal of Marxism-Leninism has contributed greatly to the inner weakness of the Party and made its continuation in power contingent upon coercion and semi-coercion rather than genuine persuasion. This inner weakness has in its turn enhanced the KSČ's subservience to the Kremlin which has become the trade-mark of Czechoslovak communism and has withstood all the temptations of the post-Stalin era. Since the effectiveness of satellite power to coerce rests in the last resort upon Soviet backing, the KSČ's failure in the battle for the mind and the inner weakness resulting therefrom necessarily increases the dependence of its leaders upon the Soviet Party chiefs. Keenly aware of the degree to which their political survival may hinge on Soviet aid, should their subjects or a rebellious Party faction rise against them, the KSČ leaders consider it a vital necessity at all times to keep within the good graces of whoever disposes of the Soviet might.

This does not mean, of course, that the members of the ruling oligarchy in Czechoslovakia follow Soviet directives solely because of this. It must not be forgotten that they are devout Marxist-Leninists and have joined the communist movement because of strong beliefs in its cause. They have worked and fought for communism their whole lives and staked their personal and political fortunes on its victory. They are fully aware of the importance of iron discipline and of the political value of unity. They know how much communism's strength depends on the strength of the Soviet Union. Therefore, there is no doubt that they see eye to eye with the Kremlin on most of the major aspects of communist ideology, policy, and strategy, and that they willingly sacrifice some of their immediate interests in the name of the unity of the communist camp.

Nonetheless, this still leaves many instances, mentioned throughout this volume, where the Czechoslovak way would have been much more to the advantage of communism in Czechoslovakia, and possibly even of communism in general, than the prescribed Soviet methods which are often unsuited to specific Czechoslovak circumstances. It is in these instances that the behavior of the KSČ leaders has been and is, more often than not, conditioned primarily by their desire to please and satisfy Moscow, an opportunistic desire dictated by their sense of weakness vis-à-vis the Czechoslovak masses and their own Party's rank and file, rather than by inner convictions.

This same weakness accounts more than anything else for the relative dearth of post-Stalin concessions in Czechoslovakia which has lagged in that respect well behind her two Central European people's democratic neighbors, Hungary and Poland. Their temperament and past experience have provided the leaders of Czechoslovak communism with a built-in tendency to gravitate toward a subtler, more civilized form of communism than is its cruder Soviet variety. Hence, when Khrushchëv's 1955-1956 emphasis on the different roads to socialism pierced the all-embracing uniformity of the Stalin era a welcome opportunity seemed to beckon for the introduction of a specific Czechoslovak way. Had the communist rulers of Czechoslovakia felt stronger at home, had they enjoyed a solid support of the majority of their Party membership and a general confidence of the Czechoslovak workers, they might have taken advantage of the discretion allowed them by the new Soviet leadership to make communism more palatable for their subjects by granting more meaningful and more lasting concessions than the few stopgap alleviations which they actually permitted. That they did not do so must, therefore, be credited primarily to their fear lest more substantial concessions might be exploited to press for further, even more sweeping reforms. They feared that more and more Party members might have joined in the liberalization stampede until it would have become impossible for the dwindling stratum of the Party faithful to arrest it.

The split personality of Czechoslovak communism, pushed by its inner weakness into the embrace of the Kremlin and yet gravitating instinctively toward its Western past, reveals itself, particularly, in the arena of formal government. While setting up a one-party monopoly of power, the KSČ leaders have sought to retain as many political institutions of the pre-communist era as they possibly could, and even to preserve such political traditions of the past as were not incompatible with the Party's supremacy. The communist Ninth-of-May Constitution of 1948 took over a great many clauses and much of the libertarian phraseology of its 1920 predecessor. Its Bill of Rights was more elaborate than the corresponding provisions of the other satellite constitutions. In spite of the incorporation of a number of eastern elements the main political provisions of the Ninth-of-May Constitution resembled the Western European constitutional pattern more than the Soviet and other satellite constitutions. The governmental framework established on its basis was parliamentary in form although it was totalitarian in actual application. In striking contrast to the general pattern prevalent behind the Iron Curtain, individual Presidency along typical Western European lines was retained in communist Czechoslovakia and the whole scheme of executive-legislative relations was copied from the prewar Constitution with only minor variations. Although deprived of every bit of political power and convened almost as rarely as its Soviet counterpart, the Czechoslovak legislature continued to differ from its Soviet equivalent in some of the formalities retained from earlier days, such as a rather regular use of standing committees and parliamentary clubs of the several permitted parties. For several years after the communist seizure of power the judiciary as well as the system of public prosecution continued to differ quite substantially from the Soviet pattern in their structure, if not in their employment as weapons of class struggle. Similarly, while emphasizing the role of the school as a principal vehicle of indoctrination, the early communist school laws adhered fairly close to native concepts of education and virtually ignored the Soviet example.

In later years the process of gradual sovietization gathered momentum and more and more facets of the Czechoslovak political system were rearranged after the Soviet fashion. Nevertheless, at the end of twelve years of communist rule, it still retains a few features which distinctly echo the pre-communist past. While the operational pattern of the Czechoslovak political system and its relationship is definitely determined by the Leninist transmission-belt theory, it remains, insofar as its formal structure is concerned, the least sovietized of the satellite systems. This continues to be true, though to a much smaller degree, even after the further major sovietization enacted by the new 1960 Constitution.

In view of the notorious submissiveness of the KSČ leaders to Moscow their comparative hesitancy in refashioning Czechoslovakia's political institutions after the Soviet image is seemingly paradoxical. It can be accounted for to a large extent by tactical considerations. Since the main concern of Czechoslovak Communists after the seizure of power in 1948 was to consolidate their position and secure, if they could, the support of a majority among the Czechoslovak people, it would not have been politic on their part to start breaking up established traditions prematurely and to sovietize too quickly. Nevertheless, at least a part of their reluctance to resort to a wholesale sovietization of Czechoslovak political institutions stems from their links, partly conscious and partly subconscious, with Western traditions which have left an indelible mark on Czechoslovak communism.

This combination of Western parliamentary form with Marxist-Leninist totalitarian substance is the only contribution of at least a certain originality which the Czechoslovak Communists have made to political theory, and even this contribution has been sharply depreciated by the stepped-up sovietization of recent years. Apart from that, the KSČ's theoreticians have followed faithfully the official Soviet line not only in the field of Marxist-Leninist ideology, but also in theoretical aspects of government. The studies of political science and law published in Czechoslovakia since the Communists took over abound in adulatory references to the appropriate Soviet authorities and are mere elaborations of the precepts developed by the Soviet science of politics from which the Czechoslovak theoreticians do not dare to depart.

Turning, finally, to the communist record in the economic sphere, one finds a mixed pattern of successes and failures. Impressive results attained in capital goods production contrast with the far more modest achievements in consumer goods output, while the results in the field of services to consumer and in agriculture must be designated as miserable. An over-all comparison of Czechoslovak economy with that of the capitalist countries at a comparable stage of development reveals that communist Czechoslovakia is still far from her avowed goal of overtaking the most advanced capitalist countries. Moreover, the communist mania for outproducing capitalism has cost the Czechoslovak man-in-the-street heavily in terms of economic and professional regimentation and neglect of his material needs. Despite several advantages in social welfare benefits, the average Czechoslovak citizen's standard of living after twelve years of communist rule appears no higher than it was before the War; and it is definitely lower than the standard of living enjoyed in comparable non-communist countries of Central and Western Europe.

On the basis of developments of Czechoslovak communism in the first twelve years of its rule, what can be said about its future prospects? While the answer must necessarily be speculative, a scrutiny of the results and trends of the twelve years under review permits at least an educated, though limited, guess.

Since the victory or defeat of communism hinges in the last resort on whether or not it can create a new species of communistic man, it is appropriate to look, first of all, at its prospects in this all-important battle for the mind. They do not look good. To be sure, a few factors helping the communist indoctrination are likely to become somewhat more effective with the passage of time. The spectacular increase in video viewing and the fact that, unlike radio, television is secure from foreign competition, are bound to enhance its value as a vehicle of indoctrination. The spread of a wired radio system and an increased output of cheaper radio sets, good only for local listening, may reduce listening to foreign broadcasts which are today the most important source of outside interference with the regime's monopoly of information. The iron laws of life expectancy will gradually remove from the scene living witnesses of the prewar era able to contradict most effectively Marxist-Leninist distortions on conditions in precommunist Czechoslovakia. The persistent efforts to recruit new teachers with a correct class profile will in due time undoubtedly raise the ratio of dependable propagandists of the new faith among the faculties and thus enable schools to do a somewhat better job of brainwashing.

But none of this is likely to conquer the overwhelming anti-communist forces deeply entrenched in the most impregnable of all fortresses, the citadel of the mind. The centuries-old Western orientation that permeates every aspect of Czechoslovak culture and is aided by the country's geographical proximity to the Free World as well as the devices of modern technology; the keen awareness of the ever-present contrast between the rosy promises and the drab reality of everyday life; the boredom inherent in indoctrination and the self-defeating nature of its excessive use; the strong Czech and Slovak nationalism that understandably turns against a doctrine advocated by men generally considered to be in the service of a foreign oppressor; persistent hopes in the ultimate defeat of communism so characteristic of a nation which has seen so many regimes come and go, hopes that may give way to fits of despondency at times of slumping fortunes but are ever ready to erupt when another chance seems to beckon—all these factors will continue to present formidable obstacles to the regime's endeavors to produce a new communist progeny. But above all, these endeavors will be thwarted in the future as they were in the past twelve years by man's attachment to, and irresistible need of, freedom which, as amply documented by the annals of modern history, may be temporarily misled or pushed underground, but never really destroyed.

Nor is it at all probable that these mighty factors operating against communism will be weakened in any decisive manner by an improvement in material well-being. When they are eventually attained, the long overdue better living standards may for a while bribe some of the more lukewarm critics into a sort of political and ideological neutralism. But they cannot overcome the resentment caused by totalitarian suppression of freedom. On the contrary, once the worst worries over the daily existence are over and somewhat more comfortable material conditions develop, freedom tends to acquire a higher priority and its absence is resented even more. This seems to be borne out by events in Soviet Russia proper where disaffection toward the regime has been gaining ground at a time of *rising* living standards and the most persistent demands for more freedom and less regimentation are heard precisely among the strata enjoying a degree of material well-being that is well above the Soviet average.

The inability to convert the great majority of Czechs and Slovaks into genuine believers in Marxism-Leninism condemns the KSČ to an indefinite reliance on coercion as the condition *sine qua non* of its continued power monopoly in the future as it did in the past. In its turn this will continue pushing the KSČ leaders, whether they like it or not, under the control of their protector, the Kremlin. The dependence of the ruling Czechoslovak oligarchs on the Soviet Party is, therefore, likely to remain the most salient trait of Czechoslovak communism in the era of Khrushchëv and beyond it, just as it was under Stalin.

This same inner weakness of Czechoslovak communism will undoubtedly prevent any meaningful democratization in the foreseeable future in the political system or in economics and culture. For the fear lest even minor concessions be exploited to press for bigger ones will not haunt the KSČ leaders any less in the future than it has in the past. Hence, whatever liberalization might occur, will be undertaken strictly within the confines prescribed or suggested by the Kremlin and will be mainly in the nature of opening safety-valves to let out excess steam rather than converting the dictatorship of the proletariat into a true communist democracy and allow the State to "wither away" as prescribed by Marxist precepts.

On the other hand, barring some drastic change of circumstances, a violent uprising against the communist regime is extremely unlikely. It seems to be more unlikely in Czechoslovakia than in any other of Moscow's European satellites. The overcautious, strictly realistic Czech mentality and a corresponding behavioral pattern (explained elsewhere in this study), which was the primary reason for the Czechoslovak *immobilisme* at the time of the Polish and Hungarian revolts, can hardly be expected to change in the near future. Therefore, as long as the Czechoslovak people remain convinced, rightly or wrongly, that Soviet troops would come to the rescue of native Communists in case of necessity, the KSČ leaders can feel relatively safe in the saddle, more so probably than their colleagues elsewhere in the Soviet orbit. In that respect Czechoslovakia presents a striking contrast: outwardly she appears to belong among the most obedient and most subdued of Moscow's satellites and one that the communist rulers seem to have the least trouble to keep under control. Yet, this seemingly unruffled surface hides a whole ocean of latent and at times rumbling anti-communism. Although no positive proof is possible, I am convinced that the ratio of genuine believers in Marxism-Leninism per capita of the population is today lower in Czechoslovakia than in most of the other satellite countries, despite the fact that the ratio of Party membership is higher than anywhere else behind the Iron Curtain.

The fate of Czechoslovak communism is thus intertwined inextricably with the fortunes of its Soviet counterpart. A collapse of communism in Russia would spell, inevitably and with little or no delay, the end of the communist rule in Czechoslovakia. Such would also be the ultimate result should the world balance of power ever be changed to the detriment of Russia so drastically as to exclude a possibility of Soviet intervention for the preservation of communist systems in other countries. Nor is it probable that Marxism-Leninism would survive in Czechoslovakia for any length of time should the very nature of Soviet communism be eventually transformed in such a manner as to preclude the use of Soviet power outside Russia.

As neither of these alternatives seems likely in the near future, Czechoslovakia will most probably remain under the rule of totalitarian communism, and without the benefit of any really meaningful relaxation, for quite some time.

BIBLIOGRAPHY

DOCUMENTARY MATERIALS

Act Relating to the School System and the Training of Teachers in Czechoslovakia, Praha, 1953.

Annuaire International de Statistique Agricole, Rome, 1937.

Annuaire Statistique de la République Tchécoslovaque, Praha, 1938.

Černá kniha kapitalistického hospodaření před únorem (Black Book of the Czechoslovak Economy Prior to February), Praha, 1948.

Československá strana lidová. Pro blaho vlasti, pro vítězství míru: úkoly pracovníků a funkcionářů československé strany lidové po X. sjezdu KSČ (The Czechoslovak People's Party. For the Welfare of the Fatherland, for the Victory of Peace: Tasks of the Workers and Functionaries of the Czechoslovak People's Party after the Tenth Congress of the KSČ), Praha, 1954.

Československá strana lidová. Pro rozkvět vlasti, pro vítězství míru: Projevy a usnesení z budovatelské konference československé strany lidové konané ve dnech 10. a 11. února 1951 (The Czechoslovak People's Party. For the Prosperity of the Fatherland, for the Victory of Peace: Speeches and Resolutions from the Conference of the Czechoslovak People's Party held on February 10 and 11, 1951), Praha, 1951.

Československý Svaz mládeže, Pionýrská organisace ČSM (The Czechoslovak Youth Union, the Pioneer Organization of the Czechoslovak Youth Union), Praha, 1955.

Cesta vesnice k socialismu, čtvrté thema roku stranického školení, 1950-1951 (The Road of the Village Toward Socialism, the Fourth Theme of the Year of Party Schooling, 1950-1951), Praha, 1950.

Dokumenty o protilidové a protinárodní politice T. G. M. (Documents on the Anti-Popular and Anti-National Policy of T. G. M.), Praha, 1953.

Dokumenty o protisovětských piklech československé reakce: z archivního materiálu o kontrarevoluční činnosti Masaryka a Beneše v letech 1917-1924 (Documents on the Anti-Soviet Conspiracy of the Czechoslovak Reactionaries: from the Archives on the Counter-Revolutionary Activities of Masaryk and Beneš in the Years 1917-1924), Praha, 1954.

Edward Beneš in His Own Words, Czech-American National Alliance, New York, 1944.

First Czechoslovak Economic Plan, Praha, 1947.

Gottwald, Klement, *Deset let. Sborník statí a projevů, 1936-1946* (Ten Years. A Collection of Articles and Speeches, 1936-1946), Praha, 1948.

————, *Kupředu, zpátky ni krok: sborník projevů předsedy vlády a dokumentů ze dnů 17-29. února 1948* (Forward, Not One Step Back: Collection of Speeches of the Chairman of the Council of Ministers and Documents from February 17 to February 29, 1948), Praha, 1948.

————, *Od února na cestě k socialismu* (From February on the Road to Socialism), Praha, 1948.

————, *O kultuře a úkolech inteligence v budování socialismu* (On Culture and the Tasks of the Intelligentsia in the Construction of Socialism), Praha, 1954.

————, *Spisy* (Works), I-III, Praha (n.d.).

————, *Za socialistický stát, za socialistické právo* (For the Socialist State, for the Socialist Law), Praha, 1950.

Gruliow, Leo, *Current Soviet Policies,* New York, 1953.

History of the Communist Party of the Soviet Union. Short Course, Moscow, 1939.

Komunistická strana Československa: Slovník lidové správy, rukovět pro funkcionáře národních výborů (The Communist Party of Czechoslovakia: An Encyclopaedia of the People's Administration, A Manual for the Functionaries of the People's Committees), Praha, 1947.

————, *Učební plány a osnovy pro rok stranického školení 1953-1954* (The Curricula and Syllabi for the Year of Party Schooling 1953-1954), Praha, 1953.

Kopecký, Václav, *30 let KSČ* (Thirty Years of the Communist Party of Czechoslovakia), Praha, 1951.

————, *Pod praporem Leninismu* (Under the Banner of Leninism), Praha, 1956.

Nationalization in Czechoslovakia, Praha, 1946.

Plánované hospodářství v Československu (Planned Economy in Czechoslovakia), Praha, Institute for Social and Economic Research of the Socialist Academy, 1948.

Postavení Československa ve světovém hospodářství (Czechoslovakia's Position in the World Economy), Praha, 1957.

Program prvé domací vlády narodní fronty Čechů a Slováků (The Program of the First Government of the National Front of Czechs and Slovaks on Native Soil), Košice, 1945.

Rok stranického školení (Year of Party Schooling), an annual publication by the Propaganda and Agitation Department of the Central Committee of the KSČ, Praha.

Sbírka nařízení Slovenské národní rady (Collection of Ordinances of the Slovak National Council), Báňská Bystrica, 1944.

Sbírka zákonů republiky Československé (Collection of Laws of the Czechoslovak Republic), Praha.

Sbírka zákonů Slovenské národní rady (Collection of Laws of the Slovak National Council), Bratislava.

School Reform in Czechoslovakia, Praha, 1948.

Slovník veřejného práva československého (Encyclopaedia of Czechoslovak Public Law), Brno, 1938-1948.

Statistical Yearbook of the United Nations, Geneva, 1958, 1959, 1960.

Statistická ročenka republiky Československé (Statistical Yearbook of the Czechoslovak Republic), Praha, 1937, 1958, 1959, 1960.

Státní úřad statistický: Deset let demokratického Československa (State Office of Statistics: Ten Years of Democratic Czechoslovakia), Praha, 1955.

Survey of Europe since the War, Geneva, 1955.

Surveys of Europe 1955 through 1959, Geneva, 1956-1960.

Svaz československo-sovětského přátelství. Pracujeme se sovětskou literaturou: jak pomáhá sovětská literatura při výstavbě našeho průmyslu a zemědělství (The Union of Czechoslovak-Soviet Friendship. We Are Working with Soviet Literature: How Soviet Literature Helps the Construction of Our Industry and Agriculture), Praha, 1954.

Těsnopisecké zprávy o schůzích poslanecké sněmovny (Stenographic Reports of the Sessions of the Chamber of Deputies), 157th Session, December 1938.

Učební plány a osnovy pro odborné školy s docházkou kratší než čtyřletou (Study Plans and Syllabi for Technical Schools with Attendance of less than Four Years), Praha, 1949.

Učební texty pro dějepis (Textbook of History), Praha, 1953.

Únor 1948. Sborník dokumentů (February 1948. A Collection of Documents), Praha, 1958.

Úřední list republiky Československé (The Official Gazette of the Czechoslovak Republic), Praha.

Ústav dějin komunistické strany Československa, *Přehled dějin komunistické strany* (The Institute of the History of the Communist Party of Czechoslovakia: An Outline of the History of the Communist Party), Praha, 1957.

———, *V bojích se zocelila KSČ* (The KSČ Strengthened in the Struggle), Praha, 1956.

————, *Za svobodu českého a slovenského národa* (For the Freedom of the Czech and Slovak Nations), Praha, 1956.

Ústava Československé socialistické republiky (The Constitution of the Czechoslovak Socialist Republic), Praha, 1960.

Ústava devátého května (The Ninth-of-May Constitution), Praha, 1948.

Vsesoiuznaia Kommunisticheskaia Partia (b) v rezoliutsiakh i resheniakh s'ezdov, konferentsii i plenumov Ts. K., 1898-1935 (The All-Union Communist Party (B) in Resolutions and Decisions of the Congresses, Conferences, and Plenums of the C. C., 1898-1935), Moscow, 1936.

Yearbooks of Labor Statistics, Geneva, 1939, 1951, 1958, 1959, 1960.

Zákony a nařízení o volbě Narodního shromáždění (Laws and Ordinances on the Election of the National Assembly), Praha, 1956.

BOOKS, MONOGRAPHS, AND PAMPHLETS

Alberty, Julius, *Úvod do vyučování dějepisu* (Introduction to the Teaching of History), Bratislava, 1959.

Bakoš, Mikuláš, *O socialistickém realizme* (On Socialist Realism), Bratislava, 1952.

Barton, Paul, *Prague à l'heure de Moscou,* Paris, 1954.

Bartošek, Karel, *Hanebná role amerických okupantů v západních Čechách v roce 1945* (The Shameful Role of the American Occupants in Western Bohemia in 1945), Praha, 1951.

————, *Američané v západních Čechách v roce 1945* (The Americans in Western Bohemia in 1945), Praha, 1953.

Bartuška, Jan, *et al., Státní právo Československé republiky* (The State Law of the Czechoslovak Republic), Praha, 1952.

Beaumier, Jean, *Od Hitlera k Trumanovi* (From Hitler to Truman), Praha, 1951.

Beckman, Rudolf, *K diplomatickému pozadí Mnichova: kapitoly o britské mnichovské politice* (The Diplomatic Background of Munich: Chapters on British Munich Policy), Praha, 1954.

Beneš, Eduard, *Demokracie dnes a zítra* (Democracy Today and Tomorrow), London (n.d.). An enlarged Czech edition of a book published in English in 1939.

————, *Paměti* (Memoirs), Praha, 1947.

————, *Problèmes de la Tchécoslovaquie,* Praha, 1936.

Bodnár, Ján, *O súčasnej filozofii v USA* (About Contemporary American Philosophy), Bratislava, 1956.

Bouček, Jaroslav, *et al., O Americe zpívam* (I Am Singing about America), Praha, 1951.

Bušek, Vratislav, *Poučení z únorového převratu* (A Lesson from the February Coup), New York, 1954.

————, and Spulber, Nicolas, *Czechoslovakia*, New York, 1957.

Černý, Václav, *Emile Verhaeren a jeho místo v dějinách volného verše* (Emile Verhaeren and His Place in the History of the Free Verse), Praha, 1955.

Československá akademie věd: Proti kosmopolitismu ve výkladech našich dějin (Czechoslovak Academy of Science: Against Cosmopolitism in the Interpretation of Our History), Praha, 1955.

Cesta k svobodě (The Road to Freedom), London, 1944.

Chalupný, Vladimír, ed., *Příručka pro nově založená družstva* (A Handbook for Newly Established Cooperatives), Praha, 1958.

Denk, P., *Anton Semjonovič Makarenko—průkopník komunistické výchovy* (Anton Semyonovich Makarenko—The Pioneer of Communist Education), Praha, 1956.

Deset let parlamentní retrospektivy (Ten Years of Parliamentary Retrospective), Ministry of Information publication, Praha, 1948.

Deset slavných let, 1945-1955. Sborník k výročí osvobození Československa sovětskou armádou (Ten Glorious Years, 1945-1955. Yearbook on the occasion of the Anniversary of the Liberation of Czechoslovakia by the Soviet Army), Praha, 1955.

Diamond, William, *Czechoslovakia between East and West*, London, 1947.

Dobrý, Anatol, *Hospodářský vývoj ČSR* (The Economic Development of the Czechoslovak Republic), Praha, 1955.

Dolejší, Vojtěch, *Třicet let bojů za socialismus* (Thirty Years of Struggle for Socialism), Praha, 1951.

Dunayev, Vladimír, *Americké Gestapo* (The American Gestapo), Praha, 1952.

Feierabend, Ladislav, *Agricultural Cooperatives in Czechoslovakia*, New York, 1952.

Fierlinger, Zdeněk, *Americký imperialism ve slepé uličce* (American Imperialism in a Blind Alley), Praha, 1952.

Foustka, Radim, *Národnostní otázka* (The Nationality Question), Praha, 1952.

————, et al., *Doplňková skripta z theorie státu a práva* (Supplementary Scripts on the Theory of the State and the Law), Praha, 1954.

Frejka, Ludvik, *26. únor 1948 v československém hospodářství* (February 26, 1948, in Czechoslovak Economy), Praha, 1948.

Friedman, Otto, *The Breakup of Czech Democracy*, London, 1950.

Gadőurek, Ivan, *The Political Control of Czechoslovakia*, Leiden, 1953.

Gallacher, William, *Britannie a komunism* (Britain and Communism), Praha, 1951.

Galuška, Miroslav, and Hoffmeister, Adolf, *Tři měsíce v Novém Yorku* (Three Months in New York), Praha, 1951.

Giraud, Emile, *Le pouvoir exécutif dans les démocraties d'Europe et d'Amérique,* Paris, 1938.

Goldman, Josef, *Czechoslovakia, Test Case of Nationalization,* Praha, 1947.

Grolig, Alois, *Úvod do theorie a metodiky národohospodářského plánovaní* (An Introduction to the Theory and Methodology of Economic Planning), Praha, 1953.

Gronský, Jan, *Prehľad štátného práva ľudovodemokratických krajin, osobitná část* (An Outline of the State Law of the People's Democratic Countries, Special Part), Praha, 1957.

——, *Prehľad ústavného a politického vývoja ľudovodemokratických krajin* (An Outline of the Constitutional and Political Development of the People's Democratic Countries), Praha, 1954.

Grulich, Bohumil, *Nová praxe našich škol s menším počtem tříd* (A New Practice of Our Schools with a Smaller Number of Pupils), Praha, 1953.

Gus, M., *Americkí imperialisti—inšpirátori mnichovskej politiky* (American Imperialists—Instigators of the Munich Policy), Bratislava, 1953.

Hájek, J. S., *Wilsonovská legenda v dějinách ČSR* (The Wilsonian Legend in the History of the Czechoslovak Republic), Praha, 1953.

Hlaváč, Miroslav, *Přehled československého práva. Stenografický záznam přednášek přednesených v Roztěži ve dnech 3.-9. ledna 1957* (An Outline of Czechoslovak Law. A stenographic Record of Lectures Delivered at Roztěž January 3-9, 1957), Praha, 1957.

Hník, František M., *Církve v čase rozhodovaní. K základům sociálně theologické orientace v československé církvi* (Churches at the Time of Decision. Concerning the Foundations of the Social Theological Orientation in the Czechoslovak Church), Praha, 1956.

Houska, J., and Kára, K., *Otázky lidové demokracie* (Questions of the People's Democracy), Praha, 1955.

Hrabánek, Jan, *The Legal Position of Journalists in Czechoslovakia,* Praha, 1947.

Hromada, Juraj, *Prehľad, československých štatných orgánov* (An Outline of Czechoslovak State Organs), Bratislava, 1955.

Jandera, Alex, *Kapitoly z dějin předmnichovské republiky* (Chapters from the History of the pre-Munich Republic), Praha, 1953.

Josten, Josef, *Oh, My Country,* London, 1949.

Kartun, D., *U.S.A. 1953. Pravda o Eisenhowerově Americe* (U.S.A. 1953. The Truth about Eisenhower's America), Praha, 1953.

Kavka, František, *Husitská revoluční tradice* (The Hussite Revolutionary Tradition), Praha, 1953.

Keprta, Josef, *Organisace a správa československého školství* (The Organization and Administration of the Czechoslovak School System), Praha, 1956.

Kerner, Robert J., *et al., Czechoslovakia,* Berkeley, 1940.

Klátil, Jan, *Národní výbory, stručný nástin jejich vývoje a organisace* (The People's Committees, a Concise Outline of Their Development and Organization), Praha, 1952.

Klokočka, Vladimír, *Základy státního práva buržoasních zemí, obecná část* (The Fundamentals of the State Law of the Bourgeois Countries, General Part), Praha, 1957.

Knapp, Viktor, *Hlavní zásady československého socialistického občanského práva* (The Main Principles of the Czechoslovak Socialist Civil Law), Praha, 1958.

Kopáč, Jaroslav, and Uher, Bohumil, *Úloha učitele v dnešní škole* (The Teacher's Role in Today's School), Praha, 1956.

Korbel, Josef, *The Communist Subversion of Czechoslovakia, 1938-1948,* Princeton, 1959.

Korbel, Pavel, *Národní výbory* (The People's Committees), New York, 1951. A mimeographed study of the Free Europe Committee.

Kozák, Jan, *K některým otázkám strategie a taktiky KSČ v době přerůstání národní a demokratické revoluce v revoluci socialistickou* (Concerning Some Questions of the Strategy and Tactics of the KSČ at the Time of the Overgrowth of the National and Democratic Revolution into a Socialist Revolution), Praha, 1956.

Král, Václav, *O Masarykově a Benešově kontrarevoluční protisovětské politice* (On Masaryk's and Beneš's Counter-Revolutionary and Anti-Soviet Policy), Praha, 1953.

Křen, Jan, *Československo v období dočasné a relativní stabilisace kapitalismu 1924-1929* (Czechoslovakia in the Period of Temporary and Relative Stabilization of Capitalism, 1924-1929), Praha, 1957.

Křížek, Jurij, *T. G. Masaryk a česká politika* (T. G. Masaryk and Czech Politics), Praha, 1959.

Křížek, Jurij, *T. G. Masaryk a naše dělnická třída. Masarykův boj proti revolučnímu dělnickému hnutí před světovou imperialistickou válkou* (T. G. Masaryk and Our Working Class. Masaryk's Struggle against the Revolutionary Workers' Movement before the World Imperialistic War), Praha, 1955.

Krofta, Jaroslav, *Kapitoly z ústav lidově demokratických zemí* (Chapters on the Constitutions of the People's Democratic Countries), Praha, 1957.

Kubalík, Josef, *Dějiny náboženství* (The History of Religion), Praha, 1955.

Kučera, Eduard, *K některým otázkám autonomie a postavení Slovenska v rámci Československé republiky* (Concerning Some Questions of the Autonomy and Position of Slovakia within the Framework of the Czechoslovak Republic), Praha, 1954.

Kučera, Jan, *Psychologie v kádrové práci* (Psychology in the Cadres's Work), Praha, 1954.

Kulski, W. W., *The Soviet Regime,* Syracuse, 1954.

Kulturně-politický kalendář (The Cultural-Political Almanac), Praha, 1958.

Kvetko, Martin, *K základom ústavného pomeru česko-slovenského* (Concerning the Fundamentals of the Czech-Slovak Constitutional Relationship), Bratislava, 1947.

Land Reforms in Czechoslovakia, New York, 1953. A mimeographed study of the Free Europe Committee.

Lenin, V. I., *Sochinenia* (Works) 1-30, Moscow, 1934-1935 (3rd edn.), 1-5, Moscow, 1941-1950 (4th edn.).

Lettrich, Jozef, *History of Modern Slovakia,* New York, 1955.

Levit, Pavel, *Správní právo, část obecná* (Administrative Law, General Part), Praha, 1954.

————, *Správní právo, část zvláštní* (Administrative Law, Special Part), Praha, 1956.

Lom, František, *Některé kapitoly z organisace socialistického zemědělství* (Some Chapters from the Organization of Socialist Agriculture), Praha, 1955.

————, *Úvod do studia ekonomiky socialistického zemědělství* (An Introduction to the Study of the Economy of Socialist Agriculture), Praha, 1954.

Macek, Josef, *Kdož jsú boží bojovníci* (Who Are God's Fighters), Praha, 1951.

————, *Z dějin českého národa* (From the History of the Czech Nation), Praha, 1951.

Meyer, Herschel D., *Musí Amerika zbrojit? Logika barbarství XX. věku* (Must America Arm? The Logic of Barbarism in the Twentieth Century), Praha, 1951.

Moore, N. E., *Economic Demography of Eastern and Southern Europe,* Geneva, 1945.

Moural, Jan, *Slovenské národní orgány* (The Slovak National Organs), Praha, 1958.

Musil, František (ed.), *Národní škola* (The National School), Praha, 1956.

Nejedlý, Zdeněk, *Klement Gottwald v boji za osvobození ČSR* (Klement Gottwald in the Struggle for the Liberation of Czechoslovakia), Praha, 1946.

Nejedlý, Zdeněk, *Nedělní epištoly* (Sunday Epistles), Praha, 1954-1955.

————, *O smyslu českých dějin* (On the Meaning of Czech History), Praha, 1953.

Newspapers and Newspapermen in Czechoslovakia, Union of Czech Journalists, Praha, 1947.

Novák, Antonín, *Byl jsem ve službách Tita* (I Was in Tito's Service), Praha, 1951.

Olivová-Pavlová, Věra, *Československo-sovětské vztahy v letech 1918-1922* (Czechoslovak-Soviet Relations in the Years 1918-1922), Praha, 1957.

Outrata, Vladimír, *Dějiny mezinárodních vztahů od roku 1870-1952* (The History of International Relations from 1870 to 1952), Praha, 1953.

Pachta, Jan, *Gottwald a naše dějiny* (Gottwald and Our History), Praha, 1948.

Paur, Jaroslav, *Education in Czechoslovakia,* Praha, 1947.

Pavlát, Vladislav, *Předmět a metoda politické ekonomie* (The Subject Matter and Method of Political Economy), Praha, 1954.

Pavlík, Ondrej, *Vývin sovietského školstva a pedagogiky* (The Development of the Soviet School System and Pedagogy), Bratislava, 1948.

Peroutka, Ferdinand, *Budování státu* (The Building of the State), 1-4, Praha, 1933-1936.

Pertold, Otakar, *Pověra a pověrčivost* (Superstition and Superstitiousness), Praha, 1956.

Plojhar, Josef, *Vítězný únor a československá strana lidová* (The Victorious February and the Czechoslovak People's Party), Praha, 1958.

Plundr, Otakar, *Soudy a prokuratura v ČSR* (The Courts and the Procuracy in Czechoslovakia), Praha, 1954.

Polišenský, Josef V., *Benjamin Franklin a první americká revoluce* (Benjamin Franklin and the First American Revolution), Praha, 1956.

Přenosil, Gustav, *Ochrana socialistického vlastnictví podle československého trestního práva* (The Protection of Socialist Ownership according to the Czechoslovak Criminal Law), Praha, 1957.

Rais, Štefan, *Do novej etapy národných výborov* (Into a New Stage of the People's Committees), Bratislava, 1954.

Randák, Karel, *et al., Demokracie, svobody, volby* (Democracy, Freedom, and Elections), Praha, 1957.

Rattinger, Bedřich, *Nejvyšší státní orgány lidově demokratického Československa: Národní shromáždění a president republiky* (The Highest State Organs of the People's Democratic Czechoslovakia: The National Assembly and the President of the Republic), Praha, 1957.

Reiman, Pavel, *Dějiny komunistické strany Československa* (The History of the Communist Party of Czechoslovakia), Praha, 1931.

Řezníček, Jiří, *Organisace plánovaní v ČSR* (The Organization of Planning in the Czechoslovak Republic), Praha, 1956.

Ripka, Hubert, *Le Coup de Prague,* Paris, 1949.

Rizga, Valerián, and Hronský, Michal, *Odměňování práce ve výrobě* (Remuneration for Work in Production), Praha, 1959.

Robeson, Paul, *Boj černochů za svobodu a mír* (The Struggle of the Negroes for Freedom and Peace), Praha, 1951.

Schmidt, Dana Adam, *Anatomy of a Satellite,* Boston, 1952.

Sinkmajer, Josef, *Ekonomika komunálního hospodářství* (The Communal Economy), Praha, 1957.

Širacký, Ondrej, *Kultura a mravnost: príspevok k analyze socialneduchovnej skutočnosti* (Culture and Morality: a Contribution to the Analysis of Social-Spiritual Reality), Bratislava, 1949.

Šlechta, Emanuel, *Klement Gottwald,* Praha, 1954.

Sobotka, Ladislav, *Učební pomůcka pro studium ekonomie socialistického zemědělství* (Textbook for the Study of the Economy of Socialist Agriculture), Praha, 1952.

Soják, Vladimír, *Boj národů lidově demokratických zemí střední a jihovýchodní Evropy za svobodu* (The Struggle of the People's Democratic Countries of Central and South-Eastern Europe for Freedom), Praha, 1957.

Spulber, Nicolas, *The Economics of Communist Eastern Europe,* New York, 1957.

Spurný, Gríša, *Únorové dny* (The February Days), Praha, 1958.

Štajgr, František, *Organisace československých soudů* (The Organization of the Czechoslovak Courts), Praha, 1953.

——, and Plundr, Otakar, *Organisace justice a prokuratury* (The Organization of the Judiciary and the Procuracy), Praha, 1957.

——, and Boura, F., *Prokurátor v občanském soudním řízení* (The Procurator in the Civil Judicial Procedure), Praha, 1955.

Stalin, Joseph, *Leninism*, I-II, New York, 1932.

Štefánek, Josef, *Česká literatura po válce* (Czech Literature after the War), Praha, 1949.

Štěpina, Jaroslav, *Rodinné právo, výklad zákona o právu rodinném s dodatkem o dědickém právu v rodině socialistické společnosti* (Family Law: an Interpretation of Family Law, with a Supplement on the Law of Inheritance in Socialist Society), Praha, 1958.

Stránský, Jan, *East Wind over Prague*, New York, 1951.

Šulc, Ludvík, *O výchově dětí v rodině a ve škole se zřetelem k spolupráci rodiny a školy* (On the Education of Children in the Family and in the School with regard to the Collaboration of Family and School), Praha, 1954.

Táborský, E., *Czechoslovak Democracy at Work*, London, 1945.

——, *The Czechoslovak Cause*, London, 1944.

——, *Naše nová ústava* (Our New Constitution), Praha, 1948.

——, *Conformity Under Communism, A Study of Indoctrination Techniques*, Washington, 1958.

Thomson, Harrison S., *Czechoslovakia in European History*, Princeton, 1953.

Towster, Julian, *Political Power in the USSR*, New York, 1948.

Uher, Bohumil, *Theorie vyučovaní na střední škole* (Theory of Instruction in the High School), Praha, 1952.

Vaníček, František, *Byli jsme v štástné zemi: denník našich rolníků ze zajezdu do Sovětského svazu, 1950* (We Were in a Happy Country: The Diary of Our Farmers on an Excursion to the Soviet Union, 1950), Praha, 1951.

Vašečka, Felix, *Buržoasný štát a církev. Typické formy spolupráce buržoasného štátu s naboženskými organizaciami se zvláštným zretelom na církevno-politickú prax predmnichovskej ČS* (The Bourgeois State and the Church. Typical Forms of Collaboration of the Bourgeois State with Religious Organizations, with a Special Reference to the Ecclesiastical-Political Practice of pre-Munich Czechoslovakia), Bratislava, 1957.

Večeřa, Jan, *Za další upevňování základních organisací strany* (For a Further Strengthening of the Party's Primary Units), Praha, 1957.

Velká říjnová socialistická revoluce a naše narodní svoboda (The Great October Socialist Revolution and Our National Freedom), Brno, 1950. Russian edn., 1951.

Veselý, Jindřich, *Kronika únorových dnů 1948* (The Chronicle of the February Days 1948), Praha, 1958.

———, *O vzniku a založení KSČ* (On the Origin and Foundation of the Communist Party of Czechoslovakia), Praha, 1953.

———, *Z prvních bojů KSČ, 1921-1924* (From the First Struggles of the Communist Party of Czechoslovakia, 1921-1924), Praha, 1958.

Vojtovič, S., *Černá Amerika* (The Black America), Praha, 1950.

Volf, Miloslav, *Naše dělnické hnutí v minulosti* (Our Workers' Movement in the Past), Praha, 1947.

Vronský, B., *Americký způsob života* (The American Way of Life), Praha, 1950.

Vyshinsky, Andre, *The Law of the Soviet State,* New York, 1948.

What They Want, Praha, 1959.

Žák, Jiří, *Exkomunikace, zázraky, sabotáže* (Excommunication, Miracles, Sabotages), Praha, 1950.

Zápotocký, Antonín, *Naše odborová politika* (Our Trade Union Policy), Praha, 1949.

———, *Po staru se žít nedá* (One Cannot Live in the Old Way), Praha, 1949.

———, *Revoluční odborové hnutí po únoru 1948* (The Revolutionary Trade Union Movement after February 1948), Praha, 1952.

Zieris, K. F., *The New Organization of the Czechoslovak Press,* Praha, 1947.

INDEX